LINGUISTIC SURVEYS OF AFRICA

Volume 3

THE EASTERN SUDANIC LANGUAGES

THE EASTERN SUDANIC LANGUAGES

A. N. TUCKER

LONDON AND NEW YORK

First published in 1940 by Oxford University Press

This edition first published in 2018
by Routledge
2 Park Square, Milton Park, Abingdon, Oxon OX14 4RN

and by Routledge
711 Third Avenue, New York, NY 10017

Routledge is an imprint of the Taylor & Francis Group, an informa business

© 1940 International African Institute

All rights reserved. No part of this book may be reprinted or reproduced or utilised in any form or by any electronic, mechanical, or other means, now known or hereafter invented, including photocopying and recording, or in any information storage or retrieval system, without permission in writing from the publishers.

Trademark notice: Product or corporate names may be trademarks or registered trademarks, and are used only for identification and explanation without intent to infringe.

British Library Cataloguing in Publication Data
A catalogue record for this book is available from the British Library

ISBN: 978-1-138-08975-4 (Set)
ISBN: 978-1-315-10381-5 (Set) (ebk)
ISBN: 978-1-138-09077-4 (Volume 3) (hbk)
ISBN: 978-1-138-09085-9 (Volume 3) (pbk)
ISBN: 978-1-315-10844-5 (Volume 3) (ebk)

Publisher's Note
The publisher has gone to great lengths to ensure the quality of this reprint but points out that some imperfections in the original copies may be apparent.

Disclaimer
The publisher has made every effort to trace copyright holders and would welcome correspondence from those they have been unable to trace.

Due to modern production methods, it has not been possible to reproduce the fold-out maps within the book. Please visit www.routledge.com to view them.

THE EASTERN SUDANIC LANGUAGES

By

A. N. TUCKER

M.A. (Cape Town), Ph.D. (London)

Published for the
INTERNATIONAL INSTITUTE OF
AFRICAN LANGUAGES & CULTURES
by the OXFORD UNIVERSITY PRESS
LONDON NEW YORK TORONTO
1940

OXFORD UNIVERSITY PRESS
AMEN HOUSE, E.C. 4
LONDON EDINBURGH GLASGOW NEW YORK
TORONTO MELBOURNE CAPETOWN BOMBAY
CALCUTTA MADRAS
HUMPHREY MILFORD
PUBLISHER TO THE UNIVERSITY

PRINTED IN GREAT BRITAIN AT THE UNIVERSITY PRESS, OXFORD
BY JOHN JOHNSON, PRINTER TO THE UNIVERSITY

CONTENTS

PREFACE vii
ACKNOWLEDGEMENTS x
BIBLIOGRAPHY xiv

INTRODUCTION

Section I. TRIBAL 1
Section II. LINGUISTIC 56

PART I
THE MORU-MADI LANGUAGE GROUP

Section I. PHONETICS 89
Section II. GRAMMAR 126
Section III. ORTHOGRAPHY 316
Section IV. VOCABULARY 341
Appendix: LENDU 380
TRIBAL INDEX 419
LINGUISTIC INDEX 428

PREFACE

THE COUNTRY AND THE LANGUAGES

BY the 'Southern Sudan' is to be understood roughly an area of some 240,000 square miles, embracing the two provinces—Upper Nile Province and Equatorial Province.[1] (The latter is a recent amalgamation of the Bahr el Ghazal with Mongalla Province.) The northern part of this country is a vast swamp, alternating with large tracts of steppe lands, which are iron-hard in the dry season and almost liquid mud during the rains. Eastward the swamps and steppes gradually give way to the highlands of Abyssinia. The south is mountainous and well wooded, leading to the Uganda escarpment and the Nile Congo Divide. The west consists of 'park land' or rolling country covered by light woods, which prevent the observer from seeing any distance except from the tops of the slight ridges which intersect the country at great intervals. To the south-west the land is richer, and tropical undergrowth more abundant. There is only one small patch of tropical rain forest to the south-east.

Owing to the Nile (Bahr el Jebel) and its tributaries, the swamps are more accessible by river steamer, during part of the year at least, than one would at first imagine. Since many of the Nilotic peoples like to live along the banks of rivers and watercourses, they may be approached in this way. Their inland branches, however, are very hard to reach, since it takes nearly the whole of one dry season to level out a 200-mile motor road, which the following wet season will entirely submerge. In the southern areas motor transport is becoming more and more possible, and roads are now being made which can outlast the rainy season. Here the main obstacle lies in the myriad small rivers and streams which intersect the country, and which, with no warning, will come down in spate and wash away the strongest bridge that local talent can erect.

The inhabitants of the Southern Sudan present a great mixture of cultures and languages. On the whole, however, language and culture are definitely linked, except in some western and south-western districts. The following are the main languages and cultural groups with which this linguistic series will concern itself:

I. *The Eastern Sudanic Languages.*
   1. The Moru-Madi group.
   2. The Bongo-Baka-Bagirmi group.
   3. The Ndogo-Sere group.
   4. Zande (and other unrelated Sudanic languages).

II. *The Nilotic Languages.*
   5. Dinka.
   6. Nuer.
   7. The Shilluk-Acholi group.

III. *The Nilo-Hamitic Languages.*
   8. The Bari dialects.
   9. The Lotuko dialects.
   10. The Topotha-Turkana dialects.

---

[1] Seligman (op. cit., p. 2) includes Dar Fur, Kordofan, Dar Nuba, and El Fung in his conception of the 'Nilotic Sudan', but the languages spoken there (with the possible exception of El Fung) lie outside the scope of this series.

11. The Nandi group.
12. The Masai group.

IV. *Unplaced Category (Western Hamitic?)*.
13. The Didinga-Beir group.

The present work will confine itself to the three main groups of Eastern Sudanic languages,[1] namely, Moru-Madi, Bongo-Baka-Bagirmi, and Ndogo-Sere. The Sudan members of these groups live in the western and southern highlands of Equatorial Province,[2] but the main body of Eastern Sudanic speakers should be sought outside the Southern Sudan in the neighbouring corners of Uganda and the Belgian Congo, and in the Oubangui-Chari and Tchad Districts of French Equatorial Africa. The Sudan representatives are obviously invaders from these parts.

The distribution of these peoples is roughly as follows (for detailed distribution see Chapter I):

Moru-Madi group.

This group extends from Amadi District of 'Mongalla' Province (Moru) in a horseshoe bend through Maridi and Yei (Avukaya, Keliko), through the north-east corner of the Congo (Logo, Lendu), north-west Uganda (Lugbara, Madi), and into the Opari District of 'Mongalla' Province (Madi).

Bongo-Baka-Bagirmi group.

This group includes the Rumbek 'Jur' and many of the so-called 'Moru' tribes. Its Sudan members are scattered between Yei and Amadi and between Amadi and Wau. The great bulk of the group, however, are to be found in the Oubangui-Chari District of French Equatorial Africa (Sara) and south-east of Lake Tchad (Bagirmi).

Ndogo-Sere group ('Belanda'-'Basiri').

These people are to be found mostly between Wau and Dem Zubeir, though a large portion of Basiri live north of the Mbomu River in Oubangui-Chari.

Other Sudanic tribes.

The Azande occupy the south-west corner of the 'Bahr el Ghazal', extending eastward as far as Maridi. The great bulk of the Azande live in the Congo. For the distribution of the smaller Sudanic tribes see Chapter I.

The term 'Eastern Sudanic languages' is used here primarily in a geographical sense; the dialects in the Southern Sudan form the eastern boundary of Sudanic speech, where it borders on the Nilotic wedge which, in turn, divides it from Hamitic speech.[3] As a group or family name, however, it is not very good, since these languages themselves are sharply divided into two opposing camps: (*a*) the Moru-Madi and Bongo-Baka groups, which have much in common with each other and with the languages of Calonne Beaufaict's *Derniers Néolithiques* (Momvu, Efe, &c.); these languages are either indigenous to the Wele basin or are among its very earliest

---

[1] For the distribution of tribes within the Nilotic, Nilo-Hamitic, &c. groups, see my article, 'Survey of the Language Groups in the Southern Sudan', *Bulletin of School of Oriental Studies*, vol. vii, pt. 4, 1935.

[2] Since the formation of Equatorial Province is very recent, and the boundaries, at the time of writing, still rather vague in places, the old terms 'Bahr el Ghazal' and 'Mongalla' Province will occasionally be used in the text to signify the north-western and the south-eastern sections of this new province.

[3] See Map 1. North of the Nilotic area there has been a great fusion of Sudanic with Hamitic, as may be seen in the multitudinous dialects of Dar Fur and Kordofan, and Hamitic influence extends westward as far as Lake Tchad at this latitude.

invaders; (b) the Ndogo-Sere group and Zande, Banda, &c. which have much in common with each other and with the languages of the later invaders of this area.

Westermann[1] places them all under the category of *Nigritische Sprachen*, except Bagirmi, which he classes under *Innersudanische Sprachen*, although he recognizes the affinity between the latter and Bongo. Delafosse uses the term *Nilo-Tchadien* for a large number of dialects in which Bongo and Bagirmi occur. At the same time all these early Wele languages have, according to most authorities, undergone varying degrees of Nilotic influence, so that Westermann's earlier classification of Moru, Madi, Bongo, &c., as 'High-Nilotic'[2] also carried with it considerable weight.

In dealing with frontier languages it is impossible to apply very strict categories; Bongo, to take an instance, though belonging to the Bagirmi group (Westermann's *Innersudanische Abteilung*) has borrowed much from the Momvu dialects, while its neighbour Baka has Mundu affinities, unpossessed by either Bongo or Bagirmi, and appertaining to the Ndogo-Sere group. In this book, therefore, the languages discussed will be described, because of their geographical position, as the 'Eastern Sudanic Languages', but they will be grouped linguistically under the names of their best-known representative dialects, thus: Moru-Madi, Bongo-Baka-Bagirmi, Ndogo-Sere.

[1] 'Charakter und Einteilung der Sudansprachen', *Africa*, 1935.
[2] *The Shilluk People*, p. 35.

ACKNOWLEDGEMENTS

THIS and the succeeding volume are published under a combined grant from the School of Oriental and African Studies, the Sudan Government, and the International Institute of African Languages and Cultures, to all of whom I am deeply indebted.

The material was obtained mostly during a linguistic tour of the Southern Sudan during 1932–3. This was my second visit to the Sudan. During the years 1929–31 I had been engaged by the Sudan Government for the purpose of studying the main 'group' languages there, helping the local authorities in the production of grammars and dictionaries for Europeans, and advising them in the application of the newly adopted Rejaf alphabet to the writing of the various group-languages in schools. It was while doing that work that I first conceived the idea of producing a comparative series on these languages, provided that I had the time to carry out the necessary investigation. To this end, on expiry of my governmental contract, the International Institute of African Languages and Cultures voted a grant of £400,[1] which was later supplemented by the School of Oriental and African Studies, who also very kindly allowed me extra leave in which to finish the research. At the same time the Sudan Government kindly promised to allow me free transport on its railways and steamers during the expedition. The various local governments, in addition, did all they could to provide me with free motor transport for my inland journeys, whenever possible. Without such generous assistance the present work would not have been possible. In this connexion Major R. G. C. Brock, Governor of the 'Bahr el Ghazal', and Mr. L. F. Nalder, Governor of 'Mongalla' Province, are especially to be thanked. Neither can I overstress the kindness and hospitality shown me by local officials and missionaries,[2] who allowed me to use their stations and their staff for the collecting of my dialectal material. During a third visit to the Sudan in the spring of 1938 I was able to check up on my tribal distribution notes and learn the latest governmental statistics.

For the presentation of the material in this book I am greatly indebted to Mr. J. R. Firth of University College, London. I had already written the Moru-Madi section when I appealed to him for criticism. The result was a rewriting of the whole grammatical section on an entirely different basis and in accordance with the linguistic theories associated with his name; this basis I have since used for the other two sections of the book.[3] To him also is due my redefining of the Sudanic, Hamitic, and Bantu languages in Chapter IV.[4] To Professor A. Lloyd James I owe an immense debt of gratitude for his thorough scrutiny of the work in manuscript form and consequent elimination of errors in style.

[1] In this connexion I should like to pay a special debt of gratitude to Professor C. G. Seligman, who was the prime mover in obtaining this grant for me at a time when money for research purposes was very difficult to find.
[2] My missionary helpers belonged to the Church Missionary Society and the Missioni Africane of Verona in the Sudan, and the Africa Inland Mission in the Congo.
[3] The principles underlying this method of presentation are also to be found clearly expressed in Professor Malinowski's book *Coral Gardens*, where they are applied to Melanesian languages, with, however, special reference to a particular aspect of culture. I am greatly indebted to the author for allowing me to see this valuable book in manuscript form while my own work was still in embryo.
[4] My original definitions (in which I was greatly helped by Professor Westermann) have already been published in my article, 'Survey of the Language Groups of the Southern Sudan'.

ACKNOWLEDGEMENTS

My material has been vastly enriched by contributions from various parts of the Eastern Sudanic area, in the form of separate monographs, answers to questionnaires, and criticisms of tentative notes of mine. Acknowledgement of these contributions is best made under the sections in which they appear in the book. Thus:

INTRODUCTION.

The following local authorities[1] have spared no trouble in subscribing towards checking, correcting, and enlarging upon my tribal statistics in Chapter I.

'Mongalla' Province.

The late Dr. K. G. Fraser and Mrs. Fraser, C.M.S. Lui, Amadi.
Major L. N. F. Brown, D.C., Amadi-Maridi District.
Mr. T. H. B. Mynors   ,,   ,,   ,,   ,,
Mr. D. Lomax   ,,   ,,   ,,   ,,
Mr. W. T. Clark   ,,   ,,   ,,   ,,
Major D. Logan Gray   ,,   Yei District.
Mr. J. Winder   ,,   ,,   ,,
Captain G. P. Cann   ,,   Opari District.
Mr. L. F. Nalder, Governor of 'Mongalla' Province.

To the last-named authority I owe a special debt of gratitude for throwing open the office files at Juba for my inspection; these files contained many items of extreme importance, which he had just received in answer to an anthropological questionnaire circulated by him throughout the province.[2]

'Bahr el Ghazal'.

Rev. Fr. Stephen Santandrea, R.C. Mission, Wau (later Kayango).
Rev. Fr. Olivetti, R.C. Mission, Kajok.
Mr. C. A. G. Wallis, D.C. Wau, Central District.
Mr. S. R. Simpson, D.C. Raga, Western District.
The late Mr. D. J. Bethell, D.C. Raga, Western District.

The last-named authority, whom I met since leaving the Sudan, was able to check my previous notes on tribal distribution and to procure for me the loan of a very valuable tribal map of the Kreish area, compiled by Mr. Hibbert, a previous D.C., besides providing me with a map of his own, on which the western section of Map 3 is based.

My population statistics were originally obtained through the courtesy of the Secretariat for Education, Khartoum, and have since been vetted by the various local authorities.

From the area outside the Sudan I have had the following assistance.

Belgian Congo.

The Belgian Government, through our Foreign Office, has very kindly provided me with the latest population figures of non-Bantu tribes in the north-east corner of the Congo.

Miss Lucy McCord and Mr. H. Stam, of the Africa Inland Mission, took great trouble to provide me with sketch-maps showing the distribution of Eastern Sudanic tribes in the Congo. These maps were a valuable addition to those already published by Czekanowski, Maes et Boone, and others, being more local in character.

---

[1] Many of my informants have since been transferred to other stations.
[2] Since incorporated in his *Tribal Survey of Mongalla Province.*

ACKNOWLEDGEMENTS

French Equatorial Africa.

I am very much obliged to the Government of Oubangui-Chari for sending me, also through our Foreign Office, statistics concerning the distribution of the Sara and Banda tribes in that area, accompanied by a very welcome map (Map 4).

I am also greatly indebted to Professor H. Labouret of Paris for obtaining for me from Fort Lamy the governmental statistics of the tribes in the Lake Tchad area.

Uganda.

My tribal statistics have been taken from the Census Returns of 1931.

In addition, Father E. Ramponi (Missioni Africane) from Gulu has very kindly given me the results of his own research into the distribution of Lugbara dialects.

PART I. THE MORU-MADI LANGUAGE GROUP.

Moru-Avukaya.

Dr. and Mrs. Fraser, at whose mission hospital at Lui I was a guest for a considerable time, were instrumental in introducing me to Moru, and allowed me to make great use of their staff, besides encroaching on their own time. Their greatest contribution, for which I shall always be grateful, was the loan of one of their leading Moru teachers, who accompanied me on my journeys through the whole Moru-Madi area, and who was invaluable in helping me with dialectal differences.

The Rev. and Mrs. F. G. Laverick, who offered me hospitality at their station at Maridi, helped greatly to put me in touch with Avukaya and the Western Moru speakers.

I should also like to thank Major L. N. F. Brown, the then District Commissioner of Amadi and Yei, for placing at my disposal members of the native police and prisoners, from whom I was able to obtain nearly all the dialects I wanted.

Since leaving the Sudan I met Mr. T. H. B. Mynors, who was busy writing a Moru grammar. We exchanged notes and he gave me a copy of his work in manuscript (which has since been circulated in the Sudan in typescript form), from which I have helped myself liberally.

Logo and Lendu.

I was only able to spend a short time in touch with Logo speakers (although the Africa Inland Mission at Aba supplied me with all the raw material I could handle while there), and my Logo section would have been very deficient but for the subsequence assistance of Miss Lucy McCord of the A.I.M. Toro, who very kindly filled in a Linguistic Questionnaire, which I had made out, and, more important still, lent me the manuscript Logo Grammar of the late Miss Mary Mozley, which proved to be a most valuable source of information.

My Lendu grammatical material was acquired similarly through the Rev. B. L. Litchman's filling in my questionnaire for that language, my time only permitting me to study its very peculiar phonetic system.

Lugbara.

Fr. Crazzolara of the R.C. Mission, Gulu, sent me some useful notes on Lugbara verbs, but unfortunately a serious illness prevented him from filling in my questionnaire. My own Lugbara field-notes were taken from natives outside their own country, and I had no means of telling whether their dialect was the purest Lugbara or not.[1]

---

[1] Comparison with the Lugbara of the New Testament shows considerable Keliko influence in my Lugbara material.

Madi.

I am greatly indebted to the C.M.S. Loka for lending me two (Pandikeri) Madi schoolboys, whom I was able to compare with Lokai speakers. In this way I was able to do some valuable dialectal work, in which I was also helped by the R.C. Mission at Loa.

Mr. P. B. Broadbent of the Civil Secretariat, Khartoum, gave me, through Professor Westermann, several of the Institute's 'linguistic guides', which had been filled in for various Sudan languages. Of these I have made particular use of the one in *Madi*, filled in by Rev. Fr. Bay of R.C. Mission, Loa; in *Keliko*, filled in by Police Corporal Yassa Akulu, under the supervision of Major D. Logan Gray; in *Kreish*,[1] filled in by Mr. D. J. Bethel, D.C. of Raga.

PART II. THE BONGO-BAKA-BAGIRMI GROUP.

Bongo.

I am, in the first place, indebted to Fr. Stephen Santandrea of the Missioni Africane, Kayango, for placing at my disposal the manuscript of an article of his on Bongo. I have unhesitatingly referred to this excellent work in order to supplement my own field-notes, and am glad to acknowledge my frequent indebtedness to the author.

'Beli.

In the same manuscript appear some notes on 'Beli, which are interesting in that they were taken on the language of the same prisoner whom I had previously examined in Wau (by kind permission of the local authorities).

Baka.

Mr. T. H. B. Mynors, during his Moru studies, had also made some notes on Baka, which he kindly passed on to me.

Sara.

I can never be sufficiently grateful to Professor D. Westermann and Dr. H. C. Melzian for giving me the notes they took on Sara Kaba during an African exhibition in Berlin in 1929. The rest of my Bagirmi-Sara material has had to be taken entirely from books, and these notes constitute the only reliable phonetic and tonetic material that I have from that part of Africa. Consequently their value in establishing my basis for comparative phonetics has been enormous.

PART III. THE NDOGO-SERE GROUP.

While at Wau I was able to do little more than take phonetic and vocabulary notes on these languages. Consequently the grammar section of Part III is built up almost entirely of comparative material collected by Father Stephen Santandrea, the manuscript of which he gave me long before it was published in typescript form in the Southern Sudan. Since then he has kept in constant touch with me and has answered numerous queries arising from his notes, besides lending me a valuable MS. on Golo.

[1] A full discussion of Kreish is to appear in a later volume of this series.

BIBLIOGRAPHY

WHERE the languages themselves are concerned, there is a surprisingly small bibliography. The following works were used mainly in the 'Introduction'. Books used in the Grammar sections are given in heavy type.

Mrs. E. O. Ashton. The Idea Approach to Swahili (*Bulletin of the S.O.S.*, 1935).
—— The Structure of a Bantu Language (ibid., 1936).
H. Barth. Sammlung und Bearbeitung Central-Afrikanischer Vokabularien. Gotha, 1862.
A. Burssens. Het Probleem der Kongoleesche Niet-Bantoetalen. (*Kongo-Overzee*, 1934.)
A. de Calonne-Beaufaict. *Azande: Introduction à une ethnographie générale des Bassins de l'Ubangi-Uele et del'Aruwimi*. Brussels, 1921.
G. Casati. *Ten Years in Equatoria*. London, 1891.
J. Czekanowski. *Forschungen im Nil-Kongo-Zwischengebiet*, vols. i and ii. Leipzig, 1917.
M. Delafosse. Essai sur le Peuple et la Langue Sara. Paris, 1898.
—— *Enquête coloniale dans l'Afrique Française*. Paris, 1930.
C. M. Doke. *Bantu Linguistic Terminology*. London, 1935.
—— *Textbook of Zulu Grammar*. London, 1931.
F. Eboué. *Langues Sango, Banda, Baya, Mandjia*. Paris, 1918.
—— *Les Peuples de l'Oubangui-Chari*. Paris, 1933.
Emin Pasha in Central Africa. London, 1888.
E. E. Evans-Pritchard. The Bongo. (*Sudan Notes and Records*, 1929.)
—— The Mberidi, &c. of the Bahr el Ghazal (ibid., 1931).
—— A Note on the Peoples of Amadi and Rumbek District (ibid., 1937).
I. L. Evans. *The British in Tropical Africa*. Cambridge, 1929.
H. Gaden. Essai de Grammaire de la Langue Baguirmienne. Paris, 1909.
M. Gaudefroy-Demombynes. Documents sur les Langues de l'Oubangui-Chari. Paris, 1906.
E. C. Gore. A Zande Grammar. London, 1931.
—— **A Zande and English Dictionary. London, 1931.**
J. A. de C. Hamilton. *The Anglo-Egyptian Sudan from Within*. London, 1935.
A. Hutereau. *Histoire des peuplades de l'Uele et de l'Ubangi*. Brussels, 1913.
O. Jespersen. *Language*. London, 1922.
—— *The Philosophy of Grammar*. London, 1924.
W. Junker. *Travels in Africa*. London, 1892.
C. R. Lagae and H. V. van den Plas. La Langue des Azande. Ghent, 1922.
P. M. Larken. Zande Notes. (S.N.R., 1923.)
J. Lukas. *Zentralsudanische Studien*. Hamburg, 1937.
—— *Die Logone-Sprache im Zentralen Sudan*. Leipzig, 1936.
—— The Linguistic Situation in the Lake Chad Area in Central Africa. (*Africa*, 1936.)
H. MacMichael. *The Anglo-Egyptian Sudan*. London, 1934.
J. Maes and O. Boone. *Les Peuplades du Congo Belge*. Brussels, 1935.
L. P. Mair. *Native Policies in Africa*. London, 1936.
A. Meillet and M. Cohen. *Les Langues du Monde*. Paris, 1924.
C. Meinhof. *Die Sprachen der Hamiten*. Hamburg, 1912.
L. Molinaro. Appunti di Grammatica della Lingua Madi. Verona, 1925.
L. F. Nalder. *A Tribal Survey of Mongalla Province*. Oxford, 1937.
H. Pedersen. *Linguistic Science in the Nineteenth Century*. Cambridge, Mass., 1931.
J. Petherick. *Egypt, the Soudan and Central Africa*.
Poutrin. *Principales Populations de l'Afrique Équatoriale Française*.

P. Ribero. Elementi di Lingua Ndogo. Verona, 1922.
Report of the Rejaf Language Conference. London, 1928.
S. Santandrea. The Belanda, Ndogo, &c. in the Bahr el Ghazal. (*S.N.R.* 1933.)
—— Il Gruppo Ndogo del Bahr-el-Ghazal (*Annali Lateranensi,* 1938).
G. Schweinfurth. Linguistische Ergebnisse einer Reise nach Centralafrika. Berlin, 1873.
—— *The Heart of Africa.* London, 1873.
C. G. and B. Z. Seligman. *Pagan Tribes of the Nilotic Sudan.* London, 1932.
R. C. Slatin. *Fire and Sword in the Sudan.* London, 1896.
F. Thonner. *Vom Kongo zum Ubangi.* Berlin, 1910.
E. Torday. African Races. (Spencer's *Descriptive Sociology.*) London, 1930.
A. N. Tucker. The Tribal Confusion round Wau. (*S.N.R.*, 1931.)
—— The Linguistic Situation in the Southern Sudan. (*Africa,* 1934.)
—— Survey of the Language Groups in the Southern Sudan. (*Bulletin of S.O.S.*, 1935.)
A. Vekens. *La Langue des Makere, des Medje et des Mangbettu.* Ghent, 1928.
M. J. W. The Belanda. (*S.N.R.*, 1923.)
A. Werner. *The Structure and Relationship of African Languages.* London, 1930.
D. Westermann. *Die Sudansprachen.* Hamburg, 1911.
—— *The Shilluk People.* Berlin, 1912.
—— Charakter und Einteilung der Sudansprachen. (*Africa,* 1935.)
J. Wils. *De Nominale Klassificatie in de Afrikaansche Negertalen.* Nijmegen, 1935.
G. Young. *Egypt.* London, 1927.

INTRODUCTION

Section I. TRIBAL

Chapter I. DISTRIBUTION OF THE EASTERN SUDANIC TRIBES.

„ II. HISTORY OF THE EASTERN SUDANIC TRIBES—THE INVASIONS OF THE WELE BASIN.

„ III. HISTORY OF THE EASTERN SUDANIC TRIBES (*continued*)—THE EFFECT OF THE INVASIONS.

Section II. LINGUISTIC

„ IV. CHARACTERISTICS OF AFRICAN LANGUAGE FAMILIES.

„ V. CHARACTERISTICS OF THE EASTERN SUDANIC LANGUAGES.

„ VI. SOME GENERAL PRINCIPLES AND DEFINITIONS UNDERLYING THE STUDY OF EASTERN SUDANIC GRAMMAR.

Section I. TRIBAL

CHAPTER I

DISTRIBUTION OF THE EASTERN SUDANIC TRIBES

1. Reference has already been made to the main groups of Eastern Sudanic speakers in and about the Southern Sudan. In this chapter each group will be analysed in detail. In the case of some tribes, attempts have been made at an exact census. In other cases only the number of *taxpayers* is given; in such cases a fair estimate of tribal strength may be obtained by multiplying the number of taxpayers by four.

THE MORU-MADI GROUP

2. This group comprises over 250,000 speakers of languages and dialects which are almost mutually intelligible, if one excepts Lendu. These languages stretch in a horseshoe bend from Amadi to Yei in Equatorial Province,[1] through the north-eastern corner of the Belgian Congo and the north-western corner of Uganda, and back again into Equatorial Province, Opari District. Both geographically and linguistically this chain of languages may be divided into three sub-groups, which can, for convenience, be called:
   i. The Northern, or Moru, dialects (Amadi and Maridi Districts).
   ii. The Central languages (Yei District and Belgian Congo).
   iii. The Southern or Madi sub-group (Uganda and Opari District).

I. The Moru Dialects (20,000 *speakers*)

3. The name 'Moru'[2] is of doubtful origin. It is used indiscriminately as an alternative name for a great many tribes and sub-tribes, and is applied even to some non-Moru-speaking tribes. The true Moru-speaking tribes are as follows:

4. The (MORU) MIZA (1,800 taxpayers) live south-east of Amadi under Chiefs Ndarago and Agangwa. There is another small section of the Miza living near the Moroägi, and a third (120 taxpayers) living and intermarrying with the Morokodo under Chief Hassan. The Miza dialect is now the language of education in the mission schools.

5. The (MORU) KEDIRU (1,300 taxpayers) live north of the Miza under Chief Wala. A branch of the Kediru nicknamed the MAKU'BA live under Chief Roba on the Tapari, in contact with the Nyangwara in the no-man's-land south of Tindalu.

6. The LAKAMA'DI live north of the Kediru on the Tali road under Sub-Chief Wura (under Chief Roba). These are the most northerly of the Moru and they live in contact with the (Bari-speaking) Mondari, with whom they intermarry.

7. The three dialects—Miza, Kediru, and Lakama'di—are so similar as to be almost identical.

8. The MOROÄNDRI[3] (850 taxpayers) live west of the Miza under Chiefs Ngere (Ngele) and Wajo.

---
[1] In what was formerly Mongalla Province.
[2] The true pronunciation is 'Moro' not 'Moru', but the latter spelling was adopted partly to avoid confusion, in missionary circles, with the South Sea Moro.
[3] In the tribal names Moroändri, Moroägi, and Morokodo it does not seem possible to omit the word 'Moro', at least, when speaking these languages. In the other tribal names the word 'Moro' may be left out at will.

INTRODUCTION. I. TRIBAL

9. The 'BĀLIMBĀ ('Böliba') (300 taxpayers) live south of the Miza adjoining Päjulu (the Bari-speaking 'Fajelu') territory under Chief Jambo.

10. These two dialects are almost identical, although 'Bälimbä has absorbed certain elements from the neighbouring Bari dialects.

11. The MOROÄGI (800 taxpayers) live west of the Moroändri on the road to Maridi in two small sections—the nearer under Chief Agangwa and the farther under Chiefs Madragi and Okupoi. A small section of the Miza is to be found living between them. A remnant of Moroägi, fugitives from the Azande, may also be found on the Tali road under Sub-Chief Mondo north of the Morokodo, and some 400 at Amadi itself.

12. The (MORU) WA'DI (325 taxpayers) are scattered about north of Maridi under Chiefs Okupoi and Madragi. Many so-called Wa'di are really Morokodo, and speak a Bongo-Baka language.

13. These two dialects are almost identical. In fact there is some doubt as to whether these people are not really one tribal unit.[1] Both these dialects are nearer to Moroändri than to Miza, but they also have much in common with Avukaya.

14. The Amadi District census for 1937 gives the following population statistics; here the number of subjects to each chief is stated, irrespective of tribe (this does not include Maridi District tribes):

Chief	Population	Tribe
Ndarago Lorola	5,675	Miza
Agangwa Warangwa (Agaŋwa Wäräŋwa)	2,302	Miza, Moroägi, Moroändri
Wajo Dengo	1,499	Moroändri
Ngere Abu (Ḍgere Ăbu)	1,398	Moroändri
Roba Koyongwa	3,274	Kediru
Wala Difo	1,962	Kediru
Jambo Loo	1,247	'Bälimbä
	17,357	

From the point of view of population, Miza is the most representative dialect of the Moru group; on the other hand, Moroändri has more in common (especially phonetically) with Madi on the one side and Avukaya on the other.

II. THE CENTRAL LANGUAGES (83,000 *speakers*)

15. The AVUKAYA[2] live principally in two sections between Maridi and Yei. The OJILA branch (750 taxpayers) lives largely between the Naam and Olo rivers, under Chief Okupoi, but reaches as far east as Chief Wajo. Another smaller section is to be found north of Chiefs Madragi and Mambe. The OJIGÄ branch (700 taxpayers) lives just north of Yei, but there is also a small section of these people, called AGAMORO living on the outskirts of Mundu country south of Maridi, and a further branch ('AJIGO') in the Belgian Congo between Aba and Faradje.

---

[1] Mynors reports that the Moroägi are only called so by the Miza, and prefer to call themselves Wa'di. Brown, however, asserts that the name Wa'di was chosen by Madragi to apply to the mixed Moroägi and Morokodo population under his jurisdiction.

[2] The name Avukaya or Abokaya is supposed by some to be of Zande origin, and various theories are current as to how it came to be applied.

16. The KELIKO or KALIKO (real name MA'DI) (1,110 taxpayers) occupy the high plateau in the southern part of Yei River District under Chief Aluma, and are grouped in the following clans: Panyana (ruling clan), Poni, Gulumbi, Ayuru, Orugu, Bora, Nyanga, Nye. There is another section of Keliko (9,138) under Chief Kalika(?) in the Belgian Congo south-east of Aba in the territory of the Alur-Lugbara.[1]

17. It is doubtful whether the BÖRI or BERRI have separate tribal existence. Logan Gray states that they live in the Belgian Congo, and gives a short vocabulary of their language. I have been unable to confirm this. It is more likely that the various scattered groups of a BÖRI clan speak either Keliko or Päjulu ('Fajelu') according to the people they live among. Mynors informs me that there is a Böri rain-makers' clan among the Moro, whose graves resemble those of Kakwa rain-makers.

18. The LOGO (some 60,000) are mostly to be found in the Congo in the triangle of country between Aba, Faradje, and Watsa[2] where there seem to be four sections of them. A few Logo are to be found in Yei District of Mongalla Province. The Belgian Government statistics concerning this tribe are as follows: 'In the territory of the Logo-Dongo (head township, Faradje) there are 75,581 inhabitants, of whom 62,941 are indigenous. They are divided into Logo-Agambi (19,976), Logo-Doka (31,510), Bari-Logo[3] (4,292), and Dongo-Tedemu (7,163).'

19. Living among the Bari-Logo, but speaking a distinct dialect of their own, are the KAZIBATI, but nothing is known of these people beyond their name.

20. The NDO (13,947) live just south of the Logo in the territory of the Alur-Lugbara, centre Aungba. Not much is known of these people, but they are said to be related to the OKABO (or OKEBU), who are blacksmiths among the Lendu and Alur, and who speak Lendu, Logo, Lugbara, and Alur, according to the people they live among.

21. Calonne-Beaufaict and Hutereau[4] both refer to scattered groups of Ndo or Ndogo ('Do' or 'Dongo' according to Hutereau), living between the Dungu and Kibali rivers. Calonne Beaufaict tries to relate these tribes to the Kreish (op. cit., p. 148), but they are far more likely to be related to the Ndo of Lugbara-Alur territory, especially as they, too, are renowned as smiths (p. 154). See, however, under 'Kreish', §231.

22. The Central languages are not so closely allied as the Moru dialects. Keliko and Logo are, on the whole, mutually intelligible, while the Agambi dialect of Logo

---

[1] Hutereau, p. 22: 'The Kaliko, who speak a dialect of Logo, extend from Aba towards the basin of the Nile.'

[2] Ibid., p. 27: 'The Logo occupy the basin of the Dungu from Faradje to the junction of the Abuku, which they occupy leaving the Dungu; from the junction of the Abuku they extend towards the south, occupying the lower right bank of the Aro, tributary of the Nzoro or Obi; thence they form the boundary of their territory by following the line of the hills Lay and Libo towards the hills Bagpwa and Tendebi; from Tendebi they extend towards the upper Oru and from that point to Faradje.'

Maes et Boone, p. 252: 'The territory of the Logo extends along the basin of the Aba above Faradje; it is bounded in the west by the meridian of Faradje; in the south it covers the basin of the Nzoro or Obi from that meridian as far as 30° 40 long. E.'

[3] Hutereau, p. 29: 'To the Lugbara may be related the Bari, riverains of the section of the Kibali included between the Nzoro and the Dungu.' Note that these Bari have nothing in common with the Bari of Rejaf.

[4] Ibid., p. 317: 'The Dongo and the Do people the basin of the Kibali above the Ambia and reach as far as the Lowa, separating the Lugbara, the Madi, and the Logo. On the left bank of the Kibali the Do have the Kebo and Alulu (Alur) as neighbours.'

is very like the Ojigä dialect of Avukaya. Ojila may be said to form a bridge between these languages and the Moru dialects, in that it is the most easily understood by Moru speakers.

The Madi Sub-group (240,000 *speakers*)

23. The LUGBARA (also called 'Lugwari') live south of the Logo with centre Aru[1] (50,844), and extend into the West Nile District of Uganda (139,348), where they are found mostly in the following counties: Logiri, Adumi, Aringa, Terego, Maracha, Offudde, Omugo, and Vurra. A few (171 taxpayers) are to be found in Yei District of the Southern Sudan; their dialect of Lugbara is very closely akin to Keliko.

24. There would seem to be four main dialects of Lugbara:
Pajulu (High Lugbara), spoken near Arua;
Oruleo-ti (Low Lugbara), the most widespread dialect;
Kulu'ba, spoken in Aringa County;
Ma'de, spoken in Logiri County.

25. The following information on the distribution of these dialects was kindly supplied me by Father Ramponi:

Aringa Sub-chiefs
Aringa, Odravo, Yumbe, Rumogi, Kei.
Dialect: Kulu'ba.

Adumi Sub-chiefs
Mbaraka, Osu, Nyio.
Dialect: similar to Pajulu.

Aiivu Sub-chiefs
Yole (Terego group), Oluko, Pajulu, Aroi.
Dialect: Pajulu.

Logiri Sub-chiefs
Logiri, Lazzebo, Bondo.
Dialect: Ma'de. (Note: Madi spoken near Rhino Camp.)

Maracha Sub-chiefs
Oluvu, Maracha, Oleba, Kabora.
Dialect: Oruleo-ti (Terego dialect, or Omugo).

Ofude Sub-chiefs
Tara, Yivu, Kisimoro.
Dialect: Oruleo-ti (see Maracha).

Omugo Sub-chiefs
Omugo, Udupi.
Dialect: Oruleo-ti.

---

[1] *Hutereau*, p. 28: 'The Lugbara occupy the entire upper basin of the Kibali river and the Obi or Nzoro river. They extend to the west towards Mount Wati and occupy the valleys in which flow the tributaries of the Albert Nile. The Lugbara who are established between the Loa (Lowa) and the Kibali take the name of Madi.' p. 321: 'The Lugbara people the territories of the upper basins of the Nzoro and the Loa; the Madi the whole basin of the Aru and the right basin of the Home.'

Maes et Boone, p. 256: 'The Lugware inhabit a territory bounded in the north by the basin of the Obi or Nzoro; in the east by approximately the 30° 15′ long. E.; in the south it covers the basin of the upper Wele or Kibali; in the west it extends as far as 30° long. approximately.'

Terego Sub-chiefs
  Terego, Ochodri, Katrini.
  Dialect: Oruleo-ti.
Vura Sub-chiefs
  Vuraa, Arivo, Ajia, Opia.
  Dialect: Pajulu.

26. The MADI[1] (pronounced Ma'di) of Uganda (40,307) are to be found in Aiivu County, West Nile District, and also in greater or lesser numbers through most of the north-east counties in Gulu District—Dufile, Adropi, Oyowi, Zaipi, Adzugopi, Laropi, Meturu, Metuli, and Moyo, the River Koshi serving as southern boundary between them and the Lugbara. The Moyo dialect is the most widespread Madi dialect in Uganda; the dialect spoken in Aiivu County is very like Lugbara.

27. The Madi further extend into the Southern Sudan into the western section of Opari District (1,022 taxpayers), but many of the Sudan 'Madi' are not of pure Madi stock, being a mixture of several totally unrelated tribes. These people speak two dialects of Madi, besides their own tribal dialects:

  MADI LOKAI in the south (2,000 speakers), and
  MADI PANDIKERI in the north (5,000 speakers).

28. The following is a tribal analysis taken from the official report on Opari District in 1932: There are seven 'Madi' chiefs in Opari District, whose tribes, taken in order from south to north, are:

Southern Madi
  Ch. Surur (population 1,200), genuine Madi related to the people of ex-Chief Rossu of Kajokaji.
  Ch. Odego (population 2,800), Lokoya (Oxoriok), related to the Lokoya of Lyria.
  Ch. Ito Gaperi (population 400), 'Fajelu' (Päjulu), related to the 'Fajelu' of Yei District.

These three tribes speak Lokai Madi, which is similar to Uganda Madi, and is the language of education in mission schools in Opari District.

Northern Madi
  Ch. Dar (population 3,200), genuine Madi related to the people of Labongo in Gulu District, Uganda.
  Ch. Iberu (population 800), Päjulu related to the 'Fajelu' of Yei District.
  Ch. Geri (population 800), Bari related to the Bari of Chief Lorilo Kombo of Central District.
  Ch. Nyani-Kuyu (population 250), Kuku related to the people of Morali, Kajo Kaji.

These four northern and eastern tribes speak Pandikeri Madi, which has more in common with Moru (Moroändri dialect) than Lokai has. I have heard of a third dialect 'BURULO said to be spoken around Nimule, but was unable to follow it up. The few words I met with were like Pandikeri.

29. The LULUBA (real name ULU'BO) (766 taxpayers) constitute the vanguard of the Ma'di penetration into Opari District, and now appear left high and dry on the

---

[1] *Maes et Boone*, p. 262: 'The Madi inhabit the valley of the Nile, on the right bank between Wadelai and the mouth of the river Aswa; on the left bank between Wadelai and the mouth of the River Kaya. There are several groups of Madi in the territory of the Belgian Congo, among the Alur and Lugware.'

Luluba Hills, forty miles south-east of Juba and west of the Lokoya, in three main villages, Lumer, Lokaliri and Larongo. Their dialect is more like Pandikeri than Lokai, with some Päjulu vocabulary since there has been much intermarrying with that tribe. Nearly all the Luluba speak Bari as a second language.

30. The Southern languages are mutually intelligible to a fairly high degree. Lugbara in many ways, however, may be regarded as a bridge between Madi and Logo.

31. All the Moru-Madi languages (with the exception of Lendu which will be discussed separately) are so closely related that any speaker of one would very soon be able to adapt himself if brought to live away from the speakers of another. Logan Gray reports that he was able to make a Lugbara chief and an Avukaya understand each other to their mutual astonishment, each speaking his own language. Hitherto, all communications between these two tribes had been carried out in Lingala, the lingua franca of the district. He also reports that a Böri of Yei District, when on a visit to Opari District, was able to talk to the Madi in his own language. My own questionings of a Moru speaker, whom I had with me on tour, brought out the fact that he found Avukaya (Ojila) and Madi (Pandikeri) the easiest languages to understand and Logo the most difficult. He himself was a Moroändri.

32. The LENDU may also be said to belong to the Moru-Madi group, yet their language cannot be understood by the other members. For one thing the divergence in pronunciation of words of common origin is too great (the Lendu having evolved a 'spitting' pronunciation of syllables containing, in many cases, consonants only), while Lendu has many grammatical constructions foreign to the other Moru-Madi languages. It is quite evident, from vocabulary evidence as well, that Momvu elements have crept in, as suggested by Czekanowski, p. 595.

33. The Lendu (151,925) live in the Congo west of Lake Albert with centre Djugu,[1] while a smaller branch of Lendu (5,985) is to be found in Alur-Lugbara territory; some have overflowed into the West Nile District of Uganda (2,670) and live mostly in Okoro County.

The real name of the tribe is 'BALE or 'BALENDRU and their language is 'BAADHA or 'BALEDHA.[2] They have often been erroneously classified as Bantu.

THE BONGO-BAKA-BAGIRMI GROUP

34. The members of this group are more scattered and diverse than those of any other language group in the Southern Sudan. They stretch from Amadi District in Southern Province in a broken line to Lake Tchad, and it is possible that there are yet further members to be discovered outside this area. Mutual understanding between the tribes is absent except over relatively small areas. By comparison of vocabulary and grammar, however, the members of this widespread group may easily be determined.

35. The BONGO in Schweinfurth's time were evidently far more numerous than now. At present they are to be found mainly in two small settlements, one, under Chief Sabun, on the Bussere River, just south of Wau (300 taxpayers) and extending south along the Bo road, and the other larger settlement farther east near Tonj, under Chief Kerasit (500 taxpayers).

[1] *Maes et Boone*, p. 98: 'The Balendu inhabit the western shores of Lake Albert, south of Mahaji; they extend approximately as far as 29° 50′ long. E. in the west, as far as 2° 30′ lat. N. in the north, and 1° lat. N. in the south.'   [2] *dh* pronounced like the *th* of English 'the'.

DISTRIBUTION OF THE EASTERN SUDANIC TRIBES

36. Major Brown also reports an isolated colony living along the Iba River from 5° 50′ N. to 6° 10′ N., calling themselves BUNGÖ. From the vocabulary he has given me there is no doubt that they are a Bongo offshoot. There is also a Bungö village headman Toi under Chief Rikita. These people speak Zande as well as Bongo.

37. Evans-Pritchard[1] gives the following sub-tribes of the Tonj Bongo: Gir, Kolongo, Dobor, Domor, Karakiti (probably the largest to-day), Mor, Gubi, Domuku, Kere, Ngudu, Kolanda, Moro, Nguru, Mbor, Muku, Dogodjo, Dawai, Kela, Bio, Landa, Mbelembe, Ngulumbeli, Lelo, Dobodo, Ngongo, Bobur, Ngboku, Ngbanguru, Ngelo, Babagimi, Gomono, Ngulupara, Mokobi, Neri, Longo.

The Gubi, Kela, and Karakiti, he adds, are probably numerically superior to the other tribes. Those tribes living along the Wau-Tonj road are much interspersed with Azande.

38. The BAKA live fairly thickly round Maridi (2,033 taxpayers) under Chiefs Nganzio, Lanzima, Bakinda, and Senambia, and extend southwards over the Congo border. There is another section of Baka north-west of Yei (380 taxpayers) under Chief Gungo, and two further isolated groups (4,000) in the Congo itself west and east of Faradje.[2] The Yei Baka are divided into eight clans under the following heads: Gungo (Chief's family), Dobo (clan Bandwa), Minjare (clan Waraga), Mavuro (clan Gwandama), Rongo (clan Shambellinga), Ndada (clan Abrahim), Gumu (clan Adalla), Gulomi (clan Mousa). A few Baka (and Mundu) are to be found under Chiefs Okupoi and Madragi north of Maridi.

39. The Baka form the southern end of a linguistic chain, stretching up through Moru country to Rumbek. Those that live in the Moru District cause most confusion to investigators, since they too have adopted the common name 'Moro'.

40. The MOROKODO live mostly on the Amadi-Maridi road just west of Amadi under Chief Hassan (625 taxpayers). A smaller section (325 taxpayers) is to be found in the region north of Maridi, under Chief Madragi, while another smaller group (100 taxpayers) live among the Ma'di near Chief Dokolo (but still under Hassan).

41. North of Amadi are four small tribes which are so intermingled as to be hard to locate accurately.

The (MORO) BITI live under Chief Dokobo, on the Tali road. The MA'DI[3] (100 taxpayers) live north of these under Chief Dokolo. The (MORO) WIRA (250 taxpayers) live farther north still, but under the same chief. The MÄ'DU live with the Lakama'di under Chief Wala. All these people are often mistaken for true Moru.

42. The languages Morokodo and Ma'di are almost identical, Biti and Mä'du are also closely allied to each other and to Nyamusa, while Wira is partly like Morokodo and partly like Lori. On the whole, however, these 'Moru' dialects are the most closely connected of all the Bongo-Baka group.

43. The NYAMUSA (900 taxpayers) live north of the Wira, also under Chief Dokolo. Their language may be regarded as a bridge between the so-called 'Moru' dialects

---

[1] *The Bongo*, p. 17.
[2] *Hutereau*, p. 27: 'The Baka of the right bank of the Atwa extend as far as the upper reaches of the rivers and streams Garamba, Kinibiti, Nakue, Bukalie, Aka.'
Maes et Boone, p. 5: 'The territory of the Abaka lies for the most part outside the Belgian Congo; it includes the region watered by the upper reaches of the tributaries of the rivers Issu-Ibba, Meridi, Jalo, and Aka, south of lat. 5° N.
[3] Not to be confused with the Madi of Opari District. See Schweinfurth, vol. i, p. 523 footnote.

and the so-called 'Jur' dialects to the north. The Nyamusa are bounded by the Atwot on the north and the Mondari on the east.

The Nyamusa are evidently the 'Bufi' of Schweinfurth and Emin Pasha.[1] Both these authorities mention another tribe, the 'Lesi' speaking a related language, but no trace of these people can be found.

44. The northern (or rather north-western) section of this linguistic chain is composed of the 'Rumbek Jur'[2] (7,268), stretching from just north-west of the Nyamusa to just south of Rumbek. They consist of half a dozen small tribes, hemmed in on the north by the Ngok Dinka and on the east by the Agar and Atwot.

45. The LORI live north-west of the Nyamusa, east of M'volo, and along the M'volo-Gnop road. The LALI and MODO, speaking an almost identical language, live close to them, exact location uncertain. The language Lori is similar to Wira and is spoken by many so-called Wa'di to the south.

46. The GBERI live west of M'volo. The almost extinct MITTU (real name WETU) speak practically the same dialect; a few families of this tribe are to be found mixed with Mundu, Babuckur, and Morokodo. The language Mittu (or Wetu), judging from the vocabularies of Schweinfurth and Evans-Pritchard, is almost identical with Morokodo.

47. By far the most numerous of the 'Jur' are the 'BELI, extending from north of Toinya Post to the Gok Dinka on the north, the Agar Dinka on the east, and the Bongo on the west. Between Toinya Post and M'volo are the SOPI (SOFI), who are probably a subsection of the 'Beli; the languages are almost identical, and are the most closely related to Bongo of all the 'Jur' languages.

48. The Amadi District census for 1937 gives the following population statistics; here again (as in § 14) the number of subjects to each chief is given, irrespective of tribe:

Amadi region—'Moru'

Chief	Population	Tribe
Hassan Nyari	2,411	Morokodo
Dokolo lo Amu	2,141	Nyamusa, Wira

M'volo region—'Jur Sofi'[3]

Chief	Population	Tribe
Korwai Kerjok	903	'Beli
Kozo Lobi	774	Modo
Yesi Lakada	520	Modo
Kondo Agoi	338	'Beli
Jok Abot	277	Modo, Lali
Doko'bo Dongoli	781	Lori

Toinya region—'Jur 'Beli'

Chief	Population	Tribe
Ndia Agar	904	'Beli and Bongo (about 50)
Ngolo Makoi	979	'Beli
Tio Mading	967	'Beli and Wetu (about 40)
Logo Dorogo	437	Gberi and Wetu (about 20)
Agok Magong	388	'Beli
Total	11,820	'Moru' and 'Jur' speakers.

[1] 'Nyamusa is the name of this district, which is inhabited by the Bufi tribe.' Emin Pasha, p. 321.
[2] Not to be confused with the Shilluk speaking 'Jur' (Luo) near Wau. The word 'Jur' means 'stranger' in Dinka, and the Dinka apply the term to all foreigners except Europeans and Arabs.
[3] The name 'Sofi' seems here to refer to a collection of tribes rather than to one tribe.

49. Such are the main members of the Bongo-Baka group in the Southern Sudan. Of late, however, some interesting information on the very confused population of the Western District of the (former province) Bahr el Ghazal has come to light:

The YULU[1] (300 taxpayers), KARA and BINGA[2] (pronounced Biŋa) (270 taxpayers), AJA (200 taxpayers), and perhaps the RUNGA (150), and NGULGULI (280 taxpayers), show remarkable vocabulary resemblance to Bongo-Baka, although no grammatical material is as yet forthcoming. These tribes are for the most part an overflow from tribes in French Equatorial Africa, the boundary of which is very near. In fact, a section of BINGA (706) is given in the French Government statistics for Oubangui-Chari as far west as the Département of Oubangui-Ouaka (a region of Bambari), the present home of the Banda tribes. The languages Binga and Yulu are more like Baka than Bongo, but the language Kara (in vocabulary at least) might almost be classified with the Sara dialects of Oubangui-Chari.

The SINYAR,[3] who live on the border of Darfur and French Equatorial Africa at Mogororo (lat. 12° N.), also show a vocabulary resemblance to Bongo-Baka. Theirs seems to be the only language in Darfur to do so.

50. Outside the Southern Sudan, enough vocabulary evidence has been collected by M. Gaudefroy-Demombynes[4] to trace this group along the Chari River in French Oubangui-Chari as far as Fort Archambault. The representatives in this area he classes under the BARMA group and they comprise the languages BARMA, BABALIA, DISSA, BULALA, and the multitudinous SARA dialects (Sara Denjé, Sara Guléi, Sara Baï, Sara Lak, Kaba, Hòro, Ngama, Valé, Télé, and Tané).

51. Delafosse[5] divides the Sara into two groups, West and East, of which he says:

West Sara, between the Chari River and the Middle Logone River. 'Under this appellation are grouped a very great number of tribes, of which the principal tribes, from east to west, are: the Horo, the Tounia, the Sara Guleï, the Sara Daï, the Sara Demi, the Mbaï, the Lake or Lag, &c. Each of these may be divided in its turn into an infinite number of sub-tribes.'[6]

East Sara, right bank of the Chari River, from 8° to 9° 5′ N. 'Their most important groups are around the depressions through which flow the Bahr Salamat and the Aouk, tributaries of the Chari. To the east they extend as far as Lake Iro, to the west they just pass the line Golkidja, Gouflé, Djinjeboa. Their colonies are extremely numerous, and each bears the name of the village it inhabits: thus one has the Sara Dagui, the Sara Ndioko, the Sara Bodo, the Sara Manga, the Sara Ngaki, the Sara Njounjou, &c.'

52. *The Kabba*, which Delafosse separates from the East Sara, have also a large number of small groups—the Kabba-Mara, the Kabba-Simmé, the Kabba-Marabiri, the Kabba-Kono, the Kabba-Boa, the Kabba-Bédoum, the Kabba-Binanga, &c., &c. They occupy the junction of the Chari with the Bahr Salamat and the Aouk. One can hardly distinguish the Kabba from the Eastern Sara, he

---

[1] Fr. Santandrea was the first to point out that Yulu was a member of the Bongo-Baka group.
[2] Hibbert, in his historical map of this area, divides the Binga into several subsections—Lali, Raja, Shalla, Moro, Ngaranja—but nothing of these is known, and the territory they once occupied, on the borders of Darfur and Dar Runga, is now uninhabited according to Bethell.
[3] From information supplied me by P. B. Broadbent and A. J. Arkell.
[4] Op. cit., which takes into account the previous investigations of Barth, Nachtigal, Decorse, and Delafosse.
[5] *Enquête Coloniale dans l'Afrique Française*, pp. 119–30.
[6] A noticeable feature of Bongo tribal organization before the arrival of the Arabs, see § 37.

states, but they differ completely from the Western Sara. He is inclined to relate them to the Dissa of Lake Iro.

53. The French Government statistics for this tribal area are as follows:

Valé (900)	Département of Ouham-Pendé in region of Batangafo. (Not listed as a Sara tribe.)
SARA (148,190)	Divided into the following tribes:
Sara Toumak (7,700)	Département of Chari-Bangoran NW. of subdivision of Koumra.
Sara Goulaye (48,190)	Départ. of Chari-Bangoran W. sub. of Koumra and also Départ. of Logone sub. of Laï (9,190).
Sara Daï (8,800)	Départ. of Chari-Bangoran sub. Moïssala and Koumra.
Sara M'baye (22,000)	Départ. of Chari-Bangoran sub. of Moïssala.
Sara Madjingaye } (11,500)	Départ. of Basin of River Sara bounded by Fort-Archambault, Koumra, and Moïssala.
Sara N'gama (7,000)	Subdivisions of Batangafo (2,500) and Moïssala (4,500).
Sara Kaba (19,700)	Region of Fort-Archambault and Départ. of Ouham-Pendé (subdivisions of Batangafo, Bouca, Paoua, and Bossangoa).
Sara Tounia (1,000)	Region NE. of Fort-Archambault.
Sara Kaba Goula } (4,600)	N. of sub. of Fort-Archambault on River Salamat.
Sara Kaba Djingé } (2,500)	Region of Kyabé, basin of River Kéita.
Sara Kaba N'démé } (5,500)	East of sub. of Fort-Archambault.
Sara Tié (3,500)	Region bounded by the rivers Salamat and Mindjick.
Sara Kaba M'banga } (5,000)	Region bounded by River Kéita in north and River Aouk in south.
Sara Kaba (1,200)	Subdivision of N'délé to the north of N'délé.

54. 'These diverse tribes', the report continues, 'inhabit the "Pays Sara", of which the centre is Fort-Archambault, and which consists in the basin formed by the confluence of the Chari River with the Rivers Salamat, Kéita, Aouk, and Sara, as well as the basins of the sources of these last-named.'

55. Finally, south-east of Lake Tchad, are the BAGIRMI (25,500), whose language also shows considerable resemblance to Bongo, as already remarked by Gaden,[1] Barth,[2] Schweinfurth,[3] and others. The Bagirmi are a very mixed race, containing both Sudanic and Arab elements.

56. Related to the Bagirmi[4] (according to Gaden, p. 2) are the KUKA on the lower course of the Wadaïan Batha, the BULALA in Lake Fitri region (according to Gaden the latter adopted the Kuka language after conquering this region), the KENGA living in the mountains in semi-independence over against the people of Wadai, the NGAMA living west of the Gribingui River, and the NDUKA on the Gribingui, whither they were driven by the Sultan of Kouti from Ba Mingui.

57. These people, though speaking closely related languages, show very great ethnological differences. The Bagirmi and Kuka have attained a fairly high level of Islamic civilization, but the other tribes, like the Sara, still live in a very primitive way.

58. Delafosse[5] gives the confines of the Bagirmi as follows: 'The empire of Baguirmi

---

[1] *Essai de Grammaire de la Langue Banguirmienne.*
[2] *Sammlungen und Bearbeitungen Central Afrikanischer Vokabularien.*
[3] *Linguistische Ergebnisse einer Reise nach Centralafrika.*
[4] See also Lukas, *The Linguistic Situation in the Lake Chad Area in Central Africa*. The author informs me from personal experience that Bulala, Kuka, and Mudogo are all practically identical and all closely related to Bagirmi.
[5] *Enquête Coloniale dans l'Afrique Française*, p. 132. I retain here his spelling of tribal names and places.

extends from Bousso and Melfi to beyond Fort Lamy, and from the right bank of the Chari to the frontiers of the Ouadaï' (Wadai Kingdom).

59. Of the other tribes in that region he says: 'The nucleus of the population of lower and middle Baguirmi consists in the Boua-Kara, the Sarouo, and the Barma, indigenous tribes closely connected to the Sara. With these one should mention the Babalia, relatively small in number now, but the descendants of a strong tribe which once occupied the regions between Lake Tchad and Djimtilo. They were driven out of their original habitat by Ouadaï raids. Besides in Baguirmi, where they live in scattered colonies, they form an important group in the neighbourhood of Kouka.'

60. 'Amidst this ethnical chaos, two tribes . . . have conserved their own characteristics, the Kotoko and the Boulala.'

61. 'The Kotoko are riverains of the Lower Chari and of the delta of the river . . . According to Decorse they are divided into three groups—the Lagouéré on the Logone where they are mixed with the Mousgou, the Semsir at Kousseri, the Soungoualkoné at Goulféï. . . . There is little to distinguish these people from the Barma. . . . They have the same customs and a language very closely related, if not identical.'[1]

62. 'The Boulala, who once played an important role in Baguirmi and Kanem, are now situated near Lake Fitri, whence they extend westwards as far as Moïto. . . . Next to them one meets groups of Kouka, who have the same origin.'

63. Professor Labouret's report on these tribes, as obtained from Fort Lamy, runs as follows:

'The tribes Kenga, Kouka, Médogo, and Baguirmi seem to have the same origin according to the Administration. The tribe Kenga would seem to be the mother tribe, originating from the mountainous regions of the Guerra and Abou-Telfame. The Kenga and associated sub-tribes live in the subdivision of Mongo; the Kouka in the mountainous country of the Adjer Médogo.

'My correspondent assures me that the Ndouka are not known at Lake Tchad. There is, however, a tribe Ndoka, but this belongs to the Banda group and lives in Dar Kouti in the neighbourhood of Ndélé.'[2]

64. The Fort Lamy statistics for these tribes are (I retain here the French spelling):

	Tribes	Subdivision	Population
1.	Kenga	Mongo	16,750
	Diongor	,,	19,350
	Bidio	,,	10,750
	Sokoro	Melfi	10,900
	Barain	,,	3,700
	Sabba	,,	6,700
	Kirdi Djonkour	Aboudeia	3,450
	,, Toram	,,	2,550
	,, Birguid	,,	1,900
		Total	76,050

[1] The linguistic aspect of this statement is not borne out by a comparison of Bagirmi with the three Kotoko dialects treated by Lukas (*Zentralsudanische Studien*)—Kuseri, Gulfei, Schoe. Vocabulary affinities are entirely lacking. Lukas, however (*Die Logone Sprache*, p. 7), classifies the Kotoko and Logone languages together as a branch of the Tchado-Hamitic group. [2] See Map 4.

	Tribes	Subdivision	Population
2.	Kouka (Aouni)	Bokoro	7,400
	„ (Koundjouroux)	Ati	8,000
	„ (Mendélé)	„	2,150
	„ (Am Dina)	Oum-Hadjer	3,550
	Médogo	Ati	4,300
	Boulala	„	17,450
	Abou Semen	„	1,800
		Total	44,650
3.	Baguirmiens	Massénya	25,500

65. The Bagirmi of Gaden is the dialect spoken in the neighbourhood of Massénya, which, according to the author, differs in only a few words from the 'provincial' dialects of Koubar (east of Massénya) and the riverain villages of the Chari. Gaden calls the language 'Tar Bârma' in contra-distinction to the 'Tar Bágrimma' of Barth and Nachtigal—which name Gaden regards as archaic. Barth's Bagirmi, which differs to a certain extent from that of Gaden (especially in verbal conjugation, where it approaches the Sara dialects), was obtained 'with the assistance of the excellent patriot and the very intelligent and pious Bu-Bakr from Bákada.'[1]

66. Of the nature of the language Gaden says: 'Although preserving all the behaviour of isolating languages, Bagirmi has entered upon the period of agglutination. Indigenous Bagirmi words are in general either monosyllabic or dissyllabic, and begin with a consonant. The great majority of them are invariable, and present the same physiognomy; only their meaning permits one to classify them as nouns, verbs, qualificatives, or elements of relation. There is a category of verbs, however, which present two different forms according to the tense they express. This is a remarkable peculiarity.'[2]

67. The Sara dialect analysed by Delafosse was obtained from a boy who was born at Goudongou, a place situated 'non loin du Bahar-Sara', kidnapped by slavers at an early age, and ultimately taken over by the French in an engagement with the Arabs. The Sara dialect analysed by Westermann and Melzian was obtained from a native of Moyen Chari in the neighbourhood of Fort Archambault, who was taking part in an exhibition in the Berlin Zoo in the summer of 1929. The two dialects are widely divergent, that of Delafosse being nearer Bagirmi.

68. Previous comparisons of languages in the Bongo-Bagirmi group have been made mainly on vocabulary evidence, but with the help of Gaden's, Barth's, and Delafosse's researches it is possible to use grammatical criteria as well, and the evidence on this point is very instructive.

69. The grammar of Bagirmi and Sara has more in common with that of Morokodo and Nyamusa than with that of Bongo and Baka, which is surprising, seeing that these eastern tribes are the farthest removed in actual distance.

70. From the vocabulary points of view, Sara has much in common with Baka, Bongo, and Yulu, while the two Western District dialects, Kara and Aja, could almost be called Sara dialects. Bongo and 'Beli, on the one hand, and Bagirmi on the other, stand in separate categories, though, of course, Bongo has fairly close affinities with Baka, and Bagirmi with Sara. Baka, as has already been stated, has many affinities with Mundu, a language outside this group.

[1] Op. cit., vol. i, p. xv.
[2] Gaden, p. 4. See also § 359.

THE NDOGO-SERE GROUP ('BELANDA'—'BASIRI')

71. This group consists of four dialects, so closely allied as to be mutually intelligible. The speakers of these dialects live largely west and south-west of Wau.

72. The NDOGO[1] (750 taxpayers) live twenty miles west of Wau, largely on the Wau–Dem Zubeir road. Their language is the accepted 'group' language for the district.

73. The SERE (also called 'BASIRI') (250 taxpayers) live west of the Ndogo, where the same road crosses the Pongo (Kpango) River. The main bulk of the Sere, however, live in French Equatorial Africa north of the Mbomu River and between the tributaries Boku and Kere. The Congo Sere (3,000–4,000) live on the opposite bank of the Mbomu River in the District Ndoruma, where they form a 'chefferie' apart under Chief Gatanga. Their language, though much subject to Zande vocabulary influence, is much nearer Ndogo than the Sere spoken in the Sudan.[2] The French Government statistics show a further small section (316) living as far west as the Subdivision Damara in the Département of Haute Sangha-M'poko, on the north bank of the Ubangi River, down stream from Bangui.

Hutereau (p. 28) notes a few families of Sere living in the basin of the Sili River (tributary of the Wele River, north-east of Amadi in the Belgian Congo).

Calonne-Beaufaict gives the following main divisions of the Sere: Agele, Adimbomu (lit. born on the Mbomu), Yakoali, Dobanda, Dabodo, Yakumbanze (op. cit., p. 95).

74. The BAI (250 taxpayers) (sometimes called 'Bari'[3] and often confused with the 'Baré') live on the Wau–Dem Zubeir road west of the Sere.

75. The BIRI (or BVIRI, commonly called 'BELANDA' or Mve-Gumba) (1,000 taxpayers) live on the Belanda circular road, which leaves Wau and after a southern detour joins the Dem Zubeir road near the Geti River. Another branch of the Biri (300 taxpayers) may be found near Dem Zubeir, and a further branch (250 taxpayers) on the road to Tembura. Their language is very like Bai.

76. The following are the main Biri clans:

(From Evans Pritchard): Fanzingo, Famangde, Mveungu, Mvegbogo, Fumono, Fairi.
(From Santandrea): Fanguru, Mbvendogo, Bambvi, Fadongo.

77. The name 'Belanda' is probably of Bongo origin and is used to denote the members of two distinct tribes, speaking totally different languages, but living together, intermarrying, and sharing the same customs, dances, &c. These two tribes are (i) the above-mentioned *Biri* (or Gamba or Mve-Gumba), who speak a Ndogo dialect, and (ii) the *Bor* (or Mve-Rodi), who speak a Shilluk dialect. Both peoples are called 'Abaré' by the Azande[4] and 'Belanda' by the Arabs.

---

[1] Calonne-Beaufaict (p. 132) confounds these people with the Gbaya-Ndogo (a Kreish subtribe called 'Nduggo' by Schweinfurth) and with groups of 'Ndogo' or 'Ndo' on the Dungu and Kibali tributaries of the Wele in Belgian Congo (p. 148). The latter are far more probably remnants of the Ndo found now among the Lendu and Lugbara (see §§ 20–1).

[2] Information from Fr. Santandrea in collaboration with Fr. Albert De Graer of the Congo Mission.

[3] Not to be confused with the *Bai* clan of the Belanda, nor with *Sara-Bai*, nor with the *Bari-Logo*, nor with the *Bari* of the old Lado Enclave.

[4] This will explain Calonne-Beaufaict's problem of the 'Abarè' or 'Bari' (op. cit., p. 116). For a fuller discussion see my article, 'The Tribal Confusion around Wau' (*S.N.R.*, 1931).

78. Scattered clusters of all four Ndogo sub-tribes may be found at intervals on the road from Wau to the Zande country and on the circular road north-west of Tembura.

It is probable that further investigation outside the Sudan will corroborate the view, held by many, that these languages are merely a sub-group within a much larger linguistic group, embracing Mundu and Bangba. (See § 85.)

ZANDE (750,000)

79. The Zande language is spoken consistently in the Southern Sudan south of lat. 6° 30′ and west of Maridi long. 29° 30′.[1] At one time Zande bade fair to oust all other Sudanic languages in the Southern Sudan—the Maridi-Amadi conglomeration, the Ndogo languages at Wau, and even a good many of the Western District languages. Since the enforced retirement of the Zande conquerors, however, these other languages have regained to a certain extent their former usage. The Azande in the Southern Sudan number 231,000 and, owing to sleeping-sickness legislation, are concentrated around Tembura, Yambio, and along the Tembura–Yambio and Yambio–Maridi roads. There is only one sub-dialect of Zande in the Sudan, spoken by the MAKARAKA (true name ADIO) (415 taxpayers), who live between Yei and Maridi in the basin of the Tori.[2] According to Hutereau another section of Dio may be found on the Mbomu River.

80. The great majority of the Azande are to be found outside the Southern Sudan in Belgian Congo.[3] The Congo Zande number over 500,000 and lie mostly to the north of the Wele River between long. 23° and 29° 30′ E. Several Zande colonies are also to be found south of the Wele, notably (*a*) a large group along the Likati River as far south as the Rubi River and Buta, (*b*) a small group along the Bima River as far as Titule, (*c*) a small group between Bambili and Amadi, (*d*) a large group south of the Bomokandi River occupying the basins of the Makongo, the Poko, and the Teli rivers, also north of the junction of the Teli and Bomokandi rivers, (*e*) a large group south-east of Dungu. In the north the Azande extend to and over the French border.

---

[1] Evans Pritchard reports that Zande is still widely spoken among the tribes east of Maridi and even among the Rumbek 'Jur'.

[2] *Maes et Boone*, p. 266: 'The Makrakra are the most eastern of the Azande. They inhabit the valley of the Tore, a tributary of the Yei, and extend to the north as far as 5° lat. N. approximately.'

[3] See Van den Plas, p. 9.

Maes et Boone, p. 34: 'The Azande inhabit a region extending from the Belgian Congo into Ubangi-Chari and the Anglo-Egyptian Sudan, and contained approximately between 23° long. E., 6° lat. N., 30° long. E., 3° ½′ lat. N. The precise limits of this area are as follows:
  (1) in the west, a line drawn from 4° lat. N., 23° long. E. to 23° 30′ long. E. on the Bomu; the Bomu; a small piece of territory on the right bank of the Shinko in the neighbourhood of Rafai, the Shinko itself as far as 5° 30′ lat. N. approximately;
  (2) in the south, the Wele, except for a narrow strip on the banks of that river occupied by the Bakango; a piece of territory between the Likati, the Wele, and 3° lat. N.; the Wele; a piece of territory between the Bima, just beyond Titule, and the Wele; the Bomokandi, the Makongo, a line covering the basin of the Poko as far as the Tely; the Tely, the Bomokandi; a line drawn from the Poko to near the Wele above Bambili, except for a piece of territory in the neighbourhood of 4° lat. and 23° long. E. occupied by the Amadi and the Mangbele; the Wele-Kibali as far as the junction of the Obi;
  (3) in the east, a line drawn from the junction of the Obi to the west of Faradje, from there towards the north as far as 5° lat. N. There are more Azande on a tributary of the Yei;
  (4) in the north, about 6° lat. N.
In the Belgian Congo a few small groups of Azande are to be found in the neighbourhood of Zobia, to the south of Dungu and between the Bomokandi and Niangara.'

DISTRIBUTION OF THE EASTERN SUDANIC TRIBES

81. The Belgian Government statistics are as follows:

Territory of the Avungara	Centre Ango	72,527 out of 72,605.	
Territory of the Avuru–Wando	Centre Dungu	175,774 ,, 177,002.	
Territory of the Avuru–Kipa–Amadi–Aba-rembo	Centre Poko	93,061 ,, 158,900.	
Territory of the Abandia	Centre Bondo	107,839 'Zandeized' Mongwandi.	
Territory of the Madjara	Centre Niangara	72,313, population largely of Nilotic origin.	

82. The Azande in French Equatorial Africa number about 21,000 and extend in scattered groups along the north bank of the Mbomu River from the Sudan border as far west as Bangassou, about long. 23. They are bounded in the north by the Banda tribes. The French Government statistics are as follows:

Subdivision of Bangassou	.	1,945
,, Rafai	.	6,886
,, Zemio	.	6,042
,, Obo	.	3,335
,, Djemah	.	2,786

'There are two main branches of Azande in French Equatorial Africa—the Avongara in the neighbourhood of Zemio and the Bandjia near Rafai.'

83. Among the Azande are to be found the descendants of a variety of conquered peoples (such as the Pambia, Barambo,[1] Huma, and Bukuru[2] on the Sudan–Congo border, and the Biri, Banda, Gbaya, Gobu in French Oubangui Chari). For a full list of Zande subsections the reader is referred to Van den Plas in Lagae's *La Langue des Azande*.

84. As a rough indication of the entire Zande language area, Van den Plas gives 23° to 30° long E. and 6° to 3° lat. N. He also gives the following as being the main dialects of Zande (and, considering the number of totally unrelated tribes comprising the Zande nation, it is a matter of surprise that the dialects are so few in number):

  i. MBOMU, possibly the purest form of the language, spoken on the Mbomu, Api, Gurba, and Bwere rivers.
  ii. SUEH–MERIDI (called by the Azande the 'English' dialect) spoken between the Sueh and Maridi rivers. It has much in common with Mbomu, certain points in common with Bamboy, and with Bile, besides certain Arab influences.
  iii. BILE spoken on the right bank of the Wele and Dungu rivers, from the confluence of the Aka River to 26° long. It is also spoken on the Bima, south of the Bomokandi, and south-west of Niangara. In the south it shows Makere influences.
  iv. BANDIYA, spoken west of long. 26°, north of the Wele River, and between Bondo and R. Rubi, also in French Equatorial Africa. This dialect has the highest percentage of foreign words.
  v. BAMBOY, less aberrant than Bandiya, spoken in the east, south of the Kibali, between the Kibali and the Dungu, on the right bank of the Dungu to the east of the Aka, and in Yei District. (The Makaraka or Adio are supposed to speak this dialect.)

Van den Plas describes Mbomu as 'la langue authentique', but Bile as 'la vraie langue Zande'.

[1] According to Van den Plas, the Pambia and Barambo languages are related to Sere (p. 16).
[2] 436 taxpayers in Maridi District; these people still speak their original Bantu language in addition to Zande.

Other Sudanic Languages

85. MUNDU is spoken by the remnants of a tribe now living amongst the Baka in Maridi (927 taxpayers) under Chiefs Ngamande (Bilal) and Sayid Adikima, and in a little colony north-west of Yei (930 taxpayers). Further colonies of Mundu are to be found in the Belgian Congo in the neighbourhood of Aba (some 2,000 speakers).[1] The language shows greatest affinity to Ndogo-Sere in vocabulary, but in grammar seems to have come under strong Baka (and even Zande) influence. It will be discussed in this series in conjunction with Ndogo-Sere.[2]

The Congo Mundu, according to Hutereau (p. 261), are historically related to the BERE, who lie farther down the Dungu River. He also mentions two smaller tribes, the TODO, riverains of the Mundu, and the DAY (or Dai), riverains of the Bere.

Kreish, &c.

86. The north-western corner of Equatorial Province[3] contains a confused mass of very small tribes. Of these the most important people are the 'KREISH' ('Kredj')—also known as KPALA and GBAYA)[4] (2,000 taxpayers). They are now divided geographically into two main sections:

(a) Eastern Kreish.

The GBAYA-NDOGO[5] (450 taxpayers) formerly lived south and south-west of Dem Zubeir, but have lately been moved on to the Raga–Said Bandas road, where they are now settled under Chief Kimandogo. Their language was reduced to writing by the R.C. Mission at Dem Zubeir, but it is not a pure dialect, being much influenced by Ndogo.

(b) Western Kreish.

The NAKA (900 taxpayers) live near Said Bandas west of the Gbaya-Ndogo, mostly under Chief Babiker. Their language' is perhaps the most representative dialect.

West of the Naka, on the River Boro, live a mixed population of 'HOFRA',[6] BOKO, KUTOWAKA, and others, all under Chief Kosho (550 taxpayers).

---

[1] *Hutereau*, p. 26: 'The Mundu live separated from their kindred of the same dialect. In the neighbourhood of Aba they are hemmed in by the Kaliko, the Fajelu, the Baka, and the Logo; to the south of Yo or Dungu they occupy a large tract of land as far as the Nzoro.'

Maes et Boone, p. 293: 'The Mundu, whose territory lies partly in the Bahr el Ghazal, occupy in the Belgian Congo a region limited in the north by 4° 45′ lat. N. approximately; in the east by the meridian 30° 10′ approximately; in the south they are bounded by the Nzoro as far as Vankerckhovenville; in the west they are bounded by a line drawn approximately from that town to the sources of the Yalo.'

[2] According to Calonne Beaufaict, Hutereau, and others, both Mundu and Sere are closely allied to Bangba.

[3] This area was recently known as the 'Western District' of the Bahr el Ghazal. In olden times it was known as 'Dar Fertit'.

[4] While every one agrees that the name 'Kreish' is a foreign one, nobody has yet discovered an acceptable indigenous name for all the people who speak the language. Bethell advocates 'KPALA', and the Kreish themselves will answer to that name, although I was told that it is the name originally given them by the Yulu. They will also answer to the name 'GBAYA', although they told me that that name properly applies only to those Kreish speakers who are not Naka. The Ndogo call them 'MANDUGBA'. In the present work the general term 'Kreish' will be used to cover all forms of their language.

[5] These are the 'Nduggo' of Schweinfurth.

[6] A nickname, probably from Hofrat el Nahas, where they worked and lived for many years. Bethell notes that these people revere copper.

87. Although Eastern and Western Kreish embrace numerous sub-dialects, each with slight but distinctive vocabulary differences, there are certain phonetic characteristics which differentiate the two main groups:

Eastern Kreish has three 'liquid' sounds—r, l, and ɽ (flapped l). Western Kreish has only two 'liquid' sounds, r and ɽ, but their relationship with the Eastern Kreish sounds is peculiar.

	Eastern Kreish		Western Kreish
	r	=	r
	romó (man)		romó
	l	=	y
	'bálà (one)		'báyà
	ɽ	=	ɽ
	éɽe (fowl)		éɽe
Note also:	y	=	y
	kóyù (house)		kóyù

Bethell further notes that the majority of Kosho's people pronounce the r sound with a uvular articulation, 'a strongly rolled gutteral r'.[1]

88. There is one small section of Kreish, the WORO (100 taxpayers), living on the Kuru River far to the south of the main body of Kreish speakers and in touch with the 'Shatt' (Thuri) and 'Dombo' (Bodho) Shilluk speakers. They are renowned hunters in the woods in that region. As may be expected, their dialect differs strongly, especially in vocabulary, from both Eastern and Western Kreish.

89. From the French side Calonne-Beaufaict reports (p. 132): 'There are several Abwaya (totem: *bokatula* spider) at Mabuturu's; they are numerous to the north of Mbomu, in the territory Zemio.'

90. The Kreish language is not confined merely to the Kreish, but has spread over other small tribes as well. It has nothing in common with Baya or Gbaya (Mandjia) in Oubangui-Chari. Poutrin, in *Principales Populations de l'Afrique Equatoriale Française*, considers Kreish a sub-section of the Banda group. I can find no correspondences in the two languages to justify this. On the contrary (as will be shown in a later volume), Kreish has a great deal in common with Bongo-Baka-Bagirmi, and may be said to be definitely related to that language group.

91. After the Kreish the BANDA are the most important people in this region (1,560 taxpayers). They live mostly between the Rivers Biri and Raga, but are obviously an offshoot of the Banda collection of tribes in Oubangui-Chari. The French Government statistics for this group of tribes are as follows:

Banda	. 87,952	Originally from the country situated between the basins of the Rivers Oubangui, Chari and Nile, but now found in the Département of Oubangui-Ouaka (48,277), subdivision of N'dele to the north (14,800), Département of Ouham-Pendé to the west (20,200), and subdivision of Damara to the south-west (4,675).
Sabanga	. 400	Département of Oubangui-Ouaka between Ippy and Ndele.
Linda	. 26,871	Département of Oubangui-Ouaka, subdivision of Ippy.
Ngapou	. 650	Département of Oubangui-Ouaka, subdivision of the Morouba.
Yakpa	. 26,000	Département of Oubangui-Ouaka, subdivision of Alindao-Kouango-Mobaye.
Dakpa	. 5,666	Département of Oubangui-Ouaka, subdivision of the Morouba.

[1] Note that Delafosse (p. 20) states that the Sara r is uvular.

Boubou	. 37,000	Département of Oubangui-Ouaka, subdivision of Fouroumbala-Kouango-Mobaye.
Yakoma	. 5,276	Département of Oubangui-Ouaka, subdivision of Fouroumbala.
N'zakara[1]	. 400	Département of Oubangui-Ouaka, subdivision of Ippy.

From the few notes I was able to take of the Sopo-River Banda, the dialect is almost identical with that described by Éboué[2] and is consequently related to Mbwaka, Banziri, and Monjombo, according to Poutrin.[3] There are several Banda dialects in the Sudan, however, and Bethell reports that one of them at least, Togbo, is almost unintelligible to the rest.

92. Mention should here be made of the GOLO (560 taxpayers), who live between the Ndogo and Wau. These people probably represent the most eastern point of Banda penetration,[4] but their language, although obviously belonging to the Banda group, has many affinities elsewhere, notably with Ndogo. In fact, Golo is fast dying out among the younger generation in favour of the latter language,[5] though many speak Kreish too.

93. Santandrea in his monograph on the tribe[6] divides the Golo into four linguistic groups:

1. The Golo who formerly lived at Kayango. These people have almost altogether forgotten their own language.
2. The Golo formerly living amongst the Belanda (Biri) and now living east of the Abushaka swamp.
3. The Golo now living west of the Abushaka swamp.
4. The Golo formerly living on the old 'sharia' encircling Wau.

94. All these sections have recently been united by Government's orders under Chief Abakar Abushaka, and extend along the Wau–Deim Zubeir road at a distance of 5 to 35 km. from Wau. There are still Golo in Zande country under Sub-chief Bakir. Santandrea estimates the total of Golo in the country at about 4,000.

95. The following Western District languages have so far not been placed:

Feroghe (850 taxpayers).
Shayu (probably dialect of Feroghe).
Mongaiyat (100 taxpayers).
Indri (or Yanderika) (100 taxpayers).
Togoyo (believed now to be extinct).

96. It is quite probable, when more is known of these languages, that the demesne of the Moru-Madi and Bongo-Baka groups will be still further enlarged. The following two points should be of interest:

97. MANGBETU has distinct vocabulary affinities with both groups, although, from the point of view of grammatical construction, it does not belong to either. Note, thus:

Mangbetu[7]	Moru		Mangbetu	Bongo	
no ru	äzu	spear	ne ngo	kɔmɔ	eye
na wi	taví	tail	ne kibi	kóbi	buffalo
mbembere	(t)ombí	locust	ne konzo	gbɔndɔ	leg
katshitshi	kásúsú	chin	ne du	'dɔ ('Beli)	thing

[1] The N'zakara speak a Zande dialect. See vocabulary in Lukas's *Zentralsudanische Studien.*   [2] *Langues Sango, Banda, Baya, Mandjia.*   [3] Op. cit.
[4] Santandrea reports: '(The Golo) strongly assert that the bulk of their tribe is still to be found in French Equatorial Africa.'
[5] This explains, as Fr. Santandrea pointed out to me, why Westermann's analysis of 'Golo' in *M.S.O.S.* 1912 is actually an analysis of Ndogo.
[6] See Preface.   [7] Examples from Vekens, op. cit.

and:

	Mangbetu	Moru	Bongo	
	ne bi	bí	mbili	ear
	ne tikwo	ti	he-ko	mouth
	ne ki	sí	kɔ	tooth
	na mo	(k)ɔmvó	hɔ́mɔ̀	nose
	ne jô	zó	rú	house
	ne ru	rú	ro	name
	ne kodo	kúrú	kɔ'dɔ	good
	ne si	(k)ɔkyɛ́	bíhi (bisi)	dog
	ne te	drí	ji	hand

98. EFE (PYGMY) presents a greater problem. Schebesta, in *Les Pygmées du Congo belge*, has already remarked considerable vocabulary correspondence between Efe and the Lendu-Logo languages, which he ascribes to mutual borrowing. On assisting the Rev. E. W. Smith in the analysis of some Efe Biblical texts, however, I noticed that there was also considerable likeness in grammatical construction, although not sufficient to include the language definitely in the Moru-Madi group.

99. The following governmental statistics of the north-east Congo tribes should be of general interest:

Territory of the	Centre	Inhabitants
Babira-Walese	Irumu	94,230
Mabudu	Wamba	174,242
Mangbetu	Isiro	122,317
Makere-Malele-Popoi	Niapu	42,680
Babua	Buta	120,160
Mobenge-Mabinza	Aketi	87,767
Babali-Barumbi	Bafwasende	69,663
Mongelima-Bamanga	Banalia	39,850
North Wanande	Beni	87,336
South Wanande	Lubero	154,917
Bakumu	Lubutu	50,164
Mamvu-Monbutu	Watsa	64,041
Logo-Dongo	Faradje	75,581
Alur-Lugware	Mahaji	160,621

CHAPTER II

HISTORY OF THE EASTERN SUDANIC TRIBES

THE INVASIONS OF THE WELE BASIN

100. The history of the Eastern Sudanic tribes, with the exception of the Azande, has to be largely a matter of conjecture, based on such doubtful evidence as physical characteristics, culture, and comparison of language; this last is a useful factor, which has, however, been much abused. Very little study has been made of the languages of the Wele and the Sueh-Maridi basins; at the best, all that one usually finds is a small vocabulary of common words, or the numbers one to ten, tucked away in an appendix to a volume of travel, and this is supplemented by uncorroborated and often misleading statements like 'the Madi language (at Dufile) . . . which is quite different from the other languages spoken in this neighbourhood, but has a definite relationship to the Makraká language';[1] or 'Sandeh and Loggo people, whose language and customs are in affinity with the Monfu.'[2]

[1] *Emin Pasha in Central Africa*, vol. i, p. 161.   [2] Casati, vol. i, p. 252.

101. Interrogation of the tribesmen themselves throws very little light on the problem. These small tribes have been subject to such violent attacks in the past, from the Azande invaders on one side and the Arab slave-traders on the other, that tribal tradition, which in Africa is so linked up with tribal lands, is practically non-existent. As Calonne-Beaufaict points out (p. 8), incidents of tribal tradition will often linger around a particular place when the tribe itself, long emigrated, will have forgotten them, so that one often obtains better historical data from the actual occupiers of the spot, even though these be in no way related to the original occupiers.

My own inquiries in the Southern Sudan resulted in the following vague statements:

Moru-Madi group:

102. The Miza claim to come from the south.

The Wadi come from the south-east; they used to live with the Madi and Lugbara.

The Avukaya come, some say from the south-west, others say from the west.

103. Recourse to the official files at Juba revealed:

The Madi Pandikeri (Chief Dar): 'These people seem to have occupied the present area for quite 200 years, and there is no one who can remember any story of migrations or of conquering their country in the past.'

The Madi Lokai (Chief Surur): 'Surur's father was Mokungu of Chief Kordunga of the Madi tribe, whose people split up, some remaining at Nimule, and some going to Chief Jakalia (present chief) in Attiak' (south of Nimule).

'The Luluba tradition is that they are the result of a fusion between the indigenous Kakajin and the immigrant Fajelu who came from Lukulu on the Yei–Kajö–Kaji road (about five generations ago).'

Bongo-Baka group:

104. The Bongo claim to come from the 'Landɛkrɛrɛ' River in the south. Tembura and Dem Zubeir seem to have been visited by them on their route to their present habitat.

The Baka come from the Belgian Congo in the neighbourhood of Dungu. They were driven north to Maridi by the Azande. Another section is supposed to have gone west and north to Tonj. Some of these came south again to Toi and Lesi.

The Morokodo, Wira, Nyamusa came from the north-east (or east) at the same time as the Mondari (a Bari-speaking tribe). The Morokodo themselves claim to have lived with the Acholi and Lokoya on the east bank of the Nile. They reached Maridi district before the Baka and settled between Maridi and Amadi. They were surrounded by the invading Azande and had to hide in caves. They assert emphatically that they have never lived with the Baka or Bongo at any period in their past history.

105. There is one big factor which is of great help in determining the past history of these tribes, and that is the very factor which is responsible for the elimination of their own tribal tradition, viz. the Zande invasions. The history of the Zande advance has been fairly accurately determined, both from Zande legend and from the accounts of eye-witnesses during the later stages, and it is by studying the course of each invading stream that one obtains a glimpse of the peoples which were swept back or engulfed. Each parcel of occupied territory has its own tale to tell, handed down from one occupier to the next, though doubtless distorted in the process. But from the sum of these conflicting scraps of legend one is finally able to obtain a hazy picture of the movements of tribes before the last eruption.

106. The following survey, which must not be regarded as complete since it only stresses the tribes concerned in this book, is obtained principally from a comparison of the historical syntheses of Calonne-Beaufaict, Hutereau, Van den Plas, and Czekanowski.

107. Most authorities are in agreement that the tribes now found in the Southern Sudan and in the Wele basin are invaders, and that the original inhabitants of the latter area at least were the Pygmies—the so-called 'Aka'.[1]

108. Calonne-Beaufaict's tentative table of invasions (which he never lived to develop) may well be cited here (op. cit., p. 245).
 A. The aborigines and the first invaders:
  1. Momvu.
  2. Shilluk tribes; Logo-Avukaya-Moru tribes.
  3. Makèrè.
 B. The first Sudanic wave (upper Mbomu):
  1. The Mayogo-Mundu-Bangba-Basiri group.
  2. The Amadi.
 C. The second Sudanic wave (lower Mbomu):
  1. The Abarambo.
  2. The Zande tribes Abèlè, Angada, Abagwa, &c.
  3. The Adio (Makaraka), Akbwambi.
 D. The Bantu invasion from the south-east:
  1. The Akarè.
  2. North Wele column, (a) Aboguru ('Bukuru', 'Babuckur'), Mabadi, &c., (b) Abangwinda, Mayeka, (c) Mobenge.
  3. The Ababua and Mobati, origin of the Mangbèlè.
 E. The Mangbetu invasion from the south.
 F. The third Sudanic wave—the Zande-Avungura (Avongara) invasion, of which the Mbomu and the Nunga branches had most effect on the Southern Sudan.
 G. The Abandya invasion. The Baza group. Aboguru, Mongbwandi, Abandya.
 H. The Arab and European infiltration.

109. Colonel Bertrand, who had access to Calonne-Beaufaict's unpublished notes, gives the following brief résumé of the invasions of this area (Preface, p. x):

110. Towards the end of the Neolithic Age, in the sixteenth century, the Momvu spread, following a direction roughly Ruwenzori–Chari. To the east, a mixing with the Shilluk-Dinka invaders produced the Bari-Logo group, while, to the west, a mixing with West African influences gave birth to the Makere. Two invasions descended upon this grouping of tribes. The first Sudanic wave (Bangba-Mayogo-Mundu, &c.), debouching from the upper Mbomu, spread south, leaving in the Bahr el Ghazal their Babukur rear-guard.[2] The Bwaka of Ubangi belong also to this group. The Bantu were the next to arrive from the west, and their vanguard, the Abangwinda, penetrated as far as the Bahr el Ghazal, to be dispersed later by the Sudanic Mongbwandi invaders from the north. At the same time the second Sudanic wave from the north reached the lower Mbomu, the Abèlè (Azande), Auro (Abarambo), and the Amadi. The third Sudanic wave, the Avongara (Azande), succeeded these, crossing the Mbomu farther west (between 24° and 25° long.) at the

---
[1] Czekanowski (vol. ii, p. 569) postulates a belt of Pygmies extending as far as Mt. Elgon on the Kenya-Uganda border. [2] Subsequently 'Bantuized' by the Abangwinda.

beginning of the eighteenth century.[1] The Momvu-Makere were driven back at the moment when stone was giving way to iron in their culture. A section of the Makere, about 1750, plunged into the forest belt to the south, developed an aristocracy under Zande chiefs there, made contacts with people of other cultures, and finally reappeared from the south under the name of Mangbetu. The Azande, who were still pressing southwards, were definitely checked by this new invasion. At the same time a branch of the Mongbandi, the Abandya, appeared north of the Wele and the Mbomu, and, after being 'Zandeized', drove the Azande themselves from the lower Mbomu, advanced south, and finally came into conflict with the Europeans north of the Congo. At the same time a new Bantu thrust, the Ababua, completely changed the tribal constitution of the area south of the Wele west of long. 26°. It was in this confusion of populations that in 1830 the last Sudanic wave, the Avongara, had its rise, and it carried on its crest this mixture of tribes into the regions which it occupied. As the Avongara swept on, however, the submerged people were assimilated into one great Zande nation, over which reigned order and the 'pax azandea'. At the end of the nineteenth and beginning of the twentieth century, European intervention arrested these migrations and stabilized the tribes in the regions where they are to-day.

111. Czekanowski's prehistory covers a wider area, which he divides into three migration zones (vol. ii, p. 568).
  i. The Nile and Great Lake area, where the invasion swept from north-east to south.
  ii. The savannah lands north of the forest belt, where the movement was from west to east.
  iii. The forest belt itself, where the last migrations were from south-west to north-east, although it may be that the Sudan tribes of the forest belt themselves came earlier from the north-west.

112. The causes of the early waves of migration are not easy to ascertain. Calonne-Beaufaict, in discussing the various Zande waves, postulates:
  (a) A drying up of the South Sahara. (This would undoubtedly have also caused the Sara, Banda, Dendi, Fan—and presumably the early Bongo—to begin their first migrations.)
  (b) Pressure of people to the north—the white 'Azudia', probably Arabs.
  (c) A tradition of conquering which was passed on to the conquered people—this being especially the case with the Avongara.

113. For the purpose of this chapter I shall use Calonne-Beaufaict's table of invasions, but discuss each section from the various points of view expressed by different authorities. Again it must be stressed that only those movements which have a direct bearing on the Southern Sudan tribes will be analysed here.

A. The Aborigines and the First Invaders
Eastern Section

114. About the year A.D. 1000, according to Czekanowski, the Bahima-Batutsi cattle-owners (of Galla stock) migrated from their Abyssinian home-lands under pressure of Semitic raids, and moved in a north to south direction. At that time the Nile–Congo Divide was peopled by scattered bands of Pygmies and, to a certain

---
[1] Their actual invasion of the Wele area, however, did not begin until the nineteenth century.

extent, by early Nilotes. The agricultural Bantu, however, had already taken up their position from the Congo to Lake Victoria, though not united in any way. The Momvu tribes were farther west at the time, but they, or their influence, extended as far south as the Aruwimi River.

115. According to Thomas and Scott this Hamitic wave from Abyssinia reached Gondokoro in the sixteenth century, bringing their cattle with them. From here they dispersed over modern Uganda, intermarried with the indigenous agricultural populations, though at the same time reducing them to a state of serfdom, and founded the kingdoms of Ruanda, Urundi, Karagwe, Ankole, and later Busoga, Bunyoro, and Buganda.

116. The Nilotic invasions (Shilluk-Acholi) from the Sudan swamps, in the same century probably put an end to the Hamitic invasion from the north-east. The first wave of Nilotes swept through Eastern Uganda, the majority settling in Kenya (Jaluo), although a Jopadhola ('Budama') rear-guard remained in Uganda. The Nilo-Hamitic Teso probably made a barrier between these and the next Nilotic wave, the Lango and Acholi, the former settling in a district north-west of the Teso, and the latter over-running (modern) Gulu and Chua districts. Then came the Alur and Jopaluo ('Chopi'), who settled south of these.

117. At about the same time the Madi and Lugbara overflowed from the Sudan, and were caught in the Acholi current and were swept into their present positions.[1] They were followed by outlying sections of the Kakwa and Kuku, who had already come from the east with the Bari.

Western Section

118. Calonne-Beaufaict (p. 146) gives the upper reaches of the Asa (southern tributary of the Mbomu) as the old home of the Momvu, who lived in symbiosis with the Pygmies. From a comparison of word-roots he notices Momvu influences in both Makere and Logo, which he regards as previous to the dispersion of their groups—one in the triangle Buta–Bambili–Bili and the other north of Doruma, towards the upper Mbomu and the Sueh. His reconstruction of Wele prehistory is as follows:

119. The country was once inhabited by small dark people with a Neolithic culture, who remained in partial occupation till the sixteenth century. Successive waves of migration emanating from the Central Sudan drove these people from an undetermined point in the Tchad–Mbomu–Nile escarpment first towards Zemio (on the French border), then towards Amadi (in Belgian Congo), the upper Nava, and the Ruwenzori. In their retreat they left behind them certain isolated islands of Neolithic civilization, which were absorbed in the sixteenth century by the pure Sudanic invaders, and which are now represented by the mixed 'Zandeized' tribes, Birri, Apambia, Abambia, Akarè, &c. The present Momvu, Wambuti, and Walese are their southern descendants, still living in interdependence with the pure Pygmies.

120. To the west, amalgamation of these people with West African migrants produced the Makèrè. In the east, fusion of the Proto-Momvu with the Shilluk invaders produced the Logo and Bari[2]-Mombutu types. Calonne-Beaufaict further notices Momvu and Mombutu influences in Kreish, and tries to link the Gbaya-Ndogo with the Ndo among the Lendu.

[1] Czekanowski further suggests an old southern course of Madi migration, perhaps contemporary with the early Baganda migrations.
[2] The Bari-Logo, not the Nilo-Hamitic Bari.

121. The main waves of Zande invasion from the north and Mangbetu invasion from the south discovered the Momvu settled between the Gada and Kibali Rivers and in the mountainous regions to the south, whence they had been ejected from the neighbourhood of Niangara.

122. The Shilluk invasions he describes as follows (p. 152): the first-known Nilotes were repulsed south of Meroe by Mashaousha deserters of Psammetichus I in 650 and 625 B.C. Their descendants, the Fung of Sennar (from whom are descended the Shilluk and Dinka),[1] emigrated by steps as far as the Bahr el Ghazal. One section went north again (1496–1659) as far as Dongola, while another section extended southwards up the Bahr el Arab. By the sixteenth century there were twenty-eight Shilluk tribes on the River Jur, under Nekongo. One band of Shilluk invaders advanced up the Sueh in the same century, and reappeared towards the end of the eighteenth century to the west of Lake Albert—the 'Alulu'.[2] Relics of this Sueh 'trek' may be found, Calonne-Beaufaict asserts, in the presence of the Dembo, Jur and Belanda, &c., in the Sueh valley. This same Shilluk movement swept with it the Bari-Logo-Mombutu-Mundu conglomeration from their home in the Sueh valley, and these in turn helped to drive the negrillos southwards. Meanwhile the Madi, coming from the north-west, had driven before them a miscellany of other tribes, which merged with the Alulu to form the Acholi and other Shilluk-speaking tribes of the Great Lake area.

123. Between the Shilluk nucleus and the primitives of the Momvu-Walesé group were some very mixed elements, (1) the Logo group, (2) the Nile Madi, (3) the Bongo.

124. Calonne-Beaufaict and Czekanowski are both inclined to underline a Nilotic strain in the Logo and especially the Madi tribal groups.[3] This would give the sixteenth century as the time of the rise of these people. Since the Bongo language group has a great deal in common with Moru-Madi (both in vocabulary and in morphology), the logical supposition is that there was once a Bongo-Madi entity, which was split by the arrival of the Shilluk invaders, and that Bongo now represents the purer element. This may further be supported by the fact that the language Bongo has affinities with Lake Tchad, whereas the Moru-Madi dialects are very localized. Finally, from what little linguistic evidence there is to go upon, there is a closer tie between Moru-Madi and Momvu-Lese than between Bongo-Baka and Momvu-Lese.

The history of these particular groups will be given separately (see Chapter III).

B. The First Sudanic Wave (Bangba-Mundu-Basiri and Amadi)

125. It must have been towards the end of the sixteenth century that the Bangba-Mundu[4]-Mayogo-Basiri pressure made itself felt. Originating near the source of the Mbomu, one column drove back the Baka and Logo, while another, passing more to the west, penetrated south to form the basis of the present Bangba, south of Niangara. The eastern fringe was caught in the tide of Shilluk invasion and swept southwards, along with the tribes the invaders had already conquered.

[1] The theory that the Fung are in any way related to the Shilluk is attacked on ethnographical grounds by Seligman, op. cit., pp. 415–22. In fact his theory (and the generally accepted one) is that the Shilluk movement was from south to north.

[2] Forerunners of the Alur?

[3] It must be admitted here that the 'Nilotic strain' is not at all obvious in the vocabulary and still less so in the grammar of these languages.

[4] Hutereau, p. 261, claims that the Mundu and Bere had a common origin and a common language—Bangba.

126. The Basiri settled north of the Mbomu, between the Kere and the Boku rivers, whence innumerable attacks from various sources have failed to dislodge them. Though often submerged they were able to retain their tribal entity and their language. A section of this people migrated into the Southern Sudan before the Zande advance. Their history will be given later.

127. The Mundu have led a harried existence, being driven backwards and forwards between the Sueh and the Yei by the ebb and flow of inter-tribal warfare. In the course of time they became more or less affiliated to the Baka, as a comparison of the two languages alone shows.

128. The Amadi originated either near the Rivers Gwan and Asa (Calonne-Beaufaict, p. 120) or north of the Mbomu (p. 136). During the same epoch as that of the Shilluk invasion (sixteenth century), they moved southwards to their present habitat, whence they made frequent, but usually abortive, expeditions south and east. One branch actually established itself on the source of the Sueh,[1] whence it was finally driven by the Azande under Bate, Tombo's son, near the end of last century. Casati noted another branch in 1880 between the Garamba and (mod.) Faradje, while Junker in 1881 noted the Amadi-speaking Niapu living under the protection of the Mangbetu.

129. These points represent the eastern limits of Amadi expansion. There is nothing in the history of the tribe nor in its language[2] to justify Logan Gray's hypothesis that the Amadi of the Congo are the parent stock from which the Madi and Moru of the Southern Sudan have sprung.[3] Calonne-Beaufaict maintains that the original name of the Amadi was 'Amago' or 'Aogo', by which they are still called by the Abarambo.

130. The Amadi, Calonne-Beaufaict continues, may be divided into two groups: (1) the true Amadi, with sub-groups Bodo, Poro, Banza, Bosé, and (2) the Vumani, who may be re-divided into (*a*) the Banda, (*b*) the Nekiri-Bodama ensemble, (*c*) other groups of minor importance. (It is to be doubted if the Banda here have anything in common with the Banda of Dar-Banda.)

C. The Second Sudanic Wave (Abarambo, Abele-Angada, Adio)

131. Of the second Sudanic wave, only the Adio section need be treated here. They are a section of a larger group, the Auro,[4] called 'Banwanda' by the Nunga Azande. They originated in the lower reaches of the Mbomu, and their migrations were in a south-westerly direction. They were checked on the Were by the Bantu Ababua, and subjected by Nindu on the Api. They are next heard of on the Bwere

---

[1] Subsequent to the departure of the Baka.

[2] Schweinfurth, vol. i, p. 523, footnote: 'The A-Madi must not be confounded with the Madi of the Mittu, nor with the Madi south of Gondokoro.' A glance at Czekanowski's 'Madyo' vocabulary will substantiate this statement linguistically. Czekanowski, as he explains, vol. ii, p. 201, uses the term 'Madyo' to distinguish these people from the 'ihnen ganz fremden Madi-Negern des Nil-Tales'.

[3] 'Notes on the component tribes which form the Amadi-speaking group' (privately circulated report). Nalder, in his chapter on tribal history, has obviously accepted Gray's theory as it stands (op. cit., p. 10). Hutereau, in trying to clear up the same point, only succeeds in confusing the issue still more, when he writes, p. 28: 'The Logware who are established between the Loa and the Kibali take the name of Madi. They do not appear to be related to the Madi of the Liwa-Angba chain, who are situated within the bend which the Wele describes between Surango and Amadi. On the contrary, many soldiers, natives of the Liwa-Angba chain, have assured me that they understand easily the natives who, living between Dufile and Wadelai on the Albert Nile, bear the name of Madi.'

[4] The Auro are themselves a branch of the Mongbwandi, coming from the Ubangi River.

River, having been scattered and then reorganized along with other tribal remnants. In order to avoid the Avongara, the Adio ascended the Bwere, and met and befriended the Baka at Yakuluku. A group of Adio (the Abadule) installed themselves next to the Mundu, while a smaller section of the Abadule pressed on to the Tori River (tributary of the Yei), where they settled, after first throwing the mixed population of that region into confusion. It is this small branch of the Adio who were, and are still, called 'Makaraka' by the surrounding Avukaya and Kakwa, but the soubriquet is often applied by these latter people to all the Azande. Calonne-Beaufaict notes that the Adio penetration must have been long accomplished by Casati's time (1880–2), since by then the Bomboi, who had followed the Adio, were also settled on the Tori.

D. The Bantu Invasions (Akare, Aboguru-Abangwinda, Ababua)

132. On the whole, the effects of the Bantu invasions are difficult to trace, since the invaders themselves were soon after subdued by the Avongara and incorporated mostly in the Zande nation. The most far-reaching thrust was that of the Abangwinda, originating probably from the junction of the Wele and Mbomu rivers and reaching almost to the Sudan border in the neighbourhood of Doruma, finally to be defeated by the Avongara under Mabenge. The spear-head of this invasion consisted in a number of small tribes, among which are to be found the Aboguru ('Bukuru', 'Babuckur'). The probability is that these tribes were either swept up *en route* by the invading Abangwinda or were themselves fugitives. Consequently their origin is difficult to determine; the Aboguru, for instance, might have come from the Likati (northern tributary of the Congo), or from the Mbomu valley (with the Bote and Mabadi, to whom they are supposed to be allied); Calonne-Beaufaict regards the area south of Yakoma (junction of the Mbomu and the Wele) as giving the clue to their origin.

133. At the present moment the Aboguru are to be found within the Zande nation between Maridi and Doruma, while another section is established next to the Mobenge on the Likati. Their own language is still spoken as well as Zande, and is a Bantu language.

E. The Mangbetu[1] Invasion

134. The term 'Mangbetu', according to Calonne-Beaufaict, is actually a family name which was later extended to cover a number of tribes speaking similar dialects —the Medje (or Maze), the Mando, the Madzu, the Mabisanga, the Makere, the Maleli, and many others (see Calonne-Beaufaict, p. 126). Their language is Sudanic and their origin probably towards the west, although their actual line of invasion was from the south, in the neighbourhood of the Aruwimi River. Their advent into the Wele area caused the Mabinza to move north-west, break through Ababua territory, and cause the Ababua themselves to appear on the Mbili River. Their eastern and northern thrust drove before it the Madjo and Momvu tribes as well.

135. By the eighteenth century they were firmly established north and south of the Bomokandi River, whence the Avongara were unable to eject them. In fact the Mangbetu adopted Zande tactics of incorporating those tribes they conquered and using them as 'buffer' states under Mangbetu protection. It was this policy, among other factors, which prevented the extermination of the Pygmies.

---

[1] Not to be confused with the Mombutu, a Momvu tribe. This mistake was first made by Schweinfurth, who used the name in too wide a sense.

136. In the second half of the nineteenth century the Mangbetu drove the Momvu out of the Bomokandi and Kibali regions into the primeval forests of the south, but were themselves forced to follow them on the downfall of Munza's kingdom in 1873.

F. The Avongara-Zande Invasion (Third Sudanic Wave)

137. The last Zande invasion was by far the greatest, and probably the greatest factor also in the scattering of the smaller Sudanic tribes of this area. The original home of the Avongara was at one time thought to be the junction of the Shinko and the Mbomu, but Calonne-Beaufaict maintains that this was merely a temporary stopping-place in their south-eastern extension, and that, by the time they reached the Shinko, they were no longer a homogeneous group. There is a tradition concerning a large lake and attacks by white people clad in garments of woven cloth, which causes Calonne-Beaufaict to suggest Lake Tchad as their origin, from which they presumably migrated, passing to the east of the Mandjia and Sara groups and west-south-west of the Banda tribes. (The latter have since moved into the Shinko area.[1]) Van den Plas, however (op. cit., p. 59), connects this legend with a Lake Taweish in Darfur (26° 30′ long. E., 12° 20′ lat. N.), from which the Azande were presumably expelled by Arabs.

138 Calonne-Beaufaict mentions also a counter-legend to the effect that the Azande, Amadi, and Abarambo had one origin, but were soon disunited by internal quarrellings. To this may be added a common Mangbetu saying that they are the brothers of the Avongara.

139. Whatever their origin, by 1800 the Avongara had crossed the Mbomu between 23° and 24° long. and were spreading, like a 'tache d'huile' along the valleys of the Mbili and the Were. Their neighbours were, on the west the Abandya, to the south and east the Abele, the Auro, and possibly the remnants of the Makere. It was from this region that the last of the Zande waves swept, following the traces of previous Abele-Angada and Auro-Abarambo invasions. Their progress was facilitated by the fact that the majority of the people they first subdued were already linguistically allied to them, and consequently easy to convert into allies. The spread of Zande rule seems marked by the following characteristics:[2] expansion under the direction of a popular hero; conservation and assimilation of the vanquished; death of the chief, followed at once by anarchy and schism, fights between would-be successors, followed by the ascendancy of one (or more) and the reassembling of the people accordingly; resumption of expansion and acquisition of new territories.

140. Of the Avongara invaders only the *Ambomu* and the *Anunga* branches have a direct bearing on the Southern Sudan. Their origin and history is as follows (the tentative dates of the activities of the various chiefs are from Calonne-Beaufaict):

141. After Gura[3] (1755-80) had established himself north of Bangaso (lower Mbomu), he sent out two expeditions under his sons, Mabenge (who reached the Wele) and Tombo (who went south-west). Meanwhile, he himself defeated a body of people on the Mbomu River (whence the name 'Ambomu'), who later amalgamated with Mabenge's forces.

142. About the year 1805 the territories of Mabenge and Tombo were divided among their respective sons, and from that date the real Avongara expansion

---
[1] After emigrating from their home in Darfur as a result of quarrels with Bagirmi sultans (Calonne-Beaufaict, p. 39).
[2] See Calonne-Beaufaict, p. xvii.   [3] Hutereau spells the name 'Ngura'.

began. Mabenge had four sons,[1] Nindu, Yapiti, Nunga, and Bogwa, and it was Yapiti and Nunga and their descendants who carried the Zande invasion into the Southern Sudan. The influence of Tombo's dynasty was confined to the west, and need not be discussed here.

The Ambomu

143. Yapiti (1805-35), Mabenge's second son, reorganized the Ambomu and led them eastwards, defeating the invading (Bantu) Abangwinda and subduing the upper Wele. His descendants imposed their law on the Amadi, the Bangba, the Abangwinda, the Sueh tribes, and even joined issue with the Mangbetu. Renzi (1835-60) and his sons Tombo and Dupwa (1860-85) reached the source of the Sueh, after fighting the Aboguru (Bukuru) and the Baka. Dupwa himself repulsed the Makaraka (Adio) and Kakwa in their own district. Bazimbi (1835-60), another of Yapiti's sons, established himself to the west of the Gurba River, whence his son Yambio[2] (d. 1904) initiated a systematic occupation of the Bahr el Ghazal, sending his son Mange against the Moru, Baka, and Golo. He also gradually overcame and assimilated into his kingdom the descendants of the other sons of Yapiti.

144. By 1880 the authority of the Ambomu extended from the watershed north of the Were to the upper reaches of the Sueh and Maridi rivers, and, after the destruction of the Mangbetu power, to the left bank of the Wele as far as the Bomokandi. The Ambomu treated as equals the Arabs and Egyptians whom they encountered, and these in return had a great respect for their organization. Hutereau (op. cit., p. 168) points out that in Schweinfurth's time the warriors of Doromo[3] (son of Ezo, son of Bazimbi) had already captured large quantities of fire-arms from the Arab traders, and cites Schweinfurth's description of an expedition directed against these Azande. In 1895, furthermore, the warriors of Doromo ambushed and annihilated a Belgian column under Captain Janssens and under-officer van Holsbeek, after Bili, his nephew, had massacred another column under Captain Bonvalet and Lieutenant Devos during the preceding year.

145. It was only towards the end of the century, after Chaltin had avenged these early setbacks, that the principal Zande chiefs Renzi, Bayoko, Bafuka, Bili, Doromo finally submitted to European authority. Bafuka, it may be noted, accompanied Chaltin in 1897 in his victorious campaign against the Mahdists at Rejaf.

The Anunga

146. Nunga was the third son[4] of Mabenge, and therefore brother to Yapiti. While on the Duma (tributary of the Were) he quarrelled with his brother Nindu[5] and led his own faction north-east, following the line of exodus of the original population on the previous invasion of the Abandya. On this march he conquered the Agabu, the Basiri (Sere), the northern Abarambo, the Apambia, and the Azenge (Dinka?).[6] The Basiri were on the Kere (north of the Mbomu) at the time, and these he drove south, settling north of the Mbomu himself. The Anunga sphere of influence, however, did not cease here, but was greatly enlarged by his sons, who conquered territory in all directions.[7]

[1] Five according to Hutereau, p. 152: Ginda, Yapate, Bogwa, Nunga, Degbia.
[2] 'Yembio' according to Hutereau, 'Mbio' according to Calonne-Beaufaict.
[3] 'Ndoruma' according to Calonne-Beaufaict.
[4] Fourth son according to Hutereau, op. cit., p. 196.   [5] 'Ginda' according to Hutereau.
[6] The last-named people are described as being totally naked and possessed of much cattle. Calonne-Beaufaict notes that 'Azenge' or 'Adjenge' is the modern Zande name for Dinka.
[7] Hutereau, pp. 197-206, gives perhaps a clearer account of Anunga activities than Calonne-Beaufaict, but both authors are cited here.

147. Bamvurugba[1] (1835–60) led an expedition, composed largely of subjugated Abarambo, Pambia, and Basiri, northwards, conquered the Shilluk-speaking Belanda (Bor), and even joined issue with the Jur (Luo) and Dinka near Wau. His son Sonango ('Solongoh' of Schweinfurth) (1860–85) drove the Sere as far as Dem Bekir. On Nunga's death Bamvurugba held sway as far east as (mod.) Tembura. Sonango called in the Arabs against his brothers, but after his death and the expulsion of the Arabs by the Egyptian government, his cousin Tembura was placed in control.

148. Zangabiru (1835–60) occupied the Kere River, and his sons extended his kingdom to the Wara in the west, the Boku in the east, the Were in the south of the Mbomu. His son Tikima plotted with the Arabs of Dem Zubeir in order to overthrow Mopoi Mokru (Zangabiru's brother), but was eventually executed by the Arabs themselves for suspected treachery. Zamoi Epira (also known as Semio), Tikima's son, managed to win back the favour of the Arabs, and was also one of the protégés of Lupton Bey, Governor of the Bahr el Ghazal. On the surrender of the latter to the Mahdists in 1883, Zamoi laid waste his eastern frontier and retreated, but returned again in 1893 with the first Belgian expedition under Van Kerckhoven, which he accompanied as far as Wadelai on the Nile in 1892.

149. Liwa (or Eliwa) (1835–60) accompanied his brother Bamvurugba on the first part of his expedition, but soon broke away and established himself at Yobo, where he subdued the Apambia. Here he was later attacked, defeated, and executed by Sonango, but his son Tembura fled to Zubeir for protection, and ultimately became the chief in the Biki-Yobo area. The other sons of Nunga (Mopoi, Yongo, Gima, &c.) played a less important role, and succumbed mostly to the intrigues of their more successful brothers.

150. By 1880 the authority of the Anunga extended over the Bangba, the Basiri, the Amadi in the east, the Birri (Momvu) north of the Mbomu, the Angada in the centre, and the Bantu Akare near Zemio.

151. Of the other sons of Mabenge and their descendants there is little to say.

Nindu went south, repulsing the Abele and the Auro, till checked by the Ababua (Bantu) barrier on the left bank of the Wele, which his son Galia eventually penetrated in 1860. The descendants of Nindu were finally overpowered by the Anunga under Zamoi Epira (with Arab help), who used them against the Ababua.

Bogwa established himself along the left bank of the lower Were over the Bangba and Basiri, and drove the Amadi south of the Wele. His descendants were eventually wiped out by Anunga under Mopoi-Bangezegino (1860–85), son of Mopoi Mokru.

G. The Abandya Invasion

152. The Abandya, according to Calonne-Beaufaict, moved parallel with the Avongara in their march to the Shinko, but were abandoned by them in the neighbourhood of Bangaso. They created in the west a confusion among the smaller tribes only equalled by that of the Avongara in the east, and even harried the western flanks of the latter, as far east as Zemio. The Abandya are a branch of the Mongbwandi, and were 'Zandeized' at a very early stage. This assimilation of Zande culture and language is said to have been intentional and undertaken with a view to building up a nation similar to that of the Avongara. It should be noted here that Calonne-Beaufaict regards the language of the Adio (which is a Zande dialect) as being related to Mongbwandi (p. 105). He also points to a similarity between the Adio and the Abaza section of the Abanday.

---

[1] 'Boruba' according to Hutereau.

H. The Arab and European Infiltration

153. The Arabs had already established themselves in Dongola, Kordofan, and Darfur by the sixteenth century, and by the end of the seventeenth century were even a part of the royal Fur dynasty. Although in touch with the Negroes to the west of Darfur at an early date, they do not seem to have concerned themselves with the southern areas until last century. Their interest in this quarter may be said to have received its first real impetus in 1819, when Mohammed Ali, Khedive of Egypt, decided to invade the Sudan. One of his expeditions reached Gondokoro in 1841, shortly to be followed by the explorers Petherick and Miani, who reached Nimule by 1860; while the first Austrian missionaries reached Rejaf in 1850. By the middle of the century Egypt controlled the Sudan as far as Fazogli, 120 miles south of Khartoum, while northern merchants, largely of Dongola stock, penetrated southwards and opened stations for the trade in ivory. The possession of fire-arms gave these traders an immense advantage over the local populations, and slave-trading very soon sprang up as a secondary activity. The trading-stations now became centres for 'razzias' in all directions, with Khartoum itself the centre of a colossal slave-trade.[1] Even though the contemporary Khedive, Said Pasha, visited the Sudan in person in 1857 and officially abolished the slave-trade, his return to Egypt was merely regarded as the signal for intensified slaving activity, which so appalled the few European ivory traders that they were glad to sell out to agents, who in turn joined the ranks of the slavers.

154. Casati (op. cit., p. 251) gives a good description of the penetration of these Arab merchants through the Bahr el Ghazal and into (mod.) Belgian Congo, which may well be cited here:

'Slave-traders and ivory merchants were the first to attempt excursions in the Makua country. Their depots were to the south of the Bahr el Ghazal, or at Ayak [north of mod. Toinya] on the Rohl River. The road which the first of them followed was on the north side of the Nile-Congo waterparting, across the countries of the Sere, Belanda and Babuker, and thence to Wando and Guruguru—by which name they used to call Mambettu-land. On leaving Ayak, caravans used to cross the Bongo territory, as far as the country inhabited by the Babuker tribe, and thence through the valleys of the Kapili and Duru rivers to the Makua; but later on Abd-el-Samath took possession of that road. The Ayak merchants were compelled to vary their itinerary, and reach the Zande region through the countries of the Moru and Abaka tribes, instead of that inhabited by the Bongo.

'The habit of using a well-known road, and the relative security that it afforded, was the reason that between Lado and the Mambettu tribes communication was kept up by the Makraka road, through the Abaka tribes, where the old road was again taken. The journey was thus very much lengthened, and in the season of the rains became a difficult and painful one, scattered over as it was with bogs, especially in the region of the Abaka.'

---

[1] Petherick is said (by Evans in *The British in Tropical Africa*) to have laid the foundation of the slave-trade in the Upper Nile, but the southern areas were so remote from Khartoum that contributions from these regions to the central market at Khartoum were negligible. Schweinfurth notes (vol. ii, p. 429) that the annual export of slaves from the Bahr el Gebel area seldom exceeded 1,000, while that from the Bahr el Ghazal varied between 400 and 600. The damage wrought by the Arabs in these areas is to be found more in the wilful laying waste of the country-side and the needless massacre of whole communities during foraging expeditions rather than in the actual slave-trading. In fact, the majority of slaves taken were retained on the spot as servants, carriers, or even as soldiers, their condition being often one of serfdom rather than one of slavery.

155. It must not be imagined that the Arabs invaded the country in the same way as the Azande, driving all before them. On the whole their influence on the ethnological features of the country, as Czekanowski rightly points out, is relatively slight. It is true that they annihilated whole villages in their vicinity, as witness the terrible havoc wrought on the Bongo, but they were too few in number and too widely scattered to set in motion another general migration. They themselves were only too anxious to preserve the *status quo*, so that each station should be surrounded by a suitably submissive people, from whom they could obtain their provisions and their ivory, both white and black. It is interesting to note in this connexion that the present distribution of tribes in the Southern Sudan differs but little from the distribution given by Schweinfurth, who visited the Bahr el Ghazal and Wele areas in 1868–71, when the slave-trade was at its height.

156. In the meantime the sensational geographical discoveries of Burton, Speke, Grant, and Baker had focussed Europe's attention on Central Africa, and when Ismael Pasha became Khedive in 1863, he found himself confronted by a growing public opinion in Europe over the horrors of the Sudan. He therefore determined to occupy the southern areas permanently and abolish the slave-trade. This, however, was only one aspect of his main project, namely the expansion of Egyptian sovereignty over all adjoining lands. In 1869 he appointed Baker Governor of the area south of Gondokoro. The latter proceeded south, and on arriving at Gondokoro in 1871 officially proclaimed the annexation of Equatoria and the abolition of the slave-trade. He even subsequently proclaimed the annexation of Bunyoro to Egypt, but, owing to financial difficulties at home, Egypt did not ratify. He was succeeded in 1874 by Gordon as Governor-General of the Equatorial Provinces, who reorganized the Egyptian administrative machine in the south, instituted an ivory monopoly, and extended chains of military stations, inaugurated by Baker, both south into modern Uganda and west into Zande and Mangbetu country. These stations in theory stood for the protection against slavers of the native populations, who in their turn were expected to supply the garrisons with grain. Owing to the corruption of the Egyptian officials (for the south was now regarded as a useful spot for the technical exile of the more unruly elements in the Egyptian administration), these military stations, unless supervised by the Governor in person, soon degenerated themselves into centres of slavery and oppression. Gordon, in addition, with the help of Gessi and Schnitzer ('Emin'), tried to extend Egyptian authority over Buganda, but in vain.

157. In the Bahr el Ghazal a new factor now arose. Here an ivory and slave trader named Zubeir had raised a private army, proclaimed himself an independent ruler, and defeated a governmental force that was sent to quell him. The Khedive did the only thing possible in the circumstances, pardoned Zubeir, and made him Governor of the Bahr el Ghazal. When, however, after a successful private war with the Sultan of Darfur in 1874, Zubeir went to Cairo to claim the governorship of that province, he was 'detained' and prevented from returning to the Sudan. His son, Suleiman, reigned in his stead but, on assuming a threatening attitude in 1877, was crushed by Gessi, 1879–80, who was appointed the new Governor of the Bahr el Ghazal. Rabeh, one of Suleiman's lieutenants, escaped and set up a kingdom in the Lake Tchad area, until brought to book by the French in 1901.

158. In 1876 Egypt could no longer bear the financial strains of Ismael Pasha's régime and went bankrupt. After this, Egyptian interest in the Sudan, especially the southern areas, languished, and Gordon, who was appointed Governor-General of the whole Sudan in 1877, found himself faced with revolt, invasion, and disintegration on all sides. In 1879, the year Ismael was deposed, he resigned, and his successor in Khartoum, Rauf Pasha, made no attempt to put down the slave-trading and corruption that now flourished everywhere. In 1880 Gessi resigned and Lupton Bey was appointed Governor of the Bahr el Ghazal. Emin was now Governor of Equatoria, and Slatin Governor of Darfur, but this small sprinkling of Europeans could make no headway against the almost universal corruption of their staff.

159. Such was the state of affairs in the Sudan when in 1881 the Mahdi raised his standard. The response from the Arabized populations in the northern provinces was almost instantaneous. Egypt, in the throes of a financial crisis, bewildered by the nationalist uprising under Arabi Pasha on the one hand and by English and French intervention on the other (both events culminating in the bombardment of Alexandria in 1882), left the Sudan to her fate, after appointing Gordon in 1884 to superintend the evacuation of the military and civil population.

160. The southern provinces were at first little affected by the Mahdist revolt, but in 1884 Gedaref and the Bahr el Ghazal garrisons surrendered, and the Emir Karamalla sent Lupton to join Slatin in captivity. Karamalla now decided to capture Equatoria, and marched south. Emin, who had been without steamer communication with the north since 1883, concentrated his forces round Lado, abandoning one post after the other. Here he was joined by Junker and later Casati, who had been exploring the country to the west. By 1885, the year of the fall of Khartoum, the Mahdists had occupied Amadi, and Emin, who was rapidly losing control of his own forces, retired to Wadelai. (Here he was finally relieved by Stanley in 1888, though the majority of his troops, who had by now settled in the country, refused to leave, and were later to become a thorn in the flesh of the Government of Uganda.) Karamalla, although the way was now open to Lado, was unable to advance, being recalled to the north, and it was not till 1890 that a Mahdist expedition under Omar Saleh ultimately reached Rejaf. The western outposts were by now also under Dervish control.

161. Meanwhile the 'scramble for Africa' among the greater European Powers, following the Berlin Agreement of 1885, was well under way, and it was not long before rival imperialists, pushing inland from east and west, began to converge on the Nile-Congo watershed. The Belgians were the first to arrive; the Congo Free State had been inaugurated in 1885, and a Belgian expedition under Van Kerckhoven established itself on the watershed in 1892. Although their leader died there, the rest advanced to Wadelai, where they persuaded the remnants of Emin's garrison to join the Belgian head-quarters at Wandi. From there they were sent on a disastrous expedition against the Mahdists in Rejaf, and afterwards left to their fate. It was not till 1897 that Rejaf was ultimately stormed by Chaltin, who thereupon occupied what was later known as the Lado Enclave.

162. In 1894 the limits of Belgian expansion eastward were settled by international agreement—roughly the Nile-Congo watershed and a strip of land to Lake Albert in the Mahaji region. (Later the Lado Enclave was leased to the King of the Belgians for life.) In the same year Britain, who had beaten Germany in a close race from the east coast, proclaimed a protectorate over Buganda, and in 1896 another over Bunyoro, through fear of French encroachment. This was no idle fear, for in 1894 the latter, having settled their southern boundary with the Congo Free State, found themselves free to expand eastwards from Ubangi. By 1896 Liotard had overthrown Dervish rule in a large part of the Bahr el Ghazal, and in 1897 Marchand left Brazzaville to complete the subjugation of the province and extend French authority as far as the Nile. An attempt by the British to rush Sudanese troops from

Uganda to the Juba River and intercept a threatened meeting between him and de Bonchamps (operating from Abyssinia), led to a violent revolt that had its repercussions throughout Uganda, lasting till 1901. In 1898 Marchand, after an epoch-making march through a hostile country, reached Fashoda at the same time that an Anglo-Egyptian force under Kitchener overthrew the Mahdists at Khartoum. The meeting of these two leaders in the Shilluk country was to result in very strained relations between England and France for a period, but in 1899 France withdrew her claims, agreeing to regard the Nile-Congo watershed as boundary (but retaining Wadai), and an Anglo-Egyptian régime in the Sudan was proclaimed. Since 1899 there have been minor boundary adjustments between the Sudan on the one hand and Uganda and the Congo on the other, the most important being the ceding of the Lado Enclave by Belgium in 1908 and of Opari District by Uganda in 1913 in return for the present West Nile District.[1]

163. The Mahdist revolt and subsequent events had little effect on tribal distribution in the southern provinces. The Dervish, and later the Belgian and French troops, were greatly augmented by the numerous levies raised among the tribesmen, but once the actual fighting was over, the tribes affected soon returned to their old abodes to contend with the Zande menace, which had a far more enduring effect. There is, however, one great ethnographic change which the Arabs, if left undisturbed, might possibly have brought about. Already in Emin Pasha's time each government and trading-post had developed into a town of mixed population, mostly of northern origin, at the moment living a parasitic existence on the surrounding tribes, but already intermarrying with these and setting up a mixed culture. Had these posts been allowed to develop in their own way, there would probably have been many repetitions of Zubeir's 'kingdom', on large and on small scales, resulting finally in a feudal system of Nubian and Danagla overlords and Central African serfs. The Mahdist revolt, in spite of the appalling excesses committed under Dervish rule, was actually instrumental in bringing this state of affairs to an end, in that it paved the way for the present Anglo-Egyptian régime.

164. European influence in the south has on the whole been one of stabilization. Slave-trading was abolished and the Zande advance was stopped. Fighting and raiding between tribes is now severely put down. The system of decentralization, brought in in 1920, has simplified government in the south, while even among the most primitive tribes, 'devolution' is being tried out in a tentative way.[2] Since the Southern Sudan is a closed area, there is no private exploitation of native labour, no transporting of natives from one part of the country to the other to work in mines or on plantations,[3] and consequently no large tribal migration.

[1] From a linguistic point of view this latter partition of territory is unfortunate, as the Madi- and Acholi-speaking minorities in Opari District are now cut off from their kindred in Uganda.
[2] Some of the 'devolutionary' practices, notably the 'Lukiko' system of native courts, are direct borrowings from Uganda, and are not founded on indigenous institutions.
[3] This cannot, however, be said for the Congo during the early days of European exploitation (before the Congo Free State was annexed to Belgium in 1908), as witness the forcing of the Momvu into the rubber plantations and consequent disruption of the tribe (Czekanowski, vol. ii, p. 467). The present system, however, is a determined attempt to follow the principles of Indirect Rule, and is 'meeting with the obstacles that have confronted it wherever it is introduced into a colonial system whose existence postulates the detachment of large numbers of the population from their traditional surroundings, and their abandonment of their normal way of life, in the interests of European economic institutions' (Mair, op. cit., p. 240).

165. The building of roads, however, is having a far-reaching effect on village distribution, since the economical and political advantages of living on a highway are now becoming apparent. In addition, sleeping-sickness legislation is an important new factor in the grouping of tribes in the western corner of the Southern Sudan and the north-eastern corner of the Belgian Congo. In the latter area even the disposition of huts within a village may be subject to governmental control.

166. Finally, present-day governmental policy will decide which languages are to live and which to die. In the north-east Congo the official language is Lingala, and the Sudanic languages are only studied at missions. In Uganda, Madi and Lugbara are also studied in mission circles. In the Southern Sudan, after a period of working in a debased form of Arabic, the government have embarked on a 'group language' policy. Zande, Madi, Moru,[1] Ndogo,[1] and Kreish[1] have been selected as the group languages from the Eastern Sudanic dialects, and officials are encouraged to use these languages in their dealings with the tribes. In addition, a series of governmental text-books in these languages for use in schools is in course of preparation. The other Sudanic languages will probably die out in course of time.

CHAPTER III
HISTORY OF THE EASTERN SUDANIC TRIBES (*continued*)
THE EFFECT OF THE INVASIONS

167. This chapter will try to give a rough outline of the effect on the Eastern Sudanic tribes of the invasions described in the last chapter. As has already been seen, most of these tribes are either original inhabitants or else among the earliest invaders. Consequently they have been subject to all or most of the 'waves', although, naturally, accurate information is only forthcoming in the last few years of their history.

THE MORU-MADI GROUP

168. According to Calonne-Beaufaict, the LOGO first appeared on the sources of the Mbomu and the Sueh, having come from the north. They were swept south by the first Sudanic wave (Mundu, Mayogo, Bere, Bangba, Basiri), and were later driven farther south by the Bangba-Bere in their march from Mbomu to Haute Bwere and the Kapili. The Baka, who were following in the tracks of the Mundu, next came upon the Logo in their temporary halting-place near Mount Bangenze and the sources of the Duru. Before these attacks the Logo retired step by step in a south-easterly direction, occupying the Aka-Garamba area, then crossing the Dungu, and finally coming to rest in the triangle Dungu–Kibali–Wele. Calonne-Beaufaict does not say at what period the Moru-Avukaya group broke away and pushed into the Maridi-Amadi district, nor does he notice the similarity between Logo, Moru, and Madi, and he does not mention the Lugbara at all.

169. Czekanowski also postulates a north–south emigration, this time in connexion with the Madi tribes, which he places in the fifteenth century coincident with the Baganda movement. The final splitting of the Madi tribe he places in the beginning

---
[1] Admitted since the Rejaf Language Conference of 1928.

of the nineteenth century, when the Azande reached Yei. A section of the dislodged Madi, according to him, went over to the right bank of the Nile and drove the Acholi on the left bank southwards. Then the Lur flooded the land in the west from Lake Albert, while the Wagaya, Nyifwa, and Jaluo moved to their present positions on the east side of Lake Victoria.

170. Of the Logo Czekanowski says (vol. ii, p. 515): 'The Logo regard themselves as a population established since the earliest times, and can only give accounts of quite small migrations. They say further that their old neighbours were the Baka and Mundu, in contradistinction to the Azande.'

171. Logan Gray, in his privately circulated 'Notes on the component tribes which form the Amadi-speaking group', gives possibly a more plausible prehistory of the Moru-Madi migration in the Southern Sudan, if one makes allowances for his one great solecism, viz. when he names the Amadi of the middle Wele as the parent stock. See § 129. He presupposes a setting-out point somewhere to the west of Lake Albert (this would not preclude a previous existence farther north), and maintains that a northern and eastern expansion along the river valleys took place simultaneously with the westward thrust of the Nilo-Hamites (Kakwa, Fajelu, Bari, Kuku, Mondari, Nyangwara). The supposed routes of the Madi tribes would then be as follows (these routes are deduced from his accompanying maps):

The LOGO remained very much where they were.

The KELIKO (or Ma'di) advanced to the upper Wele.

The MORU-AVUKAYA advanced to the neighbourhood of Maridi. The Makaraka pushing eastwards and driving the Baka before them, successfully split the Moru-Avukaya group, and the Moru took refuge in Amadi District, where they were stopped by the invading Mondari and Nyangwara.

The LUGBARA advanced over the Kaya River where they met the Kuku-Kakwa. Both invaders were turned back, the Lugbara into their present habitat, and the Kuku into the Kajö-Kaji plateau. Meanwhile, a branch of the Lugbara, having mixed with their Nilo-Hamitic neighbours, pushed onwards across the Nile to the Luluba Hills.[1]

The MADI advanced parallel to the Lugbara. The largest section settled to the north of these, a small section made its way into the Kajö Kaji plateau, and a third section advanced into Opari District.

172. If one is to postulate a Nilo-Hamitic drive across the Nile from east to west checking the Moru-Madi advance, one is also forced to postulate a period of intense miscegenation between the two invading races, since the present Bari-speaking tribes of this area—Fajelu, Kakwa, Kuku—are, both physically and culturally, much more akin to the Moru then to the Bari of the east bank of the Nile.

173. Hutereau confines himself to the period 1860–97, from the first appearance of the Azande in the Garamba basin to the capture of Rejaf by the troops of the Congo Free State. At the beginning of this period a certain tribe or clan, the AGAMBI, lived between the Aka and Garamba Rivers. For neighbours they had, on the upper reaches of these rivers, the Baka, and on the right bank of the Aka the Bukuru. An alliance with the Baka had just resulted in a crushing defeat of the Bukuru (Aboguru) when the latter were suddenly reinforced by Avongara under Dupwa. Before this

---

[1] As against this theory note that the Luluba language is much closer to Pandikeri Madi than to Lugbara, so that the Luluba may actually represent the spear-head of *Madi* invasion northwards.

new menace the Agambi wisely retreated, migrating to the left bank of the Dungu, where they speedily attained supremacy over the Logo clans already settled there. From that time onwards the position of the Agambi as regards the Logo much

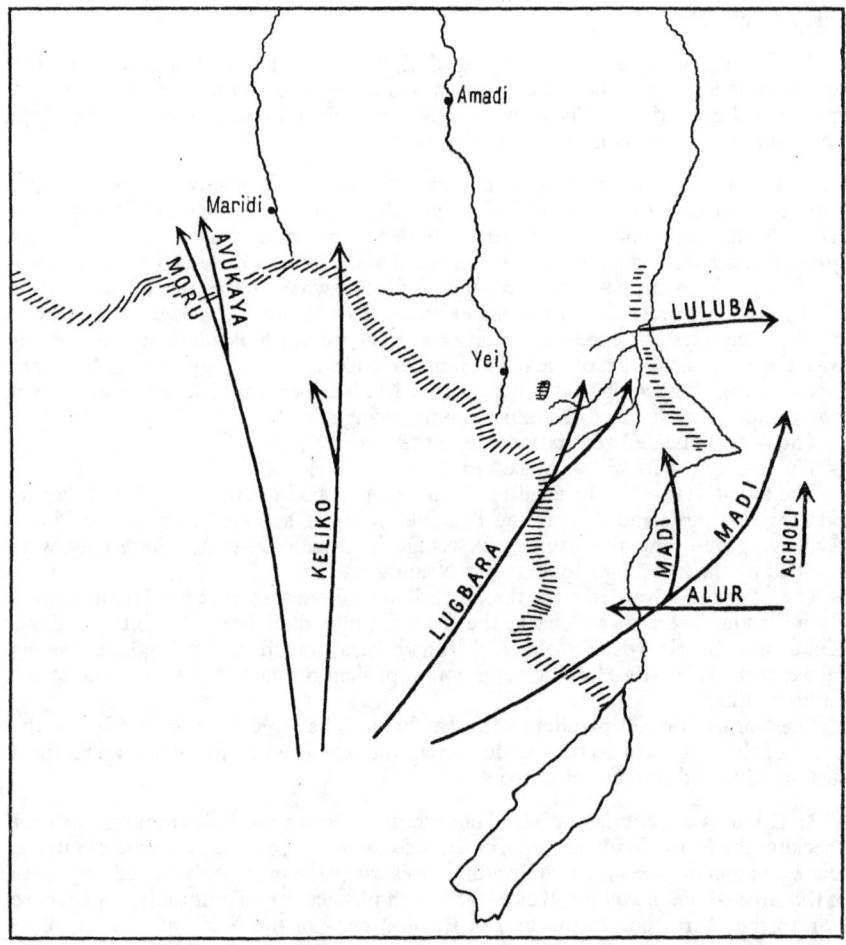

Situation as it may have been about 250 years ago, before the Kakwa, &c. had left the east bank of the Nile and before the Azande had arrived from the west. (From Logan Gray.)

resembled that of the Avongara as regards the rest of the Azande. They became the ruling clan, and decided Logo policy towards the Arab and European invaders. Under Origo they assisted the *Kuturia* (Sudani Arabs), from whom they obtained fire-arms. Under Faradje they expressed great devotion to the *Amenem Bey* (Egyptian Government) and, at a later date, equal attachment to the *Nanzara* (Mahdists). After this their allegiance wavered between the Mahdists and the government of the Congo Free State until the taking of Beden and Rejaf by the troops of the latter.

174. Of the LUGBARA Hutereau says that these people have lived up till the present day entirely independent of external influences. Apart from minor Logo and Kakwa raids from the north, a few slave expeditions by Djulu, the Alulu chief of

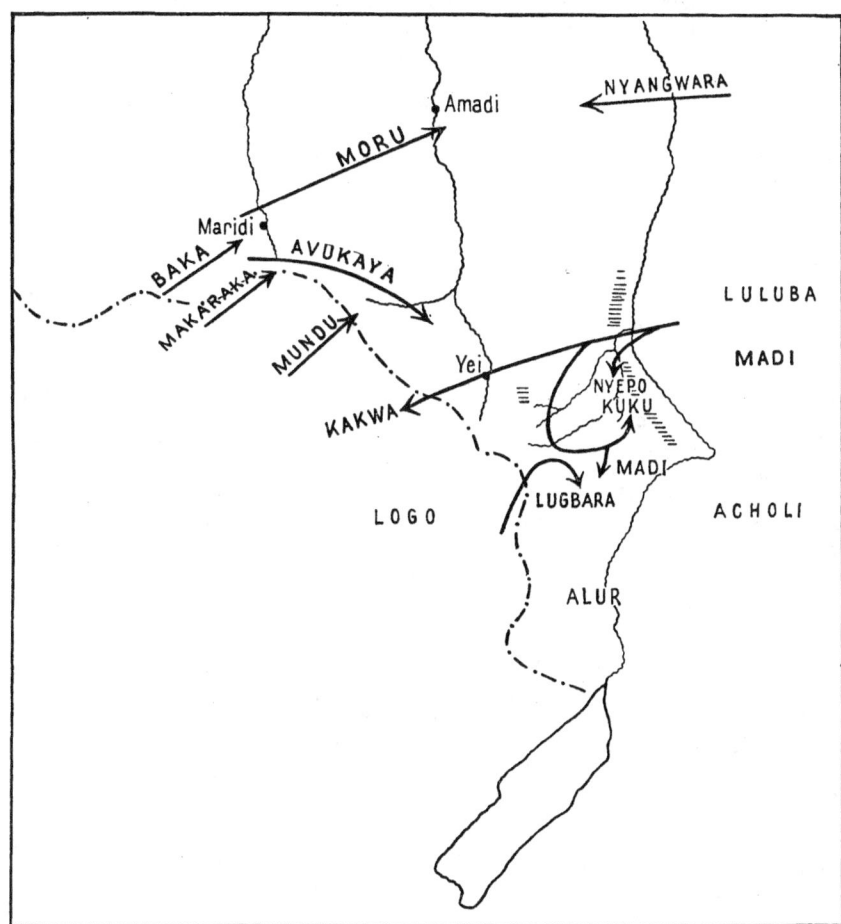

Situation as it may have been 75 years ago and substantially as it is now. The Lugbara and Kakwa turned each other back, and the Kuku and Nyepo arrived and amalgamated with Lugbara stragglers. The Makaraka drove a wedge between the Moru and the Avukaya. (From Logan Gray.)

the family Bambia, and some European reconnaissances during the occupation of the Nile enclave, their country has remained entirely closed to strangers.

175. The BARI-LOGO Hutereau maintains are probably Madi or Lugbara who descended the Lowa or the Kibali until they came into contact with the Dai, riverains of the Makua. They were later probably dispersed by the Medje-Mangbele under Abonga, followed by the Azande under Wando, Ukwa, and Bokoio (Bokoyo).

The Bongo-Baka Group

176. The BONGO were probably the first Sudanic invaders in the Southern Sudan and were well established in the neighbourhood of Tonj before the arrival of the other tribes. Their early presence is vouched for by the few tattered traditions still possessed by the latter. It is quite probable that the Bongo came from the south. Their own vague traditions point to it, while Casati in 1881 discovered near Gango on the Kibali River 'a colony of Bongo people who had settled there a long time ago, and retained the language and traditional customs of their ancestors' (p. 102). It is also probable that the Wele district was not the original home of the Bongo, but rather their southern turning-point. Their obvious linguistic affinities with the Bagirmi-Sara peoples of French Equatorial Africa indicate ultimately a northern origin.

177. The best picture of the latter history of this much afflicted tribe is perhaps given by Evans Pritchard,[1] who begins by reconstructing Bongo life before the arrival of the forces which caused their disintegration, viz. the Arabs in *c.* 1850, and the Azande (Ambomu and Anunga) soon afterwards.

178. 'The Bongo were divided into a large number of tribes who all spoke the same language but who were often separated from one another by perhaps thirty to fifty miles of uninhabited bush. Each tribe lived along the banks of a stream or in the neighbourhood of reliable water-holes, and the bush country which separated it from other tribes was waterless in the dry season and a swamp during the period of the rains. Consequently, the social and political life of each tribe was distinct from that of others. They did not act together in any undertakings. Sometimes there were inter-tribal feuds, but these were restricted by distance to two or three tribes who lived near enough to each other to make hostilities feasible.'

179. 'Then came the Arabs, who entirely altered the distribution of population as well as changed the life of the Bongo. Whole tribes left their homes and either came to live near the zeribas of the slave-raiders or sought refuge from them by migrating to Dinka country to the north-east, where they were, to some extent, protected from the Arabs. Others seem to have been completely wiped out by slavery and starvation. During this period in their history each tribe led its own isolated career. . . .'

180. 'After the Arabs came the Azande. The Bongo, politically ill-organized and completely broken by the years of Arab misrule, were unable to put up a prolonged resistance against the well-organized Zande monarchies of Gbudwe,[2] Mange, and Tembura.'

181. There is a Bongo legend, given in full by Evans Pritchard, of a united stand by Bongo under a chief Ngoli against Mange's columns, but it did not stem the Zande tide for long.

182. '. . . After the Arabs had left the country, Rikita, son of Gbudwe, moved northwards towards Minibolo and subdued one section of the Bongo, with one member of whom, Toin, he made a blood-covenant and gave him a deputyship in his territory; Gede, son of Mange, harassed Bongo country from the most eastern Zande kingdom, taking many captives, who, later, fought in his armies against the Mittu, "Jurs",

---

[1] 'The Bongo' (*Sudan Notes and Records*, 1929).
[2] Called Mbio or Bodue by Calonne-Beaufaict. Cf. § 143.

Moro, Baka, and other tribes; while the most devastating of all Zande invasions was made by Tembura's armies from the west. Tembura's brother, Selimi, crossed the Sueh and the Tonj to the banks of the Meridi, where he ordered the Gubi, Kela and other Bongo tribes, as well as the Mittu, to leave their homes on the banks of the Meridi and to come and live in Tembura's country, between the Sueh and the Iba. . . . It was only after the English occupation of the country that they returned from Tembura's kingdom to their present homes near Tonj.'

183. The BAKA, according to Calonne-Beaufaict, came from the tributaries of the Sueh, which area they evacuated before the coming of the Amadi. Whether the advance of the Mundu caused this evacuation, or whether they were caught in the first Sudanic wave while already on the move, cannot now be determined. That they followed in the wake of the wave, is however, certain. Advancing to the Nièlè (Niere?) River, they drove before them the Logo, and encountered and followed the Mundu on a tributary of the Ygba (Iba?). They were finally defeated and subdued between the Aka and the Garamba by the Avongara under Wando (grandson of Yapiti), and it is in this last area that the Congo Baka are still to be found.

184. The Sudan Baka are fugitives from here. Evans Pritchard reports (from information received from the tribesmen themselves) that they used to live along the Bima River to the south of the Were River, in peaceful relations with the Mangbetu. The latter, however, eventually drove them out of the country, in company with some Mundu and Avukaya clans. They moved to the Iba River and there split into two parties. One party went northwards to the lower reaches of the Iba, also to the Lesi, Aija, Maturungbu, and Madjuku Rivers; to this section belong the ancestors of Nganzio. They were later attacked by Azande and driven to the hills east of Maridi. The other section took a southern route to the Aka River, thence eastwards across the Yei River. They were finally turned back by the Makaraka and joined the first section in the hills west of Maridi under Bigbi. The Avukaya here joined them, coming from the Ulu River. The Baka were finally subdued by the (Zande) Ambomu under Mange, and were not restored to tribal status until the Belgian occupation of the Lado enclave.

185. The split between Bongo and Baka must have occurred at a very early date in their prehistory, since neither tribe has any tradition of their ever being one people.[1]

186. The MOROKODO-NYAMUSA group (Schweinfurth's 'Mittu'), according to Calonne-Beaufaict, must have migrated eastwards when the main body of Baka left the Sueh. (The linguistic evidence is in favour of this theory, for Morokodo-Nyamusa has points in common with Bagirmi, which Bongo, with its Logo-Momvu influences, and Baka, with its Mundu influences, have lost.) Evans Pritchard, however, is of the opinion that the starting-point of all these small tribes is far to the south, but that the 'Beli, Sofi, and Gberi came via Shambe. For a long time they lived under the protection of the Dinka chief Duwal, until misunderstandings over cattle caused them to decamp. The 'Jur' were governed by Yusef Bey Shellali from Old Mvolo during the reign of the Egyptian Government, and by the Emir Karamalla under the Mahdists. In 1898 they came for a short time under French control, when Marchand subjugated the Bahr el Ghazal. Evans Pritchard further notes that whereas once these people lived in large stockaded villages of 50–100 persons, their villages now are very small and scattered.

[1] It is true that one of Evans Pritchard's Baka informants told of Baka, Mundu, Bongo, and Bukuru all living together with the Mangbetu, and all migrating together, but even at that date they were separate tribes.

The Bagirmi-Sara Group

187. For this section Delafosse is taken as main authority.[1] It would seem that, in spite of being swamped by waves of Arab invasion from the Sahara, the main elements of the Bagirmi-Sara tribes have stood their ground. There has been a great amount of miscegenation and assimilation of Semitic culture, but there has been little or no language adoption. On the contrary, where mixed Islamic states have arisen, as in the Bagirmi kingdom, the Sudanic language has prevailed.

188. Delafosse divides the Tchad area into three zones, according to the degree of Negro preponderance (p. 135):
1. White Arabs (Oulad-Sliman).
2. Tawny ('bistrés') Arabs (near Lake Fitri, Oulad-Rachid).
3. Black Arabs (Salamat and Bagirmi, Dagana, Assalé, Oulad-Hamid, south of Bahr el Ghazal[2]).

189. The BAGIRMI empire, according to Delafosse, was founded by the Bulala, who are still to be found near Lake Fitri and near Massakory. By the end of the invasions and battles leading to the foundation of this power, the country contained nothing but a mixture of races, both Negroes and Arabs, with no common anthropological characteristics. The Bagirmi, therefore (like the Wadai), have no existence as an ethnic type. 'In addition,' he says on p. 135, 'Bagirmi has always been a great slave market, where one could find Banda, Mandja, who came there with Rabah,[3] side by side with natives from Dar Fur or Wadai, Sara, &c.'

190. Gaden's reconstruction of Bagirmi past history is as follows (pp. 2–3):
'It would be rash and moreover useless to rewrite the history of Bagirmi after Nachtigal, the reliability of whose material is really remarkable. One may add that when the hunters, who were definitely from the Kenga mountains and who are supposed to have founded Bagirmi, arrived in this country, at the beginning of the sixteenth century, they found, in the district of Koubar, which the Kukas had already crossed, people speaking a language closely related to modern Bagirmi, and probably themselves brought there by previous migrations. As for the setting-out points of these different migrations, they should probably be sought in the basins of the Bahr el Ghazal and the "Sueh".'

191. '... It is known that from these beginnings the little Sultanate created in the neighbourhood of Massénya received the name of "Bagirmi", by reason of the annual tribute of 100 head of cattle (*Baggarmia*) paid them by the Fulbe and nomad Arabs in their neighbourhood. From *Baggarmia* the Bagirmi have made *Bârma*; this is what they call themselves to-day, and they call their language "*Tar Bârma*". The form "*Bagrimma*", given by Barth and Nachtigal, does not exist now save as a memory.'

192. 'The history of Bagirmi is nothing but a long succession of war expeditions. Defensive at first against the Bulalas from Fittri, in order to free the Fulbe and cultivators of Koubar from them, then later against the Bornu and the Wadai. Aggressive against the neighbouring heathen in order to conquer territory for the new state, maintain the armed bands who constituted the power of the Mbangs,[4] and supply with prisoners the houses of the nobles and the market of Massénya, in

---

[1] *Enquête coloniale dans l'Afrique Française.*
[2] River flowing into Lake Tchad, not the Southern Sudan Bahr el Ghazal. (See Map 5.)
[3] See 'Rabeh' § 157.   [4] Bagirmi sultans.

which slaves were always the principal article of exportation. Thus Bagirmi properly understood, that is to say Massénya, only maintained itself by the continual importations of new elements. It follows that the Bagirmi language should evolve more rapidly than its near relatives.'

193. 'Having at their service only a poor language, since it was that of very primitive peasants, their political fate placed the Bagirmi rapidly in contact with people much their superiors, from whom they quickly adopted their civilization. They found it necessary to expand their language by the adoption of many new words, taken from their civilizers. They borrowed from Arabia the classes of words usually borrowed by people who become Moslems or who learn to ride horses with saddle and bridle. From Arabic also they borrowed abstract terms which the poverty of derivative elements in Bagirmi prevented from being formed within the language. The Bornu people, in whose hands rested the trade of those parts, seem to have supplied them chiefly with commercial terms. Not knowing Kanuri, we have been able to recognize only a few words of that language in Bagirmi. As for Peul (Ful), in spite of a fairly intimate contact, especially at the beginning, between the Bagirmi and the Fulbe, it has supplied Bagirmi with little. Peul is a difficult language which the Bagirmi do not speak. The Fulbe, on the other hand, have adopted a certain number of common words from Bagirmi.'

Of the other tribes Gaden says:

194. 'The Kukas say that they come from the valley of the Nile; they must then have circumnavigated Dar Fur to the east, crossed Dar Tama, then, driven from modern Wadai by the Beni Halba Arabs, must have ascended to Fittri and the Batha, passing the district of Koubar (east of Massénya), already occupied by people speaking a language related to Bagirmi, before Bagirmi itself was founded.'

195. 'The Kengas, according to themselves, must have come from the east, from a mountain called Mogoum.'

196. 'As for the Saras, of whom we have not collected any traditions, the family of their highest chief, the Mbang Day, is of the same origin as that of the Sultans of Bagirmi.'

Delafosse reports (pp. 135–6):

197. 'Tradition has it that the Kotoko[1] are the descendants of the giants So or Sao, who once inhabited the delta of the Chari and the southern shores of Lake Tchad.'

198. 'The origin of the Bulala is the cause of much discussion. According to Barth, the Bulala are of Kanuri origin, according to Nachtigal they are a section of Oulad-Hamid Arabs.'

199. The term 'Sara' (Delafosse, p. 119) has no ethnic significance but refers merely to the enclosure which surrounds a group of huts. Although the traditions of the natives themselves lead one to regard the Western Sara as autochthonous, Delafosse hypothesizes a previous western drive which expelled them from Bagirmi, which they once occupied, into the regions beyond the Chari; this without necessarily incommoding those tribes which were originally situated between the Chari and the Logone. 'This hypothesis', he says, 'seems to reconcile native traditions with the evidence of history and anthropology. In later times it is well known that

[1] See footnote to § 61.

certain tribes were driven from east to west by the journey of Rabah and in order to flee "razzias" from Wadai. Before the arrival of the Europeans, the inhabitants of the Sara plateau paid homage to the chief of the Mbandakaï. These tribes have the same customs and, from an anthropological point of view, form one ethnic group well defined and very different physically from the neighbouring tribes to the south and east. On the other hand, their language is far from being homogeneous, even if their origin should be the same. It varies from one group to another to such an extent that the natives can no longer understand each other very easily.'

200. The women of the Eastern Sara are renowned for their 'duck-bills',[1] which some authorities assert was a disfigurement expressly undertaken to discourage slavers from kidnapping them.

201. The term 'Kabba' (Delafosse, p. 129), which signifies 'comrade', again has no true ethnic significance. 'It seems, moreover', he adds, citing from notes made by M. Decorse, 'that one group of the Kabba at least must have inhabited for a long time the region called Dar-Mara, and that they also yielded to pressure from the east.'

202. 'The Sara lands on the left bank of the river (Chari) are as fertile and rich as the Sara lands on the right bank are poor and desolate. On one side one finds important villages, on the other miserable shelters hidden in the bush, the country being dotted with ruins. The reason for this state of affairs is given by the régime imposed on the natives up till very recently. The western and eastern Sara used to pay tribute in kind and in slaves to the sultans to whom they were supposed to be subject. But whilst the left bank Sara chose to deliver to the envoys of Gaourang, Sultan of Bagirmi, those amongst themselves who were less strong and consequently less capable of defending themselves, quite a different state of affairs held sway on the right bank of the river. Here "razzias" of an extreme degree of savageness took place. Bands of warriors, descending from Ndele or led by "aguids" of Wadai, overran the country with fire and the sword, razed villages, massacred women and children, and carried off as slaves the more robust men. It is to this, it seems, that one should attribute the decadence of the eastern Sara.... As a result of such a state of affairs, now ended, both industry and cattle-breeding are, practically speaking, non-existent.'

203. 'From this short study of the populations of the basin of the Middle Chari, one may conclude that there exists, immediately to the west of the river, a population with physical characteristics peculiar to themselves, namely the Western Sara, who are contiguous to the Sudanic populations Mboum, Moundang, and Toubouri; whilst, on the other hand, to the east of the river, the natives approach without doubt, at least from the anthropological point of view, the Nilotic populations.'

204. This same Nilotic *rapprochement* Delafosse notes again in the case of the Gula of Lake Iro: 'The Gula seem to be of eastern origin; they have indeed, although they are more elegant and slender, the physical type of the swamp natives of the Bahr el Ghazal.'

205. The following statistics have been taken from Dr. Poutrin's list of tribes.[2] They give a bird's-eye view of the probable tribal migrations in this area:

---

[1] Huge disks of light wood, 15 to 18 centimetres in diameter, inserted into the upper and lower lips.
[2] Delafosse, op. cit., pp. 153–65. I retain here the French spelling.

HISTORY OF THE EASTERN SUDANIC TRIBES

Barma Group

Tribe	Ethnic Group	Origin	Present Habitat	Colony
Babalia	Barma-Kotoko	Indigenous?	Left bank of Chari, below Goulfeï, Baguirmi	Tchad
Barma	(Baguirmi)	Indigenous?	Right bank of Chari, 10°–11° N.	Tchad
Kotoko	Barma (Baguirmi)	Indigenous?	Bas-Chari, delta, Bas-Logone	Tchad Cameroun
Boulala	Boulala-Kouka (Baguirmi)	Kanouri	Lake Fitri, Bahr el Ghazal	Tchad
Kouka	Boulala	Kanouri	Lake Fitri	Tchad
Baraïn			Ba-Laïri (Baguirmi)	Tchad
Kenga			E. of Baguirmi	Tchad
Saba		North	Haut-Baguirmi 12° N., 17° E.	Tchad
Sokoro			N. of Baguirmi	Tchad
Yessié	Baguirmi Arabs mixed with Negroes	East?	Left bank of Ba-Laïri (Baguirmi)	Tchad

Western Sara

Tribe	Ethnic Group	Origin	Present Habitat	Colony
Gabéri	W. Sara	Indigenous?	Ba-Illi	Oubangui-Chari
Gadago	W. Sara	Indigenous?	Haut-Tandjilé (Logone)	Oubangui-Chari
Horo	W. Sara	Regions to east of Chari	Moyen-Chari, right and left banks	Tchad
Kouang (Koung)	W. Sara	Indigenous or come from Baguirmi	Moyen-Logone-Moyen-Chari	Tchad
Laka (Lag)	W. Sara	Indigenous?	Sources of Logone, Haute-Ouahme	Oubangui-Chari
Marba	W. Sara	Indigenous	Bend of W. Logone and Tandjilé	Oubangui-Chari, Tchad
Massa	W. Sara	Indigenous Perhaps from E. of middle Chari	Logone, from Laï to Bongor	Tchad
M'Baï	W. Sara	Indigenous?	Upper course of E. and W. Logone	Oubangui-Chari
Mousgou	Massa (W. Sara)	Indigenous or E. of middle Chari	Lower course of Logone, below Bongor	Tchad
N'Dam	W. Sara	Indigenous?	Ba-Illi, Moyen-Chari	Tchad
Sara Daï	W. Sara	Indigenous?	Fort Archambault	Tchad
Sara Demi	W. Sara	Indigenous	Moyen-Logone, Ba-Illi, Bahr-Sara	Tchad
Sara Gouleï	W. Sara	Indigenous?	Bahr-Sara, Moyen-Chari	Tchad
Toumak	W. Sara	Indigenous?	Right bank of Ba-Illi	Tchad
Miltou	Sarrouo-Barma (related to W. Sara)	Indigenous	Left bank of Chari up to 10°	Tchad
Niellim	Boua (allied to W. Sara?)	Right bank of Chari, bet. Bahr-Salamat and Melfi	Togbao (Moyen-Chari)	Tchad
Seroua (Sarrouo)	Somraï (allied to W. Sara)	Indigenous	Right bank of Chari, 11° N.	Tchad
Somraï	Sarrouo (allied to W. Sara)	Baguirmi	Moyen-Logone to Ba-Illi	Tchad

Eastern Sara

Tribe	Ethnic Group	Origin	Present Habitat	Colony
Dissa	Kabba (Eastern Sara)	W. basins of Nile and Bahr el Ghazal?	Lake Iro (Koulfé)	Tchad
Doko	Massa? (Eastern Sara)	Indigenous?	Haut-Logone (W. of W. Logone)	Oubangui-Chari
Goula	E. Sara	W. Nilotic region	Lake Iro	Tchad
Kabba	E. Sara	W. basins of Nile and Bahr el Ghazal	Basins of Aouk and Salamat, right bank of middle Chari	Tchad
Sara de l'est	E. Sara	Basins of Bahr el Arab?	Basins of Bahr-Salamat and Aouk, right bank of middle Chari	Tchad
Dagba	N'Douka (Banda mixed with Sara)	Dar-Banda	Haute Ouahme, Haut-Bahr-Sara	Oubangui-Chari
Daya	Ditto	Ditto	Ditto	Ditto
N'Gama	Ditto	Ditto, E. of Gribingui	Ditto	Ditto
Maba	Ouadaï (speak a Sara dialect)	Indigenous. Perhaps from south?	Ouadaï	Tchad
Mararit	Ouadaï, Mararit-Tama (speak a Sara dialect)	South?	E. of Ouadaï	Tchad

THE NDOGO-SERE GROUP

206. Calonne-Beaufaict has already shown the Basiri as being part of the first Sudanic wave, settling north of the Mbomu, where the main body may still be found. The Sudan members of this group are obviously refugees before the attacks of the Azande, but no one is able to discover in what way the names 'Ndogo', 'Bai', 'Biri' arose, unless these were originally the names of clans or families which became exalted to tribal status.

207. The history of the Biri (Bviri, Mbe Gumba, Gamba, 'Belanda' being alternative names) is perhaps best known, and has already been set out in various numbers of *Sudan Notes and Records* by M. J. W.,[1] Dr. Evans Pritchard,[2] the present writer,[3] and Father Santandrea.[4] The following account is a summary (and condensation) of what has been written.

The Biri (or Belanda)

208. The history of the Biri is inseparable from that of the Shilluk-speaking Bor, for these two smaller tribes were united in early times to form what are now called the 'Belanda'. Since the Bor were undoubtedly the first to inhabit the Belanda area, a summary of their wanderings should be given. Though these wanderings are probably to be linked up with Calonne-Beaufaict's Shilluk invasions of the sixteenth century, there is no evidence that the Bor advanced any farther south than the sources of the Sueh. (See § 122.)

209. According to Santandrea (p. 165) the Bor, under a Dembo leader, came long ago from the north to live between the Rivers Bo and Sueh. 'The first pockets

---

[1] 'The Balanda', by M. J. W. (1923).   [2] 'The Mberidi, &c. of the Bahr el Ghazal' (1931).
[3] 'The Tribal Confusion around Wau' (1931).
[4] 'The Belanda, Ndogo, Bai, and Sere in the Bahr el Ghazal' (1933).

settled maybe along the River Sueh, and the others chiefly on the rocky hills between the two rivers, so they nicknamed each other in turn Jo Ugot = people of the mountain, and Jo Kunam[1] = people of the river. Some more pockets came maybe less than a hundred years ago, who seem to have become the ruling caste.' These were probably the 'Fujiga', (Fazuga) who played a distinguished part in Belanda history. Their setting-out point, according to M. J. W., was Lake Ambadi, north of Meshra el Rek, and their chief, according to him, was also 'Dumbo'.

210. The Biri setting-out point, according to M. J. W. was 'the country round Tembura and across the Divide, which is now in the French Congo', and they migrated before the Zande (Anunga) advance into Bor territory in the first half of the nineteenth century. This date is ascertained by Evans Pritchard by a comparison of Bor, Fujiga, and Zande genealogies. Thus:

Period (from C.–B.)	Kamum chiefs (Bor?)	Fujiga chiefs	Zande (Nunga) chiefs	
1805–35	Uziboko	Banyikongo	Nunga	
1835–60	Zaga	Bunguru	Liwa[2]	Bamvurugba
1860–85	Julukunda	Peili (Kpaile)	Tembura	Sonango
	Tuji (Tuyugi)		Renzi (Mbomu line)	

211. The Biri arrived during the reign of Zaga, while the Fujiga under Banyikongo were still at Lake Ambadi. They were well established in the Bo–Sueh area during the parallel reigns of Bunguru and Liwa. Like the Bor they lived in pockets, mostly on the hill-tops, the main clusters being as follows (according to Santandrea), reading from south to north:

Chief Udangala, near (mod.) Mupoi.
Chief Bamungede, clan Bambvi, on River Duma.
Chief Mbvongo ('Gbagida' in Zande), clan Mbve-Ndogo to north-west, also many others in this area, mingled with Ndogo, Bai, and Sere refugees.
Small tribes on the Sueh banks as far north as River Ngoni.

212. The Bor clans lay mostly to the north of the Ngoni, but intermingled with these were the Biri clans Fadongo, Fener, and Mbve-Lai, all on the River Bo. A few scattered Biri clans lived farther afield near the sources of the Bussere.

213. The two tribes seem to have lived together amicably from the very beginning; the Biri called the Bor 'Mve-Rodi' and the Bor called the Biri 'Mve-Gumba' or 'Gamba'; both tribes were known as 'Bari' or 'Abaré' by the Azande and as 'Belanda' by the Bongo and Arabs, and later by the Europeans. Their communal life, however, was not a peaceful one, for soon the Zande invaders overran the Bo–Sueh region. They were also subjected to severe Arab attacks from the north, for, as has been pointed out by others, the Basiri peoples, both in the Sudan and in (mod.) French Congo, were among the most ravaged of all these tribes by the slave-traders, their tribulations equalling, if not exceeding, those of the Bongo. Consequently, it was not an uncommon thing for whole clans to flee to the Zande invaders for assimilation and protection from the new-found horrors in the north.

---

[1] M. J. W.'s 'Kamum'. Both Evans Pritchard and Santandrea give Tuyugi as a chief in connexion with this tribe.
[2] 'Eliwa' of Calonne-Beaufaict.

214. Details of tribal adventures are too involved to set out here; Evans Pritchard's account from the Zande aspect should give a fairly general picture of the history of the next few years (p. 33):

'They were at different times and places attacked in their hill fastnesses by various Zande kings, those to the west of the Sueh by Liwa, Tembura, and other scions of the Nunga dynasty, those to the east of the Sueh by Renzi, a member of the dynasty of Yakpwati,[1] to which house they came into subjection. They were compelled either to migrate . . . further northwards, to await fresh Zande attacks, or to come down from their hills and to submit to Zande rule. In either instance their dispersion caused tribal disruption and the formation of numerous Basiri pockets widely separated from each other. . . . Where they submitted to Zande rule, as in French and Belgian territory and in Tembura and Yambio Districts of the Sudan, they tended to disperse into small groups, their own culture being maintained or absorbed by that of the Azande, according to the size of each group and its position in Zande country.'

215. With the advent of the present government, the two main sections of the Belanda have been freed from Zande interference. First the Mve-Rodi (Bor) were let free to return to their hills, while the Mve-Gumba (Biri) went to Ndokile on the Kpango. Later on, when the Azande were again threatening, the Bor under Kpaile (son of Bunguru) were brought north of the Bo River, and settled along the road there, next to the 'Jur' (Luo). The Luo would have nothing to do with them, refuting their claim to a common ancestry, even though their languages were mutually understandable; and even now intermarriage between Bor and Luo is rather rare—but that seems chiefly due to the high bride-price demanded for a Luo woman.

216. The Biri, except for a group at Dem Zubeir, are now settled along the Belanda Circular Road between Wau and Mboro, under their own chiefs (Ndokile being deposed).

The Ndogo and the Golo

217. These two small tribes suffered so heavily from the slave-raids that it is almost impossible now to ascertain their different origins. In addition, their very names have been a cause of confusion to investigators. Whether the 'Nduggo' of Schweinfurth, 'who were settled around Seebehr's Dehm'[2] were actual Ndogo or Gbaya-Ndogo cannot be said at this stage. It is obvious that the Ndogo were there once, and that Kreish-speaking Gbaya-Ndogo are the result of their fusion with the Kreish, but Schweinfurth himself, in 1871, already classifies them as Kreish.[3]

218. Of the early history of the Golo, Santandrea writes: 'Some 120 years ago we find the Golo of the Bahr el Ghazal living along the banks of streams flowing into the Bussere and Kpango ("Pongo"). They were bounded on the west by the Sere, on the south by the Biri, on the east by the Bai and Ndogo, and on the north by the Ndogo, Woro, and Gbaya ("Kreish"). . . . Later, we notice a general shifting of the Golo northwards; some joined the moving Ndogo near Deim Zubeir, and some settled a little way east, in the neighbourhood of Deim Idris, namely at Ganda, the stronghold made famous by Gessi Pasha's warlike feats. In fact, we hear that Kayango's clan had their home in the vicinity of the River Kuru, close to Ganda. As far as the Egyptian Government is concerned, most Golos were formerly attached to

---

[1] Calonne-Beaufaict's 'Yapiti'.   [2] Op. cit., pp. 220–1.
[3] Calonne-Beaufaict's attempt to link these to the Ndo of Belgian Congo has already been discussed. (See §§ 21 and 92.)

the Mamuria of Deim Bekir, some being under Deim Zubeir Mamuria, together with the Ndogo, Woro, and some Sere. Gessi Pasha met these people more or less in the positions as described above, but it should be borne in mind that almost all tribesmen had by this time dispersed over the country on account of Suleiman's[1] cruel rule.'

219. The following account of the Ndogo and Golo, whose tribal fortunes were governed by the same factors, is condensed from notes given me by Mr. C. A. G. Wallis, then D.C. of Central District, and Fr. Santandrea. The end of the slave-raiding period found the main body of Ndogo settled at Dem Bekir under the Lemgbo family, and the Golo at Dem Idris (mod. Ganda) under the Kayango family. Here the invading Anunga Azande under Zamoi[2] found them, routed them and the Sere at Mount Sarago, and besieged them near Dem Arbab. This siege was raised on their appealing to Sultan Nasir of Raga for help. For a time the two tribes lived near Sultan Nasir, but eventually quarrelled with him and moved off, the Ndogo to live at the head of the Geti and the Golo at (mod.) Kayango.[3] A second Zande invasion under Tembura was only checked by appealing to Biselli and to the Dinkas for aid, but even this did not prevent Tembura from capturing one of Lemgbo's headman, Ngomar, and transporting him south, whence he only escaped after a captivity of seven years. Since the withdrawal of the Azande, the Ndogo and Golo have lived peacefully together, although there has been a steady migration westwards during the last few years.

The Bai (or *Bari*)

220. Very little is known of the past history of this tribe. They used to live on the right bank of the River Kpango ('Pongo'), separated from the Ndogo and Golo by the River Kuru. The latter tribes were pushed against the Bai by the Zande advance and those that were not assisted by Nasir were speedily subjugated. They were not reinstated until the present government took over the administration of Wau.

The Congo Sere ('*Basiri*')

221. According to Hutereau (p. 318) the Basiri were first discovered on the Boku River by Mopoi, who subdued them and established them on the Mbomu, where for a long time they constituted one of the favourite sources of slaves for the Arabs. Several Sere families followed Mopoi Bangezegino[4] to the Sili River (tributary to the Gurba), when that chief fled from the Mbomu before the attacks of Semio (Zamoi Epira).

The Sudan Sere

222. The Sudan Sere claim to be a section of the Congo Basiri, and to have once lived between the Boku and Kere Rivers. From here they were first dislodged by the Pambia, and moved northwards. They were soon overtaken by the Azande, however, under Ikpiro,[5] and the majority submitted. A few, however, fled into the Bahr el Ghazal from a place which Santandrea gives as either Ndedegumbva or Ndedekumbva.

223. 'After they had fled from the Azande', continues Santandrea, 'they settled on the left side of the River Kpango, south of the Wau–Deim Zubeir road, not far

---

[1] Son of Zubeir Pasha. (See § 157, also *The Tribal Confusion round Wau*, p. 51.)
[2] Son of Tikima, son of Zangabiru, son of Nunga.
[3] According to Santandrea, it was at this period that the Golo split into four sections, which now underly the four Golo dialects (see § 93).
[4] Son of Mopoi Mokru.   [5] Zamoi Epira (?).

from the sources: their boundary north was the little stream Ngoku. Near there, on the other side of the Kpango, there lived a kindred tribe, small in number, the Bai, with whom they lived henceforth on very good terms. They were much harassed by Zubeir.... Again the Azande pressed them eastward. Later on Karamalla waged war on them, and it was at that time that the not numerous Sere community split into two: some took to the Azande, and settled under Tombora's[1] rule, and some followed Karamalla.... Some of these people settled definitely in the environs of Wau, but their leaders and a lot of young folk were brought over to Khartoum.'

224. 'When the Sudan Government settled definitely in the Bahr el Ghazal, numbers of Sere came back from the north.... Other bands of Sere poured down from Tombora, when they heard of their old leaders' coming. Some were prevented from doing so by their local chiefs, in spite of Government orders.... The Sere that had come from Zande country ... settled on the left bank of the River Bussere, south-west of the Biri (tribe).... From there they were brought on to the Belanda Circular Road (which goes from Wau to Mboro).' Later they were ordered to join the other Sere on the left of the River Kpango under Chief Bandas Vito Umbili.

225. 'The Sere settlement in the environs of Wau,' Santandrea concludes, 'made up chiefly of those that had come from Khartoum, is going to disappear this year (1932) to join their countrymen living near the Kpango.'

OTHER TRIBES
The Kreish (Kpala)

226. About the early history of these people Calonne-Beaufaict is justifiably reserved:

'The question of an ancient union of the groups Akbwaya (the French call them Baya), Mopwaya, &c.,[2] depends on the further study of the groups designated by the soubriquet Kreich, Kredj, given them by the Arabs. The Akbwaya proper comprise numerous tribes including the Ndogo (the Nduggo of Schweinfurth, met by him between Dem Bekir and Dem Zubeir), the Alingi (totem: the rainbow), the Aoro, &c. They extend from Djęma to the north, then along that latitude as far as 23° long., E., where Hanolet met with them. They declare that the name Kreish was given to their race, also to certain groups of fugitives from other tribes of Basiri origin (the Atogbo), Banda, Golo, Gabu, driven out by the Zande and Abandya invasions. To the south they were partly subdued after the sons of Nunga had smashed the Basiri resistance; those to the north, remaining in their country, became Moslem and founded the great villages, surrounded by ramparts, near Katuaka, notably the capital of Said ben Selis, an Arabized Kreish, at the sources of the Kotto.... It is to the north of the Mbomu where research into the migrations previous to Nunga should be profitably undertaken.'

227. Delafosse (p. 110), quoting from Modat, says: 'The Kreish were first driven south by the Fur people, then driven west by Zibeir, and finally east by Senoussi. They are now to be found at Ndélé, at Kafia Kingi, and at Dem Zibeir.'

[1] Alternative rendering of Tembura.
[2] By which he means Mèdjè Mapaya or Mokpwaya, Makèrè Mapaya, Basili Mopwaya, encountered between the Rubi and the Wele by the first Abèlè and Ababua invasions.

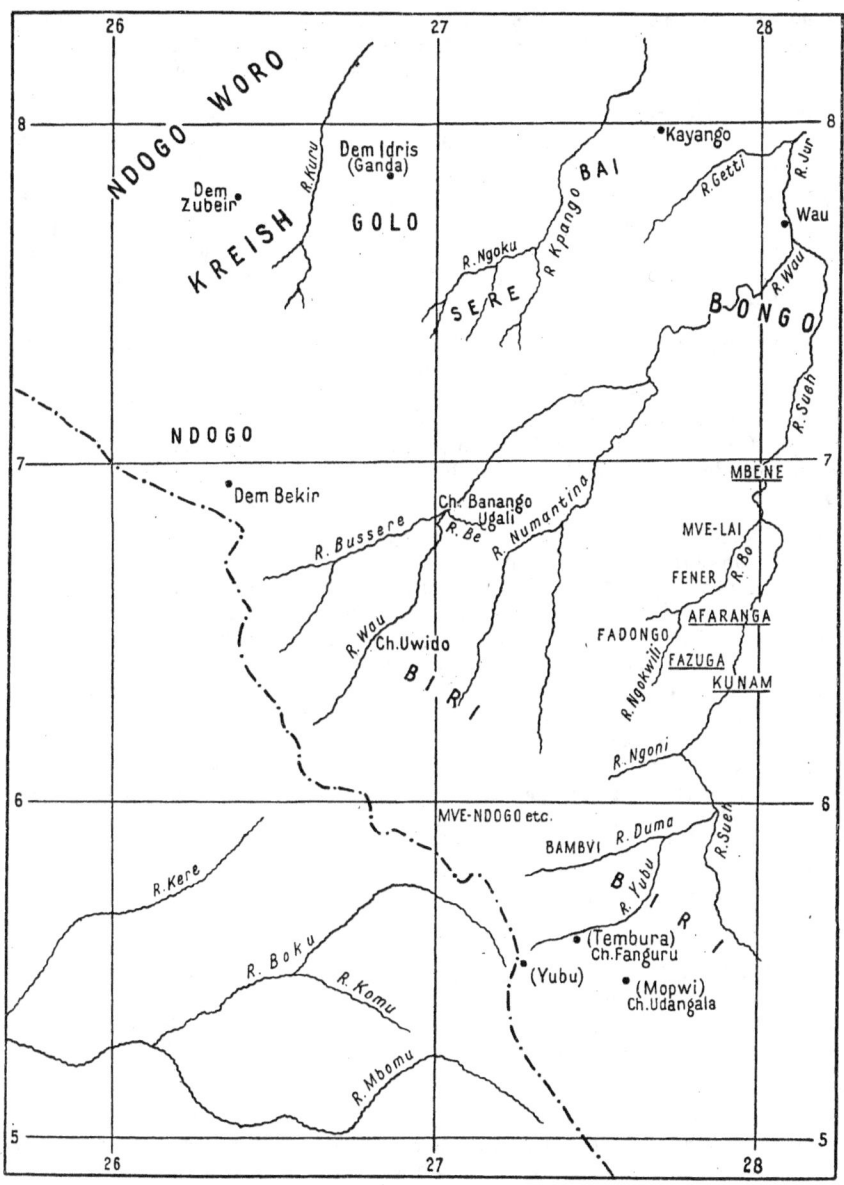

Santandrea's map to show probable distribution of the NDOGO-SERE tribes at the time of the Zande invasions. (Bor clans underlined.)

228. In Dr. Poutrin's list of tribes they are shown:

Tribe	Ethnic Group	Origin	Present Habitat	Colony
Kreish	Banda[1]	Dar-Banda	Frontier zone of Bahr el Ghazal, bet. Said Bandas, Kafia Kingi, Dem-Zubeir	Oubangui-Chari, Sudan

Note also in his list:

Golo	Pambia?	Indigenous	M'Boku-Kere (upper M'Bomu)	Oubangui-Chari

229. It seems from the above that the Kreish have occupied the region of the Sudan–French border for a very long while, and that outside pressure drove them merely over the Divide into the eastern corner of their area, where most of them are now congregated. Bethell delimits their ancestral home in a report from which the following is condensed:

230. The Kpala nation lived in a region south of the Nile swamps and the dry areas to the west (their northern boundary being roughly the line of the Boro up to Said Bandas and thence running north to take in the Migi Hills), but north of the country of the Equatorial forests and big rivers. This is confirmed by their language; there is a word for 'bridge' but not for 'boat', there is no word for 'ostrich' (which is not found roughly south of the Boro), but there is for 'giraffe' (which cannot live in thick forest).

231. Before the slave-raiding days these people must have been a considerable 'nation', consisting—like the Banda—of a number of tribes speaking varying dialects of the same language. All Babiker's present subjects, except Miyayama, were south of the Divide, their neighbours being the Zande and, on the east, the tribes of which the remnants are now under Kimandogo. They were in touch with the Zande, and most of the old men can speak Zande. Miyayama's subjects lived near a mountain called 'Mili' or 'Milah', probably the 'Méla' on the French map. Their dialect is the same as Kosho's 'Hofra', but they did not join up with Kosho as there was a hereditary feud between them. Probably the Hofra lived originally near the Divide in these parts before going to the Bahr el Arab. The Boko say their ancestral home is near Marongo Hill, near the source of the Raga River (bòkó = thick forest, which is not found in the Western District except in a few places near the Divide). The section of Kpala at present living on Khor Katta are from the Migi Hills, south of Kafia Kingi; they used, it seems, to belong to the shadowy 'Dongo empire' which once had its head-quarters at Jebel Dongo (Dango) in Darfur.[2]

The Banda

232. The Banda in the Sudan are offshoots from the immense collection of Banda tribes in Dar Banda, French Equatorial Africa. Mention has already been made of Calonne-Beaufaict's account of the Banda (§ 137), how they were driven out of Dar Fur to the south and west until they occupied the lands evacuated by the Avongara and Abandya, who had already advanced south.

233. Modat, quoted by Delafosse (p. 99) says: 'Installed primarily in the upper basin of the Kouta and, perhaps, as we have hypothesized, in a territory more northerly, this race was driven towards the south-west. It is now dispersed throughout a large tract of land bounded by 4° and 9° lat. N. and 16° and 22° long. E. Here one finds

---

[1] The grouping of Kreish with Banda cannot be supported on language evidence.

[2] Herein perhaps lies the explanation of Calonne-Beaufaict's attempt (op. cit., p. 148) to relate the Dongo of the Kibali River to the Kreish. See under NDO, § 21.

Banda tribes at Bangui (Nguéré), below the Ubangi (Mono, Ngobou, Banza), at Kafia Kingi (Ouadda), to the west of Fort-Crampel (Ngao), and on the Fafa (Bada and Ouia).'

234. Delafosse adds: 'Dar Banda, once rich and well populated, has now become, at least in its north-east section, a vast desert. Before the razzias of the slave-dealers the Banda fled, some to the west, penetrating the agricultural Mandjia who offered only a passive resistance, some to the south where they ran against the Ubangi River, forming, after the happy expression of Cureau, "une zone de compression, composée de plusieurs couches de populations échelonnées les unes derrière les autres".'

235. 'One can trace back to the seventeenth century the beginning of the foreign razzias in Banda country, razzias which lasted until our time, and which assumed sometimes the character of veritable military expeditions, under the impulse given them by the slave-trader sultans of the Upper Nile, Zubeir, Suleyman, or Senoussi, Sultan of N'Dele. Finally, the Banda country, ravaged by Rabah,[1] furnished the latter not only with slaves but also with his best soldiers.'

236. 'Fleeing from the Moslem incursions, the aborigines, abandoning their plateau, followed the natural routes which the valleys opened to them. The Tambaggo, Vidri, Marouba, Sabanga, Boubou, Linda, Dakoa, Yakpa, followed the banks of the Koto and piled themselves up on the banks of the Ubangi. Farther west, the valley of the Kouango was the route followed by the Ngapou, a fraction of the Ouadda, the Ndi, Borou or Brou, Ungourra, Mbi, Kha, Yakoua, Togbo, Langouassi. In ascending certain western tributaries of that river, several of these tribes came against the Mandjia, whom they displaced. . . . The Moria, Linda, and Kana reached with their vanguard as far as the Koumi and the Fafa. Finally, in the north-west, the large depression, where the Bamingui flows and where the Bangoran and Gribingui join to form the Chari, offered a large place of refuge for the Mbagga or G'Bagga, the Ngao, the Mbaia, and a portion of the Tambaggo. Such were the principal directions of Banda migration, but, in their flight, certain groups were split up, and this explains their diffusion. Other tribes, like the Banda-Banda, the Mbala, the Bongo,[2] &c., after victoriously resisting the Moslem incursions, were finally completely overwhelmed by Senoussi, who transported their villages to the immediate environments of N'Dele, where they disappeared. Finally, many aborigines are to be found in the "Kaga" (mountainous regions) and in the caves which are so abundant in the rocky masses of Dar Banda and Djebel-Mela.'

Of the other frontier tribes Delafosse says (p. 109):

237. 'Perhaps one ought, because of similarities of physique and language, to relate the N'sakkara to the Zande, their western neighbours.[3] They have been well studied by Comte and by the Belgian lieutenant Lalieux: according to the former author, they must have been driven from the Bahr el Ghazal; according to Captain von Wiese und Kaiserswaldau, they must have been, on the other hand, originally from the south, from beyond Wele.'

238. 'The Patri, which are often classed with the Banda peoples, belong to the N'sakkara group. They have the same origin and speak the same language.'

239. 'We have only the vaguest information about the tribes, almost entirely situated inside Sudan territory, the Karé or Kara, the Bodo, the Golo, the Basiri,

---

[1] See § 157.   [2] Not to be confused with the Sudan Bongo.
[3] See § 91 note.

the Balambo, the Pambia, and the Abomo. Of these tribes, which, with the Feroghe, the Mandala, the Binga, the Chala, and the Yulu, were once distributed along the frontier zone, there remain in French territory, after the razzias of Senoussi, no more than a few small groups, without importance and without any future, worthy only of passing reference.'

Conclusion

240. The concerted evidence of language comparison and legend seems to point to the Bongo-Baka and (later) the Moru-Madi groups' being the first invaders of the Southern Sudan, via the Wele region. That these two groups of people are ultimately of common origin is more than likely (a comparison of their characteristics as shown in Chapter V justifies such a supposition), and it is also probable that their original home lay somewhere between Lake Tchad and the sources of the Chari River. But their splitting into two groups must have taken place at a very early date—possibly before they reached the Wele area, and certainly long before the Bongo, Baka, Kreish, and 'Mittu' became separate units.

241. While in the Wele area the Bongo came into contact with the Momvu; the Moru-Madi tribes, according to most authorities, were subjected to Shilluk influence[1] during the sixteenth century. The Kreish and the 'Mittu' conglomeration were presumably by this time independently settled, since Momvu and Shilluk influence is at a minimum in these dialects.

242. The Ndogo-Sere tribes descended later upon the Wele in company with the Mundu, Bangba, Mayogo, &c., who were probably already split up into separate tribes, though recognizing a strong affinity and acting more or less in concert. The Basiri, however, settled north of the Mbomu River, while the Mundu pushed southwards and finally amalgamated with the Baka, with the result that the languages Baka and Mundu became mutually affected. The Bongo by now had reached their present position, while the Moru-Madi peoples were congregated mostly south of the Wele.

243. The history of the next three hundred years is that of a gradual penetration of the Southern Sudan area as a result of wave upon wave of invasion, from north, west, and south into the Wele area, culminating in the Avongara hordes, which poured into the Southern Sudan itself, driving before them whatever Eastern Sudanic tribes stood in their way, until held up by the Arabs and (to a certain extent) by the Dinka.[2] These same factors also stopped the flight of the Eastern Sudanic tribes, whose vanguard was now faced with three alternatives to extermination—absorption by the Azande, absorption by the Dinka, serfdom under Arab régime. The individual fortunes of all these tribes have already been discussed to the point where, under the present governments, they were restored to a certain amount of their tribal individuality.

244. As regards the part played by the Arabs, one important point stands out which Calonne-Beaufaict appears to have missed, viz. that the Arab raids from Dar Fur

---

[1] It is only fair to say, at this point, that I have been unable to find any pronounced Nilotic elements in either the vocabulary or grammar of the Moru-Madi languages. As far as vocabulary is concerned, Bongo, with its Luo contacts, has borrowed more Nilotic stems than any of the other languages of these two groups.

[2] It was probably the Dinka country, with its impassable swamps, rather than the Dinka spearmen which stopped the Zande advance.

took place 100 to 200 years before the Arab raids in the Southern Sudan and independent of the Arab pressure from the Sahara. Thus it was probably a wedge of Arab pressure from Dar Fur in the seventeenth century which sent the Sara tribes westwards and launched the Zande waves southwards, resulting in the flooding of the western parts of the Southern Sudan with the present very mixed Sudanic population. The effect of the actual Arab penetration into this area was, on the whole, not very great, and negligible compared to that in the Ubangi-Chari area.

Section II. Linguistic

Chapter IV

CHARACTERISTICS OF THE AFRICAN LANGUAGE FAMILIES

245. Before one can embark on a description of one subsection of a language family it is essential to have a clear concept of the whole family itself. Consequently, the following tentative 'definitions' of the main African language families should not be out of place here.[1]

246. It has been the custom for linguists to divide African languages into five main layers: 'Sudanic', 'Hamitic', 'Semitic', 'Bantu', and 'Bushmen'. Of these the 'Semitic' and 'Hamitic' are often classed together, while the 'Bushmen' languages are regarded by some authorities as being a subsection of the 'Sudanic' languages.[2] Consequently, for the purposes of this book, only the Sudanic, Hamitic, and Bantu languages will be defined.

Definition of a Sudanic Language

247. It would appear that linguists in the past have been content to group under the general term 'Sudanic' all Central and West African languages which cannot fit another grouping, and then to state that the main characteristic of Sudanic languages is their extraordinary divergence one from another. Thus vocabulary similarity as a criterion is possible only within a very restricted range, while other criteria allow for such anomalies as isolative languages in the north-east Congo, inflected languages (with full personal verb conjugation and noun cases) around Lake Tchad, and almost Bantu-like class systems in the Western Sudan.

248. Westermann, in *Die Sudansprachen*, pp. 14 et seq. (see also *The Shilluk People*, p. 35) set out five characteristics of Sudanic languages, which he later elaborated in his 'Charakter und Einteilung der Sudansprachen' (*Africa*, 1935). Much useful work is now being done by other investigators to sort out 'pure' Sudanic languages from those with Hamitic or Bantu admixture.[3] The definition of a 'pure' Sudanic language, however, must at this stage still be somewhat arbitrary.

General.

249. 1. Sudanic languages are monosyllabic, in that most 'words' in their simplest form consist in one syllable.

250. 2. Such syllables (or etymological roots) consist of one consonant (or consonant combination) and one vowel.

---

[1] These definitions, in a cruder form, have already appeared in my article, 'Survey of the Language Groups in the Southern Sudan' (*Bul. School of Oriental Studies*, 1935), and I am greatly indebted to Mr. J. R. Firth of University College for his valuable help in re-presenting them in their present form. As regards the data for the definitions, this was formulated with the kind collaboration of Professor Westermann, who also allowed me to use his own article, 'Charakter und Einteilung der Sudansprachen' (*Africa*, 1935), while yet in manuscript form. Other authorities consulted were: Alice Werner, *Structure and Relationship of African Languages*; C. Meinhof, *Die Sprachen der Hamiten*; De Lacy Evans O'Leary, *Characteristics of the Hamitic Languages*; Werner Vycichl, 'Was sind Hamitensprachen?' (*Africa*, 1935); Marcel Cohen, 'Les Langues dites chamitiques' (*Congr. de l'Inst. des Lang. et Civ. Afr.*, 1933).

[2] But see Lord Hailey's *African Survey*, pp. 74–5, for the latest classification into: (1) the Khoisan family (Bushman and Hottentot), (2) the Negro languages, including (a) Sudanic, (b) Bantu, and (c) Nilotic, and (3) the Hamito-Semitic family.

[3] See *inter alia* J. Lukas, 'Linguistic Situation in Lake Chad Area' (*Africa*, 1936).

CHARACTERISTICS OF THE AFRICAN LANGUAGE FAMILIES

251. 3. Sudanic languages are on the whole isolating, i.e. they make no use of internal flexion (e.g. vowel change) nor of external flexion (e.g. prefixes or suffixes). There are, however, a few nominal and verbal formal elements (agglutinative), although the 'class prefixes' of the Bantu languages and of some Hamitic languages are absent. Grammatical relationship is indicated by position in the sentence and, analytically, by the use of certain words as particles, so that, in that sense, Sudanic languages may be described as *positional* and *isolating*.

Phonetics.

252. 4. Sudanic languages are tone languages, i.e. intonation is both lexical and morphological. Lexical tone is a more important feature in Sudanic languages than in Bantu languages.

253. 5. Characteristic consonant sounds are the labio-velars **kp** and **gb** and the implosive or 'glottal' sounds **'b** and **'d**.

Morphology.

254. 6. Sudanic languages have no grammatical gender.

255. 7. Noun formatives are few, the most common being the prefix a- which forms nouns from verbal roots. In most cases compounds are formed by merely combining two or more primary words, e.g. the diminutive is formed by affixing the word for 'child'.

256. 8. The singular and plural of nouns is not normally distinguished. Where it is, number is shown by adding a noun or pronoun (usually the third person plural). The most common plural formatives of this nature are the vowels a and i or a nasal.

257. 9. There is no case in nouns. Case relationship is shown either by position in the sentence or else by association with a noun-form which can be regarded as a preposition or a postposition.

258. 10. There are no derivative verb species, except where the idea of motion towards or away from the speaker is implied, when the verb-forms 'come' and 'go' will be combined with the main verb. Similarly, combination with the verb-form 'give' shows dative relationship.

259. 11. The verb stem is invariable for person and number, which is indicated by prefixing the appropriate pronoun.

260. 12. There are no tense-forms of the verb stem, but there are tense particles, separable from the verb stem, which express more than the mere idea of time. 'Mood', as understood in classical grammar, is unknown.

261. 13. There is no specialized passive verb stem. The 3rd person plural of the verb is normally used in an impersonal passive sense (cf. the English impersonal passive construction with 'they' and the French construction with 'on').

Syntax.

262. 14. The typical sentence order is either: Subject+verb+object, or: Subject+object+verb.

263. 15. In the genitive construction the Possessor (genitive or nomen rectum) precedes the Possessed (nomen regens). This applies also to pronominal possession.

264. 16. The adjective may precede or follow the noun it qualifies.

Definition of a Hamitic Language

265. Although there seem to be relatively few languages which authorities admit to being 'pure' Hamitic languages, there is much more certainty on what constitute this family's characteristics than in the case of the Sudanic languages. For convenience the same numbering is used here as above.

General.

266. 1 and 2. Etymological roots of Hamitic words usually consist in two or three consonants. The roots themselves may be monosyllabic, dissyllabic, or trisyllabic.

267. 3. Hamitic languages are partly inflexional and partly agglutinative. Most word formatives are prefixes and suffixes, although word differentiation by means of internal vowel change ('ablaut') is by no means uncommon.

Phonetics.

268. 4. Dynamic accent (stress) plays a greater role than tone in differentiating words.

269. 5. Characteristic consonant sounds of both Hamitic and Semitic languages are the guttural sounds (Presslaute) and the so-called 'emphatic' sounds; these are typified by Arabic ح ع and ط ض ص ظ (phon.: ħ, ʕ and ṭ, ḍ, ṣ, ẓ).

Morphology.

270. 6. Hamitic languages have grammatical gender—masculine and feminine. Linked with this is the phenomenon known as *Polarity* ('linked gender'), whereby certain nouns may be masculine in the singular and feminine in the plural, or vice versa.

271. 7. There are many noun formatives.

272. 8. The singular and plural of nouns is distinguished by a multitude of formative elements, mostly suffixes.

273. 9. 'Case' relationship is often shown by suffixes, applied either to the noun or to the verb.

274. 10. Verbs may have derived species, formed mostly by suffixes.

275. 11. Person and number in verb conjugation is indicated by prefixes (as in Semitic) or by suffixes.

276. 12. Tense forms are numerous and are formed by means of prefixes and suffixes.

277. 13. In the verb paradigm there is a distinct passive stem, formed by the addition of a suffix to the root.

Syntax.

278. 14. The typical sentence order is: Verb+subject+object.

279. 15. The Possessor follows the Possessed in the genitive construction, and is usually linked to it by means of a genitive particle.

280. 16. The adjective follows the noun it qualifies.

Definition of a Bantu Language

281. The following criteria are listed below only for comparison with Sudanic and Hamitic languages. There are other Bantu criteria which fall outside these seventeen points and which would accordingly need separate treatment in a Bantu exposition. Of all the language families of Africa, the Bantu family shows the greatest consistency both in vocabulary and in structure.

General.

282. 1. Bantu languages are fundamentally dissyllabic, i.e. the etymological roots of nearly all Bantu words (when shorn of the class prefix, &c.) are dissyllabic.

283. 2. The Bantu syllable consists in consonant (or consonant combination)+vowel. It is believed in some quarters that the two vowels of a dissyllabic root are etymologically the same. Consequently, where the final vowel of a word differs from the preceding vowel, it is regarded as a suffix.

284. 3. Bantu languages are inflexional according to Doke,[1] but agglutinating according to most other authorities.[2] Prefixes are used more than suffixes or internal flexion.

Phonetics.

285. 4. Bantu languages are tone languages. (Those which are not tone languages, like Swahili, are linguae francae.)

286. 5. It is impossible to give characteristic consonant sounds for Bantu languages in general, but it interesting to note that the characteristic Sudanic sounds **kp** and **gb**, are relatively rare, and that the Hamitic gutturals and emphatic sounds are hardly ever heard.

Morphology.

287. 6. Bantu languages have no grammatical gender, although the noun class system with its concords might be compared, in its working, to grammatical gender in Hamitic languages.

288. 7. Noun formatives are of two kinds:
  (*a*) The Class prefixes.
  (*b*) Certain suffixes (the most easily detected being the verbal-noun suffixes -i and -o).

289. 9. 'Case' relationship is shown in three ways:
  (*a*) Position in the sentence.
  (*b*) Further prefixes attached to the noun.
  (*c*) Suffixes attached to the verb.

290. 10. There are many derivative verb species, formed by means of suffixes.

291. 11. The verb stem is invariable for person and number, which is indicated by prefixing the appropriate pronominal or 'concord' particle.

292. 12. Tenses are very numerous, and are formed mostly by means of prefixes and auxiliary verbs. Doke also recognizes eight 'moods'.

293. 13. In the verb paradigm there is a distinct passive stem, usually formed by means of the suffix -wa.

---
[1] Op. cit., p. 127.
[2] Alice Werner, op. cit., p. 15. This point will be elaborated in §§ 298 et seq.

Syntax.

294. 14. The typical sentence order is: Subject (with prefix)+subject concord prefix+verb tense prefix (in any)+object concord prefix (if needed)+verb stem+object (with prefix).

295. 15. The Possessor (genitive or nomen rectum) follows the Possessed (nomen regens) in the genitive construction, and is linked to it by means of the particle of relationship -a, which itself is in concordial agreement with the Possessed.

296. 16. The adjective follows the noun it qualifies and is in concordial agreement with it.

297. 17. There is one characteristic of most African languages, which has been cited as Sudanic, Hamitic, and Bantu, respectively, on various occasions, viz. the use of 'vocal images', 'onomatopoeic words', 'descriptive adverbs', 'radicals', 'ideophones' (to give some of the names by which these phenomena are known), in order to bring out or intensify the meaning of ordinary verbs and adjectives. It is quite probable that these exclamatory words are characteristic of the *Negro* element in all three language families. Therefore, their absence in any African language is more to be remarked on than their presence.

A note on the terms 'Isolating', 'Agglutinating', &c.

298. The tripartition of languages into Isolating, Agglutinating, and Inflecting was authoritatively propounded by Schleicher towards the middle of last century, and the fact that this system of language classification was adopted later by Max Müller and Whitney explains, as Jespersen points out,[1] its popularity even to the present day. Schleicher, whose quasi-mathematical formulae for these three classes are world famous,[2] had himself arrived at this division by including the Incorporating class of Humboldt under Agglutinating. Definitions as to what exactly constituted an Isolating language, &c., varied from scholar to scholar, but the following, as set out by Pedersen in his *Linguistic Science in the Nineteenth Century*, seem to give the aggregate of what was meant by the class names:—

1. *Isolating*: 'All words are monosyllabic and have no inflection of any kind. The relations which we express by means of inflection are indicated by independent words, wherever indications cannot be dispensed with entirely.'

2. *Agglutinating*: 'Here there is a mass of endings which express the relations of words, but the junction of word[3] and ending is quite clear, so that there can be no doubt as to the boundary between the two.'

3. 'In *inflectional* languages, on the other hand, it is difficult to determine the boundaries; word and ending are fused in an unresolvable unity, and internal changes in the word itself may be used to express changing relations.'

4. 'There are languages where not only the subject, but also the object, the indirect object, &c., are expressed along with the verb-form. These languages are called *incorporating*.'

299. It is to be doubted if any language is to be found which may be allotted in its entirety to any one particular class. Take, for example, a typical Bantu language, Zulu (from Doke's *Textbook of Zulu Grammar*).

---

[1] *Language*, p. 77.
[2] Isolating R R R R ; Agglutinating Rs or pR or pRs; Inflecting $pR^x s$ or $R^x s$.
[3] Jespersen, p. 76, uses 'root' as opposed to 'word' in this context: 'the formal elements are visibly tacked on to the root, which is itself invariable.'

Zulu, by the above standards, is *agglutinating*:
 ngi-thanda (I love); u-thanda (you love); u-thanda (he loves); nga-thanda (I loved); ngiyauku-thanda (I shall love), &c., &c.; uku-thand-a (to love); uku-thand-ana (to love each other); uku-thand-eka (to be lovable).

Zulu is *inflecting*:
 ngi-lala (I sleep); ngi-lele (I am asleep).
 isigubu (calabash); esigujini (in the calabash).

Zulu is *incorporating*:
 ngi-*m*-thanda (I love him); ngi-*ba*-thanda (I love them).
 abantu e-ngi-*ba*-thanda-yo (the people whom I love).

In fact, Zulu appears to be everything except *isolating*. If judged, however, by the most recurrent phenomenon, Zulu may be called agglutinating.

300. Humboldt realized the limits of this method of classifying languages twenty years or more before Schleicher propounded his formulae, and even went farther to express his doubts as to the value of such a classification.[1] In spite of these early warnings, we find Max Müller attempting to equate sociological stages in human development with Schleicher's three divisions of language, which had by now become three historical processes in the development of all properly developed languages.

301. The modern point of view is tersely expressed by Jespersen on p. 80 (*Language*), where he sums up: 'I think that the classification here considered deserves to be shelved among the hasty generalizations in which the history of every branch of science is unfortunately so rich.'

302. This view is upheld more vigorously still in the introduction to Meillet and Cohen's *Les Langues du Monde*, p. 1: 'The too notorious classification into isolating, agglutinating and flexional languages cannot be followed too exactly, and, much as it continues to be stated, it has neither scientific value nor practical utility. The only linguistic classification which has any value or utility is a genealogical one, based on the history of languages.'[2]

303. Where African languages are concerned, a fourfold classification of language processes (isolating, agglutinating, inflecting, and incorporating) may still be of value if regarded from the point of view of (*a*) the most common process, (*b*) the least common process in the language under discussion. Further, these processes should be regarded from a functional and not a historical point of view.

---

[1] 'But the languages called agglutinative have nothing in common except just the negative trait that they are neither isolating nor flexional. The structural diversities of human language are so great that they make one despair of a fully comprehensive classification' (Humboldt, quoted by Jespersen, p. 59).

[2] 'La trop fameuse classification en langues isolantes, agglutinantes et flexionelles ne se laisse pas poursuivre exactement, et, pour autant qu'elle se laisse formuler, elle n'a ni portée scientifique ni utilité pratique. La seule classification linguistique qui ait une valeur et une utilité est la classification généalogique, fondée sur l'histoire des langues.'

CHAPTER V
CHARACTERISTICS OF THE EASTERN SUDANIC LANGUAGES

304. As might be expected, the Eastern Sudanic languages show sufficient of the criteria required by the preceding 'definitions' to warrant their being classed as 'Sudanic'.

305. In the following analysis the Moru-Madi languages will be represented mostly by *Moru* (*Miza*), the Bongo-Baka-Bagirmi languages by *Bongo* (and occasionally by *Bagirmi*), the Ndogo-Sere languages by *Ndogo*, and the other Sudanic languages by *Zande*.[1]

General.

306. 1 and 2. The etymological roots of the Eastern Sudanic languages are either monosyllabic or dissyllabic. The monosyllabic roots consist in consonant (or consonant combination)+vowel.

MORU:	ya (belly)	drí (hand)	gyɛ (buy)	vo (blow)
BONGO:	hɪ	ji	gu	bu
NDOGO:	gbí	'bi	si	pfi
ZANDE:	vu	be	ngbe	vu

The composition of the dissyllabic roots varies from group to group.

307. In MORU-MADI the dissyllabic roots consist in vowel+consonant+vowel. In some dialects dissyllabic *words* often begin with a consonant, which, from an etymological point of view, is to be regarded as a prefix.

MORU:	èza (meat)	así (fire)	ɛ'bɛ (leave)	ɛmbɛ (tie)
MADI:	èza ,,	atsí ,,	ɛ'bɛ ,,	umbɛ ,,
MORU:	kàrɪ (blood)	ti'bí (fish)	kɪró (granary)	
MADI:	àrí ,,	e'bí ,,	ɛró ,,	

308. In BONGO-BAGIRMI a similar state of affairs is found.

BONGO:	bihi (dog)	mini (water)	lámgbá (burn)	tɛlɛ (swim)
BAKA:	ísì	ene	ɔmgba	ɛlɛ
BAGIRMI:	bis(i)	man(e)	nuŋgo	ŋgal(e)

309. In NDOGO-SERE the dissyllabic roots consist in consonant+vowel+liquid (l or r, &c.)+reduplicated vowel.

  NDOGO: sìlì (tail); kpérè (thorn); kilí (assemble); dɛle (return).

310. Some of the dissyllabic roots of ZANDE have much in common with Ndogo-Sere.

  ZANDE: yere (locust) boro (person) para (egg) yuru (night)

The second syllable of other roots, however, may consist in any consonant and vowel. This last vowel, as in the case of Bantu dissyllabic roots, later investigation may prove to be actually a suffix. See § 283.

  bangi[2] (eye) geda (to count) manga (to do) vunde (durra)

---

[1] Examples taken largely from Gore's *Zande Grammar*, with retention of his spelling (except in §§ 320–6) and word-division (except for addition of hyphens in places to show grammatical relationships).

[2] Should be spelt *bäŋgi* and *maŋga* in a strictly phonetic system, but the current Zande orthography is followed in this chapter, except in §§ 320–6 (the phonetic section).

CHARACTERISTICS OF THE EASTERN SUDANIC LANGUAGES

311. 3. The Eastern Sudanic languages are, on the whole, positional and isolating, as above described, although there are a large number of agglutinative elements, of which the following are prominent.[1]

312. MORU-MADI

Stem prefixes.

        MORU: **k**-úsu (bow), cf. MADI: ósù
        t-äú (fowl), cf. MADI: a'ú
        l-ɨwa (elephant), cf. MADI: ɛwa
        la-'di (to cook), cf. MADI: 'di
        k-ugu (to steal), cf. MADI: ogu

Semantic and morphological prefixes.

MORU: má 'bɪ ŋgágà. I beat the boy.   má ŋgaga **ó**-'bɪ. I'm beating the boy.
    á-'bɪ ma te. I was beaten.   **la**-'bí (a beating)
    ɔ-sá (to arrive there)   **ɛ**-sá (to arrive here)
    o-ga (to chop)   **to**-ga (to chop to pieces)
    ɔ-tɛ (to stay)   **kɔ**-tɛ (to wait)
    å-fu te. It has been broken.   **li**-fu te. It has broken.

Stem suffixes.

        LOGO: gó-**lɛ́** (back), cf. MADI: ogu
        MORU: tä-**pi** (father), cf. MADI: ata
        LOGO: ari-**á** (bird), cf. MADI: arí
        LOGO: lw-**a** (to cut), cf. MORU: ló

Morphological suffixes.

MADI: oko (woman), pl. oko-**nzi**.
    odra ra. He died.   odra-**ki** ra.   They died.
    dra (to die)   amá vu drà-**rɛ**.   We are going to die.
    mu (to go)   álɛ mu-**ka** bàru.   I want to go home.
    nyà (to eat)   lenyá lɔ̀sɔ nyà-**lɛ**.   Food is good to eat.
    ga (to chop)   tolu ga-**zo**.   Axe for chopping.
    mu (to go)   mu-re-ko-re-'e.   He who does not go.
    so (to hoe)   leti ba a so-le-re-'e. Path hoed by the people.

313. BONGO-BAKA

Stem prefixes.

        BONGO: **he**-ndó (night), cf. BAGIRMI: njo
        BONGO: **le**-'jí (beer), cf. BAGIRMI: ju
        BONGO: **n**-ónò (to hurt), cf. BAGIRMI: ony(o)
        BONGO: dɔ (to make), cf. BAGIRMI: **ta**-d(a)

Semantic and morphological prefixes.

BONGO: ma nyi 'dum(u). I eat asida. bu'du o-nyi 'dum(u). The man ate asida.
    lunduyi ná **mo**-ny(i) 'di? What did your brother eat?
    lunduyi ná **amo**-ny(i) 'di? What is your brother eating?
    kanda and **ma**-kanda = new.

---

[1] These affixes are to be distinguished from the host of separable particles, with which all these languages abound. See § 66 for Gaden's description of Bagirmi, which may well be applied to all the Eastern Sudanic languages.

BAGIRMI: ndi naŋ(e). Sit down!   met **ki**-ndi. I am sitting.
WIRA: í kú. Come!   médí **ta**-ku. I am coming.
BAKA: l-ipi tara suwali. Open the bag!   **'d**-ipi tara suwali. Close the bag!
SARA: (**n**)aga (to walk).   **'b**-aga (to stroll).

Stem suffixes.

    BITI: täbio-**ro** (lion), cf. BAGIRMI: tobio
    BONGO: mbi-**li** (ear), cf. BAGIRMI: mbi
    BONGO: ga (to chop), cf. BAGIRMI: ga-**ŋ**(a)
    BONGO: mgba (to beat), cf. BAGIRMI: mba-**l**(a)

Semantic and morphological suffixes.

BAGIRMI: deb(e) (man), pl. deb-**ge**.
    jet kab(e) or jet kab-**ki**. We are going.
BAKA: kemi ani sóó? Does the lion eat grass?
    an-**a** 'dėa? What are you eating?
    ógú zumà. Come to me!   ogu-**ni** awa. He hasn't come.

Bongo-Baka-Bagirmi has far fewer agglutinative elements than Moru-Madi.

314. NDOGO-SERE

Stem prefixes: (seemingly none). Note, however: kapfí (back), kàpfá (lake), kabaí (yaws).

Morphological and semantic prefixes.

'dáko (man), pl. **nda**-'dako.
iε (I). **nd**-ε (I myself).
iε-si. I buy. **a**-si yε. I am bought. Also 'tense' particles as in: iε-**ku**-si, iε-**ka**-si, iε-**ka**-**ku**-si, iε-**bva**-si, &c.
gbolo and **me**-gbolo (big).

There are no Ndogo-Sere suffixes. Where verb conjugation at least is concerned, Ndogo-Sere is decidedly prefix-agglutinating.

315. ZANDE

Stem prefixes. (None apparent.[1])

Semantic and morphological prefixes.

    ka-kido (to promise)   **mo**-kido (a promise)
    ka-za (to mediate)   **a**-zaro (a mediator)
    Zande (a Zande)   **a**-Zande (plural)

Also verb 'tense' particles as in: mi-**na**-manga, mi-a-manga, mi-a-mangi, mi-**ni**-mangi, mi-**ka**-mangi, mi-**na**-**ki**-mangi, &c.

Stem suffixes.

    ndu-**e** (leg)   ndu boro (man's leg)

Cf. *ndo* in Nzakara.

Semantic and morphological suffixes.

    zak-**a** (to loosen)   zak-**i** (or zäki or zeki) (to have loosened)
    nung-**a** (to travel)   nung-**u** (to have travelled)
    tind-**a** (to carry)   tind-**iro** (load)
    fu (to speak)   fu-**go** (speech)
    kit-**a** (to break)   kit-**iri** (broken)

[1] In the absence of comparative material, it is impossible to distinguish the initial element in word roots from possible etymological prefixes. Compare, however, Zande *be* and Nzakara *mbe* = arm.

CHARACTERISTICS OF THE EASTERN SUDANIC LANGUAGES 65

316. It should be noted here that from the *intonation* point of view, all these languages must be regarded as *inflectional*.

Phonetics.

317. 4. The MORU-MADI languages are tone languages in every sense of the word. Both nouns and verbs may be divided into tone 'classes', in which there is a very highly developed tonal inflection. The Moru-Madi languages are tri-tonal, i.e. there are three main tone levels at which syllables may be pronounced. (These three levels are more easily distinguished in dissyllabic words than in monosyllabic words.)

drí (hand)	tí (cow)	'bú (grave)	
drì (head)	tì (near)	'bù (rain)	
kúrú (gourd)	kúru (well)	kumú (fly)	máàwɔ (cat)
kuru (up)	kurù (ball)	kùmu (hernia)	màwɔ (cobra)

318. The NDOGO-SERE languages are also tone languages with probably as highly a developed tonal inflexion as Moru-Madi. At the present stage of investigation, however, only lexical tone has been studied.[1] Ndogo-Sere has a tri-tonal structure.

'bí (different)	yá (to go)	ká(r)á (to tear)
'bi (fruit of rubber tree)	ya (elephant)	ka(r)a (to give)
'bì (hand)	yà (meat)	ká(r)à (hoe)

319. Tone, both lexical and grammatical, does not appear to play so great a role in BONGO-BAKA as in Moru-Madi or Ndogo-Sere. The impression one has is of a tri-tonal system in course of disintegration. Tonal doublets may occasionally be found:

BAKA: ɛmɛsá. You are good.   ɛmɛsà. He is good.
'BELI: má do ŋgómá. I kill myself.   ma dó ŋgómá. I beat myself.
BONGO: 'búú (hunger)   'buu (egg)
bo'dú (pig)   bò'du (man)

320. The fact that the Azande use talking-drums is indicative of the tonal quality of ZANDE. These drums also point to a di-tonal structure.[2] Little or nothing has been done in Zande tonetics, but even lexical tone-doublets are hard to find. Note, however:

gbá (yesterday)   gúmbá (lightning)
gbâ (to-morrow)   gúmba (to speak)

321. 5. The characteristic consonant sounds kp and gb[3] are found everywhere; 'b and 'd are found everywhere except in Zande. In addition a flapped l-sound is heard throughout (usually as a variant of l or r),[4] while Ndogo and Kreish pronounce a flapped v-sound.

	MORU	BONGO	NDOGO	ZANDE
kp	ekpı (to cough)	ekpí (to help)	kpì (sour)	tikpo (salt)
gb	tómgbó (canoe)	'dugba (to catch)	gbi (to strike)	gbia (chief)
'b	'ba (home)	'be (home)	'bá (home)	
'd	la'di (to cook)	f'dí (to cook)	'dɛ́ (to speak)	
ɽ/ṿ	kíriɽí (charcoal)	ɽiŋgɛdɔ̀ (rhinoceros)	ɽiɽi[5] (sweet)	ringara[6] (country)
			ṿi (boy)	
			gɛṿɛ́ (arrow)	(Kreish)

[1] See vocabulary in Fr. Ribero's *Elementi di Lingua Ndogo*.
[2] Unless, of course, drum signalling has been borrowed from a di-tonal people and adapted to Zande. Note that the Banda drum signalling analysed by the author in the Western District is tri-tonal.   [3] Relatively rare in Moru-Madi, however.
[4] ɽ is the normal sound in Zande, alternating with r and l. It is spelt r.
[5] In Sere, where ɽ is mostly to be found.   [6] Pronounced ɽiŋgaɽa.

F

322. All these languages have a five-vowel sytsem, **a, e, i, o, u,** but the vowels **e, i, o, u** have each two varieties, 'tense' and 'lax', the use of which is largely determined by context. It is still a matter of investigation whether the varieties of **i** and **u** in Moru and Zande are not sufficiently distinct as to form different phonemes. A centralized **a** in syllables adjoining the vowels **i** and **u** is common.

There are no diphthongs nor long vowels; when two vowels fall together, the resultant sound is dissyllabic.

Examples of 'tense' and 'lax' vowels, and centralized **a**:

323. MORU

embá (moon)	mì (eye)	vo (place)	kuru (up)
ɛmba (to teach)	mɪ (you)	vɔ (to blow)	kʊrʊ̀ (ball)

må lɛ ku. I don't want it.
må sì te. I hit him.
må nì ku. I don't know.

324. BONGO

le (to dig)	í (you)	ro (name)	tu (to blow)
(t)ɛlɛ (to swim)	hɪ (belly)	rɔ (body)	tʊ (grandfather)
oŋa må. He bit me.		oŋä i. He bit you.	
é'ba 'di? You built what?		à'bä ru. He built a house.	

A further characteristic of Bongo-Bagirmi (especially in the western dialects) is the tendency to elide final vowels in words.

BONGO: tara (mouth), cf. BAGIRMI: tar(a)
nyíhí (moon), cf. BAGIRMI: nap
hómò (nose), cf. BAGIRMI: hum

325. NDOGO

sè (fish)	njí (seed)	vo (bad)	'bú (termite)
sɛ (hair)	njɪ̀ (bowels)	vɔ (five)	'bʊʊ (bamboo)

There is no centralizing of **a** in Ndogo-Sere.

326. ZANDE

(h)imò (to kill)	súŋä (to sit)
(h)ɪma (to suffer)	vʊ́ŋà (to bear)
mi ná rúndà. I am biting.	àdaɪ̯ɪ (frogs)
mi nä súŋä. I am sitting.	àdäɪ̯i (those who deny)

Morphology.

327. 6. The Eastern Sudanic languages on the whole do not show grammatical gender. The only exceptions are Bongo (alone of the whole Bango-Bagirmi group) and Zande, both of which languages show it in pronouns only.

BONGO: ba = he, him   ho = she, her
ZANDE: ko = he, him   ri = she, her   (r)u = it (animal)
       i = they, them   (i = they, them)   ami = they (animals)
                                                             ra = them ,,

328. 7. Noun formatives are few, noun compounds very common. The following are the main noun formatives:[1]

329. MORU-MADI

Prefixes.

MORU: ɔ-'bí (to beat); la-'bí (beating)

---

[1] Apart from affixed *words* as in Moru: kumba-'ba (warrior = war-man), ŋgɔ-inya (food = thing eat), in which all these languages abound.

Suffixes.
LOGO: be (to catch fish); kosia be-**le-pi-'di** (fisher, i.e. fish catcher)

330. BONGO-BAGIRMI
Prefixes.
BONGO: o-nyi (to eat)   **m**-ony(i) (food)
SARA: oji (to smoke)   **k**-wèjí (tobacco)
MOROKODO: ɛ'bɛ (to go)   **'d**-ɛ'bɛ (journey)

Suffixes (none).

331. NDOGO-SERE has no noun-forming particles.

332. ZANDE
Prefixes.
munda (to help)   **mo**-unda (a helper)
za (to mediate)   **a**-zaro (a mediator)

Suffixes.
nunga (to travel)   nung-**uro** (a journey)
mbu (to be weary)   mbu-**ġo** (weariness)

333. 8. In MORU-MADI the singular and plural of nouns need not be distinguished, though an optional suffix **-i** (**-ki** in dialects) may be used. This suffix may be attached either to the noun or to the verb (in 3rd person only).

MORU: kắrì (giraffe), pl. kärì-**ì**. But kắrì mu-**í**-te. The giraffes ran away.

MADI: oko (woman), pl. oko-**nzi** (N.B.)
odra-ra. He died.   odra-**ki**-ra. They died.

334. In BONGO-BAKA the singular and plural of nouns is usually not distinguished. In the western dialects, Sara and Bagirmi, plurality is indicated by the suffix **-ġe** attached to nouns or nominal phrases and by the suffix **-ki** attached to verbs, in the 2nd (and sometimes the 1st) person.

BAGIRMI: bisi-ma (my dog); bisi-m-**ġe** (my dogs)
    je tad(a) or je tad-**ki**.   We shall do.
    ka tad-**ki**.   You ,, ,,
    je tad(a).   They ,, ,,

335. In NDOGO-SERE and in ZANDE plurality is, as a rule, indicated by means of prefixes, **nda-** in Ndogo-Sere, **a-** in Zande. (This prefix is often omitted when the noun is already qualified by a numeral adjective. In Ndogo-Sere it may be separated from its noun by an intervening adjective.)

NDOGO: nì (woman), pl. **ndá**-nì. **ndá**-'dù táo. Three people.
    gbolo kara (big pot), pl. **ndá**-gbolo kara.
    ndá-Lemgbo ta nì-mɔ. Limbo and his wife.

ZANDE: de (woman), pl. **a**-de.
    nyanyaki kumba (strong man), pl. nyanyaki **a**-kumba.
    a-Gangura na Ngindo. Gangura and Ngindo.

336. 9. Case relationship is shown either by position in the sentence or else by association with a preposition (in Bongo-Baka, Ndogo-Sere, Zande) or a postposition (in Moru-Madi).

337. MORU-MADI

    MORU: ánya 'bi ma te dri **ya**.   He hit me on the head.
           má ga bí te ɔpí **rí**.   I paid attention to the chief.
           mɔrú fu ezá kúsu **sì**.   The Moru kill game with the bow.

338. BONGO-BAGIRMI

    'BELI: ála **do** dəma.   He hit (me) on my head.
    BONGO: 'bi'dé mini **ji** ma.   Bring water to me.
    BAGIRMI: adim-mbaŋ pia **jis**(e) Mbaŋ(a).   The attendants play with the chief.
    BAGIRMI: (N.B.) adiny Mbaŋ-**ki**.   Give it to the chief.
    BAGIRMI: omum man **jo-m-ki**.   Pour water on top of me.

339. NDOGO-SERE

  kù **ti**-lɔ é we?   How are you? (Lit. Skin on you how?)
  i bvaka nambve **ji** nda-'du.   He does services to (all) men.
  gbì í **ta** mú.   Hit him with a stick.

340. ZANDE

    mo fu e **fu** ko.   Give it to him.
    mo de e **ni** mangua.   Cut it with an axe.
    ani ndu **ku** Maridi **yo**.   Let us go to Maridi.

Zande, however, has accusative case forms for most of the *pronouns*. (Examples from Lagae.)

    mi ni-ye ka-bi **ro**.   I have come to see you.
    mo ni-ye ka-bi **re**.   You have come to see me.
    ani ni-ye ka-bi **roni**.   We have come to see you (pl.).
    oni ni-ye ka-bi **rani**.   You have come to see us.
    u na-li gi lihẽ, mo-dendi **ru**.   It is eating my food, chase it.
    ami na-ka-mera, mo-a-bi-nga **ra** te?   They (the animals) are fleeing, don't
                                                       you see them?

341. 10. There are no derivative verb species except in Zande. Motion to and from the speaker is indicated in Moru-Madi by alternations in the prefixed vowel, elsewhere by verb combinations with the verb forms 'come' and 'go'.

342. MORU-MADI

    MORU: ɛŋgá (to fly towards)   MADI: ɛdzi (to bring here)
              ɔ-ŋgá (to fly away)   dzi (to take there)

343. BONGO-BAGIRMI

        BAGIRMI: dese (bring = arrive with)
                       abse (take = go with)

344. NDOGO-SERE

        jɛ-gi-ti (bring = give come with)
        je-ia-ti (take = give go with)

345. ZANDE has an almost Bantu-like set of derived verb species:

        ti (to fall)   tisa (to cause to fall)
        pi (to lie)   piga (to lay)
        sunga (to sit)   sungada (to wait for)
        kpi (to die)   kpika (to die—of many people, &c.)
        so (to spear)   sopa (to hoe, to pierce)

CHARACTERISTICS OF THE EASTERN SUDANIC LANGUAGES 69

346. 11. The verb stem is invariable for person and number (except in Madi), but the appropriate pronoun (often contracted) is prefixed. 'Tense' prefixes, when used, stand between the pronoun and the verb stem.

There is also an auxiliary particle **ka**, which in some Moru-Madi dialects is used in the 3rd person, but which in some Bongo-Bagirmi dialects is used with the 2nd person, in certain tenses.

The plural suffix **-ki** (or **-i**) is found in some Moru-Madi dialects in the 3rd person and in the western Sara-Bagirmi dialects in the 2nd person (and sometimes in the 1st person).

347. MORU-MADI[1]

MORU:	má ɔ̀dra.	MADI:	ma dra.	I am dying.
	myá ɔ̀dra.		nyi dra.	You are dying.
	ánya **ká** ɔ̀dra.		**k-odra**.	He is dying.
	màá ɔ̀dra.		ama dra.	We are dying.
	nyàá ɔdra.		anyi dra.	You are dying.
	ànya **ká** ɔdra.		**ka ki** dra.	They are dying.

348. BONGO-BAGIRMI[2]

BONGO:	má dɔ ...	BAGIRMI:	ma tad(a) ...	I am doing ...
	í dɔ ...		(i) **ka** tad(a) ...	You are doing ...
	bá dɔ ...		ne tad(a) ...	He is doing ...
	hó dɔ ...		,, ,,	She is doing ...
	jé dɔ ...		je tad(**ki**) ...	We are doing ...
	hé dɔ ...		(se) **ka** tad**ki** ...	You are doing ...
	ié dɔ ...		je tad(a) ...	They are doing ...

349. NDOGO-SERE

NDOGO:	(i)é nju ...	I drink ...
	wó nju ...	You drink ...
	í nju ...	He drinks ...
	zé nju ...	We (excl.) drink ...
	ndóó nju ...	We (incl.) drink ...
	yó nju ...	You drink ...
	ndú nju ...	They drink ...

350.

ZANDE:	mi na manga ...	I am doing ...
	mo na manga ...	You are doing ...
	ko na manga ...	He is doing ...
	ri na manga ...	She is doing ...
	ani na manga ...	We are doing ...
	oni na manga ...	You are doing ...
	i na manga ...	They are doing ...

351. 12. There are no tense forms of the verb stem, and few tense particles in MORU-MADI and in BONGO-BAGIRMI. In both these language groups, however, existing verb forms may be intensified or given varying shades of meaning by the use of a host of postpositional particles, whose normal position is at the end of the sentence. (They are most common in Moru-Madi.)

[1] Some elements in the paradigms have had to be coined on analogy of other verbs, since, in my field notes, the verb 'to die' does not appear for all persons.
[2] Some elements in the paradigms have had to be coined on analogy of other verbs, since, in my field notes, the word 'to do' does not appear for all persons.

352. MORU: ánya ɛgwɔ 'dá ya?   Did he come back?
           ɔu, ɛgo tɛ ... or ndí ... or 'dá.   Yes, he did.
           lédr dra **gí'dá** yà?   Did the man actually die?
           a'di 'bi mi **ni** yá?   Who hit you?
           ma nyá ló'ba **ndí**.   We *do* eat hartebeest.

353.   BONGO: múgà nɛ '**du**.   *I* cut it.
           mutú fó'du **rɔ̀**.   I blew the fire.
           aí '**bá**.   Come!

354. Tenses are numerous in NDOGO-SERE and in ZANDE, and are indicated by the agglutination of a variety of prefixes in a manner reminiscent of Bantu tenses. In some ways these prefixes correspond in function to the postpositions of Moru-Madi and Bongo-Baka, but they have on the whole a more temporal significance.

355.   NDOGO: ye-si.   I buy.
                 ye-**ku**-si.   I am buying.
                 ye-**ka**-si.   I bought.
                 ye-**ka-ku**-si.   I was buying.
                 ye-**gí**-si.   I bought.
                 ye-**bva**-si.   I shall buy.
                 ye-**ku-bva**-si.   I am buying.
                 ye-**ma**-si.   If I buy.

Verbal postpositions are not at all numerous here. There are, in fact, only four main postpositions indicating (1) positive, (2) negative, (3) interrogative, and (4) exclamatory speech respectively, and may be used with almost any of the above 'tenses'.

           ye-gbi i **gi**.   I beat him.
           ye-gbi i **la**.   I didn't beat him.
           wo-gbi i gi **we**?   Did you beat him?
           dédi tómbvú jé **yo**!   Bring me a net!

356. ZANDE: mi-gumba.   I have said, I say.
                 mi-**na**-gumba.   I am saying, I say, I was saying, I had said.
                 mi-**ni**-gumba.   I say, I said.
                 mi-**ni-na**-gumba.   I am saying, I say.
                 mi-**a**-gumba.   I say, I said, I was saying, I will say.
                 mi-**na-a**-gumba.   I am saying, I say, I will say.
                 mi-**a-ni**-gumba.   I said, I had been saying, I will say.
                 mi-**na-ni**-gumba.   I said, I had been saying, I will say.
                 mi-**a-na**-gumba.   I used to say.
                 mi-**a-a**-gumba.   I used to say.
                 mi-**na-a**-gumba.   I was saying.
                 mi-**na-na**-gumba.   I used to say.

There are no verbal postpositions in Zande.

357. 13. In BONGO-BAGIRMI and ZANDE there is no passive form of the verb stem, the passive relationship being expressed by a specialized use of the 3rd person (usually plural) form.[1]

     BONGO: lamgba ru rɔ. The house was burnt. (Lit. Burned the house.)
              (Cf. fo'du lamgbá rú rɔ. Fire burned the house.)

[1] In the Sara of Delafosse alone, a passive form with suffix -**ŋga** is found. *m-usăga*. I am eaten. (Cf. *m-usa*. I eat.)

BAGIRMI: napne ji-joki ŋga. The moon is eclipsed. (Lit. The moon they tied thing.)
ZANDE: i a imo ko. He shall be killed. (Lit. They will kill him.)

358. In MORU-MADI and NDOGO-SERE, on the other hand, there is a distinct passive form of the verb, with prefix a-,[1] demanding in its conjugation a word order different from that of the active.

  MORU: á-'bɪ ma te. I was beaten.
   (Cf. má 'bɪ ŋgágà te. I beat the boy.)
  NDOGO: a-si ye. I am bought. a-gi-si ye. I was bought.
   (Cf. ye-si. I buy. ye-gi-si. I bought.)

359. 13*a*. In MORU-MADI, BONGO-BAGIRMI, and ZANDE (but not in Ndogo-Sere), the verb stem itself has two forms (aspects) according as the action of the verb is (i) incomplete, imperfect, progressive, *indefinite*, or (ii) complete, perfect, *definite*. (The imperative usually falls within the definite category.)

360. In MORU-MADI and BONGO-BAGIRMI the formal distinction lies in the pronouns and in the presence or absence of the 'characteristic' vowel[2] prefix in the verb stem. In Moru-Madi (and Bongo) also, the word order in the sentence is distinctive.

Definite Aspect

MORU:[3] má-**dʒwa** lúmvú (tɛ). I washed myself.
  mí-**dʒwa** lúmvú (tɛ). You washed yourself.
  ánya **dʒwa** lúmvú (tɛ). He washed himself.
  mà-**dʒwa** lúmvú (tɛ). We washed ourselves.
  mì-**dʒwa** lúmvú (tɛ). You washed yourselves.
  ànya **dʒwa** lúmvú (tɛ). They washed themselves.

Indefinite Aspect

MORU: má lúmvú **òdʒwa**. I'm washing myself.
  nyá lúmvú **òdʒwa**. You are washing yourself.
  ánya ká lúmvú **òdʒwa**. He is washing himself.
  mà lúmvú **òdʒwa**. We are washing ourselves.
  nyà lúmvú **òdʒwa**. You are washing yourselves.
  ànya ká lúmvú **òdʒwa**. They are washing themselves.

Definite Aspect	*Indefinite Aspect*
MADI:[3] **á-dzè** ru ra.	**má** ru dzè.
í-dzè ru ra.	**nyí** ru dzè.
(andá) **odzè** ru ra.	(andá) ká ru dzè.
àma-**dzè** ru ra.	ama ru dze.
ànyi-**dzè** ru ra.	anyi ru dze.
odzè-ki ru ra.	ka ki ru dze.

[1] If this prefix a- is to be etymologically regarded as a relic of an old 3rd person plural pronoun (cf. §§ 256 and 261), then Moru-Madi and Ndogo-Sere may be said to express the passive relationship in a Sudanic manner. There is, however, no apparent relationship between this a- and the current 3rd person pronoun forms.
[2] By 'characteristic' is meant a vowel which harmonizes, according to phonetic rules, with the vowel in the verb-root.
[3] The plural section of the above paradigms is coined on the analogy of other verbs, since, in my field notes, the verb 'to wash' is not conjugated for all persons.

BONGO

Definite Aspect		Indefinite Aspect	
m-otá i.	I see you.	ma-tä i.	I am seeing you.
otá ma.	You see me.	í-ta ma.	You are seeing me.
b-útá jɛ.	He sees us.	ba-ta jɛ.	He is seeing us.
ota jɛ iɛ.	We see them.	jɛ-ta iɛ.	We are seeing them.
otá hɛ jɛ.	You see us.	hɛ-ta iɛ.	You are seeing them.
i-ota hɛ.	They see you.	iɛ-ta hɛ.	They are seeing you.

BAGIRMI

m-ab(e).	I went.	ma-kab(e).	I go habitually.
ab(e).	You ,,	(i)-ka-kab(e).	You go ,,
n-ab(e).	He ,,	ne-kab(e).	He goes ,,
j-ab(e).	We ,,	je-kab(e).	We go ,,
ab-ki.	You ,,	(se)-ka-kab-ki.	You go ,,
j-ab(e).	They ,,	je-kab(e).	They go ,,

361. In ZANDE the two forms of the verb stem are distinguished by suffixes, **-a** for indefinite tenses and **-i** (or **-u -e -o** according to phonetic laws) for definite tenses. It should be noted in this context that the distinction in this language has also much in common with that found in Bantu[1] languages, viz.:

        -a indicating action ('imperfect').
        -i indicating state as the result of an action ('perfect').

Some typical tense forms:

Definite (perfect)		Indefinite (imperfect)	
mi-mangi.[2]	I do, I have done.	mi-na-manga.	I do, I am doing.
mi-ni-mangi.	I have done.		
		mi-ni-na-manga.	I am doing
		mi-na-a-manga.	(continuously).
mi-a-mangi.	I had done.	mi-a-manga.	I was doing.
mi-a-ni-mangi.	I had been doing.		
		mi-a-na-manga.	I used to do.
		mi-a-a-manga.	
mi-na-mangi.	I had done.	mi-na-manga.	I was doing.
mi-a-mangi.	I will do.	mi-a-manga.	I will do.
	(Distant future.)		
mi-a-ni-mangi.	I will do.		
	(Immediate future.)		

Syntax.

362. 14. The typical sentence order is: Subject+verb+object.

363. In MORU-MADI this sentence order is confined to 'definite' tenses, while 'indefinite' tenses have the order: Subject+object+verb, and passive tenses have the order: Verb+subject+agent or instrument (with postposition).

MORU:	má-zi ŋgàgà.	I called the boys.
	má ŋgàgà ùzi.	I'm calling the boys.
	ágyɛ ndá tɛ Mòndarì ya.	She was married to a Mondari.

---
[1] It should also be noted that in the majority of Bantu languages the 'action' stem of the verb has the suffix **-a** and the 'state' or 'perfect' form has the suffix **-ye** or **-ile**.
[2] Pronounced mäŋgi or even mo¡ŋgi.

364. In BONGO-BAGIRMI the sentence order is unaltered (except in Bongo itself in the 1st and 2nd person plural 'definite', when the order is: Verb+subject+object).

    BONGO: **isi** jɛ iɛ. We beat them.
       jɛ-**si** iɛ. We are beating them.
    SARA (*Del.*): m-**usa** za. I eat or ate meat.
         ma-**kusa** za. I am eating meat.
         m-**usã**ga. I am eaten.
         ma-**kusã**ga. I am being eaten.

365. In NDOGO-SERE the sentence order is only altered in the passive, when it is: Verb+subject+agent or instrument (with preposition).

    NDOGO: yi-**zu** ndu 'dáági. He killed them all.
       acu e ta sizo. He was wounded by a knife.

366. In ZANDE the sentence order is unaltered.

    mi-a-**mangi** sunge. I had done work.
    mi-a-**manga** sunge. I was doing work.

367. 15. The Possessor (nomen rectum) usually follows the Possessed (nomen regens), but in special constructions in Zande and in Moru-Madi (and in certain dialects) it precedes. The presence or absence of a linking particle depends upon the degree of intimacy in the possession.

368. When the possessor follows in MORU-MADI, it must itself be followed by a post-position.

  Possessor follows.   *Possessor precedes.*
MADI: 'bara opi **dri**. Son of the chief. ópí àdzu. The chief's spear.
            opi **a** 'bara. The chief's son.
            ópi **ni** 'bara. The chief's son.

369. In BONGO-BAGIRMI the possessor always follows.

    BONGO: soka fo'du. Smoke of fire.
       bihi '**ba** nyɛre. The dog of the chief.

370. In NDOGO-SERE the possessor always follows.

    'dè lámbva. Horn of gazelle.
    'bá **mi** Kayaŋgo. The house of Kayango.

371. In ZANDE, when the possessor precedes, it must itself be preceded by a preposition.

 Possessor follows.   *Possessor precedes.*
boro Ngindo. Ngindo's body. **ga** Ngindo boro. Ngindo's bodyguard.

372. 16. In MORU-MADI the adjective usually follows the noun it qualifies. Elsewhere it may either precede or follow.

MORU: àzu **kòzi**. A bad spear.
BONGO: 'be **kándà** or **makándà** 'be. A new house.
NDOGO: kara **meǵbolo** or **ǵbolo** kara. A big pot.
ZANDE: agude **bawe** (ten boys). **bakere** bambu. A big house.
           bawe gude. The tenth boy.

373. 17. 'Descriptive' adverbs (ideophones) are common to all the groups except possibly the Ndogo-Sere group.

MORU: bɔŋgó uní **gbírikílí**. The cloth is very black.
BONGO: lau mokonya **wakka wakka wakka**. The cloth is very black.
ZANDE: yuge na-pa **gugugu**. The wind is roaring boisterously.

CHAPTER VI

SOME GENERAL PRINCIPLES AND DEFINITIONS UNDERLYING THE STUDY OF EASTERN SUDANIC GRAMMAR[1]

A. Etymological Elements

374. African grammarians have already realized that the Greco-Latin model, as it stands, is no suitable framework on which to stretch the grammatical systems of the languages they wish to describe. There is, however, no need to go to the other extreme, and discard all classical terminology in the belief that none of it is applicable to African languages.[2] The fundamental task is to discover what forms exist in the language, then the functions of these forms in speech, after which grammatical labels may be attached accordingly. New terminology should be used only where current European terminology is unable to explain the function satisfactorily.

375. One of the characteristics of the Eastern Sudanic languages is that the form of a word very rarely gives the clue to its grammatical function. If one were confronted with the Latin word *amabunt*, one could, without being able to translate the word, assert that it is a verb, that it refers to the 3rd person plural and to future time. Such an amount of information is rarely given by an Eastern Sudanic word, chiefly owing to its lack of inflexion. And since these languages contain an overwhelming proportion of monosyllabic word-roots, one may even go further and say that it is impossible to tell, from its form, whether a given syllable constitutes a word, capable of standing alone, or a particle, incapable of standing alone. It is only by their functions that speech units may be classified, and it is soon apparent that single forms have multiple functions.

376. According to their function the Eastern Sudanic speech units may be tentatively divided into the following two etymological categories—*word-roots* and *particles*.

A *word-root* is: 'One of the ultimate elements of a language, that cannot be further analysed, and form the base of its vocabulary; a primary word or form from which others are derived.' (*Oxford English Dictionary*.)

'The irreducible element of a word; the primitive radical form without prefix, suffix or other flexion, and not admitting of analysis.' (Doke, *Bantu Linguistic Terminology*, p. 192.)

---

[1] In this chapter special reference should be made to the pioneer work of Doke in *A Textbook of Zulu Grammar* and *Bantu Linguistic Terminology*, and of Mrs. Ashton in *The 'Idea' Approach to Swahili* and *The Structure of a Bantu Language*. Collaboration with the last-named authority in the Bantu field has helped greatly in the evolving of the scheme under which the Eastern Sudanic languages are here discussed.

[2] This is a lesson that Doke, in a minor way, learnt, for his *Bantu Linguistic Terminology* now contains terms he rejected in his Zulu grammar, and rejects some of the new terms he had then coined for Zulu.

SOME GENERAL PRINCIPLES AND DEFINITIONS 75

Where Eastern Sudanic languages are concerned, it must be borne in mind that most forms complying with the above definitions are themselves capable of functioning as actual words, without the addition of further elements.

A *particle* is: 'A minor part of speech, especially one that is short and indeclinable, a relation word. Also, a prefix or suffix having a distinct meaning.' (*Oxford English Dictionary*.)

'A word of small volume, . . . which serves sometimes to modify the meaning of the principal words, and sometimes to express the relationships established between them.' (Marouzeau, *Lexique de la Terminologie Linguistique*, p. 138.)

Where Eastern Sudanic languages are concerned, it should be further borne in mind that particles, unlike words, are incapable of standing alone.

Word-roots.

377. According to their grammatical behaviour, or the behaviour of words and stems derived from them, word-roots may be studied under the following three heads:—Verbal roots, Nominal roots, Pronominal roots.

378. *Verbal roots* are roots which, with or without the aid of particles, are capable of functioning as:

379. (*a*) Verbs or nouns.

MORU: má-òdra.	I am dying.	adravo (sickness)
BONGO: m-onyi.	I eat.	mony(i) (food)
NDOGO: ie-zo.	I eat.	izozo (food)
ZANDE: mi-yamba.	I call.	moyambu (servant)

380. (*b*) Verbs or adverbs ('descriptives', Doke).

MORU: pe (to crow)	gogo-pe-te (cock-crow)
BONGO: m-onya-ro (I stop)	kada-nya-ro (late)
NDOGO: ie-iŋgɛle (I ran)	ti-ŋgɛle (quickly)
ZANDE: ti (to fall)	uru ti (sunset)

381. (*c*) Verbs or adjectives ('qualificatives', Doke) or adverbs.

MORU: ma-mba-te. I grew.   agó àmba-go (an old man).   amba (often).
BONGO: m-ɛ́mɛ́mɛ̀. I am good.   makɛmɛ kírɛ́ (a good arrow).   kamakeme (well).
NDOGO: ni nə nikila. This woman is bad. nikila ni (a bad woman). nda mu zə megbolo nikila. Those trees are very big.
ZANDE: gberă (to be bad).   gbegberẽ bodu (a bad man).   gbegberé (badly).

382. (*d*) Verbs or prepositions.

MORU: oso (to resemble)	oso . . . ronye (like)
BAGIRMI: tak(a) (to receive)	tak(a) (like)
ZANDE: fu (to give)	fu ko (to him)

383. (*e*) Verbs or postpositions.

LOGO: dre (to stay)	miri dra-**dre**. The chief died.
BAGIRMI: kor(o) (to be tired)	tat ŋgas **kor**(o) (to break a thing completely)
NDOGO: ie-**ġi**. I come.	yi-bia-**ġi**. He refused.

384. (*f*) Verbs or verbal auxiliaries.

LOGO: ma-dre.	I stay.	ma-**dre**-nyale.	I am eating.
BONGO: má-dɔ.	I do.	má-dɔ-ndɛ́rɛ̀.	I am walking.
NDOGO: ie-**ġi**.	I come.	ye-**ġi**-si.	I bought.

385. (*g*) Verbs or conjunctions.

    MORU: anya eke (he says). eke (that . . .)
    NDOGO: dɛle (to return). iɛ-'dɛ cɔ ji gi, kadɛle yi-bia-gi. I told him so but he refused.
    ZANDE: ya (to say). ya (that . . .).

386. (*h*) Verbs or nouns or prepositions or conjunctions.

    MORU: ata (to speak); ata (word); tana (because of); tana (because).

387. *Nominal roots* are roots which, with or without the aid of particles, are capable of functioning as:

388. (*a*) Nouns.

    MORU: ledr (person)
    BONGO: bo'du
    NDOGO: 'du
    ZANDE: boro

389. (*b*) Nouns or adverbs ('descriptives', Doke).

    MORU: ŋgäkyi (night)   ŋgäkyisi (by night)
    BONGO: hetɔrɔ̀ (sky)   tɔro (loudly)
    NDOGO: kpɔ (strength)   tikpɔ (tightly, strongly, &c.)
    ZANDE: uru (sun)   na uru (daily)

Also words like 'to-day', 'to-morrow', where the same form may be used as a noun or as an adverb.

390. (*c*) Nouns or adjectives ('qualificatives').

    MORU: ma mɔru-i. I'm a Moru.   lá'bí mɔrɔ́rɔ (Moru custom)
    BONGO: gi (child)   gi fo'du (small fire)
    NDOGO: gɔ (hunger)   siiŋgi tagoto (hungry lion)
    ZANDE: irapupo (dumb man, lit. owner of dumbness)   irapupo toro (dumb spirit)

391. (*d*) Nouns or prepositions.

    BONGO: dɔ (head)   dɔ koŋgo (on the road)
    NDOGO: muu (head)   (me)muu mbata (on the stool)
    ZANDE: ri (head)   ri gangara (on the top of the hill)

392. (*e*) Nouns or postpositions.

    MORU: drì (head)   liti drì (on the road)
    BAGIRMI: bʊra (net)   j-ab bʊra. We went on walking.

393. (*f*) Nouns or conjunctions (or prepositions).

    LOGO: ŋgá (thing)   ŋgá (because)
    BAGIRMI: jo (head)   jo (because) (because of)
    NDOGO: cɔ (word)   tacɔ (because, lit. with word)
    ZANDE: pai (thing)   pai sa (but, lit. one thing)

394. *Pronominal roots* are roots which, with or without the aid of particles, can function as:

SOME GENERAL PRINCIPLES AND DEFINITIONS

395. Pronouns or qualificatives or descriptives.
    MORU: ɔ́nɔ́ (this, it); dɔ́fɔ́ ənɔ́ (this stick); nòa (here)
    BONGO: nà rá 'bìná (it is here); ba gimá na (this boy); 'bina (here)
    NDOGO: ŋinə (this); ni nə (this woman); eno (therefore)
    ZANDE: gini ku kpi? (which died?) gini sunge? (what work?) sa gini? (why?)

396. Pronouns or qualificatives.

    MADI: ama.   We.   ama boŋgo.   Our cloth.
    BONGO: je.   We.   boŋgo je.   Our cloth.
    NDOGO: ze.   We.   bvu-ze.   Our father.
    ZANDE: ani.   We.   baŋgir-ani.   Our eyes.

397. It is to be doubted whether there are any Adjectival or Adverbial roots in the Eastern Sudanic languages.

Particles.

398. According to their morphological behaviour, particles may be studied under the following two heads:
    Inseparable particles and separable particles.

399. *Inseparable particles* are directly attached to word-roots or stems, and may not be separated from them by other intervening words or particles. They function as:—

400. Prefixes.
    MORU: **ku**su (bow), cf. MADI: ósu
    BONGO: **hen**dɔ́ (night), cf. BAGIRMI: njo
    NDOGO: **ka**pfí (back) (?)
    ZANDE: de (woman), cf. NZAKARA: **n**de.

401. Suffixes.
    MORU: kizwe (pig), cf. MADI: izo
    BAGIRMI: mba**la** (to beat), cf. BONGO: mgba
    ZANDE: tue (ear), cf. NZAKARA: tu.

402. *Separable particles* are not necessarily directly attached to word-roots or stems, but may be separated from them by other intervening words or particles. They function as:

403. (*a*) Prepositions.
    MORU: mí-pa ma **nì** zɔ́ òmɔ-nI. Help me in building a house. ɔmɔ = build.
    BONGO: **ji** ma (to me)
    NDOGO: **ji** gba (to the chief)
    ZANDE: **ni** mangua (with an axe).

404. (*b*) Postpositions.
    MORU: ndâ **bɛ** (with him)
        má-'bI nda **te**. I beat him.
    BONGO: m-ʊmgbá gimá **rə**. I beat the boy.
    NDOGO: ye-gbi i **gi**. I beat him.
    ZANDE: Yambio **yo**. (In, to, from, &c., Yambio.)

405. (*c*) Linking particles.
    MADI: opi **ni** bara (the chief's son)
    BAGIRMI: bel **an** Paca (prisoner of the Patia's)
    NDOGO: 'bá **mì** Kayaŋgo (Kayango's home).

406. (*d*) Verbal auxiliaries.

    MORU: ánya **ká**-tudú. He is sleeping.
    BONGO: ma-**rɔ**-minɔ. I am weeping.
    NDOGO: yi-**ka**-baka i. He made it.
    ZANDE: mi-**na**-manga. I am doing.

407. (*e*) Conjunctions.

 MORU: ... **oko** má-ndré läbí kʊ tɛ̀. ... but I don't see a water-buck.
 BONGO: í muny mihi **ɔra** kėnjí? Are you eating meat or fish? má 'bi sékin jii, **ke** yí ŋa kebí nɛnɛ. I give you a knife, that you may cut the rope with it.
 NDOGO: ... **ka** yi-bia-gi. ... but he refused.
 ZANDE: **ka** mo-susi ngbanda rago. ... If you pass beyond the boundary. ...

408. (*f*) Conjunctions or Prepositions or Descriptives.

 BONGO: í rɔ mínɔ **dijí-'di**? Why are you crying? (Lit. for what?)
    má rɔ minɔ **dijí** njûr. I am crying for poverty.
   ,, ,, ,, **dijí** boma do ye rɔ. ... because my father is dead.
 NDOGO: gɔ (like); gɔ-ŋinɔ (as); gɔ-ŋinɔ (thus, i.e. like that)
 ZANDE: mo ndu ka yamba Kereboro (**ba**)mbiko mi na kpi nyemu ka fu ngua fu ko. Go and call Kereboro because I want to give medicine to him.
   mi na u (**ba**)mbiko ngua kaza. I am recovering on account of the medicine.

B. Parts of Speech

409. As can be seen from the foregoing, any one form may have a great variety of functions. Since, in the majority of cases, the form of a word is no criterion, the various parts of speech must be determined by their function in the sentence. The problem is how many parts of speech should be recognized.

410. Jesperson (*A Philosophy of Grammar*, p. 91), speaking for languages in general, maintains that 'the following word-classes ... are grammatically distinct enough for us to recognize them as separate 'parts of speech', viz.

(1) Substantives (including proper names).
(2) Adjectives.
 In some respects (1) and (2) may be classed together as 'Nouns'.
(3) Pronouns (including numerals and pronominal adverbs).
(4) Verbs.
(5) Particles (comprising what are generally called adverbs, prepositions, conjunctions—co-ordinating and subordinating—and interjections). This fifth class may be negatively characterized as made up of all those words that cannot find any place in any of the first four classes.

411. Doke, from the results of investigations in a number of Bantu languages, has decided (*Bantu Linguistic Terminology*, p. 28) that the following classification of 'parts of speech' is essential in studying a Bantu language. His classification is based partly on functional and partly on formal (i.e. type of prefix used) grounds:

 I. Substantive: (1) Noun.
       (2) Pronoun: (*a*) Absolute.
            (*b*) Demonstrative.
            (*c*) Enumerative.
            (*d*) Qualificative.

SOME GENERAL PRINCIPLES AND DEFINITIONS 79

II. Qualificative: (1) Adjective.
      (2) Relative.
      (3) Numeral.
      (4) Possessive.
III. Predicative: (1) Verb.
      (2) Copulative.
IV. Descriptive: (1) Adverb.
      (2) Ideophone.
V. Conjunction.
VI. Interjection (including vocatives and imperatives).

412. In Eastern Sudanic languages classification will have to be almost entirely functional. It is true that certain particles, &c., are attached to forms only under specific grammatical conditions, but they are not necessarily the sole criteria of these conditions. With this aspect duly considered, the parts of speech deemed necessary for the study of Eastern Sudanic languages are as follows:[1]

413. 1. *Noun*: 'A word used as the name or description of a person or thing' (*Oxford English Dictionary*).
'A word which signifies the name of anything concrete or abstract' (Doke, p. 152). Nouns are formed from Nominal or Verbal roots:

MORU:	drí (hand)	lägú (laughter)	(vb. gu)
BONGO:	ji	mínyí (smell)	(vb. inyi)
NDOGO:	'bi	bagɛɛ (building)	(vb. gɛɛ)
ZANDE:	be	ngara (bravery)	(vb. ngara)

414. 2. *Pronoun*: 'A word used instead of a noun substantive, to designate an object without naming it, when that which is referred to is known from context or usage, has been already mentioned or indicated, or, being unknown, is the subject or object of inquiry' (*Oxford English Dictionary*).
'A word which signifies anything concrete or abstract without being its name' (Doke, p. 178). Pronouns are formed from Pronominal roots.

MORU:	ma (I)	à'di (who?)
BONGO:	ma	yeki
NDOGO:	ie	'di
ZANDE:	mi	da

415. For purposes of easy reference the term *Substantive* (as in Doke) will be occasionally used to cover both Noun and Pronoun.[2] This is a purely arbitrary use of the term.

416. *Qualificative pronouns* (i.e. qualificative forms used substantivally: see Doke, p. 181) are formed from the same roots as Qualificatives. (See § 419.)

MORU:	maro (mine)	kadŭna (a good one)
BONGO:	'bama	makùnya (a bad one)
NDOGO:	ìmɛ	toi (a good one)
ZANDE:	gimi	wene-e (a good one)

---

[1] The order in which they are presented here is not necessarily the same as that in which they are discussed in the grammar sections.
[2] Doke unfortunately fails, in his definitions, to make a satisfactory differentiation in function between 'Noun' (p. 152) and 'Substantive' (p. 205).

417. There are certain pronominal forms (interrogative, demonstrative, &c.) which may function both as pronouns and as qualificatives (see Part I, Chapter VII). The term Pronoun (and Substantive) will cover these forms only in their first function.

MADI:	iŋgo (which one?)	'dɔ (this one)
BONGO:	bándá	nà
NDOGO:	ŋgá	ŋinɔ
ZANDE:	gini	gere

418. 3. *Adjective*: 'A word standing for the name of an attribute, which being added to the name of a thing describes the thing more fully or definitely' (*Oxford English Dictionary*).

'A word which qualifies a substantive' (Doke, p. 44).[1]

Adjectives are formed from nominal or verbal roots.

Numerals are included under adjectives.

MORU:	ŋgaga **kadoro** (a good boy)	mapa **nji** (five loaves)
BONGO:	**makùnya** kɨrɛ̀ (a bad arrow)	a'ji **moto** (three men)
NDOGO:	**ŋgu** 'ba (a new house)	nda-u'du **tao** (three people)
ZANDE:	**bakere** bodu (a big person)	agude **bawe** (ten boys)

419. For purposes of easy reference, the term *Qualificative*[2] (as in Doke) will be used to cover not only adjectives but also relative and possessive forms and those pronominal forms mentioned in § 417 (interrogative, demonstrative, &c.) when used to qualify substantives.

MORU:	täpi **maro** (my father)	ledr '**dɔ** (this man)
BONGO:	dɔ̀ **ma** (my head)	ba gimá **na** (this boy)
NDOGO:	'bá **mɛ** (my house)	ni **nɔ** (this woman)
ZANDE:	**gi** bambu (my house)	**gi** aboro **re** (this person)

420. 4. *Verb*: 'That part of speech by which an assertion is made, or which seems to connect a subject with a predicate'[3] (*Oxford English Dictionary*).

'A word which signifies an action connected with a substantive (i.e. noun or pronoun) or the state in which a substantive is' (Doke, p. 217).[4]

Verbs are formed from Verbal roots only.

MORU:	ny-**ekyi**. Come!	ópí **drà**-te. The chief is dead.
BONGO:	**ai** ('ba).	nyéré **we**-rɔ.
NDOGO:	**gi**.	gbá **ci**-gi.
ZANDE:	mo-**ye**.	gbia **kpi**.

421. For purposes of easy reference the term *Predicative*[5] will be used (as in Doke) to cover all words or phrases as have 'the quality of predicating, affirming or asserting' (*Oxford English Dictionary*) or denying or inquiring. There is, however, no part of speech that can be labelled '*Copulative*',[6] since predicative constructions involve

---

[1] The only differentiation Doke makes between Adjective and Qualificative is in the formation and not in the function.

[2] The term is not used here in as embracing a sense as in the *Oxford English Dictionary*: 'A word, as an adjective or adverb, attached to another word to qualify it.'

[3] The *Oxford English Dictionary* definition does not quite fit Eastern Sudanic languages, as under such a definition 'linking particles' (see Part I, § 717) would have to be classed as verbs.

[4] Doke's definition is further framed to exclude Bantu imperatives and infinitives; the former he classes as interjections and the latter as nouns. His example is not followed here.

[5] Doke fails in his definitions to make any differentiation in function between 'verb' (p. 217) and 'predicative' (p. 173).

[6] 'A word which does the work of a predicative, and which is formed directly from some other part of speech'. (Doke, p. 82.)

SOME GENERAL PRINCIPLES AND DEFINITIONS 81

parts of speech already defined, viz. verbs, nouns, pronouns, adjectives, also adverbs. In some cases predication is affected by juxtaposition, in others with the aid of particles or auxiliaries.[1]

Examples of non-verbal predicatives:

(Nouns) *(Pronouns)*
MORU: má mɔ̀rʊ-i. I'm a Moru. mí a'dì yà? Who are you?
BONGO: má boŋgò. I'm a Bongo. yí yéki?
NDOGO: iɛ á ndɔgò. I'm a Ndogo. wɔ a 'di we?
ZANDE: mi **nga** zande. I'm a Zande. da **ŋga** mo?

(Adjectives) *(Adverbs)*
MORU: ma kadoro. I am well. íŋgwa yà? Where are you?
BONGO: 'bè na makanda. The house is new. má o. I am here.
NDOGO: boŋgo a bvibvi. The cloth is black. keji (**ku**) nɔ. The road is here.
ZANDE: ko **du** bakere. He is big. ko wari? \
wari **du** ko?/ Where is he?

422. 5. *Adverb*: 'A word that modifies or qualifies an adjective, verb or other adverb' (*Oxford English Dictionary*).

'A word which describes a Qualificative, Predicative or other adverb with respect to manner, place and time' (Doke, p. 44).

Adverbs are formed from Verbal, Nominal, or Pronominal roots, and, in the case of Descriptive Adverbs (Ideophones),[2] from roots which often contain sounds not found in other kinds of words (see § 373; also Part I, § 759 et seq.).

(Verbal) *(Nominal)* *(Pronominal)*
MORU: vo-ni-te (at night-fall) kovole(se) (afterwards) eŋwa? (where?)
BONGO: kamakitigɔ (strongly) bıhı (down) 'baki (there)
NDOGO: ti-ŋgɛle (quickly) ti-kpɔ (strongly) kazɔ (there)
ZANDE: gbegbere (badly) ni-pai (greatly) erẽ (here)

423. There are, further, many phrases to be found which, though they in themselves are not adverbs nor contain adverbs, yet are composed of the same component parts as go to the formation of adverbs, and have the same function. For such phrases the term *Adverbial expression* or *Adverbial* will be used. Compare:

(Adverb) *(Adverbial)*
MORU: kunduä-**si** (behind) kusu **si** (with a bow)
BONGO: di**jí**-'di? (why?) di**jí** 'boo (because of hunger)
NDOGO: **ti**-kpɔ (fast, hard) **ti** ndu (on them)
ZANDE: **ni**-ba-sa (immediately) **ni** baso (with a spear)

424. *Preposition*: 'An indeclinable word or particle serving to mark the relation between two notional words, the latter of which is usually a substantive or pronoun. The following substantive or pronoun is said to be "governed" by the preposition' (*Oxford English Dictionary*).

'Prepositions are indeclinable words which, besides other uses, are placed before

---

[1] Some of the latter could be labelled '*Copula*' on the strength of the *Oxford English Dictionary* definition, 'That part of a proposition which connects the subject and predicate', but nothing would be gained by doing so here.

[2] 'A vivid representation of an idea in sound. A word, often onomatopoeic, which describes a predicate, qualificative or adverb in respect to manner, colour, sound, smell, action, state or intensity' (Doke, p. 118). Doke divorces the Ideophone from the Adverb, including both under the wider classification of 'Descriptive'. His example is not followed here.

substantives and pronouns to define their relation to other words' (Bradley, quoted by Doke).

Prepositions are formed from Verbal or Nominal roots or from Particles. They are relatively rare in Moru-Madi.

    MORU: oso ... ronye (like); le ... ya (as far as); ni (from).
    BAGIRMI: tak(a) (like); de ro-m-ki (next to me), cf. ro (= body); se (with).
    NDOGO: giti (towards), cf. gi (= come); gbi tai (in the room), cf. gbi (= belly); ta (with).
    ZANDE: ku (to), cf. ku (= give); be (from), cf. be (= hand); ni (with).

425. *Postposition*: 'A particle or relational word placed after another word, usually as an enclitic; especially a word having the function of a preposition, which follows instead of precedes its object' (*Oxford English Dictionary*).

Postpositions are formed from Verbal or Nominal roots or from Particles, and they may be used after both Substantives and Verbs. They are very common in Moru-Madi, but relatively rare in the other languages.

After substantives:
    MORU: zo **ya** (in the house), cf. ya (= belly); mi-**ri** (to you).
    BAGIRMI: kuj-iny-**ki** (in his hut).
    ZANDE: gbata **yo** (in or out of the pot).

After verbs:
    LOGO: dra-**dre** (he died), cf. dre (= to be); ma-ali-**dí** (I'm just coming).
    BAGIRMI: ma-tad-**jo** ŋgas ena. I'll do that thing again. Cf. jo (= head).
    NDOGO: agbi i **g̣i** (he was beaten), cf. gi (= to come).

426. *Conjunction*: 'An uninflected word used to connect clauses or sentences, or to co-ordinate words in the same clause' (*Oxford English Dictionary*).

Conjunctions are formed from Verbal or Nominal roots or from Particles.

    MORU: tana (because) (cf. to say);   ŋga (because) (cf. thing); oko (but).
    BAGIRMI: jo (because) (cf. head); to (if).
    NDOGO: kadɛle (but) (cf. to return);   tacɔ (because) (cf. word); ka (if).
    ZANDE: ya (that) (cf. to say);   pai sa (but) (cf. thing); ka (but).

427. *Interjection*: 'A natural ejaculation expressive of some feeling or emotion, used or viewed as a Part of Speech' (*Oxford English Dictionary*).

'An isolated word which has no grammatical bearing upon the rest of the sentence' (Doke, p. 130).

    MORU: owa! (expression of disapproval)
    BAGIRMI: a!
    NDOGO: akoo!
    ZANDE: ai!

428. As stated earlier, the terms 'Substantive', 'Qualificative', and 'Predicative' are used here, not as parts of speech in themselves (as in Doke) but as collective names for groups of parts of speech with similar but not identical functions. A fourth collective term would doubtless be very useful for all those parts of speech which Jesperson rather vaguely classes as 'particles' (see § 410), for, in the Eastern Sudanic languages especially, many adverbs, prepositions, postpositions, and conjunctions, both in form and in their relationship functions, are very closely allied.

    MORU: From **kundu** (= back):
        zɔ **kundu** (behind the house) (lit. house's back)
        kundu-äsi (behind) (adverb)

SOME GENERAL PRINCIPLES AND DEFINITIONS 83

    From **ta** (= to say):
        tana-'di (why?)
        tana ama du. For we are many.
        nda ye **tana** ma. He did it for my sake.
LUGBARA: **si** (a particle)
        dru-**si** (to-morrow) a'di-**si** (why? lit. what with)
        amani ovule obiro ri-**si**. For we are many.
    Compare these examples with the construction:
        usu **si** (with a bow)
BAGIRMI: From **jo** (= head):
        ma-put-**jo** ta. I'll pass again.
        jo sandukniki. On the box.
        dob-ena ŋgëlali, **jo** morbo. The road is bad because of mud.
        jo nam eli, je-mbileny(a). If it is not fat, we'll exchange it.
    Compare the last three examples with the construction:
        jo-ma (my head)
NDOGO: From **ta** (a particle) and **cɔ** (= to say):
        igi **taco** wo.   He is coming for you.
        tacɔ-ɛ?   Why?
        tacɔ mù ni ɛ gi. Because the rain fell.
    Compare these examples with the construction:
        co-tiri **ta** cɔ Sere. Story (lit. word of Tiri) in the language of Sere.
ZANDE: mbata (first, beforehand) fu (to)
        mbata fu (before) (conjunction)
        tipa-rani (for us)
        tipa-gine? Why?

    Other grammatical terms needing definition are:

429. *Verbal auxiliary*: 'A formative element which serves to differentiate the various tenses, &c. in verbs' (Doke, p. 57).

This term is reserved for such elements as precede the verb stem. Elements which follow it are either Suffixes or Verbal Postpositions.

Verbal auxiliaries are formed from Verbal roots or from Particles.

    MORU: ma-**te** enya uwi. I am grinding grain. Cf. te (to stay); ánya ká-tudù.
        He is sleeping.
    BAGIRMI: m-**et** kab(e). I am walking. Cf. etu (to be); **ka**-tad(a). You did.
    NDOGO: ie-**gi**-si. I bought. Cf. gi (to come); ie-**ba**-si. I shall buy.
    ZANDE: mi-**a**-manga. I do.

430. *Linking particle*. A particle which stands between two words and serves to associate them.[1]

        MADI: opi **a** bara (the chief's son)
        BONGO: gimá '**ba** nyɛ́rɛ́ (the son of the chief)
        NDOGO: ɓi (**mì**) gba (the son of the chief)

431. *Affix*: 'Affixes are additions to roots, stems and words, serving to modify their meaning or use. They are of two kinds, prefixes, those at the beginning, and

---

[1] A linking particle differs from a preposition in that it must always be preceded by a substantive, whereas a preposition may be preceded by any part of speech, or may begin a sentence.

suffixes, those at the end of the word bases to which they are affixed' (*Oxford English Dictionary*).

'An element which is capable of being attached to or incorporated with a word, in order to modify its function, meaning, value, &c. According as it is initial, medial or final, it is termed prefix, infix or suffix' (Doke, p. 45).

Neither definition is comprehensive enough for Eastern Sudanic languages, since in the study of these languages account should also be taken of affixes whose existence can be proved only by etymological means. For example, the **he** in Bongo **hendə** (night) is here regarded as a prefix, because the corresponding word in Bagirmi (**njo**) has no initial syllable; the Bongo word, however, cannot be said to differ in 'function, meaning, value, &c.' from the Bagirmi word on account of this prefix. Similarly, the **-pi** in Moru **täpi** (father) is here regarded as a suffix, because the corresponding word in Madi is **ata**, but the Moru word cannot be said to differ in 'function, meaning, value, &c.' from the Madi word on account of this suffix.

432. For the purpose of this book, affixes will be discussed under two heads:

Stem affixes: Elements which are incorporated with certain words or stems in certain languages, but which do not appear to modify them in function, meaning, value, &c., since corresponding words or stems in related languages are without these elements.

Morphological or Semantic affixes: Elements which are capable of being attached to or incorporated with a word or stem, in order to modify its function, meaning, value, &c. (Doke's definition of 'affix'.)

Only prefixes and suffixes will be discussed in this work. Infixes do not occur.[1]

433. *Prefix*: 'An affix attached to the beginning of a word or stem' (Doke, p. 174). Stem prefixes are formed from particles only.

       MORU: **k**oto (ant-hill), cf. MADI: oto
       BONGO: **b**íhi (dog), cf. BAKA: ísì
       NDOGO: **kà**pfá (lake) (?)

Morphological, &c. prefixes are formed from nominal roots or from particles.

    MORU: **ŋg**ɔinya (food), cf. ŋga (thing)   lɔŋgɔ (a song)
    BONGO: **a'ji** mony (food), cf. a'ji (thing)   minyi (a smell)
    NDOGO: **iz**ɔzɔ (food), cf. i (thing)   **nda** 'du (people)
    ZANDE: **ira**dī (thief), cf. ira (owner)   aboro (people)

434. *Suffix*: 'An affix attached to the end of a word or stem' (Doke, p. 206). Stem suffixes are formed from particles only.

       MORU: bi (ear), cf. LUGBARA: bí-**le**
       BONGO: mbi-**li** (ear), cf. BAGIRMI: mbi
       ZANDE: tu-**e** (ear), cf. NZAKARA: tu

Morphological, &c. suffixes are formed from nominal roots or from particles.

     MORU: kila-**'ba** (warrior), cf. 'ba (person); kila'ba-**ı** (warriors)
     BAGIRMI: ŋgon-**ne** (girl), cf. ne (woman); ŋgan-**ge** (children)
     ZANDE: ina-**pase** (knowledge), cf. pai (matter); nungu-**ro** (a journey)

---

[1] The prevalence of prefix and suffix *combinations* may often give one the impression that there are infixes in these languages.

PART I

THE MORU-MADI LANGUAGE GROUP

CONTENTS

Section I. PHONETICS		89
Chapter I. Vowels		89
,, II. Consonants		100
,, III. Intonation		111
,, IV. The Comparative Phonetics of Moru-Madi		114
Section II. GRAMMAR		126
Chapter V. Nouns		126
,, VI. Personal Pronouns		138
,, VII. Other Pronouns and Pronominal Adjuncts		144
,, VIII. The Genitive Constructions		159
,, IX. Prepositions and Postpositions		166
,, X. Verb Classes		177
,, XI. Verb Conjugation		180
,, XII. Verbs in Sub-dialects		195
,, XIII. The Function of Verb Stem Prefixes		204
,, XIV. Auxiliary Verbs and Particles		219
,, XV. Verb Suffixes		234
,, XVI. Verb Postpositions		247
,, XVII. Relative Constructions		262
,, XVIII. The Tonal Conjugation of Verbs		270
,, XIX. Adjectives		282
,, XX. Predicative Constructions		290
,, XXI. Reduplication in Verbs and Adjectives		305
,, XXII. Adverbs and Adverbial Phrases		307
,, XXIII. Conjunctions		313
Section III. ORTHOGRAPHY		316
Chapter XXIV. Suggestions for the Spelling of Moru-Madi		316
,, XXV. Word Division		320
,, XXVI. Specimen Texts (in Moru, Logo, Lugbara, Madi)		327
Section IV. VOCABULARIES		341

PART I
THE MORU-MADI LANGUAGE GROUP

1. In dealing with the Moru-Madi languages and dialects, the following contractions of language names will occasionally be made in the text to save space:

Moru dialects		Central languages		Madi dialects	
M.	Miza	AVU.	Avukaya (general)	Lo.	Lokai
K.	Kediru	Jl.	Ojila ⎫ (dialects)	Pa.	Pandikeri
L.	Lakama'di	Jg.	Ojiga ⎭	Bu.	'Burulo
Ä.	Moroändri	KEL.	Keliko	Lul.	Lulu'ba
'B.	'Bälimbä	LUG.	Lugbara		
Äg.	Moroägi	LOGO (L.)	Logo proper		
W.	Wa'di	LOGO (A.)	Agambi dialect		

Owing to the great divergence of LENDU, both in pronunciation and in grammar, from the rest of the group, this language will be discussed separately in an appendix

A NOTE ON THE SCRIPT USED

2. In order to show dialectal variation, a narrow phonetic notation with tone marks is used in connexion with all material collected on the spot. Much language material, however, as already stated in the Preface, has been received from outside sources, and this material cannot be retranscribed into a narrow phonetic and tonetic system. For the sake of uniformity (for every contributor to this work has his own manner of spelling), all such material will be transcribed here in accordance with suggestions for a practical Moru-Madi orthography, details of which are to be found in Section III. Further, to prevent confusion, and also to show where my own researches end and where those of my collaborators enter, contributions from outside sources will be printed in *italics*.

Italicized material in this book will therefore represent:

in MORU: extracts from Mr. T. H. B. Mynor's *Moru Grammar*.
      ,, ,, answers to Professor Westermann's 'Linguistic Guide'.
      ,, ,, the New Testament.

in MADI: extracts from Father Molinaro's *Grammatica della Lingua Madi*.
      ,, ,, answers to Professor Westermann's 'Linguistic Guide'.
      ,, ,, Madi Bible History *Ofo Oleree* (Lokai dialect).
      ,, ,, the New Testament (Pandikeri dialect).

in LOGO: extracts from Miss M. Mozley's MS. Logo Grammar and Miss Lucy McCord's answers to my questionnaire.
      extracts from the New Testament.

in LUGBARA: extracts from the New Testament.

in KELIKO: ,, ,, answers to Professor Westermann's 'Linguistic Guide'.

in LENDU: ,, ,, Rev. B. L. Litchman's answers to my questionnaire.
      ,, ,, the New Testament.

In Section III will be found specimens of connected text in the principal Moru-

THE MORU-MADI LANGUAGE GROUP

Madi languages. These are all written in the suggested orthography and according to suggested rules for word division.

For the sake of reference the two spelling-systems used in this book are set out below:

Proposed alphabet for Moru-Madi (italicized material)	Phonetic values of each letter, including dialectal variations (non-italicized material)
a	a
ä	ä (ö)
b	b bv
'b	'b
c	ts tsʷ tʃ
d	d
dr	dr
'd	'd
e	e ɛ (ɪ)
f	f
g (gy)	g gy gʸ gʷ
gb	gb
h	h x
i	i ɪ
i (ɪ)	ɪ
j	dz dzʷ dʒ
'j	'j
k (ky)	k ky kʸ kʷ
kp	kp
l	l (ɽ)
m	m
n	n
ny	ny
ŋ	ŋ
o	o ɔ (ʋ)
p	p pf
r	r
ḷ (ɽ)	ɽ
s	s sʷ ʃ
t	t
tr	tr
u	u ʊ
v	v
w	w wʸ
y	y
'y	'y
z	z zʷ ʒ

SECTION I
PHONETICS
CHAPTER I
VOWELS

3. There seem to be five categories of vowel sound in Moru-Madi, which may in a practical orthography, be represented by the letters *a, e, i, o, u*. With the exception of **a**, however, each category covers two main varieties of vowel sound, which may be tentatively called 'tense' and 'lax'. Thus:

Tense vowels	i	e	o	u
Lax vowels	ɪ	ɛ	ɔ	ʊ
Neither tense nor lax	a			

In addition there is a central vowel which, because of its etymological and phonetic relationship to **a**, is here written *ä* (although in previous systems it has been written *ö*).

4. There appears to be a principle of vowel harmony governing the distribution of the 'tense' and 'lax' varieties of vowels—tense vowels and lax vowels being seldom intermingled in the same word or indeed in the same short phrase. This principle appears to be more operative in Moru than in Madi. At the same time there seems to be considerable latitude allowed as to which variety of vowel should predominate in any given sentence. It will be evident from this that an accurate phonetic analysis of these languages is extremely difficult, in as much as it is often impossible to say whether some words are to be represented lexicologically as having tense or lax forms. Note the following tense and lax alternation of vowel in the second person pronoun (**mɪ** or **mi**) and the negative particle (**ku** or **kʊ**):

Tense context: mí-mvú ku.   You don't drink.
Lax context: mí kʊ́ kàdo.   You are not good.

5. Vowel harmony, however, cannot fully account for the two varieties of vowel sound, for there are certain words in the vocabulary of every Moru-Madi speaker which, when spoken in isolation, have a tense vowel, just as there are other words in his vocabulary which, when spoken in isolation, have a lax vowel. These words, however, are inclined to vary from dialect to dialect, and in some cases, from individual to individual. Note the following examples of 'doublets' in which it is essential to distinguish tense from lax in MORU (Miza):

Tense: mì (eye)   kúrú (gourd)   vo (place)
Lax: mɪ (you)   kʊrʊ̀ (ball)   vɔ (to blow)

6. Thus, although the Moru-Madi languages may be described as having *five* main categories of vowel sound, there are actually *ten* main vowels in the speech of any one speaker, who will not necessarily fully agree in his use of these sounds with any of his neighbours.

7. The following vowel chart indicates the tongue positions for these ten vowels in the pronunciation of a typical MORU (Miza) speaker. Except for the central vowel, these tongue positions may be regarded as being typical for the bulk of Moru-Madi speakers.

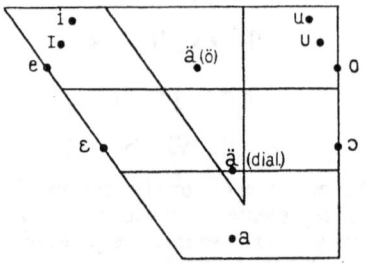

It is to be noted that in the *i* and *u* vowel categories the tense variety is the more common in words spoken in isolation, but that in the *e* and *o* vowel categories the lax variety is the more common.

The Vowels in Detail

THE *i* VOWELS. *Most common variety* **i** *(tense)*
Less common variety ɪ *(lax)*

8. In most *i*-words, when pronounced in isolation, the vowel has a tense quality. Its acoustic effect is somewhat like that of the vowel in English 'feet'—but considerably retracted. Examples:

MORU (M.)	OJILA	LOGO	LUGBARA	MADI (Lo.)	
tí	tí	ti	ti	ti	(to give birth)
si	si	sì	di	sî	(to beat)
mì	lifí	mí	mí	mí	(eye)

9. Some words, when pronounced in isolation, seem to contain the lax variety ɪ, although, when used in a tense vowel context, they employ the tense variety i. The acoustic effect of ɪ is very like that of the vowel in English 'fit'. Examples:

MORU (M.)	OJILA	LOGO·	LUGBARA	MADI (Lo.)	
drɪ̀	drɪ̀	drɪ̀	drɪ̀	drɪ̀	(head)
ɛrɪ	rɪ	rɪ	ri	rɪ	(to hear)
sɪ	tsɪ	tʃi	tsi	sɪ	(to bite)
ɪ'dwɪ	edrɪ	kɪ'di	igbɪ	e'bwé	(cold)

(Note how this vowel varies with **i** and **e** in some dialects.)

THE *u* VOWELS. *Most common variety* **u** *(tense)*
Less common variety ʊ *(lax)*

10. In most *u*-words, when pronounced in isolation, the vowel has a tense quality, somewhat like the vowel in English 'pool'. Examples:

MORU (M.)	OJILA	LOGO	LUGBARA	MADI (Lo.)	
fu	fu	fu	fu		(to kill)
gu	gu	gu	gu	gu	(to laugh)
mu	mu	mu	mu	mu	(to go, run)
kuru	uru	kuru	urubgí	oru	(up)

Miss Mozley records a fronted **u**-sound (approaching the vowel of '*vü*' in French) in LOGO in words like *vuna* (ground), *vuse* (after), *vule* (to).

VOWELS

11. Some words, when pronounced in isolation, contain the lax vowel ʊ, with quality similar to that in English 'pull'. This vowel alternates with u in tense vowel contexts and with ə in lax vowel contexts.

MORU (M.)	OJILA	LOGO	LUGBARA	
kʊ́rʊ́	ʊ́rʊ́	kórwá		(well)
kʊ́mè	ʊ́mè	kómɛ	ɔ́ŋwì	(brains)

(ʊ-words are not nearly so numerous as ɪ-words.)

THE *e* VOWELS. *Most common variety* ɛ (*lax*)
Less common variety e (*tense*)

12. In most cases of *e*-words pronounced in isolation the vowel has a lax quality similar to the vowel in English 'shell'.

MORU (M.)	OJILA	LOGO	LUGBARA	MADI (Lo.)	
ndrɛ	ndrɛ		ndrɛ	ndrɛ	(to see)
	fɛ	fɛ	fɛ	kɛ	(to give)
ɛlɛ̀	ɛlɛ		wɛ̀	'dɛ	(to swim)
ɛ́ndrɛ̀	andrɛ	ándrɛ́	ándräpɪ	ɛndrɛ	(mother)

13. Some words, when pronounced in isolation, contain the tense vowel e, which is similar in pronunciation to French *é*. This vowel alternates with ɛ and ɪ.

MORU (M.)	OJILA	LOGO	LUGBARA	MADI	
kyémbá	embá	ɪmbá	bìra	ebá	(net)
èza		za	èza	èza	(meat
lédr	édr				(person)

(e-words are relatively scarce as compared to ɛ-words.)

THE *o* VOWELS. *Most common variety* ɔ (*lax*)
Less common variety o (*tense*)

14. In most cases of *o*-words pronounced in isolation the vowel has a lax quality, somewhat like the vowel in English 'law'.

MORU (M.)	OJILA	LOGO	LUGBARA	MADI (Lo.)	
vɔ	vɔ	ávɔ	vɔ	vò	(to blow)
ŋgɔ	ŋɔ	ŋwa	myu	ŋɔ̀	(to break)
zʷɔ́	dʒwɔ́	dʒɔ́	dzɔ́	dzɔ́	(hut)

15. Some words, when pronounced in isolation, contain the tense vowel o, pronounced as in French 'eau', which alternates with ə and ʊ.

MORU (M.)	OJILA	LOGO	LUGBARA	MADI (Lo.)	
kótó	ótó	kótóa	ɔtɔ́gɔ	ótó	(termite)
tòkó	okó	tɔkwá	okó	okó	(woman)
vo	vo	vora	vo	vo	(place)

(Words containing o are relatively common as against words containing ə, and several doublets may be found. Cf. **vo** and **vɔ** above.)

THE VOWEL a

16. This vowel is similar to Italian a in quality, its tongue position lying between that of Italian a and that of the vowel in English 'but'. It is not at all like the vowels in English 'cat' or English 'father'. The following examples are common to all Moru-Madi languages:

má (I), drà (to die), pa (foot)

THE CENTRAL VOWEL ä (ö)

17. In all the Moru-Madi languages there is a central vowel with a pronunciation considerably closer than that of the English central vowel in 'colonel'. The Rejaf Conference (1928), in dealing with the proposed orthographies for Bari and the Nilotic languages, recommended that the letter ö should be used to indicate central vowels, as this letter was already in use in mission literature.[1] Later, when the Rejaf principles came to be applied to the Nilotic languages, it was found that these languages contained more than one kind of central vowel, and it was recommended that the diaeresis should be used with other vowel letters to indicate these centralized vowels. In the light of this recommendation, it has been decided in this present work to represent the Moru-Madi central vowel by the letter ä rather than by ö because:

(1) in the great majority of instances of this pronunciation, its derivation from a is obvious;
(2) there is a certain amount of inconsistency between dialects in the use of the central vowel as against a, so that the two symbols should be as close in form as possible.

e.g. ma = I.   mǎ-nì ku = I don't know (MORU)
           (m)á-nì ku = I don't know (MADI)

To write *mö-ni ku* in Moru would be misleading.

18. There are other cases of central vowel in Moru-Madi, where the sound does not seem to be related to **a**.

Compare MORU o'bwǎ; MADI bwi; LOGO 'bu = to shoot.

In most dialects this central vowel has the same quality as the central vowel which is related to **a**, and will accordingly be written *ä* except in such dialects as make a difference in pronunciation.

OTHER CENTRAL VOWELS

19. In (MORU) WA'DI there is a central vowel ö, while ä is much more open than in the other Moru dialects.

e.g. kwögú (back), cf. ädrú (buffalo).

Occasionally in other languages centralized forms of other vowels are heard:

MORU (K.) lèsi (fire), MORU (M.) èdrë (to stop), LOGO läri or lëri (drum). Such instances are rare enough to be ignored for the most part in this present work.

VOWEL HARMONY

20. There are four main kinds of vowel harmony in Moru-Madi, each governed by specific sound rules.

1. *Tense and lax harmonizing.*

21. As stated earlier, the tendency in Moru-Madi is against the juxtaposition of tense and lax vowels. Consequently many words and particles have two phonetic

---

[1] The first missionaries in the Southern Sudan were to a large extent Austrian. Mitterrutzner used the letter *ö* for the sound in his Bari grammar, because to him and his compatriots it sounded most like the *ö* in German. Note that the Logo missionaries in the Congo represent the sound by *a*.

VOWELS 93

values according to their neighbouring words or particles. Take the following examples from MORU (Miza):

Tense contexts		Lax contexts	
i and ɪ : mí-zi ŋgàgà.	Call the boys.	mí-'bɪ ŋgàgà.	Beat the boys.
u and ʊ: má ku dìtɔkó ì.	I am not a woman.	má kʊ́ ɔnzíró.	I am not bad.
e and ɛ : ny-ékyi nòa.	Come here.	ny-ɛ́sà tè.	You arrived.
o } and ɔ: kòzi-ro } u } kòzi-ru }	(bad).	ɔ̀ka-rɔ	(red).

22. It should be remarked here, however, that the above observations refer to a tendency and not to a rigid sound law, and that every allowance should be made for individualisms on the part of the speakers. Consequently much of the following material will not accord with the 'rules' just put forward.[1]

2. *Complete harmonizing.*

23. Another form of vowel harmony is found in the Miza dialect of MORU and the Pandikeri dialect of MADI in the vowels of pronouns before Class III verbs, i.e. dissyllabic verbs beginning with a consonant. Here, in most cases, the vowel of the 1st and 2nd personal pronoun is made to agree altogether with the first vowel of the verb stem.

Examples from MORU (Miza):

má-lasà ŋgwa.	I wash the child.	nyá-lasa ŋgwa.	Wash the child.
mó-lɔ́sɛ bɔŋgó tɛ̀.	I sewed the cloth.	nyó-lɔsɛ bɔ̀ŋgɔ.	Sew the cloth.
mí-lii-te.	I wept.	nyí-lii-te.	You wept.
mú-túri ndá tùrì.	I fear him.	nyé-turì ma.[2]	Fear me.
		nyé-leru asi.	Light the fire.
		nyé-lɛwa-tɛ.	You turned.

Examples from MADI (Pandikeri):

| mɛ́-lɛgwɛ̀ aíse aga dì. | I am lost in the bush. |
| mú-lukwɛ̀ ɔpɪ ra. | I paid the chief. |

24. Complete harmonizing before Class III verb stems is also found in these two languages in the case of the passive prefix, which before monosyllabic stems is a or ä.

MORU (M.): á-pè kɪlá'bái tɛ.	The warriors were defeated.
ä-zí ma Dɛŋgò.	I am called Dengo.
but u-kugu paráta tɛ.	The money was stolen.
MADI (Pa.): ú-luŋgwé mà Äyurù.	I am called Ayuru.

25. In Pandikeri Madi, furthermore, the 3rd person auxiliary particle ka is similarly harmonized before Class III verbs. In Moru Miza it is only harmonized before dissyllabic verb stems beginning with a vowel (Class II verbs).

MADI (Pa.): ópí ku-luŋgwé nyi'ɪ. The chief is calling you.
MORU (M.): ánya kú-ùmú, but ánya ká-tumu. He is running.
ánya kɛ-ɛzi. He must bring it.

In other Moru dialects the auxiliary rɔ is similarly harmonized before Class II verbs.

MOROÄNDRI: ndá rú-ùmu, but ndá ró-tumu. He is running.

[1] In addition, one should take into account the fact that the investigator himself often finds it difficult to decide which of two very similar vowel sounds is the more common in use. For example, should one write *etsa* or *ɪtsa*, *golo* or *gulʊ* in cases where the speakers themselves seem to vary according to their own moods?   [2] Irregular harmonizing.

3. The Centralization of a ('Umlaut').

26. This phenomenon resembles closely Indo-Germanic 'Umlaut', though it applies only to the vowel a. This sound normally occurs in both tense and lax contexts, but cannot occur before certain words and particles containing the tense vowels i or u; the central vowel, which is here written ä, is found in this context.

Examples from the pronoun forms nya (you) and ma (I) in MORU (M.):

nyá ɔ'du ɔyé yà?	What are you doing?	nyä́-ŋgu.	Smell it.
má-lɛ ku.	I don't want it.	mä́-nì ku.	I don't know.
má-sɔ gìni.	I hoed the ground.	mä́-fu-te.	I killed him.
má-sì-te.	I bit it.	mä́-sì-te.	I hit him.
nyézu ŋgágà ma-rɛ. Send the boy to me.		nyévɔ kwìnì mä-rì. Throw the stone to me.	

Examples with the passive prefix a in MORU:

á-'bɪ ma te.	I was beaten.	ä́-zí ma te.	I was called.
á-gyɛ ndá tɛ.	She was married.	ä́-fu gárà te.	The pot was broken.

27. In AVUKAYA centralization is also found in syllables which *follow* the vowels i and u. Thus:

óló-wa (axe), but 'bì'bì-wä (bat).
lɔrɪ-'ba (blacksmith), but rú-'bä (body).

Note also the tribal names: 'Bälimbä, Odʒigä, and Ulu'bo.

28. Sometimes the result of centralization is a totally different vowel—e or o for the most part. Compare:

LOGO:	läti	MADI:	leti	MORU:	liti = path.
LOGO:	atá	KELIKO:	atäpi	MORU:	täpi or tepi = father.
MADI:	anyu	MORU:	känyú	LOGO:	*kenu* = sesame.
MADI:	adzí	MORU (Ä.)	ädzí	MORU (Äg.)	odzí = yesterday.

29. In the MADI dialects centralization of a is much rarer than elsewhere, but, even in this language, a before i or u is often pronounced with a different voice quality—a hollow breathy quality reminiscent of the Nilotic 'breathy voice'.[1]

MADI (Lokai)

läri (drum) a̰ri in Lulu'ba.
amvu (field) a̰mbu in Lulu'ba, a̰mvu in 'Burulo.
o̰ŋú (fly) a̰ŋú in Lulu'ba.
ɪtɔ́ (hare) itó̰ in Lulu'ba, itó̰ in 'Burulo.

'Breathy' voice quality, however, will not be represented elsewhere in this present work.

30. The vowels e and o do not appear to cause the centralization of a neighbouring a sound, but occasional instances seem to indicate that centralization can occur before the lax vowel ɪ—e.g.

mä́-dɾɪ (to me, on me); Moróändrɪ (pronunciation of so-called 'Öndri' or 'Endri'). Consequently ä cannot be regarded as the 'tense' form of a in the same way as e may be regarded as the 'tense' form of ɛ, or u the 'tense' form of ʊ, &c.

---

[1] This phenomenon is explained at length in *Practical Phonetics for Students of African Languages*, by Westermann and Ward, pp. 204 and 210. In the above examples the diacritic ̰ indicates 'breathy' voice.

4. 'Characteristic' vowels.

31. It often happens that a monosyllabic word stem under certain conditions, governed largely by grammar, will take a vowel prefix. Some other word stems are dissyllabic and invariably begin with a vowel. The quality of this initial vowel, whether prefixed according to grammatical and semantic rules, or inherent in the word stem itself, depends on the quality of the vowel in the word-root, although there is not necessarily a complete identity in vowel quality as discussed in §§ 23–5.

These initial vowels are here called 'characteristic' vowels, because they are characteristic for each type of word stem.

32. The best illustrations of characteristic vowels are to be found in verb conjugation, as the rules governing the use of these vowel prefixes are fairly easy to define. In MORU (Miza) the system is as follows:

Verbs may be divided into three classes:

Class I: monosyllabic verbs which employ the 'characteristic' vowel prefix only in certain tenses (here called the 'Indefinite' tenses).[1]

Class II: dissyllabic verbs which are always conjugated with a 'characteristic' vowel prefix, i.e. it is part of the stem.

Class III: dissyllabic verbs beginning with a consonant. (Since these employ no characteristic vowel, they may be ignored here.)

The relation between root vowel and characteristic vowel is as follows:

	Root vowel	Characteristic vowel
Class I verbs:	tense	u-
	lax	ɔ-
Class II verbs:	tense	u- o- ä- e- i-
	lax	ʊ- ɔ- a- ɛ- ɪ-

Note that in Class I verbs there are only two possible characteristic vowels, but that in Class II verbs there are ten possible characteristic vowels. Examples:

Class I: tense: ù-mu (to run)　　ù-mvu (to drink)　　ù-si (to strike)
　　　　　　　　　　　　　　　　　　　　　　　　　　　ù-pi (to open)
　　　　lax: ɔ̀-nya (to eat)　　ɔ̀-vɔ (to blow)　　ɔ̀-sɪ (to bite)
　　　　　　ɔ̀-ŋga (to fly)　　　　　　　　　　　ɔ̀-'dɛ (to dive)
Class II: tense: u'du (to sleep)
　　　　　　　　äŋgu (to smell)　　áti (to hold)
　　　　　　　　ekyi (to come)
　　　　　　　　imu (to run hither)　　iti (to tell)
　　　　lax: ɔzɔ̀ (to give)
　　　　　　ata (to speak)　　àba (to travel)　　a'bu (to shut up)
　　　　　　èdrɛ (to stop)　　ɛrɪ (to hear)　　ɛŋga (to fly hither)
　　　　　　ɛmbɛ (to tie)

Dialectal variation in the characteristic vowel.

33. The MORU dialects seem to fall into three groups as regards characteristic vowels. The system just described fits Miza, Kediru, and Lakama'di. For Moroändri, 'Balimbä, and Moroägi a different system of vowel harmonies is in use. Wa'di and Avukaya have yet another (and simpler) system.

[1] See §§ 338 et seq.

	-ÄNDRI	WA'DI	AVUKAYA (Jl.)
Class I: tense:	u-mu (to run)	ä-mu	
	ù-mvu (to drink)	ä-mvu	mvu
	ù-pi (to open)	ä-pi	pi
lax:	ɔ̀-vɔ (to blow)	a-vɔ́	vɔ
	ɔ-sɪ (to bite)	a-sɪ	tsɪ
Class II: tense:	ù'du (to sleep)	ä'du	(k)o'du
	äŋgù (to smell)	äŋgù	äŋgù
	äti (to hold)	äti	äti
	ämu (to run hither)	ämu	
lax:	ádrɛ (to stop)	ádrɛ	ádrɛ
	ɪdɛ (to break)	adɛ	ɛdɛ
	ɔmbɛ (to tie)	ambɛ	ambɛ
	ɔba (to travel)		
	àta (to speak)	ata	ta

Characteristic vowels in the Central and Southern languages.

34. In the Central languages there is no characteristic vowel for Class I verbs (cf. Avukaya above). In MADI the characteristic vowel is o- before tense stem vowels and ɔ- before lax stem vowels.[1] Where Class II verbs are concerned, the most common characteristic vowel is a- in the Central languages (before both tense and lax stem vowels), and in MADI: e- or -o before tense stem vowels and ɛ- or u- before lax stem vowels.

In all these languages, however, the phonetic principles underlying characteristic vowel quality are not fully understood, and other vowels are also much in use.

	MADI (Lo.)	LUGBARA	LOGO
Class I: tense:	o-mu (went)	mu	
	o-di (forged)	di	di
	o-ndro (sucked)	ndru	*ndro*
lax:	ɔ-sí (bit)	tsi	tʃi
	ɔ́-ndrɛ́ (saw)	nɛ	no
	ɔ-ga (chopped)	ga	ga
Class II: tense:	ɛdzí (brought)	dzi	
	ɔtsi (gnawed)	tsi	tʃi
	ori (feared)	ourisi	*tiri*
	ogu (stole)	ugu	kugu
	edre (was)		adre
	egwe (forgot)	avi	*avi*
	ɛŋgwé (returned)		àndʒɪ
	etsá (arrived)	atsa	atsa
lax:	ɛrɪ (heard)	rɪ	arɪ
	ɛ'bɛ (left)	ɛ'bɛ	
	édrɛ (stopped)	édrɛ	ádrɛ
	ɛkɛ (gave)	ɪfɛ	afɛ
	ɛdɛ́ (made)	idɛ	lɛdɛ
	uŋgwɛ (called)	mvɛ	vi
	ukwɛ (paid)	ufɛ	fɛ
	umbɛ (tied)	umbɛ́	lambɛ́

[1] The grammatical rules governing the use of the characteristic vowel in Madi verbs are different from those in Moru. In Madi the characteristic vowel occurs only in the 3rd person and when no object precedes the verb.

VOWELS 97

Class II verbs are not so common here as in the Moru dialects, and it will be noticed that many verbs which are Class II verbs in Madi are Class I verbs in the other Southern and Central languages.

The vowels in Class III verbs.

35. Class III verbs, which are not very common in any language, are of the pattern: consonant+vowel+consonant+vowel. Comparative research establishes that the second syllable of such a verb is the etymological root of the word and that the first syllable is a prefix, the vowel of which stands in harmonic relationship to the vowel of the root. This relationship is similar to that of characteristic vowels and the word-root, but is not necessarily identical. Note the following examples from MORU (Miza):

    Class III: tense: lifu (to be broken); cf. u-fu (to kill)
                 lulu (to hurt), kugu (to steal)
                 mätu (to pray), tärִi (to saw); cf. ír̥í (knife)
                 leru (to kindle), dembí (to hide)
          lax: lɔgɔ (to give back), kɔtɛ (to wait); cf. ɔ-tɛ (to stay)
                la'di (to cook), latrı (to curse); cf. ɔ-trı (to curse)
                lala (to lay)
                lɛdzi (to talk), pɛrɛ (to spread)

Characteristic vowels in nouns.

36. In all nouns of the pattern: vowel+consonant+vowel, or consonant+vowel +consonant+vowel, the vowel in the first syllable is in harmonic relationship with that in the second syllable on the same phonetic principles as the vowels in Class II and Class III verbs. Examples from MORU:

  tense: ätu (arrow)   udrú (buffalo)   gìní (earth)   kundu (back)
    lax: àrı (bird)   ópí (chief)   lɔrɛ́ (baboon)   kɔ́drá (bamboo)

COALESCENCE AND ELISION OF VOWELS

37. When a word normally ending in a vowel is immediately followed by a word beginning with a vowel, the former vowel is often elided. Examples from MORU (Miza):

ma äzú bè (I have a spear) is often pronounced mäzú bè.
drì-ù'bǎ (headache)   ,,   ,,   dru'bǎ.
tóri ézi ta (a dream brought news) is often pronounced tórézi ta.
nyá a'di u'di yà? (What are you digging?) is often pronounced nyâ 'du'di ya?
nyédɛ andí vumír̀ɔ (Dress yourself)   ,,   ,,   nyédandí vumír̀ɔ.

Sometimes coalescence between the two vowels results:

    MORU: má ŋgàgà ùzi (lit. I boys call) is often pronounced má ŋgàgòzi.
    LUGBARA: mi amvúpi (your sister)   ,,   ,,   mɛmvúpi.

38. Cases like the foregoing are the results of rapid speech and need not be recognized in orthography. There are, however, certain occasions when the vowels of pronouns are always elided, even in slow speech, and the rules for this elision should receive attention, both in a scientific treatise and in a practical orthography. These special occasions arise when the pronouns precede nouns or verbs which begin with a vowel.

H

Pronouns+nouns.

39. Where the pronoun possessor precedes a noun beginning with a vowel in MADI, the vowel of the pronoun is elided, but the tone of the pronoun syllable is often transferred to the first syllable of the noun. E.g.

    MADI (Lo.): má (I)   ɛndrɛ (mother)   m-ɛ́ndrɛ (my mother)
              nyí (you)   amvóti (sister)   ny-âmvóti (your sister)

Where the linking particle à intervenes between a pronoun and its noun, the vowel of the pronoun is either completely harmonized or elided, but the tone of both syllables is retained.

           má à pa   or mâpa (my leg)
           nyí à pa   or nyá à pa or nyâpa (your leg)

Pronouns+verbs.

40. Here again distinction must be made between Class I verbs (monosyllabic verbs which take a 'characteristic' vowel only in certain tenses) and Class II verbs (dissyllabic verbs beginning with a characteristic vowel). Distinction must also be made between the behaviour of pronouns in the 'Definite' tenses (of which the past tense is a typical example) and the 'Indefinite' tenses (of which the present continuous tense is a typical example).

Definite tenses.

41. In MORU the pronoun vowel is always elided before Class II verbs, though the characteristic vowel of the verb adopts the tone of the pronoun syllable. Class I verbs, having no characteristic vowel in these tenses, do not cause elision; the behaviour of pronouns before Class III verbs has already been discussed (§ 23).

MORU (M.)
    Class II verbs.   Class I verb.
       m-ózò ŋga ndá-rì.   I   gave it to him.   má-sì-te.   I   bit.
       ny-ózò   You   ,,   ,,   mí-sì-te.   You ,,
       ány-ozò   He   ,,   ,,   ánya sì-te.   He ,,
       m-ɛsa-te.   I   arrived.
       ny-ɛsa-te.   You ,,
       ány-ɛsa-te.   He   ,,
       m-ɛsa-te.   We ,,   Class III verb.
       m-ú'du-te.   I   slept.   mí-lii-te.   I   wept.
       ny-ú'du-te.   You ,,   nyí-lii-te.   You ,,
       ány-u'du-te.   He   ,,   ányä lii-te.   He ,,

42. In MADI there is either elision or complete harmonizing of the vowel in the 1st and 2nd person pronoun before Class II verbs. The tone of the pronoun syllable is often transferred to the characteristic vowel of the verb. In the 3rd person there is no sound change. Class I verbs do not cause sound change, and the behaviour of pronouns before Class III verbs has already been discussed (§ 23).

MADI (Lo.)
    Class II verbs.   Class I verb.
         m-emu-ra.   I   came.   (m)á-mu-rá.   I   went.
         ny-emu-ra.   You ,,   (ny)í-mu-rá.   You ,,
         emu-ra.   He   ,,   àni òmu-rá.   He ,,

VOWELS

mɛ́-ètsa-ra or m-êtsa-ra.	I arrived.	
ny-ɛ́bɛ́.	You stop it.	Class III verb.
		(Pandikeri dialect).
m-ɛ́gwè nyí-si kừrừ.	I haven't forgotten you.	mɛ́-lɛgwè nyí-si kừrừ.
ny-ɛ́gwe má-si rá yà?	Have you forgotten me?	nyɛ̀-lɛgwè má-si rá yà?
bá ɛgwè ledzó sɪ dì.	They have forgotten it.	'bá legwè le'jó sɪ dì.

Indefinite tenses.

43. In MORU the 'characteristic' vowel is found with Class I and Class II verbs in these tenses, and the vowel of the pronoun, when it precedes, may (1) remain unaffected, (2) undergo complete harmonizing, (3) be elided, though the tone of both the pronoun syllable and the verb characteristic vowel is retained. These same processes may also affect the 3rd person auxiliary particle **ka**.

In the following examples from MORU (M.) the pronoun vowel is not affected:

Class I verbs:	má-ɔ̀dra.	I am dying.
	nyá-ú'di na ɔ'duta yà?	Lit. You-dig it why?
	ndá-ká-ubi nȧ.	He is pushing it.
Class II verbs:	má-abȧ.	I am walking.
	nyá-áta ɛ́ŋʊnyɛ?	Lit. You-say how? (How do you say it?
	ánya ká-atȧ.	He is talking.

In the following examples the pronoun vowel is harmonized or elided:

Class I verbs:	mú-ùmu or m-ûmu.	I am running.
	nyú-ùmu or ny-ûmu.	You are running.
	ánya kú-ùmu or ánya k-ûmu.	He is running.
	ánya kɔ́-ɔ̀dra or ánya k-ɔ̂dra.	He is dying.
	ŋgàgà kɔ́-ɔ̀dzʷɪ or ŋgàgà k-ɔ̂dzʷɪ.	The boys are playing.
	lédri k-ɔrɨ vùru.	The people are sitting down.
Class II verbs:	m-ɔ́ì. I am going. m-ɔi.	We are going.
	nyɔ́-ɔ̀ì íŋwa yà? or ny-ɔ̂ì íŋwa yà?	Where are you going?[1]
	nyé-ɛkpí ɔ'dɔta yà?	Why are you coughing?
	nyi-íbi na ɪ̀ŋwa yà? or ny-íbi ...	Where are you pushing it?
	kɔkyɛ́ k-ɔ́ì ɔ̀dranɪ.	The dog goes to die.
	arɨ́ kɛ́-èŋgá or arɨ́ k-êŋgá.	The bird flies here.

44. In MADI Class I verbs have no characteristic vowel in the Indefinite tenses, but the tone of the pronoun is affected. Before Class II verbs the vowels of the pronouns are either harmonized or elided. The vowel of the 3rd person auxiliary particle **ka** is elided when it immediately precedes the verb stem, which in such cases always has a characteristic vowel.

Class I verbs:	mâ-mu.	I am going.[2]
	nyì-mu.	You are going.
	ànì k-ômu.	He is going.
Class II verbs:	*m-emu-ra.*	I shall come.
	ny-emu-ra.	You will come.
	k-emu-ra.	He will come.
mɛ́-ètsa ɔ̀bừ rȧ or m-êtsa ...		I shall arrive to-morrow.
mɛ́-ɛ̀mu ɔ̀bừ rȧ or m-êmu ...		I shall come to-morrow.

[1] Compare ny-ói-te. You have gone. (Definite).
[2] Compare (m)á-mu-rá. I have gone. (Definite).

45. In the other languages elision is not the general rule, but seems to depend on the mood of the speaker. It only occurs before Class II verbs, when it does occur, since Class I verbs are never given a characteristic vowel.

    LOGO: *mi-ali* or mi-k-ali (for mi-ko-ali). Come!
       ma-ali. I come. *ma-are tecile.* I am walking.
   LUGBARA: *mi-eto ma.* Save me. mɪ-ɪmu. Come!
       ma-aii-ra. I will.
   KELIKO: mí-ámú or m-ɛ́mú. Come!

CHAPTER II

CONSONANTS

46. The following table represents the sum total of consonants recorded, including dialectal variations. The consonant system for any one language will be much simpler. (See remarks on practical orthography for the group, Section III.)

	Labial			Alveolar				Palatal	Velar			Laryngeal
	Bi-labial	Labio-Dental	Dental	Retroflex	Sibilant	Semi-sibilant			Pre-velar	Velar	Labio-velar	
Explosives	p b		t d						ky gy	k g	kp gb	ʼ
Implosives	ʼb			ʼd				ʼj ʼy				
Fricatives		f v			sʷ zʷ s z	ʃ ʒ				(x)		h
Affricates		(pf) (bv)		tr dr	tsʷ dzʷ ts dz		tʃ dʒ					
Nasals	m		n					ny		ŋ		
Liquids, &c.				r l ɽ				y			w	

THE CONSONANTS IN DETAIL

47. The following examples, except where otherwise stated, are taken from the MIZA dialect of MORU. The descriptions of the sounds, however, apply in the main equally well to the other languages in which they occur. The distribution and inter-dialectal relationship of the Moru-Madi speech-sounds will be discussed in a later chapter.

Labial consonants: **p, b; f, v; ʼb, m.**

48. p is pronounced with little aspiration; **b** is more fully voiced than in English. On the whole the pronunciation of these consonants is as in French. **f** and **v** are also pronounced as in French, i.e. the **v** is more voiced than in English.

 p and **b** occur before front vowels (**i, e, a**) and **f** and **v** occur before back vowels (**o, u**). Examples:[1]

   Before front vowels: u-pí (to open)   bí (ear)
          kapírì (tail feathers)
          kɔ̀pɛ (guinea fowl)   bɛ (with)
          ɔ-pá (to help)   bà (breast)

[1] This system holds for most of the Moru dialects and for Madi. In the Central languages

CONSONANTS

Before back vowels: kufú (shoulder)   tivu (beard)
fofo (lake)
ɔ-fɔ (to go out)   ɔ-vɔ́ (to throw)

In LOGO the affricates **pf** and **bv** are sometimes heard as alternatives to **f** and **v**. (See § 108.)

pfu or *fu* (to kill).   bvɪ̀drɪ and *vudri* (down).

49. The implosive consonant **'b** is pronounced with very little implosion and is hard for foreigners to distinguish from exploded **b**, though it is usually pronounced with more muscular effort.[1] **m** is pronounced as in English; there is a slight tendency to nasalize open vowels after it.

'b and **m** occur before all vowels.

'bí (hair)	mì (eye)
'bɪ̀'bɪ (star)	mɪa (guinea-worm)
	kúmè (brains)
ɛ'bɛ (to leave)	ɛmɛ́ (to heat)
'bà (village)	lama (side)
'bàdrɪ̀ (tribe)	mätu (to pray)
'bɔlɔtò (soft)	mɔ́dɔ́ (really)
kɛ'bo (hoe)	
a'bʊ (to shut up)	mʊ́rè (dung)
'búdr (grave)	kùmú (fly)

Dental consonants: **t, d, n**.

50. **t** and **d** are articulated with the tongue tip against the teeth as in French. Sporadic instances of alveolar **t** that were observed would appear to be due to idiosyncracies of pronunciation and to have no semantic significance. It was not possible to determine whether the normal value of **n** is dental or alveolar. **t** is pronounced with little aspiration and **d** is more fully voiced than in English.

t, d, and **n** may occur before all vowels.[2]

ätí (to hold)	u-dí (to forge)	uni (black)
ɔ-tí (to count)		kítɔnɪ (scorpion)
te (postposition)		
tɛsì (outside)	kɔdɛ̀ (cotton)	
ta (word)	ɔ-da (to pour)	ana (that)
täbírí (hunger)		
kɔtɔ́ (navel)	dɔfɔ̀ (club)	ɔnɔ́ (this)
koto (anthill)	kàdo (good)	noa (here)
kʊ́tʊtí (bank)		
ätú (arrow)	nyedu (rat)	

Alveolar consonants (liquid): **r, l, ɽ**.

51. **r** is rolled as in Scotch; **l** is always pronounced 'clear' as in French and German. **ɽ** is a flapped l-sound, which in some dialects is merely a variety of **l** heard before

and in Moroändri, **f** and **v** occur before all vowels (cf. § 138.) Note that the Miza words fɛ̀rɛ̀ (few) and taví (tail) are importations from Moroändri. The true Miza-Kediru forms are more like sɛ̀rɛ̀ and (t)azʷí (see §§ 107 and 146). Note also that the preference for bɔŋgɔ́ over vɔŋgɔ́ (= cloth) lies in the fact that the word is of foreign origin.

[1] See 'A note on the implosives' (§§ 73–6).
[2] The syllables **ne** (nɛ) and **nu** (nʊ) seem to occur only as variations of **lɛ** and **nyu**. Thus: 'to want' is nɛ or lɛ in Logo, but lɛ elsewhere; 'sesame' is änú in Avukaya but (k)änyú elsewhere.

i and u. In Moru, however, it has an independent existence and has to be distinguished from l.

r, l, and ɽ (in Moru) may occur before all vowels.

riŋgo (sinew)	lú'búlí (blue)	kɔɽi (basket)
kärí (giraffe)	rwali (rope)	äɽí (poison)
täbírí (hunger)	líti (path)	täɽi (to cut)
turì (to fear)	lii (to cry)	ɛɽi (to come)
		kíriɽí (charcoal)
tɔrí (dream)	lìwa (elephant)	gàɽɪ (left hand)
àrɪ (bird)		bɪɽí (lips)
	leru (to light)	
pɛrɛ (to spread)	lèzɔ (twins)	
lara (to spread)	lasa (to bathe)	ɽatararo (hard)
		dámgbáɽá (stick)
	lärí (drum)	
kɪró (granary)	ɔ-ló (to cut)	guɽó (cat)
aróà (hippo)	loo (thirst)	ɽo (verb postposition)
kʊrú (mud)		kuɽukosú (elbow)
u-rú (to take away)	ulu (to love)	äɽú (to swear)
luru (green)	Luú (God)	täɽú (water-rat)
vurú (earth)	lúkù'du (water-pot)	

Cognate words in l and r (but not ɽ) are found throughout the group.

Alveolar consonants (retroflex): **tr, dr, 'd.**

52. The sounds **tr** and **dr** are invariably pronounced wrongly by Europeans, who use either the typical English pronunciation of 'tray' and 'dray' (where the **r** is not rolled) or the Scotch pronunciation of the same words (in which the **t** and **d** are *dental*). In Moru-Madi **tr** and **dr**, the **t** and **d** element, as well as the following rolled element, are alveolar and slightly retroflex.

In LUGBARA the rolled element is not so strong as in the other languages, and in the pronunciation of some speakers is entirely absent, so that all one hears is an alveolar **t** and **d** followed by slight friction.

dr occurs before all vowels and is very common, but **tr** occurs in only a few words. A front vowel after **dr** is very often not pronounced, especially when the syllable is unaccented, but the **r**-element in such cases is never syllabic (as in Lendu). E.g. MORU:

ledr or ledrɪ (person); mådr or mådrɪ (to me).

53. The implosive **'d** (like the implosive **'b**) is pronounced with very little implosion. The retroflex tongue position is in fact a more distinguishing feature than the manner of articulation, which occasionally hardly seems implosive at all.[1]

'd occurs before all vowels.

Examples of **tr, dr,** and **'d**:

	'bàdrì (tribe)	u-'di (to dig)
ɔ-trí (to curse) (M.)	drí (hand)	tɔ'dɪ (new)
	ɛdrɛ́ (to stand)	ɔ-'dɛ́ (to dive)
atrá (foreigner) (M.)	làdra (tongue)	ɔ-'da (to insult)

[1] Miss L. E. Armstrong notes a similar phenomenon in Somali (see 'The Phonetic Structure of Somali', *M.S.O.S.* 1934) for which she uses the symbol ɖ. (See also §§ 73–6.)

CONSONANTS

tra (tense particle) (Jl.)
trɔ (with) (Madi)

drɔ (verb particle) (Madi)

udrú (buffalo)

'dɔ (this)
i'dʊ (absent)
u'du (to sleep)

Alveolar consonants (sibilant and semi-sibilant): **s, z; c, j**.

54. This group of consonants is subject to so much inter-dialectal variation that each main language will need separate treatment. (See also under sound-change, §§ 119–26, 140–5.)

MORU: **s z, ts^w dz^w**.

55. s and z are pronounced as in English, except that the z is fully voiced. These sounds occur before all vowels.

sí (with)
sí (tooth)
ɔ-sɪ (to bite)
ɔ-sɛ́ (to shut)
ɔ-sá (to arrive)
ɔ-sɔ (to bear twins)
kúsu (bow)

azi (another)
u-zí (to call)
ɛzi (to bring)
zɛvɔ̀ (buttocks)
ɔ-zá (to milk)
ɔzɔ̀ (to give)
làkazʊ (pot)
äzú (spear)

56. ts^w and dz^w are pronounced by some people with the tongue position for 'its' and 'adze', but by others with a tongue position approaching more than of 'itch' and 'edge'. In addition there is a slight accompanying labialization, a faint w-element, heard throughout the sound, especially when the sound is followed by a front vowel (**i** or **e**). This w-element is not a semi-vowel w following the consonant (for such a sound see § 83). Before back vowels the w-element is not heard.

ts^w and dz^w occur in corresponding words in all Moru dialects except Moroändri. (See § 144.)

Before front vowels: kɛts^wi (seed)
ɪts^wí (bowels)
ts^wɛ̀ (tree)
lets^wɛ (warana)
ts^wɛké (fish-spear)

u-dz^wɪ (to forget)
u-dz^wɛ́ (to burn)

Before back vowels: katsó (long)
tsurutsuru (wet)

odzo (equal)
odzú (to wash)

These sounds do not occur before **a**, but occasionally **a** is added as a suffix to syllables containing these consonants. In the following examples the w-element is the result of contraction of the back vowel before such a suffix:

katswá (long: alternative to katsó)
tswà-rì (thin)
ɔdzwá (to wash: alternative to odzú)

In an ideal orthography the letters *c* and *j* may conveniently be used for the sounds ts^w and dz^w, and such has been done here with Moru material obtained from outside sources. The w-element in these sounds need not be represented.

MADI: s z, ts dz.

57. s and z are pronounced as in Moru, except that before back vowels a slight w-glide is sometimes heard. z never occurs before the vowel u.

sí (to build) zi (another)
sɛ (to smoke) zɛlédrì (buttocks)
sá (to clean) zá (to milk)
lɔsɔ (good) àzʷɔ (long)
so (to dress) zo (to hide)
osù (bow)

Madi s and z words correspond to Moru s and z words, but there are also many Moru s and z words which correspond to ts and dz words in Madi.

58. ts and dz have a tongue position somewhere between the sound of 'its' and 'adze' and the pronunciation of *c* and *g* in Italian words like 'cinque' and 'giorno'. Before back vowels a slight w-glide is sometimes heard, but there is no w-element in the sounds before front vowels, and they do not correspond to tsʷ and dzʷ in Moru, though they often correspond to Moru s and z. ts never occurs before the vowel u.

tsí (to bite) dzí (to bring)
  dze (to wash) (to buy)
ɔtsé (dog) dzɛ́rɛdzɛ́rɛ̀ (fast)
tsɛtsɛ (slow)
tsa (to arrive) dzaligó (old)
tsoma (to soak) dzɔ or dzʷɔ (hut)
  adzú (spear)

In an ideal orthography the letters *c* and *j* may conveniently be used for the sounds ts and dz, and such has been done here with Madi material from outside sources.

LOGO: s (ʃ) z (ʒ), ts (tʃ) dz (dʒ).

59. The sibilant alveolar consonants in Logo (and also in Lugbara, Keliko, and Avukaya) are similar, both in articulation and in occurrence, to those in Madi, except that before the vowels i and ɪ there is a tendency to pronounce them with a retracted tongue position, the resultant sounds approaching somewhat the sounds in English 'she', 'leisure', 'church', 'judge'. There is, however, a good deal of individual variation in pronunciation, as the following examples show.

60. This phenomenon is less apparent with the fricatives:

Before i (y) *and* ɪ:
sì (to build) or ʃì zi (to call) or ʒi
kosia (fish) or kòʃya azi (another)
sì (with) ʃi (to split) azi (work) or aʒi
sì (to tear) tɪʃɪ (to write) kɪzya (pig)
sɪnya (sand) ʃɪŋgwa (ground-nut)

Before other vowels: sɛ́ (to smoke) za (meat)
  asɔ (to dress) zɔ (to milk)
  ísú (four) zu (to hide)
  kísù (bow)

In an ideal orthography the letters *s* and *z* could, without ambiguity, be used to cover both sorts of fricative sound, and such has been done with Logo and Lugbara material obtained from outside sources.

61. With the affricates this phenomenon is more marked and is to be noticed occasionally before other vowels (with the exception of a).

Before i (y) *and* ɪ:

atsí-kelá (charcoal)	atʃí-fá (firewood)	dzi'da (frog)	adʒi (to wash)
	kutʃí (thorn)		lidʒí (left hand)
tsí-kɔ (blunt)	tʃitʃi (sharp)		
ŋgátsi (night) or	ŋgătʃi		
	kútʃìku (chin)		

Before other vowels:

tsa (to arrive)	tʃɛtʃi (hot)	tadzá (to spread)	
àtsɔ ⎫ (hoe) àtswa ⎭		kɔdzɔ ⎫ doctor kɔdzwa ⎭	dʒɔ ⎫ hut dʒwa ⎭
		kɪdzúrúkwá (termite)	kɪdʒúrúkwá

In an ideal orthography the letters *c* and *j* could, without ambiguity, be used to cover both sorts of affricate.

Palatal consonants: **ny, y; 'j 'y.**

62. ny is pronounced as in French 'baigner'. It occurs in all languages in cognate words.

kínyì (crocodile)	ɔ-nya (to eat)
ɔ-nyí (to divide)	inyè (thus)
nyenye (mosquito)	kănyú (sesame)

63. y is pronounced as in English 'yes'. It occurs in all languages, but y-words in Moru do not correspond to y-words in Madi, and vice versa.

MORU: ɔ-yɛ (to do)	ɔ-yó (to clean)	ya (belly)	
MADI: eyí (water)	yo (absent)	yu (to untie)	yeì (to answer)
LOGO: iyí (water)	yɔ (absent)	aya (iron)	

64. 'j is a pure palatal sound pronounced implosively. The implosion is stronger than in 'b and 'd. This sound occurs in the MADI dialects and in KELIKO.

Examples from MADI (Lokai): 'jì (to light); o'ja (war); 'jó (to speak); o'ju (horn).

65. 'y is y pronounced with a slight glottal 'catch' (see § 76). The sound occurs in LOGO (also in Avukaya and Moru Wa'di) and corresponds to Madi 'j in cognate words.

Examples from LOGO: to'yó (thin); ko'yá (horn).

66. There are no pure palatal explosives in the Moru-Madi group. The velar explosives **k** and **g** are often palatalized before front vowels (see § 67), while in some of the dialects the alveolar affricates have a more palatal tongue position than in the main dialects. Thus:

MADI	sa (tail)	is pronounced almost	ekyá	in LULU'BA.
,,	dzó (house)	,,	,,	gyɔ	,,	,,
,,	dzuru (country)	,,	,,	gyuru	,,	,,

Velar consonants: **k (ky), g (gy); ŋ.**

67. k is pronounced with little aspiration and g with a considerable amount of voice. ŋ is pronounced as in English 'singing' but is a relatively rare sound outside the compound ŋg.

Before front vowels (i, ɪ, e, ɛ) a very fronted (*pre-velar*) variety of k and g is usually heard in MORU MIZA, the tongue position of which is often actually palatal.

These sounds may be conveniently written *ky* and *gy*, if it is felt that a spelling distinction is needed.[1]

Before front vowels:	kukyí (thorn)	gyií (water)
	ɛkyì (to arrive)	tägyí (smell)
	ŋgäkyí (night)	ɛgyɪ (to write)
	kɔkyɛ́ (dog)	ɔ-gyɛ́ (to buy)
	kʷɔkyɛ̀ (bush)	
	kyɛ́-tɛ́ (finished)	

Note: tsʷɛkɛ́ (fish-spear) is the only apparent exception to this rule.

Before other vowels:	tɔká (bellows)	agà (enclosure)
	ɔ-kɔ́ (to catch)	ɔ-gɔ (to return)
	tòkó (woman)	gólo (river)
	kʊ́mè (brains)	nyagʊrà (short)
	kumú (fly)	ugu (to steal)

Examples of **ŋ**: íŋwa (where?), -ŋwa (diminutive ending).

68. A distinction must be drawn between **k-** (**ky-**) as part of a word root and **k-** as a prefix. In the latter instance the palatal variety is not so common, nor is the fronting of the sound always so strong; it is sometimes absent altogether. In the following examples **kʸ** will indicate a semi-fronted variety. Note before back vowels an occasional labialized variety, indicated **kʷ**.

Before front vowels:

kizwe (pig)	kʸìnì (skin)	
	kʸianɔ (formerly)	
kɪtɔ́ (hare)	kʸɪrɔ́ (granary)	
kìla (war)	kʸégà (crab)	kyémbá (net)
kɛtsʷi (seed)	kʸɛ'bo (hoe)	kyɛ́rá (medicine)
		kyɛmbɛ (neck)

Before other vowels:

kʊ́rʊ́ (gourd)	kʷɔyi (vulture)
kurʊ́ (mud)	kʷɔ́nyí (nail)
kótó (termite)	kʷɔmvɔ́ (nose)
kɔ̀ba (jackal)	kʷɔyí (horn)
kàya (knee)	
käbi (lizard)	

Note: **ky** and **gy** in word roots correspond to **ts** and **dz** in other Moru dialects, but the prefix **k-** is absent in such dialects. (See §§ 141–2.)

Labio-velar consonants: **kp**, **gb**; **w**.

69. The dual-articulation explosives are to be found in all the Moru-Madi languages, but very seldom in related words. The sounds are slightly lip-rounded, and **gb** is sometimes pronounced implosively.

w is pronounced as in English, but is occasionally fronted before front vowels, when it is pronounced like the *u* in French 'huit'.

MORU:	kìtìkpara (stool)	táwi (very)
	ekpɪ (to cough)	wʸítì (iron)
		wɪtɛ (dry)
		lìwa (elephant)
		wá (beer)

[1] To write these sounds *c* and *j*, as is done in some text-books, causes much confusion with the sounds **tsʷ** and **dzʷ**, which are also denoted by these letters in the same books.

MADI: otsokpɔ̀ (chin)   logbi (beads)   awowia (wild dog)
      ɔkpó (hard)   logbɔtó (yaws)   ɔwó (to cry)
      kpôdu (all)
      ɛ̀kpadrú (many)
LOGO: kìtìkpala (stool) gbíɛndúsì (the bush) ówá (beer)   wa'wà (to yawn)
LUGBARA: kpʊkpɔ (hard)   gbà (to beat)   owa (beer)

Laryngeal consonants: ' h.

70. Whether the glottal explosive (') is to be regarded as a speech sound or an extra-linguistic accident is a debatable point. It occurs as initial element in some dialects in words consisting merely in a vowel. E.g.

'belly' = 'a   in Southern and Central languages.
           ya   in the Moru dialects.
'to make' = 'ɛ   in Madi and Lugbara.
            yɛ   in the Moru dialects.

It also occurs in some dialects to separate two vowels which might otherwise merge into a diphthong.

'fowl' = (t)äú   in Moru.
          ä'ú   in the Central languages.
          a'ú   in Madi.
'to yawn' = aʊ   in Moru.
            'wa'ú in Lugbara.
            'o   in Madi.

It also occurs as glottal element in implosives. (See §§ 73–6.)

71. The **h**-sound is probably also extra-linguistic. It is sometimes heard in front of words beginning with a vowel.

MADI: hɔ̀'ja and ɔ̀'ja (war); hini and ini (black).

A velarized form of this sound is sometimes heard at the end of a word, especially on a stressed syllable with the vowel -a.

LUGBARA: 'báh   or 'bá (person)   oátáh or átá (pool)
KELIKO: zah   or za (meat)   mbah or mba (moon)
LOGO: móndyah or *mundia* (person)

72. In MORU MIZA there are a few words in which a velarized **h** (alternating with the velar fricative **x**) seems to occur as a speech element. This sound sometimes corresponds to **k** elsewhere.

íhwi or íxwi (wild dog); cf. íku in Moroändri
hwá or xwá (no!); cf. 'á in Moroändri, hɛ̃ in 'B.
hwɨlɨ or xwɛ̀lɛ̀ (drinking pipe)
bukúhúhwè or bukúxúxwè (thunder)
Note also in Avukaya: härägägä or xärägägä (lizard)
and in the Pandikeri Madi New Testament: *hwi* (to enter), *hwe* (tree).[1]

A note on the implosives. 'b, 'd, 'j, 'y.

73. The term 'implosive' is not a very happy one, as these sounds may, on occasions, be pronounced *explosively*. To understand in what way these sounds differ from normal **b**, **d**, **j**, and **y**, one should understand the physical processes underlying the articulation of the latter.

[1] Lokai Madi has *kwi* and *kwe* for these two words.

74. In normal **b, d,** and **j** (including **dz** and **dʒ**), a closure is made in the mouth at the lips, teeth, or teeth-ridge, and air is pressed against the closure. This air, during the process, is set in vibration in the larynx by the vocal chords through which it is forced, and this vibration is termed 'voice'. The sounds are thus 'voiced' sounds. Finally, at a given time, the closure is released and the explosion is heard.

75. In **'b, 'd,** and **'j** the closure is made roughly as for **b, d,** and **j** (except that **'d** is alveolar and **'j** palatal). The larynx is now forced down over the column of air in the throat, and this air is set in vibration by the vocal chords, again producing 'voice'. The difference between the two forms of 'voicing' is that in **b, d,** and **j** the air is forced from the lungs through the larynx, while in **'b, 'd,** and **'j** the column of air is more or less stationary, while the larynx moves down over it. When the time comes for the release of the oral closure, if the pressure of air within the mouth is less than that outside the mouth, the sounds are *implosive*; if the pressure of air within the mouth is greater than that outside the mouth, the sounds are *explosive*; if the pressure is equal, the sounds are neither implosive nor explosive, but mere articulations without breath force.[1]

76. In normal **y** there is no complete closure in the mouth, and the sound is voiced throughout. In **'y** there is again no complete closure in the mouth; consequently there comes a time when the larynx ceases to descend, and breath is forced through it from the lungs for the articulation of the following vowel. This gives the impression of a slight glottal 'catch', as of **y** preceded by the glottal explosive, and in some dialects, as will be seen in a later chapter, the glottal explosive itself serves for this sound. (See § 133.)

Consonant Combinations

1. Nasal Compounds

77. The following combinations of voiced consonant preceded by cognate nasal stop are frequent. As before, examples are taken from Moru-Miza, except where otherwise stated. It must be borne in mind that the nasal elements in these compounds rarely have syllabic value.

Labial compounds: **mb, mv, (nv).**

78. mb: (ky)ɛmbɛ (neck) tombí (locust) ìmba (moon)
  mv: u-mvu (to drink) kɔmvó (nose)
  nv: kɔnvɔlɛ (back again)

Very often the nasal is not pronounced before **v**, but the preceding vowel may be nasalized.

ũvu, kɔ̃vó or kɔvó, kɔ̃vɔlɛ or kɔvɔlɛ.

This form of pronunciation is more common among the Central languages than in Moru or Madi.

Dental and alveolar compounds: **nd, ndr.**

79. nd: ndiriŋwà (girls); andi (self); ndá (he); kándà (fence)
  ndr: indri (goat); lendr(i) (shadow); ɔ-ndrɛ́ (to see); ɔ-ndrɔ́ (to suck)

Whether **nd** is a true dental sound is doubtful. Examples of it are rare both in Moru and in Madi, and these mostly correspond to **ndr** in other languages.

---

[1] These conclusions were arrived at on the strength of kymograph experiments Mr. R. T. Butlin and I made at the School of Oriental and African Studies, on a similar series of sounds (b, d, j, g) heard in Swahili. These sounds have already been called implosive by Doke. (*Phonetics of the Zulu Language*, p. 291).

CONSONANTS

Alveolar sibilant and semi-sibilant compounds: **nz, nj, (ndz^w, ndz, ndʒ)**.

80. Here it is best to treat each main language separately:

    MORU (M.) 'buänză (cloud)   kɪnzú (termite)   onzí (Ä.) (bad)
               ṅdz^wí (five)   ɔ-ndz^wì (to untie)   ɔ̀ndz^wɛ (white)
      MADI: nza (thick)   ɔnzú (thin)   n(d)zɛtɛ (mud)
                 undzí (bad)   ɛ́ndzɔ́ (lies)   ndzɛ (to undress)
                 andzí (heavy)   'bɔrɔn(d)zí (children)
      LOGO: kánzi (basket)   kìndzɔ̀ (lies)   kɔ̀nzi or kùndʒi (bad)
                 kɪndʒí (to untie)   lɛndʒì (heavy)   àndʒimva (children)
  LUGBARA: ndzɔ̀ (lies)   ɔ̀ndzi or ùndʒi (bad)

In all languages, except Moru, there is much variation in the second element of these nasal compounds; in Madi it alternates between **dz** and **z**, and in Logo and Lugbara **z**, **dz**, and **dʒ**.

Velar and labio-velar compounds: **ŋg, (ŋgy), mgb.**[1]

81.   **ŋg**: ŋga (thing)   sɪŋgɔ (sand)   äŋgù (to smell)
           läŋgyi (heavy)   ŋgyi-úŋgyi (thick)
   mgb: tomgbo (canoe)   kätumgbu (rhinoceros)   lɛmgbɛrɛ (termite)

2. COMPOUNDS WITH THE SEMI-VOWELS w AND y

w-compounds

82. w-compounds are to be found in all languages, but are best regarded under two main heads:

    I. Compounds consisting in consonant+semi-vowel **w**.
    II. Labialized consonants (i.e. in which the w-element is an integral part of the sound and not a following sound.)

I. *Type*: *consonant*+**w**. Three kinds:

83. (*a*) Compounds caused by the addition of a vowel suffix (usually -**a**) to words ending in a back vowel. Most common in Logo.

       LOGO: bòŋgo or bòŋgwa (cloth)   tɔ̀kɔ or tɔ̀kwa (woman)
               mɔ́gɔ́ or mɔ́gwá (grave)   dʒɔ́ or dʒwá (house)
               koto or kùtwa (navel)   lo or lwà (to cut)
       MADI: iŋgo or iŋgwa (what?)   bwí (to shoot), cf. 'bú in Logo.
       MORU: katsɔ́ or katswá (long)   ndrɔ or ndrwa (year)
               ɔ-dzú or ɔ-dzwá (to wash)   kídru or kídrwe (vein)
               kizu or kizwe (pig)   o-'bwä (to shoot)

Note also that the suffix -**i** of predication often has this effect. Mynors records a pronunciation of *tokwi* for *toko i* (it is a woman).

84. (*b*) Compounds not traceable to such causes. There are no such compounds in Logo, but many in Madi. It is to be noted that they are all compounds with **k**, **g**, or **ŋ**.

       MADI: ikwí (bowels)   gwɛ̀ (to burn)   iŋgwi (white)
               kwà (bone)   -ŋgwa (diminutive ending)
       MORU: kwa (to gnaw)   -ŋgwa and -ŋwa (diminutive endings)

---

[1] Logically, the nasal element should be written **ŋm**, as it is also a labio-velar sound, but *m* may be used here without ambiguity. (Note that *n* should not be used, as that represents a dental or alveolar sound.)

85. (*c*) Compounds in which the **w**-element is sometimes present and sometimes not. These are not compounds with **k, g,** or **ŋ**.

    MADI: swá and sá (to clean)   kúdzwέ and údʒê (brains)
            dzwe and dzè (to marry)
            εrwa (medicine), cf. (ky)εra in Moru.
            ùdrwe (urine), cf. (k)ʊdrε elsewhere.
    MORU: ɪ̀'dwɪ and ɪ'dɪ (cold)

II. *Type: labialized consonant.* Two kinds:

86. (*a*) Sounds in which labialization is an essential element and without which the sounds do not occur. (Here the **w** is written small, to indicate that it is not the second element in a compound, and may accordingly be ignored in an ideal orthography. (See § 56.) Such sounds occur only in MORU.[1]

    MORU: ɪtsʷí (bowels); u-dzʷέ (to burn); ɔ̀ndzʷε (white)

87. (*b*) Sounds in which labialization is caused by assimilation of a following back vowel. (Here again the **w** is written small to indicate that it is the result of assimilation and not the second element in a compound, and may therefore be ignored in an ideal orthography.) This assimilation does not always occur.

    LOGO: korokʷo (knee)   mʊndʷɔ́ (maize)   áŋgʷɔpí (how many?)
    MORU: vɔŋgʷɔ́ (cloth)   zʷɔ́ (hut)   kɔ́zʷɔ́ (witch)   ŋgʷɔ́nya (food)

and with the k-prefix:

    kʷɔdra (bamboo)   kʷɔi (vulture)   kʷɔzí (bad)

y-*compounds*

88. y-compounds occur only in LOGO. They, too, are best regarded under two main heads:

    I. Compounds consisting in consonant+semi-vowel **y**.
    II. Palatalized consonants (i.e. in which the **y**-element is an integral part of the sound and not a following sound).

I. *Type: consonant*+**y**.

89. There is only one kind of semi-vowel compound, and it is caused by the addition of a vowel suffix (usually -a) to words ending in a front vowel.

    LOGO: *kari* or *kàrya* (leprosy)   *lidri* or *lìdrya* (pot)
          drɪ̀'bi or *drɪ̀'bya* (hair)

Sometimes the vowel suffix is assimilated to -ε.

    LOGO: *apikifi* or *àpεkifyε* (bee)   *dili* or *dɪlyè* (spear)
          kodri or *kʊdryε* (urine)

Note the following irregular y-compounds in words that normally end in a back vowel (and where one would naturally expect a **w**-compound).

    LOGO: *mondo* or *móndya* (person)   kɪzya (pig), cf. (k)izo elsewhere.
                                     kɔ́zya (rain), cf. ɔzɔ elsewhere.

II. *Type: palatalized consonant.*

90. Palatalized consonants result when the vowel suffix is attached to a word ending in a front vowel after a *velar* consonant (**k** or **g**). In such cases no semi-vowel is

---

[1] But see under 'five' in Vocabulary.

heard, but the articulation point of the tongue is pre-velar (**ky** and **ġy**) or sometimes even post-alveolar (**tʃ** and **dʒ**). See § 143.

LOGO: *kabiliki* or kébɪlɪ̀kyà (sheep)   *kaligi* or kalígyέ (leopard)
mbiligi or ambɪlɪdʒa (lizard)

In this context compare the palatalized variants of **k** and **ġ** found in Moru before front vowels in general (§ 67). Since the semi-vowel **y** never occurs after velar consonants, the palatalized velar consonants may without ambiguity be written *ky* and *gy*.

CHAPTER III

INTONATION

91. Moru-Madi intonation should be discussed under three heads—Lexical, Morphological, and Syntactic intonation. In this chapter all examples (except where otherwise stated) are taken from the Miza dialect of MORU.

Lexical tone.

92. The Moru-Madi languages are *tone* languages, i.e. relative voice pitch is as important an element as vowels and consonants in the formation of words. There are three main tone levels, which may be marked in the following ways (the letters *ka* representing here a syllable):

        High level tone   **ká**
        Mid level tone   **ka** (unmarked)
        Low level tone   **kà**

The interval between each tone level is approximately a major third for any one speaker, but the absolute pitch of any syllable is not the same for all speakers, i.e. they do not all speak in the same *key*.

93. The following pairs of words from the Miza dialect of MORU give a clue as to the lexical function of tone:

drí (hand)	'bú (grave, hole)	tí (cow)	έdɛ (to clean)
drɪ̀ (head)	'bù (rain)	tì (near)	ɛdɛ (to make)
kumú (fly)	tí'bí (grandfather)	kɔ̀kyέ (dog)	la'bí (beating)
kùmu (hernia)	tì'bì (fish)	kɔkyὲ (bush)	la'bɪ (custom)

Examples from other languages:

    MOROĀNDRI: kuré (mud)   AVUKAYA: odrá (bamboo)   ɔkyέ (dog)
                       kurè (boil)   òdra (beer)   ɔkyὲ (bush)
          MADI: drí (hand)   LOGO : kɔkyí (dog)
                       drɪ̀ (head)   kɔkyɪ̀ (bush)

Morphological tone.

94. Grammatical tone study requires a narrower method of transcription. Words undergo a decided tone 'inflexion', which is to a great extent due to tonal assimilation of other words and particles in juxtaposition. The following two extra tone marks are thus necessary:

        Mid-high level tone   **kḁ** (between mid and high)
        Mid-low level tone   **ka̤** (between mid and low)

These two tone levels are purely *relative* levels. Whereas one can distinguish a high tone word from a mid or a low tone word when spoken in isolation, the mid-high and mid-low tones are only discernible in relation to other levels in the phrase under discussion. When spoken in isolation, words containing these tone levels usually fall automatically under the three main tonal categories mentioned above. E.g.

así (fire); lerú (to light); ɔ'dʊ́ (what?). But:
nyá ɔ̀'dʊ lerú yà? má àsi lĕru. What are you lighting? I'm lighting a fire.

95. There are many particles which have tone levels entirely dependent on the words they precede or follow, and which, since they are never pronounced in isolation by the natives, must be regarded as 'neutrals' from the point of view of tone. Examples of these are the particles, **ri** and **te**.

mă-rí (to me)	mă-zi ŋgàgà te.	I called the boys.
mí-ri (to you)	mă-zi ànya rɔ́ tè.	I have already called them.
ányä-ri (to him)		

Also the characteristic vowel in verbs:

má-ɔ̀dra. I am dying.   lédr ni ɔdrà-rɔ. Man is mortal.

96. Other forms have a definite tone value which influences the tone of adjoining words, although the forms themselves are not necessarily pronounced by the natives in isolation. Note the influence of the negative particle **ku** on the tone of the verb stem in:

mă-mvú ku. I didn't drink it.   Cf. mă-mvu-tè. I drank it.

Note also the influence of the subject pronoun when immediately preceding the verb stem in:

má-úzì-na. I am calling him.   Cf. má ŋgàgà uzi. I am calling the boys.

97. As may be seen from the above examples, Moru-Madi tones are normally level. Rising and falling tones are relatively rare, and may usually be attributed to the coalescence of two vowels of different pitch. Such tones are indicated by a combination of tone marks:

Falling tones: kâ (high to low), kâ̄ (high to mid), kā̂ (mid to low)
Rising tones: kǎ (low to high), kā̌ (mid to high), kǎ̄ (low to mid)

Examples: kûmu (he runs; from ká-ùmu).
kôŋga (he jumps; from ká-ɔ̀ŋga).
mǎ (or màá) ŋgàgà uzi. We are calling the boys.

98. Since, as has been said earlier, no one speaker speaks necessarily in the same 'key' as another, it would be unprofitable to try to reproduce Moru-Madi intonation in staff notation—for, even if the particular key of this notation fitted the voice of a given Moru-Madi speaker, the chances of its fitting the voices of the readers of this book are very slender. To show, therefore, the actual pitch relationship between syllables in a narrow tonetic transcription, a tonic sol-fa transcription is appended here in places. The 'doh' is intended to represent the normal mid level tone of the speaker's voice, and which the reader may interpret as the tone that lies approximately midway in pitch between the highest and lowest pitches which he normally uses in conversation.[1] The other notes will give the relative rise and fall of the voice above and below this middle note. This system will be used mostly in the chapter on the tonal conjugation of verbs (Chapter XVIII).

[1] A gramophone record taken of a group of Moru boys at Lui reciting the Lord's Prayer aloud reveals, on analysis, that the 'doh' for the majority of the boys on this occasion was in the neighbourhood of middle C.

99. The intonation signs will then have the following relative values, within about half a tone, in terms of tonic sol-fa (the letters *ka* representing a syllable):

Level tones	Falling tones	Rising tones
ká (r re) m f	kâ m–l₁	kǎ l₁–m
kȧ de r (re)	kâ m–d	kǎ d–m
ka d	kâ d–l₁	kǎ l₁–d
kà t₁		
kà (t₁) ta₁ l₁ si₁ s₁		

Examples from this chapter (§§ 94–7) with approximate musical values.

nyá ɔ̇'dʊ lerʊ̇ yà?	m t₁ d d r l₁	What are you lighting?
má àsi lɛ̌ru.	m l₁ d t₁ d	I am lighting a fire.
mǎ-zi ŋgàgà te.	m d l₁ l₁ d	I called the boys.
mǎ-zi ànya rɔ̇ tė.	m d l₁ d r l₁	I have already called them.
má-ɔ̀dra.	m l₁ d	I am dying.
lédr ni ɔdràrɔ.	m (d) d d l₁ d	Man is mortal.
mǎ-mvú ku.	m m d	I didn't drink it.
mǎ-mvu-tė	m d r	I drank it.
má-úzì-na.	m m l₁ d	I am calling him.
má ŋgàgà ùzi.	m l₁ l₁ l₁ d	I am calling the boys.
mǎ ŋgàgà ùzi	l₁–m l₁ l₁ l₁ d	We are calling the boys.
kûmu. kôŋga.	m–l₁ d m–l₁ d	He runs. He jumps.

Examples from Chapter I with approximate musical values.

(§ 21)	mí-zi ŋgàgà.	m d l₁ l₁	Call the boys.
	mí-'bɪ ŋgàgà.	m d l₁ l₁	Beat the boys.
	má ku ditɔkɔ́ ì.	m d d d m l₁	I am not a woman.
	má kʊ̇ ɔnzírɔ́.	m r d m m	I am not bad.
	nyékyi nòa.	m d l₁ d	Come here.
	nyɛ̀sȧ-tė.	r r l₁	You arrived.
(§ 23)	má-lasà ŋgwa.	m d l₁ d	I wash the child.
	nyá-lasa ŋgwa.	m d d d	Wash the child.
	mó-lɔ̀sɛ̇ bɔŋgó tɛ̇.	m r r d m r	I sewed the cloth.
	nyó-lɔse bòŋgɔ.	m d d l₁ d	Sew the cloth.
	mú-túri ndá tùrì.	m m d m l₁ l₁	I fear him.
	nyé-turì ma.	m d l₁ d	Fear me.
(§ 43)	ndá ká-ubi nȧ.	m m d d r	He is pushing it.
	nyá-áta ɛ́ŋʊnyɛ?	m m d m d d	How do you say it?
	ánya ká-atȧ.	m d m d r	He is talking.
	mûmu. nyûmu.	m–l₁ d m–l₁ d	I am running. You are running.
	nyɔ̀ì íŋwa yà?	m–l₁ m d l₁	Where are you going?
	nyɛ̂kpí ɔ'dɔta yà?	m–d m d d d l₁	Why are you coughing?
	nyíbi na iŋwa yà?	m d d r d l₁	Where are you pushing it?
	kɔkyé kɔ́ì ɔ̀dranɪ.	d m m–l₁ l₁ d d	The dog goes to die.

Syntax tone.

100. The question of sentence intonation in Moru-Madi has had very little investigation, but one aspect, in which it differs widely from European languages, may be mentioned here. Whereas in English the tone pattern of an interrogative sentence may differ fundamentally from that of a statement, in the Moru-Madi languages the tone patterns are fundamentally the same. The question may be accompanied by a significant gesture or a general raising of the voice, but the tone relationship of the syllables within the sentence is unaltered. To put it in musical terms—the *tune* remains the same, though the key, the tempo, and the general expression may be violently altered.

To take a specific example, the English sentence 'Thè money is stolen', when used as a question, will have a totally different tune from that accompanying the sentence when used merely to state a fact. In the Moru sentence 'úkugu paráta tɛ', the first and fifth syllables will always be the highest in pitch, no matter in what context the sentence appears.

101. This principle applies not only to sentences containing varying emotions but also to sentences, such as co-ordinate or subordinate clauses, conditionals, &c., whose syntactic relationship in English demands a peculiar intonation.

Compare, for instance, the tone patterns in the English sentences: 'I can see the tree' and 'I can see the tree, but I can't see the waterbuck.' In Moru 'I can see the tree' is rendered 'má-ndrɛ́ tsʷɛ ndɪ́' in both contexts, with variations in the actual pitch of each syllable, but not in the main outline of the tune with its lowest note always on 'tsʷɛ'.

CHAPTER IV

THE COMPARATIVE PHONETICS OF MORU-MADI

Vowels

102. Vowel variations between dialects are so complicated that they cannot be fully set out here. The behaviour of the 'characteristic' vowel has already been discussed (§§ 31–6). Where the vowels of word-roots are concerned, the following general remarks must suffice:

103. On the whole there is correspondence of vowel *category* (see § 3) between languages, but within each category tense vowels do not necessarily correspond to tense vowels, nor lax vowels to lax, although the lax vowel ɪ would appear to be consistent in a large number of words. E.g.

mɪ (you); 'bɪ̀'bɪ (star); drí (hand); drɪ̀ (head)

where the lax vowel is to be found in most languages when these words are spoken in isolation.

104. ɛ in MORU and MADI often corresponds to **a** in the Central languages.

MORU (M.)	LOGO		
zɛ	za	(excrement)	
kyɛ̀ or tsʷɛ	fa	(tree)	(fɛ̀ in -ändri)
ɛpɛ	ápá	(honey)	

105. ɔ in MORU and MADI often corresponds to **u** in the Central languages.

MORU	LUGBARA		MADI	LUGBARA	
kɔmvó or ɔmvó	umvú	(nose)	zô	zù	(to hide)
kónyí or ónyó	ʊnyʊka	(nail)	'jó	dʒu	(to say)
ɔ̀-ndrɔ	ndru	(to suck)			

THE COMPARATIVE PHONETICS OF MORU-MADI

CONSONANTS

106. The consonantal correspondences in cognate words are best shown from the point of view of MADI, in which language sound-change is least apparent.

Labial consonants: **p, b; f, v; 'b, m.**

107. Madi **p** and **b** (before front vowels and a), **f** and **v** (before back vowels), have correspondences throughout the group.

MADI	LUGBARA	LOGO	AVUKAYA	MORU	
òpɛ	opé	kòpɛ	òpɛ	kɔpé	(guinea-fowl)
pá	pá	pá	pá	pá	(foot)
òba	òba	bóá	òba	kòba	(jackal)
bí	bíle	bí	bí	bí	(ear)
ófúdrɔ̂	ɔfɔra	tófɔ́rókɔ́	ɔfɔ̀	tórɔ́fɔ	(ashes)
lɔfwarà	fɔrɔró	*fora*		fɔrɔla	(yellow)
vò	vo	vo	vo	vo	(place)
vó	vɔ́	vo	vɔ	ɔ-vó	(to blow)

Note that **f** and **v**—*not* corresponding to **f** and **v** in Madi—occur before front vowels in the Central languages and Moroändri. (See § 144.)

108. In a few instances **p** in one dialect corresponds to **f** in another.

MADI	MORU	KELIKO	
ápara	fäfä	atafara	(lake)
áfù	u-pi		(to open)

In LOGO the affricates **pf** and **bv** are sometimes heard as alternatives to **p (f)** and **b (v)**.

pfu and *fu*	(to kill)	bvìdrɪ and *vudri*	(down)
pfɔró and *fora*	(yellow)	màbvɔyɔ	(stupid)
topfa and tófɔ́rókɔ́	(ashes)		
pfarapfara	(blue)		

In LULU'BA the Madi nasal compound **mv** is regularly represented by **mb**.

MADI	LULU'BA	
mvu	mbú	(to drink)
amvu	ambu	(field)
òmvɔ	òmbɔ	(nose)

109. Madi **'b** and **m** (before all vowels) have correspondences throughout the group.

MADI	LUGBARA	LOGO	AVUKAYA	MORU	
'bi	'bi	'bi	'bi	'bi	(hair)
'bà	'bà	'bà	'bà	ɔ-'ba	(to put)
'bù		'*bu*	'bù	'bukúrú	(sky)
mí	mí	mí		mì	(eye)
má	má	má	má	má	(I)
mú	mú		lämu	u-mú	(to run)

110. In MADI (Lokai) implosive **'b** often alternates with normal **b** in the pronunciation of many speakers.

LOKAI	PANDIKERI	
'bará or bará	'borá	(child)
'bà or bà	'bà	(to put)
ɔ'bʊ́ or ɔbʊ́	ɔ'bú	(to-morrow)

Note, however, the differentiation between 'b and b in words like the following in Lokai:

'bà	(home)	bà	(breast)
'bí	(hair)	bí	(ear)
e'bí	(fish)	ébì	(lion)

111. In a few instances 'b in one dialect corresponds to b or gb in another.

MADI	LUGBARA	AVUKAYA	MORU	
bwí	gbí	'bú	o-'bwǎ	(to shoot)
lu'bule	iríbìli	ibi-ru		(green)
e'bwé	igbɪ			(cold)

Dental consonants: **t, d, n.**

112. Madi **t, d,** and **n** are found throughout the group.

MADI	LUGBARA	LOGO	AVUKAYA	MORU	
tí	tí	tí	tí	tí	(cow)
tè	tɛ	tɛ	tɛ	ɔ-tè	(to stay)
adó	adʊ	odo	dɔ̀	ɪdó	(fat) (sb.)
ɛdɛ́	idɛ	lɛdɛ	ɛdɛ	ɛdɛ́	(to make)
ɪna	ńná	íná	ńná	ńná	(three)
nì	nì	nì	nì	u-nì	(to know)

Alveolar consonants (liquid): **r, l, (ɽ).**

113. Madi **r** and **l** (before all vowels) have correspondences throughout the group.

MADI	LUGBARA	LOGO	AVUKAYA	MORU	
rú	ru	ru		ru	(self)
robí	aroà	aríwà	arúà	aróà	(hippo)
erì	írì	írì	ärrì	ärrì	(two)
arí	aría	àrɪá	àrɪwa	àrɪ	(bird)
àlʊ	àlʊ	àlɔ	àlɔ	àlɔ	(one)
lɛi	lɛ	*le*	lɛ	lɛi	(milk)
lɛ	lè	lɛ	lɛ́	ɔ-lɛ	(to want)
läri		leri	läri	läri	(drum)

114. Before certain vowels, however (notably **i** and **u**), there is often a great deal of dialectal alternation between **r** and **l**, which includes the flapped ɽ and occasionally even 'd.

Alternation between **l** *and* ɽ.

axe	= tólú (in Madi)	túlu (in Lugbara)	kólóŋwá (in Miza)
		kòbáɽú (in Logo)	óɽóvá (in -ändri)
		káɽú (in Keliko)	óɽóvá (in Ojila)
			ólówá (in Ojiga)
water-rat	= alú (in Madi)	älú (in Lugbara)	täɽú (in Miza)
		tälú (in Logo)	älú ⎫ (in Avukaya)
			aɽú ⎭
knife	= ílí (in Madi)	ílí (in Lugbara)	íɽí (in Miza)
		älí (in Logo)	ílígó (in Avukaya)
		íɽí (in Keliko)	

Alternation between **r** *and* **l** *(and* ɽ*).*

body	= rú (in Madi)	rú'ba ⎫ (in Logo)	lúmvú (M. K. L.)
		rumva ⎭	rúmvú (Ä. Äg. W.)

THE COMPARATIVE PHONETICS OF MORU-MADI 117

wind = äri (in Madi) alí (in Lugbara) ɔ̀lɪ (in Miza)
         ɔ̀lɪ (in Keliko) ɔ̀ʈɪ (in 'Bälimbä)
                 iʈi (in Ojila)

Alternation between l (*or* ɭ) *and* 'd (*or* d).
person = lídri (in Madi)   lédr (in Miza)
                ɭédr (in 'Bälimbä)
                'dédr (Äg. W.)
grandmother = dada (in Lulu'ba)   làdra (M. K. L.)
                dède (Ä. Äg. W. Jl.)

Alveolar consonants (retroflex): **tr, dr, 'd**.

115. With the exception of some of the Madi dialects (see § 117) **tr** and **dr** are to be found throughout the group.

MADI	LUGBARA	LOGO	AVUKAYA	MORU	
	tri	*tatri*	trí	ɔ-trí	(to curse)
drà	drà	drà	drà	ɔ-drà	(to die)
indrí	ndrí	ndrí	ndrí	indrí	(goat)

116. There is a tendency in LUGBARA to eliminate the r-element in **tr** and **dr**, although the consonants remain slightly retroflex and are often followed by slight friction (cf. the pronunciation of 'train' and 'drain' in southern English).

LUGBARA	MADI	MORU	
tu or tru		ɔ-trí	(to undress)
dusì or drù	drúzí		(to-morrow)
ndɛ or ndrɛ	ndrɛ	ɔ-ndré	(to see)

This tendency is especially strong after **n** where it is not confined to Lugbara.
fence = kándà (in Miza) kándrà (in 'Bälimbä)
always = ɔndɔrɔ-ndɔrɔ or ɔndró-àlɔ (in Miza)

117. In all the sub-dialects of MADI, including Lulu'ba, **tr** and **dr** in Lokai correspond to *dental* **t** and **d**. Thus, except in a few words, which themselves vary according to the speaker, Lokai **tr** and **t** are represented by dental **t** in the other Madi dialects, and Lokai **dr** and **d** by dental **d**.

LOKAI	PANDIKERI	'BURULO	LULU'BA	
drí	dí	dí	dí	(hand)
údru	údu	udu	o'do'dú	(frog)
drà	dà		da	(to die)
trɔ	tɔ			(with)
ndrɛ̀	ndɛ̀		ɔndɛ	(to see)
ándra	ándasí	anda	anda	(face)

118. Implosive **'d** is found in all languages.

MADI	LUGBARA	LOGO	AVUKAYA	MORU	
ko'dú	ku'dú	ko 'dú	o'dú	u'dú	(to sleep)
'da	'dá	'da	'da	ɔ-'da	(to insult)
'dí	'di	'di	'di	'dó	(that)

In LOKAI MADI the implosion is often so slight as to be hardly discernible, but the articulation point of the tongue is never dental, so that there is never any actual confusion with dental **d**.

Alveolar consonants (sibilant and semi-sibilant): **s, z; c, (ts), j, (dz)**.

119. Madi **s** and **z** are found throughout the group.

MADI	LUGBARA	LOGO	AVUKAYA	MORU	
sì	sì	sì	sì	sì	(with)
sɛ	sé	sé	sé	ɔ-sɛ	(to smoke)
isu	isù	ísú	sú	sú	(four)
èza	èza	za		èza	(meat)
zì	àzi	aʒi	àza	àza	(other)

120. In some dialects **s** and **z** are pronounced with a **w**- element of varying degrees of strength in some words.

excrement = zɛ (in Madi and Moru)   zʷɛ (in Avukaya)
to milk   = za (in Madi Lokai)   zwa (in Madi Pandikeri and Lulu'ba)
          ɔ-zá (in Moru)   zwa (in Avukaya)
to clean = sa (in Madi Lo.)   swa (in Madi Pa. and Lul.)
fat   = osede (in Madi Lo.)   swede (in Madi Pa.)

Note: long = azʷó (in Madi Lo. and Pa.), (k)atsó and (k)atswá (in Moru and the Central languages).

121. Before the vowel **i** (ɪ) LOGO occasionally has ʃ, corresponding to Madi **s**, and ʒ corresponding to **z**. (See § 60.)

to write = sì (in Madi)   tíʃɪ (in Logo)
to call = u-zí (in Moru) zi or ʒi (in Logo)

122. **ts** and **dz** have variations within the Madi sub-group itself. In all the sub-dialects of Madi, including Lulu'ba,[1] **ts** and **dz** in Lokai often correspond to **s** and **z**. Thus Lokai **ts** and **s** are represented by **s** in the other Madi dialects, and Lokai **dz** and **z** by **z**.[2]

LOKAI	PANDIKERI	'BURULO	LULU'BA	
atsí	así	así	así	(fire)
àtsɔ	àsɔ	àsɔ	àsɔ	(hoe)
ru itsi	esi ru		esu riŋɔ	(to meet)
adzú	azú		adʒú	(spear)
dzó	só		dʒó	(hut)
dzí	zí			
ódzó	ózó		ózó	(wizard)
ɛndzó	ɛndzó		ɔzɔ	(lies)
undzí	undʒwí		ndʒwé	(bad)

123. Outside the Madi sub-group these sounds correspond roughly to **s** and **z** in the Moru group, but to **ts** and **dz** in the Central languages.

MADI	LUGBARA	LOGO	AVUKAYA	MORU	
etsá	atsá	atsá	atsá	ɛsá	(to arrive)
ru itsi		ru kisu	su		(to meet)
ɛdzí	dzí		adzi	ɛzɪ	(to bring)
ódzó	udzɔgɔ	kɔdzwa	odzɔ	kózʷó	(wizard)
ɛndzó	ndzɔ̀	ndzɔ̀	ɔ̀ndzɔ̀	ɛn(d)zɔ	(lies)

[1] Lulu'ba sound-relationships, however, are less regular.
[2] See, however, § 147.

124. In the Central languages the variations tʃ and dʒ are met with before certain vowels. (See § 61.)

MADI	LUGBARA	LOGO	KELIKO	AVUKAYA	MORU	
tsí	tsi	tʃi	tʃi	tsi	ɔ-sɪ	(to bite)
lɔtsì	tʃitʃi	tʃitʃi	tʃitʃi	tʃitʃi	si-ɔsì	(sharp)
atsí	atʃí	atsí	atsí	atʃí	así	(fire)
dzɔ́	dzɔ́	dʒwá	dʒɔ́	dʒwɔ́	zʷɔ́	(hut)
adzú	àdzu		àdzu	adʒú	äzú	(spear)
undzí	ɔndzí	kundʒí	ɔnzí	wondʒí	ɔnzí	(bad)

125. There are certain words in which Madi (Lokai) **ts** and **dz** correspond to **k** and **g** elsewhere under certain conditions. (See under 'palatalization', § 141.)

    dog = ɔtsɛ́ (in Lokai Madi)   ɔkɛ́ (in Pandikeri Madi)
    rhinocerus = idzidzì (in Lokai Madi)   igigì (in Pandikeri Madi)
    brothers = ádrîinzi (in Lokai Madi)   adiŋgì (in Lulu'ba)

126. Note the following irregular correspondences:

MADI (Lo.)	MADI (Pa.)	LULU'BA	LUGBARA	LOGO	AVUKAYA	MORU	
tsʷinya	tsʷinya	ɪŋá		sɪnya	sínyá	sɪŋgɔ	(sand)
tso	tso	otʃwà	tsɔ̀	syà	tsɪ	ɔ-sɪ	(to sneeze)
lèdzu	lèdʒu					lèzɔ	(twins)
ìzɔ̀	ìdzɔ̀	ɛzɔ	ɪzɔ̀gɔ	kɪzya	ɪzɔ	kizwe	(pig)

Palatal consonants: **ny, y, 'j, ('y)**.

127. Madi **ny** has correspondences throughout the group.

MADI	LUGBARA	LOGO	AVUKAYA	MORU	
nya	nyá	nyá	nya	ɔ-nya	(to eat)
ínyɔ́	kínyu	ínya	ínyà	kínyì	(crocodile)
anyu	anyu	känyi	änú	kånyú	(sesame)

128. Madi **y** corresponds to **y** in the Central languages, but to **g** in Moru (except where it is an incidental glide between two vowels).

	MADI	LUGBARA	LOGO	MORU	
	aya	aya	aya	kàgwa	(iron)
	eyí	iyí	iyí	gyìí	(water)
but note:					
	a(y)íse		*kaisa*	kä(y)i	(grass)
	mɛ(y)á			mɪa	(guinea-worm)
	lɛ(y)á	lìwa	lìwa	lìwa	(elephant)

129. Madi implosive **'j** corresponds to **y** in Moru and **dʒ** (or **dz**) in Lugbara. Elsewhere the corresponding sound is **'j** or **'y**.

MADI	LUGBARA	LOGO	AVUKAYA	MORU	
o'ju	údze	ko'yá	ɔ'yɛ	kʷɔyí	(horn)
à'ja			à'ya	kàya	(knee)
'jo	dʒu			lɛdzi	(to speak)
le'jɔ́	ɪdʒɔ́	edʒo			(word)
'jì	edze	'di	'ji		(to light)

It might be noticed here that Madi ' also corresponds to Moru y. (See § 133.)

THE MORU-MADI LANGUAGE GROUP. I. PHONETICS

Velar consonants: k, ġ; ŋ.

130. Madi k and ġ correspond to k and ġ elsewhere, except when labialization or palatalization influences are present (see §§ 136-47).

MADI	LUGBARA	LOGO	AVUKAYA	MORU	
ka	eka	ká	kakà	ɔká	(red)
kʊ	ku	ko	ko	ko	(neg. particle)
ɪgá	gara	kígga	ɪgará	kyégà	(crab)
gá	ga	ga	ga	ɔ-ga	(to chop)
agɔ	agopi	agó	agó	àgo	(man)
ŋgoru	ŋgà	ŋga	ŋga	ɔ-ŋgá	(to fly)

131. ŋ alternates with **ny** and **ŋg** in the various languages, and there would appear to be no systematic correspondence.

MADI	LUGBARA	LOGO	AVUKAYA	MORU	
ŋɔ̀	nyú	ŋwa	ŋɔ	ɔ-ŋgó	(to break)
óŋa	ónyà	kóŋwà	oŋwa	káŋwà	(termite)
íŋgwá	ŋgáyà	ɪŋgayà	aŋguya	íŋwaya	(where?)
ɪŋgo		aŋgo'di		ɪŋgɔ	(which?)

Labio-velar consonants: kp, ġb, w.

132. Although the labio-velar explosives are found everywhere, there is very little correspondence between dialects, and those words which do correspond undergo considerable variation. **kp** may correspond to **k(w)** and **p**, while **ġb** may correspond to **ġw** and **'b**. **w** is found in a few common words.

MADI	LUGBARA	KELIKO	AVUKAYA	MORU	
otsokpɔ̀	íkpíkpi	ótsókɔ̀	ítʃíkì		(chin)
ɔkólɔ̀	ɔkélè	ɔkélè	kpu	ɛkpɪ	(to cough)
	kítíkpara	kítíkpara	kìtìkpara	kitìkpara	(M.) (stool)
			kɔtɔkpá	kɔ̀tɔ̀para	(Ă.)
bwí	gbí	'bu	'bu	o-'bwá	(to shoot)
	gbe	gbɛ	'bú	'bwä	(egg)
ówá	ówa	ówa		wá	(beer)
wé	wé	wè		ɔ-wyá	(to sweep)
ɔ̀'wɪ-ra				wɪ-tɛ	(dry)
	wítì	wítì		wyítì	(iron)

Laryngeal consonants: ', h.

133. The glottal explosive in Madi, when not extra-linguistic, corresponds to **y** in Moru and **'y** or **'** elsewhere.

MADI	LUGBARA	LOGO	AVUKAYA	MORU	
'oɛ	'ɛ	'o	'ɛ	ɔ-yé	(to do)
'a	'ya	'a	'a	ya	(belly)

Compare § 129, where Madi **'j** also corresponds to Moru **y**; the correspondences in the other languages, however, are different.

134. As already mentioned in § 72, there are a few words in which **h** in Madi Pandikeri corresponds to **k** in Madi Lokai.

    tree = *hwe* (Pa.)   *kwe* (Lo.)
    to enter = *hwi* (Pa.)   *kwi* (Lo.)

Similarly **h** in Moru Miza sometimes corresponds to **k** elsewhere.

    wild dog = íhwi (Miza)   íku (Moroändri)

Nasal compounds: **mb, mv; nd; ndr; nz, nj (ndz, ndʒ); ŋg; mgb.**

135. Although on the whole the nasal compounds have correspondences throughout the group, there are many words in which the nasal element is missing in some languages.

MADI	LUGBARA	LOGO	AVUKAYA	MORU		
ɛmbɛ	ombɛ	kyɪmbɛ	ɛmbɛ	kyɛmbɛ	(neck)	but
ebá	bìra	kyɩ̀mba	embá	kyémbá	(net)	
ɔ̀mvɔ	umvú	komvó	ɔmvó	kʷɔmvó	(nose)	but
				kovó (K.)		
	indi	*tandi*		andí	(self)	
líndrɪ	éndr	líndrɪ	lɛndrɪ	lendr	(shadow)	but
lɛdrá	édrè	làdra	làndra	làdra	(tongue)	
éndzó	ndzɔ̀	kɩ̀ndzɔ	enzo		(lies)	but
undzí ⎫	ùndʒi ⎫	kùndʒi ⎫		kɔzí (M.) ⎫		
ondzí ⎭	ɔ̀ndzi ⎭	kɔ̀nzi ⎭	wɔ̀ndʒi	ɔnzí (Ä.) ⎭	(bad)	
idzú	udzúrúkó	kɪdzú	idʒuruku	kɪnzú	(termite)	
oŋgó	ŋgɔ	ŋgɔ	ŋgo	ɔ-ŋgɔ	(to sing)	but
ruŋa				róŋga	(island)	
mgba	gbà	'bɛ̀			(to beat)	
oŋgoli	nyɛmgbɛlɛ		màgbɛlɛ		(rope)	

Labialization and Palatalization in Word Stems

Labialization.

136. In MORU MIZA, when k-, g-, or z- precedes o or ɔ, one usually hears an intrusive w between the consonant and the vowel. This glide sound is not heard in most of the other Moru dialects.

bamboo = kʷódrá (in Miza)   kódrá (in K., L., Äg., W.)
nose   = kʷɔmvó (in Miza)   kwamvó (in Wa'di)   omvó (elsewhere)
cloth = vɔŋgʷó (in Miza)   bɔŋgó (elsewhere)
house = zʷó (in Miza)   zó or zá (elsewhere)

137. In some languages this phenomenon has undoubtedly led to sound-change in the following vowel:

bamboo = ɔ̀dra   (in Madi Lo.)   kwèda (in Madi Pa. and Lul.)
all   = tsúnɪ (in Moru K.)   tswénɪ (in Moru M.)
to shoot = 'bu (in Logo)   'bwi (in Madi)
egg   = 'bu   (in Logo)   gbe (in Lugbara)
thin   = rórè   (in Moru M.)   rwarwè (in Moru K.), orwé (in Madi)
yellow = afɔrɔ̀ (in Lulu'ba)   lɔfwarà (in Madi Lo.), lofarà (in Madi Pa.)

kw, gw, and **ŋw** *in word roots.*

138. In the Central languages and in Moroändri the combination velar consonant+semi-vowel w is never found in word roots. Instead, one hears a labial fricative (**f** or **v**).

MADI	LUGBARA	KELIKO	LOGO	AVUKAYA	MORU (Ä.)	MORU (M.)	
kwà	fa	fa	fa	fa	fa	ko(w)à	(bone)
		fa			ɔ-fá	ɔ-kwa	(to gnaw)
kwá	ufa	fa	fa	fa			(to clean)
'baráŋgwa	mvá	mvà	mvá	mva	mvà	ṅgwá	(child)
		màdà-va	tsaá-mvá	bíá-vá	gaá-vá	gɪɽí-ŋwá	(small)

Note that Moroändri is the only *Moru* dialect to show this form of sound-change. In this dialect, therefore, as in the Central languages, f and v may occur before all vowels. (Cf. § 48, also § 144.)

139. In LOGO, when the suffix -a is added to words ending in -ko or -g̈o, contraction often takes place, the resultant sounds being kwa and g̈wa. Here there is no sound-change to f and v.

LOGO: tedrago or tédrágwá (rat); toko or tokwa (woman)
See § 83 for further examples.

Palatalization.

140. As already mentioned (§§ 67–8) the consonants k, g̈, and w, when occurring before a front vowel in Moru, often show the results of palatalization, the tongue position of k and g̈ being pre-velar, if not sometimes actually palatal. This form of palatalization is to be found in the Moru dialects Miza, Kediru, Lakama'di, 'Bälimbä, also in Avukaya and occasionally in Logo and Lulu'ba.

dog = kɔkyɛ́ (in Miza)   ɔkyɛ́ (in Avukaya)   kɔkyi or *kokia* (in Logo)
to marry = ɔ-gyɛ́ (in Miza)   gyɛ (in Avukaya)   gyɛ (in Logo)
iron = wyítɪ (in Miza)   wítɪ (in Keliko and Lugbara)

141. In other languages the palatalizing process has resulted in the alveolar affricates ts (tʃ) and dz (dʒ) for the explosives k and g̈ in such contexts. Such languages are Madi (Lokai dialect), Lugbara, Keliko, and the Moru dialects Wa'di and Moroändri.

Palatalization is least apparent in Madi Pandikeri.

MADI (Pa.)	MADI (Lo.)	LUG-BARA	KELIKO	LOGO	AVU-KAYA	MORU (M.)	MORU (Ä.)	
ɔké	ɔtsé			kɔkyi	ɔkyé	kɔkyé	ɔtsé	(dog)
okí	otsí	utʃʷí	kutsé	kutʃí	ukyí	kukyí	utsʷí	(thorn)
ekí	ekí					ėkyi		(to come)
				ŋgắtʃi	ŋgắtʃi	ŋgắkyi	ŋgắtsi	(night)
kyi (Lul.)			kéki	etʃí	etʃí		ătʃí (W.)	(to walk)
legí	ledzí	idzí	idzí	lidʒí	ɽidzí			(left hand)
agíni	adzíni	adze	ágyɛ / adzɛ	ägyia	ägyí		ädzí	(yesterday)
gè	dzè	(ogba)	dze	gɛ	gɛ	ɔ-gyé	ɔ-dzʷé	(to buy)
gyè	dzʷè	(ogbwa)	gye / dze	gyɛ	gyɛ	ɔ-gyé	ɔ-dzé	(to marry)
aŋgí	andzí	ändzí	ändzí	lɛndʒì	ländzi	läŋgyi	ländʒi	(heavy)

Note also:
| iyí | eyí | iyí | iyí | iyí | | gyìí | idzí | (water) |

It will thus be seen that while some of the ts and dz words in Lokai Madi correspond to s and z words in Pandikeri Madi and Moru (see §§ 122–5), others correspond to k and g̈ words in Pandikeri and ky and g̈y words in Moru Miza (and to ts and dz words elsewhere).

142. In those languages which take the prefix k- in nouns, the palatalization of this k- by a following front vowel is not so uniform nor so complete as that of k in a word root. (kʸ here stands for the semi-palatalized variety. See § 68.)

MORU MIZA	MOROÄGI	MORU WA'DI	LOGO	
kyɛmbɛ	kɛmbɛ	kʸɛmbɛ	kyɪmbɛ / kembe	(neck)
kyémbá	kyémbá	kʸɪmbá	kʸɪmba	(net)
kʸini	ini	kʸini	kʸini	(skin)
kyégà	kégà	kɪgà	kígga	(crab)

143. In LOGO, as already mentioned (§§ 89-90), when the suffix -a is added to a noun or verb ending in -i, the resultant glide sound -y- often has a palatalizing effect on a preceding velar consonant, so that one hears ky or even tʃ and gy or even dʒ, while the vowel suffix itself is often assimilated to -ɛ.

    kokia or kɔkyá (dog)   *kabiliki* or kébɪlɪ̀kyà (sheep)
    kalɪgɪ or kalígyá / kalígyɛ́ } (leopard)   *mbiligi* or ambɪlɪdʒa (lizard)

It is probable that many of the ky- and gy- words of Moru Miza have arisen in this way. Compare:

    dog   = kɔkyɛ́ (in Moru)   kɔkyá or *kokia* (in Logo)
    forest   = kɔ̀kyɛ (in Moru)   kɔ̀kya (in Logo)
    to buy   = ɔ-gyɛ́ (in Moru)   gɛ or *gia* (in Logo)

Note also:

    to sweep = ɔ-wyá (in Moru)   we (in Madi)

kw, gw, and ŋw *before a front vowel*.

144. It has already been shown (§ 138) that the combination of velar consonant and semi-vowel w in Madi and Moru is represented by a labial fricative in the Central languages (and Moroändri). When this combination is followed by a front vowel, palatalization is found in Moru, the resultant sound being an alveolar affricate with slight accompanying labialization (tz^w and dz^w; see § 56).

In the Central languages (and Moroändri) the sounds are as in § 138 (f and v). The Madi dialects (including Lulu'ba) undergo no sound-change.

MADI	LUGBARA	KELIKO	LOGO	AVUKAYA	MORU (Ä.)	MORU (M.)	
ikwí	fí	fí	fí	fí	ɪfí	ɪts^{w}í	(bowels)
kwí	ɪfɪ	ɪfɪ	kífɪ	efɪ	efi	kɛts^{w}i	(seed)
kwɛ	fɛ	fa	fa	fɛ	fɛ̀	ts^{w}ɛ̀ / kyɛ }	(tree)
				lɛfɛ	lɪfɛ	lɛts^{w}ɛ	(warana lizard)
ɛk(w)ɛ	ɪfɛ	afɛ̀	afɛ̀	afɛ	ɔfɛ	ats^{w}ɛ (Äg.)	(to give)
gwɛ̀	vɛ̀	vɛ̀	vɛ́	vɛ̀	u-vɛ́	u-dz^{w}ɛ́	(to burn)
iŋgwi	ímvɛ̀	imvɛ	ɛmvɛ	amvɛ	ɔ̀mvɛ	ɔ̀ndz^{w}ɛ	(white)

with one notable exception:

    índʒ^{w}í   ńdʒwí   ńdz^{w}í   ńdz^{w}í   (five)

cf. (u)mbú in Lendu.

145. The following are the forms that this palatalization of labialized velar consonants takes in the various MORU dialects:

KEDIRU	LAKAMA'DI	MOROÄGI	WA'DI	'BÄLIMBÄ	
etʃ^{w}í	ɪts^{w}í	itsí	ets^{w}í	es^{w}í	(bowels)
kɛtʃ^{w}i	k^{y}ɛsi	kɛts^{w}i	kɛts^{w}i	esi	(seed)
ts^{w}ɛ̀	ɪsé	ts^{w}ɛ	ts^{w}ɛ	ɪsé	(tree)
	lɛsɛ	ts^{w}a	r̥ítsó	r̥ɪtsɛ	(warana)
u-dze	u-zɛ̀	ä-dze	ɛdzé	u-z^{w}e	(to burn)
ɔ̀ndʒ^{w}ɛ	ɔ̀ndʒ^{w}ɛ	andz^{w}ɛ́	ándz^{w}ɛ	ɔ̀ndʒ^{w}ɛ	(white)
ńdz^{w}í	ńdz^{w}í	ńdz^{w}í	idʒi	ńdz^{w}í	(five)

146. Thus the Moru sounds ts^w and dz^w before a front vowel are related to kw and gw in Madi and to f and v elsewhere. From which may be seen that f and v may occur before all vowels in the Central languages (and Moroändri), but that

when they occur before front vowels or the vowel a, they do not correspond to **p** (**f**) and **b** (**v**) in Moru and Madi. (See § 107.)

That the two Miza words, fɛrɛ (few) and taví (tail), (mentioned in footnote to § 48) are probably borrowings from Moroändri, is indicated in the dialectal forms sɛrɪ and az^wi, found preserved in the 'Bälimbä dialect.

Other palatalized forms.

147. In the following examples only LULU'BA seems to give a clue as to the velar origins of the sounds concerned. Note that in Madi the Lokai forms mostly have **s** and **z** and the Pandikeri forms **ts** and **dz** (instead of vice versa, see § 122); Moru has **s** and **z**.

LULU'BA	MADI (Lo.)	MADI (Pa.)	LOGO	AVUKAYA	MORU (M.Ä.)	
ɔké	sì	tʃʷì	sì	sì	ɔ-sî	(to tear)
ekyá	sâ	ètsʷa				(tail)
kyì	asì		ʃì		ɔ-si	(to divide)

LULU'BA	MADI (Lo.)	MADI (Pa.)	LUGBARA	KELIKO	MORU (M.Ä.)	
ugyɛ	kudzʷɛ́	udʒê				(brains)
ɛgya	túbídʒo		tíbídʒò		làkaza ⎫ làkazu ⎭	(pot)
-ŋgi	-nzi	-ndʒi	-nzi	-ndzɪ		(plural suffix)

INTONATION

148. Little may be said about comparative tone study in Moru-Madi, seeing that the tone system for any one language is still to be fully worked out. All languages seem to have three main tone levels—high, mid, and low. Rising or falling tones are usually the result of coalescence of vowels of different pitch.

Lexical tone.

149. On the whole there is a tendency for cognate words, when their grammatical contexts are similar, to have the same tone level throughout the dialects. Thus:

the monosyllabic words drí (hand), bí (ear), pá (foot), má (I) are pronounced in isolation with *high* level tone in all languages;

the monosyllabic words drì (head), bà (breast), zè or zà (excrement) are all pronounced in isolation with *low* level tone;

in the dissyllabic words àrɪ or arí (bird), así or atsí, &c. (fire), täü or a'ú, &c. (fowl), the last syllable invariably has a higher tone than the preceding syllable;

in the words kúsù or ósù, &c. (bow), kárà or arà (python), aróà or aríwa, &c. (hippo), the last syllable invariably has a lower tone than the preceding syllable;

in the words ópí (chief), ílí or íṛí (knife), koto or ótó (anthill), the two syllables are of equal pitch.

Note, however, the following tonal anomalies:

MADI	LUGBARA	LOGO	KELIKO	MORU	
'a	'à	'á	'à	ya	(belly)
mí	mí	mí	mí	mì	(eye)
ɛndrɛ̀	ándrǎpɪ	ándré	ɛ́ndrǎpi	ɛ́ndrɛ̀	(mother)
ébî	ɛbì			ìbì	(lion)
ɔ̀dra	ódrá	ódrá	kɔdra	kódrá	(bamboo)

Morphological tone.

150. In all the Moru-Madi languages there are particles, the tone values of which are entirely dependent on the words they precede or follow, just as there are other forms which have a definite tone value which influences the tone of adjoining words.

E.g. Note variation in pitch of **ni** and **'bo** in LUGBARA (cf. § 95):

ädzu ɔpí **ní** (name of the chief)   ámvárí **mí-ni** (your field)
àmà-nya ìza **'bò**. We ate the meat.   má-atsá **'bɔ**. I have arrived.

Note also the effect of the negative particle **ku** in LUGBARA (cf. § 96):

mí-**mu**-'bo? Did you go?   má-**mù** ku. I didn't go.

Morphological tone is dealt with more fully in the tonal conjugation of verbs (Chapter XVIII).

Syntax tone.

151. The same principles underlying the tonal pattern of Moru sentences will be found to underly the intonation of the other members of the Moru-Madi group. The tonal pattern of the sentence is determined according to the inherent tones of the words themselves and their morphological relation one to another. Sentence intonation may be superimposed upon this original tone pattern, and the actual musical intervals between consecutive syllables may be widened or narrowed as the occasion demands, but the primary relationship is always preserved, i.e. a high tone syllable is always relatively high and a low tone tone syllable always relatively low, no matter in what context the sentence is used.

SECTION II
GRAMMAR
CHAPTER V
NOUNS

Form

152. Moru-Madi nouns have many forms. The simplest form is monosyllabic, consisting in consonant (or consonant combination)+vowel. The following examples are common to all languages:

    drì (head)   mí (eye)   bí (ear)   pá (foot)

Vowel prefixes.

153. As a comparative measure of noun-forms it is convenient here to take LOGO, in which language the above monosyllabic form is most common. Compared with the Logo forms, however, certain nouns in other languages begin with a characteristic vowel,[1] which may be regarded as a prefix:

LOGO	MORU	MADI	
drú	udrú	odrú	(buffalo)
mba	ìmba	ímba	(moon)
nì	inì	inì	(snake)

154. In all languages, however, there are many dissyllabic nouns with the form: vowel+consonant+vowel. Note the following common examples:

    ɔpi (chief)   agɔ (man)   a(t)sí (fire)   ándrè or éndrè (mother)

Consonant prefixes.

155. As a comparative measure of noun-forms it is convenient here to take LUGBARA, in which language the above dissyllabic form is most frequent. Compared with the Lugbara forms, certain nouns in other languages begin with a consonant prefix (k-, t-, l-). The following is the distribution of these consonant prefixes:

k- *prefix*: found in most of the MORU dialects (M., K., L., Äg., W.), also in LOGO and KELIKO. Absent in LUGBARA, the MADI dialects, and in two MORU dialects (-Ändri and 'Bälimbä).

LOGO	MORU (M.)	MORU (Ä.)	MADI	LUGBARA	
(k)úsu	kúsu	úsu	ósù	ósù	(bow)
kyɪmbɛ	kyɛmbɛ	embɛ	ɛmbɛ	ombɛ	(neck)
ɔlɛ	kulɛ	ɔlɛ	olɛ	olè	(evil eye)

t- *prefix*: found in LOGO and in some MORU dialects (M., K., L.). The Moru dialects -Ägi and Wa'di have **k-**. The other languages have no consonant prefix.

LOGO	MORU (M.)	MORU (W.)	MORU (Ä.)	MADI	LUGBARA	
(t)ä'ú	täú	kä'ú	äú	a'ú	a'ú	(fowl)
te'í	teí	kä'í	täí	a'í	a'í	(salt)
tälú	tärú	kärú	äɾú	alú	älú	(water-rat)
tɔkwá	tòkó	akó	okó	okó	okó	(woman)

---

[1] For definition of characteristic vowel see § 31.

NOUNS

1- prefix: found mostly in MORU (all dialects), MADI, and LOGO. Least common in KELIKO, LULU'BA, and LUGBARA.

MORU	MADI	LOGO	KELIKO	LULU'BA	LUGBARA	
lendr	líndrɪ	líndrɪ	ɪndrɪ	indi	(l)éndr	(shadow)
läri	läri	leri	äri	ari	äri	(drum)
lìwa	lɛá	lìwa	(l)ìwa	èwa	èwa	(elephant)
làdra	lɛdrá	làdra	àdra	lɛda	ídrà	(tongue)
làdra	ada	adrǎpi	ɪdrǎpi	dadâ	ɪdrǎpi	(grandmother)

Prefixes with semantic function.

156. Most of the prefixes already discussed seem to have no semantic function, i.e. in those languages where they are used, the words do not differ in essential meaning from the corresponding words in those languages where they are not used. In most languages, however, the prefix 1- is also used to form nouns from verbal roots. In some languages this function is performed by a vowel prefix.

Examples from MORU:

'bɪ (beat)   la'bí (a beating)   (k)ugu (laugh)   lägú (laughter)
gyɛ (marry) lagyɛ́ (marriage)   trɪ (curse)   látrí (a curse)
(dial. dzɛ) (dial. ladzɛ́ or lɛdzɛ́)   'da (swear)   la'dɔ (blasphemy)

Examples from MADI:

mgba (beat) lamgba (a beating)   'i (grind)   lo'i (grinding)
to (dance)   lató (a dance)   'jo (speak) le'jó (word)
nya (eat)   lenya (food)

Examples from LUGBARA:

dʒu (speak) idʒó (word)   nya (eat)   ɪnya (food)
le (love)   ale (love sb.)

Examples from LOGO:

nya (eat)   lényá (food)   le (love)   male'dia (love sb.)

The following sentences show how such verbal nouns are used:

MORU: mí-ŋgɔ lɔŋgɔ   Sing! lit. You sing song.
Anya ăa ma go laǎa.   He reviled me a reviling.
*Matindi tri Ayaŋwa go **latri**.*   Matindi cursed Ayangwa a cursing.

MADI: {Lo.: Nyí lɔŋgɔ́ ɔ̀ŋgɔ́ wa ya?   Má lɔŋgɔ́ ɔŋgɔ́ wà.} Can you sing a
{Pa.: Nyí-ŋgɔ lɔŋgɔ́ wa ya?   Má-ŋgɔ́ lɔŋgɔ́ wà.} song? I can.

MADI: {Lo.: Má **lató** òto.} I dance a dance.
{Pa.: Má-to lató.}

LULU'BA: mɔ'j(ɔ) e'jɔ́ ni. I speak words.

Noun Suffixes

157. Most noun suffixes have semantic or grammatical functions. For the purpose of easy reference they are listed here alphabetically, the languages in which they occur being shown in brackets.

-a (LOGO)

158. Many nouns in Logo have a suffix -a, which is not usually found in other languages. In Logo, too, alternative forms of the noun without this suffix are very common. Its function seems to be one of imparting definiteness to the noun in question. E.g.

arí or ariá (bird)   *kari* or kariá (blood)
fí or fɪa (bowels)   kɔtɔ or kɔ́tóa (termite)

Before this suffix final close vowels in the noun stem often alternate with the semi-vowels **y** and **w**:

dili or *dɪlyɛ*[1] (spear)   *tɔkɔ́* or *tɔkwá* (woman)
lidri or *lɪ̀drya* (pot)   *dʒɔ́* or *dʒwá* (hut)

k and **g** before a front vowel in the word stem are usually palatalized before this suffix. (See Section I, § 90.)

kabiliki or *kǎbilíkya* (sheep)   *kɔkyí* or *kokia* or *kɔkyá* (dog)
ambiligi or *ambilidʒa* (lizard)   *ogi* or *ɔgia* or *ɔgyà* (baboon)
kaligi or *kalígyɛ*[1] (leopard)

159. The following are the only examples of this kind of suffix that could be found in the MORU dialects:

ndrɔ or ndrwa (year); kídru or kídrwe (vein); kizu or kizwe (pig).

It is, however, probable that the words kɔkyé (dog) and kɔkyé (bush) show assimilated suffixes.

-e or -ɪ (MORU and LOGO)

160. This suffix is used to show plurality. E.g. kɪlá'bá, pl. kɪlá'báɪ (warrior) in Moru. For further discussion see under 'Plurality', § 191.

-ka (MADI)

161. This suffix is used to form nouns from verbal roots. For further discussion see under 'Infinitive', § 544.

E.g. MADI (Pa.) *odza-ka* (blasphemy); *vote-ka* (faith).

-kɪ (LUGBARA and KELIKO)

162. This suffix is used to show plurality, and corresponds thus in some respects to the -ɪ of Moru. E.g. 'ba, pl. 'bákɪ (person), in Lugbara. For further discussion see under 'Plurality', § 191.

-ni

163. This particle is found in LOGO, LUGBARA, MADI, and LULU'BA. Its function is uncertain, and it may be attached, not only to nouns and pronouns, but even to verbs and adverbs.

LOGO: *Nzambe 'ba yi-ni.* God created water.
    Aii adre-ki adi-ni no. (Mk. iii. 2.) They watched him (lit. they were him watching).
    ... *adre ta nidi-ni ri.* (Mk. iv. 14.) ... soweth the word (lit. is word that sowing).
    Kadre niti-ni. It came to pass (lit. happened thus).
    Tebiri are ama o-ni. We are hungry (lit. hunger is us harming).

LUGBARA: *'Ba Farisai-ni, 'Ba Yahudi-ni pie dria.* (Mk. vii. 3.) The Pharisees and all the Jews.
    Eri-ni ti co-ria. (Mk. viii. 33.) When he had turned about.
    Musa azi emi-ndra ŋgo-ni ya? (Mk. x. 3.) What did Moses command you? (lit. Moses commanded you-to what?)
    Azi-ni ŋga-iŋgi-ra. (Mk. xiv. 57.) And there arose certain.
    'Ba azi-ni ka jo-ni ko, ka-ni adripi-ni, ka-ni amvipi-ni ... (Mk. x. 29.) There is no man that hath left house, or brethren, or sisters ...

[1] -a alternates with -ɛ after **y**.

MADI: ma or ma-**ni** (I or me)
má nya-odrupi-**ni** ndrɛ-ra. I will see your brother (lit. I your brother see-will).
idzú ɔnya warage-**ni**. The white ants ate the paper.
nyi-zí akimu-**ni**. Ask the doctor.

LULU'BA: mo-kwέ mí-ní gurú-**ni**. I'll give you money.
ny-ó'jó gela-ti-**nɪ**. You speak a foreign language.
mɔ-só anyukwá-**ni** ɛkyí si. I shoot game with a bow.
mó-'jo mí-ní Óló'bó-ti-**nɪ**, anyí no-**nì**. I speak Lulu'ba-language to you, that you may know.
así kɔ́dɔ́ ma-**ni**. The fire burns me.
(Cf. así kɔ́dɔ́ dʒó. The fire burns the house.)
no-mbwí òwà-**ni**? Are you drinking beer?
ámbu kwɔ, mó-mbú i-**ni**. I am not, I am drinking water.
álɛ Olu'bo-go-**nì**, álɛ Óríó-gó ko. I want a Lulu'ba, I don't want a Lokoya.

For further discussion of this suffix see § 581.

-nzi (MADI)

164. This suffix is used to show plurality in nouns denoting persons, e.g. *oko*, pl. *okonzi* (woman). For further discussion see under 'Plurality', § 195.

-pi

165. This particle is found, with varying functions, in most of the Moru-Madi languages. In MORU, LUGBARA, and KELIKO it is found, though not consistently, as the final syllable in terms of relationship.

MORU	LUGBARA	KELIKO	cf. MADI	
tǎpi	átá	atǎpi	átá	(father)
ädrúpi	adrúpi	adrúpi	adrúpi	(brother)
ämvúpi	ämvúpi	ämvúpi	amvótì	(sister)
έndrὲ	ándrǎpɪ	έndrǎpi	ɛndrɛ̀	(mother)
tí'bí	a'bipì	ä'bipì	á'bî	(grandfather)
làdra	ɪdrǎpi	ɪdrǎpi	ada	(grandmother)

166. In the Central languages—LOGO, KELIKO, AVUKAYA—and also in LUGBARA, this particle is used after verbs with 'relative' force.

Examples from Logo:

ago acale-pi. The man who arrived. *ta-konji-ole-pi* (sinner, lit. word-bad-do-er). See under verbs, § 653. An interesting parallel to this suffix is the *-er* suffix in the English words—*father, mother, brother, sister*, which also occurs in words like *doer, singer, tin-opener*.

167. In MADI (Lokai dialect) and in LUGBARA this particle is further used as a linking particle between two nouns, where it corresponds to 'and' in English. In this context it is used in conjunction with a post-position.

Examples from MADI:

Petro-pi Andrea tro. Peter and Andrew.
Farisei-pi Skribi aɪ Sacerdoti tro. Pharisees and Scribes and Priests.
Ba elf isu-pi okonji aɪ boronji tro. Four thousand people with their wives and children.

Examples from LUGBARA:
Yakobo-pie Yohana be. James and John.
Karani-pie 'ba-Farisaini be. Scribes and Pharisees.
Eri-ŋga za-mva ma ati-pie andri be iji. (Mk. v. 40.) He took the girl's father and mother.

Note that in Moru and Logo the plural suffix -i is used in this context. (See § 192.)

-ri (LUGBARA)

168. This suffix is very common in Lugbara (and Keliko) after nouns and pronouns, where its function is uncertain.

e-ri (he or she); *eyo-'ba-ri* (the beginning, lit. things making).
Okpo eri-ni ovu mani-ri be to. (Mk. i. 7.) Who is mightier than I (lit. strength his is mine with great).
Aílɛ-rí sɛ. Aile is pulling (it).
ínyá-rí ùndʒi. The food is bad.   'bá 'dá-rì mʊkɛ. That man is good.

It is found mostly, however, in relative constructions. (See § 654.)

'ba-ori-ri-pi-ri (Mk. iv. 3.) A sower (lit. man-seed-sow-**pi-ri**).

-ti (MADI)

169. This suffix occurs mostly in the PANDIKERI dialect of Madi, where it corresponds to -pi in Lokai.

Yakobo-ti Yohana tro. James and John.
Turo-ti Sidoni tro. Tyre and Sidon.
Ani koko ati-ti endre tro za dri. (Mk. v. 40.) He took the father and mother of the girl.

But note also in LOKAI MADI: amvótì (sistér).

-za, -zɔ

170. This suffix is much used for the formation of abstract nouns from verbal roots. (See further §§ 570–1.)

LUGBARA: *Endrilendri dra-za ni a.* (Matt. iv. 16.) In the shadow of death (lit. shadow death of in).
'Ba-omi-za. (Mk. v. 27.) A crowd (lit. people pressing).
MORU: (ŋga) bɔŋgɔ́ lɔsɛ́-zɔ́ (needle; lit. cloth sewer).
LOGO: bɔŋgwá lasɛ́-za.
Compare MORU: *Ta-kozi onja-za.* (Mk. i. 4.) For the remission of sins.

COMPOUND NOUNS

171. Moru-Madi shows that well-known Sudanic trait of being able to build up an endless number of new words by combining existing words. Here are some typical examples:

MORU: gilu (thirst, lit. water-pain; cf. LULU'BA iyí-vwí); drì'bí (hair, lit. head-hair); arioba (guinea-fowl, lit. bird-walk); kıla'ba (warrior, lit. war-man); pakususu (heel, lit. foot-chin); tazevoondre'ba (witness, lit. word-bottom-place-see-man).

LOGO: dri'bi (hair); tili'bi (beard, lit. mouth-hair); *nyaladira* (kitchen, lit. food-cook-place).

MADI: a'úkɛlɛ (egg, lit. hen-egg); dzuruga (country, lit. land-belly); dzurugo (foreigner, lit. land-man).

NOUNS

PREFIXED NOMINAL FORMS

172. In many noun compounds certain nominal forms, when used initially, have special functions. These forms may be regarded as nominal prefixes, although in other contexts they may often be found as separate words, and as such differ from the prefixes already discussed in §§ 153 et seq.

di (or 'di) (MORU)

173. di is prefixed to personal nouns (and sometimes to adjectives) to indicate a class or type rather than actual persons. In this respect it somewhat resembles the English suffix *-kind* in *womankind*, &c.

    má ku (di-) tɔkɔ́ ì.   I am not a woman.
    di-toko ezi tiza go.   Woman bring firewood.
    di-adravoro azaka . . . fera. (Mk. vi. 5.) A few sick folk.

Note also: *'di-aza eki ku.* Nobody has come. (aza = other.)
Note also in LUGBARA: *mi-ovu di-alaro.* (Lk. v. 13.) Be thou clean.
Note in LOGO: *'dia* = 'people'.

ŋga, ŋgə (MORU, LUGBARA, KELIKO)

174. ŋga may be translated by 'thing' in most Moru-Madi languages. It may also occur as an indefinite pronoun (see § 237). As a nominal prefix it is used in Moru as an alternative to la- to form nouns from verbal roots. Note the following verbal nouns in the MORU dialects:

	food	*cursing*	*loving*	*cutting*
M.:	lenya, ŋgɔinya	latrí, ŋgɔ́otrí	ŋgälu	ŋgɔ́ɔ́lɔ̀là
Ä.:	ŋgɔinya	latrí, ŋgóatrí	ŋgólɛ	ŋgóàlàlà
W.:	ɽınya	latrí, ŋgáatrí	ŋgálɛ	ŋgáàlɔ̀lɔ̀
Jl.:	nyasá	latítrí, ŋgátítrí	ŋgálèlè	ŋgámvamva

and in the Southern and Central languages (note that ŋga appears in LUGBARA and KELIKO as a *suffix*):

	insult	*laughter*	*beating*
MADI: Lo.:	là'da	lagu	lamgbá
MADI: Pa.:	là'da	logu	lamgbá
LUGBARA:	ò'daŋgara	òguŋgara (àguɲa)	gbaŋgara
KELIKO:	'dàŋgara	gùŋgara	gbaŋgara

ta (MORU, LOGO, LUGBARA)

175. ta may be translated by 'word' or 'thing' or 'matter' in most Moru-Madi languages. As a nominal prefix it is used to form abstract nouns from various roots. Note that in LUGBARA the form appears as a *suffix*:

    MORU: *ta-oma* (faith); *ta-mawe* (blasphemy); *ta-kozi* (sin).
    LOGO: *ta-ka'i-le* (faith); *ta-i-Nzambe-ɖa-zo* (blasphemy); *ta-konji* (sin); *ta-i-utukufu-aɖea-ro* (praise).
    LUGBARA: *aü-ta* (faith); *aɖa-ta* (blasphemy); *le-ta(a)* (love); *inzi-ta* (praise); *eda-ta* (confession).

SUFFIXED NOMINAL FORMS

176. In many noun compounds certain nominal forms, when used finally, have special functions, being used to denote sex, size, &c. These forms may be regarded as nominal suffixes, although in other contexts they may often be found as separate words, and as such differ from the suffixes already discussed in §§ 157 et seq. It is not convenient to classify these forms alphabetically; classification is best made according to function.

Forms denoting Sex

177. Sex may be shown in nouns by suffixing the appropriate word denoting 'male' or 'female'—thus forming a compound noun. The usual word for males is **ago** (man) or **ata** (father), and for females **(t)oko** (woman) or **ɛndrɛ** (mother). Examples:

MORU:	kɔkyɛ́-ágó (male dog)	kɔkyɛ́-tòko (female dog)
	ɪndrɪ-tégó (male goat)	ɪndrɪ-ɛndrɛ (female goat)
	täú-gógó (cock)	täú-ɛndrɛ (hen)
MADI:	ebi-ágo (male lion)	ebi-okú (female lion)
	endri-go ⎱ (male goat) endri-ata ⎰	endri-endre (female goat)
	aú-logo (cock)	aú-okú ⎱ (hen) aú-ɛndrɛ ⎰
LUGBARA:	ebi-ágɔ (male lion)	ebi-okú (female lion)
	aú-logo (cock)	aú-okú (hen)

178. In some of the Southern and Central languages, a special suffix **-zi** is used to indicate the women folk of a tribe or sect. The men are either indicated by the normal form **ago** or not at all.
Thus in MADI:

Madi(go) and *Madizi* (Madi man and Madi woman)
Bari(go) and *Barizi* (Bari man and Bari woman)

In LOGO: *ago avuzi*, and in LUGBARA, *auzi* = widow.
In the MORU dialects this distinction is not made. Compare:

So-and-so (man) is a foreigner.   *So-and-so (woman) is a foreigner.*
MADI: Dɛŋgú ni dʒúrú-go.   Ámonà ni dʒúrú-**zi**.
LUGBARA: „   ri 'bá-àta   „   ri àta-**zi**.
KELIKO: „   ri 'bá-àtra.   „   ri 'bá-àtra-**zwi**.
MORU: Ayélè àtra i.   Itó àtra i.

In MADI the suffix **-zi** may sometimes be applied to the higher animals as well:
    ibi-izi (lioness), alternative word to ibi-okú.

Note that in LULU'BA **-izi (na)** is the regular female suffix for all animals, while in MADI (Pa.) **izi** means 'woman'.

179. In the MORU dialects certain animals have irregular sex names which probably indicate their age as well. These terms are mostly used by hunters. The following outstanding examples from the MIZA dialect may be noted:

Regular forms:

    mui-ágó and mui-tòko (hyena); kɔrɔnya-ágó and kɔrɔnya-tòko (leopard); ihwe-ágó and ihwe tòko (wild-dog); gòrɔ-ágó and gòrɔ-tòko (wild-cat); arɛ̀àbà-gógó and arɛ̀àbà-ɛndrɛ (guinea-fowl); timélé-gógó and timélé-ɛndrɛ (sheep).

In the following examples the males take the suffix **mäü**. The females take the regular suffix **toko** or **ɛndrɛ**:

    ibi-mäü (male lion); kí-mäü (male crocodile); kǎrì-mäü (male giraffe); lòrɛ-mäü (male baboon); kɔria-mäü (male monkey); aróà-mäü (male hippopotamus).

NOUNS

In the following examples the male suffixes are highly irregular. The female suffix is usually **ɛndrɛ**:

lìwa-mäú or bìrà (male elephant); udrú-mäú or mängù (male buffalo); yáŋgá-gʊrʊ (male oribi); kógwá-gʊrʊ (male digdig); lɛbá-gɔ̀rɪ (male bush-buck); lɔ́'ba-túbì (male hartebeest); lä'bí-malɪga (male water-buck); tärú-mɔmba (male field-rat); taago-ráŋgá (kɛ́tó in 'Bälimbä) (male goat—alternative to ɪndrɪ-tɛgo).

In the following examples the female forms are irregular:

lìwa-gʊrà (dialects 'B. and Ä.); liwa-jala (M.) (female elephant).
udru-manda (dialects 'B. and Ä.) (female buffalo).
indri-ntrupi (Ä.) (female goat).
lɔ́'ba-gɔ̀gɔ or gwègwɛ (M.) (female hartebeest—alternative name to lɔ'ba-ɛndrɛ).

Forms denoting Size

Augmentative.

180. The form **ago** (man) may also be suffixed to indicate abnormal size. This use of **ago** is most common in Madi; in Moru the suffix is not used as an augmentative. Examples from MADI:

ílí (knife)   ílí-go (big knife) (ílí-agó in Lugbara and Keliko)
kwe (tree)   kwe-go (big tree)   evo (bush)   evo-go (big bush)
lea (elephant) lea-go (big elephant)

Note also the word for 'thumb' in most languages, obviously derived from the word for 'hand':

drí-ágó (Moru); drí-àgɔ (Avukaya); dri-gagɔ (Logo); drɪ-agɔ (Lugbara and Keliko).

In most languages words are also to be found in which the suffix **-go** is permanent, and has no augmentative function.

'knife' = írí (M., K., L.); iligo (Ä., 'B., W., Avukaya)
'wizard' = (k)ózó (Moru and Madi); udzɔgɔ (Lugbara and Keliko)
'pig' = (k)ɪzɔ (in most languages); izɔ̀gɔ (Lugbara)
'rat' = idrɛ (Madi); edragɔ (Lugbara, Keliko, Avukaya); tédrá(gwá) (Logo)

Note also in LOGO: *li* and *ligu* (knife); *ba* and *bago* (string).

181. In the following rare instance the word for 'woman' is used in an augmentative sense:

LOGO: fa-kadrɛri (AVUKAYA: fa-andrɛ) = big tree (lit. tree-mother)

Diminutive.

182. The normal diminutive form is obtained by suffixing the word ŋgwá (dial. mvá) (= child). In the MORU dialects there is a further diminutive ending ŋwá (dial. vá), with a slightly different function. The rules for use of these two diminutive forms are as follows:

ŋgwá (mvá) is used especially for diminutives which indicate the young of a species. Thus:

(M.) täú-ŋgwá; (Ä.) äú-mvá (chicken) from (t)äú (fowl).

ŋwá (vá) is used for diminutives in general and for pet names. This form is the more common of the two.

(M.) gúlʊ-ŋwá; (Ä.) gúlʊ-vá (stream) from gúlʊ (river).

Compare: kɔ̀kyéŋwá (little dog) and kɔ̀kyéŋgwá (puppy).

Note the following names of children:

Litiŋwa (from liti = road); Ɔdraŋwa (from ɔdra = die); Tombiŋwa (from tombi = locust); Kituŋwa (fron kitu = day). These names are all connected with incidents surrounding the children's birth.

The above-stated distinction is not always logically observed even in Moru. Thus:

   àrɪ (bird), arɪ́ŋwá (fledgeling); drí (hand), drɪ́ŋwà (fingers).

183. In the Southern and Central languages this distinction is not made at all, and the form **ŋgwa** (or **mva**) is used in all cases.

	chicken	small knife	small elephant	finger (little)
Lo.:	a'u-a-ŋgwa	ílí-à-ŋgwa	lèa-ŋgwa	drɪ-a-ŋgwa
Pa.:	a'u-a-ŋgwa		làa-ŋgwa	di-ŋgwa
LUGBARA:	a'u-mva	ílí-mvà		dri-mva
KELIKO:	a'u-mva	ílí-mvà		dri-mva
LOGO:			liwa-mva	dri-ga-mva

184. The diminutive form is not found with nouns only, but may occur with adjectives also. E.g.

 MORU: tsʷàrè-ŋwa (Ä. sɛrɛ-va) = narrow, from tsʷa = long.
 LOGO: { (L.): *ca, caca, ca-mva* = small. *anyi, anyi-mva* = near.
    { (A.): *bia, biabia, bia-mva.*

In most languages, too, words are to be found in which the suffix is permanent, with no specialized diminutive function, although the words to which they are attached invariably represent small objects.

'bird' = àrɪ (M., K., L.); àrɪŋwa (Äg.); àrɪŋgwa ('B., W., Madi); àrɪva (Ä., Keliko); àrɪwa (Avukaya).
'axe' = túlú or kólú (Central and Southern languages), kólóŋwá or ólóvá (Moru dialects); olowa (Avukaya).
'small' = gɪrɪŋwa (M.); gaává (Ä.).

185. The genitive construction may occasionally be used to show smallness. (This is the normal process in Lendu.)

  MADI: lɛa ni bara (young elephant, lit. elephant's child).
 LENDU: *zho dza mgba.*
 MADI (Pa.): a'u ni 'bòndzî (chickens, lit. fowls' children).

The Personal Form

186. In MADI and the Central languages (but not in Moru) **'ba** is a monosyllabic noun meaning 'man' (*homo* not *vir*). In all the Moru-Madi languages, however, **'ba** may be suffixed to noun or verb stems or to phrases to indicate the doer of an action, the person exercising a trade or profession, a member of a clan or village[1], or the person who owns or is affected by something. In such cases **'ba** may be termed a 'personal suffix', as it can be applied only to persons.

 MORU: *toka'ba* (blacksmith, from toka = smithy)
    loŋgo'ba (song-maker at a dance, from oŋgo = to sing)
    ländri'ba (soothsayer, from ländri = divination)

---

[1] Hence the number of village and sectional names like Aŋgu'ba, Läsi'ba, Maku'ba. Note also Ulu'bo (Lulu'ba).

pidio'ba'ba (maker of mortars, from pidi = mortar, o'ba = make)
'bädri'ba (chief, from 'bädri = country)
boŋgo'ba (person wearing clothes—term of scorn, from boŋgo = clothes)
aba'ba (traveller, from aba = to travel)
miaku'ba (blind man, lit. eye-without-man)
ŋgaamba'bai (rich people, lit. things-much-people)
MADI: *o'ja'ba* (warrior, from o'ja = war); *aci'ba* (traveller)
LUGBARA: *ägubi'ba* (warrior).
LOGO: *äbi'ba* (victim of a curse)
LENDU: *ndru'ba* (wizard)

Note the following and compare with the relative construction, § 659:

	warrior	*liar*
MORU:	kɪlá'bá, pl. kɪlá'bà(ì)	usú'bá
LOGO:	kʋmbà'bá, pl. kùmbà'bà'dɛ	kɪndzɔ'bá
LUGBARA:	ägubi'bá, pl. 'bá-àgùbìnì	ɪndzɔ'bá
KELIKO:	ʋmbà'bá, pl. 'bá-ʋmba'ba-á'dì	ʋndzɔ-a-'bá
AVUKAYA { Jl.:	ʋmbà'bá	indzɔ('bá)
{ Jg.:	ɔmbà'ba	ʋndzɔ

Where there is an object, this object precedes the form. Compare:
MORU: *ce-oga-'ba* (wood-cutter); *zo-omu-'ba* (house-builder); *ŋga-uŋgi-'ba* (load-carrier).
MADI (Opari): *kwe-'ba* (woodman); *zo-'ba* (house-expert); *teri-'ba* (porter).

Locative Forms

187. The form **vo** (place), besides being capable of acting as an independent noun, may be suffixed to many words in MORU to indicate a place associated with some action or some thing, or to indicate a state of health. E.g.

pa-vo (path, lit. foot-place); *ti-vu* (chin, lit. mouth-place); *adra-vo* (sickness, from ɔdra = to die); *zɛvɔ̀* or *zɛlévɔ̀* (buttocks, from zɛ = excrement).

In LOGO the form **ra** is suffixed:

boŋgo-ji-ra (lit. clothes-wash-place); *ŋga-laḍi-ra* (lit. food-cook-place); *vo-ra* (place)

188. Another locative form, most common in the Central languages, is **lɛ** (or **rɛ**), attached mostly to words denoting certain parts of the body.

MORU	MADI	AVUKAYA	LOGO	LUGBARA	
ugú	ogu	ugúlé	gólé	ògurɛ	(back)
zɛ (lé)vɔ̀	zɛlédrì	zɛvɛrè			(buttocks)
págálé		gálé	(pa)'alɛ	'alɛ	(sole)

In LENDU **lɛ** appears as an optional *prefix* to nouns denoting all parts of the body:

(le)dz (back); (le)dʒɔ (head); (le)bi (ear).

Note the use of **le** in adverbs of place in all languages:
MORU: *kuru(le)* (above); *vuru(le)* (below); *ko(n)vole* (back again).
LOGO: *nole* (A.) *nile* (here); *tugule* (behind); *'ale* (inside); *aŋgole?* (whither?).
MADI: *na(le)* (there).

For the part played by **le** in post-positions, see § 298.

NUMBER
General remarks on noun plurals.

189. In most cases the plural of a noun is not formally indicated, the context being sufficient to show whether the noun concerned refers to one person or object or more than one. Certain nouns, however, have definite plural forms, often accompanied by changes in tone. The words for 'boy' and 'girl' are to be particularly noted in the Moru dialects.

		boy	*boys*	*girl*	*girls*
MORU	M.:	ŋgágà	ŋgàgà	ŋgúti	ndiriŋwà
	K.:	ŋgágà	ŋgàgà	ŋgútíɲɔ	ndiríngwà
	L.:	ɲágà	goníɲà	ndríàka	ndiriŋwã
	Äg.:	ndărɔ́ŋgwa		ŋguti	ndɪrfakwá
	W.:	ndrĩ̀ŋgwa	ndríŋgwà	ŋgwătíŋgɔ́	àkuŋgwa
	'B.:	ŋgwágà	ŋgwàgà	ŋgútí	diiŋgwà
	Ä.:	mvágà	mvàgà	mbătì	ndirivă

190. Words with suffixed nominal forms (as discussed in §§ 176 et seq.) often show tonal change in these endings in the plural.

MADI   Lo.: aú-ɛ́ndrɛ, pl. aú-ɛndrê (hen); aú-ŋgwá, pl. aú-bɔ̀rɔ̀ndzî (chicken)
       Pa.: aú-ɛ́ndɛ   au-ɛndê   aú-a-ŋgwa   aú-ni-'bɔndʒî

MORU   M.: kɔkyéŋgwá, pl. kɔkyéŋgwà (puppy); kɔ́lɔ́ŋwá, pl. kɔlɔ́ŋwà (axe)
       Ä.: ɔtsémvá   ɔtsémvà   ɔɾóvá   ɔɾóvà

MORU   M.: 'bérɛ́ŋwá, pl. 'bérɛ́ŋwà (hill); kɪtó, pl. kɪtóŋwà (hare)
       L.: 'bérɛ́ŋó   'bérɛ́ŋgwɔ̀   kɪtóŋgó   kɪtóŋwà
       Ä.: úníva   únívà   ɪtógó   ɪtógò
       'B.: kúní   kúníŋgwà

AVUKAYA: flígó, pl. flígò (knife)
MORU: Karí'bá pl. Karí'bà (a clan name).

Plural Suffixes -ɪ and -kɪ

191. An optional plural suffix -ɪ (-i after tense vowels) is to be found in MORU and LOGO. In LUGBARA and KELIKO the suffix is -kɪ. These suffixes are used whenever the speaker wishes his hearers to understand quite definitely that the noun in question is in the plural. This method of indicating the plural is most common in Lugbara. Examples:

LUGBARA and KELIKO: 'bá (person), pl. 'bákɪ
MORU: lédr (person), pl. lédrɪ; kărì (giraffe), pl. kăriì
LOGO: *ago* (person), pl. *agoɪ*; *toko* (woman), pl. *tokoɪ*; *ndri* (goat), pl. *ndrii*

This suffix may terminate noun phrases of a relative character in Logo:

ndri-liki-i-le-pi-ăi-i (goat-herds), *ăia-ma-dre-le-le-pi-ăi-i* (the people whom I like)

192. In MORU and LOGO the plural suffix is often used to join two nouns, where it corresponds to 'and' in English. Here it is usually found in conjunction with a postposition. Other languages use -**pi**. (See § 167.)

MORU: *Yakobo-i Yoane be.* James and John.
LOGO: *Tura-ɪ Sidona be.* Tyre and Sidon.
     Idri mva ni ata-ɪ andre be. (Mk. v. 40.) He took the girl's father and mother.

193. The plural suffixes are not always confined to nouns, but may be attached to verbs or verbal auxiliaries in sentences where the subject is plural.[1]

MORU:	ma-pɛ lɛ́dr Ndarágɔ̀ rɔ r̥ɛ.	I defeated the people of Ndarago.
	kɪlá'bá-ɪ pɛ̀-ɪ tɛ r̥ɛ̀.	The warriors have conquered.
	mí-'bà kɛ́dr.	Stop him (lit. you make stop).
	mí-'bà kɛ́dr-ɨ.	Stop them (lit. you make stop-ɪ).
	kǎrɨ mu-te.	The giraffe ran away.
	kǎrɨ mu-í-te.	The giraffes ran away.
	má-ndrɛ lɔ̀rɛ te.	I saw the baboon . . . or baboons.
	lɔré ndrɛ́-ɪ ma te.	The baboons saw me.
	lɔré nya-í mɔndú mí-rɔ ku.	The baboons did not eat your sweet-potatoes.
	anya zi-i mi adi ya?	What do they call you?

Attached to the auxiliary particle **ka**:

anya ka-ɪ toga.   They are cutting.
anya ka-ɪ ce oga.   They are cutting wood (lit. wood-cutting).
but: ŋgàgà k-ôdzwɪ. The boys are playing. lɔré k-ôdzwɪ. The baboons are playing.

194. In the Southern and Central languages the plural suffix **-ki** is used with verbs—even in languages like Madi, where it is not used with nouns in the ordinary way. Note its use after **ka**.

MADI:	*odra-ra.*	He died.	*odra-ki-ra.*	They died.
	k-odra-ra.	He will die.	*ka-ki-dra-ra.*	They will die.

		The boys went	*They are going*	*They will go*
MADI	Lo.:	bɔrɔndzí óvɔ-kí-ra	ká-kí-vòvò	ka-ki-mu-ra
	Pa.:	'bɔndzí vɔ(-kí)-ra	aí kó-vóvò	
LUGBARA:		andziri mu-kí-'bò		
KELIKO:		anziri mu-kí-gɪ		

In LUGBARA and KELIKO this plural particle is used even with the 1st and 2nd person in certain tenses.

	We went	*You (pl.) went*	*They went*
LUGBARA:	ama-mú-kí-'bo	emi-mú-kí-'bo	kò-mú-kí-'bo
KELIKO:	áma-mù-kí-gɪ		kò-mu-kí-gɪ
Cf. MADI:	*ama-mu-ra*	*anyi-mu-ra*	*omu-ki-ra*

Note the following uses of **-ki** in LOGO:

adi aca ama no.	He arrived to see me (lit. he arrived my see).
adi aca ama-ki no.	He arrived to see us.
adi aca-ki ama no.	They arrived to see me.
toko ali-ki ama no.	The women came to see me.
ma-are ama jo-ki si.	I build my houses (lit. I-remain my houses build).
ma-si-ki ama jo.	I and others build my house.
ago osi-ki ai jo ɪ.	The man and others is building his house.

Note also: *lau ama-**ki**-a'di* (our country) and compare

MORU (Ă.:) ɔpɪ nda-**ka**-rɔ (their chief)

---

[1] Mrs. Frazer maintains that the -i particle should be used in all plural sentences in Moru, either with the noun or with the verb.

Plural Suffix -**nzi**

195. Certain nouns in MADI form their plural by the addition of **-nzi**. These nouns are mostly terms of relationship.

E.g. *oko*, pl. *okonzi* (woman)

This suffix cannot be used after the feminine suffix **-zi**.

Madizi (Madi woman), pl. *Madi okonzi*; ebizi (lioness), pl. ebiokú.

Note the presence of **-nzi** in the following irregular plurals in the Southern languages, and compare with § 189.

		boy	*boys*	*girl*	*girls*
MADI	Lo.:	bará	bòrònzi	zá	índzòndzi
	Pa.:	'borá	'bòndʒî	zá(ŋgwa)	ídʒôndʒɪ
	'Bu.:	'bora	'boronzi		
LUGBARA:		ŋgótí(ŋa)	ànziri(ŋa)	ìzɔŋa	ìzɔnzi
KELIKO:		m̀vá	anzi'bá	ìdʒɔŋa	ìdzwóndzɪ

		brother	*brothers*	*sister*	*sisters*
MADI	Lo.:	adrúpi	ádrîinzi	amvótì	avôndzi
	Pa.:	adäzi	adindʒì	ambázì	ambôndʒi
LUGBARA:		ädrúpì	adrù		
LULUBA:		adíŋá	adiŋgì		

CHAPTER VI

PERSONAL PRONOUNS

196. The term 'personal pronoun' is applied to:
(A) forms of personal reference used in isolation or as the object of a sentence;
(B) forms of personal reference used as possessor in the genitive construction;
(C) forms of personal reference used in conjunction with post-positions;
(D) verb prefixes which indicate person.

A

197. The personal pronouns taken in isolation are remarkably consistent throughout the entire group.

The *first person* is   má (I, me)   pl. àma (we, us).
The *second person* is mí (thou, thee)   pl. àmi or ìmi (ye, you) in most languages,
but   nyí   pl. anyí in Madi and
   ni   pl. ni   in Lendu and the Ojila[1] dialect of Avukaya.

The *third person* is, for the most part, a form of andá or anyà. Thus:
ánya (he, him) pl. anyá (they, them) in MORU (M., K., L.)
ndá or ndínà   pl. ndáka or ndíka in MORU (Ä., 'B., Äg., W.)
ànda or àni   pl. andápi or à'ɪ in MADI
náni   in LULU'BA
ani or *adi*   pl. *aii*   in LOGO
anya   pl. *anyai*   in LOGO (Agambi)

[1] In the Ojiga dialect the form is **mi**.

In some of the Central languages the word for 'person' is used:

'bá or ani	pl. 'bá (kɪ)	in KELIKO
'bá	pl. 'bá(kɪ)	in LUGBARA
'bá	pl. 'bá	in LOGO

In nearly all languages the demonstrative may be used as the 3rd person pronoun. In AVUKAYA this is the normal form, although it literally means 'that man'.

gúlà   pl. gúlèi   in AVUKAYA

Third person pronoun **í (yí)**, pl. **i (ií)** (*Referring pronoun*).[1]

198. This form of 3rd person pronoun is used only to refer back to the speaker or subject of a previous sentence. Hence it is tentatively called here 'referring pronoun'. Examples:

MORU: (M.) ánya ɛkyɛ **i** tɛ kadʊ.   He says he is well.
     (Å.) ndá si **i** adróvɔrɔ.   He says he is ill.
Cf.   ndá si **ndá** adróvɔrɔ.   He says he (i.e. the other man) is ill.
LOGO: *ama adrupi ta **i** adre draro.*   My brother says he is ill.
    *ama madre ta **ako'di** adre draro ko.*   My mother says he is not ill.

Compare also in MORU:

yí te mòyùru. He is poor.   ií te mòyùru. They are poor. Here the information originates from the people concerned.
ánya te mòyùru. He is poor.   anyá te mòyùru. They are poor. Here the information originates from a disinterested quarter.

Pronouns as object.

199. When personal pronouns are used as the object of a verb, their forms are unchanged.

LOGO: *adi no ma.*   He sees me.   *adi no mi.*   He sees you.
    adi no adi.   He sees him.   *má-ʃi ani.*   I split it.

The normal 3rd person pronoun, however, is often omitted when the sense is quite clear.

MORU: mí-'bí kù ya?   Didn't you beat him?

This rule is very important. Absence of an object pronoun indicates that the object is obvious to the speaker and hearer. When, however, the verb is used without reference to any specific object, an indefinite pronoun or the **na** (dial. **le**) particle is given the sentence position of the object. (See §§ 237, 257.)

Note the following idiomatic use of the third person pronoun in MADI and LOGO:

MADI: *zo ma-dri k-endre opi dri **ani**.*   My house is like the chief's.
    *any-eŋgo m-etede-le-re-e **ani**.*   Sing as I have taught.
LOGO: *ma-le äli muruŋgu **nda**-di ko, ma-lɛ ca-di **nda**.* I don't want a big knife, I want a small one.

B

200. When used as possessor in genitive constructions, the personal pronouns occasionally undergo sound-change if the word immediately following begins with a vowel.

MADI: *ma pa* (my leg)   *nyi drɪ* (your head)   *ani ti* (his cow)
    ama mi (our eyes)   *any-endre* (your mother)   *aɪ ata* (their father)
KELIKO: *ŋo i pa gi.* (He) broke his leg.

[1] Not found in Madi.

In LOGO and AVUKAYA (and a few neighbouring Moru dialects) the pronominal form contains a prefix a-.

LOGO: *ama dri* (my head)　　*ami dri* (your head)　　*adini dri* (his head)
　　amaki dri (our heads)　*amiki dri* (your heads)　*aiiki dri* (their heads)
AVUKAYA: ama ru (my body)

Compare also in LOGO:

Ago fe ei indri ma-dri.　　The man gave his (own) goat to me.
Ago fe adi indri ma-dri.　The man gave his (the other man's) goat to me.

Note that in Moru the possessive pronoun does not precede the thing possessed. (See next paragraph.)

C

201. When used in conjunction with post-positions, personal pronouns occasionally undergo sound-change, particularly if the post-position contains the tense vowel **i**. Examples from MORU:

má-rɔ (of me, my); mí-rɔ (of thee, thy); ánya-rɔ (of him, his); ɪ-rɔ (of him, his) (referring)

àma-rɔ̀ (of us, our); àmɪ-rɔ̀ (of you, your); ànya-rɔ̀ (of them, their); ɛ-rɔ (of them, their) (referring)

mǎ-rí (to me); mí-rí (to thee); ányä-rí (to him); í-rí (to him) (referring)
amǎ-rí (to us); amí-rí (to you); ànyǎ-rí (to them); i-rí (to them) (referring)

Thus: tǎpí marɔ̀ (my father)　　tǎpí ányarɔ̀ (his father)
　　nyɔ́zɔ mǎrí. Give it to me. nyɔ́zɔ ányärí. Give it to him.
　　Askeri eke toko ɪro mu-te, yi-le o'bi na. The soldier says his wife has run away, he wants to beat her.
　　ndá ɛkyɛ nyɔ́zɔ̀ **iri**. He says you must give it to him.

D

202. When used as subject of a verb, personal pronouns undergo considerable sound-change. The laws governing such sound-change are best discussed with reference to each person separately.

FIRST PERSON

The normal form.

203. In most languages the pronoun stands at the head of the phrase unaltered.

MADI: má-mu.　　I go.　　amá-mu or amá-vɔ̀vɔ̀.　　We go.
LUGBARA: má-mu.　I go.　　ama-múmu.　　　　　　We go.
LOGO: *ma-le ami.*　I love you.　*ama-yi ami.*　　　　We hear you.

The form with low tone.

204. In MORU the plural subject pronoun has no initial vowel and is low in tone. Only this tone difference distinguishes it from the singular form.

MORU (M.) (Ä.) má-nya ɛ̀za. I ate meat. mà-nya ɛ̀za. We ate meat.
　　(M.) má ŋgàgà ùzi. I call the boys (lit. I boys call). màá ŋgàgà ùzi. We call the boys.
　　(Ä.) má-rɔ́ mvàgà ùzi.　　mà-rɔ́ mvàgà ùzi.

PERSONAL PRONOUNS

This plural low-tone form alternates with the normal plural form in the Central languages.

LUGBARA: má-nya-drài̱. I have eaten it.   àmà-nya-'bɔ́. We have eaten it.
KELIKO: má-nyà-gɪ.   mà-nya-gɪ.
LOGO: mà-nya-drɛ̀ or *ama-nya-dre*.
AVUKAYA: mà-nya-trà.
LUGBARA: má-rì ézà nyalɛ. I eat meat (lit. I am meat eating).
   mà-rì ézà nyalɛ. We eat meat.
AVUKAYA: má-rɪ à'wa nyà.   mà-rì a'wa nyà.
LOGO: *má-o.* I do.   *mà-o.* We do.

The form with elided initial consonant.

205. In MADI (Lokai dialect only) the singular subject pronoun has no initial consonant (**m-**) in the 'definite' tenses.[1] The full pronoun is usually found in the plural, though the contracted form may be found here too.

Lo.: á-mu-rá. I went.   ama-mu-ra, or à-vò-ra. We went.
Pa.: mǎ-mu-rá.   àmà-vò-ra.

This phenomenon is not found in the Subjunctive, however: *ma-no-dro ta* (that I may see something).

The form with elided vowel.

206. The pronoun vowel is elided before a Class II verb, i.e. a verb which begins with a vowel, this vowel replacing the vowel of the pronoun.

MORU: m-ésá-te. I have arrived.   m-ɛsá-tè. We have arrived.
m-ú'du-te. I have slept.
MADI: m-ésá-rá. I have arrived.   *am-emu-ra.* We have come.

Note that the initial consonant **m-** is retained before such verbs in Madi.

The form with centralized vowel.

207. Before the tense vowels **i** and **u** in the verb stem, the vowel of the pronoun is centralized in most languages. (See § 26.)

MORU: mǎ-mvú ku. I didn't drink it.   mä-mvú ku. We didn't drink it.
mǎ-sì-te. I hit him.
Cf. má-sì-te. I bit him.
MADI Lo.: á-nì kʊ. I don't know.
Pa.: mǎ-nì kʊ.
LUGBARA: mǎ-ni kù.
KELIKO: mǎ-ni ku.

SECOND PERSON

The normal form.

208. In most languages the pronoun stands at the head of the phrase unaltered.

MADI: nyí-mu. You go.   anyí-mu or anyí-vɔvɔ. You go (pl.)
LUGBARA: mi-mu.   imi-múmu.
LOGO: *mi-no ma.* You see me.   *ami-le ma.* You (pl.) love me.

The form with low tone.

209. In MORU the plural subject pronoun has no initial vowel and is low in tone. Only this tone difference distinguishes it from the singular form.

mí-zi ŋgàgà te. You (sg.) called the boys.   mì-zi ŋgàgà te. You (pl.) called the boys.

[1] The 'definite' tenses correspond largely to the past and perfect in English. (See §§ 338 et seq.)

This plural low-tone form alternates with the normal plural form in the Central languages.

>LOGO: *mì-kofe ŋga aii-dri nyale.* Give ye food to them to eat.
>*mì-li noa.* Go (ye) and see.

The form with elided initial consonant.

210. In MADI (Lokai dialect only) the singular subject pronoun has no initial consonant (**ny-**) in the 'definite' tenses. The full pronoun is usually found in the plural, though the contracted form may occur too.

>Lo.: *í-mu-ra.* You went. *anyi-mu-ra* or *ì-vù-ra.* You (pl.) went.
>Pa.: nyí-mu-rá. ànyì-vò-ra.

Note also in LUGBARA: í-mu-'bò. You went.

The form with elided vowel.

211. The pronoun vowel is elided before a Class II verb, i.e. a verb which begins with a vowel, this vowel replacing the vowel of the pronoun. (Note that this rule does not always apply to the Central languages.)

>MADI: ny-ɛmú. Come!
>KELIKO: m-ɛ́mú or mí-ámú.
>LUGBARA: mɪ-ɪmʊ.
>MADI: *ny-emu-ra.* You have come. *Any-emu-ra.* You (pl.) have come.

Note that the initial consonant **ny-** is retained before such verbs in Madi.

The **nya-** form.

212. In the MORU dialects the subject pronoun itself is **nya** (dial. **na**) before any verb which is conjugated with its 'characteristic' vowel, i.e. before Class II verbs which always begin with a vowel, or Class I (monosyllabic) verbs which have a characteristic vowel prefix in the 'indefinite' tenses.[1]

When immediately preceding Class II verbs, the pronoun vowel is elided as in § 211.

>M., K., L.: ny-ɛ́sá-te? Have you arrived?   ny-ɛsá-te? Have you (pl.) arrived?
>Ä., Äg., 'B.: n-ásá-te?   n-asá-te?
>Jl.: n-atsɛ-tra?
>M.: ny-ú'du-te? Have you slept?
>Ä.: n-ú'du-te?

>Compare thus: M., K., L.: ny-ɛ́mbɛ̀ èba. Tie the rope! Class II.
>Äg.: n-ɛmbɛ èba.
>Ä., 'B., Jl.: n-ómbɛ èba.
>W., Jg.: n-ambe èba.

>and: MORU (all dialects): mí-nya èza. Eat meat! Class I.
>AVUKAYA (Jl., Jg.): mí-nya a'wá.

When the pronoun is separated from the verb by an intervening object (as in the 'indefinite' tenses), the form of the pronoun is **nya** in Miza, **mɪ** or **na** in the other dialects.

>M., K., L.: nyá a'd(i) ɔ̀yɛ ya? What are you doing? (lit. you what do *ya*).
>Ä.: mɪ-rɔ a'di ɔ̀yɛ ya?
>'B.: nɔ-rɔ a'di ɔe ya?

---

[1] The 'indefinite' tenses correspond roughly to the imperfect and progressive tenses of English. (See §§ 338 et seq.)

Note the following irregular alternations of the two pronominal forms elsewhere:
AVUKAYA: mí-ra.   Go!   na-raa-trá. You will go.
KELIKO: nyí-mù.   You (sg.) are going.   mi-lélè. You (pl.) are going.
    mí-mu-gí. You (sg.) went.

Third Person

The normal form.

213. The 3rd person pronoun is often omitted. When present, the normal form is usually found and there is no eliding of consonants in Madi.

MORU { M.: ánya nya èza. He ate meat.   ànyá nya èza. They ate meat.
     { Ä.: ndá nya èza.   ndàá nya èza.
  KELIKO: *kini i mu ku.* (He) says he will not go.

In MADI (Lokai dialect only) the verb always has a 'characteristic' vowel in the third person in the 'definite' tenses, and this is occasionally found in AVUKAYA also

MADI { Lo.: (ànì) òmu-ra. He went.   *omu-ki-ra* or *ɔvɔ-kí-ra.* They went.
     { Pa.: (andá) mu-ra.   à'ɪ vɔ(-kí)-ra.
  AVUKAYA: gúla ɔvó lesí. He blows or blew the fire. (Definite.)
       gúla lesí voá. He is blowing the fire. (Indefinite.)

The form with elided vowel.

214. The pronoun vowel is elided in some languages before a Class II verb, i.e. a verb which begins with a vowel, this vowel replacing the vowel of the pronoun. Note that in some languages this elision is not present.

MORU { M.: ány-ɛsa-tè. He has arrived.   any-ɛsa-tè. They have arrived.
     { Ä.: ndá asa-tè
     M.: ány-u'du-te. He has slept.
     Ä.: ndá ú'du-te.

Where the referring pronoun **i** occurs before a Class II verb, a semi-vowel **y** is usually heard.

    MORU (M.): ánya ɛkɛ y-ékyi a'da. He says he will come.
          anyá ɛkɛ y-ekyí a'da. They say they will come.

The form with centralized vowel.

215. Before the tense vowels **i** and **u** in the verb stem, the vowel element of the pronouns **anya** and **nda** tends to be centralized in the MORU dialects.

M.: ányä zi ŋgàgà te. He called the boys. ànyä zi ŋgàgà te. They called the boys.
Ä.: ndä́ zi mvàgà te.   ndä́ä zi mvàgà te.

The ka particle.

216. In about half the Moru-Madi languages the third person is indicated by a particle **ka** in the 'indefinite' (progressive) tenses. The particle is distributed throughout the group as follows:

	Languages using *ka*	Languages not using *ka*
Moru dialects:	Miza, Kediru, Lakama'di, Ägi.	Moroändri, 'Bälimbä, Wa'di.
Central languages:		Avukaya (Ojila and Ojiga), Keliko, Logo, Lendu.
Southern languages:	Madi (Lokai, Pandikeri), Lulu'ba.	Lugbara.

As can be seen, this particle is not found in the Central languages and languages with affinities to these.

Examples: (Note that before vowels the particle is subject to sound-change).

MORU
- M.: zó k-ûdzʷɛ. The house is burning.   Ä.: zó rú vɛ.
- K.: zó kú-àdze.   'B.: zó rú ze.
- L.: zó kú-ùze.   W.: zó èdʒe-gä.
- Äg.: zó kú-ùdze.   Jl.: dzó ábí vě.

Cf.   M.: zó dzʷè-te. The house was burnt. (Definite.)

MORU (M.): lédr ka wá m̀vu. The people are drinking   Ä.: ledr rɔ wá mvu.
beer (lit. people beer drink).

MADI
- Lo.: bá ka ìra m̀vu.   KEL.: 'bárìpì ıwa m̀vu.
- Pa.: 'bá kú-mvú ówá.   LUG.: 'bá-kí ówá m̀vu.

For further examples see under verbs, § 496.

The kɪ (or ɪ) particle.

217. As has already been remarked, the plural particle kɪ is much used in the third person in the Southern and some Central languages (see §§ 193–4). In the 'definite' tenses the particle follows the verb stem. In Moru the particle is ɪ.

The man sees me   *The people see us*

MADI
- Lo.: orʊgʊ óndré má   bá òndrɛ (-kí) àma
- Pa.: orʊgʊ ndè ma   'ba ndɛ àma

LUGBARA: arógù ndrɛ ma   'ba-ri ndrɛ-kí àma
KELIKO: arógù ndɛ ma   'ba-ri-pi ndɛ-kí ama
MORU: ... ndrɛ mà tè   ... ndrɛ-ɪ mà tè

In the 'indefinite' tenses the particle follows the **ka**.

He washes himself   *They wash themselves*
(lit. he his body washes)

MADI
- Lo.: ká ná-ru dzè   ka-kı ru dzè
- Pa.: andá ku-dʒwé ru   a'ı kú-dʒwé ru

LUGBARA: ırı é dʒì   kó ru odʒì
KELIKO: érí é dze   kó ru-kó-pi dʒì
MORU: ànya ka toga. (He cuts.)   ànya ka-ɪ toga. (They cut.)

The plural particle is not so much used in the indefinite tenses.

CHAPTER VII

OTHER PRONOUNS AND PRONOMINAL ADJUNCTS

218. The following pronominal forms have for the most part two main functions—they may act as pronouns standing alone in the sentence, or they may act as qualifiers, following nouns or other pronouns.

They will be discussed under the following heads:

A. Demonstrative forms (two kinds).
B. Interrogative forms (two kinds).
C. Reflexive, reciprocal and emphasizing forms (two kinds).
D. Indefinite forms (nine kinds).
E. Relative pronoun (Moru only).
F. Pronominal particle **na**.

A. Demonstrative Forms

219. There are two sorts of demonstrative, which have to be carefully distinguished. One is concerned with the distance from the speaker and is formed with **n-**. (This may be called the 'near and far' demonstrative.) The other indicates intimacy with the speaker or person addressed and is formed with **'d-**. (This may be called the 'reference' demonstrative.) The distribution of these forms throughout Moru-Madi is as follows:

  I. *'Near and far' demonstratives*   II. *'Reference' demonstrative*
  nə and **na** M., K., L., Keliko.   **'də** M., K., L.
  ni and **na** Ä., 'B., Äg., W., Avukaya,   **'di** Ä., 'B., Äg., W., also all
      Logo.   Central and Southern
  (**'di**) and **na** Madi.   languages except:
               lɛ Lulu'ba.

The demonstratives may be used either as pronouns standing alone, or as qualifiers following the substantive they qualify.

I. *'Near and far' demonstratives*.

220. Two degrees of distance are indicated in the **n-** demonstratives.
 ni (dial. **nə**) denotes nearness and may be conveniently translated 'this, here'.
 na denotes relative remoteness and may be conveniently translated 'that, there'. Extreme remoteness may be indicated by emphasizing the **na** form = 'that, yonder'.

The demonstratives have specific plural forms. They are also often to be found combined with the **'di** (dial. **'də**) form, but this latter element does not modify the spatial relationship.

Examples from MORU:

   M.: ə̀nə, pl. *koi* (this)   **ana**, pl. *kai* (that)
   Ä.: **ìnɪ**   **ìna**

M.: bɔŋgó ənó ȧni kʊ́ ə̀dzwà-nɪ. This cloth cannot be mended.
 dófó ənó lédr ezà-zá (sɪ) na. This stick is for punishing the man with.
 m-ítì tà ənə mi-ri. I tell you this (lit. I tell word this you to.)
 mi-zi mano koi eki-nɪ ma-vo. Call these people to come after me.
Ä.: **néné** tàvi ti rù. This is the tail of a cow.
Jl.: odzíla nə̀ dó. This man is good.
M.: mán (i) **ana** ópí ɪ. Yonder person is a chief.
 ma-sa-na 'bereŋwa se ana ya gɪ-ɖa ya? Shall I be able to reach yonder hill.
 tu se kai si opi dra-gwo. In those days the chief died (lit. days which those in chief died).

Note occasional use of relative pronoun **se** with demonstrative. (See § 254.)

Examples from LOGO:

 ago niɖi (this man)   *ago nii* or *ni* (these men)
  nini (A.)
 dili niɖi (this spear)   *dili nii* or *ni* (these spears)
 ndri niɖi (this goat)   *ndri nii* or *ni* (these goats)
 ago naɖi (that man)   *ago nae* or *naɪ* (those men)
 dili naɖi (that spear)   *dili nae* or *naɪ* (those spears)
 ndri naɖi (that goat)   *ndri nae* or *naɪ* (those goats)
 ago naɖi or *naale* (yonder man)   *ago naae* (yonder men)
 dili naaɖi or *naale* (yonder spear)

II. *'Reference' demonstrative.*

221. The principal function of the **'d-** demonstrative is to refer to something or some one already mentioned or understood.
Examples:

   What is it? (What is this?) *What are they? (What are these?)*
MORU {M.: **'dóó** a'di yà?   kòyi ò'di i yà?
   {Ä.: **'dí**'di a'di yà?   **'dí'bá** à'di i yà?
MADI: **'dí** a'du ya?
LUGBARA: **'dɪrɪ** a'du ya?
KELIKO: **'dɪrɪ** a'du ya?

and the answer:
   It is a chair   *They are stools*
MORU {M.: **'dó** gíti i, *or* ɔnɔ gíti i kòyi kitipara ì
   {Ä.: **'dí** kíti ì   **'dí'bá** kitipara ì
LUGBARA: **'dɪrɪ** adʒú opɪ nì. } It is the spear of the chief.
KELIKO: **'dɪrɪ** ópɪ àdʒu.
LULU'BA: mar(i) izi lɛ She is my wife (lit. my wife that).

  This is my father's cloth
MORU (Ä.): **'di** bòŋgo tǎpi marɔ rɔ
MADI: **'di** bòngo m-áta dí i
LUGBARA: **'dɪrɪ** má-tépí boŋgó ì
KELIKO: **'di** má-tépi à bòŋgɔ ì

  I hit him (lit. *that-one*)
LUGBARA: má-gba-rɛ **'díni**
KELIKO: mä-vi **'díni**
LOGO: ma-'bɛ **'díni**
LENDU: ari di. Cook it.

Do you want to buy it? (lit. *you-want thing this to buy*)
MORU M.: mí-lɛ ŋgá **'dó** ògyɛ-nɪ yà?
  Ä.: mí-lɛ ŋga **'di** ɔdzɛ?
  W.: mí-lɛ ŋga **'di** adzé-lé yà?
  Jl.: mí-lɛ ŋga **'di** gyi-lɛ yà?

MORU: ny-ozo **ɖo märi**. Give me that one.
KELIKO: fe mani **ɖa-ri**.
MORU (M.): ny-ozo iɾi **ɖo ma-ri**. Give that knife to me.
LULU'BA: mo'dí ágwína lê. That big man.

222. It may also be used in a purely demonstrative sense, especially in antithesis with **na**. One can easily see, however, that the form in **'d-** is the more intimate of the two.

  This man is good; that man is bad
   {M.: lédr **'dó** kàdɔ lédr **aná** kʷòizi
MORU {Ä.: lédr **'di** àndiro lédr **aná** ònziro
   {W.: dedr **'di** àndiro ɪná-**'di** kòziro

In MADI, according to Molinaro, the **'d-** form is always used as a 'near' demonstrative, and the **na** form as a 'far' demonstrative. It is probable that this phenomenon needs further investigation in that language.

MADI: *zo ɖii loso.* This house is good.
boronzi ɖii ogu. Those boys are thieves.
kwe naa azo. That tree (or post) is tall.
amvonzi naa ole-ki ro ko. Those sisters do not love each other.

223. The reference demonstrative, when suffixed to nouns, often corresponds in function to the definite article 'the' of English.

LUGBARA: má-gba mva-'dì-rì. I beat the child (in question).
LOGO: *ma-no waraga aɖea-aɖea.* I see the paper (in question).
adre ta niɖi-ni ri. (Mk. iv. 14.) He soweth the word.
LULU'BA: bwi anyukwa-lɛ. Shoot the animal.

224. It may also be suffixed to personal pronouns for the sake of emphasis. (Compare English 'You there!')

MORU { K.: nyá-'di iŋwa yà? Where are you? (lit. you-that where?)
'B.: ná-'də iŋgɔlɛ̀?
Äg.: ná-'də iŋgɔ yà?
LOGO: *aɖi* and *akoɖi* = him (lit. man that).
LULU'BA: mi-lɛ̂, pl. mí-lɛ́ = You there.

225. In the Central languages it occurs as final element in certain forms of verbal noun and in certain kinds of adjectives. (See §§ 535 and 692.) Examples from LOGO:
azi-o-le-pi-ɖi (worker); *ɖia-le-so-le-pi-ɖi-i* (a crowd); *azi-o-le-ɖi* (working); *ɖia-ɖia-le-zo-le-pi bi-ɖi-i* (a big crowd).
ago dra-le-pi-ɖi (a dead man); *kokia aiko-le-pi-ɖi* (a sleeping dog).
toko tani-ɖi (a good woman); *toko deri-na tabe-ilena-ɖi* (a jealous woman).

B. INTERROGATIVE FORMS

226. There are two sorts of interrogative. One is formed with 'd- and may be translated by 'Who?' (What person?) or 'What?' (What thing?). This is here called the 'General' interrogative. The other has the form ŋgo or ŋo and may best be translated by 'Which?' This is here called the 'Selective' interrogative. Thus:

I. *'General' interrogatives*   II. *'Selective' interrogative*
à'di (who?) à'du or à'do (what?)   ŋ(g)o (which?)

The interrogatives may be used either as pronouns standing alone, or as qualificatives following the substantives they qualify. They may also be used in the formation of adverbs. Occasionally they are used in non-interrogative sentences, in which case they correspond to 'whoever', 'whatever', &c., in English.

I. *'General' interrogatives.*

227. In most languages the form à'di is used with reference to persons and the form à'du or à'do with reference to things. In some of the Moru dialects, however, à'di is to be found in both contexts.

	Who are you?	*Who is there?*	*Who will go?*
MORU:	mí a'di ya?	à'di lau ya?	
MADI:	nyí a'dí ià?	a'di ina?	a'di kómó-ni yà?
LUGBARA:	mí a'di a?	a'di-ri 'da nià?	a'dí amú-lá-ni yà?
KELIKO:	mí a'dí a?	a'di-ri 'dá nià?	a'dú-rí mú-ni yà?
LOGO:	mí a'di ià?		
AVUKAYA:	mí a'dú ià?		

LULU'BA: mírí ru à'di? What (lit. who) is your name?
LUGBARA: 'Ba ɖi iri tro aɖi ye eyoni ati eri-ni leleri ya? (Mt. xxi. 31.)
Whether of them twain did the will of his father?

148   THE MORU-MADI LANGUAGE GROUP. II. GRAMMAR

	Whom do you want?	Whom did you see?	To whom did you give money?
MORU:	mi-le aďi ya?	mi-ndre aďi ya?	ny-ozo parata aďi-ri ya?
MADI:	nyi-le aďi-i ya?	anyi-ndre aďi ya?	(ny)i-ke pesa aďi(-i)-ni ya?
KELIKO:	mi-le aďi-ri?	mi-ndre aďi?	mi-fe farata si-aďi ani?

	What do you want?	What is this?	What are you doing? (lit. you what do?)
MORU {M.:	mi-le aďi ya?	'dóó a'di yà?	nyá ə'du əyɛ yà?
MORU {Ä.:		'di'dí a'di yà?	mí-ró a'di əyɛ yà?
MADI:	nyi-le aďo ya?	'dí a'du ya?	nyí à'də 'ɛ?
LUGBARA:		'dırı a'du yà?	mí-gá à'du ɛlɛ yà?
KELIKO:	mi-le aďu?	'dırı a'du ya?	mí à'də ɔlɛ̀ yà?
LULU'BA:			min(i) owé a'do-ni?

LOGO: aďo tai tani-ďi ma-koo ya? (Mt. xix. 16.) What good thing shall I do? (Cf. LUG.: ma-ŋga-ye eyo onyiro sini a?)

In the interrogative adverb (= 'Why?') the form à'du is usually found. Note here that it precedes substantives.

           Why are you crying?
MORU { M.: nyá-li ə'du ta yà? (lit. you-cry what word?)
       Ä.: mí-ró aú ɔ̀ŋgɔ ə'du ta ya? (lit. you noise sing what word?)
MADI { Lo.: ny-ówó à'du-sì? (lit. you-cry what-with?)
       Pa.: ny-óú à'du-sì?
LUGBARA: mí-ówá à'di-sì?
KELIKO: mí-ŋgɔ a'du-sì?
LULU'BA: ləú a'do? (lit. crying what?)

           Why is the boy crying?
LOGO: mvaago adre ŋgole aďo-sı ya?
LENDU: mbga kadzz aďu jo? (lit. boy cry what word?)

Non-interrogative use: (Note retention of interrogative particle ya.)
LOGO: aďo ŋgo ya mi-dre lele ďi-se. (Mt. vi. 81.) What things ye have need of.

II. 'Selective' interrogative.

228. The use of the form ŋgo (or ŋo) seems usually to indicate that one out of a number of persons or objects is to be selected. It would thus correspond to English 'which' rather than to 'what'.[1] In Moru this interrogative is sometimes preceded by the relative pronoun se.

MORU: ma-pi-na sanduku se eŋgo-nye ya? Which box shall I open? (lit. I-open-shall box that which?)
LOGO: 'Dia aŋgo-ďi ya ďia nii iri ďiise? (Mt. xxi. 31.) Whether of them twain?
KELIKO: ɛri zo ŋgo-ni? What did he say?
LUGBARA: Emi ago ŋgoa-na, kabilo eii toro? (Lk. xv. 4.) What man of you having a hundred sheep?
        Musa azi emi-ndra ŋgo-ni ya? (Mk. x. 3.) What did Moses command you?
MADI (Pa.): 'Di maďi ŋgo-ni? (Mk. iv. 41.) What manner of man is this?
MADI (Lo.): e'bu losoree iŋgo i? Which is the good piece of work? (lit. work good which is?)

[1] Note that in Lugbara and Keliko this form is less 'selective' than in the other languages and often corresponds to 'What?'.

OTHER PRONOUNS AND PRONOMINAL ADJUNCTS

Non-interrogative use:
    LOGO: *'Dia aŋgo-ɖi ya ko-fe.* (Mt. x. 42.) Whosoever shall give.
    LUGBARA: *Afa iŋga-pi depi drinia ri.* (Mk. x. 32.) What things should happen unto him.

229. This form is more in use than the 'general' forms in the building up of interrogative adjectives and adverbs.

Adjectives.
    MORU: *tá-ŋwà-nyɛ yà?* How many?
    MADI: *au nyi-dri iŋgo-pi?* How many chickens have you? (lit. chickens you-on how-many)
    KELIKO: *anziŋa-ri imu-ki ŋgopi?* How many boys have come?

Adverbs.
    Where are you going?   *Where do you come from?*
  MORU M.: nyó-ɔ̀i íŋwa yà?   ny-ékyi niŋwa yà?
    Ä.: mí-ró-ɔi íŋgwa yà?   n-áʈi níŋgwa ya?
    Where are you carrying that box? (lit. you box that carry where)
    M.: nyá sandùku 'dóó uŋgyi gaŋ́wa ya?
    Ä.: mí-ró sandùku 'dí undzi iŋ́(g)wa ya?
    Where are you carrying that box from?   *Where are you?*
    M.: nyá sandùku 'dóó iŋgyi niŋwa yà?   mí gaŋ́wa yà?
    Ä.: mí-ró sandùku 'dí ändzi níŋ́gwa yà.
    Where are you pushing it?
    M.: nyá-ubí-na íŋwa yà?
    Ä.: mí-ró-úbì-nà ɛ́ŋwa ya?
    'B.: ná-ró-ùbi-na ɪŋgɔ̀-lɛ-rɔ yà?
    Äg.: nǎ-dudu íŋǵwɔ yà?
    Jl.: mí-ze áníka áŋgo-lɛ́-ró ya?
    How do the Moru catch fish? (lit. people Moru fish catch how)
    M.: lédr Mɔrɔ́-rɔ ká ti'bi ùru 'bo-íŋwa-nyɛ̀ ya?
    Ä.: lédr Mɔrɔ́-rɔ ró i'bi ùru 'bo-iŋwa-tí ya.
    M.: bérazí má-rɔ adɔ (bo) gɔ-éŋwa-nyɛ̀ a? How fares my friend?
    When will So-and-so go?
  MADI { Lo.: Oyúru kómu etú-íŋgɔ-si yà?
       { Pa.: Lúgumà kúmu a'dɔ̀-ŋgǎ-nì.
  LUGBARA: 'Búgá lamú ŋgo-tú yà?
  KELIKO: Kutu mu íŋgo-tú yà?
    LOGO: *aŋgu ya, aŋgo-le ya*   = where? whither?
        aŋgu-tu ya   = when?
        aŋgini ya, aŋgo-ti-ni ya = how?

C. REFLEXIVE, RECIPROCAL, AND EMPHASIZING FORMS

230. Pronouns of this nature may be grouped under two heads:
  I. Type **ro, ru, romvo, lomvo**, with mostly reflexive or reciprocal function.
  II. Type **andi, andivo, tandi, indi, ndi**, with mostly emphasizing function.

These forms may be used either as pronouns standing alone, or as qualifiers following the substantive they qualify. They have also further uses which will be explained in the text.

I. *Type ro, ru, romvo, lomvo.* (*Reflexive and reciprocal*)

231. The most common reflexive-reciprocal pronoun is a form of **ro** = 'body'. Sometimes it is combined with the form **vo** = 'place'.

MORU: má-tri **lómvó** má-rɔ tɛ.   I undressed myself.
má **lúmvú** má-rɔ ɔ̀dzwa.   I am washing myself.
mi-fú **rù** ku.   Don't fight each other.
mà **lúmvú** ùfú ädrupi ma-rɔ bɛ.   I fight with my brother (lit. we body fight brother mine with).
Baya óndó-àló ká **rú** (or **lúmvú**) ufú ädrúpi ndá-rɔ bɛ.   Baya always fights with his brother.

AVUKAYA Jl.: ledr 'da **lumvu** te.   The man washed himself.

LOGO: ago iri nda fu **ru** dre, aii dra-le.   The two men killed each other (lit. men two they kill body, they die).
mvaagoi adre **ru** coa.   The boys are beating each other (lit. boys are body beating).
mvai adre **ru** ɖa.   The children cursed each other.
ama **ro** ja.   We tease each other.
anyi **ro** ti aɖosi ya?   Why do you quarrel.
le **ru** (to love one another); bu **ru** (to fight).
kibe **ru** (to gather together).
kimo **ru** (A.) (to crowd together).

It will be noticed from the above that this form is preferred in Logo for reciprocal action. For reflexive action see § 235.

Other languages:

	I am washing myself	*Wash yourself*	*He washed himself*
MADI { Lo.:	má má-**ru** dzè	nyi-dze **rú** pl. ànyi-dze **ru**	andá odzè **ru** ra
Pa.:	má-dʒwe (ma-)**ru**	dʒwe **rú**	andá odʒwè **ru** ra
LUGBARA:	má má(-**ru**) odʒì	mí-dʒi mi-**ru**-'ba[1]	ɪrɪ dze ɪ-**ru**-'ba 'bo
KELIKO:	má má dze	í-dzi mi-**ru**-'ba	ɪrɪ dzé ɪ-**ru**-'ba ge

232. ro, lomvo, &c., have other functions besides those mentioned above. For example:

MORU: ndá gá kué té ma-**lomvo**.   He told a lie against me.

(See also under Postpositions, § 304.)

MORU: zo maro gi-**ro**.   My house is wet. (gi = water.)
adravo maro ndi kozi-**ro**.   My illness is bad.

(See also under Predicatives, § 723.)

                The bananas have turned red   *Food is good to eat* (lit. food body eats well)

MADI { Lo.: rabolo kákí **ru** étsó éká   lényá ká **rò** nyà lɔsɔ
Pa.: rabolo kákí **ru** kétʃóro eka   lényá kúnyá **rɔ̀** lɔsɔ
MORU: 'búgʊ zá **ro** tɛ ɔ̀kà-**rɔ̀**

---

[1] The form ru'ba, found in Lugbara and Keliko, is a compound of **ru** = body and **'ba** = person.

MADI: *karede* (< *ka ro ede*). It is done.
karanzo (< *ka ro anzo*). It is good, it profits.
osi ro. It is written.
LOGO: *tedi ru da* (was saved); *pa ru da* (was delivered).
lede ru da (was cleansed); *nji ru da* (was opened—of eyes).
MORU: *bɔŋgó ɛndzɪ ru te*. The cloth is spoilt.

II. Type *andi, andivo, tandi, indi, ndi* (*Reflexive and emphasizing*)

233. This form sometimes serves as an alternative to *ro*, &c., but its function is usually more emphasizing than reflexive. It is not used outside pronominal constructions.

MORU: *ma andivo moi ku Maridi ya.* I myself am not going to Maridi.
ma-le Indarago andivo(-na) ondrenɪ. I want to see Ndarago himself.
waraga ono ni andivo mɪro. This paper is your very own.
äzu ono ndi ndaro. This spear is truly his.
anya eke kusu ono andivo ɪro. He says this bow is his very own.
andivo ru ndaro aɖi ya? What is his actual name?

ma-'bi mi andi. I *will* beat you.
ma-ndre Indarago andi. I *will* see Ndarago.
moi andi Amadi ya ondo. I *will* go to Amadi to-morrow.

With reflexive force:

M.: *ny-ɛ́dɛ andívə mírɔ̀.* Dress yourself.
(Cf. Ă.: *n-adɛ rʊ̀mvʊ́ mɪ̀rɔ̀*)
M.: *lédr 'bä andívə frɔ te.* The man shot himself.
(Cf. Ă.: *lédr 'bä i te*)

Examples from LOGO:

akoɖi do-dre aɖi ai-tandi. He took it himself.
L.: *ama(-ni)-tandi* } I myself.
A.: *ama(-ni)-ati* }

Examples from LUGBARA:

ɖi azita nabi be indi. (Mt. vii. 12.) For *this* is the law and the prophets.
vilerisi oko eri dra indi. (Mt. xxii. 27.) Finally the woman (she) died herself.

And from KELIKO:

ma Kelikú î tàndi. I personally am a Keliko.

234. In LENDU the form *ndi* is used throughout with referring, reflexive, reciprocal, and emphasizing functions.

Referring: *ma-jo por ndi ku the.* My brother says he is ill.
(Cf. *zha por ke ku the na ŋga.* My mother says he is not ill.
Reflexive: *ike hwi-ŋgue ndi ndiro.* The man killed himself.
bwetsznzo thi ndi-ma. The boys are beating themselves.
Reciprocal: *aro kpa ce-ŋgue ndi-ma.* The two men slew each other.
kpa ndi-ma thu. The children curse one another.
Emphasizing: *ke ɖu-ŋgue ndi ndiro.* He took it himself.

235. In all languages the normal personal pronoun (for the 1st and 2nd person) and the referring pronoun (for the 3rd person) may be used instead of the reflexive, reciprocal, and emphasizing forms given above. Examples:

1st and 2nd person—
- MORU: (preferred in reciprocal sentences)

mu-túri **àma** tùrì.	We fear each other.
m-ulú **àma** tàwì.	We love each other very much.
ma-pá **àma** te.	We helped each other.
mɪ-pá **àmɪ**.	Help each other.
mɪ-'da **àmɪ** ku.	Don't insult each other.

- LOGO: (preferred in reflexive sentences)

ma-fu **ma**.	I hurt myself.
ama-fu **ama**.	We hurt ourselves.
mi-fu **mi**.	You hurt yourself.
ami-fu **ami**.	You hurt yourselves.

Note also

ma-o **ma**.	I do it myself.
mi-o **mi**.	You do it yourself.

- KELIKO:

má **má** dze.	I wash myself.
mɪ **mɪ** dze.	You wash yourself.

3rd person (referring pronoun)—
- MORU: (used in reflexive and reciprocal sentences):

ŋgágà 'bi **i** tɛ.	The boy beat himself.
lédr dzwà **i** te.	The man washed himself.
lédr 'bä **i** tɛ.	The man shot himself.
ópí ạ̄ɾu **i** te.	The chief took an oath.
anyá túri **yi** tùrì.	They fear each other.
lédr Mɔ̀rɔ-rɔ ká **i** ɔpa.	The Moru people help each other.
ŋgaga ká kàlà ɔ̀pɛ **i̇**-vɔya.	The boys are (mouths) quarrelling with each other.

- LOGO (not used in reciprocal sentences):

aďi (or *anya*) *fu* **i**.	He hurt himself.
ai (or *anyai*) *fu* **ai**.	They hurt themselves.
ago nda fu **i** *dra-le*.	The man (he) killed himself and died.
mva-agoɪ adre **aii** *coa*.	The boys are beating themselves.
nda (or *anya*) *o* **i**.	He does it himself.

- LUGBARA: ɪrɪ é dʒì. He is washing himself.
- KELIKO: érí e dze. He is washing himself.

D. INDEFINITE FORMS

236. There are nine sorts of indefinite pronoun in Moru-Madi, corresponding roughly to the following forms in English:

I.	ŋga or ta	corresponding to	'something', 'anything', 'it'.
II.	aza or azi or zi	,,	'any', 'other', 'more', 'some'.
III.	ruka	,,	'other', 'more'.
IV.	aki, adee	,,	'different', 'other', 'more'.
V.	anjoko, ambi, mbi	,,	'the rest', 'the others'.
VI.	nani	,,	'some one'.
VII.	alo	,,	'a certain', 'some one'.
VIII.	anda, nde	,,	'a certain'.
IX.	'ba (or ba)	,,	'they', 'one'.

I. *The forms ŋga and ta (afa and kɔ in Lugbara).*

237. A transitive verb is seldom used without an object, expressed or understood. Whereas in English one says 'I am eating', 'I am talking', &c., Moru-Madi speakers prefer to say 'I am eating *food*', 'I am talking *words*'. Where no specific object may be attached to the sentence, the two indefinite or general forms **ŋga** (= 'thing') and **ta** (= 'word') are much used.[1]

MADI: *anyi-'jo ta.*   Speak! (pl.) (lit. ye-say word).
  má-tó tà ra.   I danced (lit. I-danced word).
  má tà to.   I am dancing (lit. I word dance).
  okwe mani ta ko.   He did not give me anything (lit. gave me thing not).
LOGO: *mi-laɖi ŋga.*   Cook! (lit. you-cook thing).
  aɖi laɖi ŋga konji.   He cooks badly.
  aɖi le ŋga nya-le.   He wants to eat (lit. he wants thing to eat).
  ŋga o (to work); *ŋga ko* (to sweep); *ŋga to* (to dance).[2]

Examples from other languages (verbs **gu** or **kugu** = to steal, **'i** or **ui** = to grind, **ə** or **'ɛ** or **'yɛ** = to do):

	I do not steal	*Stop grinding*
MORU (Ä.):	m-úgu ŋgá ku	n-a'bɛ ŋg(a) úl
LUGBARA:	mú-kugu ŋgá kɔ	m-ɛ'bɛ 'i-ŋga-ra
KELIKO:	m-úgu ŋgá ku	
AVUKAYA Jl.:	m-úgu ŋgá-'dì kɔ	MADI Lo.: ny-ɛbɛ ta 'í-ka
AVUKAYA Jg.:	mú-kugu ŋgá ku	MADI Pa.: ɛ'bɛ ŋgá 'í-ka

I am not doing anything
  LOGO: mó-ó ŋgá kò or *ma-adre ta ko.*
  KELIKO: má-ɔ ŋgá kò
  AVUKAYA: má-'yɛ ŋgá kɔ
  LUGBARA: má-'ɛ̀ ko ku
  eri nya-ni afa ko.   He did eat nothing.

238. **ŋga** and **ta** are also used in most languages in the formation of verbal nouns.

	loving	*a cook*
MORU M.:	ŋgá-lù	ŋgá-la'dí-'ba (lit. thing-cook-man)
MORU Ä.:	ŋgá-lɛ	
MORU W.:	ŋgó-lɛ	
AVUKAYA:	ŋgá-lè(-lè)	('bà-)ŋgá-la'dí-lé-bè-rì
KELIKO:	ala-ŋga-ra	('ba-)ŋga-a'di-pì-nì
LUGBARA:	ala-ŋga-ra	
LOGO:	*ta-konji* (sin)	('ba-)ŋgá-la'dí-lí-pì-'dì

239. In MADI an emphasizing pronoun may be formed by means of **ŋga** and the possessive pronominal form.

  a-jo ma-ŋga ma i.   I said it myself.
  k-emu ana-ŋga.   He is coming himself.
  any-ede anya-ŋga anyi i.   Do it yourselves.
  aɪ ori-ki aɪa-ŋga vuru.   They themselves sat down.

---

[1] Note, however, that absence of object-word does not indicate absence of object, but rather that the object is obvious to both speaker and hearer. See § 199.
[2] Note also in LOGO: *ari-* (object) *gu* (verb) = to laugh.
  ti- (object) *zi* (verb) = to ask.

240. In LOGO ŋga is used as subject to certain verbs which have no specific subject.

ŋga ketekete (it is clear)   ŋga kitu-ru (it is sunny)
ŋga wa-le (to dawn)

241. In most languages **ta** and **ŋga** are used to introduce sentences giving cause or reason.

I go back because there is no food
LOGO: ma-gɔ andʒélé **ŋgá** nyanya 'da-yɔ̀
KELIKO: ma-gɔ vúlé **ŋgá** nyanya 'da-yɔ̀
LUGBARA: ma-gɔ vúlé **akɔ** nyanya yɔ̀
MORU: **ta-na** = because

II. *The forms aza, azi, zi.*

242. These forms may perhaps be rendered in English by 'some, more, another or others of the same category as that already discussed'.

MORU: *mi-ge täi **aza**.* Bring some salt.
  *mí-'dà **azi** kù.* Don't insult other (people).
  *ma-le indri **aza** oje-nɪ mä-ri.* I want to buy another goat for myself.
  *täpi-**azi*** (uncle, lit. other father)
  *endre-**azi*** (aunt, lit. other mother); *toko-**azi*** (co-wife)

Note also: *'dí-**az(á)** orívɪá láu ya?* Is any one there? (lit. person other present there)

*'dí-**az(á)** í'dú nɔ̀a.* Nobody is here.
(M.): *lédr **àza** nì àrɪ ɔ̀kwa ku.* } Nobody can catch a bird (lit. man other knows
(Ä.): *'dí-**azä** nì kù tè àrɪ ɔ̀kɔ-nɪ.* } bird catch not)

  *anya ozo ŋga-**aza** ku märi.* He gave nothing to me.
MADI: *pesa **zii** iya.*   There is no more money.
  zii ole-ra, zii ole ku.   Some fled, others did not.
LUGBARA: *'ba **azini** yo-ra.* (Matt. xxvii. 49.) The rest said.
  ***azini** ŋga-iŋgi-ra.* (Mk. xiv. 57).   And there arose certain.
LOGO: *azi* = more (adjective)
  azina or *aziɖi* = more (pronoun)
KELIKO: *'ba **ji** imu ko.*   Nobody has come.

243. These forms may be used in a reciprocal sense, especially in MADI.

The boys are quarrelling with each other
Lo.: bɔrɔnzi kúzá bá-**àzí** trɔ
Pa.: 'bɔnzi kudʒwa 'bá-**àzí** tɔ
KELIKO: andziri utäko 'bá-**àzi** bɛ

III. *The form ruka.*

244. This form may perhaps be rendered in English by 'some, more, another or others in addition to that already mentioned'.

MORU: *ätu maro iɖu amba, ny-ozo **ruka**-na mä-ri.* My arrows are not many, give me some others.
  ***ruka**-na oi-go losi ya, **ruka**-na oi-go aba-nɪ.* Some went to work, some went to hunt.
LOGO: *a**ruka**-na* (some); *a**ruku**-'ba* (some people).

OTHER PRONOUNS AND PRONOMINAL ADJUNCTS

IV. *The forms aki, adee.*

245. These forms may perhaps be rendered in English by 'some, more, another or others of a different category to that already mentioned'.

> MORU: *mano ono ädrupi maro idu, anya ledri **aki**.* This man is not my brother, he is another man.
>
> *ri iro go gi-alo vo **aki** ya.* (She) remained herself alone in another place.
>
> MADI: *lenya dii onzi, ny-ekwe mani **adee**.* This grain is bad, give me another sort.
>
> *nyi-kwe kikwasi bara **adee** ni.* Give the pin to another boy.

V. *The forms anjoko, ambi, mbi.*

246. These forms may perhaps be rendered in English by 'the others or the rest of the category of which part has already been mentioned'.

> MORU: *ma-nya eza te tandrube, oko yau-ono **anjoko**-na ŋgwa-te.* I ate the meat yesterday, but now the rest of it is rotten.
>
> *And they went and told it unto the residue.* (Mk. xvi. 13.)
>
> MORU: *ago ànya oi-gwo pei tana gwo **anjoko**-nai ri.*
> LOGO: *aii dreki njı-zo dreki ta-za aiiki **ambii** dri.*
> LUGBARA: *yi ŋga-mu a-le eyo olo 'ba **mbi**-le matia.*

VI. *The form nani (= 'some one').*

247. This form has so far been recorded only in Moru.

> MORU: ***nani**-ŋwa ye ta do te onziro.* Some one has done this thing badly.
>
> Note that the form in za or zi is usually preferred:
>
> *endaro di-aza tembi ma ndi.* (Lk. viii. 46.) Somebody hath touched me.

VII. *The form -alo(-sa).*

248. The form alo (= 'one') may be used to indicate 'some one, a certain one, a single one'.

> MADI: *oko **alo-alo** ka ba enya enyanya si.* Some woman is harming the people with evil.
>
> *bara **alo** odra okolo si ra.* One of the boys is dead from coughing.
>
> ***alo-alo** o'jo dini.* Somebody said that.
>
> *andre ba **alo-sa** ko.* I haven't seen a soul.
>
> *la'bi **alo-sa** esuro ko.* There isn't a single buck.
>
> ***alo-sâ** emú ko.* Nobody has come.
>
> *ɔpi **sa** emú ko.* No chief has come.
>
> LUGBARA: *'ba **alo** va ma-rua ra.* (Lk. viii. 46.) Somebody hath touched me.
>
> *auzi alioro **alo** ŋga emu-ra.* (Mk. xii. 42.) There came a certain poor widow.
>
> LUGBARA: *agu **alo** eri ovu agupi anzi iri.* } (Lk. xv. 11.) A certain man had two
> MORU: *man-aza **alo**-di, ŋgwai be ritu.* } sons.

VIII. *The forms anda, nde.*

249. In LOGO the form anda is preferred to alo, and in LUGBARA nde is sometimes used in similar contexts.

> LOGO: *taitoko **anda** lemerero aca-dre.* (Mk. xii. 42.) There came a certain poor widow.
>
> *dia **anda** dreki ŋga-zo kuru.* (Mk. xvi. 57.) And there arose certain (people).

LUGBARA: *'ba **nde** ovu anzi iri be ra.* (Mt. xxi. 28.) A certain man had two sons.
*eri ndre 'ba **nde** ru erini Matayo.* (Mt. ix. 9.) He saw a man named Matthew.

Note also: *'ba **nde** dria ka-ndre oko mile.* (Mt. v. 28.) That whosoever looketh on a woman.

IX. *The form 'ba (or ba).*

250. In MADI the form **'ba** or **ba** (-'people') is often used in an impersonal sense in verbs where no specific subject is indicated. (Cf. **ŋga** in Logo, § 240.)

        ba k-o'jo.   One says. It is said. (Cf. *On dit. Si dice.*)
        ba o'jo-ki.   They said. It was said. (Cf. *On a dit. Si disse.*)
(Opari Madi) **ba emu ko.**   Nobody has come.
(Torit Madi) **madi emu koro.**

E. RELATIVE PRONOUN (se)

251. MORU alone has a relative pronoun. This pronoun is often used in conjunction with the verb postposition **bɛ** (see § 643), but the latter element is not always present.
Examples without **bɛ**:

má-lɛ ŋgàgà **se** *ni kala ɪŋgɪlɪsɪ té.* I want a boy who knows English.
lărí **sé** *Mìza kó-òtʊ na, ăzi 'mùrɪ'.* The dance which the Miza dance is called 'muri'.
M.: *nda* **sé** *ká ŋgá kùgù, kòzirɔ.* Those who steal things are bad.
Ă.: *nda* **se** *rɔ ŋga ùgù, òndzirò.*

Examples with **bɛ**:

lédr **sé** *fù ìbì* **bɛ**, *ädrúpi márò.* The man who killed the lion, was my brother.
lédr **sé** *àtra fu* **bɛ** ... The man whom the foreigner killed ...
tɔkó lédr **sé** *áfu* **bɛ** *anarɔ, ɔi-tɛ.* The wife of the man who was killed, ran away.

252. Unlike other pronouns, **se** may not be followed by a postposition, nor be one of the elements in the genitive construction. Note the following rendering of the English forms 'to whom', 'whose', &c.

la'bi se mi-'bu pa-na (or *pa anyaro*) *be, mu-te.* The water-buck whose leg you shot (lit. who you shot his leg) has run away.
mano se m-ozo-na parata liwa-si ro anya-ri eŋgware ya? Where is the man to whom I shall give money for the ivory? (lit. man who I-shall-give money elephant-tooth for him-to where).
liti se mi-'ba kagwa be nda-dri, adu-na kadoro. The road on which you put iron-stone will become good (lit. road which you-put stone it-on, will-become good).

253. se or **tu se** (lit. the day which) may sometimes be used as a conjunction = 'when'.

se moi-be Wala rige, ma-'bu lo'ba te. When I went to Wala's, I shot a hartebeest.
se moi-na Ŋgeɪɪ rige, ma-le ledri anyaro ondreni cini. When I go to Ngeli's, I want to see all his people.

254. se is also much in use in introducing demonstratives or other qualifying agents.

    ndi mui ăe-go bu se ana ya.   And the hyena fell into that pit.
    tu se kai si opi dra-go.   In those days the chief died.
    ma-pi-na sanduku se eŋgonye ya?   Which box shall I open?
    lédr **sé** *waragà bɛ ɛsa-te.*   The man with the letter has arrived.

OTHER PRONOUNS AND PRONOMINAL ADJUNCTS

F. The Pronominal Particle na (dial. a, nɛ, ni, lɛ, la)

255. In all Moru-Madi languages a pronominal particle is to be found, usually standing after the word to which it is connected. This particle is to be found in various forms (**na** or **a** in Moru, Madi, Logo, **lɛ** in Avukaya, **la** in Lugbara).

The following are its main functions:

After verbs.

256. When occurring after a verb, the particle may refer to something already mentioned, and may thus act as an object pronoun.[1]

    MORU M.: mɪ-ndrɛ **na** ɛŋgware ya?   Where did you see him (or it)?
        'B.: ma-lɛ a'ba **na**. ⎫
        W.: ma-lɛ ä'bwä **nä**. ⎬   I want to put it down.
        Jl.: ma-lɛ a'ba **lɛ**. ⎭
    LULU'BA: wɛ lɛ́ ku. Don't do it.   vʊ lɛ́ ku. Don't blow it.
    MADI: *ny-oŋgwe-a.* Call him.

            I can't do it
        MORU: mǎ-nì ɔ̀yɛ-**na** ku.
        MADI ⎰ Lo.: á-nì 'wɛka-**na** ku.
            ⎱ Pa.: mǎ-nì ɛka-**na** ku.
        LUGBARA: mǎ-nì ɛ́-**lǎ** ku.

257. Like **ŋga** (see § 237) it may be used with a transitive verb where no specific object is indicated.

    MORU: má-tɔ̀dzwa-**na**.   I am washing.
          nyá-tùmvu-**na** yà? Are you drinking?

After nouns.

258. When occurring after a noun it may act as a possessive particle, referring to a possessor already mentioned. (Cf. referring pronoun **i**, §§ 200–1.)

    MORU: *mano se mi-ndre be lau, ädrupi-na dra-te.* The man you saw there, his brother is dead.
        m-usu vo-na ku te. I couldn't find it (lit. I found its place not).
        bɔŋgó ɔnɔ́ áni ádzwà-nà ndi. This cloth can be washed (lit. cloth this knows its washing indeed).
    MADI: *endre-na* (his mother: alternative to *ani-endre* or *endre ani-dri*).
        endre-ki-na (their mother: alternative to *aɪ-endre* or *endre aɪ-dri*).
        onyo pa-na ra. He broke his leg.
        owi ti-na ra. He opened his mouth.

259. It may also act merely as an emphasizing particle.

    MORU: ta-**ná** dzʷè-te. ⎫
    AVUKAYA: ta-**lá** vi-tra. ⎬ I have forgotten it (lit. the matter has escaped).

Note also: ta-na = because (in Moru).

    MADI: *ny-owo Rubaŋa Opi nyi-dri na ndraga.* Bow before the Lord thy God (lit. you bow God Chief your before). (Cf. *nyowo ma-ndraga.* Bow before me.)

---

[1] Miss Mozley, for LOGO, gives **na** and **ni** as alternative object pronouns for the third person (singular and plural), but gives no examples of their use.

After pronouns.

260. When occurring after a pronoun it has an emphasizing value.

  MORU: *toko andivo-na dra-te.* The woman herself is dead.
    ma-ndre Indarago andivo-na ku. I do not see Ndarago himself.

After adjectives and other qualifiers.

261. **na**, &c., is used to give a pronominal value to qualificatives.

  MORU: *aza(-na)* (another one)   *azaka(-na)* (others)
    ruka(-na) (another one, others)
    anjoka(-na) (the rest)
    käti(-na) (the first)   *riri(-na)* (the second).

    I want a good one really
  MORU M.: má-lɛ kàdʋ́-na àyan
    Ä.: má-lɛ andí-na yù
    W.: má-lɛ andí-na a̍'dò
    Jl.: má-lɛ tàndi-lɛ i̍'dì

  LOGO: *tandi-na* (another one)   *aruka-na* (some—pronoun)
                azi-na (more—pronoun)

  ma-na
  ama-ka (A.) } (mine)   *amaki-a* (ours)
  mi-na
  ami-ka (A.) } (yours)   *amiki-a* (yours)
  aďea-aďea   *aiki-a*
  aďi-ka, anya-ka (A.) } (his)   *aďiki-a* } (theirs)
              anyaki-a (A.)

  Fa niďi ma-na, mi-na aŋgua ya? This stick is mine, where is yours?

As independent word.

262. Occasionally **na** can stand alone.

  MORU M.: **na** ɔ'du! What! (Exclamation of surprise.)
    Ä.: **na** a'dí!

Anomalous position of na, &c., in the sentence.

263. One outstanding feature of **na** is that it does not conform to the rules which govern other pronouns regarding position in the sentence. Thus:

(*a*) The plural particle **ki** precedes **na** instead of following it.

    MADI: *endre ki-na* (their mother).

(Cf. *aii-ki adrupi* (their brother) in LOGO.)

(*b*) In the intimate genitive **na** follows the thing possessed instead of preceding it.

  MADI: *endre-na* (his mother); cf. *m(a)-endre* (my mother); but note *ná-ru* (his body)
  MORU: *toko-na* (his wife)

(*c*) **na** follows the postpositions instead of preceding them.

  MORU: *sɪ-na* (with it); cf. *äzú sì* (with a spear); *mä-ri* (to me)
  LOGO: *le-na* (inside it); cf. *'ba le* (in the village); *ama-drɪ* (for us)

(*d*) **na** as object follows verbs in the 'indefinite' tenses instead of preceding them.

  MORU: *má 'bú u'di.* I am digging a hole (lit. I hole dig).
    nyá-u'di **na.** You are digging it.

CHAPTER VIII

THE GENITIVE[1] CONSTRUCTIONS

264. Westermann maintains that the typical Sudanic genitive construction consists in possessor plus thing possessed (nomen rectum plus nomen regens). This may still be found in some dialects of Moru-Madi, or in especially intimate constructions.

265. There are two main forms of genitive construction:

I. The possessor (nomen rectum) precedes the thing possessed (nomen regens) with or without an intervening particle. This conforms with Westermann's criteria for Sudanic languages and is most common in the Southern and Central languages,

e.g. MADI: ópí àdzu (the chief's spear).

II. The possessor follows the thing possessed, but is itself followed by a postposition.[2] This construction is more used in the Moru dialects, the former construction being used to express intimate possession only,

e.g. MADI: adzu ɔpí drí (the spear of the chief).

I. Possessor plus Possessed (*nomen rectum plus nomen regens*)

266. Where there is no intervening particle, this construction is identical in Moru with the 'compound noun' construction already discussed in § 171. It is used for especially intimate genitive relationship, like parts of the whole, members of the body, &c.

e.g. MORU: liwa-si (ivory), i.e. elephant tooth.
tsʷɛ-gò̝rì (tree-branch)
tsʷé-dr (tree-top)
kɪtó-drì (hare-head)
lä'bí-kɔyɪ (water-buck-horns)
MADI: leà-sí (ivory)
LENDU: *bwetsiki-jo* (man-head)
bi-jo (buffalo-head)

267. In the Southern and Central languages it occurs much more frequently and in less intimate contexts.

I am So-and-so's son	*The chief's spear*
MADI (Pa.): ma Súméin 'bura-ì	ópí àdʒu
LUGBARA: ma Gbágbé ŋgoti	ópí àdʒu
KELIKO: má Álúma mvá	ópi àdʒu

It occurs very often in the name of the language:

má-ta Lògò-ti. I speak Logo, i.e. Logo-mouth.
má-ta { Ɔdzílä-ti. / Ɔdzíga-ti. I speak Avukaya.
má-tá Wa'dí-ti. I speak Wadi.

---

[1] By 'genitive' must be understood a relationship that is not necessarily always one of possession. Expressions like 'pitcher of water' (MADI Pa.: *kudo ei dri*, Mk. xiv. 13) or 'rivers of living water' (MORU: *gulu gi adri ro*, Jn. vii. 38) may be rendered in the same way as the more conventional 'spear of the chief'. Similarly, MADI: *amvu opi dri* may mean 'a field of the chief' or 'a field for the chief'.

[2] It has been suggested that this postposition is fundamentally a noun in apposition to the *nomen regens*, whereby the old Sudanic construction is maintained. I have no reliable evidence to support this theory.

	ma-dza Mà'dí-ti.	I speak Keliko.
	ma Lúgbàrà-ti dʒu.	I speak Lugbara.
	mo-'jó Ólú'bó-ti ni.	I speak Lubu' ba.
	má-tra 'Balɛ-dhà.	I speak Lendu.
(but)	nyá-ta kàlà Morò.	Speak Moru!
	má-ta ka Ăgi (rɔ).	I speak Ăgi.
	má-ta úlí Odzíla ká.	I speak Avukaya (alternative).

It is also found with personal pronouns in intimate constructions (except in Moru):

    MADI: má-lɛ m-ata-i.   I love my father.
    LUGBARA: álɛ má-tépí.
    KELIKO: má-lɛ má-täpì.   *ji i-ti.* (He) opened his mouth.
               gbakí mà-drì.   They hit my head.
    LULU'BA: ɔsí má-pá 'ɔ.   It bit my leg.

In Moru it occurs only idiomatically in such expressions as *ma andivo* (I myself), *Ndarago andivo* (*na*) (Ndarago himself).

Possessive Pronoun Prefix a-

268. In LOGO and AVUKAYA (and a few neighbouring Moru dialects) there is a specific possessive form of the pronoun with prefix a-. This prefix is only distinguishable in the first and second person singular.

    LOGO: *ama-dili* (my spear)   *ama-adrupi(ɪ)* (my brother(s))
             ami- „ (your „)   *ami-* „
             aɖi-ni-dili (his spear)   *aɖi-ni-adrupi(ɪ)*
             amaki-dili (our spears)   *amaki-* „
             amiki- „ (your „)   *amiki-* „
             aiiki- „ (their „)   *aiiki-* „
    AVUKAYA: *ama-ru* (my body).
    MORU WA'DI: *ama-rúmvu.*
    MORUĂGI: má rɔ áma-'bu o'di. I'm digging a hole for myself (lit. I am my hole digging).

Compare:

	My head	Your head	His head	Our heads	Your heads	Their heads
LOGO:	ámä-drì	ámi-drì	'bá'dini drì	àmaki-drì	àmiki-drì	'bá'diki drì
AVUKAYA Jl.:	ámä- „	áni- „	gúläri „	àmä- „	àni- „	gúlèi „
AVUKAYA Jg.:	ámɔ- „	ámi- „	„ „	„ „	àmi- „	„ „
KELIKO:	mâ- „	mî- „	'bá'dà „	amä- „	imi- „	'ba'dà „
LUGBARA:	mâ- „	mî- „	'ba'da „	ama- „	imi- „	'bá'de „
LENDU:	ma-jo	ni-jo	ke-jo ndi-jo	ko-jokpar	ni-jokpar	kpa jokpar ndima „

This a- form in LOGO is also used to express other relations. Note the following:

    aɖi le ama no-le.   She wants to see me (lit. she wants of me the seeing).
    aɖi aca ama no.   He arrived to see me.
    „ „ *amaki no.*   „   „ us.

and in AVUKAYA:

    gúla 'dɔ̀ àma pàá.   He *will* help me (lit. he will my help).

Internominal Linking Particles
-à-

269. In the Southern and Central languages the particle **à** is often interposed.

MADI: ópi a bara. The chief's son.
  kudo a zele. The bottom of the pot (or under the pot).
LOGO: akoǎi a ŋga. His things.
  ǎia irini-be-ǎi a jo na (into a strong man's house, lit. man strong a house in).
  ai adrupi Pilipo a toko-ɪ (his brother Philip's wife).
LUGBARA: èrì gba má à dri. He hit my head (or he hit me on the head).
KELIKO: ǎipa-pi opi a amvu áa. They are hoeing the farm for the chief (or the chief's farm).

The vowel of the pronoun possessor is often assimilated to this vowel:

	My leg	Your leg	His leg	Our legs	Your legs	Their legs
MADI Lo.:	má à pa	nyá à pa	nà à pa	àmà pa	ànyà pa	à'ɪ à pa
MADI Pa.:	má à pa	nyá à pa	andá à pa	àmà pa	,,	à'ɪ à pa
LUGBARA:	má à pa	mí pa	ɪrɪ a pa	àmà pákɪ	ìmì pákɪ	ɪmɪ ɛ pákɪ
KELIKO:	má à pa	mí ì pa	ɪrɪ a pa	àmà pa	ìmì pa	kópɪ à pa

270. In MADI this linking particle also occurs in the object relative construction, with the verb-form as 'thing possessed.'

bara ny-oŋgwe-le-ra-rɪ-'ɪ (<nyi-a-uŋgwe, &c.). The boy whom you called.
ma'dí dzurugo à dí-lé-rì'ɪ. The man whom the foreigner killed.
(Cf. ma'dí ebi dí-ré-re'i. The man who killed the lion.)

-ni-

271. Another intervening particle in these languages is **ni** or **ri**. On the whole, constructions with intervening particles are preferred to those without, even in intimate genitive.

MADI: leá **ni** sí (ivory); ópi **ni** 'bara (son of the chief)
  tí **ni** zè (cow dung); ópí **ní** àdʒu (the chief's spear)
  kwe **n**-andraga (the front of the tree; or, in front of the tree)

	How many hands have you?	I have two.
MADI Lo.:	nyá à drí sí yà?	má à drí ri
MADI Pa.:	nyí **ni** dí sí yà?	má **ni** dí ri

  (Lit. Your hands, how many? My hands two.)
LOGO: Logo **ni** ti yokoǎo. The slave has no cattle (slave's cattle not).
  ago **ni** dili (the man's spear); aǎi **ni** adrupi(e) (his brother(s))
  ago **ni** dri (,, ,, head)

(This construction is most popular in the 3rd person singular in Logo. Note, however:

  ama adrupiɪ = my brothers,
  aiiki adrupiɪ = their brothers,
  ǎiaki adrupiɪ = the men's brothers.)

LULU'BA: The regular construction in Lulu'ba is with **ri**:

My ear	Your ear	His ear	Our country
ma **ri** bí	mi **rí** bí	náni **rí** bí	ama **rí** júrú

My face	Your face	His face
má r-ándà	mí r-ánda	íni r-ánda

	My sheep	*Your sheep*
	má rí indí(ni)	mí rí indí(ni)

cow dung: tí rí wɔ́rɔ̀; elephant dung: ɛwá rí zie

272. In MADI the particle **ni** also occurs in certain sentence constructions with the verb-form as the 'thing possessed'.

má-à-dzɔ ɛ̀sì ópí **ní** kwi-lɛ arù korò. My house is not worthy for the *chief to enter*.

(Cf. bárá 'dii ɛ̀sì kwi-lɛ màdri iti kʊ. These boys are not worthy to enter my house.)

ma (LUGBARA) **ve** (KELIKO)

273. Alternative linking particles are **ma** in Lugbara and **ve** in Keliko.

LUGBARA: *Oko Simonini* **ma** *andri*. (Mk. i. 30.) Simon's wife's mother.

Simoni pie Andorea be pie yi **ma** *jo*. (Mk. i. 29.) The house of Simon and Andrew.

Eri azini olo eyo baputizi-ni 'ba **ma** *asi ojazu, yi* **ma** *eyo onzi wuzuri indi*. (Mk. i. 4.) And preach the baptism of repentance for the remission of sins. (Lit. He also said things baptism-of, people's hearts to-turn, their things bad to-forgive also.)

Eri ŋga baputizi fe yidri yi alia **ma** *ru Yorodani*. (Mk. i. 5.) Lit. He then baptism gave them-to water in of name Jordan.

'Ba alo toni ewa afufuni enyi okuri **ma** *alia ko*. (Mk. ii. 22.) Lit. Man one puts beer fresh bottle old's inside not.

Yi ŋga zi tinia eyo ɖiri **ma** *efini*. (Mk. iv. 10.) Lit. They then asked him things these (their) meaning (from efi = to understand).

KELIKO: *mi* **ve** *boŋgo-ri* (your clothes), *mi* **ve** *pa-ri* (your feet), *opi* **ve** *ja-ri* (the chief's house).

II. POSSESSED PLUS POSSESSOR (*nomen regens plus nomen rectum*)

274. This construction demands a postposition,[1] but there is no continuity throughout the languages of any one form of postposition. The following are the main particles used:

MORU: **rɔ** (= body?)
AVUKAYA : **tra** or **ka(tra)**
MADI (Lo.): **drì** (Pa.): **dì** (= head?)
LULU'BA: **ri**
MADI ('Bu.): **ni**
LUGBARA and KELIKO: **ni**
KELIKO: **'de, vɛrɛ**
LOGO: **a'dɪa, ni a'dɪa**
LOGO (A.): **ka, ni ka**.

275. In MORU this construction is used almost exclusively for both intimate and non-intimate genitive.

	knife	knives	head	hand	hands
my	ílí ma-rɔ	ilíí ma-rɔ	drì má-rɔ	drí ma-rɔ	drí má-rɔ
your	mí-rɔ	mí-rɔ	drì mí-rɔ	mí-rɔ	mí-rɔ
his	{ ánya-rɔ { ndá-rɔ	{ ánya-rɔ { ndá-rɔ	{ drɪ ánya-rɔ { drɪ ndá-rɔ	{ ánya-rɔ { ndá-rɔ	{ ánya-rɔ { ndá-rɔ
his (own)	'ı-rɔ	'ı-rɔ			

---

[1] I have occasionally found instances in the Central languages where there is no postposition in evidence. Note also kàlà Morò = the language of the Moru.

THE GENITIVE CONSTRUCTIONS

	knives	heads	hands	chief
our	ilí àma-rɔ̀	drì àma-rɔ̀	drí àma-rɔ	ɔpí àma-rɔ̀
your	{ àmɪ-rɔ̀ { ìmɪ rɔ̀	{ àmɪ-rɔ̀ { ìmɪ rɔ̀	{ àmɪ-rɔ { ìmɪ-rɔ	{ àmɪ-rɔ̀ { ìmɪ-rɔ̀
their	{ àinya-rɔ̀ { ndàka-rɔ̀	{ ànya-rɔ { nda-rɔ	{ ànya-rɔ { nda-rɔ	{ àinya-rɔ̀ { ndàka-rɔ̀
their (own)	'ɛ-rɔ			

e.g. *nda pi kala e-ro go.* He opened his mouth.

Note reflexive sense:

lédr 'bä andívɔ 'ɪ-rɔ te.   The man shot himself (i.e. his body).
má andívo má-rɔ ɛdɛ.   I am dressing myself.
má lómvó má-rɔ̀ ɔ̀trì.   I'm undressing myself.

Note: after the interrogative pronouns the postposition is **ri-**

boŋgo ono adi-ri ya?   Whose are these clothes?

276. In MADI it is used especially to denote non-intimate genitive, and is used much in predicative constructions.

sí leà drì (an elephant's tooth; cf. Moru: *si liwa rɔ*).
adzu ɔpí drí 'è. It is the chief's spear.
*aɪ kaki amvu opi **dri** so.* They hoe the field of (or for) the chief (lit. they are field chief of sowing).

But note, however:

	My name	Your name	His name	
MADI	Lo.: rú má-drí'í Pa.: . . . má-dí	. . . nyi-dríì . . . nyi-dí	. . . na-dríì . . . na-dí	

	My mother	Your mother	His mother	The mother of a man
MADI	Lo.: iǎ ma-dri Pa.: . . . má-dî	. . . nyi-drî . . . nyí-dî	. . . 'di-drî . . . ná-dî	ái méndɛ̀ } mo'dí-le'dì

277. In LOGO the particle is **na** when referring to the 1st and 2nd person singular, **a'dia** when referring to the 3rd person singular (whether pronoun or noun), and **a** when referring to the plural—all persons.

*míri má-**na**.*   My chief.   *míri amáki-á('dí).*[1]   Our chief.
   „   *mí-**na**.*   Your „   „   *amíki-á('dí).*   Your „
   „   *agú'di **a'dia**.*   His (i.e. that man's) chief.   „   *'bá'diki-á('di).*   Their „

278. This form is found, too, when the possessive is used without an antecedent, i.e. pronominally.

Fa nidi mana; mina aŋgua ya?   This stick is mine; where is yours?
Mana yokodo; nidi adiadia.   Mine is missing; this is his.
Fa nii amakia; amikia (di) aŋgu ya?   These sticks are ours; where are yours?
Amakia(di) yokodo; mii aiikiadii.   Ours are missing; these are theirs.

279. In the Agambi dialect of LOGO the postposition is **-ka** throughout the singular and **a** throughout the plural. Thus:

		mine	yours	his	ours	yours	theirs
LOGO	(L.):	*mana*	*mina*	*adiadia*	*amakia*	*amikia*	*aikia*
	(A.):	*amaka*	*amika*	{ *adika* { *anyaka*	*amakia*	*amikia*	{ *adikia* { *anyakia*

---

[1] Pronounced *amákyá, amíkyá, 'bá'dikya.*

Compare AVUKAYA:

    mǎ di 'bú ámáka. I'm digging a hole for myself (lit. hole mine).

280. The genitive postposition in LOGO has sometimes an adjectival function:

dili Logo aḍia.	A Logo spear.
(Cf. Logo ni dili.	A Logo man's spear).
dri dru aḍia.	A buffalo head.
(Cf. dru ni dri.	A buffalo's head).

but not necessarily always:

Kokia adre fa ti aḍia nya.	The dog is eating a cow-bone.
Arugu kugu dre fa kokia aḍia.	The monkey stole the dog's bone.
Dílya mírì 'dia.	The chief's spear.
Drɪ má-na ('dì).	My head (alternative to ámä-drì)

Sometimes the **ni** linking particle is inserted.

ma-no waraga Kilima **ni** aḍɪa.	I see Kilima's paper.
(A.) ma-no waraga aḍi **ni** ka.	I see his paper.

281. Further examples from Southern and Central languages:

		My field	Your ...	His ...
MADI	Lo.:	ámvú má-**drí**-'ì	... nyí-drí'ì	... aní-drí'ì
	Pa.:	„ má-**dí**-'ì	... nyí-dí'ì	... andá-dì
LUGBARA:		ámvárí mâ-ni	... mí-ni	... ìrì-nɪ
KELIKO:		ámvúri má-vénì	... mí-véni	... ìrì-vénì

		Our field	Your ...	Their ...
MADI	Lo.:	... àma-drí'ì	... ànyi-drí'ì	... a'í-drí'ì
	Pa.:	... ama-dí-ì	... anyi-dí-ì	... ai-dí-ì
LUGBARA:		... àma-vɛni	... ìmi-vɛni	... koo-vɛni
KELIKO:		... àmà-veni	... mì-veni	... ko-vénì

	My bow	Your bow	His bow
LUGBARA:	úsu mâ-ni	úsu mí-ni	úsu 'bá'dà-ni
KELIKO:	„ má-vènì	„ mí-vènì	„ 'bá'dè'dɛ-veni
LOGO:	kɪsu má-na-'dì	kisu mí-na'dì	kisu 'bá'di-'bà'dì
AVUKAYA (Jg.):	úsu ámá-kà	úsu ámí-ka	úsu 'bádèdè-kà
			„ gúlà'dì-ka

	Our chief	Your chief	Their chief
LUGBARA:	mɔkɔtɔ ama-ní	... imi-ní	... 'bána'dià-ni
KELIKO:	... má-vɛnɛ	... mí-vɛnɛ	... 'bá'da'bé-vɛnè
LOGO:	... amáky-ɛ̀'dí	... amíky-ɛ̀'dí	... 'bá'diky-ɛ̀'di
AVUKAYA (Jg.):	... amá-ka-rɪ	... aní-ka-ri	... „

                      My dog

KELIKO:	otsógó má-nì or otsógó má-vérè
LOGO:	kɔkyé ámá-na ('di) or má-kɔkyé
AVUKAYA { Jg.:	ɔké ámá-ka-trá
Jl.:	ɔkyé má-ka-trá

282. It must not be supposed that every language has evolved hard-and-fast rules for the application of the various genitive constructions. The constructions are in many cases interchangeable, without involving any apparent change in meaning:

	Bird's head	Cow urine
MORU:	kitó drì, drì kitó rɔ	kʊdr tí rò
AVUKAYA:		tí odre, odré ití
LOGO:	arí drì, drı arí a'dia	ti kodriɛ, kodriɛ ti 'dia (or 'dɛ)
KELIKO:	arívǎ drì, drı arıva mà'de	kɔdrɛ tí mà'dɛ
LUGBARA:	aríé drì, drì aría ní	ʊdre tí nì

Cow liver

LUGBARA: ti ogo, ogo ti ni
KELIKO: ti ogo, ogo ti   (note absence of postposition)
LOGO: ti togo, togo ti.

Note, however:

	Chief's spear	A spear of the chief's (?)
MADI { Lo.:	ɔpı adzu or	adzú ɔpı drí'e
Pa.:		,, ,, di i
LUGBARA:	ópí àdʒu	adʒú opi nì

	The chief's son	It is a son of the chief
MADI { Lo.:	ópı ni (or a) bara	bara ɔpí dri i
Pa.:	ɔpı ni 'bora	'borá ɔpí di i

I am the son of a chief

LUGBARA: ma ópí à ŋgʊti.
KELIKO: ma ópi ni mvá.

283. When two genitives come together the tendency is to vary the constructions. Occasionally one of the particles is dropped:

	Spear of chief	Spear of my chief
LUGBARA:	ädzú ɔpi **ní**	ädzú ɔpí mà-**ni**
KELIKO:	,, mɔkɔtɔ	,, mɔkɔtɔ ma-**ní**

This is the cloth of my father

MORU (Ă.): 'dí boŋgo tǎpi ma-rɔ rɔ (note double postposition)
MADI (Pa.): 'di boŋgo má-ta 'dí i
LUGBARA: 'dırı má-tǎpi bɔŋgɔ ì (my father = má-tǎpì or tǎpi ma-nì)
KELIKO: 'di má-tǎpi à bɔŋgɔ ì

	Give my mother's cloth to me	My brother's goat died
MORU (Ă.):	na-azɔ bɔŋgó ndrúpi má-rɔ rò mä-ri	indri adrupi ma-ro ro dra-te
MADI { Lo.:	nyɛ́kwɛ bɔŋgó m-ɛ́ndrè **drí**'i madri	(Torit): *m-adrupi a endri odra-ra*
Pa.:	nyɛ́kɛ mání m-ɛ́ddɛ a bɔ̀ŋgɔ	(Opari): *endre m-adrupi **dri** odra-ra*
LUGBARA:	mífe (mani) m-andrip(i) a bɔ̀ŋgɔ	
KELIKO:	mífe mani m-andrìpi a bɔ̀ŋgɔ-rì	ma-adrepi a ndri dra-gi.

MORU (M.): *kokye uni toko đasi odrupi ma-ro ro ri dra-te* (note triple postposition). The black dog of the chief wife of my brother is dead.

284. Where the pronominal particle **na** is used as possessor, it always *follows* the thing possessed, whether the possession is intimate or not. See § 263.

MORU: *mano se mɪ-ndrɛ-bɛ lau, ädrupi-**na** dra-te.* The man you saw there, his brother is dead.

*toko-**na** dra-te.* His wife is dead.

MADI: *ru **na**[1]* (his body)   *ru **kina*** (their bodies)
*mi **na*** (his eyes)   *mi **kina*** (their eyes)
*endre **na*** (his mother)   *endre **kina*** (their mother)

alternative to:

endre ani dri   *endre aɪ dri*

CHAPTER IX

PREPOSITIONS AND POSTPOSITIONS

285. As said before, the majority of case relationships, which in English are shown by prepositions, are here shown by postpositions and suffixed particles. While it is impossible to state whether these were all once original words bound to their nouns in the manner of Sudanic genitives, there are several postpositions about whose fundamental meaning there can be no doubt. Where the form can be used as a noun, the near English noun-equivalent is given. For the sake of easy reference, the postpositions found in Moru-Madi languages will be listed alphabetically.

Since prepositions play a very small part in the Moru-Madi languages, they will be treated at the end of the chapter.

POSTPOSITIONS

286.   **'a** (AVUKAYA), *see* **ya**.

aku, ako.

287. This postposition corresponds roughly, in function, to the English preposition 'without'.

MORU: *ma-go-na tenye opi ondre **aku** ya?* Shall I just return without seeing the chief?

*anya gye ŋguti maro go tenye lakaza **aku**.* He just married my daughter without any dowry at all.

It is used largely to express the *negative* of possession (see § 741).

MADI: *opi boronzi **ako**.* The chief has no sons.
LOGO: *ma adre ŋganya **ako** ro.* I am without food.
MORU: *kiano, ledri Moru-ro boŋgo **aku**, oko yau-ono ndaka boŋgo be.* Long ago the Moru had no clothes, but now they have them.

288.   **alia** (LUGBARA), *see* **ya**.

---

[1] Or **ná-ru** (the only exception to be found).

bɛ

289. This postposition occurs in all the languages of this group except Madi (and Lulu'ba) (*see* **tro**), and corresponds in certain circumstances to English 'with' (accompanying).

I (lit. *we*) *go with my brother*
MORU: m-ɔi ädrúpí márɔ̀ **bɛ**
AVUKAYA: ma-ni ámȧ̈drúpì **bɛ**
LOGO: ma-ni-lyɛ́ mǎ-ádrípì **bɛ̀**
KELIKO: 'bǎ mu-lɛ má-ádrípì **bɛ̀**
LUGBARA: ama-mu-lɛ má-ádrípì **bɛ̀**

MORU (Ä.): má kɪlá-rɔ́ ndá **bɛ**. I am angry (lit. warlike) with him.
(M.): mí-'ba yɔ̀sɔ́ ku ányà **bɛ**. Don't hate him (lit. don't make bitterness with him).
má 'be drɪ tɛ ndâ **bɛ**. I met him.
Jl.: ma-isu ru-ní **bɛ**. I met you.
KELIKO: andziri utä ko'bá-àzi **bɛ̀**. The boys are quarrelling with each other.
LOGO: *mi-ali yi be*. Bring the water (lit. come with water).
ama-ate (adre) irinyi be. My father is strong (lit. remains with strength).
MADI: *azeni waraga-ga ma-be.*[1] Yesterday I was in school (lit. school-belly me with).

Note also in Moru:

ŋgäki be (last night)
meri be (last rainy season)

290. It also corresponds to 'and' when it joins nouns (not verbs). Here it is often assisted by the particles **-ɪ** (§ 192) and **-pi** (§ 167).

MORU: *Yakobo-i Yoane be.* James and John.
LUGBARA: *Yakobo-pi-e Yohana be.*
LOGO: *Yakobo-ɪ Yoane be.*

My mother and my brother have gone	*We saw a sheep and a goat*
MORU: ndrúpi márɔ ndí udrúpi márɔ (**bɛ**) ɔ̀ɪ-tɛ̀	*ma-ndre timele ndi indri be.*
KELIKO: mándrépi-ri mádrípí **bɛ** mùkí-gɪ	*ama-ndrɛ-ki kabilo ndri be.*
LUGBARA: mándrépi mádrúpi **bɛ** kó mùkí-'bo	
LOGO: *mi-zi Kaŋgi boi azina be.*	Call Kangi and the other boy.
MORU: *nyezi tiza asiro märi ndi gi be.*	Bring me firewood and water.

291. The postposition **bɛ** may also be used in predicative constructions showing possession. (Cf. verb 'to have' in English.) (See § 712.)

LOGO: *miri adre tie be.* The chief has cattle.
MORU: ma äzú **bɛ̀**. I have a spear (lit. I spear with).
Ayaŋwa (ɔrɪ-via) ŋgwa be ya? Has Ayangwa any sons?
má mànyèrù **bɛ**. I have scabies.
má dr(ì)-ù'bǎ **bɛ̀**. I have a headache.
má yá-lú **bɛ̀**. I have stomach-ache.

[1] Normally, Madi uses the particle **tro**.

The last three examples may also be rendered:

mànyèrù nya ma tɛ.	Scabies has eaten me.
drɪ márɔ ku'bu'bǎ.	My head aches.
ya márɔ lulu.	My stomach hurts.

Note the double use of **be** in the following:

My friend has a dog and a monkey
KELIKO: márózíì usógó **bɛ** uzí **bɛ**
LUGBARA: márózíì utsɔgɔ **bɛ** arógu **bɛ**
MORU (Ă.): bɛrâzí márɔ ɔ̀tsɛ lɔ̀re **bɛ**

Note that in MORU the postposition has a different function when attached to verbs (see § 643).

ŋgónya sé mà-nya **bɛ**. The food which we ate.

drɪ̀ (or drì) (= 'head')

292. This postposition, corresponding to 'on' in English, alternates with **ya** in some languages. The exact difference in meaning is hard to find.

MORU (M.): äzú márɔ 'dɛ-tɛ líti **drɪ̀**.	My spear fell into the road.
kɪlá'bá azi kɛkyi-te amǎ-**drɪ̀**.	The other warriors came against us.
tswé **dr.**	On the top of the tree.

A dream brought news of my father to me
MORU { M.: tɔri ɛzi ta tǎpi ro mǎ-**drɪ̀** (tɛ)
        { Ă., B.: órí lɔbɛ „   „   „
AVUKAYA: ɔva rɪ amata ka ani mǎ-**drɪ̀** (dra).

I know how to cook (lit. I know cooking its head indeed(?))
M., Ă., B., Ăg.: mǎ-ni là'dɪ **drɪ̀-nà** ndɪ (*or* te)
W., Jl.:   „   „   **drɪ̀-nà** (*or* lè) trá.

Compare:

	Sit down	*(He was made) chief over the people*
MORU:	(mí-rɪ̀ vù-**rʊ**)	(á'ba ndá te) ópí-ró lédrɪ **drɪ̀**
AVUKAYA:	ɔrɪ vù-**drɪ**	
MADI { Lo.:	nyi-ri vu-**dri**	ópí lakí **drɪ'ɪ̀**
{ Pa.:	rɪ vu-**di**	ópí lakí dí ì
LOGO:	mi-ko-liri vu-**dri**	ópí 'bádrɪ ɔ̀**drɪ**-nɪ̀
LUGBARA:	mi-ri va-**a**	
LULU'BA:	akɔ̀rɪ̀ vu-**a**	

Note also the genitive postposition **dri** in Madi (§ 274).

drí, ndrí, ní, rí

293. This postposition is easily confused with **drɪ̀** (= on) already discussed, and there is a certain amount of overlapping. It corresponds roughly to 'to', 'from', 'for' in English.

Give me something	*What did you buy for me?*
MORU { M.: nyózɔ ŋga mǎ-**rí**	M., K.: nyégé na-ɔ'dú mǎ-**ri**
{ Ă.: náza ŋgáza mä-**ndri**	'B.: nájɛ na-a'dí mǎ-**rí**
	Ă.: nádʒé na-ɔ'dí mǎ-**dŕ**
LULU'BA: ɪ-rɔpa má-**rí** ŋga (Pay me)	Ăg.: nádʒé na-a'dí mǎ-**drí**
	Jl.: ná'dɔ a'du-giá má-**drí**

PREPOSITIONS AND POSTPOSITIONS

Give me a book
LUGBARA: (m)í-fɛ má-**drí** buku
KELIKO: mí-kàfɛ ma-**dri** ,,
LOGO (A.): mí-afɛ ma-**drɛ** ,,

Note, in LOGO, ama-**drí** = for us, to us.
ama-**drì** = my head.

Further examples from MORU (Miza):

mí-ga bí mä-**ri**.	Listen to me (lit. you cut ear me for).
má-ga bí te ɔpí **rí**.	I listened to the chief.
ndá mù-te ni ìbì **ri**.	He ran away from the lion.
má-lɔsɛ òyɛ tăpi må-rɔ **ri**.	I'm working for my father.
nyézi må-**ri**.	Bring it to me.

294. It may be used in predicative constructions to show possession.

MORU: *parata ɔri-via mä-ri*. I have some money (money is present to me).
ŋgɔ-inya idu mä-ri. I have no food (food is absent to me).
MADI: *ma-dri endri 5 aa (be, ci)*. I have five goats.
opi dri boronzi iyo. The chief has no sons.

Note also this idiomatic use of **rí** with the infinitive form of verbs in MORU:

ɔnyá-ní må-**rí** i'du.	I shall not eat (it).
,, mí-**ri** ,,	You ,, ,,
,, ányä-**ri** ,,	He ,, ,,
(lit. eating to me is not)	
ɛmé-ní mí-**rí** i'du.	You shall not boil it.
ʊmʊ-nɪ ndä-**ri** i'du.	He cannot run.
ɔɪ-nɪ Maridi ya i'du mä-**ri**.	I can't go to Maridi.
ma-le ku Ayaŋwa ri wa omvu-nɪ.	I don't want Ayangwa to drink beer.

295. By means of a further locative postposition **ga**, the 'having' is extended beyond the individual to include his family, household, village, or even country.

MORU: *ɛpɛ ɔri-vɪa mɪ-rɪga?* Have you any honey (chez-vous)?
Matindi kyi-te täpi rige. Matindi has gone to his father's village.
anya go-go 'bäru i-rige. So he returned to his own home.
parata idu mä-rige. I have no money (chez moi).
LOGO: *ti yokoďo ama-drika*. I have no cow (lit. cow is absent chez moi).

Long ago there were no foreigners (English) in Madi country
MADI { Lo.: andé ɛzɛ, ma'di vù **dri** mundú yo.
     { Pa.: andánì ɛzê, vu **di-gé** 'diá ɪŋlísì yo.

296. In MADI the equivalent particle is usually **ni**, and this is to be found as an alternative to **dri** in Lugbara and Keliko.

Give me something   *Hoe the field for me*
MADI { Lo.: nyíkwe má-**ní** ta[1]   *nyiso ma-**ni** amvu*
     { Pa.: ɛkɛ ma-**ni** ŋga
LUGBARA: ífɛ má-**ní** ŋga
KELIKO: mífɛ má-**ní** ŋga

[1] Note, however, in Madi Lokai the occasional use of **dri**.

	They forgot the words	*I did not forget you*
MADI	Lo.: ledzó ɛgwè 'bà **ní** rá	nyɛ́gwè má-**ní** kʋrʋ̀
	Pa.: le'jó lɛgwè 'bà **ní** dì	nyélɛgwè má-**ní** kʋrʋ̀
	(lit. The word escaped from them.)	(You escaped from me not)

Bring me my mother's cloth

MADI	Lo.: nyɛ́kwe bɔŋgɔ́ méndrè drí'i mà-**dri**
	Pa.: nyɛ́kɛ má-**ní** mɛ́dde a bɔ̀ŋgɔ
LUGBARA	mífɛ ma-**ni** mandripi a bɔ̀ŋgɔ
KELIKO	mífɛ ma-**ni** mandripi a bɔ̀ŋgɔ rì

297. ga (MADI, LUGBARA), *see* ya.

lɛ

298. This postposition occurs mostly in compounds. It corresponds roughly to 'at', but its locality implication is indefinite.

LOGO:	adi 'ba **le**.	He is at the village.
MORU:	ma-ndre ini te täbi ze**le**.	I saw a snake under the basket.

I will return (back)   *Will you come back?*

LOGO:	ma gò àndʒɛ-**lɛ**.	LUGBARA:	m-ɛ́mu vu-**lɛ**?
KELIKO:	má ígò vu-**lɛ**.	KELIKO:	mí-mu vu-**lɛ**?
AVUKAYA:	má gò vu-**lɛ**.	MADI:	ny-ɛŋgwí vú-**lɛ́**?

Note also the use of **lɛ** as a suffix in certain nouns:

pagalɛ (sole), &c. Cf. § 188.

299. lomvu (MORU), *see* ro.

na (LOGO, LENDU)

300. This is the most common locative postposition in these two languages.

The chief will arrive at Aba to-morrow

LOGO:	opi dre cazo Aba **na** tudru
LENDU:	pi di kasi Aba **na** bu

	My father is in the field	*My mother is in the house*
LOGO:	ama-ata (adre) amvu **na**	ama andre adri jo **na**
LENDU:	aba ku nzagu **na**	zha ku adza (no particle here)

LOGO:	mi-ali bongo ji-le yi **na**.	Go and wash the clothes in the river.
LENDU:	rasu ku da **na**.	There is a crocodile in the river.

301. ni (MADI), *see* drí.

rɛ (MORU)

302. This postposition corresponds to English 'to' with the implication of 'towards' 'in the direction of'. It is to be differentiated from rí (corresponding to 'to' in other contexts).

nyézu ŋgaga ma-**rɛ**.	Send the boy to me.
(Cf. nyɛ́vɔ kwíní mä-**ri**.	Throw the stone to me.)
nyugu ke'bo ono Ayaɲwa **re**.	Take this hoe to Ayangwa.

303. rí (MORU), *see* drí = to.

ro, ru, lomvo, &c. (= 'body')

304. These forms, which in other contexts act as reflexive and reciprocal pronouns (see § 231), when used as postpositions, correspond to 'against' in English.

He told a lie against me
MORU: ndá gá kué té ma-**lomvu**
KELIKO: ire úlí úndzɔ má-**rù** gɪ

You told a lie against us
MADI ⎰ Lo.: nyídzo ɛ́ndzɔ ma-**trɔ̀**
      ⎱ Pa.: nyéli ɛ́ndzɔ máni-**rù** gɪ

MORU: kɛnjì ta te mi-**lomvu**. (He) broke conventions (lit. words) against you.
má-'ba yɔ̀sɔ́ ndá-**lúmvù** (or -bɛ). I hate him (lit. make bitter against him).
mi-'ba luku'du miro tiṛi **lomvo**. Put your pot by the wall.
muɖu zo ya indri **lomvo**. I sleep in the hut with the goats.
KELIKO: ŋga mǎ-**ru** gì. (It) flew towards me.
LUGBARA: ma-li mí-**ùmv-ɛlɛ** ga. I go to you.

si or sì or sè

305. This postposition corresponds to 'with' (instrument) or 'from' in English.

The . . . shoot game with a bow	*The Zande stab game with a spear*
MORU (Ä.): Mɔrú fu ezá úsu **sì**	Makaraká fu ezá äzú **sì**
AVUKAYA ⎰ Jl.: Adzila bu-íkä à'wa úsu **sì**	,, 'di-ikä ädʒú **sì**
⎱ Jg.: Odʒugu bu-ika'de à'wa úsu **sì**	,, 'di-ika'de ädʒú **sì**
KELIKO: Kelikó 'di zá úsu **sì**	,, 'di zá ädzú **sì**
LOGO: Logo 'bukɪ zwǎ kúsu **sì**	,, 'dikɪ 'dilya **sì**
LUGBARA: Lúgbàrà gbɪ ezá úsu **sì**	,, 'dikɪ ädʒú **sì**

LULU'BA: mɔ-dí mini dí **sì**. I hit you with (my) fist.
mɔú vwí **sì**. I'm crying with hunger.
mó-kyi awala **sì**. I stroll along (lit. I go with walking).

Take this knife to kill the hen with (it)
MORU: mí-ru ílí 'do, mí-lɔ tǎu **sɪ**-na. (Note: na following **sɪ**.)
MADI (Pa.): 'du ílí 'di'i, lì **sì** à'ú do.

He cut the tree with an axe	*They built the house of mud*
MORU: *anya ga ce go koloŋwa **si***	*anya mo-i zo go gini **si***
KELIKO: *ga tepi-ri ubolu **si***	*bi-ki jo-ri otretre **si***
MADI: *oga kwe tolu **si** ra*	*aɪ osi-ki zo oto **si** ra*

Note also:
MORU: áfu gárà te dɔ́fɔ́ **sè**. The bowl is smashed with a stick.
ɛ́ndzwì bɔ̀ŋgó te àsɪ **sì** . . . mí-**sì**. The cloth is spoilt by fire . . . by you.
tu se kai si opi dra-go. In those days the chief died.
M.: nyá-áta ɛ́ŋunye kala Mɔrú **si** yà? How do you say that in Moru?
nya-ta kala Miza **si**. Speak Miza.
K.: má-ta ka Kädíru **si**. I speak (Moru) Kediru.

306. In most languages (but not in Madi), when **si** denotes separation, i.e. corresponds to 'from' in English, it is usually combined with other particles.

MORU: ópí pa ŋgútí tɛ **nì** udrú **sí** (or **rí**). The chief saved the girl from the buffalo.

MORU: *ŋguti ḍa-go ce* **dri-si**. The girl fell from the tree.
m-ego-na Tali ya-si ondo. I shall return from Tali to-morrow.
atá mírò dzʷè-te mǎ-**drɪ-sì**. I forgot your words (lit. words your escaped me-from).

LOGO: *mi-do waraga vu*-**dri-sɪ**. Take the paper off the ground.
(A.): *tai vi ma-se dre.*⎫ I forgot it.
    tai ja ma-se da.⎭

LUGBARA: *ma-ri ouri-si ópí sì.*⎫ I am afraid of the chief.
KELIKO: *má-dri ŋgáro mírì* **si**.⎭

	They forgot the words	I have not forgotten you
MADI { Lo.:	bá ɛgwè ledzó **sɪ** dì	m-ɛ́gwe nyí-**sɪ** kừrừ
Pa.:	'bá lɛgwè le'jó **sɪ** dì	mé-lɛgwe nyí-**sɪ** kừrừ

307. Many adverbs are built up with the help of this particle.

MORU: *ŋgäkisi* (by night); *emba ono si* (this month); *kitusi* (by day).
ŋgäki ono si (to-night); *emba azi si* (next month).
kandra si (from in front); *biɼisi* (from beside).
nosi (this side); *tasi* (across).

LOGO: *ŋgacisɪ* (by night)   *kitusɪ* (by day)
nolesɪ (from here)   *dalesɪ* (from there)
aḍosɪ ya (why?)   *ḍisɪ* (because)

MADI: *eniagasi* (by night)   *etuatsi* (by day)
drusi (to-morrow)   *oḍósì* (why?)

ti (= mouth) LOGO; **tia, tinia,** LUGBARA; **tisi** MADI

308. This postposition is most common in LUGBARA, where it corresponds to **ri, dri, si, laga, lomvo,** and many others in other languages.

Ask of me whatsoever thou wilt (Mk. vi. 22)
LOGO: *Mi-ko-zi aḍo ŋga ya mi-dre-le-le-ḍi ma-ti*
LUGBARA: *Mi-zi ma-tia afa mi ni le-le-ri*

And he began again (people) to teach by the sea side (Mk. iv. 1)
LUGBARA: *Dika eri 'ba 'ba imba miri tia*
MADI (Pa.): *Ani kedo bini-ka meri tisi*

And he asked him (Mk. v. 9)
LUGBARA: *Eri ŋga zi tinia*
LOGO: *Dre ta lizi-zo akoḍi ti*

LUGBARA: *Eri ŋga yo yi-tia.* (Mk. vii. 9.) And he said unto them.
ŋga yo 'ba eri-ni ma-tia. (Mk. x. 23.) And saith unto his disciples.
Dika eri ŋga fo Turu matia. (Mk. vii. 31.) And he departed from (the coasts of) Tyre.

trɔ, tɔ (MADI)

309. This postposition in MADI is equivalent to **be** in the other languages, and corresponds to 'with' (accompanying) in English. Here it is usually assisted by the particle **-pi** (§ 167) or a plural pronoun.

m-endre aɪ madrupi tro omu-ki-pi. My mother and my brother have gone.
ny-amvoti-pi amvoti ma-dri tro. Your sister and my sister.
ama-ndre bilo-pi endri tro. We saw a sheep and a goat.

PREPOSITIONS AND POSTPOSITIONS

I (lit. *we*) *go with Zira*	*The boys are quarrelling with each other*
Lo.: amá-vu Zíra **trɔ**	bɔrɔnzi kúzá bá àzí **trɔ**
Pa.: mà-vɔ́ Zíra **tɔ**	'bɔnzi kudʒwa bá àzi **tɔ**

My mother and my brother have gone
Lo.: mɛ́ndrɛpí madrúpi **trɔ̀** ɔvɔkí-pí
Pa.: mɛ́ndɛpí mádúzi **tɔ̀** vɔ̀-pí

My friend has a dog and a monkey
Lo.: márɔ́zfı̀ ni ɔ̀tsɛ lɔ̀rɛ **trɔ̀**
Pa.: márɔ́zfı̀ ni ɔ̀kɛ dʒɔ̀mi **tɔ**

This particle occasionally occurs in Moru in conjunction with **be** in plural constructions:

MORU: *mi-ki **trɔ** ama be.* Go together with us.

310. The postposition **trɔ** may also be used (in MADI) in predicative constructions showing possession (cf. verb 'to have' in English).

MADI: *nyi boronzi isu **tro**.* You have four boys (lit. You boys four with).
*opi lenya **tro**.* The chief has food.

vu (= 'ground')

311. This postposition, which is usually amplified by others, implies residence in a given place, and thus corresponds sometimes to 'at' in English.

LOGO: *mi-kali ma-**vu**-la.* Come to me (on a visit).
*mi-ko-tai ta-konji **vu**-le-se.* Leave sin (lit. leave word-bad-place-from).

Come to me here (where I am)	*I go to you*
AVUKAYA { Jl.: ná-ni má-ŋgá nòlè	má-ni ni-**vóla**
{ Jg.: ná-ni má-**vólɛ** nòlè	má-ni mi-**vóla**
LOGO: mí-kàlì ma-**volɛ** nòlè	má-li mi-**vólè**
LUGBARA: mí-mú ma-**vɔ**	ma-mɪli mi-**vólɛ**-'dì

MORU: *anya ekyi-go ma-**vo**.* He came after me.
*udu maro **vo**-si, ma-le lazanɪ.* After my sleep I want to wash.

And his disciples follow him (Mk. vi. 1)
MORU: *Ago taeri'bai ndaro deindi nda-**vo***
LOGO: *'Dia ai tayilepïdii dreki-lizo adi-**vuse***
LUGBARA: *'Ba eri-ni ŋga-mu eri-**vutia***

yá, ǵa, 'a, alia (= belly)

312. These forms are the most common locative postpositions in Moru-Madi. In the MORU dialects the form is **ya**.

MORU: mí-sá-na itú Marıdi **yá** yà?	When will you arrive at Maridi?
má-'ba enyá te lakáza **yá**.	I put the food into the pot.
ánya 'bi ma te drì **ya**.	He hit me on the head.
ndá ɔi ku lòsè **ya**.	He has not gone to work.
má-'dɛ ndí líti **ya**.	I took to the road (lit. I fell the road in).
agé ndá tɛ Mòndarì **ya**.	She married a Mondari (lit. was-married she Mondari in).
M.: m-ɔ́i ɔ'déni gyi **ya**.	I'm going to dive in the water.
L.: m-úikyí ɔ'déni gyi **ya**.	
Ä., 'B.: ma-rɔ-ɔi ɔ'délé dʒi **ya**.	

313. In the Central languages the form is 'a, and in the Southern languages ga. Occasional alternatives in ge are also to be heard, and Lugbara has an alternative form in alia.

AVUKAYA:	máni á'dɛlɛ lumvá ấ.	I shall dive in the water.
LULU'BA:	mo'dí àká 'jo 'a.	The man is in the house.
MADI:	búk ɔlú sandúk'a. } buk sanduk aga. }	The book is in the box.
	m-emu lenya ga.	I've come to dinner.

Other examples:

The chief will arrive at Yei to-morrow   *Against me* (lit. *my body in*)

LUGBARA: mɔkɔtɔ atsa Yei ga drùsì   má-ru gá
KELIKO: mɔkɔtɔ ítsá Yei ge drù   má-ru gá
AVUKAYA { Jl.: mɔkɔtɔ atsa Yei á
           { Jg.: mɔkɔtɔ netsa Yei a
LOGO: mɔkɔtɔ anétsá Yei 'a kıdru[1]

The warriors came against me   *He has not gone to work*

MADI { Lo.: ɔ'já'bá kɛvu má-ru gá   ani omu ɛ̀bù gá ku
     { Pa.: ɔ'já'ba ɛvɔ má-ni-ru gé   ándá mu i'bu gɛ ku

He hit me on the head   *The thing is forgotten in my heart*

MADI { Lo.: òmba ma drì ga   tà ɛ́gwɛ̀ má-así gä dì
     { Pa.: mbá ma dì ge   ŋgá lɛgwè má-ni-así gí dì

Yesterday I was in the school   *Put salt in the food*

MADI: azeni ma-be waraga ga   nyi-'ba ai lenya ga
LUG. and KEL.: áze mà skul gä.   mi-'ba azi tibi aga

LUGBARA: yi ye de yi alia. (Lk. v. 7.) They began to sink in the sea.
           yi efo oguru alia. (Lk. v. 2.) They came out of the boat.

314. Postpositions are often preceded by the linking particles. (See § 269.)

LUGBARA: yi-agi ovupi oguru azini **ma alia** ri. (Lk. v. 7.) Their partners who were in the other ship.
           mi-fi yi aliro **ma alia**. (Lk. v. 4.) Launch out into the deep (water).
MADI: ori kwe (**a**) zele. He sat under a tree.
      omba ma (**n**-)andraga. He stood beside me.

Compound Postpositions

315. As may be expected, shades of meaning may be expressed by combining postpositions with each other or with other particles. The following selection should be illustrative:

MORU (Ä.): náṛi má-**laga**	Come towards me.
LOGO: ŋga má-**laga**	It flew towards me.
LUGBARA: ,, má-ndɪ-**gá-sì**	,, ,, ,,
LOGO: ma-liri anyi mesa **laga**.	I sit beside the table.
mi-da yi **lana**.	Pour water into it.
MORU: mí-ru èza ku **nì** kòkyɛ **rɪgɪ**.	Don't take the meat away from the dog.
ázu ndá te Ndaragù **rɪgɪ**.	He was sent to Ndarago's place.
(Cf. ,, ,, **rɛ**.	He was sent to Ndarago.)
ny-olofo taro kiro **zelesi**.	Take out the hive from under the granary.

[1] Note in Logo the form **na** is usually preferred (§ 300).

PREPOSITIONS AND POSTPOSITIONS 175

316. The foregoing list of postpositions must not be regarded as complete. Only the most widespread and representative examples have been given. In the following table, arranged alphabetically according to their English equivalents, are all the postpositions in the main languages which have been discovered up to date.

	LOGO	MADI	MORU	LUGBARA
above	drile			
across			tasi	
after	vuse			vutinia
against	ru, ro		rɔ, lomvu	be
alongside			biɾi	tia
among		agaga	lako	le
at	vu		via, vɔya	
at	lɛ			ria
at the door of			kala, tisi	
„ foot of			pa	
because of	dise			risi
before	kandra	andraga	kandra	milia
behind	tugu	oguga	kundu	vutinia
beneath		zelega	zɛlɛ	ŋgokoa
beside	laga	mara(ka)ga	laga, rige	
between	kofula	lofoaga	kɪtɔreya	eselia
by	se	sɪ̀	sɪ̀	bi, si
for	te			vu, rusi, vurisi
from	vulese, ase	sɪ	dri-si	rua
in	'a, na, lena	'a, ga	ya	'a, na, alia
in (rest)	ledi	iledi (= 'voila'!)		
into	lana			a
on	drì, mi	drɪ̀	drɪ̀	rua
on this side of			nosi	
outside			teze	liarisi, ruania
over	drise			
to	drí, se	ni	rí	tinia, dri, tia
towards	vule		rɛ	vu
with	bɛ	trɔ	bɛ	be
with (instrument)	se, asa	sɪ̀	sɪ̀	si
without	ako	ako	akɔ, akʊ	

PREPOSITIONS

317. There are very few prepositions in Moru-Madi, and these usually work in conjunction with certain postpositions. The most common in MORU is **ni**, corresponding to English 'from', 'with', 'in'.

Combined with **si** or **ri**:

MORU: má-pá ndá te **ni** ìbì **ri** (or **si**). I saved him from the lion.
ndá mù te **ni** ìbì **si** (or **ri**). He ran away from the lion.
ópí pa ŋgútí tè **nì** ùdrú **sí** (or **rì**). The chief saved the girl from the buffalo.
má-rú-na äzú mìrɔ 'da **nì** mi-rɪgɪ. I shall take your spear away from you.

MORU: *ŋgaga turi turi ni udru ri.*   The boy is afraid of the buffalo.
      mui dra-te ni tăbiri ri.   The hyena died of hunger.
      waraga esa-te mare ni mi-re.   A letter reached me from you.
      mbara-na para { *ni mi-ri.* / *mi-drisi.* }   His strength is greater than yours.

Combined with **ya**:

MORU: *ndi anya efui-go taasi ni lukuău ya.*   And they came out from the pot.
      mekyi ni Maridi ya.   I come from Maridi.

Combined with **dri** or **ru**:

MORU: *iri mı-ro (kado) para ni ɔno drisi.*   Your knife is better than this one.
    (Knife your good excelling from this)
LOGO: *amba jo ni maligu mina-ăi ru se.*   This house is bigger than yours.
    (Excels house in big yours it)

Note, however, in LOGO:

    Kiju lasua amba ni.   The white ant's bite is more serious.
    amba lăti angodi mvu ni ya?   Which path is further?

Combined with **via** (see § 576):

MORU: *nda turi turi nì ɩ́kyɩ́-vìa.*   He is afraid to come.
      ɔ́pí pa ndá te nì àsí rɪ ɔ̀za-vìa.   The chief saved him from being burned by the fire.
      anya ŋga-go ni uău-via.   He got up from his sleep.

Note also the 'linking particle' **ni** in the genitive construction (§ 271). This construction, however, is foreign to Moru.

Other prepositions are:

318.   **Kitore** (MORU) = amidst

    iri maro ăa-te kitore kuni roya.   My knife has fallen among the rocks.
    'ba Matindi ro kitore 'ba Jebule ro 'ba Jamuni be.   Matindi's village (is) between Jebule's and Jamuni's villages.

         le (MORU) = as far as

319. *ugu nda te twa le Juba ya.*   He was taken away as far as Juba.
      anya ri-te noŋa mada le meri si.   He stayed here until the dry season.

         loto (MORU) = near

320. *musu lă'bi te loto golo ti.*   I found a water-buck near the river.
      musu gi te loto golo ya.   I found water near by in the river.

         oso (MORU) = like

321. *mi-na oso lei ronye.*   Her eyes are like milk (Moru flattery).

         anyi (LOGO) = beside

322. *ma-liri anyi mesa laga.*   I sit beside the table.

         tana (MORU) = because of

323. *nda ye losi te tana ma.*   He did work for me.

CHAPTER X

VERB CLASSES

324. Moru-Madi verb stems have the same forms as the noun stems. There are three main forms of verb stem, and verbs may be divided into three classes according to their form, each verb class being conjugated in a distinctive manner. The clue to verb class may be found in the Imperative Singular.

325. Class I verbs are monosyllabic verbs which normally have no 'characteristic' vowel prefix. (Rules for the appearance of this prefix will be given later (§ 437).)

e.g. MORU: mí-**mu**. Run!
mí-**mvu** gyǐ. Drink water!
mí-**nya** èza. Eat meat!
MADI: nyi-**mû**. Go!
nyi-**mvú** eỉ. Drink water!
nyi-**dze** rú. Wash yourself!
LOGO: mí-kò-**li**. Go!
mí-kò-**nya**. Eat it!
mí-**se** bá. Pull the rope! (away).
LUGBARA: í-**mù**. Go!
í-**mvù** yi. Drink water!
mí-**dʒi** mí-ru'ba. Wash yourself!

326. Class II verbs are dissyllabic verbs of the pattern *vowel plus consonant plus vowel*, the first vowel of which is 'characteristic'.

MORU: ny-ɛ'**bɛ**. Stop!
ny-í**mu**. Run! (towards me).
MADI: ny-ɛ**bɛ**. Stop!
ny-ɛ**mú**. Come!
ny-ɛkɛ mání ta. Give me something!
LOGO: mí-à**li**. Come!
ny-asɪ eba. Pull the rope! (towards me).
LUGBARA: m-ɛ'**bɛ**. Stop!
mɪ-ɪ**mu**. Come!

327. Class III verbs are dissyllabic verbs of the pattern *consonant plus vowel plus consonant plus vowel*, the initial consonant (and sometimes the whole initial syllable) being here regarded as a stem prefix. For conjugation purposes these verbs may be grouped with Class II verbs.

MORU: nyá-**la'di** èza. Cook meat!
nyó-**lɔsɛ** bòŋgɔ. Sew the cloth!
MADI: *anyi-ko'du diadro*. Sleep on!
LOGO: mí-ka-**la'di** zà. Cook meat!
mí-**tà'bu** tì. Shut your mouth!

328. On the whole class correspondence in cognate verbs is fairly high throughout the Moru-Madi dialects, but it is by no means a general rule. Note the following:

The goat is lost = indrí **dzʷe**-te. Moru. Class I
indrí **ègwè**-di. Madi (Lo.). Class II
indí **lɛgwɛ**-di. Madi (Pa.). Class III

To cook	= **la'di** in Moru and Logo.	Class III
	'di in Madi and Lugbara.	Class I
To travel	= **tʃi** or **etʃi** in Lugbara.	Class I or Class II
	tetʃi in Logo.	Class III
To steal	= **oġu** or **uġu** in the South and Central languages.	Class II
	kuġu in the Moru dialects.	Class III

Verb Prefixes

329. Verb prefixes differ from noun prefixes in that they may often be attached to originally simple verb stems within a given language. When thus attached they have semantic and grammatical function.[1]

e.g. MORU: ópí **sa**-te Amádi yá. The chief arrived at Amadi (implying that the chief is travelling away from us). *Class I.*

ópí **esá**-te Amádi yá. The chief arrived at Amadi (implying that the chief is travelling towards us). *Class II.*

LOGO: ma-**si**-dre boŋgo. I tore the cloth (implying that there is only one tear). *Class I.*

ma-**lasi**-dre boŋgo. I tore the cloth (implying that there are many tears). *Class III.*

These prefixes will be discussed in greater detail in Chapter XIII.

Verb Suffixes

Many of the verb suffixes are identical in form with the noun suffixes mentioned in Chapter V.

-a

330. Some verbs in LOGO have a suffix -a, before which a final front vowel will alternate with **y** and a final back vowel will alternate with **w**.

lo or lwà (to cut)   si or sya (to sneeze)
tsɔ or tswa (to hit)   lasí or lasíá (to tear)

k and ġ before a front vowel are usually palatalized in such words.

gi or gyɛ[2] (to buy)

The following are the only examples found in the MORU and MADI dialects, and they are doubtful:

	MORU	MADI
To shoot	'bwä	bwi cf. 'bu in Logo.
„ wash	dzwá	dze cf. dzu in Moru (K.), dʒi in Logo.
„ sneeze	sì	tso cf. otʃwa in Lulu'ba.

-I MORU, -KI MADI, LUGBARA, LOGO, &c.

331. The plural suffix and its application to verbs has already been discussed in Chapter V. e.g.:

MORU: lɔré nya-**í** mɔndú.   The baboons ate the sweet potatoes.
LOGO: aii ri-**ki** ŋgakisia ko. They do not sow seed.
LUGBARA: ama-mú-**kí**-'bo.   We went.
MADI: aɪ epa-**ki** limi ani-dri. They seized his belongings.

---

[1] Verb prefixes, therefore, fall under the category of 'Morphological and semantic affixes' as against 'Stem affixes' discussed in the Introduction, § 432.

[2] -a alternates with -ɛ after y.

VERB CLASSES 179

-pi *Central languages*

332. In the Central languages this suffix has a 'relative' function. (See § 653.)

LOGO: *ago dre-le-**pi**-ḋi.* The man who died.
KELIKO: 'ba kemirú 'dí-í-**pi**-ri. ⎫
LUGBARA: 'ba òbì 'di-lé-**pi**-ri. ⎭ The man who killed the lion.

-nɪ, -lɛ, -rɛ, -ka, -ŋga

333. These suffixes are, from the grammatical point of view, best classed as 'infinitive' suffixes. (See §§ 530 et seq.)

MORU: má-lɛ́ ku ɔ̀dra-**nɪ**. ⎫
AVUKAYA: má-lɛ drà-**lɛ** kù. ⎭ I don't want to die.

MADI: má-mu 'bá ndrɛ-**rɛ**. ⎫
LUGBARA: má-mu 'bá ndɛ-**lɛ**. ⎭ I go to see the people.

MADI: á-nì la-**ka** na kʊ. ⎫
LUGBARA: má-ni là-**ŋga**-ra ku. ⎭ I don't know (how) to read it.

-ra'a LOGO; -ria LUGBARA; -via, -vɔya MORU

334. These suffixes are, from the grammatical point of view, best classed as 'participial' suffixes. (See §§ 574 et seq.)

MORU: *má-ndrɛ ndá tɛ ù'du-**via**.* I saw him sleeping.
LOGO: *ma-dre ŋga nya-**ra'a**.* I remain (food) eating.
LUGBARA: *yini emba be-**ria** miri alia.* Casting nets into the sea (lit. they nets casting sea in).

-za, -zo, -zu

335. These suffixes usually indicate the purpose for which anything stands. (See §§ 563 et seq.)

MORU: *kodra zo omu-**za**.* Bamboos for house building.
LOGO: *yi saani ji-**zo**.* Water for washing plates.
MADI: *pa aci-**zo**.* Legs for washing.
LUGBARA: *pari 'bani usuru obe-**zu**.* Place for receiving people's taxes.

All these suffixes will be discussed more fully in Chapter XV.

336. From the foregoing it is evident that the stems of Moru-Madi verbs cannot always be formally distinguished from noun stems. Compare the following nouns with the verb forms just discussed:

LOGO: zɔ or zwa (hut)
MORU: írí pl. irí-ì (knife)
LUGBARA: 'bá pl. 'bá-kɪ (person)
MORU: täpi (father)
MORU: *eki-**ni** 'bäru ni kadu para.* ⎫
MADI: *eŋgwi-**ka** zo-ga cwi.* ⎭ Coming home is pleasant.
LOGO: *azi o-leḋ-i adre tani.* Working is good.
AVUKAYA: ugú-**lɛ́** ⎫
LUGBARA: ògu-**rɛ** ⎭ (back) (cf. ugú in MORU).
LOGO: *ŋga-laḋi-**ra*** (kitchen) (cooking place).
MORU: bɔŋgó lɔsɛ-**zɔ** ⎫
LOGO: bɔŋgwá lasɛ-**za** ⎭ (needle) (cloth sewer).

One is justified, however, in classifying these neutral forms under 'nouns' and 'verbs', because in the context, what are here termed 'verbs'—even in their simplest forms—are clearly distinguished, by positional and syntactical relations, from what are here termed 'nouns'.[1]

337. Verbal constructions may be of the following kinds:

(a) Verb root—contextually defined.
   MORU: má **dra.** I die.   LOGO: *ma si boŋgo.* I tear the cloth.

(b) Particle+verb root—the particle may or may not be a prefix.
   MORU: má **ɔdra.** I am dying.   LOGO: *ma lasi boŋgo.* I rend the cloth.

(c) (a) or (b)+particle—the particle may or may not be a suffix.
   MORU: ópí **drà-te.** The chief is dead.   LOGO: *akoǎi li-dre yi mvu-zo.* He has gone to drink water.

(d) Auxiliary verb (which itself may have pattern *a*, *b*, or *c*)+verb stem, with or without particles.
   LOGO: *ma adre teci-le.* I am walking.

CHAPTER XI

VERB CONJUGATION

ASPECT

338. In dealing with Moru-Madi verbs one must banish the narrow 'tense', or rather 'time', conception which governs European verb conjugation. When precise time is to be indicated in a statement (like 'yesterday' or 'to-morrow' or 'long ago') the appropriate adverb is used.

339. The most important feature in Moru-Madi verb conjugation is *Aspect*. There are two aspects, and the position of the verb-forms in the word order of the sentence is indicative of the aspect of the action described by the verb. Thus:

1. Word order = Subject+verb+object: the verb action is *complete*, *momentary*, '*perfect*', DEFINITE.
2. Word order = Subject+object+verb: the verb action is *incomplete*, *progressive*, '*imperfect*', INDEFINITE.[2]

340. Aspect may also be indicated on occasions by specific forms of the verb stem, these forms varying from language to language. Thus in MORU Class I verbs have a characteristic vowel in the Indefinite conjugation but none in the Definite conjugation, while in MADI Class I verbs have a characteristic vowel in the 3rd person in the Definite tenses, but not in the Indefinite tenses (except when there is no object).

341. The preceding and following particles, &c., often indicate 'time' in a general sense, but usually emphasize or enlarge upon the above two fundamental aspects,

---

[1] To take a simple example from English, the neutral forms *beat*, *beats*, may be classified as 'noun' or 'verb' forms, but solely according to their positional and syntactical relations.

[2] These conclusions were arrived at independently by Miss Mozley (for Logo) and myself (for Moru and Madi).

VERB CONJUGATION

or else indicate purely relative or dependent action. There are no 'moods' as understood by European grammar (but see § 342).

Note the following 'times' expressed in the Definite Aspect in LOGO (from Miss Mozley):

adi ali ama no agia.	He came to see me yesterday.
adi ali ama no andru.	He came to see me to-day.
adi ali ama no udru.	He will come to see me to-morrow.

342. Under each aspect are found various forms of conjugation which correspond in function to some of our tenses and moods. In the following paradigms, therefore, the tense signatures 'present', 'past', and 'future', and the mood terms 'imperative', 'dependent', 'subjunctive', &c., will be used, to save the coining of new terms— but the English labels should not be taken too literally. The paradigms are taken from Moru (Miza), Madi (Lokai), Logo, and Lugbara, as being most representative of the Moru-Madi languages. Only the principal conjugational particles will be given below, so as not to overload the tables. A full discussion of all the known particles is to follow in a separate chapter.

343. The transitive conjugation with an expressed object shows best the characteristics of the two aspects. Where there is no expressed object, the word order often fails as a criterion, while sound assimilation between verb stem and particle tends to blur the pattern. The intransitive conjugation will therefore follow the transitive in each case.

Moru (Miza)

TRANSITIVE CONJUGATION

DEFINITE ASPECT. *Formal characteristics.*

344. Word order = Subject+verb+object.

Class I verbs have no 'characteristic' vowel (except in 3rd person future and subjunctive).

Vowels of pronouns elided before Class II verbs, and 'harmonized' before Class III verbs.

2nd person pronoun prefix is **mɪ** (Class I verbs), **ny(a)** (Class II and III verbs). Plural suffix **-ɪ** may follow verb stem in 3rd person.

No auxiliary particle for 3rd person (except in 3rd person subjunctive).

Many postpositions.

Negative expressed by postposition **ku**.

345. *General form* (Present or past time or no time expressed).

Class I.	má-zi ŋgàgà.	I called the boys, or I call ...
	mí-zi ,,	You ,, ,, You call ...
	ányä zi ,,	He ,, ,, He calls ...
	mà-zi ,,	We ,, ,, We call ...
	mì-zi ,,	You ,, ,, You call ...
	ànyä zi ,,	They ,, ,, They call ...
Class II.	m-ɛ́mɛ gìi.	I heated the water, or I heat ...
	ny-ɛ́mɛ ,,	You ,, ,, You heat ..
	ány-ɛmɛ ,,	He ,, ,, He heats ...
	m-èmɛ ,,	We ,, ,, We heat ...
	ny-èmɛ ,,	You ,, ,, You heat ...
	àny-ɛmɛ ,,	They ,, ,, They heat ...

Class III.
má-kanda tsʷɛ.	I shook the tree, or I shake ...
nyá-kanda ,,	You ,,	,,	You shake ...
ánya kanda ,,	He ,,	,,	He shakes ...
mà-kanda ,,	We ,,	,,	We shake ...
nyà-kanda ,,	You ,,	,,	You shake ...
ànya kanda ,,	They ,,	,,	They shake ...

Note 'harmonizing' in **mɔ́**-lɔgɔ ku. I didn't give it back. **mí**-lifu te. I am broken, &c., &c. (See § 23.)

346. *General form with postpositions.*

mǎ-**zi** ŋgàgà **te.**	I (have) called the boys.
mǎ-**zi** ŋgàgà **ku.**	I didn't call the boys.
ópí **pa** ma **tɛ.**	The chief helped me.
Mókó sɔ̀ ŋgà **ku-te.**	Moko did not hoe anything.
mí-sì ndá **'da yà?**	Did you bite him?

Note also occasional plural suffix to verb stem:

ànya **zi-i** mi aḋi ya?	What do they call you?
ànya **so-i** ämvu go opi ri.	They hoed the farm for the chief.
ànya **mo-i** zo go gini si.	They built the house of mud.

347. *Future form.* (Note characteristic vowel in 3rd person of Class I verbs.) Optional suffix: **(n)a**. Optional postposition: **'da** (sometimes **ndi**). No negative form.

Class I verbs.

mǎ-**zí-na** ŋgàgà **'da.**	I shall call the boys.
má-**yɛ́-na** lɔsi **'da.**	I shall do the work.
ma-**'bi** mı **andi.**	I shall certainly beat you.
mí-**ndrɛ-na** àma ɔndɔ.	You'll see us to-morrow.
mí-**sá-na** itù yà?	When will you arrive (there)?
mí-**gɛ́-na** ɔ̀'du yà?	What will you sell?
ánya əpá ma **'dǎ.**	He will help me.
ópí ə**'bí-(n)a** mí **'dá.**	The chief will beat you.
Makaraká **úfú-na** àma **ndi.**	The Azande will kill us.

Class II verbs.

m-**ozo-na** indri Hakimo ri ondo.	I'll give a goat to Hakimo to-morrow.
m-ɛ́**'bé-na** Lúì ('da) ɔndɔ.	I shall leave Lui to-morrow.
ny-**ɛ́gɛ́-na** ɔ'du yà?	What will you buy?

(Owing to lack of material, intransitive verbs are used here.)

ány-**u'dù-a-'dǎ.**	He will sleep.
ndá ɛ̀kɛ̀ y-**ékyí-a-'da.**	He says he will come.
anyá ɛ̀kɛ̀ y-**ekyí-a-'dǎ.**	They say they will come.

Class III verbs.

má-**la'dí-na** tɔ́rɔ́mɔ́ **'dá.**	I shall cook maize.
toko **kidi-na** toromo ḋa ondo.	The women will plant maize to-morrow.

Note that the negative of the general form is used to indicate negative future time:

mǎ-**mvú ku.**	I shall not drink it, or I did not drink it.
m-**oi ku** Maridi ya ondɔ́.	I shall not go to Maridi to-morrow.

VERB CONJUGATION

348. *Subjunctive form.* (Note 3rd person auxiliary particle: **ka** or **k**+characteristic vowel in Class I, **k-** in Class II, **ka-** in Class III.)
 Negative postposition: **ku**.
 Subjunctive postposition: **rə**.
 Class I.
   mí-'dɛ ma-**sə** vɔ̀.   Let's hoe the place.
   ma-**nya** eza ku.   I am not to eat meat.
   mi-**nya** eza ku.   You are not to eat meat.
   ma-ta-te ndä-ri, ndá **k-ɔ̀yɛ** ta ku ínyɛ.   I told him he must not do so.
   mí-'ba ánya **k-ɔ̀sɔ̀** gìnɪ.   Let him hoe the ground.
   mí-'ba ndá **k-ɔ̀nya** ku.   Don't let him eat it.
 With reduplication:
   mí-'ba ndá **k-ənyá** ɔnyà.   Make him eat.
 With postposition:
   ny-ékyi nòa, má-**ndrɛ̀** mì rə.   Come here that I may see you.
 Class II.
   m-iti.   Let us tell.
   m-ɛ́zi.   I must bring it.
   ndá ɛkɛ ny-ɔ́zɔ̀ i-ri.   He says you must give it to him.
   ánya **k-iti**. Let him tell.   anya **k-iti**. Let them tell.
   ányá **k-ɛzi**. He must bring it.
   ányá **k-ɛzi** ku. He must not bring it.
  Class III.   mä-**mätù** Lùú.   Let us pray to God.

349. *Imperative form.* (Identical with 2nd person of Subjunctive, and also with 2nd person of General form.)
   Class I.   mí-**zi** ŋgàgà, pl. mì-zi ŋgàgà.   Call the boys.
                mí-**yɛ** lɔsì ku.   Don't do the work.
 With reduplication:
                mí-'**bɪ** ɔ'bɪ.   Beat him.
 Class II.   ny-**émbɛ́** ɛba.   Tie the rope.
                ny-**ɛ́'bɛ̀** ánya.   Leave him.
 With reduplication:
                ny-**émbɛ** ɛmbɛ.   Tie it.
 Class III. nyá-**la'di** tɔ̀rɔ́mɔ́, pl. nya-la'di tɔ̀rɔ́mɔ́.   Cook the maize.
             nyé-**turì** ma.   Fear me.
             nyé-**leru** àsi, pl. nyè-**leru** àsi.   Light the fire.
             nyɔ́-**lɔgɔ̀** ánya kɔ̀nvɔ́lɛ́.   Give it back to him.

INDEFINITE ASPECT. *Formal characteristics*.
350. Word order = Subject+object+verb.
 Class I verbs have 'characteristic' vowel **u-** or **ə-** (see § 32).
 2nd person pronoun prefix is **nya** for all verbs.
 Vowels of pronouns unaffected by following sounds.
 Auxiliary particle **ka** for 3rd person.
 Plural suffix **-ɪ** may follow auxiliary particle **ka**.
 No postpositions. Verb suffixes in dependent forms.
 Negative particle **ku** precedes verb.

351. *General form.*

Class I.	má ŋgàgà ùzi.	I am calling the boys.
	nyá ,, **ùzi.**	You are ,, ,,
	ánya ká ,, ùzi.	He is ,, ,,
	màá ,, ùzi.	We are ,, ,,
	nyàá ,, **ùzi.**	You are ,, ,,
	ànya ká ,, ùzi.	They are ,, ,,
Class II.	má gìí ɛ́mɛ́.	I am heating water, &c., &c.
Class III.	má tórómó la'dì.	I am cooking maize, &c., &c.

Note when **na** is used as object, it follows the verb (see § 263).

Class I.	má-úzì **na**.	I am calling him.
	nyá-ubí **na** íŋwayà?	Where are you pushing it?
	Aílɛ ká-ɔsé **ná**.	A. is pulling it (away).
Class II.	Aílɛ ká-ɛsé **ná**.	A. is pulling it (towards me).
Class III.	má-tubwä **na**.	I am shooting.

352. *Negative.*

Class I.	máá kʊ̀ lómvó márɔ̀ ɔ̀trɪ.	I am not undressing myself.
	nyáá kʊ̀ lómvó mírɔ̀ ɔ̀trɪ.	You are not ...
	ánya ká kʊ̀ lómvó 'érɔ̀ ɔ̀trɪ.	He is not ... &c., &c.

Note when **na** is used as object, it follows the verb, which loses its characteristic vowel.

má ku nyà **nà**. I'm not eating it.	má ku mvù **nà**. I'm not drinking it.
nyá ku nyà **nà**. You're ,,	nyá ku mvù **nà** You're ,,
ánya ká ku nyà **nà**. He is ,,	ánya ká ku mvù **nà**. He is ,,

353. *Dependent forms* (object and verb only).

Suffixes **-nɪ, -za, -vìa**.

má-lɛ kú mí ɔ̀'da-**nɪ**.	I don't want to insult you.
*ma-le kodra zo o**mu-za**.*	I want bamboos for building a house.
má-ndrɛ ánya te, tɔkɔ ɪrɔ ɔ̀'**bɪ-vìa**.	I saw him beating his wife.

and with **na**:

má-nì ɔ̀yɛ **na** kʊ.	I don't know (how) to do it.

MORU (MIZA)

INTRANSITIVE CONJUGATION

354. As has already been stated, the intransitive conjugation gives a less clear picture of Moru-Madi verbs than the transitive, for the following reasons: (*a*) the characteristic reversal of the sentence order between Definite and Indefinite forms can only be observed in transitive verbs with expressed object; (*b*) the behaviour of the characteristic vowel is often hard to determine in an intransitive verb owing to assimilation with particles which, in the transitive conjugation, are kept apart by the intervening object word.

In the following paradigms attention should be paid to such assimilations, especially in the Indefinite forms.

Moru (Miza)

DEFINITE ASPECT.

355. *General form* (with or without postposition).

Class I.
    má-sá-tè. I arrived (there).
    mí-sá-tè. You ,, ,,
    ànyá sá-tè. He ,, ,,
    ma-sá-tè. We ,, ,,
    mɪ-sá-tè. You ,, ,,
    anya sá-tè. They ,, ,,

Class II.
    m-ɛsá-tè. I arrived (here).   m-ói-te. I have gone, or I went.
    ny-ɛsá-tè. You ,, ,,   ny-ói-te. You ,, ,, You ,,
    ány-ɛsá-tè. He ,, ,,   ány-ɔi-te. He has ,, He ,,
    m-ɛsá-tè. We ,, ,,   m-ɔi-te. We have ,, We ,,
    ny-ɛsá-tè. You ,, ,,   ny-ɔi-te. You ,, ,, You ,,
    any-ɛsá-tè. They ,, ,,   any-ɔi-te. They ,, ,, They ,,

Class III. mí-lifu te. I am broken in spirit.

356. *Future form.* (Note characteristic vowel in 3rd person of Class I verbs.)

Class I. *ma-sa-na* Tali ya itu ya? When shall I arrive at Tali?
    mí-**sá-na** itù yà? When will you arrive (there)?
    ópí ɔ**sá-na** ɔndɔ. The chief will arrive to-morrow (there).
    ànya ɔ**dra-na**-'dá. They will die.

Class II.
m-oi-na Maridi ya ondo. I'll go to Maridi to-morrow.
ny-**ékyi-na** etú yà? When will you come?
ny-**ɛ́sá-na** itu niwa yà? When will you arrive here?
ány-**ekyí-a**-'dá. He will come.
ópí e**sá-na** ɔndɔ. The chief will arrive to-morrow (here).
ma-ma ma-ro-be, nda **eki-na**-*ndi*. I hope he will come.

357. *Subjunctive form.* (Note 3rd person auxiliary particle k(a)-.)

Class I.
má-**ru**. I must take it away.   mä-**ru**. Let us take it.
ánya **k-uru**. He must take it away.   anya **kä-ru**. Let them take it.[1]
ny-ɛ́'bɛ **k-ɔ̀rɪ**. Let him be.
mi-'ba ku **ka-đe** *vuru*. Don't let it fall down.

With reduplication:
mí-'bá **k-umu** úmù. Make it run.

Class II. mɪ-'dɛ m-**ói**, or *m-oi amaro*. Let's go.
    ny-**oi** miro. You may go.
    mí-'ba ánya **k-oi**. Make (or let) him go.
    mí-'bà **k-ɛdrɛ**-i. Make them stop.

Class III. mä-**kúgu** kú drì-ɔndrɔ̀. Let's not steal to-day.
    m-ɛ́rɛ te ŋgága **ká-lii**. I heard a boy cry.

With reduplication:
    mí-'ba gí 'dú **ka-la'di**-la'di. Make that water boil.

---

[1] Owing to lack of material, transitive forms with unexpressed object are used here.

358. *Imperative form.*

Class I.	mí-**mu** ku.	Don't run!
	mí-**mu** ùmù.	Run!
Class II.	ny-ɔ́ì, pl. ny-ɔ̌ì.	Go!
	ny-**ékyɨ** nòa, pl. ny-ekyɨ nòa.	Come here!
	ny-**ímu** umu.	Run (to me)!
Class III.	nyá-**lasa** ku.	Don't wash it.
	*nye-**tori** ku.*	Be not afraid.

INDEFINITE ASPECT.

359. *General form.*

Class I.	má ɔ̀dra.	I am dying.
	anyà k-ɔ̀dra.	They are dying.
	*ŋgaga **ka**-ɨ oji.*	The children are playing.
	*asi **ka**-uje.*	The fire burns.
	*gogo **ka**-ope.*	The cock crows.
Class II.	nyá-**áta** ɛ́ŋʊnyɛ kala Mɔrʊ́ si yà?	How do you say (it) in Moru?
	nyó-ɔ̀ì íŋwa yà?	Where are you going?
	m-ɔ́ì.	I am going.
Class III.	má-**tu'du**.	I'm going to sleep.
	nyá-**tu'du**.	You're ,, ,,
	anya ká-**tu'du**.	He is ,, ,,
	*täu **ka**-kere.*	The hen cackles.

360. *Dependent forms* (verb only).

má-lɛ̀ ku ɔ̀dra-nɪ. I don't want to die.
ndá ɔ̀zɔ̀ parátà tɛ mä-ri, **ukyí-zá-ná** Amádi yà. He gave money to me, in order to go to Amadi.
má-ndrɛ ndá tɛ u'du-via. I saw him sleeping.

Madi (Lokai)
TRANSITIVE CONJUGATION

DEFINITIE ASPECT. *Formal characteristics.*

361. Word order = Subject+verb+object.
Class I and III verbs have characteristic vowel in 3rd person.
Plural suffix **-ki** follows verb stem in 3rd person.
No auxiliary particle for 3rd person (except in Subjunctive).
Vowels of pronoun prefixes elided before Class II verbs.
1st and 2nd person pronoun (singular) prefix have no initial consonant before Class I verbs.
Many postpositions.
Negative expressed by postposition **ku** or **koro**.

362. *General form.*

Class I.	(m)á-**ndrɛ** nyi.	I see (or saw) you.
	(ny)í-**ndrɛ** ma.	You see ,, me.
	orʊgʊ ɔ́ndrɛ́ ma.	The monkey sees me.
	àmà-**ndrɛ** nyi.	We see (or saw) you.
	ànyì-**ndrɛ** ma.	You ,, ,, me.
	bá ɔ̀ndrɛ-**kí** àma.	The people see us.

VERB CONJUGATION

Class II. *m-ede e'bu.*[1]   I do (or did) the work.
         ny-ede ,,   You do ,,   ,,
         ede ,,   He does ,,   ,,
         am-ede ,,   We do ,,   ,,
         any-ede ,,   You ,,   ,,   ,,
         ede-ki ,,   They ,,   ,,   ,,

Class III. No transitive examples to hand, but note:
    boronzi okoḍu-ki koro. The boys are not asleep.

363. *General form with postpositions.*
    a-no ta ra.   I saw something.
    ono ta ra.   He saw something.
    ɔ̀sɔ tà kʊ.   He is not hoeing anything.
    ɔ̀sɔ tà kʊ-rʊ̀.   He did not hoe anything.
    aɪ oto-ki ta ko endro.   They do not dance to-day.

364. *Exhortative form.* (Idiomatic use of 3rd person of General form.)
onya ta.   Let's eat.   *osa-ta.*   Let's hoe—said to one person.
onya-ki ta. Let's eat. *osa-ki ta.* Let's hoe—said to more than one person.

365. *Subjunctive form.* (Note 3rd person auxiliary particle **k-**. Initial consonant of pronoun not elided. Otherwise like general form.)
Negative postposition **ko.**
Subjunctive postposition **dro.**
Class I.   *ma-no (dro) ta.*   That I may see something.
      nyi-no ,, ,,   That you may ,,
      k-ono ,, ,,   That he ,,   ,,
      ama-no ,, ,,   That we ,,   ,,
      anyi-no ,, ,,   That you ,,   ,,
      k-ono-ki (dro) ta.   That they ,,   ,,
*nyí-zí akimu ni, mà-**nya** drɔ̀ èza.* Ask the doctor if I may eat meat.
*nyi-'dù ílí, nyi-**lí** a'ù dro.* Take a knife so that you may cut the chicken.
Class II.   *am-ede ta.*   Let us do something.
      am-eŋgo leŋgo.   Let us sing a song.
      am-ogu ta ko.   Let us not steal anything.

366. *Imperative form.* (Identical with 2nd person Subjunctive.)
Class I.   *nyi-no ta,* pl. *anyi-no ta.*   See!
      nyí-zí akimu-ni, pl. *nyi-zí akimu-ni.*   Call the doctor.
Class II. *any-ede e'bu anyi-dri.*   Do (pl.) your work.
      ny-oŋgwe` 'ba.   Call the man.
Class III. *nye-konyi ma.*   Help me.

INDEFINITE ASPECT. *Formal characteristics.*
367. Word order = Subject+object+verb.
    Class I verbs have no characteristic vowel.
    Auxiliary particle for 3rd person = **ka.**
    Plural suffix **-ki** follows auxiliary particle **ka.**
    No negative form. ('Definite' negative form used.)
    Postposition **ra** for future tense.
    Verb suffixes in dependent forms.

---
[1] This paradigm is not actually given in full by Molinaro, but is coined here on the analogy of other paradigms.

368. *General form.*

Class I.
má èza **nya**. — I am eating meat.
nyí ìyi **mvu**. — You are drinking water.
Oyúru **ká** ledzó **dzò**. — Oyuru is speaking words.
'bá kà ìra **m̀vu**. — The people are drinking beer.

Class II.
ópí ká nyi **uŋġwέ**. — The chief is calling you.
oko **kakí** ecakwi **azi**. — Women bring firewood.

369. *Future form.*

Class I.
ma	ta	**no-ra**.	I shall see something.
nyi	,,	,,	You will ,, ,,
ka	,,	,,	He will ,, ,,
ama	,,	,,	We shall ,, ,,
anyi	,,	,,	You will ,, ,,
ka-ki	,,	,,	They will ,, ,,

má nya-adrupi-ni **ndrɛ-ra**. — I shall see your brother.
ɔ'bó amá era **mvu-rá**. — To-morrow we shall drink beer.

Class II.
má ópí **úkwè-ra**. — I'll pay the chief.
ma e'bu **ede-ra**.[1] — I'll do work.
nyi e'bu **ede-ra**. — You'll do work.
ka e'bu **ede-ra**. — He'll do work.
ama e'bu **ede-ra**. — We'll do work.
anyi e'bu **ede-ra**. — You'll do work.
ka-ki e'bu **ede-ra**. — They'll do work.

Note when the particle (n)a is used as object, it follows the verb.

mé-έdέ-a-rá o'bú. — I'll do it to-morrow.

370. *Dependent forms* (object and verb only).

Suffixes: -rɛ -ka -lɛ -zo

ɔŋga-kí léti **sɔ̀-rɛ**. — Let's go and sweep the road.
á-nì waraga **là-ka** ku. — I do not know (how) to read a book.
á-ma **ndzì-lɛ** kwɛ. — I tried (in vain) to lift it.
tolu kwe **ga-zo**. — Axe for chopping wood.

Madi (Lokai)

INTRANSITIVE CONJUGATION

DEFINITE ASPECT.

371. *General form* (with or without postposition).

Class I.		Class II.	
a-dra-ra.	I died.	m-emu-ra.	I came.
i-dra-ra.	You died.	ny-emu-ra.	You came.
odra-ra.	He ,,	emu-ra.	He ,,
ama-dra-ra.	We ,,	am-emu-ra.	We ,,
anyi-dra-ra.	You ,,	any-emu-ra.	You ,,
odra-ki-ra.	They ,,	emu-ki-ra.	They ,,

Class II.
m-êtsȧ-rȧ. — I have arrived.
lúkudɔ́ **ɛdrà-ra**. — The pot broke.

Class III. boronzi **okoďu-ki** koro. — The boys are not sleeping.

[1] This paradigm is not actually given in full by Molinaro, but is coined here on the analogy of other paradigms.

VERB CONJUGATION

372. *Subjunctive form.*

Class I.
  ma-dra-dro. That I should die.
  nyi-dra-dro. ,, you ,, ,,
  k-odra-dro. ,, he ,, ,,
  ama-dra-dro. ,, we ,, ,,
  anyi-dra-dro. ,, you ,, ,,
  k-odra-ki-dro. ,, they ,, ,,
  nyi-jo k-omu. Tell him to come.

373. *Imperative form.*

Class I.   nyi-dra, pl. anyi-dra. Die!
Class II. ny-ɛmú, pl. àny-ɛvɔ̀. Come!
Class III. pl. anyi-kodu diadro. Sleep on!

INDEFINITE ASPECT.

374. *General form* (ra = future postposition).

Class I.		Class II.	
ma-dra.	I die.	m-emu-ra.	I'll come.
nyi-dra.	You die.	ny-emu-ra.	You'll come.
k-odra.	He dies.	k-emu-ra.	He'll come.
ama-dra.	We die.	am-emu-ra.	We'll ,,
anyi-dra.	You ,,	any-emu-ra.	You'll ,,
ka-ki-dra.	They die.	ka-ki-emu-ra. } ká-kì-ɛvə.	They'll ,,

As can be seen, the past and the future tenses have identical forms in the 1st and 2nd persons of Class II verbs, which are not distinguished even in intonation. Thus:

	I have arrived	*I'll arrive to-morrow*
MADI {	Lo.: mé-ɛtsá-ra.	mé-ɛtsá ɔ̀bu ra.
	Pa.: m-ɛ́sa-rá.	m-ɛ́sá ɔ̀'bu ra.

Class III. (Examples from Pandikeri.)
  za odra ko, koduko. (Mk. v. 39.) The damsel is not dead but sleepeth.
  ɔpi ku-luŋgwé. The chief is calling.

375. *Dependent forms* (verb only).
  amá-vù **drà-rɛ**. We are going to die.
  á-lɛ **mù-ka** bàru. I want to go home.
  á-'bì **sì-lɛ** kwɛ. I try (in vain) to write.
  . . . ani **ni-zo**. So that he should know (them).

LOGO
TRANSITIVE CONJUGATION

DEFINITE ASPECT. *Formal characteristics.*

376. Word order = Subject+verb+object.
Class I verbs have no 'characteristic' vowel.
Vowels of pronouns elided before Class II verbs.
Plural suffix **-ki** follows verb stem in 3rd person.
Many postpositions.
Negative expressed by postposition (a)ko.
Auxiliary particle **ko** in 'Volition' form.

377. *General form.*

Class I.
- má-sɩ ani. — I split it.
- ma-si ama-jo-ɩ. — I am building my house.
- ago do waraga. — The man takes (or took) the paper.
- ma-si-ki ama-jo. — I and others are building my house.
- ama-vo-ki ŋga ami-dre. (Mt. xi. 17.) — We have piped (thing for you).

Class II.
- mi-au-dre lä'bi ya? — Have you skinned the water-buck?

Class III.
- ama-pa **loga** ma. — My foot hampers me.
- ma-**kutu** ti-le. — I spill the cow-milk.
- adi ladi ŋga konji. — He cooks food badly.

378. *General form with postpositions.*
- ma-**nya** ŋga **dre.** ⎫
- ma-**nya-dre** ŋga. ⎭ — I have eaten food.
- odrógú **tsɩ** ma **drɛ̀**. — A mouse bit (or is biting) me.
- kalígyá **nyà** kʊkyá mána **drɛ̀**. — A hyena ate my dog.
- ma-**nya-dre** ŋga e. — I am eating food (at the moment of speaking).
- mi-nɔ má **dré à**? — Did you see me?
- ma-**nya-ru** ŋga. — I shall eat food.

379. *Imperative form.* (Same as 2nd person of General form.)

Class I.
- mi-**nda** ama-boŋgo. — Look for my cloth.
- mi-do tau'bu. — Take the eggs.

Class II.
- mì-**ado** faraŋga ma-dri. (Mk. xii. 15.) — Bring me a penny.

Class III.
- mi-**ladi** ŋga. — Cook (something)!

380. *Volition form* (with auxiliary particle **ko**).

Class I.
- mi-**ko**-o ado ya? — What will you do?
- ma-**ko**-o ta ko. — I shall do nothing.
- mà **ko**-gi ya? (Mk. xii. 15.) — Shall we give?

Class II.
- mà-**k-ado** ado ŋga ya? (Mk. xix. 27.) — What shall we have?

Class III.
- ma-**ko-ladi** tau ya? — Shall I cook a chicken?

381. *With postpositions.*
- ... adi **ko-fe-ro** adi-märi **ka**. (Mt. xviii. 34.) — ... till he should pay his debt.
- ... ma-**ko-pa-ro** ama-märi mi-dri we-i. (Mt. xviii. 26.) — ... and I will pay thee all my debt.
- mì-**ko-kusu** akodi di. (Mt. ii. 8.) — When ye have found him.

382. *Volition Imperative.*

Class I.
- mí-kɔ̀-**nya** kɔ. — Don't eat it.
- mi-**ko**-ta. — Say it.

Class II.
- mi-**k-aji** akodi ma-vuna nole. (Mt. xvii. 17.) — Bring him hither to me.

Class III.
- mi-**ko-ladi** tau. — Cook a chicken.

INDEFINITE ASPECT. *Formal characteristics.*

383. Word order = Subject+object+verb.
No characteristic vowel.
No 3rd person auxiliary particle (except in the Subjunctive).
Negative expressed by postposition (**a**)**ko**. Subjunctive by **ro**.
No other postpositions. Auxiliary verbs much used.
Verb suffixes in dependent forms.

384. *General form.*
    má zá **nya**.   I'm eating meat.
    kidrú má ami **nə̀** vɛlɛ́?   To-morrow shall I see you again?
    má sandúku **dɔ**.   I'm carrying a box.

385. *Subjunctive form.* (Note **ko** auxiliary in 3rd person.)
    ... ma boŋgo **ji** ako **ro**.   ... So that I could not wash the clothes.
    ... a'di **ko-ji ro**.   ... So that he can wash them.

386. *Dependent forms* (object and verb only).
Suffixes **-le, ŋga-ra, -zo**.
    ma-le yi **mvu-le**.   I want to drink water.
    ma-lɛ **àgu-ŋga-ra**.   I want to laugh.
    akoði li-dre yi **mvu-zo**.   He has gone to drink water.
    aði ali ama no.   He came to see me.

387. *Progressive forms* (Subject+auxiliary verb[1]+object+dependent form of main verb *without suffix*).[2]
    má-**nıɽı** owa **mvu**.   I am drinking beer.
    mundia **are** *mbi za*.   The people are burning the grass.
    aði liri ta fe.   He is talking (lit. he is words giving).
    boi {**are** / **adre**} *saani ji*.   The boy is washing plates.
    ma-o ama-jo si.   I am building my house.
    täbiri **are** *ama o we.*   We are very hungry (lit. hunger is us harming much).
    täbiri **are** *ama o ko.*   We are not hungry.

Note, however:
    má-**drɛ́** búku **gyê**.   I *bought* a book.

Logo
INTRANSITIVE CONJUGATION

DEFINITE ASPECT.

388. *General form.*
    Class I.   *ma-li udru.*   I (shall) go to-morrow.
                ma-ò. I do. *ma-ó.* We do.
                lia vi. The wind blows.
                mbi ve. The grass burns.
    Class II.   *mi-adre ago togo mbamba-ði be.* (Mt. xxv. 24.) Thou art a hard man.
                aði ali ama no.   He came to see me.
                ma-ali di.   I'm just coming.
                do aga.   Fat melts.
    Class III.   *ma-kayi iri.*   I'll sleep two (nights).
                äzi tocwa.   The work is tiring.
                mi-tusu aŋgini ya? (Mt. xviii. 12.) How think ye?

---

[1] The subject is joined to the auxiliary verb according to the Definite Conjugation.
[2] The suffix is only used when the verb is intransitive. See §§ 395 and 540.

389. *Imperative form.*
Class I.   mi-ŋga kuru.   Get up!
Class II.   mi-ali.   Come!
Class III.   mi-kai.   Sleep on.

390. *Volition form.*
Class I.   ma-ko-li-ro.   That I may go.
Class II.   aii k-ali-ki ma-vule.   They shall come to me.

391. *Volition Imperative form.*
Class I.   mi-ko-li.   Go!
Class II.   mi-k-ali.   Come!
Class III.   mi-ko-liri kiri.   Be quiet!

INDEFINITE ASPECT.

392. *General form.* There is no formal difference in the Intransitive verb between the 'Definite' and 'Indefinite' general forms. Thus most of the forms in § 388 may equally well be used here.

393. *Subjunctive form.*
mi-ali mi-no-ro.   Come that you may see.
ama-pa loga ma-ali ako ro.   My foot hinders (me) so that I can't come.

394. *Dependent forms* (verb only).
ďia-nda le aiko-le.   So-and-so loves sleeping.
za-ra'a.   Burning.

395. *Progressive forms* (Subject+auxiliary verb+dependent form *with suffix*).
Class I.   mvamva ádrɛ́ ŋgɔ̀-lɛ.   The baby is crying.
             ma-o li-le.   I am going.
             ma-nya ŋga, ma-are pi-zo.   I eat food until I am satisfied.
             ma-kayi iri, m-ara nji-zo. I'll sleep two nights and return.
Class II.   mundia dre aiyi-ra'a . . . While men slept . . .
             ago adre ali-le ai-'ba na. The man comes to his village.
Class III.   aďi are teci-le.   He walks.
Note also: aďi are ali-le da (or dre). He has come.

Whereas transitive verbs very often do not employ suffixes in the progressive forms, the intransitive verbs always employ them.

LUGBARA
TRANSITIVE CONJUGATION

DEFINITE ASPECT. *Formal characteristics.*

396. Word order = Subject+verb+object.
Class I verbs receive no characteristic vowel.
Initial consonant in 1st and 2nd pronoun sometimes elided, usually not.
Pronoun occasionally omitted in the imperative.
Auxiliaries: **ma** (subjunctive), **ka** (conditional).
Plural suffix **-ki** occasionally found.[1]
Suffix **ni**.
Postpositions '**bo, ra, da, ko** (neg.).

[1] Not found in the New Testament language.

VERB CONJUGATION

397. *General form.*
  Class I. *isu eri so pa miri tia.* (Lk. v. 2.) Then he stood (lit. set foot) by the lake.
  eri ndre oguru iri. (Lk. v. 2.) He saw two ships.
  ma-zi emi. (Lk. vi. 9.) I ask you.
  Class II. *yi oko e'bi oŋgolomuro ambo.* (Lk. v. 6.) They caught fish, a great multitude.
  eri ejo eri-dri. (Lk. v. 13.) He stretched forth his hand.

398. *Imperative form* (same as 2nd person General form).
  Class I. *mi-so emba.* (Lk. v. 4.)   Let down (your) nets.
  emi-le emi-juru. (Lk. vi. 27.)   Love your enemies.
  emi-du koli mani. (Mt. xi. 29.)   Take my yoke.
  Class II. *mi-eto ma.* (Mt. xiv. 30.)   Save me.
  mi-ece mi kuhani vu. (Lk. v. 14.)   Show thyself to the priest.
  mi-iju mi-dri. (Lk. vi. 10.)   Stretch forth thy hand.
  emi-oja eri-dri azini indi. (Lk. vi. 29.) Offer to him the other also.

399. *General form with postpositions.*
  yi ko dria ra. (Lk. v. 11.)   They forsook all.
  mi-lu oko ḍiri ra ya? (Lk. vii. 44.)   Seest thou this woman?
  aiitaa mini eri pa mi 'bo. (Lk. xviii. 42.) Thy faith (it) hath cured thee.

400. *General form with suffix.*
  Te ama oko-ni afa alo-ni ko. (Lk. v. 5.) But we have caught not one thing.
  mi-fe-ni ma-dri yi alo-ni ko. (Lk. vii. 44.) Thou gavest me no water.
  mi-efi-ni odo ma-dri a ko. (Lk. vii. 46.) Thou didst not pour oil on my head.

401. *General form with auxiliaries.*
  Opi, ma-ma-aii ndretaa mani. (Lk. xviii. 41.) Lord that I may receive my sight.
  eri ma-azi yi ko. (Lk. viii. 31.) That he should not command them.
  yi ka-ye ḍini ra. (Lk. v. 6.) When they had done this.

INDEFINITE ASPECT. *Formal characteristics.*
402. Word order = Subject+object+verb.
  Class I verbs receive no characteristic vowel.[1]
  Auxiliary particles: **adri, ovu, ŋga, ka, ko.**
  No auxiliary for 3rd person.
  Suffixes: **ni, lɛ, ka, ŋga, zu, za, zo, ria.**
  Postpositions: **ra, 'bo, ko** (negative).

403. *General form.*
  Class I. *'ba dria yi mi ndru.* (Mk. i. 37.) All people (they) seek thee.
  'ba . . . ewa afufuroro le ko. (Lk. v. 39.) No man (having drunk old wine) desireth new (wine).
  mi pati-ola ji-ni ko. (Rom. xi. 18.) Thou bearest not the (tree-)root.
  'ba Karanini 'ba Farisaini be yi eri ndro. (Lk. vi. 7.) And the Scribes and Pharisees watched him.
  Class II. *emi eyo ega emi-asi a ŋgonia?* (Lk. v. 22.) What (word) reason ye in your hearts?
  emi ma omve Opi, Opi aḍisia? (Lk. vi. 46.) Why call ye me, Lord, Lord?

[1] In my own field notes, Class I verbs are often given a characteristic vowel. (See § 434.)

404. *Dependent forms* (object and verb only).
  *ma-pa **oji-zu**.* (Lk. vii. 44.) To wash my feet (with).
  *ori erini **ri**.* (Lk. viii. 5.) To sow his seed. (*ri* = sow.)
  *yi le mi **ndre**.* (Lk. viii. 20.) They desire to see thee.
  *eco mini ma-rua '**ba-za-ro** alaro.* (Lk. v. 12.) Thou canst make my body clean.

405. *Progressive form* (with suffix lɛ).
  márì ézà **nya-lɛ**. I am eating meat.
  ma mí ùmvɛ-**lɛ-ga**. I am calling you.

406. *Constructions with auxiliaries* (Subject+auxiliary+object+dependent form).
  *eri **ka** Yesu **ndre-ra**.* (Lk. v. 12.) When he saw Jesus.
  *emi **ka** afa mani yo-leri ye ko indi.* (Lk. vi. 46.) (But) ye do not the things which I say.
  *yi **ka** oguru yini **adi** yi tia 'bo.* (Lk. v. 11.) When they had brought the ships from the water.
  *yi **ŋga** eyo erini **inzi** indi.* (Lk. viii. 25.) And they obey his word.
  *ama **ŋga** emba so yi a.* (Lk. v. 5.) We will let down the net into the sea.
  *ofo **ko** eri-rua **mbe-le** kocici.* (Lk. v. 13.) And the leprosy left his body immediately.
  *eri **ovu** 'ba **imba-ria**.* (Lk. v. 17.) As he was teaching the people.
  *De 'ba-oŋgolomuro yini **ovu-ria** eri **omi-ria** cici.* (Lk. v. 1.) (Lit.) As the people they were him pressing all.

LUGBARA
INTRANSITIVE CONJUGATION

DEFINITE ASPECT.

407. *General form.*
  Class I. *yi **bi** eri-vuti.* (Lk. v. 11.) They followed after him.
    *eri **su** mile vaa.* (Lk. v. 12.) He fell on his face.
    *ama-**zo** miri tia adasi.* (Lk. viii. 22.) Let us go over unto the other side of the lake.
    ama-**mú-kí**-'bo. We went.
    emi-**mú-kí**-'bo. You went.
    kò-**mú-kí**-'bo. They went.
  Class II. *De eri **ovu** aku alo a.* (Lk. v. 12.) When he was in a certain town.
    *emi-**emu** oguo vule ya?* (Lk. xxii. 52.) Be ye come out as against a thief?

408. *Imperative form* (same as General form).
  Class I. *mi-**mu** leti mini a.* (Lk. v. 14.) Go (in) thy way.
       *emi-**ndre**.* (Lk. vii. 34.)   Behold.
  Class II. *mi-**ovu** di alaro.* (Lk. v. 13.)   Be thou clean.
       *emi-**emu** ma-va.* (Mt. xi. 28.)   Come unto me.

409. *General and Imperative form with postpositions.*
    *yi **emu-ra**.* (Lk. v. 7.)   And they came.
    *ma-**aii-ra**.* (Lk. v. 13.)   I will.
    *eri **aii-da**.* (Lk. v. 16.)   And he prayed.
    *eri **oro-'bo**.* (Lk. viii. 24.)   He arose.
    *mi-**mu** ma-vurisi **ra**.* (Lk. v. 8.) Depart from me.
    *mi-**ro ko**.* (Lk. v. 10.)   Fear not.

VERB CONJUGATION

General form with suffix.
Te eri **dra-ni** ko. (Lk. viii. 52.)   For she is not dead.
ma **emu-ni** 'ba alaro omve ko. (Lk. v. 32.) I came not to call the righteous.

410. *General form with auxiliaries.*
yi **ma-emu** yi aza ko. (Lk. v. 7.) That they should come and help them.
eri azi eri-tia, **ma-yo** 'ba azini tia ko. (Lk. v. 14.) And he charged him to tell no man (i.e. that he should not speak to other men).
Eyo-onzi mini **ma-ovu** ko-zaro. (Lk. vii. 47.) Thy sins be forgiven.
Te Simoni Petero **ka-ndre**-ra. (Lk. v. 8.) When Simon Peter saw it.
Mi-**ka-le**-ra. (Lk. v. 12.) If thou wilt.

INDEFINITE ASPECT.

411. *General form.*[1]
Class I.   Te mini yi **nya** yi **mvu** indi. (Lk. v. 33.) But thine eat and drink (indeed).
Class II.   Te eri **oduko**. (Lk. viii. 52.) But (she) sleepeth.

412. *Dependent forms* (verb only+suffix).
                nya-ka. Food.

413. *Progressive form* (with suffix lɛ).
      ma-**ovu-le** 'ba onzini-risi. (Lk. v. 8.) I am a sinful man.
      ma-**mu-lɛ**. I am going.

414. *Constructions with auxiliaries* (Subject+auxiliary+dependent form of main verb).
Eri **ka** eca jo vu. (Lk. viii. 51.)   When he came into the house.
eri **ŋga** eca dini. (Lk. v. 1.)   And it came to pass.
mi **ŋga ovu** 'ba 'ba-oko-piri. (Lk. v. 10.) Thou shalt become a fisher of men.
yi **adri ovu** meleki ageia. (Lk. vii. 25.) They are in the king's courts.

CHAPTER XII

VERBS IN SUB-DIALECTS

415. As may be seen, verb conjugation is not the same in the four main languages of the group, although very nearly so. Thus: Moru forms its future from the 'Definite' form, while Madi from the 'Indefinite'. The characteristic vowel is used in Moru Indefinite conjugation, but in Madi Definite conjugation (third person only), while in Logo it is absent altogether. The second person pronoun is 'nya' in Moru in the Indefinite conjugation, and 'mi' in the Definite. In Madi it is 'nyi' and in Logo and Lugbara 'mi' throughout. The verb infix ka accompanies the third person Indefinite in Moru and Madi, but not in Logo or Lugbara.

Similar deviations are to be found among the dialects of each principal language.

---

[1] The general form of the Indefinite Construction is indistinguishable from that of the Definite Construction in the Intransitive Conjugation—except in intonation.

Moru Dialects (including Avukaya)

416. Verbs in Kediru and Lakama'di are conjugated as in Miza for the most part. In the other dialects, Moroändri, 'Bälimbä, Moroägi, Wa'di, and especially Avukaya, elements are to be found which bear a fairly close resemblance to Logo.

DEFINITE ASPECT.

417. In Class I verbs there is great conformity throughout the dialects with Miza.

E.g. MOROÄNDRI: mǎ-zi mvàgà (te). I called the boys.
  mí-zi ,, ,, You ,, ,,
  ndá zi ,, ,, He ,, ,,
  mä-zi ,, ,, We ,, ,,
  &c. &c. (see § 345).

What are you doing? *What are you digging.* *Go!*

AVUKAYA (Jl.): mí-'ɛ adúla yà? mí-'di àdula yà? mí-ra![1]
WA'DI: mí-'ɛa ä'di ya? mí-'di ò'di yà?

Where will you throw the water away?

M.: mí-da-**na** igyí íŋwa yà?
Ä.: mí-da-**na** idzí íŋwa yà?
'B.: mí-da-**na** idʒí íŋgóléro yà?
Äg.: mí-da-**na** idʒí íŋwa yà?

418. In Class II and Class III verbs the 2nd person pronoun is **n-** rather than **ny-**. Note also that the characteristic vowel is often **a-** rather than **ɛ-** in Class II verbs.

Class II.

MOROÄNDRI: m-ámɛ idʒi te. I heated the water.
  n-ámɛ ,, You ,, ,,
  ndán-amɛ ,, He ,, ,,
  m-àmɛ ,, We ,, ,,
  n-àmɛ ,, You ,, ,,
  ndàn-àmɛ ,, They ,, ,,

  n-ámɛ idʒí. Heat the water!

AVUKAYA (Jl.): n-ázɛ ɛnika aŋgolé yà? Where are you pushing it?
  n-ámá lùmvu dà-lɛ aŋgolé yà? Where are you going to throw the
WA'DI: n-ɔ̀i idʒí ɔdɔ-nɛ íŋwa yà? water?

Class III.

MOROÄNDRI: ná-kanda fɛ. Shake the tree.
  ná-la'di däbäli. Cook the grain.
  ná-lasa mva. Wash the baby.
  ná-leru àsi. Light the fire.
  nó-lɔgɔ̀ ndá kòvólɛ̀. Give it back to him.

AVUKAYA { Jl.: ní-losɛ́ bɔ̀ŋgɔ. Sew the clothes.
  { Jg.: mí-losɛ bɔ̀ŋgɔ. ,, ,,

Compare the Ojiga form with Logo: mí-lɛsɛ bɔ̀ŋgɔ.

---

[1] But: **na-raa-trá**. You will go.

VERBS IN SUB-DIALECTS

In some Class III verbs pronominal forms alternate.

Translate it into ...	*Lay the wood across.*	*Hide it.*
M.: nyó-lógò kala-Miza ya.	nyá-là tsʷɛ̀.	nye-dembí.
Ä.: nɔ-lógò kala-Moroändri ya.		nä-läpi.
Ag.: mí-lagʊ kala-Moroägi ya.	mí-lala tsʷɛ̀.	nyɛ́-lăpi or mɪ-läpi.
W.: mí-lagwa Wa'di-ti 'a	mí-lala tsʷɛ̀.	mɪ-läpi.
Jĺ.: mí-lɔgo Odzɪla-tí 'a.	mí-la(la) fɛ.	mi-läpi.

419. In the Subjunctive form the 3rd person auxiliary **k-** is lacking, although the verb has a characteristic vowel for the 3rd person.

Ä.: n-ádrɛ nána má-ndrɛ̀ mì rɔ. Come here that I may see you.

He must take it away.   *He must not bring it.*
Class I. M.: ányà k-uru.   Class II. ánya kɛ-ɛzi ku.
       Ä.: ndá uru.   ndá azi kù.

INDEFINITE ASPECT.

420. Here the divergences between Miza, Kediru, and Lakama'di on the one hand, and the other dialects on the other hand are more noticeable, the main features being:

   I. An auxiliary particle **rɔ** (cf. Logo **adre**) in Ä., 'B., Äg.
   II. 2nd person pronoun **mɪ** (not **nya** or **na**) in Ä., Äg.
   III. No 3rd person auxiliary particle **ka** in Ä., 'B., W., and Avukaya.

Examples (cf. § 351).

MOROÄNDRI: má-ró mvàgà ùzi. I am calling the boys.
           mí-ró   „   ùzi. You are   „
           ndá-ró   „   ùzi. He is   „
           mà-ró   „   ùzi. We are   „
           mɪ-ró   „   ùzi. You „   „
           ndà-ró   „   ùzi. They „   „

421. I. Auxiliary particle **rɔ**. Compare:

I am digging a hole.
Ä.: má-rɔ 'bú ú'dì.   M., K., L.: má 'bú u'di.
Äg.: má-rɔ 'bú o'di.
'B.: m-ɔrɔ 'bú ò'dì.

I am dying.
Ä.: má-ró ɔ̀dra.   M.: má ɔ̀dra.

422. II. 2nd person pronoun.

What are you digging?
Ä.: mɪ-rɔ a'd(i) u'di yà?   M., K., L.: **nyá** a'd(i) u'di yà.
                             B'.: **n**-ɔrɔ   „   „

Why are you digging it?
Ä., Äg.: **mí**-r(ɔ) ú'di na a'dita yà?   M., K., L.: **nyá** u'di na ɔ'duta yà?
                                           'B.: **n**-ǎr-ú'dì na tana'di ya?

Where are you going to throw that water away?
Ä.: **mí**-r-ói idzí 'di ɔdá ɪŋwa yà.   M.: **ny**-ɔí igyí 'dó ɔda ɪŋwa yà?
                                         'B.: **ná**-r-ói ìdzi 'di dà-lɛ íŋgólérɔ yà?

Note also in WA'DI:

ná niá a'di ɔ-lɛ yà? What are you doing?

423. III. Absence of **ka** auxiliary for 3rd person. (See also §§ 216, 496.)

The chief is calling you.	*The people are drinking beer.*
Ä.: ópí rɔ́ mɪ ùzi.	lédr rə wá m̀vu.
M.: ópɪ ká mɪ ùzi.	lédr ka wá ùmvu.

They are dying.	*Luguma is talking.*
Ä.: andá rɔ́ ɔ̀dra.	Lúgumà rɔ́ ledzi.
M.: anyà k-ɔ̂dra.	Lúgumà ka lɛdʒʷi.

Madi Dialects

The Pandikeri dialect differs from the Lokai dialect in the following important points:

DEFINITE ASPECT.

424. The verb has no characteristic vowel.

There is no elision of the consonant in 1st and 2nd person pronoun.

The plural pronoun subject is differentiated from the singular by intonation alone (as in Moru).

Altogether the verb conjugation is nearer Moru than Lokai.

Lokai	*Pandikeri*		Cf. *Moru*		
á ndrɛ nyi (ra)	má ndɛ̀ nyi (ra)	I saw you	má ndrɛ́		mɪ
í ndrɛ ma	nyí ndɛ̀ ma	You saw me	mí	,,	ma
orʊgʊ ɔ́ndrɛ́ má	orʊgʊ **ndɛ̀** ma	The man saw me	ánya	,,	,,
àmà ndrɛ nyi	mà ndɛ̀ nyi	We saw you	mà	,,	mɪ
ànyì ndrɛ ma	nyì ndɛ̀ ma	You saw me	mì	,,	ma
bá ɔ̀ndrɛkí àma	'bá ndɛ̀ àma	The people saw us	ànya	,,	àma

Further examples:

	A bee stung me.	*The white ants ate the paper.*
Lo.:	laŋú ətsi ma trɔ̀.	idzú ɔnya warage nì.
Pa.:	laŋú si ma tɔ.	idzú nya warage nì.

425. In the imperative the pronoun is not used:

Lokai	*Pandikeri*	
nyi mvú eí	mvú iyí	Drink water.
nyi té má	té má	Guard me.

INDEFINITE ASPECT.

426. Word order = Subject+verb+object (i.e. same as in the Definite conjugation). The intonation is different, however, and the 3rd person has an auxiliary prefix **ka-** (alternating with **ku-**).

Examples:

Lokai	*Pandikeri*	
má èza **nya**.	má **nyá** èza.	I am eating meat. (Past = má nya èza ra.)
nyí ìyi **mvu**.	nyí **mvú** iyi.	You are drinking water.
Oyúru ká ledzó **dzɔ̀**.	Lúgumà ká-'jó lè'jo.	So-and-so is talking words.

Compare also:

	The chief is calling you.	*The people are drinking beer.*
Lo.:	ópí ka nyi uŋgwɛ̀.	bá kà ìra m̀vu.
Pa.:	ópí ku-luŋgwɛ̀ nyi'i.	'bá kú-mvú ówá.

	The child sucks the breast.	*To-morrow we shall make (drink) beer.*
Lo.:	bará **ká** bà **ndro**.	ɔbɔ́ amá erá **mvu** rá.
Pa.:	'borá **kú-ndu** ba.	ɔ'bɔ́ ama '**ɛ́** ówá rà.

427. The verb follows the Subject, however, in the infinitive, &c.

	I want to buy a cow.	*I go to see the people.*
Lo.:	ma lɛ ti **dzɛ**-lɛ.	má mu bá **ndrɛ**-rɛ.
Pa.:	ma lɛ ti **ɡɛ**-lɛ.	má mu 'bá **ndɛ**-rɛ.

428. The LULU'BA verb, as far as can be determined, is conjugated like the Pandikeri verb as regards sentence order, but like the Lokai verb in other respects.

429. *Definite aspect.*

Class I.	í-**mbì** éwà?	Are you drinking beer?
	yá-**mbu** mú ku, á-mbu yí.	I'm not drinking 'mu', I'm drinking water.
	no-**mbú** iyi.	Drink water!
	mo'dí-ní **sí** dʒo (oli) 'o.	The people built a house.
Class II.	asi ədə dʒó 'ɔ.	The fire burnt the house.
	əkyέ má-rí-bòŋgo.	He tore my shirt.

430. *Indefinite aspect.*

Class I.	mo'dí **kosí** dʒó ni.	The people are building a house.
Class II.	así **kɔ́dɔ́** dʒó.	The fire is burning the house.

LOGO DIALECTS

431. The most noticeable way in which the AGAMBI dialect differs from the other Logo dialects is in the Volition Imperative, where the prefix **a-** (instead of **ko-**) is added.

Class I.	*fe* (to give).	*mi-a-fe.*	Give!
Class II.	*ada* (to show).	*mi-ada.*	Show! (< *mi-a-ada*).

432. There is also a difference shown in the postposition used to indicate past time.

	I have eaten food.	*I have finished.*
L.:	*ma-nya ŋga **dre**.*	*ma-o akele **dre**.*
A.:	*ma-nya ŋga **da**.*	*ma-o landele **da**.*

It has already been stated that the Agambi dialect has much in common with the Ojiga dialect of Avukaya.

KELIKO

The Keliko verb, in its general forms at least, is very like the Lugbara verb. Compare the following examples:

433. DEFINITE ASPECT.[1]

	I ate meat.	*I didn't eat it.*	*The man saw me.*	*The people saw us.*
KELIKO:	má-**nya** èza **ɡɪ**.	á-**nyà** kuɛ.	aróɡù **nde** ma.	'barɪpɪ **ndɛ-kí** ama.
LUGBÁRA:	má-**nya** èza '**bo**.	á-**nyà** ku.	aróɡù **ndrɛ** ma.	'barɪ **ndrɛ-kí** àma.

[1] It should be noted in this context, that in the Keliko and Lugbara analysed by me, the consonant element in the pronoun is often omitted as in Madi. This does not occur in the language of the Lugbara New Testament.

		Drink water.	Look after me.

KELIKO: í-**mvù** yi.   mí-**ndɛ** ma-tɛlɛ.
LUGBARA: í-**mvù** yi.   mí-**ndrɛ** ma-valɛ.

KELIKO: *ăipa **tu-ki** uŋgo andru ku.*   They do not dance to-day.
*dumba-gu-ri **ǎi** ligi.*   The hunter killed a leopard.
*dumba-gu-ri **fe** mani jaa.*   The hunter brought me meat.
*ăipa **ji-ki** mi ăǎu?*   What do they call you?
*a-**ndre** mi gi.*   I saw you.
*ma-**nya** a'bogo-ri koye.*   I did not eat the bananas.
*ama-**nya-ki** a'bugu.*   We eat bananas.
*i-**ji** eri.*   Ask him.
*mi-**ru** ko.*   Don't be afraid.

434. INDEFINITE ASPECT.[1]

	Why are you crying?	The chief is calling you.	They are dying.
KELIKO:	mí-**ŋgə** a'du-sì?	ópí-rɪ mi **zi**.	'bá-**kí drà**.
LUGBARA:	mí-**ówá** à'di-sì?	ópí-rɪ mí **ìzi**.	'bárɪpì **adrà**.

	I shall see your sister.	To-morrow we'll make beer.
KELIKO:	ma mí-ávupi **ndɛ-rà**.	druse ama ɛ́wâ '**ä**.
LUGBARA:	ma-rɪ m-ɛmvúpi **ndrɛ-ra**.	druse ama íwâ **la-ra**.

	I go to marry a wife.	I do not know (how) to read a book.
KELIKO:	má-mu okó **dzɛ-lè**.	má-ni wáraga **la** ku.
LUGBARA:	má-mù okó **ogbwa-lɛ**.	má-nì wáraga **là-ŋga-ra** ku.

KELIKO: *ma sandúki '**dú**.*   I am carrying a box.
*ama marakonyu **jɛ-lɛ**.*   We sell groundnuts.
*au-ri undu **nya**.*   Chickens eat corn.
*'ba-ri uŋgo **tu**.*   The people dance.
*ma-le ɛri **ndre-le**.*   I want to see him.

COMPARISON OF VERB CONJUGATION

435. In order to give a composite view of the dialectal variations already described, the verbs 'to wash oneself' and 'to go' are set out below as specimen paradigms of transitive and intransitive verb respectively.

TRANSITIVE VERB PARADIGM

DEFINITE ASPECT.
Past.

	MORU		LUGBARA
	Miza	-ändri	
I	má-dʒwa lúmvú márɔ tɛ.	má-dzɪ lúmvú márɔ tɛ.	má-dʒè ma 'bo.
You	mí-dʒwa lúmvú mírɔ tɛ.	mí-dzɪ lúmvú mírɔ tɛ.	
He	ánya-dʒwa lúmvú 'írɔ tɛ.	ndá-dzɪ lúmvú 'írɔ tɛ.	ɪrɪ dʒe fru'bá 'bo.
We	mà-dʒwa, &c.	mà-dzɪ, &c.	
You	mì-	mì-	
They	ànya-	ndaká-	kó odʒe èru'ba ra (*or* 'bo).

[1] It should be noted in this context, that in the Lugbara analysed by me, Class I verbs often have a characteristic vowel in the Indefinite forms as in Moru. This characteristic vowel does not occur in the language of the Lugbara New Testament.

VERBS IN SUB-DIALECTS

Imperative.

sg. mí-dʒwà {andívɔ mírù. / lúmvú mírɔ̀.}   mí-dʒwà lúmvú mírɔ̀.   mí-dʒe mí ru'ba.
pl. mì-dʒwà, &c.   mì-dʒwà, &c.   mi-dʒe, &c.

	MADI		KELIKO
	Lokai	Pandikeri	
I	á-dzè ru ra.	má-dʒwè ru ra.	á-dze má ru'bá ge.
You	*i-ze ro ra.*		
He	(andá) odzè ru ra.	(andá) odʒwè ru ra.	ɪrɪ dzé ɪru'ba ge.
We	*ama-ze ro ra.*		
You	*anyi-ze ro ra.*		
They	ódze rukí ra.	ódʒwe rúkí ra.	k-odze koru'ba ge (*or* ra).

Imperative.

sg. nyi-dze rú.   dʒwe rú.   í-dzɪ mí ru'ba.
pl. anyi-dze rú.   nyi-dʒwe rú.   ɪmɪ-dzɪ, &c.

INDEFINITE ASPECT.

Present.

	MORU		LUGBARA
	Miza	-ändri	
I	má lúmvú márɔ òdʒwa.	má-rɔ́ lúmvú márɔ òdzɪ.	má má(ru) odʒè.
You	nyá lúmvú mírɔ òdʒwa.	mí-rɔ́ ,, mí ,, ,,	
He	ánya ká lúmvú írɔ òdʒwa.	ndá-rɔ́ ,, ɪ ,, ,,	ɪrɪ e dʒè.
We	mà lúmvú, &c.	mà-rɔ́, &c.	àmá ma odʒè.
You	nyà....	nyà-rɔ́....	
They	anyá ká....	ndaká-rɔ́....	kó ru odʒè.

Infinitive (I want to wash myself).

má-lɛ lúmvú márɔ òdʒɔ-nɪ.   má-lɛ lúmvú márɔ òdzɪ-lɛ.   má-lɛ má ódʒe-lɛ́.

Present.

	MADI		KELIKO
	Lokai	Pandikeri	
I	má máru dzè.	má-dʒwe rù.	má ma dze.
You	nyí nyaru dzè.	nyí-dʒwe rù.	mí mi dze.
He	ká náru dzè.	andá k-udʒwé rù.	érí é dze.
We	amá ru dzè.	mà-dʒwe rù.	ámá ámá dze.
You	anyí ru dzè.	nyì-dʒwe rù.	
They	kaki ru dzè.	a'í k-údʒwé rù.	kórukópɪ dze.

Infinitive (I want to wash myself).

á-lɛ ru dzɛ-lè.   má-lɛ ru dʒɛ-ka.   má-lɛ́ mà dʒe-lɛ.

INTRANSITIVE VERB PARADIGM

DEFINITE ASPECT.

Past.

	MORU DIALECTS			AVUKAYA
	Miza	-ändri	Wa'di	Ojila
I	mǎ-mù-tè.	mǎ-mù-tè	mǎ-mu-trá.	má-ra-trá.
You	mí-mù-tè.	mí-mù-tè.		
He	ánya-mù-tè.	ndá-mù-tè.		
The boy . . .	ŋgágà mu-te.			
The boys . . .	ŋgàgà mu(-í)-te.			

Future.

I	mǎ-mú-nà-'da.	mǎ-mú-nà-'da.	(See infin.)	má-ràà-tra.
You	mí-mú-nà-'da.	mí-mú-nà-'da.		ná-ràà-tra.
He				gúla arà-tra.

Imperative.

| sg. | mí-mu. | mí-mu. | mí-mu. | mí-ra. |
| pl. | mì-mu. | mì-mu. | mì-mu. | mì-ra. |

Subjunctive.

 mí-'dɛ mɔì. Let's go.
 ánya kwɔì. Let him go.
 nyé'bɛ kòrɪ. Let him be.

INDEFINITE ASPECT.

Present.

	MORU DIALECTS			AVUKAYA
	Miza	-ändri	Wa'di	Ojila
I	mú-ùmu.	má-ró-ómu.	mǎ-lǎmu / mǎ-àmu-gä	má-rà-'á
You	nyú -ùmu.	mí-ró-ómu.	mí-àmu-gä	mí-rà-'á
He	ánya kú-ùmu.	ndá-ró-ómu.	ndínà mu-gä	gúlà rà-'á
The chief	ópí ká tumu.	ópí rò tumu.		
The people are sitting down.				
	ledri k(á t)ərì vùru.	ledri r(ó t)ərɪ vùru.		

Infinitive.

(I don't want to die).
 má-lɛ ku ɔdra-nɪ. má-lɛ ku ɔdra-lɛ. má-lɛ àdrà-lɛ kù. má-lɛ drà-lɛ kù.
          (I arrive to go).[1]
          má-tsa àmu-lɛ.

Compare:

	Miza	Kediru	-ändri	'Bälimbä	-ägi
I am walking	má-abà.	má-abà.	má-r-óba.	m-óróba.	má-rɔ-ɔbá.

---

[1] This is the Wa'di manner of forming the future tense. The verb 'tsa' ('atsa' in 3rd person) is conjugated in its *definite* form, followed by the *indefinite* infinitive of 'mu'.

VERBS IN SUB-DIALECTS
SOUTHERN AND CENTRAL DIALECTS[1]

DEFINITE ASPECT.
Past.

	MADI LOKAI	MADI PANDIKERI	LUGBARA	KELIKO
I	á-mu-rá.	mǎ-mu-rá.	má-mu-'bò.	má-mu-gí.
You	i-mu-rá.	nyí-mu-rá.	í-mu-'bò.	mí-mu-gí.
He	ànì òmu-rá.	andá mu-rá.	eri mu-'bò	eri mu-gí.
We	à-vừ-ra.	àmà-vò-pi.	ama-mú-kí-'bo.	ama-mu-kí-gɪ.
You	ì-vừ-ra.	nyì-vò-pi.	emi-mú-kí-'bo.	
They	ovu-ki-ra.	à'ɪ vò-pi.	kòmu-kí-'bo.	komu-kí-gɪ.
Have the boys gone?				
	bɔrɔndzí òvu-rá?	'bɔndʒí vɔkí-ra?	andziri mu-kí-'bo?	andziri mu-kí-gɪ?

Imperative.

sg.	nyi-mú.	mú.	í-mu.	í-mu.
pl.	ányí-vò.	nyi-vò.	imi-mó-kî.	imi-mó-kî.

Subjunctive.

Let me go.
nyébé mà-mu.   'ba má-mú.

Let us go.
nyiba óvừ.   'ba ma-vừ.   mé'bé àmà-mu-kì.   méku 'bá mù-ki.

Let him go.
nyébé kòmu.

Exhortative.

Let's go {ómu-kî. / óvɔ-kî.}   ávɔ-kî.   áma-mú-kì.   'bá mo-kî. / 'bá le-kî.

INDEFINITE ASPECT.
Present.

	MADI LOKAI	MADI PANDIKERI	LUGBÁRA	KELIKO
I	máà-mu.	mǎ-mu.	má-mu.	mǎ-mu.
You	nyɪ̀-mu.	nyi-mu.	mi-mu.	nyí-mu.
He	ànì kó-òmu.	ndä-mu.	erɪ mú.	èrɪ̀ mu.
The chief	ópí kò-òmu.	ópí k-òmùmù.	ópí lamu.	ópírì-mumu.
We	ama-vòvò.	amá-vòvò.	ama-múmu.	ama-lélè.
You	anyí-vòvò.	nyi-vóvò.	imi-múmù.	mi-lélè.
They	ká-kí-{vòvò. / mumù.}	a'í k-óvóvò.	kórɪ mùmù.	kô-lélè.
The people...	{na bà kó-vòvò. / na kó-mùmù.}	bá kó-vóvò.	'bá-kí mùmù.	'bá-rɪ̀-pi ko-lélè.

Future.

I	má-mu má-mu-rá.	ma-mu má-mú-ra.	ma-mu-la-rá.	ma-mu-rá.

[1] Note alternation of **mu** with **vo** (Madi) and **le** (Keliko) in the plural.

Future.

	MADI LOKAI	MADI PANDIKERI	LUGBARA	KELIKO
I'll go to-morrow.	ɔbɔ́ ma-mu-rá.	ɔ'bɔ́ ma-mu-rà.	drusi ma-mú-lá-rá.	drú ma-mu-rá.
He'll go to-morrow.	andrâ kóòmu ɔ̀'bo.	andá kúmú ɔ̀'bo.	erɪ mú-lá drusi.	érí mú drù.
The chief will go.	ɔpí komu-ra.	ɔpí kɔ́mù-ra.	ópi mu-la-rá.	ópí-rí mu-rá.

CHAPTER XIII

THE FUNCTION OF VERB STEM PREFIXES

436. Stem prefixes are of two sorts. Some are added to existing verb stems as conjugation elements in certain tenses, e.g. má sɔ̀ gini (I hoe the ground) and má gini ɔ̀-sɔ (I am hoeing the ground). Others help to compose verb stems as such, the verbs being thus in Class II or Class III according as the prefix is a vowel or a consonant+vowel. In many cases these stem prefixes have a discernible semantic value, but not in all cases. In this chapter the following vowel prefixes are discussed:

- A. Characteristic vowel in Class I verbs.
- B. Characteristic vowel in Class II verbs *(a) Directional, (b) Plural action, (c) Causative, (d) Other verbs.*
- C. The Passive vowel prefix.
- D. The Infinitive vowel prefix.

and the following consonant prefixes:

- A. Plural action prefixes.
- B. Causative prefix.
- C. Intensive prefix.
- D. Neuter-passive prefix.

Vowel Prefixes

A. THE CHARACTERISTIC VOWEL IN CLASS I VERBS

437. As already mentioned (§ 32) Class I verbs, in certain languages, take characteristic vowel prefixes under certain conditions, morphologically defined. Thus in MORU, verbs conjugated according to the Indefinite Aspect have a characteristic vowel **u-** (before tense stem vowels) or **ə-** (before lax stem vowels and **a**).

e.g. má-sə̀ gini. I hoe the ground. DEFINITE.
má gini ə̀sɔ. I am hoeing the ground. INDEFINITE.

In the Definite aspect the characteristic vowel is found in the 3rd person future only.

e.g. ánya ɔpá ma 'dà. He will help me.

In the Subjunctive 3rd person it also occurs, preceded, in Miza, by the auxiliary **k-**. See § 500.

M.: ányà k-**uru**. He must take it away.
Ä.: ndá **uru**.

In MADI the characteristic vowel is found in the 3rd person only, and in constructions in which no object (or particle **ki**) precedes the verb. Thus it appears always in the Definite Aspect, but only in the Indefinite aspect in the singular and when there is no object. The vowels are **o-** (before tense stem vowels) and **ə-** (before lax stem vowels and **a**).

e.g. **ono** ta. He sees something. **ono**-ki ta. They see something. DEFINITE.
ka ta no. ,, ,, ka-ki ta no. ,, ,, INDEFINITE.
odra-ra. He died. **odra**-ki-ra. They died. DEFINITE.
k-**odra**. He is dying. ka-ki-dra. They are dying. INDEFINITE.
k-**odra**-dro. That he die. k-**odra**-ki-dro. That they die. SUBJUNCTIVE.

B. THE CHARACTERISTIC VOWEL IN CLASS II VERBS

438. The characteristic vowel of Class II verbs is usually **i** or **e** (for tense stem vowels) and **a** and **ε** (for lax stem vowels), and it is always pronounced in all forms of the verb. Class II verbs may be coined from Class I verb roots under the following conditions:

(a) Directional Verbs

439. When the speaker wishes to indicate that the action of the verb is in a direction towards himself or towards the doer of the action, the verb stem acquires a characteristic vowel prefix, **i, e, ε** (**a** in dialects), and is conjugated as a Class II verb.

Examples from MORU (Miza):
mäfátis **esá**-te Lui yá tandróbè. The D.C. reached Lui (here) yesterday.
z^wó **έ'dέ**-'da mä-drì. The house will fall down on me.
ndá ká **ibi**-ná márı. He is pushing it towards me.

440. When he wishes to indicate that the action of the verb is in a direction away from himself, or when he is not concerned with the direction, the verb root is simple (monosyllabic, Class I) and the characteristic vowel, which is now **u-** or **ə-**, is used only in the Indefinite Aspect or in the 3rd person future.

mäfátis **sa**-te Amádi yá tandróbè. The District Commissioner reached Amadi (not here) yesterday.
z^wó **ə'dε**-'da ndä-drì. The house will fall down on him.
ndá ká-**ubi**-ná mì-rı. He is pushing it towards you.

See § 450 for paradigm of the two verbs **sa** and **εsa** = to arrive.

441. Contrast the following:

Speaker is inside the house and says:

    Pull it into the house.   *Pull it out of the house.*
    M.: ny-**έsε** zó yasì.   mí-**sε** tεsì.
    Ä.: n-**áse** ,,   mí-**sε** ivè.

Speaker is outside the house and says:

    Pull it into the house.   *Pull it out of the house.*
    M.: mí-**sε** zó yasì.   ny-**έsε** tεsì.
    Ä.: mí-**sε** ,,   n-**ásε** ivè.

442. Further examples from MORU:

DEFINITE.
Imperative.

Class I

mí-bì láù.	Push it over there.
mí-ŋgyi láù.	Carry it ,, ,,
mɪ-dà vʋrʋ.	Throw it away.
mí-vɔ kwíní ndǎrì.	Throw the stone to him.
mɪ-sɛ sanduku.	Shut the box.
mí-kɪ teze.	Go outside.
mí-'dɛ kʋ vùrʋ.	Don't fall down.
mí-zu ŋgaga Amadi ya.	Send a boy to Amadi.

Class II

ny-íbì noa.	Push it here.
ny-íŋgyi nòa.	Carry ,,
ny-éda vʋrʋ.	Pour it down (on me).
ny-ɛ́vɔ kwíní märi.	Throw the stone to me.
ny-ɛ́sɛ́ sandúkù.	Shut the box.
ny-ékyi noa.	Come here.
ny-ɛ'dɛ kʋ mädrì.	Don't fall on me.
ny-ézu ŋgága marɛ.	Send a boy to me.

Perfect.

Class I

zwó 'dɛ-tɛ vùrʋ.	The house fell down.
M.: ánya ŋgyi-te Amádi yá.	He carried it to Amadi.
Ä.: ndá **ndzi** ,, ,,	,, ,,

Where did you push it? (away).
Jl.: mí-ze aníka áŋgoléró yà?

Class II

zwó ɛ'dɛ́-te mǎdrì.	The house fell down on me.
M.: ánya **iŋgyi**-tɛ màrɛ.	He carried it to me.
Ä.: ndá **ändzi** ,, ,,	,, ,,

Where did you push it? (towards).
Jl.: n-**áze** aníka áŋgoléró yà?

Class I	Class II
What will you sell for me with this money?	*What will you buy for me . . . ?*
M., K.: mí-**gɛ́** na ɔ'dú mǎrí parátà ónó si yà?	ny-**ɛ́gɛ́** na ɔ'dù mǎrí . . .
Ä.: mí-**dzɛ́** na ɔ'dí mǎdŕ ,, ní ,,	n-**ádzɛ́** ,, ɔ'dí mǎdŕ . . .
'B.: mí-**gyɛ** ,, a'dí mǎrí ,, 'dí ,,	n-**ágyɛ** ,, a'dí mǎrí . . .
Äg.: mí-**dʒɛ** ,, a'dí mǎdrí ,, ní ,,	n-**ádʒɛ** ,, a'dí mǎdrí . . .

INDEFINITE.

Class I (away from speaker).	Class II (towards speaker).
Whither are you carrying that box?	*Whence are you carrying that box?*
M.: nyá sandúku 'dóó **uŋgyi** gáŋwa yà?	nyá sandúku 'dóó **iŋgyi** nìŋwa ya?
Ä.: mí-ró ,, 'dí **undʒi** ɪŋwa yà?	mí-ró ,, 'dí **ändʒi** ,,

He is carrying a box (away from me).
M.: ánya ká sandúku u**ŋgyi**.
Ä.: ndá ró   ,, **undʒi**.

He is carrying a box (towards me).
ánya ká sandúku **iŋgyi**.
ndá ró   ,, **ändʒi**.

Where are you pushing it? (away).
M.: nyá-**ubí**-na íŋwa yà?
Ä.: mí-ró-**úbì**-na έŋgwa yà?
'B.: ná-ró-**ùbi**-na ɪŋgòlɛrɛ yà?
Äg.: nǎ-dudu íŋgwɔ yà?

Where are you pushing it? (towards).
nyí-**íbi**-ná ɪŋwa yà?
mi-ro-**äbì**-ná ɛŋgwa yà?
ná-ró-**ǎbi**-nǎ ɪŋgòlɛrɛ yà?
ná-ró-**äbi**-ná íŋgwɔ yà?

443. Examples from MADI:

         Class I. **mu** = to go (pl. və)

		(Reduplicated)
To-morrow I'll go.	*The chief will go.*	*I'll go.*
Lo.: ɔbó ma-**mu**-rá.	ɔpí k-**omu**-ra.	má-**mu** má-**mu**-rá.
Pa.: ɔ'bó ma-**mu**-rá.	ɔpí k-**ómù**-ra.	ma-**mu** má-**mú**-ra.

The boys are going.	*We are going.*
Lo.: bɔrɔndzí k-**ɔ́vʊ̀**.	amá-**və̀-və̀**.
Pa.: 'bɔndʒí k-**úvó**.	ama-**vɔ́-və̀**.

         Class II. **emu** = to come (pl. ɛvo)

		(Reduplicated)
I'll come to-morrow.	*The chief will come.*	*I'll come.*
Lo.: m-**ɛ́mú** òbu ra.	ɔpí k-**emu**-ra.	má-**àmu** m-ɛmu-ra.
Pa.: m-**ɛ́mú** ò'bu ra.	ɔpí k-**emu**-ra.	m-**emu** m-**emu**-ra.

We will come.	*The locusts are coming.*
Lo.: am-**emu**-ra.	ombí k-**ɛvò**.
Pa.:	ombí k-**eki**.

Come!	*The chief came.*
Lo.: ny-**ɛmú**, pl. àny-**ɛvə̀**.	ɔpí **emu**-ra.
Pa.: **ɛmʊ**, pl. (à)ny-**ɛvə̀**.	ɔpí **emu**-ra.

444. Examples from LULU'BA:

    Class I

kyíí. Go!

í'dέ k-**omú** mi-ra. The mouse runs to you.
a-tə boŋgo 'o. I put on clothes.

mó-**tó** bòŋgo-nì. I am putting on clothes.

    Class II

èkyí wá.   Come here!
mäfátis **ekí** yó? Has the D.C. arrived?
(adi) **ekí** kú.   He has not arrived.
í'dέ k-**emu** ma-ra. The mouse runs to me.
m-**ɛtwa** bòŋgɔ kàlɛ 'o. I took off clothes.
m-**ɛ́twέ**-ri bòŋgɔ kàlɛ-nì. I am taking off clothes.

445. In LOGO the characteristic vowel of Class II verbs is **a-**. Thus:

Class I	Class II	Class I	Class II
li (to go)	*ali* (to come)	*do* (to take)	*ado* (to bring)
nji (to go away)	*anji* (to come back)	*ca* (to arrive (there))	*aca* (to arrive (here))
go (to go back)	*ago* (to come back)	*fo* (to go out)	*afo* (to come out)
		si (to go in)	*asi* (to come in)

There seems little difference in conjugation, except in the Volition Imperative, in which the **ko** infix loses its vowel.

Class I. mi-ko-**li**. Go!
Class II. mi-k-**ali**. Come! (not mi-ko-ali). (Cf. Ä.: n-áli nana. Come here!)

446. Further examples in Logo:

The motor-car left here and will reach Aba to-morrow.
Class I. *Larua ŋga-dre agia dre* **ca**-*zo Aba na tudru.*
The motor-car left Aba and will reach here to-morrow.
Class II. *Larua ŋga-dre Aba agia dre* **aca**-*zo nole tudru.*

Class I. *mi-ko-se fa ma vulese.*	Pull the log away from me.	
Class II. *mi-ase fa ma vuna.*	,, ,, towards me.	
Class I. *mi-ko-si koro le na.*	Climb down into the well.	
Class II. *mi-asi fa le se ma vuna.*	,, ,, the tree to me.	
Class I. *mi-ko-mba fa nidi drina.*	,, up this tree.	
Class II. *mi-k-amba koro lese*	,, ,, out of the well.	

Class I and Class II. *mi-**do** nole se. mi-k-**aji** todia.* Take this food away. Bring it back.

Class II and Class I. *mi-**ado** yi aruka madri. mi-ko-**go** aba.* Bring me some water. Take it back.

Class I–II. *mi-ko-**li**. mi-k-**ago**.* Go away. Come back.

Class II–I. *mi-k-**ali** nole. mi-ko-**go**.* Come here. Go back.

447. In LUGBARA (and KELIKO and AVUKAYA) the characteristic vowel of Class II verbs is usually **a-**, although **ε-** (or **ɪ-**) is to be found occasionally.

The chief will come.	*Come!*
LUGBARA: ɔpí-r(i) **amu**-la-ra.	mɪ-ɪmʊ̀, pl. ɪmɪ-ímʊ̀
KELIKO: ɔpí-r(i) **amu** (-lɛ)-ra.	mí-ámʊ́, pl. ìmì-ímʊ́-kɪ.
KELIKO: *mu.* Go!	*imu.* Come!
i-mu ku. Don't go.	*imu ku ye.* Don't come.

448. Where the first person is concerned, the **a** of **ma** and the characteristic vowel **a-** often merge, so that directional distinction is impossible.

	Class I	Class II
	I'll go back.	*I'll come back.*
LUGBARA:	**màgɔ̀** vʊlɛ.	**màgɔ̀** ndɔ̀.
KELIKO:	**màgɔ̀** vʊlɛ.	má-ígɔ̀ vúlɛ.
LOGO:	**magu** andʒɪlɛ.	**magɔ** andʒɪlɛ.
AVUKAYA:	máni **àgʊ̀** lɛ.	**mágɔ̀** vʊlɛ.

THE FUNCTION OF VERB STEM PREFIXES

General examples:

449. Example with verb 'sɛ' = to pull.

	Class I	Class II
Imperative:	Pull the box (away from me).	Pull the box (towards me).

MORU (M.): mɪ-sɛ sandúkù.   ny-ɛ́sɛ́ sandúkù.
AVUKAYA
(Jl. and Jg.): mi-sɛ   „   n-asɛ.   „
MADI { Lo.: nyi-sɛ́ „ or nyi-kû.   ny-ɛ́sɛ́ „ or ny-ɛ́kû.
       { Pa.:   sɛ́   „ or kû.   ɛ́sɛ   „ or ɛ́ku.
LUGBARA: mí-sɛ̀ „   mí-ásɛ „
KELIKO: í-sɛ̀ „   m-ɛsɛ (or mɪasɛ) sandúkù.
LULU'BA: **tu** iba (pull the rope).   ɛtu iba (pull the rope).
LOGO: mí-se eba.   ny-asɪ eba.

Past: He pulled it (away from me).   He pulled it (towards me).

MORU { M.: sɛ-tɛ.   ɛsɛ-tɛ.
       { Ä.: sɛ-tɛ.   asɛ-tɛ.
MADI { Lo.: ɔsɛ-pí.   ɛsɛ-ra.
      { Pa.: sɛ-pí.   ɛsɛ-ra.
LUGWARA: sɛ-'bò.   asɛ-'bo.
KELIKO: sɛ-gɪ.   ɛsɛ-gɪ.
LULU'BA: m-ɛtú-r(i) ìbà ni. (I pulled the rope.)

Present: So-and-so is pulling it   So-and-so is pulling it
             (away from me).   (towards me).

MORU { M.: Aílɛ ká-ɔsɛ́ ná.   Aílɛ ká-ɛsɛ́ ná.
       { Ä.: „ ró-ɔsɛ́ ná.   „ ró-asɛ́ ná.
MADI (Lo.): „ k-ɔ́sɛ a.   „ k-ɛ́sɛ a.
LUGBARA: „ rɪ sɛ.   „ r-ɛsɛ. (< rɪ-asɛ).
KELIKO: „ sɛ.   „ kà-ásɛ.

450. Example with the verb '(t)sa' = to arrive.

	Class I	Class II
Future:	When will you arrive at Maridi? (away)	When will you arrive here? (towards)

M., K.: mí-sá na itú Marìdi yá yà?   ny-ɛ́sá na itú niwá yà?
Ä., 'B.: mí-sá na ätú Marìdi yá yà?   n-ása na ätú nɛ̈nɔ yà? (niyɛ yà.)
Äg.: mí-sá na a'ditú Marìdi yá yà?   n-ása na a'ditú niyɛ yà?
Jl.: ná-atsà Marídi ála áŋgutú yà?   ná-'d-átsá aŋgutú nɔŋgó yà?

The chief will arrive at Loka to-morrow.   *The chief will arrive at Yei to-morrow.*
              (away)   (towards)

MORU (M.): ópí ɔsá-na Loka ya ɔndɔ.   ópí esá-na Yei ya ɔndɔ.
AVUKAYA { Jl.: mɔkɔtɔ atsa Loka la.   mɔkɔtɔ atsa Yei a.
        { Jg.: mɔkɔtɔ n(i) atsɛ Loka le. mɔkɔtɔ n-ɛtsa (< ni-atsa) Yei á.
LOGO: { mɔkɔtɔ ní tsa kɪdru Lókà na.   mɔkɔtɔ { an-ɛ́tsá Yei 'a kɪdru.
                                              { ání átsá
LUGBARA: mɔkɔtɔ tsá Lóka gá drùsì.   mɔkɔtɔ atsa Yei ga drùsì.
KELIKO: mɔkɔtɔ tsa-lɛ drù Lókà ga.   mɔkɔtɔ ɛ́tsá Yèì ge drù.

		Class II
		I have arrived (here).
MADI	Lo.:	mé-ɛtsá-rá.
	Pa.:	m-ɛ́sà-rá.
LULU'BA:		m-ɛ́sà-ti.
AVUKAYA:		mátsa-trá.[1]
LOGO:		mátsá-drɛ̀.[1]

451. Example with the verb 'ŋga' = to fly.

	Class I	Class II
	The bird is flying (away).	*The bird is flying towards me.*
LUGBARA:	arívía ŋgà-ga.	arívía eri ŋga mävu.
KELIKO:	arívá ádré ŋga lïŋgà.	arívá adr(e) aŋga.
LOGO:	aría ŋga-ra-lɛ.	aría aŋga-ra-lɛ.

(b) Plural Action Verbs

452. In MADI plurality of action is shown by a prefix **o-** or **u-** (i.e. the verb is a Class II verb).

e.g. **tsɪ** (bite) **ətsɪ** (gnaw)

Indefinite aspect.
- Lo.: ɔtsé ká ezá **tsɪ**.   The dog is biting the meat. Class I.
- Pa.: ɔké k-**úsí** ma.   The dog is biting me.

but:
- Lo.: ɔtsé ká kwa **ótsí**.   The dog is gnawing a bone. Class II.
- Pa.: ɔké k-**ósí** kwà.   ,, ,, ,,

Definite aspect.
- Lo.: ɔtsé **ətsɪ** ma ra.   The dog bit me. Class I.
- Pa.: ɔké **sɪ** ma rá.   ,, ,,

but (note difference in tone):
- Lo.: ɔtsé **ətsí** kwà ra.   The dog gnawed the bone. Class II.
- Pa.: ɔké **əsí** ,,   ,, ,, ,, ,,

Imperative.
- Lo.: nyi-tsi. Bite!   ny-ətsí. Gnaw!
- Pa.: si.   əsí.

e.g. **ŋə** (to break) **oŋə** (to break up)

Indefinite.
- Lo.: baráŋgwá ká kwɛ̀ **ŋə̀**.   The boy breaks the stick. Class I.
- Pa.: 'boràŋgwá k-**úŋú** kwɛ̀.   ,, ,, ,,

but:
- Lo.: baráŋgwá ká kwɛ̀ **oŋə̀**.   The boy breaks the stick into pieces. Class II.
- Pa.: 'boràŋgwá k-**úŋú** kwɛ̀.   (No difference in Pandikeri.)

Definite.
- Lo.: baráŋgwá **əŋò** kwe rá.   The boy broke the stick. Class I.
- Pa.: 'boràŋgwá **ŋò** ,,   ,, ,, ,,

but:
- Lo.: baráŋgwá **uŋò** ,,   The boy broke up the stick. Class II.
- Pa.: 'boràŋgwá **əŋò** ,,   ,, ,, ,, ,,

[1] Impossible to tell superficially whether form is má-tsa or m-átsa. (See § 448.)

THE FUNCTION OF VERB STEM PREFIXES

Imperative.
Lo.: nyɪ-ŋɔ̀. Break it!   nyu-uŋɔ̀. Break it up!
Pa.: ŋə.   ,,   əŋɔ̀.   ,,   ,,

(c) Causative Verbs

453. Mynors notes a few instances in MORU where the e- prefix gives the verb a causative rather than a directional meaning.

Class I	Class II
o-ŋga (to get up)	eŋga (to raise up)
o-mba (to grow up)	emba (to bring up)
o-ca (to be tall)	eca (to nourish)

(d) Other Class II Verbs

454. In MORU there are a great many verbs belonging to Class II in which the initial vowel does not appear to be a prefix, but part of the root, which is therefore dissyllabic. Such verbs may have any vowel in the vowel system in the initial syllable—viz. **u, ə, i, e, ɛ, a** and also **o, ä, ɪ**—according to the Moru laws of vowel harmony.

455. Examples from MORU:

Characteristic vowel **i** or **ɪ**.
  ny-íti märi. Tell me.   m-ídɛ-te. I cleaned it.

Characteristic vowel **e** or **ɛ** (dial. **a** or **ɔ**).
  ny-éndzwɛ bòŋgó tɛ.   You spoilt the cloth.
  ɔpí ɛdʒwɪ kàlà márɔ tɛ.   The chief asked me.

  I am heating the water.   *I let go of him.*   *Leave him alone.*
  M.: má gíí ɛ́mɛ́.   ma ánya ɛ'bɛ.   ny-ɛ́'bɛ̀ ánya.
  Ä.: má-ró ìdʒi ámɛ.   má-ró ndá ɛ'bɛ.   n-á'bɛ̀ ndá.

  Tie the rope.   *Why are you coughing?*   *Come here.*
  M.: nyé-émbɛ́ èba.   nyé-ɛkpí ɔ'du-ta yà?   ny-ékyi nòa.
  K., L.: nyé-émbɛ́ èba.   (pl. ny-ekyi nòa.)
  Ä.: nó-(ə)mbɛ èba.   mɪ-rɔ-ɛkpí a'di-ta yà?   n-áli nana.
  'B.: nó-(ə)mbɛ èba.   nǎ-r(ɔ)-ɛ́kpɛ́-na a'di-ta yà?   n-ǎkyi nɛnɔ.
  Äg.: n-émbɛ èba.   nǎ-ɛ́kpe a'di-drí à?
  Jl.: n-ɔ́mbɛ mbàgɔ.   ní-íkpu a'dɔ-drí yà?
  Jg.: n-ambɛ mbàgo.
  W.: n-ambɛ eba.

Characteristic vowel **a** (dial. **ə**).
  Go! (lit. Travel).   *Speak Moru.*   *What did you say?*
  M.: ny-ábà.   ny-áta kala Moró.   ny-átá-t(e) ɔ'dú yà?
  Ä.: n-ɔ́bà.   na-áta kala Moró.   n-áta-t(e) ɔ'di yà?

Characteristic vowel **ə** (dial. **a**).
  Where are you going?   *I went.*   *You went.*   *He went.*   *Go!*
  M.: nyó-əì íŋwa yà?   m-ói-te.   ny-ói-te.   ány-əi-te.   ny-ɔ́ì, pl. ny-ɔ́í.
  Ä.: mí-rɔ́-əì íŋwa yà?   m-ói-te.   n-ói-te.   nd-ói-te.   n-ɔ́i.

	Pay him.	Untie him.
M.:	ny-ózò ŋga ndǎrì.	ny-óndzʷi ánya.
Ä.:	n-ázò ŋga ndǎrì.	n-óndzʷi ndá.

M.:	nyá ɔ'du ɔzò yà?	What are you giving back?
	má ilì ɔzò.	I'm giving a knife back.

Characteristic vowel **u**.

	I slept.	You slept.	He slept.
M.:	m-ú'du-te.	ny-ú'du-te.	ány-u'du-te.
Ä.:	mú-ú'du-te.	nú-ú'du-te.	ndá-ú'du-te.

Characteristic vowel **ä**.
M.: m-ǎti-te. I held it.

456. Some verbs are not consistent in their obedience to class rules in all dialects:

Class I (in Wa'di and Ojila only).   Class II.

M.:	ny-ózò ŋga ndǎrì. Pay him.	ny-ózò ŋga märi. Pay me.
Ä.:	{ n-ázò / n-ófɛ̀ } nda.	n-ófɛ̀ ma.
W.:	mí-tsɛ̀ ŋga ṅdinàdri.	n-átsɛ̀ ŋga mädri.
Jl.:	ní-fɛ̀ gʊla drı.	n-áfɛ̀ madri.

M.: ndá ɔzɔ boŋgó ko tɛ märigɛ. He did not give me a cloth.

Other verbs again are invariable, no matter what the direction of the action may be. E.g. MORU:

mí-zi ndâ.	Call him (to come to me).
ny-ɔ́ì, pl. ny-ɔ́í.	Go (away from me).
ny-áka } lòzò. ny-úgu }	Take it far away.

Examples from MADI

457. Examples of non-directional Class II verbs are rare in Madi. Note, however, the following:

any-**ede** ebu anyi-dri.	Do (pl.) your work.
am-**ede** ta.	Let us do something.
any-**eŋgo** kareaga.	Sing (pl.) lustily.
am-**eŋgo** leŋgo.	Let us sing a song.
am-**elegi**.	Let us pray.
am-**ogu** ta ko.	Let us not steal (anything).
any-**olo** ciri.	Be quiet (pl.).

458. Many of the corresponding verbs in the Pandikeri dialect belong to Class III.

	I paid the chief.	The pot broke.
Lo.:	m-**úkwɛ̀** ɔpı ra.	lóku'dó **ɛdrà** ra.
Pa.:	mú-**lukwɛ̀** ,,	,, **lɛdà** ra.

	I am lost in the bush.	The goat is lost.	The goat is not found.
Lo.:	m-**ɛ́gwɛ̀** aíse aga dì.	indrí **ègwè** dì.	indrí **ésu** (ro) korò. (Note reflexive.)
Pa.:	mé-**lɛgwɛ̀** ,, ,,	indí **lègwè** dì.	indí **ésú** korò.

THE FUNCTION OF VERB STEM PREFIXES 213

Call your brother quickly.
Lo.: ny-**ùŋgwė** nyí-adrúpi ni ɛzɛzɛ.
Pa.: **lúŋgwɛ́** nyá-adǎzi ni ɛzɛzɛ.
Lulu'ba: m-**úŋgw(ɛ)** osí 'o. (I have called the chief.)

The chief is calling you.
Lo.: ópí ka nyi **uŋgwė**.
Pa.: ,, k-**uluŋgwé** nyi'ɪ.

Give me something.	*He did not give me a cloth.*
Lo.: ny-**íkwɛ** mání ta.	**ɛ́kwɛ́** mání boŋgó koro.
Pa.: (ny)-**ɛkɛ** mání ta.	**ɛkɛ** ,, ,, ,,
Lulu'ba: m-**umbɛ** 'ɔ̀. I tied it.	m-**unji** 'ɔ̀. I untied it.

459. In the other Central languages the two classes of verbs are not so clear. As may be expected, the Ojila dialect of Avukaya, being spoken in the Moru area, shows more tendency towards verb classes than the Ojiga dialect, which is influenced by Logo. Keliko also shows a few traces.

Examples:
	Cook meat.	*Don't cry.*
LUGBARA:	mí-**à'di** za.	mí-**əwə** kɔ.
KELIKO:	mí-k-**à'di** za.	mí-**àŋgə** kɔ.
LOGO:	mí-ka-**la'dí** zȧ.	mí-kɔ-**ŋgə** kɔ. (Class I in Logo).
Cf. MORU:	nyá-**la'di** èza.	

	The goat is lost.	*Call your brother quickly.*
LUGBARA:	indí **àvɪ**-'bo.	m-**úmvɛ** (< mí-**umvɛ**) médrúpi mbèlè.
KELIKO:	indí-rí **àvɪ**-ge.	

Give me something.
LUGBARA: (m)í-**fɛ** mání akozí (Cl. I).
KELIKO: mí-**fɛ** mání ŋga (Cl. I) or mí-k-**àfɛ̀** madri (Cl. II).
LOGO: {mí-**áfɛ̀** / ny-**áfɛ̀**} madrɛ buku (Cl. II). (Give me a book.)

He did not give me a cloth.
LUGBARA: ɪr(ɪ) **ɛfɛ** mání boŋgó kù.
KELIKO: ɪr(ɪ) **ɛfɛ** ,,   ,, kùɛ.

AVUKAYA (Jl.):	mí-**ɛdɛ** or n-**édɛ**.	Do it.
WA'DI:	mí-**áŋga**.	Pick it up.
Äg.:	ny-**ɛ́ŋga**.	

460. It may be that all non-directional, &c., verbs of Class II were once governed by a similar functional rule, and were related to verbs in Class I—but this is mere supposition. It is true that in some of the Southern and Central languages the verbs of Class II are all directional, but it is equally true in Moru that there are many verbs in this class which cannot possibly be given a directional significance. It must also be borne in mind in Moru, that only the vowels **i, e, ɛ** (a in dialects), can have a directional, &c. meaning, whereas Class II verbs in general include the vowels **ɪ, ə, o, u, ä** as well.

C. THE PASSIVE VOWEL PREFIX

461. Moru-Madi verbs have a passive form, obtained by prefixing a vowel to the stem. This vowel in MORU is:

Class I. **á-**.
Class II. Characteristic vowel with high tone (i.e. the stem is unaltered except for tone).
Class III. A 'harmonized' vowel, i.e. a vowel of the same quality as the first vowel of the verb stem (see § 24), with high tone.

The passive verb may be followed by a postposition.
The sentence order in a passive sentence is as follows: passive verb+'sufferer'+verb postposition+'agent' (if any).

462. Examples from MORU:

Class I verbs:

á-'bɪ ma te.	I am (or was) beaten.
á-za zó te.	The house is (or was) burnt.
á-nya ŋgóinyà tɛ.	The food was eaten.
á-pè kɪlá'báɪ tɛ r̥ɛ.	The warriors were defeated.
ă-zí ma Deŋgò.	I am called Dengo.
á-gyɛ ndá tɛ Mòndarì ya.	*She* married (lit. was married by) a Mondari.
(Cf. ndá gyɛ Mondárì tɛ.	*He* married a Mondari.)
ă-fu gárà te dòfó sì.	The bowl was smashed by a stick.
ä-ru-aɖa ni anya rige.	(Lk. viii. 18.) From him shall be taken away.

With reduplication (note characteristic vowel in second part):

I'm crying because I'm beaten (... *have been beaten*)

M.:	ma-líí tana	á'bɪ ma ə'bì.
L., K.:	m-íli	á'bɪ ma ə'bì.
Ä., 'B.:	ma-rɔ-áŋgwa tana	á'bɪ ma ə'bì.
W., Äg.:	ma-ŋgau	,, á'bɪ ma'bì.

Class II verbs. Here the characteristic vowel with a high tone is used *instead of* **á-**, but the sentence order is the same.

éndzwì bòŋgó tɛ àsɪ sì ... mí sì.	The cloth is spoiled by fire ... by you.
ézu ndá te márɛ.	He was sent to me.
(Cf. á-zu ndá te Ndaragù rɛ. Class I.	He was sent to Ndarago.)
ozo-na aza ɖa anyä-ri. (Lk. viii. 18.)	To him shall (more) be given.

Class III verbs. Here the passive prefix 'harmonizes' with the first vowel of the verb stem (see § 24).

ú-kugu paráta márɔ té.	My money is stolen.
á-lara ɪnyá tɛ.	The grain is spread out.

463. In the Southern and Central languages passive verb forms are less used, and a specialized form of the 3rd person plural active is often found instead. The sentence order is usually the same (unless an indefinite subject, like **'ba**, precedes the verb).

		A man has been killed.	*Two goats have been stolen.*
MADI	(Torit):	'ba oɖi-ki maɖi ra.	ogu-ki endri eri ra.
	(Opari):	oɖi-ki maɖi alo ra.	ogu-ki endri ra.
	KELIKO:	ɖi-ki 'ba-ago dre.	ogu-ki ndri-i iri gi.

THE FUNCTION OF VERB STEM PREFIXES 215

I am called So-and-so.   *I was beaten.*

MADI ⎧ Lo.: adi m-**oŋgwe** Lúgumà-e.   ⎧ bá ká mà **mgba**.
      ⎨ Pa.: **ú-luŋgwé** mà Ăyurù.   ⎨ ma'dí-zì **ómgbá** mánì.
      ⎩ (Passive.)   mo'dí áka **m̀gbá** mánì.
LUGBARA: **zi-kí** mà Araba-i.   **gba-kí** ma 'bò.
KELIKO: **zi-kí** mà Ayélè.   'bá-zi **gbà** mà gɪ.

With reduplication:
 MADI (Lo.): ɔmgba-kí ma mgbà.   I was beaten.
 LULU'BA: ómgbá mɔ-mgbà.   ,,   ,,
 AVUKAYA: ótsa mà tsa-tsà.   ,,   ,,

Compare:
 MADI ⎧ Lo.: dzʷè (to marry a woman)   ódzè (to marry a man)
      ⎨ Pa.: gyè   ágè

Note sentence order in:
 LUGBARA: indrí-ri **ésu-kí** ku.   The goat is not found.
 KELIKO: indí-ri **ésu-kí** kùé.   ,,   ,,   ,,
 LULU'BA: kó 'dɔ min(i) **ɔ̀si**.   You were not bitten.

Examples of passive forms:
 LUGBARA: **á-nya** ìza 'bó.   The meat is eaten.
 LOGO: **a-nya**-dre.   It is eaten.
 LUGBARA: **u-gúgu** ma-parata ra.   My money was stolen.
 AVUKAYA: **u-gúgu** paráta amá-ka tra.   ,,   ,,
 LUGBARA: **a-pi**-'bo.   It is broken.
 KELIKO: **a-fu**-gɪ.   ,,   ,,

464. In LOGO the passive stem is used more than in the other Central languages.
 Why is the boy crying?   *Because he is beaten.*
 mvaago adre ngo-le adose ya?   **acoa** adi dre dise. (Passive.)
                                   Because he is being beaten.
                                   aii dre adi **coa**-le dise. (Plural active.)
 If you go there, you will be killed . . . beaten. (Plural active.)
  mi-ko-li nale di, aii **ko-fu** mi dra-le . . . aii **ko-coa** mi.
 If you had gone there, you would have been killed.
  mi-li-dre nale dre di, **afu**-dre mi. (Passive.)
  afu adi dre dili se.   He was killed by a spear.
  ati ma dre kiono.   I was born a long time ago.
  (Cf. ma-ti mva dre.   I gave birth to a child.)

Compare:
 To him shall be given. From him shall be taken away even that he hath.
 (Mt. xiii. 12.)
 LOGO: **a-ko-fe** akodi dre.   **a-ko-do** ŋga akodi drekase.
 LUGBARA: 'ba ŋga azini **fe**-ra.   'ba ŋga **pa** afa erini ovule eri-be ri.
 He shall be called a Nazarene. (Mt. ii. 23.)
 LOGO: **a-zi** akdoi dia Nazareta adea.
 LUGBARA: kini 'ba ŋga eri **omve** 'ba Nazari.

D. THE INFINITIVE VOWEL PREFIX (LOGO)

465. According to Miss Mozley the infinitive verb receives a prefix **a** when it stands alone (i.e. is not dependent on a previous verb).

a-liri vudri. To sit down.

A-ko-gi bedaia Kaisala adea, a-ko-gi ko ďi aŋgoďi togi-e ya? (Mk. xii. 14.) Is it lawful to give tribute to Caesar, or not (lit. to-give tribute Caesar to, to-give not that which lawful-is)?

Compare, however, § 535.

Consonant Prefixes

A. PLURAL ACTION PREFIXES: t-, l-

466. These prefixes are best studied in LOGO. When an action is directed against a plurality of objects, or when a plurality of actions is directed against an object or situation, the verb describing such actions is a Class III verb beginning with the consonant **t-** or **l-**. Class III verbs of this nature may be coined from existing Class I or Class II verb roots and stems. E.g.

Plurality of objects.

Class I. *ago do waraga.* The man takes the paper.
Class III. *ago todo waraga.* The man takes the papers.
Class II. *toko aji sandu.* The woman returns the box.
Class III. *toko leji sandu.* The woman returns the boxes.
Classes I and III. *boi do ŋga toba-le.* ⎫
Classes III and I. *boi todo ŋga ba-le.* ⎬ The boy takes the things to put them away.
Classes III and III. *boi todo ŋga toba-le.* ⎭

Plurality of actions.

Class I. *ma-si-dre boŋgo.* I tore the cloth (once).
Class III. *ma-lasi-dre boŋgo.* I tore the cloth (into shreds).
Class I. *benderendi nda ci-dre ama-drikanji.* The mouse bit my finger.
Class III. *benderendi nda teci fa dre.* The mouse gnawed the wood.

Compare LOGO *teci* (to walk) (Class III) with MORU *ekyi* (to come) (Class II).

467. Mynors gives the following examples of plural action from MORU:

Class I	Class III
o-vo (to throw)	*lovo* (to throw one by one)
u-mu (to run)	*lämu* (to run round in circles in a dance)
o-si (to slit)	*tosi* (to cut into strips)
o-ke (to pull in half)	*toke* (to pull to pieces)
o-ga (to chop)	*toga* (to chop to pieces)

Compare MIZA *tär̲i* (to saw) with dialect form *r̲i* (to cut).

Note also:

W.: *mä-gbí làmu-gä.* I'm just walking about. Cf. M.: *u-mú* = to run.
Jl.: *mä-gbí làmu-ä.* „   „   „

468. In the MORU dialects the **t-** form is often used to indicate action over a large field or lasting over a long time. As for as can be seen, such forms occur only in the *Indefinite* tenses.

The people are sitting on the ground.
M.: ledri k-ərì vùru, or ledri ká tərì vùru.
Ä.:   „   r-ərì   „   „   ró tərɪ   „

The grass is burning.	Cf. *The house is burning.*
M.: käí kú-ùdzwé, or käí ka **tudzwɛ**.	zó kú-ùdzwɛ.
Ä.: äí rú-**ùvɛ**. äí rɔ tuvɛ.	zó r-úvɛ.

The bird flies (*away*).   *The bird flies* (*hither*).
M.: arí kó-ə̀ŋga, or arí ká təŋgà.   arí kɛ́-ɛ̀ŋga, or arí ká-tɛŋgà.
K.:   „   -àŋgà   „   „   „   „   „
'B.: arıŋgwá ró-ə̀ŋga ... ró təŋgà   ... rá-àŋgà ... ró-taŋgà.
Ä.: arɪvá   „   „   ... ró-   „   „

This prefix construction is often indistinguishable from the progressive construction formed with the auxiliary verb 'tɛ' (= to stay, remain), except where an object intervenes. (See § 525.)

ma-t(e) ɔi.	I am going.	nyá-tùmvu na yà?	Are you drinking?
má-t(ɛ) abà.	I am walking.	ma-t(e) ɔdzwa na.	I am washing.
(Ä.: máró t(ɛ) ɔba.)		má-tubwä na.	I'm shooting.

but:
    ma-t(e) enya **uwi**. I am grinding grain.

469. Plural action verbs with **t-** and **l-** are not common in the Southern languages. Lugbara occasionally makes use of a prefix in **l-**. From MADI I have obtained only the following doubtful example: (verb = **ni** = to know).

    Lo.: má-**tìnì** tswɛ-tswɛ.   I know it haltingly.
    Pa.: má-**lɛní** ɛsésé.   „   „
    (Cf. ma-ni koro = I don't know.)

Note also:
The chief runs.
MORU { M.: ópí ká tumù.
        { Ä.: ópí rɔ tumu.
    LUGBARA: ópí lamu. Cf. WA'DI: má-lǎmu. I run.

In MADI plural action is denoted by Class II verbs beginning with the vowel **o-**. (See § 452.)

B. CAUSATIVE PREFIX l-

470. In MORU and LOGO, too, the **l-** form is occasionally used in a *causative* sense.

MORU: *o-fo* (to go out).	*lofo* (to take out).
MORU: má-**gá**-zò. I refuse.	má-**lága** anya zò. I forbid them.
LOGO: ma-**ga** ŋga dre. „	ma-**loga** aii dri re. „ „

C. INTENSIVE PREFIX k-

471. **k-** forms are not very common in Moru-Madi. The following have been noted in MORU:

Class I   *Class III*
ɔ-tɛ (to stay)   kɔtɛ (to wait)
o-vo (to blow)   kovo (to fan, to blow up a football or tyre)

D. NEUTER-PASSIVE PREFIX: la- or l-

472. The neuter passive verb stem is obtained by prefixing to the verb root a syllable beginning with the consonant l-. The vowel of this prefix is irregular.

Whereas the passive construction indicates that there is an agent to the action, the neuter-passive construction merely expresses a passive state without implicating an agent or instrument. The following examples from Moru should make this difference plain: (note the *active* sentence order in the neuter-passive).

M.: ǎ-**fu** gárà te.   The bowl has been broken (by some one). *Passive.*
M.: gára **li-fu**-te.   ⎫
W.:   ,, **lä-fu**-tra. ⎬ The bowl has broken (nobody implicated). *Neuter-passive.*

ǎ-**fu** má te.   I am hurt (by some one). *Passive.*
mí-**lifu**-te.   I am broken (in spirit). *Neuter-passive.*
bɔŋgó **lɛwà**-te. The cloth is torn. *Neuter-passive.*

Mynors gives: *o-da* (to pour)   *lada* (to fall—of water)
                o-pi (to turn)   *lepi* (to revolve)

473. This construction is most common in the Moru dialects and least common in the Central languages.

In LOGO the unchanged verb stem is often used in a neuter-passive sense. E.g.:

*saani **ji**-dre.*   The plates are washed.
*sandu ŋ**gi**-da.*   The box is opened.
*boŋgo **gi**-da wei.*   The cloth is sold, all of it.

Note, however, in Logo:

*agomva **toro** ago dre.*   The boy woke the man up.
*ago nda **laro**-dre.*   The man woke up.

474. Sometimes in Moru, too, and elsewhere, the verb is unchanged in the neuter-passive.

                The house was burnt.   *The stick was broken.*
M., K., L.:   zó **dzʷè**-te.   dófó **la-ŋgɔ̀**-te.
'B.:   zó **ze**-te.
W.:   zɔá **dʒè**-tra.   lóró **ŋɔ̀**-tra.
Ä.:   zó **vè**-te.   dófó **la-ŋgɔ̀** te.
Jl.:   dzóá **vè**-tra.   lóró **ŋɔ̀**-tra.

Sometimes verbs with the l- prefix may be used actively.

           The meat is cooked.   Cf. *Cook the meat.*
MORU (M.): ezá **lá'dí**-té.   nyá-**lá'dí** èza.
LOGO: ɪzá **la'di**-drì.   mí-ka-**la'dɪ** zà.
AVUKAYA: á'wá **la'di**-trá.   'ba ŋgá **la'dí**-lɛ-bè-rì. (One who cooks.)

Note also in MADI (Pandikeri).

           lóku'dó **lɛdà**-ra.   The pot broke.
           mo'di **lɛdà** ni.   The man broke it.

475. Some of the neuter-passive verbs in Moru, like other Class III verbs, are able to prefix an extra passive vowel on occasions.

ə-**trɪ** = to curse, as in mí-**trɪ̀** ma kʊ. Don't curse me.

⎰ M.: nyá ma **ə̀trɪ** ɔ̀'dutaya? Why do you curse me?
⎱ Ä.: míró ma **ə̀trɪ** à'ditaya?   ,,   ,,   ,,

THE FUNCTION OF VERB STEM PREFIXES 219

latrɪ = to curse, to be accursed.
In passive: **á-trì** ma tɛ. ⎫ I am cursed (accursed).
á-látrí ma tɛ. ⎭
o-nji = to discharge.
landzɪ = to leave. As in tokó márò **landze** tɛ. My wife left me.
In passive: parata máro **á-landzé** tɛ. My money is spent.

476. It should be noted at this point that in LENDU the normal passive is formed with a prefix **le-**.
ma-go-'blo. I gave birth.
ma-lego-ŋgue 'blo drrdrrnjina. I was born long ago.
ke le-'bi-'bi. He is being beaten.   *ke le-'bi-ŋgue.* He was beaten.

OTHER CLASS III VERBS

477. There are a fair number of dissyllabic verbs in each language in which the consonantal element of the first syllable seems fixed, and the only grounds for regarding it as a prefix at all is in the fact that the same root occurs in related languages without this element. Typical examples of these verbs are:

MORU: lerú (to kindle); cf. LOGO *turu*
lɔgò (to give back); cf. LOGO *go*
la'dì (to cook); cf. MADI 'dì
lɔsɛ (to sew); cf. LUGBÁRA tsí
lasa (to wash)

LOGO: *lande* (to be tired); cf. o-lande-le = to get tired, leave off work.

MADI (Pa.): lɛgwe (to get lost); cf. MADI (Lo.): ɛgwe
luŋgwɛ (to call)   ,,   ,,   uŋgwɛ
lukwɛ (to pay)   ,,   ,,   úkwe

MORU: kugu (to steal); cf. MADI ogu   LOGO kugu.
kanda (to shake).

MADI: ko'dú (to sleep); cf. MORU u'dú.

CHAPTER XIV
AUXILIARY VERBS AND PARTICLES

478. The auxiliary forms in Moru-Madi occupy a position between the subject of the sentence and the verb, this position being usually immediately after the subject. Many auxiliaries are formed from verbal roots which themselves may be used as independent verbs in other contexts. Some verbal roots may function as independent verbs in one language but only as auxiliary verbs in another. Where the form has a verbal as well as an auxiliary use, the approximate English equivalent of the verb will be given. There are also many auxiliaries which seem to be formed from particles only. For the sake of easy reference, the auxiliaries will be discussed here alphabetically. The auxiliaries occur mostly, but not exclusively, in Indefinite constructions, the sentence order being Subject+auxiliary+object+verb.[1]

[1] In most cases the auxiliaries themselves are *definite* in aspect, while the verbs they assist are in a dependent *indefinite* form.

a (LOGO—Agambi, KELIKO)

479. This auxiliary is used in the Volition Imperative in the Agambi dialect of LOGO, and corresponds to **ko** in the main Logo dialects. (See § 431.)

   LOGO (A.): *mi-a-fe.* Give!
   KELIKO: mí-à-ŋgɔ kɔ. Don't cry.

480. adre, adri, are. See **dre.**

   'ba (= to make, to put). Causative auxiliary.

481. This auxiliary occurs in all languages, and implies usually the enforcing of one person's will on another. Occasionally it implies permission (when it may be translated by 'let').[1] The verb that follows this auxiliary occurs either in the *subjunctive* (Definite aspect with **k-** in 3rd person), or the *infinitive* (Indefinite aspect with suffix **-nɪ** or **-lɛ**).

Examples with the Subjunctive:

MORU:

mí-'bà ndá **k-ɛdr**.	Stop him. (Make him stop.)
mí-'ba (ánya) **k-əì**.	Let him go.
mí-'ba ndá **k-ənya** ku.	Make him stop eating (lit. Make him that he eat not).
mí-'ba ánya **k-ɔ̀sɔ̀** gìni.	Let him hoe the ground.

With reduplication:

mí-'ba ndá **k-ənyá** ənyà.	Make him eat.
mí-'bà **k-umu** ùmù.	Make it run.
mí-'bà gí 'dʊ́ **k-usi** usi.	Make that water boil.
mí-'bà èza **ka-la'di** la'di.	Cook the meat (lit. Make the meat cook).

   Don't forget it (lit. Let talk of it escape not).
   M., L., 'B.: mí-'bà ta-na **k-udzʷe** kú.
     Ă.: mí-'bà ta-na **uvi** ku.
     Jl.: mí-'b(a) ulí-la **uvu** kó.

(Note absence of **k-** particle in certain Moru dialects. See § 500.)

Examples with the Infinitive:

MORU:

má ndá ɔ'ba **ɛ́drɛ̀-nɪ**.	I am stopping him.
má-'ba **ɛdr** tɛ.	I stopped him. (Suffix elided.)
má-'ba gìí tɛ {**la'di-nɪ.** / **usi-nɪ.**}	I made the water boil.
má-'bà ndá lɔŋgó əŋgɔ̀.	I made him sing (lit. a song sing).
ɛ́ndrɛ́ 'ba ŋgwa (te) lɛí **əndrə-nɪ.**	The mother suckled the baby (lit. Mother made child milk to-drink).

With reduplication:

má-'bà ndá **turi-nɪ̀** turi.	I made him fear.

LOGO:

ma-'ba mvaago yi **mvu.**	I make the boy drink water.

With reduplication:

ma-'ba do **aga-le** agaga.	I put the fat to melt.

Cf. LENDU: mgba-i bu ba mgba **nju.** The mother suckles the baby (lit. Child-mother makes milk child suck).

[1] See also the auxiliaries **ɛ'bɛ** and **'dɛ.**

AUXILIARY VERBS AND PARTICLES

Examples of 'ba as a finite verb:
MORU: mí-'ba ndí ku bòŋgɔ ya. Don't dirty the cloth (lit. Put dirt not cloth on).
má-'ba enyá tɛ lakaza ya la'dí-nɪ. I put food in the pot to boil.

'da, 'do or do (= to become). (Central languages) (MORU)
482. This auxiliary is always used with the *Indefinite* construction. It sometimes refers to past time. (Cf. **dre** in LOGO.)[1]

                A hyena ate my dog.
LOGO: iŋgílya dó mákɔkyɛ́ **nyà-lɛ**.
LUGBARA: lubogú **'dú** mɔtsógò **ànyà-lɛ**.
AVUKAYA { Jl.: lòbògò **tro** ɔ̀kyɛ mà-kà-tra **nyà-lɛ́**.
         { Jg.: lòbògò **do** ɔké ámá-ka-trá **nyà-lɛ́**.

483. In AVUKAYA it is used mostly to stress the certainty of future happenings.
Jl.: gúla **'dɔ̀** àma pà-á. He will help me.
na-**'dɔ áni-á** aŋguta ya? When will you come?
ná-**'dɔ** a'du **giá** mádrí paláta **'dú** si ya? What will you buy (or sell) for me with this money?

I'll beat you to-morrow.   *The chief will beat you* (pl.).   *You'll see us to-morrow.*
Jl.: ma-**'da** ní **tswa** andru.   kúmú a'**dó** aní **tswà** (tra).   ná-**'da** amá **ndrɛ** idrù.
Jg.: ma-**'da** mí **tswa** andru.   míri a'**dɔ** amí **tswà** (tra).   ná-**'dɔ** amá **ndrɛ** idrù.

It is sometimes used to describe habitual action:
Jl.: má-**'dɔ́** a'wá o'**buà** úsu sì. I shoot game with a bow.

Note also in MORU (only example to hand):
óndó mà-**'daà**-gwo ɔ́i ní Amádi yá. To-morrow I shall go to Amadi.

dre, adre, (a)re, ra (LOGO), **ra** (LENDU), **dre, re** (KELIKO), **adri** (LUGBÁRA) (= to abide, to be).

484. This verb is used as an auxiliary in the Central languages (including Lugbara), and is always followed by indefinite forms of the verb (usually the infinitive form, with or without a suffix).[2] Its functions are as follows:

(a) To indicate progressive action in present time (LOGO and KELIKO).

LOGO: ma-**re** linya **nya**.   I am eating food.
KELIKO: má-**drɛ** nyɛ **nya**.   ,, ,, ,,
LOGO: *mi-**adre** aɖo o ya?*   What are you doing?
*ma-**adre** teci-le aŋgia.*   I'm just walking about.
*ma-**adre** ŋga a.*   I'm hoeing (something).
*ma-**adre** ŋga laɖi.*   I'm cooking (something).
*ma-**adre** mondo i.*   I'm grinding grain.
*mi-**adre** za laɖi ya?*   Are you cooking meat?
*koko, ma-**adre** za laɖi ko.*   No, I'm not cooking meat.
*ma-**adre** kosia laɖi.*   I'm cooking fish.
*mi-do tau-'bu tovo-le, ma-**dre** ŋga **nya-ra'a**.* Take the eggs to boil while I am eating (food).

[1] Miss Mozley notes that **ado** (to become) is used in Agambi Logo with the same function as **dre**, but gives no examples.
[2] When there is an object (which precedes the verb) the verb usually has no suffix here. When there is no object, the verb usually has a suffix.

(b) To indicate habitual action in present or past time (LUGBARA, LOGO, and LENDU).
> LUGBARA: *Eri adri ombi nya.* (Mk. i. 6.) He used to eat locusts.
> LOGO: *Dre tombi nya-zo.* „ „ „ „
> LUGBARA: *Oce yiḋi adri joloko anzi ni mesa etiari nya.* (Mk. vii. 28.)
> LOGO: *Kokiaɪ mesa zona dre-ki anjieki a koronyo nya-zo kania.* But even the dogs eat the children's crumbs under the table.
> LUGBARA: *Eri ŋga yi imba dika, erini adri-le imba-le-ri-le.* (Mk. x. 1.) And he taught them again, as he was wont to teach.
>> LOGO: *agoe adre-ki aḋo o ya?*   What do the men do?
>> *agoe adre-ki ka'wa liki.*   The men hunt animals.
>> *tokoe adre-ki lidi laḋi.*   The women cook porridge.
> LENDU: *bwetsimba ḋoḋo.*   The boy is sleeping.
>> *bwetsimba ra-ḋoḋo nzz.*   The boy sleeps every day.
>> *nzo ka-ra wa mbu?*   Do children drink beer?
>> *nzi, nzo ra wa mbu nzi.*   No, children do not drink beer.

(c) To indicate action in past time (LOGO, KELIKO, LUGBARA).
>> *I chop (or chopped) the tree.*   *I bought a book.*
> LOGO: ma-drɛ fa gà. (vb. = ga.)   má-drɛ́ búku gɛ̂. (vb. = gɛ.)
> (Cf. KELIKO: má fa gà-rɛ.   má búku gɛ̀-rɛ.)
> LOGO: *Tiza adre maleke-ni o we.* (Mk. vi. 26.) The king was very sorry (lit. Sorrow was the king affecting greatly).
>> *aḋi are ali-le-da* (or *-dre*). He has come.

>> *The cat caught a mouse.* (vb. = ru.)
> LOGO: gònza (adrɛ́) tédrégò rù.
> KELIKO: ndrógó (adrɛ́) édrágo ru-rì.
> LUGBARA: *Etu-zu ondre-si, eri adri fo aku a amve.* (Mk. xi. 19.) When even was come, he went out of the city.

(d) It is very often to be found in LOGO in sentences describing action subsequent to what has just happened. Here the main verb has the suffix zo.
> LOGO: *'Dialezolepi bi-ḋii we dreki ru kebe-zo aḋi-vuna, kadre nitini aḋi si kalumgba na, dre liri-zo yi na.* (Mk. iv. 1.) And a very great crowd collected around him, so that he entered into a ship, and sat in the sea.
> *Aii adreki aḋini no.* (Mk. iii. 2.) And they watched him.
> *Dranyano aḋi dre aiiki zi-zo, aii dre ata-na tai-zo, aii dreki li-zo aḋi-vuse.* (Mk. i. 20.) At once he called them, and they left their father, and came after him.
> *aii dre-ki ama no-zo nale.* (Mt. xxviii. 10.) And they shall see me there.

485. Note the following sentences where **dre**, &c., is used as a main verb.
> LOGO: *ma-dre ta ko.* I'm not doing anything.
> *mi-adre ago togo mbambaḋi be.* (Mt. xxv. 24.) Thou art a hard man.
> LUGBARA: *Eri be afa erini dria, afa erini adri-zu-ri dria.* (Mk. xii. 44.) She cast all her possessions, everything that there was.

drɪ or adrɪ (MORU, MADI)

486. Whether this auxiliary has the same derivation as Logo **adre** is hard to say. It occurs in the Moru and Madi dialects with the meaning of 'still, yet'. It may be preceded by the **rə** particle in Moroändri.

AUXILIARY VERBS AND PARTICLES

I am still tying it. *I am still biting it.*
M.: má-dr(ɪ)-ɛmbɛ́ nà.   M.: má-dr(ɪ)-ə̀sɪ na.
Ä.: márɔ́ dr(ɪ)-əmbɛ́ la. K.: má-drə-àsɪ na.
W.: ma-dr-əmbɛ́-gá nà.
Jl.: ma-dr-əmbɛ́ la.

The meat is being cooked.
Ä.: ezá rɔ́ drɪ̀ la'di.
Jl.: a'wá drɪ̀ la'di ya.

Note:
He is not dead; he is still alive (lit. he remains human).
MORU: dra ku; drɪ̀ lédri-rɔ́.
MADI (Lo.): ɔ́drà kúru; adri ɔ́lɔ lídri.
LUGWARA: írí drà ku; ɪrɪ drɪ̀ ídɪ-ru.

'dɛ (= to let, allow) (MORU)

487. Fundamentally, the difference between **'dɛ** and **'ba** is that the former applies more to exhortation, while the latter more to enforcement or permission.
In Moru this distinction is maintained to a great extent.

mɪ-'dɛ mɔ̀ì.   Let's go.   (A invites B to go.)
mí-'ba {mɔ̀ì.   Let us go.} (A and B ask permission of some one else.)
       {mǎrí-ɔ́ɪ-nɪ.   ,,   ,, }
mɪ-'dɛ́ ma-ŋgɔ́ lòŋgɔ̀.   Let's sing a song.
mí-'ba ma-ŋgɔ́ lòŋgɔ̀.   Allow us to sing a song.
mí-'dɛ ma-sɔ vɔ̀.   Let's hoe the place.
mí-'ba ànya k-ɔsɔ gini. Let *him* hoe the ground.

Note that **'dɛ** seems to be followed always by the Subjunctive.

ɛ'bɛ (= to leave alone)

488. This auxiliary alternates with **'ba** (and **'dɛ** in Moru) in sentences of exhortation, and may occasionally be used in a causative or permissive sense. It is followed by the Subjunctive.

Let's sing.   *Let us (allow us to) go.*   *Let him go.*
MORU: mɪ-'dɛ́ ma-ŋgɔ́ lòŋgɔ̀.   mí-'ba m-ɔ̀ì.   mí-'ba ndá (k)ɔi.
MADI {Lo.: any-ɛ́'bɛ́ ɔ́ŋgɔ-kí lòŋgɔ̀.   nyí-ba ɔ́vʊ̀.   ny-ɛ́'bɛ́ k-òmu.
     {Pa.: ny-ɛ́'bɛ́ ákʊŋgó-kí loŋgó.   ny-ɛ́'bɛ́ mà-mu.   'ba k-omu.
LUGBARA: ɪm-í'bɛ́ àmaŋgo íŋga.   m-ɛ́'bɛ́ àmà-mu-kì.   m-ɛ́'bɛ̀ wamú.
KELIKO: mí-m-ú'bá ŋgɔ̀-ki ŋgo.   mé-k-u'bà mù-ki.

Note:
MORU: ny-ɛ́'bɛ́ k-ərɪ.   Leave him alone (i.e. let him be).

eco[1] (LUGBARA)

489. This auxiliary differs from most in that it is impersonal, i.e. it is preceded by no subject pronoun. Its main function is to indicate potentiality, but it may also indicate seemliness or worthiness. It is used with the Indefinite construction.

Eco mini ma-rua ba-za-ro alaro. (Lk. v. 12.) Thou canst make my body clean.
Eco Setanini Setani dro-za-ro ŋgoni ya? (Mk. iii. 26.) How can Satan drive out Satan?
'Ba nde vu econi ko; te Muŋgu vu eco dria. (Mt. xix. 26.) With men this is impossible, but with God all (things) are possible.

[1] Probable pronunciation **etso.**

Econi 'bani ewa afufuro 'ba-zu zu okuri a ko. (Lk. v. 37.) No man putteth new wine into old bottles (lit. it beseems man beer new to put bottle old in not).
Econi mini fi-za-ro jo mani a ko. (Lk. vii. 6.) I am not worthy that thou shouldst enter under my roof (lit. it beseems thou shouldst-enter house mine in not).
Baka jijimani 'ba-diri-dri econi mani avu-za-ro ayu-za-ro ko ani. (Mk. i. 7.) The latchet of whose shoes I am not worthy to stoop down and unloose.

esi (= to be proper) (MADI) su (LOGO)

490. Like the Lugbara **eco** this Madi auxiliary seems to correspond to the Latin word 'decet'. It is followed by the infinitive (suffix **lɛ**) or the 'purpose' construction (suffix **zo**).

These boys are dirty; they are not worthy to enter (my house).

MADI { Lo.: bárá dii andí trɔ̀; **ésì** kwi-lɛ màdri iti kʊ. (kwi = enter.)
       Pa.: 'borá 'di andí tɔ; **indʒwí** ándâ ní kwi-zɔ́ zʊ̀ gà.
            kokwé mádí zo ga kò.
            (let them not enter . . .)

My house is dirty; it is not worthy for the chief to enter.

MADI { Lo.: má à dzɔ andí trɔ̀; **ésì** ópí ní kwi-lɛ (or dzɔ́) arù korò.
       Pa.: má à zɔ andí tɔ̀; **indʒwí** ópí ní kwi-zɔ́ zʊ̀ gà.
LOGO: **su** *ma-ko-liri jo na.* I must stay at home.

491. fɛ (KELIKO). See kwɛ.

fo (= to go out) (MADI, &c.)

492. This auxiliary is used in the Southern Languages for strengthening the past negative. It corresponds closely to the English auxiliary 'didn't', when spoken with emphasis. It is used with the Indefinite construction, and the verb is usually followed by the particle **si**.

Didn't you eat anything?   *I didn't.*

MADI { Lo.: í-**fo** tá nyá-**sì** koro yà?   á-nyà kʊrʊ̀, or á-**fu** tá nyá-**sì** koro.
       Pa.:   mǎ-**fu** ŋgá nyá-**sì** koro.

I didn't go.   *I didn't sleep.*

MADI { Lo.: á-**fò** ya-**sì** koro.   má-**fo** u'dúkɔ-**ka-sí** ko.
       Pa.: má-**fo** mʊ̀-**sì** koro.   má-**fo** u'dúkɔ-**si** kʊrʊ.
LUGBARA: má-**fo** mʊ̀-lɛ́ kʊ.
KELIKO: má-**fo** mʊ̀-lɛ́ kʊ.

The probability is, in Madi at least, that the assisted verb is in verbal noun form (note 'u'dúkɔ-ka') followed by the postposition **sì**. Thus: 'I didn't go out from sleeping'.

go (LOGO)

493. This auxiliary is used only in sentences describing action or state subsequent to something that has happened before, where it seems to alternate with **dre** (see § 484 *d*). Compare this with the Moru verb postposition **gʷo** (§ 603) and conjunction **ago** (§ 765).

Mi-dre ami-läti do-zo, dridri mi-go adre-le adrupi-ro ami-adrupi be. (Mt. v. 24.)
  Go thy way, first be reconciled to thy brother (lit. be brother-like).
Lia ake-dre, ŋga go adre-le si we. (Mk. iv. 39.) And the wind ceased and there was a great calm (lit. things then became calm very).
aii iri niiki za go adre-le alo? (Mt. xix. 5.) And they twain shall be one flesh?
tai ve-le-ro ɖise ɖi ago niɖi go adre-le konji amba . . . (Mt. xii. 45.) And the last state of the man is worse . . .

AUXILIARY VERBS AND PARTICLES

ġbi or ġi (MORU, AVUKAYA)

494. This particle is used in the sense of 'just', 'merely' in the main Moru dialects.
I'm just walking about (in reply to question, 'What are you doing'?)

    M.: má-ġyí a'ba.
    Ä.: ma-rɔ ġi ɔba.
    W.: mä-ġbí lämu-gä.
    Jl.: mä-ġbí làmu-ä.

495. In AVUKAYA and related dialects it is used for ordinary progressive action.

AVUKAYA: má-ġɪ sandúku pí yä.	I am opening a box.
gúla ġí sandúkù ɛdɛ.	He is carrying a box.
gúlà ġ(e) ä'dúkwa.	He is sleeping.
(Cf. má-ä'dúkwà.	I am sleeping.)
má-'dɔ ġbí dzi ɛlɛnɔ.	I am washing it.
oma bí vɛ.	The grass is burning.
WA'DI: käi (ġbí) edzí-gá.	The grass is burning.

The k- particles

(a) Third person particle ka (MORU, MADI).

496. As has already been mentioned (§ 216), the 3rd person in the Indefinite tenses is indicated in certain languages by an introductory particle **ka**. This particle, when immediately preceding a verb stem, often harmonizes in with it, but is never part of it, as it may be separated from the verb by an intruding object word. It probably occurs in the indefinite tenses only. (See, however, § 499.)

497. In the MORU dialects the particle is found in the Miza sub-group (Miza, Lakama'di, Kediru) and in Ägi. It is not used in the Moroändri sub-group (-ändri, 'Bälimbä, Wa'di) nor in Avukaya.

The following examples, which were intended primarily as an intonation test (hence their improbable context), illustrate very well how the **ka** harmonizes with the characteristic vowel of a verb when it immediately precedes it, but how it is unaffected when preceding a stem beginning with a consonant.

The guest is running.

M.: kùmu **kú**-ùmù.		Ä.: ùmu **rú**-ùmù.
L.: ,, **kó**-ùmù.		'B.: ,, **ór**-tóùmù.
Äg.: ,, **ká**-tumù.		W.: kwòmu òumu-gä.
		J.: ùmu mgbí rà'a.

The fly is running.

  M.: kùmú **ká**-tumu.   Ä.: úmú **ró**-tumu.
  L.: úmú **ká**-tumu.
  Äg.: úmú **kó**-ùmu.

When it occurs before an object, it is also unaffected.

ledri ka kuku o'be tana-adi ya?	Why are the people making a noise?
ledri ka liti oso.	The people cut a road.
ledri ka ämvu oso.	The people hoe a farm.

Note occasional use of plural particle **-i** with it.

  ŋgaga ka-i oji.   The children are playing.

498. This particle is much in use in the Southern languages (i.e. Madi dialects and Lulu'ba) but not used in the Central languages (Logo, Keliko, Lugbara).

MADI: *'ba ka liti so.* The people cut a road.
'ba ka amvu so. The people hoe a farm.
etu k-efo. The sun is rising. *etu k-oďe.* The sun is setting.
etu k-osusu. The sun is shining. *erivi k-olwe.* The wind is blowing.

The chief is going. *They will die.*

MADI { Lo.: ópí kó-òmu.   andá-pí k-ódrà-ni, or ká-kí dra-ra.
       Pa.: ópí k-ómumù. à'ɪ k-oda-ra.

LULU'BA: í'dé k-ómumù. así k-ódó dʒó. The fire burns the house.
(the mouse runs) (Cf. asi ɔdɔ dʒo 'ɔ. The fire burnt the house.)

The chief is calling you.
Lo.: ópí ka nyi uŋgwɛ̇.
Pa.: ópí ku-luŋgwé nyi'i. (Note assimilation. See § 25.)

Further examples from Southern and Central languages (note the use of the plural particle **ki** as well). Compare p. 203.

The people are going. Cf. *The boys went.*

MADI { Lo.: 'bákàrɪà kə kə-vòvò.   bɔrɔndzí óvɔ (kí) pí . . . rá.
       Pa.: 'bâkú vòvò.   'bɔndʒí vɔ-pí . . . rá.

LUGBARA: 'bákí mùmù.   andziri mu-kí-'bò.
KELIKO: 'bárɪpɪ ko-lélè.   andziri mu-kí-gɪ.

The boys are going to the field.   Observation: It is probable that the

MADI { Lo.: bɔrɔnzi k-óvù ámvú ä.   **ko-** in Keliko conjugation is the
       Pa.: 'bɔndʒí k-úvó ámvʊ ge.   3rd person pronoun itself (see

LUGBARA: andziriki mù ámvʊ̇ gà.   vocabulary) and not an auxiliary
KELIKO: andzeri kó-mú ámvú gé.   particle.

(b) **k-** in the Subjunctive (MORU and MADI).

499. The Subjunctive is something of an anomaly. Its form is *definite* in that the word order is: Subject+verb+object, but at the same time the third person is reinforced by the particle **k-** or **ka** and the characteristic vowel (in Class I verbs).

The Subjunctive is used in sentences expressing permission, compulsion, or doubt. It very often follows the auxiliary verbs *'ba, ɛ'bɛ, 'dɛ* (= to make, to let. See §§ 481, 487–8). In MORU, further, it occurs often in subordinating clauses of time and condition, and in MADI (Pandikeri) in sentences describing action subsequent to what has just happened.

Examples from MORU.

500. Note the absence of **k-** in Moroändri, although the characteristic vowel is used for the third person as in Miza.

Class I.   ma-nya eza ku.   I must not eat meat.
           mǎ-ru.   I must take it away.
           anya kä-ru.   Let them take it.
   M.: ányà k-uru.   }   He must take it away.
   Ä.: ndá uru.   }
   M.: ánya k-urú kù. }   He must not take it away.
   Ä.: ndá urù kù.   }

AUXILIARY VERBS AND PARTICLES 227

Class II.   mέ-εzi.   I must bring it.
M.: ánya kε-εzi. }
Ä.: ndá azi.   }   He must bring it.
M.: ánya kε-εzi ku. }
Ä.: ndá azi kù.   }   He must not bring it.
ánya k-ɔì.   Let him go.
Class III. mä-mätu Lùú.   Let us pray to God.
mo-kúgu ko.   Let us not steal.
m-έrε-te ŋgága ká-lii.   I heard a boy cry.
mí-'ba gí 'dú ka-la'di-la'di.   Make that water boil.

Other examples:

m-ata-te ndäri, ndá k-ɔyε ta ku ínyε. I told him not to do that (lit. I said to-him, he must-do word not so).

Anya se bi be ta ere-za, anya k-oga bi. (Mk. iv. 9.) He that hath ears to hear (things), let him hear.

Ondre-ni ànya-ri oko k-ondre-i te oko. (Mk. iv. 12.) That seeing, they may see.

Ondro nda k-embe ledri ratararo te kutu. (Mk. iii. 27.) Except he will first bind the strong man.

Compare (no k- prefix in 1st person):

Ocini am-eri ya nai ya. (Mk. v. 12.) That we may enter into their bodies (lit. bellies).

501. In subordinating clauses of time and condition:

Ondro toko koi vo gi-ro ya oko, kito ru tavi udru ro go. When the woman went to the place of water, the hare took the buffalo's tail. (Moru folk-tale.)

Anya go go 'bäru ndrindri, uki kilazi anyaro kufu anya te. He went home quickly, lest his enemy should kill him.

Examples from New Testament:

Ondro ăi-aza kata-te amiri, ... (Mk. xi. 3.) And if any one says unto you, ...

Ago ondro ăi-toko konji-na ago ndaro, ... (Mk. x. 12.) And if a woman shall put away her husband.

Mì-'ba ăi-aza aloăi kodo ami ku. (Mk. xiii. 5.) Take heed lest any man deceive you (lit. Do not let any man deceive you).

Ago nda kefu-te ni kolomgbo ya oko, ... (Mk. v. 2.) And when he came out of the ship, ...

Ago anya kondre Yesu te lozo oko, ... (Mk. v. 6.) But when he saw Jesus afar off, ...

Oko ànya kere-i-te oko, ... (Mk. iv. 15.) But when they have heard, ...

But note:

Ago tandrulesi, kitu ci-te oko, ... (Mk. i. 32.) And at even, when the sun had set, ...

Ondro ma-tembi-gi alo boŋgo ndaro te oko, ... (Mk. vi. 28.) If I may touch but his clothes, ...

Ondro mi-ni oye-na te oko, ... (Mk. ix. 22.) If thou canst do anything, ...

502. Examples from MADI (Lokai).

(Note absence of k- in 1st and 2nd person).

k-omu.   He must go.   nẏ-έbέ k-ɔmu. Let him go.
k-omu-ki.   They must go.
k-ono ta.   He must see the thing.

k-ono-ki ta. They must see the thing.
ama-legi. Let us pray.
am-ede ta. Let us do something.

503. Examples from MADI (Pandikeri).
maḋi ani bi tro, ani keri. (Mk. iv. 9.) He that hath ears, let him hear.
za kadri enzoko. (Mk. v. 23.) That the girl may become well.
ma-'jo anyini iyo ecandi ma ko. (Mk. v. 7.) I adjure thee that thou torment me not.

504. Subsequent action sentences:
Ani kedo bini-ka meri tisi, moro retundro kemu ani-dri, ani kohwi i'bo a, kolo meri a. (Mk. iv. 1.) And he began to teach by the sea, and a great multitude came to him, so that he entered into a boat, and sat in the sea.
Ezeze ani koŋgwe ai; ai e'be atani Zebedi, ai kavoko ani. (Mk. i. 20.) And straightway he called them; and they left their father Zebedee, and went after him.

505. After the verbs ə'ba, &c. = 'make', 'let', note that the k- particle is to be found in *Keliko* (where the 3rd person particle is normally absent). In Moru, however, the dialectal distinction still holds. (See also § 497.)

	Let him go.	*Let me go.*	*Let us go.*
MADI {Lo.:	nyέbέ k-òmu.	'ba má-mú.	'ba ma-vò, or nyí-ba óvò.
Pa.:	'ba k-omú.		
KELIKO:	méfὲ kà-mu.		'bá lekî.

Compare:
MORU { M.: mí-'ba ndá k-ɔi.
       Ä.: mí-'ba ndá ɔi.
LUGBARA: m-έ'bὲ wamú.
MORU: mí-'ba ánya k-ɔ̀sɔ̀ gìnɪ.   Let him hoe the ground.
M.: mɪ-'ba ta ná k-udzwe kú.   Don't forget it (lit. don't let word of it
Ä.: ,, ,, uvi ,, escape).
LULU'BA: kwe ŋgwé k-ɔndɔndɔ.   Let the child suck.

In Madi the Subjunctive can occur after the verb 'to want':
MADI { Lo.: álɛ mátâ ni ra. I want to speak.
       Pa.: málɛ máta ni rà.

506. Examples from LOGO:
Note that the Subjunctive has the *Indefinite* form, with 3rd person auxiliary **ko**.
... *ma boŋgo ji ako ro.*   ... so that I should not wash the clothes.
... *mi-no ro.*   ... so that you should see.
... *a'di ko-ji ro.*   ... so that he may wash them.

(c) **ka** LUGBARA.

507. This particle is used in LUGBARA in subordinate clauses of condition or time. It is not a subjunctive particle, however (see **ma**, § 517), and may be used with all persons.

With Indefinite construction:
ka eco mini afa ye-za-ro, ... (Mk. ix. 22.) If thou canst do anything, ...
'Ba nde ka-dra-ra, ka tini mva ko, ... (Mt. xxii. 24.) If a man should die, having no child, ...

Ma-ka va boŋgo erini su-le-ri-di, ... (Mt. ix. 21.) If I touch the hem of his garment, ...
Mile mini indiria ka mi asi oja oja, ... (Mt. v. 29.) If thy right eye offend thee, ...
Eri ka 'ba koŋgolokoro ḋiri ombe oko, eri ŋga di jo erini eza ndo. (Mk. iii. 27.) When he has bound the strong man first, then he will spoil his house.
Eri ka-fo oguru alia, ... (Mk. v. 2.) When he came out of the ship.
Ondre be, etu ka-ḋe 'bo, ... (Mk. i. 32.) At even, when the sun had set.
Eri ka Yesu ndre, ... (Mk. v. 6.) When he saw Jesus, ...
Yi ka eyo eri 'bo, ... (Mk. iv. 15.) When they have heard the word, ...

With Definite Construction:
Yi ka-eri ḋini, ... (Mt. xxii. 22.) When they had heard these (things), ...
Yi ka-ye ḋini ra ... (Lk. v. 6.) When they had done this.

(*d*) ka LENDU.

508. In LENDU there is a volition particle 'ka', but the imperative prefix is a-. The particle ka is found in Indefinite constructions and does not seem to be used in subordinate clauses.

a-ri-r. Cook (something).
ma ka ka aḋu ri. What shall I cook?
a-ri o. Cook a chicken.
ni-dza-ndrrtszja dhe 'blo, ni ka ve-r nji mgba? Your cow is dead, what will you do?
ma ka ve nja ritsz nji-nzi. I shall do nothing.

The volition particle in Lendu is not to be confused with the 'ka' of interrogation.

ni ka aḋu ri? What are you cooking?
ma za ri. I am cooking meat.

(*e*) ko LOGO, ka KELIKO, LUGBARA (?); *Volition particle.*

509. This particle expresses futurity combined with willingness or desire or intention. The examples should make this plain:

LOGO (Note *definite* construction).
ama-ti dra-dre; ma ko-o aḋo ya? My cow is dead; what shall I do?
ami-ti dra-dre; mi ko-o aḋo ya? Your cow is dead; what will you do?
ma-ko-o ta ko. I shan't do anything.
Ago Ninewe aḋea ko-ŋga-ki kuru. (Mt. xii. 41.) The men of Nineveh shall rise.

When used with a Class II verb, the vowel of the particle is replaced by the characteristic vowel of the stem.

akoḋi k-aca nole tudru ko, akoḋi k-aca natu. He won't arrive here to-morrow, he'll arrive the day after.

	I split it.	*I'll free you.*	*You'll free me.*
LOGO:	má-ʃì ani.	má-kʊ-tri mí.	mɪ-kʊ-trɪ má.
KELIKO:	má-ka-sì ani.	má-ka-trɪ mí.	a-ka-trɪ mà (passive).

510. This particle is very often used in the imperative, especially where willingness is understood.

Class I.	*ama-ko-ŋgo loŋgo ya?*	May we sing?
	koko, ami-ko-ŋgo loŋgo ko.	No, don't sing.
Class II.	*mi-k-ali wa.*	Do come.
	mi-k-ali ma be.	Come with me.

Class III. *su ma-ko-liri jo na.*   I must stay in the house.
   ami-ko-liri kiri.   Be quiet (pl.).
   mi-laďi ŋga!   Cook something.
   ma-ko-laďi aďo ŋga ya?   What shall I cook?
   mi-ko-laďi tau.   Cook a chicken.

Compare with Keliko:

	Cook the meat.	Don't call him.	Don't eat it.	Don't go.
KELIKO:	mí-kà-'di za.		mí-kà-nya kʊ.	mí-kà-lɪ ko.
LOGO:	mí-ka-la'dí zá.	mí-ku-zi kɔ.	mí-kə̀-nya kʊ.	mí-kə̀-li ko.

	Don't cry.	Sit down.
KELIKO:	mí-à-ŋgɔ kɔ.	mí-rɪ or mí-kə-rɪ
LOGO:	mí-kə-ŋgɔ kɔ.	mi-ɽiri or mí-kə-lɪrɪ
LUGBARA:		mí-rɪ or mí-ka-rɪ

511. It also corresponds in function to the Subjunctive in Moru. (Note that here **ko** occurs for all persons, and that the sentence construction is *definite*.)

 LOGO: **ko-yi**-wa. (Mk. iv. 9.) Let him hear.
 *Nitini ŋga no-ra'a, aii **ko-ni**-ro.* (Mk. iv. 12.) That seeing (things), they may know.
 *mà-**ko-si**-ro aii le na.* (Mk. v. 12.) That we may enter into their bodies.
 *mì-le ma-**ko**-o ami-dre aďo-ta ya?* (Mt. xx. 32.) What will ye that I shall do unto you?
 ... *mì-**ko-kai**-ro akoďi dre.* (Mt. xxi. 32.) ... that ye might believe him.
 ... *mà-**ko-no**-ro kai-le.* (Mk. xv. 32.) ... that we may see and believe.

512. Like the **ka** of Lugbara and the Subjunctive **k-** of Moru, this particle may often be found in subordinate clauses of condition or time.

 LOGO: *Ago **ko-dra**-dí, mva yo,* ... (Mt. xxii. 24.) If a man should die, having no children, ...
 *Ma-**ko-tabe** akoďi a boŋgo kodia di.* (Mk. v. 28.) If I may touch but his clothes, ...
 *Yendrose, kitu **ko-ndi**-di,* ... (Mk. i. 32.) At even when the sun had set, ...
 *I-**ko-no** Yesu rararo di ra ŋguse,* ... (Mk. v. 6.) When he saw Jesus afar off, ...
 *aii **ko-yi** di,* ... (Mk. iv. 15.) When they have heard, ...
 *aii **ko-yi** niďi dre di,* ... (Mt. xxii. 22.) When they had heard these (things), ...

(*f*) **ko** (= to take) (MADI).

513. Molinaro (p. 54) mentions an auxiliary verb **ko** (= to take) as a means of reinforcing past action in Lokai Madi, but gives only one example without context:

   oko-'jo = He said.

  kwɛ, ki, fɛ (= to put) (LULU'BA, KELIKO). *Causative auxiliary.*

514. This seems to be the normal causative auxiliary in LULU'BA. It may be followed by the infinitive (**ri**) or subjunctive. E.g. From **ndo** = to suck.

  *andení **ki** ndú-ri ŋgwáni.*   The mother suckles the child.
  kwɛ ŋgwá kə̀ndəndə̀.   Let the child suck.
  „ „ kə̀ndə ebà.   Let the child suck the breast.
  „ „ ndɛní kəndə́ndò.   Let the mother suckle the child.

In KELIKO the auxiliary is **fe**, but it is not very often used.

 KELIKO: m-ɛ́fɛ̀ kàmu. Let him go.

AUXILIARY VERBS AND PARTICLES

li (LENDU). *Causative auxiliary.*

515. This is an alternative auxiliary to **ba**.

bwetszmgba da zho.   The boy drinks water.
ma-li bwetszmgba zho da.   I make the boy drink water.

Note the use of both auxiliaries in the following:
tsz(kpar) r-nyi nyi.   The cattle are running.
nzi ni-ba tsi lir tsz nyir.   Don't let the dog make the cattle run.

liri, nili, ri (= to live) (LOGO).

516. This verb is an alternative to **adre** in its progressive capacity.

LOGO: má-**nɪʈɪ** owá mvu. I am drinking beer.
Cf. KELIKO: má-**drɛ** lewá mvu.
LOGO: *aði liri ta fe ðia dri.* He is talking to the people.

In the Agambi dialect, according to Miss Mozley, the auxiliary has the form **iri**, **ori**, or **ri**.

ma (LUGBARA)

517. This particle is used in subjunctive sentences. It occurs in all persons.

LUGBARA: *mi-le ma-**ma**-ye mi-vu aðinia?* (Lk. xviii. 41.) What wilt thou that I shall do unto thee?
*Curuðo mi-fe atibo mini **ma-mvi**.* (Lk. ii. 29.) Now lettest thou thy servant depart (lit. give thy servant that he depart).
*'Ba bile be, **ma-eri** eyo ðiri.* (Mk. iv. 9.) Lit. He ears with let (him) hear things these.
*Yini ndre-zu yi-**ma-va** ko, yini eri-zu yi-**ma-ni** efini ko.* (Mk. iv. 12.) Lit. They in seeing they might perceive not, they in hearing they might know the meaning not.
*Mi-pe ama ti ezo ðiri ma alia, ama-**ma-fi** yi-ru a ani.* (Mk. v. 12.) Lit. You send us swine these into, that we may enter their bodies in, them.
*Mi-emu mi-dri ti ru ani a, ru ani **ma-ati** ani, eri **ma-ovu** idri-ro ani.* (Mk. v. 23.) Come and lay thy hands on her body, that her body may be healed, that she may be alive.

ŋga (LUGBARA)

518. This auxiliary is used in sentences describing action subsequent to what has previously happened.[1] It occurs always in the Indefinite construction.

*'Ba tre di oku yi vunia to, eri **ŋga** fi o'bo alia, eri **ŋga** ri yi dria ani.* Many people gathered about him, so that he entered into a boat, and sat in the sea. (Mk. iv. 1.)
*Yi **ŋga** eri **ndre**, kani eri **ŋga** 'ba ðiri ati.* And they watched him, whether he would heal that man. (Mk. iii. 2.)
*Eri **ŋga** yi omve coti; yi **ŋga** yi-ata ko-ra, yi **ŋga** mu vutinia.* And he called them straightway; and they left their father, and followed him. (Mk. i. 20.)

Consequently it may often have a future significance:

*Ma-**ŋga** mooni fe mii ko.* I won't give you mine. (Lit. I **ŋga** mine give you not.)
*Ma-**ŋga** mi 'du ra.* I'll carry you. (Lit. I **ŋga** you carry shall) (extract from folk tale.)
*Te etu **ŋga** eca-ra.* (Mt. ix. 15.) But the day will come.

[1] Compare **dre** in Logo, **k-** (with subjunctive) in Madi, and postposition **go** in Moru.

ŋga (= to rise) (MADI)

519. This auxiliary is used in Madi to strengthen the past positive, though whether it is to be regarded as the antithesis of **fo** is doubtful. It may be followed either by the simple verb root or by the form with contracted pronoun prefix.

I was talking.   *He ate.*
Lo.: má-ŋgá dzo-ra (or *a-ŋga a-jo-ra*).   *oŋga onya-ra.*
Pa.: má-ŋgá 'jo-ra.

o (= to do, to put) (LOGO)

520. This auxiliary has two main functions in Logo.

(*a*) As a *causative* auxiliary it is more popular perhaps than **'ba**, though its function is the same, and it is followed by the infinitive.

mi-o do aga-le.   Melt the fat. (vb. = aga.)
*ma-o ti-le **kutu**.*   I let the milk spill. (vb. = kutu.)
(Cf. *ma-kutu ti-le.*   I spill the milk.)
ago o si-ki ai jo e.   The man gets others to help him (lit. man makes build-plural his house) build his house.

And idiomatically:

adi o tai ali-zo.   He is about to come (lit. he makes words so that he comes).
za adre ra-le ra ra.   The cattle are running.
mi-ko-loga kokia, adi ko-o za ra-le ako.   (Forbid the dog that he will not make the cattle run.) i.e. Don't let the dog chase the cattle.
ma-o ake-le dre. }
(A.) *ma-o lande-le da.* } I have finished (lit. made (it) end).
mi-o-dre azi nda ake-le ya?   Have you finished the work?

(*b*) As a *progressive auxiliary* it seems to differ little in function from **adre** or **liri**, except that it is not used quite so extensively, and is confined to continuous present action.

ma-o jo si.   I am building a house.
ma-o li-le.   I am going. (Note 'le' suffix.)
Compare Moru 'Bälimbä: ndáná ó teu'dù.   He is sleeping.

rə (*Moroändri* sub-group)

521. This particle occurs in the Indefinite construction in Moroändri, 'Bälimbä, and Ägi, and is probably related to the **adre** of Logo (especially its slurred forms). It describes progressive action.

Ä.: má-ró wá m̂vu.   I am drinking beer.

What are you doing?	*I am walking.*	*I'm digging a hole.*
Ä.: mí-ró a'di əi yà?	má-ró-(ə)ba.	má-rə 'bú ú'dì.
'B.: n-óró a'di əi yà?	m-óró-(ə)ba.	m-óró 'bú ò'dì.
Äg.: mí-rá a'di a yà?	má-rə-əbá.	má-rə 'bú o'di.

It is significant that this particle seems confined mostly to those Moru dialects which do not use the 3rd person particle **ka**.[1] Compare:

He is blowing the fire.
M.: ánya **ká** así òvɔ.
Ä.: ndá **ró** así òvɔ.

---

[1] Ägi, however, uses both, and Avukaya neither: Äg.: ndá-**rà ká** así òvɔ. Jl.: gúla lesi voá. He is blowing the fire.

AUXILIARY VERBS AND PARTICLES 233

522. When immediately preceding a verb, the vowel of the particle often harmonizes with the characteristic vowel of the verb.

The grass is burning.
Ä.: äí rú-ùvɛ.
'B.: äí ɔ́rɔvɛ.

Further examples from Moru dialects:

Why are you digging?	*Why are you coughing?*
Ä.: mí-r-ú'di na 'dita yà?	mɪ-rɔ-ɛkpí a'dita yà?
'B.: n-ǎr-ú'di na tana'di ya?	n-ǎr-ɛ́kpé na a'dita ya?
Äg.: mí-r-ʊ́'dì na a'dita yà?	nǎ-ɛ́kpe a'didríä'?
M.: nyá-ú'di na ɔ'duta yà?	nyé-ɛkpí ɔ'duta yà?
Jl.: mí-'di a'dɔdrí yà?	ní-íkpu a'dɔdrí yà?

Where are you going to throw the water away?
Ä.: mí-r-ói idzí 'di ɔdá íŋwa ya?
'B.: n-ár-ói ìdzi 'di dà-lé íŋgóIɛrɔ yà?
Äg.: n-ói ìdʒí ɔdɔ-nɛ íŋgwɔ yà?
M.: ny-ói igyí 'dó ɔdá íŋgwa yà?
Jl.: ná-niá lùmvu dà-lɛ áŋgolɛ́ yà?

rɪ (AVUKAYA)

523. This auxiliary seems to have the same function in Avukaya as **dre** or **liri** in Logo, although it is not so common. Note that **ri** is one of the forms in the Agambi dialect of Logo. See § 516.

Jl.: gúla **rɪ** à'dù 'yɛ ya?	What is he doing?
Jg.: mí-**rɪ** à'dù 'yɛ ya?	What are you doing?
Jl.: gúla **árí** gùa.	He is laughing.

524. su LOGO. See **esi**.

tɛ (= to remain) (MORU)

525. This auxiliary has already been referred to under the heading of plural action (§ 468). There is no proof that the plural action prefix **t-** is not a contraction of this auxiliary verb. In the following examples there can be no doubt that the auxiliary is being used:

I am sleeping.	*He is sleeping.*	*I am washing (it?)*
M.: má-t-u'dù.	ánya ká-t-u'dù.	má-t(e)-ɔ̀dzwa na.
Äg.: mɔ-te-u'dù.	ndána ká-te-u'dù.	má-rɔ́ tɛ-adzi na.
'Ä.: má-rɔ́ t-u'dù.	ndârɔ́ t-u'dù.	má-rɔ́ t(ɛ)-ɔ̀dzwi na.
'B.: mɔ-te-u'dù.	ndáná ɔ́ te-u'dù.	má-rɔ́ tɛ-ɔ̀gyi na.

M.: *ma-t(e) enya uwi.* I am grinding grain (vb. = uwi).
anya ka-te-ladi. He is cooking.
ma-ndrɛ anya te anya ka-t-aba liti ya. I saw him (he was) walking along the road.
gyí te ti-usí-ní. The water is just on boiling.
kitu ka-te-efu. The sun is rising.
kitu ka-te-o'de (or *oci*). The sun is setting.
kitu ka-t-oka. The sun is shining.
oli ka-te-oli. The wind is blowing.

te (LUGBARA)

526. This particle occurs mostly in subordinate or subsequent clauses of time.

Etao te ca Ewa bu, ... When the Hare arrived at the Elephant's, ...
Te ca yi tia a alo, ... When (they) arrived at the other side of the water, ...
Ama-ŋga-be, te aci isu ŋgoa? But if we throw (it away) where shall we find fire?

tsa (= to arrive) (WA'DI)

527. Like the *'də* in Avukaya, this auxiliary is used to emphasize the imminence of future happenings. It is followed by the Infinitive.

    mi-**tsa** aɾi-lɛ́ ä'ditú yà?   When will you come?
    míri **atsá** mɪ a'bí-lɛ́.   The chief will indeed beat you.

ye (= to do) (LUGBARA)

528. This auxiliary seems to correspond in function to o in Logo, but examples are rare.

Za-mva mani ye dra-ra. (Mk. v. 23.) My little daughter lieth at the point of death.

CHAPTER XV
VERB SUFFIXES

529. The following particles are attached directly to the verbal root or stem in accordance with grammatical and syntactic rules. When an object is used with these verbs, it invariably precedes the verb. Consequently all verbs employing suffixes have the Indefinite Aspect.

These suffixes often coincide in function with many European verb suffixes, like the infinitive suffix *-en* in German, the participial suffix *-ing* in English. Consequently for classification purposes, terms like 'infinitive', 'participle', 'gerund', &c., will be used, although, here again, the English labels must not be taken in too literal a sense.

A. THE INFINITIVE SUFFIXES
MORU
-nɪ (dial. -nɛ, -lɛ, -rɪ)

530. These suffixes, under certain circumstances, do indeed correspond very closely in function to the 'infinitive' particles in European languages. They correspond also to the 'gerund' suffix (*-ing*) of English.

Examples from MORU (Miza):

    *ny-ozo gi märi umvu-**nɪ**.*   Give me water to drink.
    *ny-ózó ŋga mắrí ɔndré-**ní**.*   Give me the thing to look at.
    *má-'ba enyá tɛ lakázá yá la'dí-**nɪ**.*   I put food in the pot to cook.
    *ópí pa ma nì zó ɔ̀mɔ-**nɪ**.*   The chief helped me to build a house.
    *m-átà tɛ ndärí ku ta 'dó ɔyɛ́-**nɪ̀**.*   I told him not to do that.

After **be**:

    bé mắri ɔ̀yɛ-**nɪ**.   I must do it. (Lit. It is to me to do.)
    bé mírí ku ɔ̀yɛ-**nɪ**.   You must not do it.
    bé giní ɔ̀sɔ-**nɪ**.   The ground must be hoed.
    bé kú giní ɔ̀sɔ-**nɪ**.   The ground must not be hoed.

VERB SUFFIXES

531. The following examples are for comparison with the forms in other Moru-Madi languages. Cf. § 542 et seq.

After verbs of motion:

M.: ànya koi aba-**nı**. They are going to hunt. m-oi ku anya uzi-**nı**. I'm not going to call him.
moi uḏu-**ni**. We are going to sleep. m-ɔi ɔ̀dra-nɪ. We are going to die.
Ä.: mǎ-r-ɔ́ı ù'du-lɛ. I am going to sleep.

After causatives (where the infinitive alternates with the subjunctive):

| má-'bà tɛ ɛdr-**nı**. | I made him stop. |
| má-'bà ndá turi-**nɨ** turi. | I made him fear. |

After verbs of knowing:

M.: mǎ-ni ndí là'di-**nı**. I know (how) to cook (i.e. I can cook).
bɔŋgó ɔnɔ́ ǎni kʊ ɔ̀dzʷà-**nı**. This cloth cannot be washed (lit. cloth this knows not washing).
Ä.: lɛ́dr-àza nì ku tɛ̀ arɪ ɔ̀kɔ-**nı**. Nobody can catch a bird (lit. person-other knows not *te* bird catching).

After verbs of wanting:

má-lɛ ɔɪ-**nı** 'bǎru. I want to go home.
ma-le anya ondre-**ni**. I want to see him.
opi le ku märi oi-**ni** läri ya. The chief doesn't want (for) me to go to the dance.

After adjectives:

ŋgʷɔ́nyá kadó ɔ̀nya-**nı** (or ɔ̀nya-**rı**). Food is nice to eat.

After prepositions:

nda 'ba ànya **ni** vo ondre-**ni**. (Lk. vii. 21.) He gave them sight (lit. he put them to earth seeing).

Gerund or Verbal noun form (cf. **la-** and **ŋga-** forms, §§ 156 and 174):

ori-**nɪ** vuru kadoro. To sit (or sitting) down is nice.
eki-**ni** 'bäru ni kadu para. Coming (or to come) home is very pleasant.
oi-**nɪ** Maridi ya iḏu mä-ri. I won't go to Maridi (lit. going to Maridi is not for me).
umu-**nɪ** ndä-ri iḏu. He cannot run.

532. Where there is an object, the infinitive particle may often be omitted, especially after verbs of motion.

M.: m-oi ŋgoinya **onya**.	I am going to eat food.
M.: m-édé m-ɔ́ı léti ɔ̀tɔ.	Let's go and sweep the road.
Ä.: má-r-ɔ́ı lédr ɔ̀ndrɛ.	I'm going to see the people.
Ä.: má-ɾɪ-tɛ̀ átá mírɔ àrɪ.	I have come to hear your words.
Note: ḏitoko koi boŋgo **oja-ni**.	The women are going to wash clothes.
M.: mǎ-ni waraga ùzi ku.	I don't know (how) to read a book.
lɛ́dr-aza nì àrɪ ɔ̀kwa ku.	Nobody can catch a bird.
ndá lɛ lósi ɔyɛ́ ku.	He doesn't want to do work.
kye **oga** losi ago ro.	Cutting trees is men's work.
ŋgoinya **la'di** losi ḏitoko ro.	Cooking food is women's work.

After the verb ε'bε (= to leave off) the infinitive particle is not used.

M.: ny-έ'bέ ŋg(a) úì. Leave off grinding (something).
Ä.: ny-έ'bέ aba. } Leave off walking.
Ä.: n-á'bέ əba. }
Ä.: n-á'bε əmvə si. Stop sneezing.

There are also a few verbal noun forms which have no suffix.

    ata = to speak = speech.   ạɾu = to bless = blessing.

533. Comparison of Moru dialects:

    I want to catch the mouse.   *I'm going to dive in the water.*

M.:} má-lέ nyedu ɔkó-**ní**.   m-ɔ́ì ə'dέ-**nɪ** gyi yá.
L.:} ,,   ,,   ,, -**ní**.   m-úì ə'dέ-**nɪ** ,,
K.:} ,,   ,,   ,, -**nε**.
Ä.:} má-lέ nyedu ɔkó-**nε**.   ma-rɔ ɔi ə'dέ-**nέ** dʒi ya.
'B.:}   ,, ,, -**lέ** ,,
Äg.:} má-lέ εdra ɔkó-**lε** (or- **nε**).
W.:} ,, kɪdra ako-**lε**.
Jl.:} ,, éndragó lòkó-**lε**.   má-ni-á 'dε-**lε** lumvá á.

    I don't want to die.   *I don't want to insult you.*

M.: má-lέ ku ɔ̀dra-**nɪ**.   má-lε kú mí ɔ̀'da-**nɪ**.
Ä.:}   má-lε kú mí ɔ̀'da-**lέ**.
'B.:} má-lε k(u) ɔdrà-**lε**.   ,, ,, 'da-**lέ**.
W.:}   má-lε mí a'dá-**lε** kʊ.
Jl.:} má-lε drà-**lε** kù.
Jg.:} ,, àdrà-**lε** kù.   ,, ,, 'da-**lε** ,,

(Note alternation in position of negative particle **ku**. See §§ 583, 607.)

The Infinitive Suffix
LOGO (and AVUKAYA)
-lε

534. The Logo and Avukaya infinitive suffix is similar to that found in Moru Wa'di and occasionally in Moroändri.

    LOGO: *ma-tibi tejina o-le.*   I try for the first time to do it.
            ma-ni boŋgo di-le ku.   I do not know how to sew.
            mi-do ŋga 'ba-le.   You take the food to put away.
            aḍi le ama[1] no-le   She wants to see me.
    AVUKAYA: *má-lε arígù-lε.*   I want to laugh.

535. The verbal noun form often requires a further suffix **'di**.

    LOGO: *azi o-le-ḍi adre tani.* Working is good (lit. work to-do).
          *ŋga **kugu-le-ḍi** konji.* Stealing is bad (lit. thing to steal).
          *amvu **a-le-ḍi** adre azi ago aḍia.* Hoeing fields is men's work.
          *ŋga **laḍi-le-ḍi** adre azi tokoi a'dia.* Cooking food is women's work.
          *ma-le ŋga **a-le-ḍi** ko.* I don't like (things) hoeing.
          *ḍia nda le **aiko-le**.* So-and-so likes sleeping.
          *agoe le za **bu-le**, kosia **be-le-ḍi** be.* Men like hunting animals and catching fish.

---

[1] Note a- prefix in pronoun. See § 268.

but not in AVUKAYA:

 ŋgá-lὲ-lὲ dɔ́. Loving is good. arí dɔ. Laughing is good.

536. The infinitive is much used in these two languages after the auxiliaries **adre, liri, o,** &c. (Logo), **ri, do** (Avukaya), to indicate progressive action.

 LOGO: *aďi are teci-le.*   He is walking.
   mvamva **ádrέ** ŋgɔ̀-lɛ. The child is crying.
   ma-o li-le.   I am walking.
 AVU. { Jl.: oma **ri** vé-lέ.   The grass is burning.
    { Jg.: oma **ri** vé-nì.

537. This construction may also refer to past action,[1] when it may be followed by a postposition.

 LOGO: *aďi are ali-le da* (or *dre*). He has come.
   akoďi dre ŋga-le dise. (Mt. xxviii. 6.) He is risen.
   ɪŋgílya **dó** ma-kɔkyɛ nyà-lɛ. A leopard has eaten my dog.
 AVU. { Jl.: läbägu **tro** ɔ̀kyέ màkàtra nyà-lɛ. A hyena has eaten my dog.
    { Jg.: läbägu **do** okέ ámákatrá nyà-lɛ.

538. Sometimes, in describing progressive action, the progressive auxiliary is absent.

 LOGO: ma(i) pà-**li** pà.   I am hammering.
 AVU. (Jl.): mání sandúki trɔ̀-lɛ. I am carrying a box.
   máni áni (ámi in Jg.) ʒì-lɛ. I am calling you.

539. The infinitive is further employed in describing a series of actions. Here, too, there is no auxiliary.

 LOGO: *mi-ali, boŋgo do, li-le, ji-le yi na.* Come (and) take the clothes (and) wash (them) in the river.
 I killed a man and he died.
 LOGO: mǎ-fu míndέ ádrà-lɛ.
 AVU. (Jg.): má-'dí 'bá drà-lɛ.

540. When there is an *object*, the infinitive suffix in the dependent verb is usually omitted. This occurs chiefly after the auxiliaries **adre, o,** &c., and after verbs of motion.

 LOGO: má-**drέ** mi ʒì.   I am calling you.
   mundia are mbi za.   The people burn the grass.
   aďi liri ta fe ďia dri. He talks (lit. is words giving) to the people.
   ma-o jo si.   I am building a house.
   ma-mʊ tòkwa **gyɛ**.   I go to marry a wife.
   aďi ali ŋga gi.   He comes to sell food.
   mi-ali boŋgo do.   Come and take the clothes.
   aďi aca ama **no**.[2]   He arrived to see me.

   What are you doing? *I am eating meat.* *I want to beat you.*
 LOGO: mí-**rá** à'dò-ŋg(a) ɔ yà? má-**drí** za nyà. má-nὲ mi **tswa**.
 AVU. { Jg.: mí-**rɪ** à'dʊ̀ 'yɛ yà? má-**rɪ** à'wa nyà. má-lɛ mi **tswa**.
    { Jl.:   má-**rɪ** à'wa nyà. má-lɛ ni **tswa**.

Note also in LOGO: *ma-kicoa li mi-be ko.* I cannot go with you.

[1] More probably a present state which is the result of action in the past.
[2] Cf. *aďi le ama no-le* in § 534.

Infinitive Suffixes
MADI
-rɛ, -ka, -lɛ

541. There are three infinitive forms in Madi, whose use is contextually defined In function, however, they all correspond to **nı** and **lɛ** of Moru and Logo.

-rɛ

542. After verbs of motion the dependent verb has suffix **rɛ**. (Note that this suffix persists even when there is an object.)

I am going to sleep.	*We are going to die.*	*I go to see the people.*
Lo.: mâ-mú o'dúkɔ-**rɛ**.	amá-vù drà-**rɛ**.	má-mu 'bá ndrɛ-**rɛ**.
Pa.: má-mú o'dúkɔ-**rɛ**.	ama-vó dà-**rɛ**.	má-mu 'bá ndɛ-**rɛ**.

Let us go and sweep the road.	*I have come to hear your words.*
Lo.: ɔŋga-kí léti sɔ̀-**rɛ**.	m-ɛ́mú nya-ledzó ɛrɪ-**rɛ**.
Pa.: avɔ̀-kí léti sɔ̀-**rɛ**.	m-ɛ́mú nya-le'jó-ni ɛrɪ-**rɛ**.

Note also in Opari Madi:

| e'bu 'ba dri kwe ga-**re**. | It is men's work to cut trees. |
| e'bu okondzi dri lenya ɖi-**re**. | It is women's work to cook food. |

-ka

543. The verbal noun form has suffix **-ka**. This form is also used after verbs of knowing, wanting, the verbs **ɛ'bɛ** and **fo,** and in negative constructions.

544. Gerund or Verbal noun:

Torit Madi:

kwe ga-**ka** e'bu 'ba dri.	Cutting trees is men's work.
anya ɖi-**ka** e'bu oko dri.	Cooking food is women's work.
eŋgwi-**ka** zoga cwi.	Coming home is pleasant.

545. After verbs of knowing.

I can do it.	*I can't do it* (lit. I know, &c.)
Lo.: á-nì 'wɛ-**ka** na rà.	á-nì 'wɛ-**ka** na kʊ.
Pa.: mǎ-ni ɛ-**ka** na rà.	mǎ-ni ɛ-**ka** na kʊ.

I can't read it.	*I can't read a book.*
Lo.: á-nì la-**ka** na kʊ.	á-nì wáraga là-**ka** ku.
Pa.: má-nì la-**ka** na kʊ.	má-nì wáraga là-**ka** ku.

546. Verbs of wanting.

I want to go home.	*I don't want to go home.*
Lo.: á-lɛ mù-**ka** (or mù-lɛ́) bàru.	(m)á-lɛ mu-**ka** (or mu-**si**) barú ku.
Pa.: má-lɛ mù-**ka** 'bäru.	má-lɛ mu-**ka** 'bärú ku.

I want to work.	*He doesn't want to work.*
Lo.: á-lɛ ébù è(dɛ)-**lɛ**.	ólɛ ébu ɛ-**ka** ku.
Pa.: má-lɛ f'bu ɛ́-**ka**.	anda lɛ f'bu ɛ-**ka** ku.

Note in Opari Madi:

| ma-le ani ndre-**re**. | I want to see him. |

547. After ɛ'bɛ (= to leave off).

Stop shouting (sg.). *pl.*
Lo.: ny-ɛ'bɛ ɔzá-**kà**. àny-ɛ'bɛ ɔzá-**kà**.
Pa.: ɛ'bɛ odʒwá-**kà**. àny-ɛ'bɛ ɔdʒwá-**ka**.

Stop sneezing (nose). *Stop grinding (thing).*
Lo.: ny-έ'bέ ɔ̀mvɔ́ tsi-**ka**. ny-ɛ'bɛ ta 'í-**ka**.
Pa.: έ'bέ ɔ̀mvɔ́ tsi-**ka**. ɛ'bɛ ŋga 'í-**ka**.

Note an alternative with the verbal noun in l- (see § 156): This verbal noun construction may be used instead of the -ka form in Madi:

Lo.: nyɛbɛ **lo'i**. Stop grinding.
Pa.: ɛ'bɛ **lo'i**.
ɛ'bɛ **ledzó**. Stop talking.
améni **lóŋgó** ra. We have learned singing (to sing).

548. After **fo** (= to go out).
Lo.: má-fo u'dúkɔ-**ka** si ko. I didn't sleep (lit. I went out to-sleep from not).
Pa.: „ u'dúkɔ si koro.

-lɛ: *in other contexts*

549. This suffix occasionally alternates with **ka**.

I tried (in vain) to lift it. *I try (in vain) to write.*
MADI { Lo.: á-ma ṅdzì-**lɛ** kwɛ. á-'bì sì-**lɛ** kwɛ.
Pa.: má-ma ŋ̀gì-**le** kpɛ. má-'bì tʃwi-**lɛ** kpɛ.

I am waiting (thing) to eat.
MADI { Lo.: má-tɛ a nyá-**lɛ** ti, or má-tɛ a nyá-**ká** tì.
Pa.: má-té ŋgá nya-**lɛ̀**, or má-té ŋgá nya-**kà**.

550. After adjectives.

Food is good to eat.
MADI { Lo.: lenyá lɔ̀sɔ nyà-**lɛ**.
Pa.: lenyá lɔ̀sɔ nyà-**lɛ**.

INFINITIVE SUFFIXES
LUGBARA and KELIKO
-le (or -la), -ŋga (or ŋa), -ka (or -taa)

551. These two languages show such similarity in infinitive forms that they may be discussed together. After certain verbs, and in sentences denoting progressive action, the suffix is -lɛ. Here similarity with Logo is apparent, though Lugbara usually retains this suffix even when there is an object.

-lɛ (or -la)

552. After verbs of motion.

I go to marry a wife. *I have come to hear your words.*
LUGBARA: má-mu̇ okó ogbwa-**lɛ**. ma-ímú mí-ɪdʒó-'di arı-**lɛ**.
KELIKO: ma-mʊ okó dzɛ-**lɛ**. ma-ímú mí-ɪdʒó yí.

I go to see the people. *Let's go and sweep the road.*
LUGBARA: má-mu 'bá ndɛ-**lɛ**. ámúkí léti à-**lɛ**.
KELIKO: má-mu 'barıpı ndrɛ. 'bá-mu léti fa.

	I am going to sleep.	*We are going to die.*
LUGBARA:	má-mu lá-lɛ́.	àmákí-mu òdà-là ra.
KELIKO:	má-mu u'dúkɔ.	ámá-mú drà gɪ.
KELIKO:	*ma-mu inya nya.*	I am going to eat food.
	ma-i ji-le ko.	I am not going to call.

553. After verbs of wanting and waiting.

	He doesn't want to work.	*I want to go home.*
LUGBARA:	f-lè àkò ɛ́-lɛ́ ku.	má-lɛ mú lisoga.
KELIKO:	ɪ(-rɪ)-lɛ ŋga a(-ra) ku.	má-lɛ mú 'bàru.

I am waiting to eat (something).
LUGBARA: má-tɛ àko nya.
KELIKO: má-tɛ ŋgá nyà(-lɛ́).

554. Progressive action (with or without auxiliary).

LUGBARA:	má sandúki 'dú-lɛ́.	I am carrying a box.
	má lítsɔ wɛ-lɛ.	I am sweeping the veranda.
	ma-pà-li pà.	I am hammering.
	ɪzá 'dí-lɛ.	The meat is cooking.
	ma-ovu-le 'ba onzini-risi. (Lk. v. 8.)	I am a sinful man.
KELIKO:	mvá ádrɛ́ ŋgò-lɛ.	The child is crying.

	I am going.	*The grass is burning.*
LUGBARA:	ma-mu-lɛ́.	ásɛ́ rɪ vɛ-lɛ.
KELIKO:	mä-mu-lɛ mu.	ásɛ́ rɪ vɛ(-nì).

	What are you doing?	*I am calling you.*	*I am eating meat.*
LUGBARA:	mí gá-à'du ɛ-lɛ yà?	ma mí ùmvɛ-lɛ-ga.	má-rì ɛ̀zà nya-lɛ.
KELIKO:	mí à'dɔ ɔ-lɛ́ yà?	má mì zì-lɛ.	má zá nya.

555. As in Logo, this construction may also refer to past action. Cf. § 537.

LUGBARA:	lubogú **'dù** m-otsógò ànyà-lɛ.	A hyena has eaten my dog.
	ɪzá 'dɪ-lɛ-ga.	The meat is cooked.

556. The infinitive may also be used to describe a sequence of action.

I killed a man and he died.
LUGBARA: má-'dí 'bá drà-lɛ.
KELIKO: mǎ-fu 'bá dà-lɛ.

-ŋga

557. The gerund form is ŋga(-ra) in Keliko only, but this form is also used after adjectives and after certain verbs in both languages. For Lugbara gerund see § 562.

558. Gerund or Verbal noun.

KELIKO:	*peti ga-ŋga-ra ri ago ve-ni.*	Cutting trees is men's work.
	inya reva-ŋga-ra oku a-ni.	Preparing food is for women.
	imu-ŋga-ra 'beti-ri anyisi.	Coming home is pleasant.

559. After adjectives:

Food is nice to eat.
LUGBARA: ínyá rɪ mǔkɛ̀ nyà-**ŋga-ra**-ga.
KELIKO: ésá rɪ mǔkɛ̀ nyà-**ŋga-ra**-ga.

VERB SUFFIXES

560. After verbs of knowing (Lugbara only).

	I can't read it.	*I can't read a book.*
LUGBARA:	má-nì là-ŋga-ra ku.	má-nì wáraga là-ŋga-ra ku.
KELIKO:	má-ni là ku.	má-nì wáraga là ku.

561. After ɛ'bɛ (Lugbara only).

LUGBARA:	mɛ́'bɛ ɔmvó so(-ŋa).	Stop sneezing.
	mɛ́'bɛ 'i-ŋga-ra.	Stop grinding.
	mɛ́'bɛ odʒɔ(-ŋa).	Stop shouting (sg.).
	ìmɛ'bɛ odʒɔ-ŋga-ra.	Stop shouting (pl.).

Note also occasional forms elsewhere, such as:

KELIKO and LOGO: má-lɛ àgu-ŋga-ra. I want to laugh.

-ka (or -taa)

562. In LUGBARA the gerund form is -ka[1] or -taa.

LUGBARA: *mi-fe nya-ka eri-dri.* (Rom. xii. 20.) Feed him (lit. give eating to him).
mi-aii ndre-taa mini. (Lk. xviii. 42.) Receive thy sight.

B. THE z- SUFFIXES

563. These suffixes in Moru and Madi correspond to the infinitive particle in English only when some purpose is expressed. In Logo and Lugbara z- forms are found in dependent non-purpose clauses as well.

-zá MORU

564. Examples:

ma-le kwɔdra zɔ ɔmu-za. I want bamboos for building a house.
ndá ɔzɔ̀ parátà tɛ märi, ukyí-zá-ná Amádi yà. He gave me money in order to go to Amadi.
dɔ́fɔ́ (ɔ)nɔ́ Dzɔrɔmı ɔ'bí-zá sı-na. This stick is for beating (or to beat) Joromi with (it).
mɔ́zɔ̀ ip̣í ɔnɔ́ te miri, tàu ɔ̀lɔ-aza sı-na. I give you this knife to cut the chicken (with it).
nda kecu-za-na. (Mk. iii. 2.) That they might accuse him.

-zo MADI

565. Examples:

. . . ani ni-zo.	(. . . so that he should know them).
pa aci-zo.	(legs for walking [to walk with]).
tolu kwe ga-zo.	(axe for chopping wood).

-zo LOGO

566. Examples:

akoďi li-dre yi mvu-zo. He has gone to drink water.
aďi do-dre ami-ďili za 'bu-zo. He has taken your spear to hunt game (with it).
mi-ali yi be ama-drika ji-zo. Bring water (lit. come water with) to wash my hands.
mi-da yi saani ji-zo. Pour the water for washing plates.
ma-ali-dre ama-amvupi no-zo. I have come to see my sister.

---

[1] This suffix seems to alternate with -za. See § 571.

-zu LUGBARA

567. Examples:

Yi ŋga ti ici 'ba-Herodiani be, eri dri ja-zu. (Mk. iii. 6.) They took counsel with the Herodians (how they might) destroy him.

'Ba yi adri tala iji, 'ba-zu afazu alia ya? (Mk. iv. 21.) Do men buy a candle, to put under a bushel?

'ba ka-zu eri omi-zu ko. (Mk. iii. 9.) So that they should not throng him.

Yi isu-ni eyo omvi-zu tinia ko. (Mk. xiv. 40.) They found no word to reply to him.

okpo 'ba azini ni eri etali-zu yo. (Mk. v. 4.) Lit. strength man any for him to-tame was-not.

568. In both LOGO and LUGBARA this suffix is used in dependent sentences. In Logo the verb is usually assisted by an auxiliary (**dre, are, o,** &c.).

LOGO: *ma-nya ŋga, ma-are pi-zo.* I eat food until I am satisfied.

ma-kayi iri, ma-ra nji-zo. I sleep twice before I return.

adi o ta-i ali-zo. He is about to come (lit. he makes plans to come).

*dre adre-zo nale Erode **dre** dra-zo ka.* (Mt. ii. 15.) And stayed there till Herod died.

*adi **dre** nji-zo nalese.* (Mt. xii. 9.) And when he was departed thence.

LUGBARA: *Erini fi-zu oguru alia, . . .* (Mk. v. 18.) When he was come unto the ship, . . .

Yini 'ba-tre ko-zu, . . . (Mk. iv. 36.) When he had dismissed the multitude, . . .

Erini eri ndre-zu, . . . (Mk. v. 22.) When he saw him, . . .

Odu yini andri pa-zu yi-dri ŋga eca-ra. (Mk. ii. 20.) The day when they shall take the bridegroom from them shall come.

Pari 'ba-azo-beri-diri la-zu-ri. (Mk. ii. 5.) Bed (lit. place) on which the sick of the palsy lay.

Yi ka pari erini ovu-zu-ri ndre-ra. (Mk. vi. 55.) When they saw the place where he was.

Eyo, erini ovu-zu jo a, ŋga ku-ra. (Mk. ii. 1.) The news, that he was in the house, spread.

'Ba mani le-zu eri-dri, ma-fe-ra. (Lk. iv. 6.) To whomsoever I will I give (it).

Eri co bile eri-zu. (Mt. xi. 15.) Let him (ears) hear.

569. In both languages, too, this particle is found in co-ordinate sentences, especially those that describe sequence of action. Consequently it is much used in narrative.

LOGO: *adi turu tala, **dre** ŋga ao-zo jo na, **dre** nda-zo we.* (Lk. xv. 8.) She lights a lamp and sweeps (in) the house, and searches much.

*adi **dre** fo-zo **dre** ŋgo-zo.* (Mt. xxvi. 75.) And he went out and wept.

*aii **dre**-ki mondu ba-zo si-le, **dre** nya-zo.* (Mt. xii. 1.) And they began to pluck the ears of corn, and to eat.

LUGBARA: *eyo olo-zu, orindi onzi dro-zu indi.* (Mk. i. 39.) And preached the word, and cast out devils.

Eri ŋga fi pari-'bani-oku-zu-ri a, 'ba imba-zu. (Mk. i. 21.) He entered into the synagogue (lit. place for meeting people) and taught people.

Eri ŋga-ni tala i, azini ko-ni jo ale, ndru-zu okposi? (Lk. xv. 8.) Does she not light a candle and sweep the house out, and search well.

-zo (all languages)

570. In all languages verbal nouns (noun instruments) may be formed by means of this particle. Thus from the verb stems **lɔsɛ** (to sew) and **pa** (to hammer) are derived:

	needle (i.e. cloth sewer)	*hammer* (i.e. thing beater)
MORU:	(ŋga) bɔŋgó lɔsɛ́-**zɔ̀**.	ŋgá ŋgá-útu-**ru**.[1]
AVU. { Jl.:	ítá lɔsɛ́-**zɔ**.	ŋgá ipá-**zó**-la.
{ Jg.:	ítá lásɛ́-**zɔ**.	ŋgá ipá-**zó**-la.
LOGO:	bɔŋgwá lasɛ-**za**.	(ŋgá) ípa-**dzó**-nà.
KELIKO:	ŋgá itsi-**zɔ**.	ŋgá pa-**zò**-nì.
LUGBARA:	(sendáni) bɔŋgó gbī-**dʒó**.	ipa-**dʒó**-là.

-za LUGBARA

571. In LUGBARA another sort of verbal noun is formed with the suffix **-za**.

le-za (love). *asi te-za* (hope).
mi-fe eri-dri afa-mvu-za. (Rom. xii. 20.) Give him drink.
Mvi 'ba ni eri emu afa-nya-za nya-zu azini afa-mvu-za mvu-zu. (Mt. xi. 19.) The Son of man came (food) eating and (drink) drinking.

Compare these forms with the Gerund in **-ka** and **-ŋga-ra** (§§ 562 and 557).

-za-ro LUGBARA

572. This form seems to be used after certain verbs, notably **eco** (to be able) and **ovu** (to be).

LUGBARA: *Baka jijimani ba ɖiri dri econi mani avu-za-ro ayu-za-ro ko ani.* (Mk. i. 7.) The latchet of whose shoe I am not worthy to stoop down and unloose. (*econi* = to be able.)
Econi ani yini nyaka nya-za-ro ko. (Mk. iii. 20.) So that they could not eat bread.
Eco Setanini Setani dro-za-ro ŋgoni ya? (Mk. iii. 23.) How can Satan drive out Satan?
Ngori aga-ra ya? Yo-za-ro 'ba-azo-beri matia, . . . (Mk. ii. 9.) Which is easier? To say to the sick of the palsy, . . .
'Ba azini indi, dri eri-ni ovu ondri-za-ro. (Mk. iii. 1.) And there was a man there, his hand was withered. (*ovu* = to be.)
Eri ŋga ejo-ra, dri-ni ŋga ati-za-ro. (Mk. iii. 5.) And he stretched it out, and his hand was healed.
Eyo onzi mini ma-ovu wu-za-ro. (Mk. ii. 5.) Thy sins be forgiven.
Eri ovu fe-za-ro ma-dri. (Lk. iv. 6.) For that is delivered unto me.
Erini ovu-zu si-za-ro. (Lk. iv. 10.) For it is written.

For **-za** with adjectives see § 704.

C. The Participial Suffixes

573. Participles are formed with the aid of the particles **vu** and **ra**, which both indicate primarily 'at the place of' and hence 'at the time of'.

-via (-vɔya) MORU

574. The Moru participle suffix is **via** (Miza) **vɔya** (-ändri).[2] These suffixes may be used in a purely spacial adverbial sense:

ndá ɔ̀rı-**vìa** (or **vɔ̀ya**) noà. He lives here (lit. he lives place here).
täú'bu ɔ̀rı-**vɔ̀ya**? Are there any eggs? ɔ̀rı-**vɔ̀ya**. Yes, there are.

---
[1] This is an overlapping in function of the 'result' particle **dro**. See § 595.
[2] = **vu-ya** = in the place.

575. But they also occur participially:

má-ndrɛ ndá tɛ ù'du-**vòya**. I saw him sleeping.
ndá drà-te kɪló òyɛ-**vòya**. He died while fighting.
má-ndr adrúpɪ márɔ te, tòkɔ ɛrɔ ò'bɪ-**vìa** (or ká tòkɔ ɛrɔ ò'bɪ). I saw my brother beating his wife.
mέrɛ ŋgága (te) {lí-**vìa**. / ká-lii.} I heard a boy crying.
'ditòkó ká lɔŋgó òŋgɔ, ɪnyá wĭ-**vìa**. The women sing while grinding grain.
tăpí márɔ̀ u'dù-**vòya**. My father is sleeping.
ánya ŋgwónyă ònya-**vìa**. He is eating.

Note in the following sentence there is no participial form:
ánya ndrɛ ádrupí ndárɔ ăfu-tέ. He saw his brother killed.

576. Gerund forms after a preposition:

hakím pa ŋgágà te, **ni** ɔdrá-**vìa**. The doctor saved the boy from dying.
nyέ-tɛŋga tăpi márɔ kú **nì** u'dú-**vòya**. Don't wake my father from sleeping.
nyá-laga ndá **nì** (or **zŏ**) ònya-**vìa**. Stop him from eating it.
ópí pa ŋgútí tɛ **ni** ini rɪ ɔsi-**vìa**. The chief saved the girl from being bitten by a snake (lit. from the snake, biting).
ópí pa ndá te **nì** àsí rɪ òza-**vɪa**. The chief saved him from being burned by the fire.
ópí pa zɔ te **nì** ùdzwé-**vìa**. The chief saved the house from burning.

Note that the '**vu**' particle in Logo and Lugbara has merely a locative significance:
LOGO: *mi-kali ma-**vu** la*. Come and see me (where I am).
Cf. LUGBARA: *mi-mú ma-**vɔ***. Come to me.

-ra and -ra'a LOGO

577. ra = place. Note its use in the following compounds:

*boŋgo-ji-**ra***. Place where clothes are washed (lit. cloth-wash-place).
*ŋga-lad̆i-**ra***. Kitchen (lit. food-cook-place).

ra'a = in the place. This form is used as a participial suffix to verbs.
e.g. *za-**ra'a***. Burning.
*Yoane dre ali-le ŋga nya-**ra'a** ko, ŋga mvu-**ra'a** ko d̆ise*. (Mt. xi. 18.) John came neither eating nor drinking.
*ma-liri ami-be yekalu na, ta tada-**ra'a** kitu vuse kolia*. (Mt. xxvi. 55.) I sat with you in the temple, teaching daily.

In subordinate temporal clauses ('while' clauses) the auxiliary **dre** is used with this construction.

*mi-do tau-'bu tovo-le, ma-**dre** ŋga nya-**ra'a***. Take away the eggs to boil, while I am eating.
*mundia **dre** aiyi-**ra'a**, akod̆i kari'ba dre ali-zo*. (Mt. xiii. 25.) While men slept, his enemy came.

-ria LUGBARA

578. The Lugbara participial suffix is very like that in Logo, both in form and in function.

*Erini aga-**ria** miri tia . . ., eri ŋga Simonini ndre, azini Andarea . . ., yini emba be-**ria** miri alia*. (Mk. i. 16.) As He was walking by the sea . . ., He saw Simon and Andrew . . ., casting nets into the sea.

*Orindi onzini eri rua ase-**ria**, oyo-**ria** oduko uru si,* . . . (Mk. i. 26.) The bad spirit having torn his body and having cried with a loud voice, . . .
*Te 'ba nde yini oduko-**ria*** . . . (Mt. xiii. 25.) While men slept . . .

It may be attached to the auxiliary as well:

*Suru Muŋgu ni eri ovu dini, 'bani ka ŋga-**ria** ori ri-**ria** nyaku a.* (Mk. iv. 26.) The Kingdom of God is, as if a man should cast seed into the ground.

Or to the postposition:

*Aŋgo azini yini emi aii-le ko-**ria**,* . . . (Mk. vi. 11.) Whosoever shall not receive you, . . .

D. OTHER SUFFIXES

-I, -KI

579. The plural suffix has already been discussed (§§ 193–4) in relation to nouns. Where verbs are concerned the suffix is **-i** in Moru and **-ki** elsewhere.[1] In the Definite Aspect it is attached to the verb stem, but in the Indefinite Aspect it is attached to the verb auxiliary (if any). In most languages it occurs only in the 3rd person, but in Lugbara[2] and Keliko it may occur in the 1st and 2nd person as well. Examples:

Definite Aspect.

MORU: *ànya **to-i** läri ku ondro.*   They do not dance to-day.
MADI: *mundro **emu-ki**-ra.*   Strangers came.
LOGO: *aii **aca-ki** ama no.*   They arrived to see me.
LUGBARA: *ama-**mú-kí**-'bo.*   We went.

Indefinite Aspect.

MORU: *anya **ka-i** vure ope.*   They are holding a discussion.
MADI: *okonzi **ka-ki** loseri so obo.*   The women will plant grain to-morrow.
LOGO: *tokoe **adre-ki** ado o ya?*   What are the women doing?

Note in KELIKO:

*ama-**mvu-ki** iyi.*   We drink water.
*anziŋa-ri **ko-ki** uduka ye.*[3]   The boys are not sleeping.
*ama-'**di-ki** ariŋa-ri.*   We killed fowls.

-na MORU

580. One function of the **na** particle is as suffixed complement to the verb when no definite object is expressed. Here it is often difficult to distinguish from the **na-** pronoun. (See § 255.)

M.: *má-tòdzwa-**na**.*   I am washing (something?).
Ä.: *márɔ́ tɔ̀dzwi-**na**.*
M.: *má-drɪ ɔ̀sɪ-**na**.*   I am still biting.
má-dr-ɛmbɛ́ { **-na** / **-la**   I am still tying.
*nyá-ú'di-**na** o'duta yà?*   Why are you digging?
*anya ka ledri ufu-**na**.*   He kills men (i.e. his present occupation is man-killing).

---

[1] Note in Logo the *noun* plural suffix is **-ɪ**, not **-ki**.
[2] Not found in the New Testament language.
[3] Suffix attached to negative particle.

Compare LOGO: *aďi are teci-le.*   He is walking.
    ma-adre teci-le aŋgia.   I am just walking.

The **na** particle is also found in the future construction. (See under **'da**, § 628.)

-ni LOGO, LUGBARA, MADI, LULU'BA

581. It has already been shown how the particle **ni** may be attached to nouns or pronouns in these languages. It may also be attached to verb stems (Definite or Indefinite). Its function is uncertain.

Examples from LOGO:

mbia vé-**nì**.   The grass is burning.
yi-lavo are amaki o-ni.   We are thirsty (lit. water-thirst is us afflicting).

Examples from LUGBARA:

ópí drà-**nì** (or -**'bó**).   The chief is dead.
Yohana eri emu nya-ni enya ko, azi-ni mvu-ni ewa ko. (Mt. xi. 18.) John came neither eating nor drinking (lit. John he came eating food not, and drinking beer not).
Emi-ji-ni mele ka-ni emvea . . . ko. (Mt. x. 9.) Provide neither gold nor silver.
Te ama-oko-ni efa alo-ni ko. (Lk. v. 5.) But we have taken nothing.
Ma-ni-ni ago . . . ko. (Mk. xiv. 71.) I know the man . . . not.

Examples from MADI and LULU'BA.

MADI: andápí kódrà-**nì**.   They will die.
  Lo.: á-lɛ má-tâ-**ni** ra.   I want to speak.
  Pa.: má-lɛ má-ta-**ni** rá.
LULU'BA: mɔ 'jé 'jó-**ni**.   I speak words (lit. I words speak).
  'ba ani à'do 'bá-**ni**?   What are the people doing?
  'bá ani kó-ɔ̀tɔ-**ni**.   They are dancing.
  ki asi-n(i) ovú-**nì**.   Go and blow the fire (lit. go fire blow).

-a LOGO

582. As in the case of nouns (see § 158) many verbs in Logo have a suffix **-a**, which is not usually found in other languages. In Logo, too, alternative forms of the verb without the suffix are very common. The function of this suffix is uncertain, but it seems to be most in evidence when the verb stands alone.[1] e.g.:

LOGO: lo and lwà (to cut)   tsɔ and tswa (to beat)
  ŋo and ŋwa (to break)   zɔ and zwa (to milk)

With sound-change:

    gi and gyɛ (to buy)

Compare also: ndrɛ and ndra (in Moru) = to see.
    'bú (in Logo) and 'bwä (in Moru) = to shoot.
    sì (in Moru) and sya (in Logo) = to sneeze.

---

[1] The present writer came across it mostly when filling in the verb section of the vocabulary. It was also much in evidence in the vocabulary collected by Miss McCord—more than in the sentences she collected.

CHAPTER XVI

VERB POSTPOSITIONS

583. As already stated, postpositions are used mostly in the Definite Aspect, where they have the following positions (examples from MORU):

(a) At the end of a sentence.

mä-ni-**te**.	I know.
má-ndrɛ ló'ba **ǵʷo**.	I saw a water-buck.
ma-ni ɔyɛ-na **ndi**.	I know how to do it.
ma-'bo liwa aloďi **te**.	We shot one elephant.

(b) After the verb, but followed by the rest of the predicate.

mói-**te** tsoȧ.	I went out.
m-ɛzí-**ǵʷo** tokó máro rí.	I took it to my wife.
mǎ-ni-**ndí** là'di-ni.	I know how to cook.

(c) After the object, but followed by the rest of the predicate.

má-ndrɛ ndá **te** ù'du-vòya.	I saw him sleeping.
adrupi maro ge ti **te** ritu.	My brother bought two cows.
ma-ye losi **te** tandrube.	We did work yesterday.

Compare in LOGO:

ma-fu le'bi **dre** or ma-fu-**dre** le'bi. I killed a water-buck.

584. Some postpositions may be used with Indefinite constructions as well as with Definite constructions. Such are:

yà, drá, wa (Madi), **ni**, and others.

There are also several particles which act as postpositions in some contexts, but which precede the verb stem in other contexts. Such are:

ku, dro, ǵa.

Some postpositions are found only in principal sentences, others are found only in subordinate sentences, while others still occur in both kinds of sentences.

For the purpose of easy reference the Moru-Madi verbal postpositions will be arranged in alphabetical order, irrespective of language, and the various functions of each will be discussed in turn.

585. a AVUKAYA. See **ǵa**.

586. ako, aku. See **ko**.

bɛ, 'bɛ, bi. Central languages (MORU).

587. The Central languages seem to use this particle in emphatic replies to questions (cf. **ndi** in Moru).

LOGO:	má-nɔ mì **'bɛ**.	I can see you.
	ma-si ama-jo **'be**.	I certainly do (or did) build my house.
KELIKO:	má-nɔ̀-**bi**.	I see.
	mä-i-**bi**.	I know.
AVUKAYA:	ma-nyá ärú **bɛ**. ⎫	We *do* eat water-rat.
WA'DI:	ma-nyá koṛú **bé**. ⎭	

(Cf. M. and Ä. ma-nyá ló'ba **ndi**. We do eat water-buck.)

For the function of **bɛ** in Moru (relative function) see Chapter XVII.

'bo LUGBARA, MORU

588. This is the normal 'past time' postposition in LUGBARA, but it may also be used as a 'perfect' state indicator, to imply that an action is finished.

má-atsá-'bɔ.	I have arrived.
ódrógú tsì mà 'bo.	A mouse bit me.
ópí drà-'bɔ.	The chief is dead.
'bárɪ òdra-ki-'bo.	They died.
àmà-nya ìza 'bó.	We have eaten the meat.

In MORU this particle is found in the Indefinite construction only.

How do the Moru catch fish?

M.: ledr Mɔróra ká ti'bi ùru-'bo ìŋwanyì yà?
Ä.: ledr Mɔróra ró i'bí ùru-'bo ìŋwatì yà?

'blo LENDU

589. In Lendu this particle seems to be used exclusively when there is no object.

ma-dza-ndrrtszja the-'blo.	My cow has died.
iszle go-'blo.	The woman gave birth.
mgba le-go-ŋgue-'blo tszbajo.	A child has just been born.
dike ce-'blo.	The man woke up.

ca[1] MORU

590. The following examples explain the use of **ca** in Moru:

mi-'bi ma ca (oko), m-eki-a-ndi mi-vo. Although you beat me, I'll follow you.
ma-du-ca ŋgoinya aku, ma-ye losi a-ndi. Although I am (exist) without food, I'll do work.

And in a predicative construction:

käbi ca onje, ndi edo iro be. Although the lizard is white, he has oil (Moru proverb).

dí[2] LOGO

591. This particle is used often with the idea of assuring some one that an action will take place.

ma-ali-dí. I am just coming.
ma-li 'bu dí. I'll go and shoot it at once.

It is very common in dependent sentences conveying the idea of 'as soon as':

yi ko-liva-dre-dí, mi-'ba täu'bu tove-le. As soon as the water boils, put the eggs in to boil.
täu ko-liŋga we dí, mi-kago aba. When the fowl is big, bring it back.

It is also used in sentences implying 'as, like as':

mi-ko-o niɖi ŋgoro (= *ŋga ro*) *ma-dre tada-le mi-dre-dí tini.* Do this as I have shown you.

---

[1] From Mynor's grammar. Probable pronunciation ts^wa. See notes on orthography, Chapter XXIV.

[2] From Miss Mozley's grammar. It is therefore impossible to state here whether the **d** is explosive or implosive.

VERB POSTPOSITIONS

592. In LOGO, too, the conditional relies almost entirely on the use of the final particle **di**—helped sometimes by the volition auxiliary **ko**.

mi-ado täu-'bu di, ma-gi-ru. If you'll bring eggs, I'll buy them.
mi-ko-li nale di, aii ko-fu mi dra-le. If you go there, you will be killed (lit. they will kill you to die).
kabiliki avi ami-drika-se di, ami-ata ko-coa mi. If you lose the sheep (lit. if the sheep gets lost from 'chez-vous') your father will beat you.
mi-ko-mvu lojo nadi di, mi-ko-dra. If you drink that poison, you will die.
mva ko-ŋgo-di, ma-ko-fe ti-le adi-dre ko. If the child cries, I won't give it milk.
mva ko-ŋgo ko di, ma-ko-fe ti-le adi-dre. If the child does not cry, I'll give it milk.

And in past condition (note double use of '**dre**'):

mi-li-dre nale dre-di, afu-dre mi. If you had gone there, you would have been killed.
kabiliki avi-dre ami-drika-se dre-di, ami-ata coa-dre mi. If you had lost the sheep, your father would have beaten you.
mi-ko-mvu lojo dre-di, mi-dra-dre. If you had drunk the poison, you would have died.
mva ko-ŋgo-dre-di, ma-fe-dre ti-le adi-dre ko. If the boy had cried, I would not have given him milk.
mva ko-ŋgo-dre ko-di, ma-fe ti-le adi-dre. If the boy had not cried, I would have given him milk.

dì MADI

593. This particle seems to occur only in Madi, and only with certain verbs, notably the verb '**egwe**' = to escape, get lost, be forgotten.

	The sheep is lost.	*I am lost in the bush.*
MADI Lo.:	bɪlä ɛ́gwɪ-**dì** (or **rà**).	mégwè aísé-aga **dì** (or **rà**).
Pa.:	,, lɛ́gwɛ-**dì** (or **rà**).	mélɛgwè ,, **dì**.

They forgot the words.

(They got lost from the words.)	(The words escaped them.)
Lo.: bá ɛgwè ledʒó-sɪ **dì**.	ledʒó ɛgwè bàní **dì** (or **rá**).
Pa.: 'bá lɛgwè le'jó-sɪ **dì**.	le'jó lɛgwè 'bàní **dì**.

dr(ì) MORU

594. This postposition is used in sentences to show that the action of the verb is not completed at the time of speaking.

má-'bí ndá ku-**dr̀**.	I haven't beaten him yet.
gìf la'di ku-**dr̀**.	The water isn't yet boiled.
or la'di-**dri** ku.	

dro, ro

595. Sentences with this particle show the result of an action, whether actual or merely contemplated. Thus this particle occasionally overlaps in function with the 'purpose' suffix -**zo** (see §§ 563 et seq.).

dro or **ro** usually occurs as a postposition to the subjunctive form of the verb. In Logo it may be used in the Indefinite Aspect. In Lugbara it seems to occur only in conjunction with the suffix -**za** (see § 572).

MORU: *Ayaŋwa ozo ŋgoinya go märi, ma-nya-**ro**-be.* Ayangwa gave me food, so that I might eat.

MORU: *ta se ono ma-pe-te miri, ny-adu-ro-be-ya iďwi-si.* This thing I have told you so that you may be joyful.
moi-na Maridi ya ondo, mandre vure miro ro.[1] I shall go to Maridi tomorrow to see your case.

I gave him poison so that he should die.
MORU: má-zo ärí tɛ ndäri, tànà ndá kòdrà-rɔ.
MADI { Lo.: má-kwɛ láka èrwà, kòdrà-**dro**.
       Pa.: má-kɛ láka èrwà, andá aní dà-**zɔ**.
LUGBARA: má-fè ɪrɪnɪ kɪsù, wa dra-**rʊ́** sɪ ra.
KELIKO: má-fè ɪrɪnɪ kɪsù, erɪní dra-**zwâ** nɪ.

Come here so that I (or we) may see you.
MORU (Ä.): n-ádrɛ nána, má-ndrè mì rɔ.
MADI { Lo.: mì-mba àŋgwé nà lɛ, mà-ndrɛ-**dro** nyi.
       Pa.: édé na dʊ́, àmà-ndɛ nyi.
LUGBARA: mí-àdrè ànvɛ 'dà, má-ndrɛ mì.
KELIKO: mí-adré 'dá, má-ndrɛ mì.
LOGO: *mi-ali, ma-no-ro.*

Take this knife to cut the chicken with.
MORU: mí-ru ílí 'do, mí-lɔ tàù sɪ na.
MADI { Lo.: nyi-'dù ílí, nyɪ-lɪ a'ù **dro**.
       Pa.: 'du ílí 'di'i, lì-sì à'ú **do**.
LUGBARA: í-'du íli, à'ʊ́ li-**zo**.
KELIKO: mí-agyí ílì 'dìrì, a'ú li-**dʒʊ́** àni.

Further examples from LOGO:
aďi zu sabuni, ma boŋgo ji ako ro. He hid the soap, so that I could not wash the clothes.
mi-k-ado saani, aďi ko-ji-ro. Bring the plates so that he can wash (them).
mi-k-ali ma-vuse, ma-k-ala-ro ami ďia-be-le-pi-ďii-ro. (Mk. i. 17.) Follow me and I will make you fishers of men.
ama-pa loga, ma-ali ako ro. My foot prevents me from coming.
aďi loga ma-ali ako ro. He prevented me from coming.

596. Combined with **ka**, this particle forms phrases in LOGO that are best rendered in English by 'until'.
LOGO: *mi-li ko, ma-ago-ro-ka.* Don't go until I return.
mi-nya ŋga nyano ko, kitu ko-ndi-ro-ka. Don't eat now until the sun sets.
mi-liri boŋgo ko-yo-ro-ka, mi-do-ro 'ba-le jo na. Wait until the clothes dry, before you start putting them in the house.

597. In LENDU **ro** is sometimes used with sentences showing cause or reason (cf. **zo**, § 563).
LENDU: *ma-gbogbo, furira ma-jo ke ti sz-ŋgue-ro.* I am laughing because my brother has been stung by a bee (lit. I laugh, reason my-brother he bee bitten-has-been).

dro, do

598. In the Southern languages this particle corresponds to Moru **ri** in permissive sentences (cf. § 631). Here its dialectal variant is **do**, but the latter is not a postposition.

[1] Or: *vure miro ondre-nɪ* (infin.).

VERB POSTPOSITIONS

Ask the doctor if we may eat meat to-day.

MADI { Lo.: nyí-zí akimu-ni, mà-nya-**drò** èza.
Pa.: ,, ,, **dó** amá-nya èza.
LUGBARA: imi-zí akimu, mà **dò** èzá nya-ra.
KELIKO: mi-dzi ,, rɪ, **də** ma dzá nya-ra.

The doctor says you may drink water.

MADI { Lo.: akímu kodzo, nyí-mvù-**dro** eí.
Pa.: ,, ku'jó də ànyí-mvu iyí.

ga, a AVUKAYA, KELIKO, LUGBARA (MADI)

599. This postposition is very common among the Central languages (excluding Logo) and in one or two of the MORU dialects that have come under Central influence. It is not used in Moru proper.

It occurs only in the Indefinite Aspect and usually denotes progressive or habitual action.[1]

AVUKAYA (Jl.): má-'dɔ́ a'wá ó'bu-ǎ úsu sì. I shoot game with a bow.
gúla lesi vo-á. He is blowing the fire.
gúla árí gù-a. He is laughing.

Compare:

	I am talking.	*I'm just walking.*	*He is going.*
OJILA:	má-tà ata-'a.	mä-gbí làmu-ä.	gúlà rà-'a.
WA'DI:	má-tà àta-**ga**.	mä-gbí lomu-**gä**.	ndínà mu-**gä**.

	The grass is burning.	*I'm still tying it.*
OJILA:	oma (gí) vɛ-'á.	
WA'DI:	käi (gbí) edzí-**gá**.	ma-dr-ɔmbé-**gá**-nà.

600. In KELIKO and LUGBARA the **ga** usually follows an infinitive suffix.

KELIKO: 'ba-ri leti ga-le-**ga**. The people cut a road.
'ba-ri amvu a-le-**ga**. The people hoe the field.
mí à'dɔ́ ɔ́-lɛ-**ga** yà? What are you doing?
ésá-rɪ mʊ́kɛ̀ nyà-ŋga-ra-**ga**. Food is nice to eat.
LUGBARA: drusi má mi ndrɛ-lɛ-**ga** 'dì? Shall I be seeing you to-morrow?
ɪzá 'dɪ-lɛ-**ga**. The meat is cooked.
ínyá-rɪ mʊ́kɛ̀ nyà-ŋga-ra-**ga**. Food is nice to eat.

Note also in LUGBARA:

mí-**gá** à'du ɛ-lɛ yà? What are you doing?

For the function of **ga** in MADI (Relative function of time or place) see Chapter XVII.

ge, gɪ KELIKO, MORU

601. This is the normal particle for the past in KELIKO.

má-atsá-**ge**. I've arrived.
mä-mu-**gɪ** (or **ra**). I've gone.
mà-nya za **gɪ**. We ate the meat.
'bári ɔ̀dràki-**gɪ**. They died.
bogu nya otsógó mávérè **gɪ**. A hyena has eaten my dog.

Compare the particle in the following Moru greeting:

nyú'du-'dá yà? mú'du-**gù**. Have you slept? I have.

---
[1] Compare **ga**, **a** as noun postpositions, § 312.

602. In MORU **gɪ** has a different function. Combined with **tɛ, 'da, ku,** it corresponds to English 'really', 'actually', and ultimately has a potential force.

lédr dra-**gí-'dá** yà? Did the man actually die?
mí-ti ta-na **gɪ-'da** ya? Did you mind? (Lit. did you really hold word of it?)
mí-tí-**na** tà-nà **gɪ** ku yà? Won't you mind?
má-yɛ-**gí-nì**. I just did it (for no reason).
ma-ndrɛ-**gɪ**-te. I see that. (It is evident.)
ma-sa-gɪ-ɖa Maridi ya ya? Can I reach Maridi?
musu 'ba miro gɪ-ɖa ya? Shall I find your village?
kado te musu gyi ku-te, ma-ye-gɪ aŋgwonye ya? Supposing I haven't found water, what am I to do?

In the following sentences, note how the Moru often uses simple tenses where we say 'can' and 'can't':

mí-ndrà lä'bí anà **gì-'dá** yà? Can you see that water-buck?
hwâ, má-ndrá kʊ̀. No I can't.
mí-ndrà tsʷɛ 'dèsì àna **gɪ-'da** yà. Can you see that big tree?
ɔʊ̀, má-ndrá tsʷɛ **ndí**, oko má-ndrá lä'bí kʊ-tɛ. Yes, I can see the tree, but I can't see the water-buck.
mí-ndrá lä'bí tsʷè zèlɛ áná **gí** kʊ yà? Can't you see the water-buck under the tree?
ɔʊ̀ yáʊ̀-ɔnɔ́ má-ndra-tɛ̀. Yes, now I can see it.

g(w)o MORU (Narrative)

603. This postposition is used in MORU when a sequence of events is being described, either in past or in future time.

ini si ndá te, ndí drà-**gò**. A snake bit him (and) he died.

Narrative in the past:

tandróbɛ mói-te tsóà, águ má-ndrɛ ló'ba **gwò**, ndí má-bwä-**gwò**, ndí drà-**gwò**,
Yesterday I went out, and I   saw a hartebeest, and I   shot (it) and (it) died,
   mézí-**gwo** tokó máru rí, adí   la'dí-**gwo**,   águ má-nya-**gwò**.
(and) I took (it) to my wife, and she cooked (it) and   I ate it.

Narrative in the future:

ɔ́ndɔ́   má-'daá-**gwo** ói ní Amádi yá, águ má-gé-na tɔ̀rɔ́má ('da),
to-morrow   I shall go   to Amadi, and I shall buy maize,
águ mózɔ-ná **gwo** tokó máru rí, ndí ánya la'dí-na **gwò**, águ ma-nyá-na **gwò**.
and I'll give it   to my wife, and she   will cook it, and we'll eat it.

In most of the other languages, narrative sequence is given by means of infinitive and other particles.

ka LOGO

604. This particle occurs in subordinate clauses of temporal condition (cf. English 'until'), but it may also be used in imperative or exclamatory sentences.

mi-no-ka! (Mt. ii. 13.) Behold!
mi-k-adre nale ma-ko-ta ta mi-dri ka. (Mt. ii. 13.) Be thou there until I bring (lit. say) thee word.
Dre adre-zo nale Erode dre dra-zo-ka. (Mt. ii. 15.) And was there until the death of Herod.

kpɔ, kyə MADI, LULU'BA

605. This particle occurs in MADI in emphatic sentences, and corresponds in meaning to English 'quite', 'utterly'.

The chief is definitely dead . . . quite dead.		*He has eaten it entirely.*	
Lo.:	ópí ɔ̀drà kpɔ́.	onya **kpwo**.	
Pa.:	,, dà kpɔ́.		
LULU'BA:	ánya-'ɔ, kyɔ̀wɔ̀.	I've eaten it entirely.	
	mokí márò **kyo**.	I'm definitely going (lit. I went my body quite).	

ku, ko (Negative)

606. This particle is universal (with the exception of Lendu) and is used mostly with the *Definite* form of the verb, unless a distinct progressive negative is to be shown, when it may be used with the Indefinite form.

Use in the Definite Aspect.

607. ku follows the verb as a postposition. Tense particles are not usually employed in negative sentences, but when they are, they follow **ku**.

Examples from MORU:

mí-mvú **ku**.	Don't drink, or Don't drink it.
nyú'dú **ku**.	Don't sleep.
mǎ-mvú **ku**.	I am not to drink (it).
	I am not drinking (it).
	I do not drink (it).
	I shall not drink (it).
	I did not drink (it), &c., &c.

má-kandá tsʷɛ **ku**. I didn't shake the tree.
enyɛ'dɔ́ lédr drà-te ya? hwa, ánya drà **ku**. Is the man dead? No he isn't.
mǎ-'bwä lä'bí te, ɔ̀kɔ̀ ánya drà **ku-te**. I shot a water-buck, but it didn't die.
má-'bí ndá **ku-drì**. I haven't beaten him yet.

Note the subtle difference:

mǎ-nì ɔ̀yɛ-na **ku**. I can't do it (said before trying).
mǎ-nì ɔ̀yɛ-na **ku-te**. I can't do it (said after trying).

Note also the choice of positions in the Moru sentence (cf. § 583):

má-lɛ **kù** mí ɔ̀'da-nɪ. } I don't want to insult you.
má-lɛ́ mí ɔ̀'da-nɪ **ku**. }

This is not possible in Logo:

ma-le yi mvu-le **ko**. I don't want to drink water.

Examples from MADI (and LULU'BA).

608. Note that the pronoun often has no initial consonant (as in the General form. See § 362).

MADI { Lo.: (m)á-lɛ **ku**. } I don't want it.   á-mù **ku**. } I'm not going.
       { Pa.: má-lɛ **ku**. }   mǎ-mù **ku**. }

MADI { Lo.: Rubaŋa drà-rɛ-**kù**-rè'ɪ. } God is immortal.   á-yà **ku**(-rʊ). } I didn't
       { Pa.: Lubaŋa dà-rɛ-**ku**-rɪ'ɪ. }   má-mù **ku-rù**. } go.

LULU'BA: atí ki ɔ̀da-'ɔ. Is your father dead?   ád(i) ódá **ko**. He is not dead.
          Mofótis ekí-o? Has the D.C. come?   (adí) ekí **ku**. He has not come.
          ɔʊ **kú**. Don't cry.   á-lɛ ɔ́ŋgó **ku**. I don't want to sing.
          á-lɛ **kwɔ́**.[1] I don't want it.   ámbu **kwɔ**. I'm not drinking it.

---

[1] Probably **kwɔ** = **ku** + ɔ (past time postposition).

Other languages:
	I don't want it.	*I won't eat it.*
LUGBARA:	má-lɛ kʋ.	má-nya kʋ.
KELIKO:	má-lɛ kʋ.	má-nya kʋ.
LOGO:	ma-lɛ ko.	

609. When past time is to be indicated, the various time postpositions are added in all languages (with assimilation).

	So-and-so is not hoeing.	*So-and-so did not hoe.*
MORU:	Mókó sɔ̀ ŋgà kʋ.	Mókó sɔ̀ ŋgà kʋ-te.
MADI Lo.:	Anyánzó ɔ̀sɔ tà kʋ.	Anyánzó ɔ̀sɔ tà kʋ-rʋ.
MADI Pa.:	,, sɔ ŋgá kʋ.	,, sɔ ŋgá kʋ-rʋ.
LUGBARA:	Abírígí àsò la kʋ.	Abírígí sɔ̀ kʋ.
KELIKO:	,, a ŋgà kʋ.	,, a ŋgà kʋ̀-ɛ.

	The goat is (or was) *not found.*	*He did not give me a cloth.*
MORU:	úsú ìndri kʋ.	ndá ɔzɔ boŋgó kʋ-te mä-rigɛ.
MADI Lo.:	indrí êsu-ro ko-rò.	ékwɛ mání boŋgó kʋ-rʋ̀.
MADI Pa.:	indí ésú kʋ-rʋ̀.	ɛke mání boŋgó kʋ-rʋ̀.
LUGBARA:	indí-ri ésu-kí kʋ.	ɪr(ɪ) ɛfe mání boŋgó kʋ̀.
KELIKO:	indí-rɪ ésu-kí kwĕ.	ɪr(ɪ) ɛfɛ mání boŋgó kʋ̀-ɛ.

Use in the Indefinite Aspect.

610. When the negative is used with the *Indefinite* construction, it precedes the verb.

MORU: má kʋ {mvʋ́ / nyá nà.}   I am not to {drink / eat it.}   I am not {drinking. / eating.}
nyá kʋ ,, ,,   You are not to ,,   You are not ,,
ánya ká kʋ ,, ,,   He is ,, ,,   He is ,, ,,

má-tà-tɛ ndärí kʋ ta 'do ɔyé-nì.   I told him not to do it.
(I told to him not thing that to do.)

M.: máá kʋ andí vʋ-má-r(ɔ) ɛ̀dɛ̀.   Ä.: má-ró kʋ . . .   I am not dressing myself.
nyáá ,, ,, mí ,, ,,   mí-ró ,,   You are not dressing yourself.
ánya ká ,, 'ɛ ,, ,,   ndá-ró ,,   He is not dressing himself.

LOGO: ma ko (k)aiko.   I am not sleeping.

611. In negative predication kʋ precedes the complement in Moru:

mí kʋ́ kàdo.	You are not good.
má kʋ ɔndzíró.	I am not bad.
má kʋ ('di)tɔkó ì.	I'm not a woman.

This is not the case, however, in other languages.

	You are not good.	*I am not bad.*
MADI:	nyi lɔsó ko.	má ɔndzí ko.
LULU'BA:	mi osú-na kʋ.	ma ndʒwé-na kʋ.
LUGBARA:	mi múké kʋ.	má ɔdʒí kʋ.
KELIKO:	mi múké kʋ.	má ɔdʒí kʋ.
AVUKAYA:	mí sú kʋ.	

Further examples from Logo:
>   *adi konji **ko-ro**.* He is not bad.
>   *yi ko-ve **ko**.* The water is not hot.
>   *nini **ko** andi.* (A.) This is not the same.

ako, aku

612. In LOGO this postposition is much in use in the negative of subjunctive sentences. Elsewhere its function is uncertain.

> LOGO: *mi-ko-loga kokia, adi ko-o za ra-le **ako**.* Don't let the dog make the cattle run (lit. you-prevent dog, he makes cattle to-run without).
> *adi zu sabuni ma Madamu boŋgo ji **ako** ro.* He hid the soap so that I could not wash Madam's clothes.
> *ama-pa loga ma-ali **ako** ro.* My foot prevents me from coming.
> LUGBARA: . . . *econi ani Yesuni fi-za-ro **aku** alesi mboro **ko**.* (Mk. i. 45.) . . . insomuch that Jesus could no more openly enter into the city.
> MORU: *mí-'ba ta lɛí rɔ kùdzʷè **ku** ɛzì **àku**.* Don't forget to bring the milk (lit. you-make talk milk of escape not to-bring without).

613. na MORU. See **ra**, § 628.

ndi MORU; indi LUGBARA

614. This postposition is often used in replies to questions, and may be represented in English by words like 'indeed', 'certainly'.

> MORU: *ánya dra-**ndí** yà?* Is he actually dead?
> *ɛnyɛ'dò lɛ́dr dra-**ndí** yà?* Was the man dead? (when you got there).
> *mí-'bwä lä'bí **ndí** yà? ɔu, mǎ-'bwä-**ndi**.* Have you ever shot a waterbuck? I have indeed.
> *mí-ni-'dǎ yà? mǎ-nì-**ndi**.* Do you know it? Yes I do.
> *ma-nyá ló'ba **ndí**.* We *do* eat hartebeest.
> *má-ti tànà **ndi**.* I *do* mind.
> *má-tí-**na** tànà **ndi**.* I *shall* mind.
> *mí-ndrà ma gí-'dá yà? má-ndrà mɪ **ndi**.* Can you see me? I can.
> *ma-ma ma-ro-be, nda eki-na-**ndi**.* I hope he will come.

In LUGBARA it may occur in commands as well as in statements. Its function is always emphatic.

> LUGBARA: *'ba yo-ra **indi*** (Mt. v. 31). It hath been said (lit. people have said indeed).
> *Econi emini azi ŋgazaro Muŋgu dri afa-nyakuari dri **indi** ko.* (Mt. vi. 24.) Ye cannot serve God and mammon.
> *Eri dra **ndindi**.* (Mt. xv. 4.) Let him die the death.
> *Emi-fe 'ba dri toko **indi**.* (Mt. x. 8.) Freely give (to people).
> *Mi-ye diri, eri ŋga ye-ra **indi**.* (Lk. vii. 8.) 'Do this' and he doeth it.

Compare the forms **andi** and **indi** as emphasizing pronouns, § 233.

ndo LUGBARA

615. The function of this postposition is similar to that of **ndi**.

> *Odu asi-zu eri ŋga eca-**ndo**.* (Mt. xxiv. 14.) And then shall the end (lit. day of ending) come.

ndrə MADI

616. This particle is used only to emphasize verbs of wanting.

I want very much to speak.

MADI { Lo.: álɛ mátâ-ni **ra**.
Pa.: málɛ máta-nɪ { **rå**.
ndrə̀.

ni MORU, MADI, &c.

617. In both MORU and the Southern languages this postposition is used in sentences which point out the doer of an action.

MORU: *adi fu-**ni** ya? mä-fu-**ni**.* Who killed him? I did.
*adi 'bi mi **ni** ya?* Who hit you?
*adi le boŋgo todi **ni** ya? ma-le-**ni**.* Who (is it who) wants new clothes? I do.
*anya ka ledri ufu-**ni**.* He is (the one who is) killing men.
*a'dɔ lifu-**ni** ya? mä-fu-**ni**.* Who broke it. I did.

M., Ä., 'B., L.: *tắpí máro drà-te; mä-fu ánya ndá(na) } **ni**.* My father is dead; I killed him.
*ma-lìí (tana) täbírí fu ma **ni**.* I'm crying because hunger killed me (i.e. I am hungry).
*ŋgónya sè mà-nya-bɛ, ndrúpi máro la'di-**nì**.* The food which we ate, my mother cooked it.

MADI { Pa.: *lóku'dó lɛdà-ra; madi lɛdà-**ni**.* The pot is broken; the man broke it.
Lo.: *lenya anyi anya-le-re-e, mendre odze-**ni**.* The porridge which you ate, my mother made it.

	Who will go?	*So-and-so will go.*
MADI { Lo.:	adi kómú-**ni** yà?	Ɔyúru kómu-**nì**.
Pa.:	a'dí kúmú-**ni** yà?	Lugúmà kúmú-**nì**.
LUGBARA:	a'dí amú-lá-**ni** yà?	'Búgá lamu-la-**nì**.
KELIKO:	á'dúrí mú-**ni** yà?	Kútú mu-**nì**.

'o LULU'BA

618. This is the normal 'past-tense' postposition in LULU'BA.

mi-i'bwi anyukwá '**o**?   Did you shoot the animal?
ɔké ɔsí má '**ə**.   A dog bit me.
má-gà-'**ə**.   I am just going (lit. I have gone).
iyí-vwí o ru-ma '**ə̀**.   I am thirsty (lit. water-hunger does my body).

oko MORU

619. This postposition succeeds all other postpositions, and is used at the end of dependent clauses (time or conditional) only. Even here it may be omitted occasionally.

MORU: *ondro anya ka-i-ogo 'bäru enye **oko**, anya usu avo go.* When they were returning home thus, they found the corpse.
*moi-be Juba ya **oko**, ma-gye-na boŋgo todi ami-ri.* If I go to Juba, I'll buy you new clothes.
*mä-zi ami te ca **oko**, nyere ku-te alona.* Although I called you, you did not hear.

pa MORU

620. Mynors gives this peculiar suffix in Moru enumeration of high numbers. When a man wishes to represent the number 60 (= 3 × 20), he says:

nya ma pa, ago nya mi pa, ago nya man-oďo pa. (Lit. eaten me, and eaten you, and eaten that man also.)

Note also:

ny-oi ku-te oko, m-oi-pa ku. If you don't go, I won't go.

pi MADI (Central languages)

621. This particle occurs only after verbs of motion (away from speaker).

	My father is gone.	*He pulled it* (away)	Cf. *He pulled it* (towards).
MADI Lo.:	mátá ɔŋga-**pi**.	ɔsɛ-**pí**.	ɛsɛ-**ra**.
Pa.:	,, ŋga-**pi**.	sɛ-**pí**.	ɛsɛ-**ra**.

The boys went (have gone)

Lo.: bɔrɔndʒí ɔ̀vɔ(-kí)-**pi**, or . . . ɔ̀vɔ(-kí)-**ra**.
Pa.: 'bɔndʒí vɔ-**pí**, or . . . vɔ-**ra**.

For the function of **pi** in LOGO and LUGBARA and KELIKO (Relative function) see Chapter XVII.

ra, tra, dra, (d)re, 'da

622. Variations of this particle occur in almost every language, where they may be used for indicating either past or future time.

Past time.

623. They are the normal postpositions for past time in MADI, LOGO, AVUKAYA, and some of the Moru dialects (notably Ägi, Lakama'di, and Wa'di), and are used in the Definite Aspect.

	I have arrived.	*I know.*	*The chief is dead.*	*They died.*
MADI Lo.:	mé-ɛtsá-**rá**.	ma-ni-**ra**.	ópí ɔdra-**ra**.	bá ɔdrakí-**ra**.
Pa.:	m-ɛ́sá-**rá**.	mä-nì-**ra**.	ópí dà-**ra**.	à'ɪ dà-**ra**.
LOGO:	má-tsá-**drè**.	ma-nì-**drè**.	míri drà-**drè**.	
AVU. Jl.:	má-tsa-**tra**.		kumu drà-**tra**.	
Jg.:	má-tsa-**trá**.			

Did the chief beat you?

MORU L.: ópí 'bi mi **rá** yà?
Äg.: ɔpí 'bi mi **trá** ya?
Jl.: kumu tsɔ mi **trá** ya?

Did you see me?	*Yes I did.*
Jl.: mí-ndrɛ̀ ma **trá** ya?	ɛ̀, mà-ndrɛ mì **tra**.
LOGO: mí-nɔ má **dré** à?	ɛ̀, má-nɔ mì **drè**.

The box fell.

W.: sandúku a'dɛ-**tra**.
Jl.: sandúku 'dɛ-**tra**.

	I told you.	*I forgot* (lit. the matter fled from me).
LOGO L.:	ma-ta mi-dri **re**.	tai vi ma-se **dre**.
A.:	ma-ta mi-dri **da**.	tai ja ma-se **da**.

In LOGO it may occasionally be used in the Imperative.
   *mi-k-ali-**dre** ka.* Come at once.
   *mi-ko-o-**dre** niḍi ka.* Do this at once.

624. In KELIKO and LUGBARA the corresponding particle is an occasional alternative to **gi** and **'bo** respectively.
  KELIKO: mókótó drà-**(d)rɛ**. The chief is dead.
      mi-mu-**rá** (or **gí**) ya? Did you go?
  LUGBARA: ma-nyó-**ra**. We *do* eat it. (Emphatic habitual.)

625. In LUGBARA, further, it is much used in subordinate or co-ordinate sentences.
*Etu ka ḍe-**ra**.* (Mt. xx. 8.) When even was come.
*eri yo-**ra** . . .* (Mt. ix. 9.) And he saith . . .
*ka yi ndre-**ra**.* (Lk. xviii. 43.) When they saw it.
*'ba nde ka dra-**ra**.* (Mt. xxii. 24.) If a man die.

Or in narrative:
*'ba-ori-ripiri eri fo-**ra**.* (Mt. xiii. 3.) A sower went forth.
*aria yi emu yi ga yi nya-**ra**.* (Mt. xiii. 4.) And the fowls came and devoured them up.
*Te 'ba Farisaini yi fo-**ra**.* (Mt. xii. 14.) But the Pharisees went out.
*Eri ŋga uru eri so pa **ra**.* (Lk. vi. 8.) And he arose and stood forth (lit. set foot).

626. In most of the MORU dialects the corresponding particle **'da** is used only in questions and replies to questions. In the latter case it varies with other postpositions.
  M.: ánya ɛgʷɔ-**'dá** ya? Did he come back?
    ɔu, ɛgo-**'dá**. (or -ndí or -tè). Yes, he did.
    mí-ni-**'dà** yà? Do you know it?
    ɔu, mǎ-nì-ndi. Yes I do.
    mí-sì ndá **'da** yà? Did you bite him?
    ɔu, má-sì-**'da**. Yes I did.

Future time.
627. LOGO is the only language which does not use this particle in a future sense.
In most languages (omitting Moru for the moment) this particle, when implying future time, is used in the *Indefinite* Aspect, with or without an auxiliary. Sometimes the verb stem is given a suffix (**la** in Lugbara, **lɛ** in Avukaya).

       They will die. *I shall do it to-morrow.*
 MADI {Lo.: ká-kí-dra-**ra**. mɛ́-ɛ́dɛ́-a-**rá** ó'bú.
    Pa.: à'ɪ k-uda-**ra**. ma-ɛ-ɛ(-**ra**) o'bú.
 LUGBARA: kóri drà-**la-rà**. ma-'ɛ(-la)-**ra** drù.
 KELIKO: kópi drà-**ra**. ma-ódɛ́-**rá** drù.

    Shall I see you to-morrow?
  KELIKO: dru má mi ndrɛ-**rá**?
  AVUKAYA: udrú má **ná** ni ndrɛ-**lɛ́-trá**?

LUGBARA: *afa dria ovu-zu zi-zaro, yi ŋga yi eda-**ra**.* For all things that are covered, they shall be revealed.
*azini ka ovu opi-zaro, 'ba dria **ŋga** nyi-**ra**.* (Mt. x. 26.) And if hid, all men shall know them.
*eri **ŋga** dri ja-**ra**.* (Mt. x. 39.) He shall lose his life.
*paŋga erini eri **ŋga** isu-**ra**.* (Mt. x. 41.) He shall receive his reward.

Note thus the difference between past and future in MADI (cf. § 374):
Class I.
 a-no ta ra. I saw something.   *ma ta no-ra.* I'll see something.
 ono ta ra. He saw something.   *ka ta no-ra.* He'll see something.
 ono-ki ta ra. They saw something.   *ka-ki ta no-ra.* They'll see something.

 a-dra-ra. I died.   *ma-dra-ra.* I'll die.
 odra-ra. He died.   *k-odra-ra.* He'll die.
 odra-ki-ra. They died.   *ka-ki-dra-ra.* They'll die.

Class II.
 m-ede ebu ra. I did work.   *ma ebu ede-ra.* I'll do work.[1]
 ede ebu ra. He did work.   *ka ebu ede-ra.* He'll do work.
 ede-ki ebu ra. They did work.   *ka-ki ebu ede-ra.* They'll do work.

 m-emu-ra. I came.   *m-emu-ra.* I'll come.
 emu-ra. He came.   *k-emu-ra.* He'll come.
 emu-ki-ra. They came.   *ka-ki-emu-ra.* They'll come.

628. In MORU the future is expressed by **'da** (**tra** in dialects) and a form of the *Definite* Aspect. This form differs from the general form in that the characteristic vowel is used in the 3rd person of Class I verbs.[2] The verb stem may also be followed by a suffix **-na** or **-a**.

 MORU: má-**ndrɛ́** mɪ **'dá** udrú yà?   Shall I see you to-morrow?
    ànya ə̀-**dra-na-'dá**.   They will die.
 AVU. (Jl.): ma-**'da**[3] ní tswa andru.   I'll beat you to-morrow.
    ná-**'də** a'du giá ya?   What will you buy?
    kúmú a-**'dó** aní tswa (**tra**).   The chief will beat you.

Sometimes the **na** particle is used alone.
 MORU: mí-**ndrɛ́-na** àma ɔndɔ.   You'll see us to-morrow.
    mí-**sá-na** itù Marídí ya ya?   When will you arrive at Maridi?
    Makaraká **ú-fú-na** àma ndi.   The Azande will kill us.

   Where will you throw the water away?
    M.: mí-**da-n(a)** igí íŋgwa yà?
    Ä.: mí-**da-na** idʒi íŋwa ya?
    'B.: mí-**da-na** idʒi íŋgólɛ́rə yà?

629. Note the difference between past and future in MORU:
Class I.
 má-yɛ lɔsì **'da**. I did the work.   má-yɛ́ (-na) lɔsì **'da**. I'll do the work.
 ánya **pa** ma **'da**. He helped me.   ánya ə-**pá** ma **'dá**. He'll help me.

Class II.
 ány-**u'du-**'da. He slept.   ány-**u'dù**(-a)-**'dá**. He'll sleep.

Compare: *Did the chief beat you?*   *The chief will beat you.*
 MORU { M., Ä., 'B., K.: ɔ́pí **'bɪ** mi **'dá** yà?   ɔ́pí ə-**'bí** (-n)a mi **'dá**.
      Äg.: ɔ́pí **'bɪ** m̀i **trá** yà?   ɔ́pí ə-**'bí**-a mɪ **tra**.

---
[1] Paradigm coined on analogy of other paradigms from Molinaro.
[2] It somewhat resembles the Subjunctive form, except that there is no k- particle. See §§ 387 and 499.
[3] **'da** or **'də** (= become) is an auxiliary verb here. See § 483.

And with auxiliary **'də** in AVUKAYA:

    The hyena ate my dog.   *The chief will beat you.*

AVU. (Jg.): lòbògò **do** ɔkɛ́ amaka **trá** nyalɛ.   míri a-**'də** amí tsoa **tra**.

ri MORU, MADI, LUGBARA

630. This particle, in principal sentences, corresponds to the 'wa' of Logo (§ 640) and is used in polite imperative or permission.

    nyɛdrɛ-rɪ.   Please stop.
    mǎ-mvu-rɨ yà?   May I drink it?
    mɔi-ri.   I'm going (if I may).

m-ú'du-rɨ yà? May I sleep? *yau ono ny-uďu-ri.* (Mk. xiv. 41.) Sleep on now. ányä 'du-**rɨ** yà? May he sleep?

631. Attached to the Subjunctive, it corresponds in function to one of the uses of '**dro**' in the Southern languages (cf. § 598).

ny-ádzi kàlà akímu rɔ, kode má-nya èza **rí** yà. Ask the doctor, whether I may eat meat.

akímu ɛkyɛ, nyí-mvù gyɨ̌ rɪ. The doctor says you may drink water.

For the function of **rɪ** in MADI and LUGBARA and KELIKO (Relative function) see Chapter XVII.

632. ro LOGO (see **dro**).

ru LOGO

633. This postposition is used in LOGO in sentences denoting future time. It differs from the future particles in other languages in being attached to the Definite general form.

lenjise ma-nya-ru ŋga. This evening I'll eat something.

ʈɛ MORU

634. This particle has been found only in conjunction with the verb (ə)pɛ = to conquer.

    ma-pɛ lédr Ndarágɔ rɔ **ʈɛ̀**.   We defeated the people of Ndarago.
    kɪlá'bárɪ pèɨ-tɛ-**ʈɛ̀**.   The warriors have conquered.
    ápè kɪlá'bárɪ tɛ-**ʈɛ̀**.   The warriors were defeated.
    lɔse ďɔ pɛ ma **ʈɛ**.   The work is too much for me.

ʈə MORU

635. This postposition is used in sentences to indicate that the action is already completed at the time of speaking.

    mǎ-zi ànya **ʈə́**-tè.   I have already called them.
    má-ndra-**ʈə́**-tɛ.   I have already seen it.

te MORU

636. This particle is confined to the Moru dialects Miza, -ändri, 'Bälimbä, and Kediru, where it is the most-used of the past tense particles.

    mä-ni-**te** (or **-ndi**). I know.   mà-nya èza **tɛ**. We ate the meat.
    ópí drà-**tɛ**. The chief is dead.   ànya drà-**te**. They died.

mǎ-'bwä lä'bí **te**, ɔ̀kɔ̀ ánya drà ku-**tè**. I shot a water-buck, but it didn't die.

Variations of it occur occasionally in Lugbara and Lulu'ba.

LUGBARA: má-ndʒì-**ʈɪ** (or **-'bo**.) I lifted it.

     mí-ndrɛ̀ ma **tsí**-è? è, mà-ndrɛ mì **tsɪ**. Did you see me? Yes I did.

LULU'BA: mésa-**ti**. I have arrived.

637. In MORU **te** may also be used with the Subjunctive.

*opi **kondre** vure mi-ro **te** oko, ma-le tana eji-nɪ mi-ri.* When the chief has seen your case, I want to ask you about it.

*Ago nda **koi-te** anya ufu-ni oko Kito eke:* ... And he was going to kill them when the Hare said: ...

trə MADI

638. This particle occurs only in emphatic or ejaculatory statements in Madi.

   I ate the food all up.[1] *The mouse bit my finger.*
  Lo.: á-nya linyá **trəa**. ídré ɔtsí má-a-drɨ **trɔ̀**.
  Pa.: má-nya linyá **təa**. ídé sɪ má-nɪ-dí **tə**.

   A bee stung me. *A splinter has stuck into my finger.*
  Lo.: laŋú ɔtsɪ ma **trɔ̀**. kwɛ ɛsí má-à-drí gá **trɔ̀**.
  Pa.: laŋú sɪ ma **tɔ̀**. kwɛ lɛswí má-nɪ-dí gá **tɔ̀**.

wa MADI (Potential)

639. This particle is used with the Indefinite construction. In the negative it follows or is assimulated into the negative particle and is not joined to the verb stem. In the Pandikeri dialect it is separated altogether from the verb stem.

   Can you sing a song? *Yes, I can sing a song.*
  Lo.: nyí lɔŋgó **ɔ̀ŋgɔ́-wa** yà? ɔ̌, má lɔŋgó **ɔ̀ŋgɔ́-wà**.
  Pa.: nyí-**ŋgɔ́** lɔŋgó **wa** yà? ɔ̌, má-**ŋgɔ́** lɔŋgɔ **wà**.

   Can you speak Madi? *No, I can't speak Madi.*
  Lo.: nyí Madí-tɪ **dzɔ̀-wa** yà? má Madí-tɪ **dzò kwɛ**.
  Pa.: nyí-**'jó** Ma'dí-tɪ **wa** yà? má-**'jó** Ma'dí-tɪ **kpɛ́**.

   Can he hoe? *No, he can't hoe.*
  Lo.: áni ká tá **sɔ-wa** yà? ká tà **sɔ̀ kwɛ**.
  Pa.: andâ **k-úsɔ́** ŋgá **wa** yà? **k-úsɔ́** ŋgá **kpɛ̌**.

No other language seems to have this particle. Logo demands an auxiliary verb with dependent clause.

mi-kicoa motoka no nale ya? ma-kicoa. ma-kicoa ko. Can you see that motor-car? I can. I can't.

wa LOGO, LULU'BA

640. In LOGO the particle is one of politeness, equivalent almost to 'please', and is used with the 'volition' construction.

  *mi-k-ali-**wa**!*   Do come!
Cf. LULU'BA: ɛ̀kyí-**wá**!   Come! (implication uncertain).

In LOGO, again, this particle may be used in a permissive sense.

  *ma-si-**wa**? mi-ko-si **wa**.* Shall I come in? Yes, please do.
  *ko-yi-**wa**.* (Mk. iv. 9.) Let him hear.

Altogether its function is very similar to that of **rɪ** in MORU. (See §§ 630-1.)

---

[1] Or 'I ate all the food' (with **trəa** as an adjective)? Compare LUGBARA:
  má-nya ìza **drà ɨ̀**. I ate all the food.

yà, (à) (Interrogation)

641. In nearly all the Moru-Madi languages, interrogation is indicated by the optional particle **yà** or **a**, which succeeds all other particles and usually ends the sentence, though it may be followed by adverbial phrases, &c. Examples of this suffix will be found throughout this book, and need not be given here.[1] It should be remembered, in passing, that the intonation pattern of a Moru-Madi interrogative sentence usually ends on a low note.

ya MORU

642. An imperative may be made more emphatic by adding an almost exclamatory particle **ya**.

ny-eṛi ya! Come!   *ny-imu ya!* Run!

CHAPTER XVII

RELATIVE CONSTRUCTIONS

bɛ[2] MORU (Relative postposition)

643. The Moru relative construction places more emphasis on the relative pronoun **se**[3] than on the postposition (which may often be omitted). In this way Moru differs from the Central and Southern languages (with the possible exception of Madi Pandikeri). In Moru, further, the relative phrase may be terminated by a demonstrative or the particle **na**.

Present time (Indefinite):

Gi aloďi ni wute-dri-eri ya se ka ŋga obe ma-be **ono** au. (Mk. xiv. 20.) It is one of the twelve that dippeth (food) with me.
Mano se ka laďa o'da ono aďi ya? (Lk. v. 21.) Who is this which speaketh blasphemy?
atá **sé** ɔpı **k-átá-bɛ** kɔzıru. The words which the chief says are bad.
lărí **sé** Mìza kɔ́-ɔ̀tʊ-**na**, ắzi 'mùrı'. The dance which the Miza dance is called 'more'.

Past time (Definite):

lédr **sé** fù ìbì bɛ, ädrúpi márɔ̀. The man who killed the lion is my brother.
ŋgágà **sé** mí-**zi**-bɛ́, f'dú láù. The boy whom you called is not here.
ŋgónya **sé** mà-**nya**-bɛ. The food which we ate.

---

[1] Logo has instances in which **ya** is used in non-interrogative sentences, viz. in conjunction with the interrogatives **ngo** and **'do** when these are used non-interrogatively. See also §§ 227–8.
Mi-ko-zi **aďo** ŋga **ya** mi-dre le-le-'ďi ma-ti. (Mk. vi. 22.) Ask of me whatsoever thou wilt.

[2] It is probable that **bɛ** is closely related to the **pi** of Logo, &c. Note that in the Ojiga dialect of Avukaya the corresponding particle is **bɛ** or **bi**.

[3] See §§ 251–3.

Subjunctive (Definite):
  ŋga se mi-le-be miri[1] ***ono.*** (Mk. vi. 22.) Whatsoever thou shalt wish of me.
  The Subjunctive form is often used in reference to simple past time.
  *Ago nda de-gwo ŋga teki, anya se **k-oye** ta ďo **be** ondre-ni.* (Mk. v. 32.) And he looked about, to see her who had done this (thing).
  *ti'bi se lowa-ro du ànya **k-uru-i-be ana.*** (Lk. v. 9.) The draught of fishes which they had taken.

Passive:
  tɔkó lédr sé áfu-bɛ aná rɔ, ɔi-tɛ. The wife of the slain man went away.

644. The difference between subject and object relative is shown only by the word order. Notice also that the relative pronoun itself may not be followed by a postposition. (See § 252.)
  lédr sé fù ìbì bɛ. The man who killed the lion.
  lédr sé àtra fu-bɛ. The man whom the foreigner killed.
  *Anya se cini **k-oďe** kwini se ana-dri, lifu-na-ďa jiŋijiŋi; oko anya se kwini **k-eďe** dri-i-ge **ana,** onji-na anya ďa oso durufu ronye.* (Lk. xx. 18.) Whosoever shall fall upon that stone, shall be broken; but on whomsoever the stone shall fall, it will grind him like powder.

Observation: In the following sentences **bɛ** is not a relative particle:
  lédr sé waragà bɛ ɛsa-te. The man with the letter has come. (See postposition, § 289.)
  bé mǎrí ɔyɛ-nɪ. I must do it. (See § 729.)

645. In MORU the relative construction may be used in temporal or conditional clauses. The complete construction is: **tu se . . . be** (= the day that . . .), but incomplete forms are more common.
  se moi-be Wala lä'bu rige, mä'bu lo'ba te. When I went to Wala's, I shot a hartebeest.
  se moi-na Ŋgeri rige, male ledri anyaro ondrenɪ cini. When I shall go to Ngeri's, I want to see all his people.
  moi-be Juba ya oko, magyena boŋgo toďi miri. If I go to Juba, I'll buy you new clothes.
  moi-be-te Juba ya oko, magye boŋgo toďi te amiri. If I had gone to Juba, I would have bought you (pl.) new clothes.

The Relative Particles (Southern and Central Languages)

646. The relative construction in Moru, as has already been seen, is formed with the aid of the particle **bɛ**. In the other languages it is formed by means of a relative particle attached to an infinitive form (and in Madi a 'purpose' form as well) of the verb. The relative particle in MADI is **rɪ** (sometimes followed by the predicative particle **ɪ**) and in LOGO is **pi** (usually followed by the reference particle **'di**).

The relative particle in the Southern and Central languages, though always used in the indefinite conjugation, may be separated from the infinitive stem by intervening words and particles.

THE RELATIVE IN MADI

647. There are four constructions with relative particle in Madi, which may follow any of the infinitive forms in **-rɛ**, **-ka**, or **-lɛ** or the purpose form in **-zo**, and from which it may be separated by the negative postposition **ko**, the past time postposition **ra**, or any adverb or adverbial phrase.

[1] *märi* (?)

(a) *Relative form* -rɛ-rɪ (-'ɪ).

648. This form is used when the subject of the relative clause is singular.

I gave water to the dying man (i.e. man who was dying).

MADI { Lo.: má-kwɛ eí madí **dra-ré-rɪ** ní.
Pa.: má-ke iyí mo'dí **dà-rɛ-rɪ** ní.

(Cf. MORU (Ä.): má-zwi dʒwi lédr ɔ̀drà-drà ri.)

lenya **'di-re-rɪ-ɪ** (cook [one who cooks food]).
mu-re-ko-rɪ-ɪ ([one] who does not go).

(b) *Relative form* -ka-rɪ (-'ɪ).

649. This form is used when the subject of the relative clause is plural.

ba leti, **so-ka-rɪ-ɪ** *omvuki ewa ra.* The men who are hoeing the road have been drinking beer.
okonzi **roti-ka-rɪ-ɪ** (squabbling women).
eca-ka *azeni* **rɪ-ɪ**. They who arrived yesterday.

In PANDIKERI MADI, however, rɛ is used.

Those who steal things are bad.	*Lawyers* (men who deal with words).
Lo.: bá ta **ògu-ka-rɪ** ùndzi.	bá ti **édrɪ-kà-rì-'ɪ**.
Pa.: 'bá ŋgá **ogu-ré-rí** indʒwi.	'bá ti **edì-rɛ-rì-'ì**.

Compare in TORIT MADI:

kwe ga-re-rɪ-ɪ (cutter of trees).	*kwe ga-ka-rɪ-ɪ* (cutters of trees).
zo si-re-rɪ-ɪ (house builder).	*zo si-ka-rɪ-ɪ* (house builders).
kudo ede-re-rɪ-ɪ (potter).	*kudo ede-ka-rɪ-ɪ* (potters).
madi aci-re-rɪ-ɪ (traveller).	*madi aci-ka-rɪ-ɪ* (travellers).
madi teri azi-re-rɪ-ɪ (porter).	*madi teri azi-ka-rɪ-ɪ* (porters).

(c) *Relative form* -lɛ-rɪ (-'ɪ).

650. This form is used when the action of the relative clause is passive, or when the relative is the object of a verb. Note also the linking particle **a** (see § 270).

Compare thus:

The man whom the foreigner killed is my brother.

MADI { Lo.: madí dzurugo **à dí-lɛ́-rì'ɪ**, madrúpi'ì.
Pa.: mo'dí dʒúrúgó **à 'di-lɛ-rɪ'ɪ** má àdázì'ɪ.

The man who killed the lion is my brother.

MADI { Lo.: ma'dí ebi **dí-ré-re-i**, ...
Pa.: mo'di ìbì **'di-rɛ-rí**, ...

Other examples from MADI:

cupa **ze-le-rɪ-ɪ** *dii*. This washed bottle. **dra-le-ko-rɪ-ɪ** (immortal).

When the agent or author of the action is mentioned, it is joined to the verb by a genitive construction:

leti ba **a so-le-rɪ-ɪ** *ekwa.* The path, hoed by the people, is large.
bara **ny-oŋgwe**[1]**-le-(ra)-rɪ-ɪ** *iyo.* The boy, called by you, is not here.

[1] nyi-a-uŋgwe.

RELATIVE CONSTRUCTIONS 265

(d) *Relative form* -**zo-rɪ-ɪ**.

651. This is the form when a 'reason' for the action of the verb is being given or demanded.

(*lejo*) **ma-mu-zo** *baru* **rɪ-ɪ**, *mendre avo*. The reason why I went home was my mother was ill.
(*lejo*) **memu-zo** *ko* **rɪ-ɪ**, *mendre avo*. The reason why I didn't come was my mother was ill.
nyi-zi, ani a **mu-zo** *ei ga ko* **rɪ-ɪ** *aďo*. Ask him why he has not gone to the water.

Note also:

    opi emu-zo-rɪ-ɪ ŋga.   When the chief has returned.
    etu nyemu-zo-rɪ-ɪ.   The day on which you return.

(e) *Relative form* -**re-ǵa**.

652. In MADI (Lokai) the particle **ǵa** follows the infinitive form of the verb to indicate place where, or time when, an action occurred. (Compare noun postposition **ǵa** = belly, § 312.)

    mendre olo-re-ǵa (where my mother lives).
    nyi-ďe-re-ǵa (where you fell).
    etu efo-re-ǵa (where the sun rises).
    lenya nya-re-ǵa (while eating food [or where he was eating]).
    ma-mu-re-ǵa (while I was going [or where I was going]).

Note also in MADI (Pandikeri):

    Lofo ondrwe la-ǵa. (Mk. vi. 35.) Now when evening had fallen.

THE RELATIVE IN THE CENTRAL LANGUAGES

pi

653. The relative particle **pi** is used when the relative is the subject of the clause. It is attached to the infinitive verb form in **-lɛ** but to no other verb form. It is often strengthened by the reference demonstrative **'di**. (See § 225).

When the relative is the object of the clause, the particle **pi** is not used.

Examples from LOGO:

Subject relative: ago **dra-le-pi-'di** (a dead man).
              kokia **aiko-le-pi-'di** (a sleeping dog).

ago **dra-le-pi-ďi** *adre ama adrupi e*. The man who died was my brother.
ago **aca-le-pi** *agia ďi*. The man who arrived yesterday.
mi-kamu mvaago **ŋgo-le-pi** *nda ďi madre*. Send me the boy who is crying.
akoďi **ďe-le-pi** *kira . . . niďi dre*. (Mt. xxi. 44.) Whosoever falls on this stone.
akoďi e tai-ni **yi-le-pi-ďi**. (Mt. xiii. 20.) (It) is he that heareth the word.
kosia **be-le-pi-ďi** (fisher, i.e. fish catcher).
boŋgo **di-le-pi-ďi** (tailor, i.e. cloth sewer).
kinzo **ta-le-pi-ďi** } (liar, i.e. evil speaker).
tolonyo **ta-le-pi-ďi** }
ru **fu-le-pi-ďi** (warrior, i.e. body killer).
azi **o-le-pi-ďi** (worker, i.e. work doer).

Object relative:

Ma-ko-laďi kope, mi-dre 'bu-le-ďi ya? Shall I cook the guinea-fowl which you shot?
Togi e ko ya ma-o ŋga mana ŋgoro ma-dre le-le-ďi tini? (Mt. xx. 15.) Is it not lawful for me to do what I will with mine own (things)?
Mi-ko-zi aďo ŋga ya mi-dre le-le-ďi ma-ti. (Mk. vi. 22.) Ask of me the things you wish.
ŋga fe-le-ďi. A gift.
ŋgae mì-adre-ki no-le ďii no-le. (Mt. xiii. 17.) Those things which ye see. (Note reduplication.)

654. The relative construction of Lugbara is similar to that of Logo. For the subject relative **-pi(-ri)** is added to the verb root (rarely to the infinitive).

Examples from LUGBARA:

*Eri ŋga ba dri olu dria, 'ba eri ye-**pi-ri** ndre-zu.* (Mk. v. 32.) And he looked round about, to see her who had done this (thing).
*'Ba dria alo alo oďe-**pi** oni ďa-ri ma-dria **ri**, yi ŋga yi onyo nyiŋgiriki.* (Lk. xx. 18.) Whosoever falls on that stone, he shall be broken.
*'Ba ďi-ri Muŋgu oďa-**pi-ri** eri aďi-ni a.* (Lk. v. 21.) Who is this which speaketh blasphemy (lit. man this God insulting he who?).
*Yi aku yi agi ovu-**pi** oguru azini ma alia **ri**.* (Lk. v. 7.) They beckoned unto their partners who were in the other boat.
*'Ba eri-ni ovu-**pi** eri be **ri** ndi.* (Lk. v. 9.) All that were with him (lit. people his being him with themselves).
*Eri ndre oguru iri pa so-**pi** yi ku tia **ri**.* (Lk. v. 2.) He saw two ships standing (lit. feet planting) by the lake.
*'Ba Farisaini azini 'ba azitaa imba-**pi-ri** yi ri ageia, yi **ni** emu-**pi** aku ... indi.* (Lk. v. 17.) There were Pharisees and doctors of the law sitting by, which were come out of every town of ...

655. For the object relative **-ri(-le)** is added to the infinitive or **-zu** stem of the verb, and the verb is preceded by the genitive linking particle **ni**.

*Econi mani ye-za-ro afa mani-ri be ma **ni le-le-ri-le** kwia?* (Mt. xx. 15.) Can I not do with my things what I will?
*Mi-zi ma-tia afa mi **ni le-le-ri**, ...* (Mk. vi. 22.) Ask of me the things you wish.
*kini 'ba dria eri **ni ďe-le** eri-dria **ri**, eri ŋga eri ere irifurale.* (Mt. xxi. 44.) But on whomsoever it shall fall, it will grind him to powder.
*Emi-ndre onyiro eyo emi **ni eri-le-ri** ďi.* (Mk. iv. 24.) Take heed what ye hear (lit. you observe well the things you hear).
*e'bi emba alia ri yi **ni oko-le-ri**.* (Lk. v. 9.) Fishes in the net which they had taken.
*Mi-olo yi-tia eyo amboro Muŋgu **ni ye-le** mi-be **ri**.* (Mk. v. 19.) Tell them how great things the Lord hath done for thee.
*kile Musa **ni azi-le-ri-le**.* (Lk. v. 14.) As Moses commanded.
*'Di eyo ma **ni efo-zu-ri**.* (Mk. i. 38.) For therefore came I forth (lit. That is the reason I came for).
*eyo baputizi-ni ... yi ma eyo-onzi **wu-zu-ri** indi.* (Mk. i. 4.) Baptism ... for the remission of sins (lit. word of baptism, they might sins thereby remit indeed).

RELATIVE CONSTRUCTIONS

656. In some of the Central languages, notably KELIKO and LUGBARA, relative particles often follow the subject or object of a verb in a non-relative sentence.

	They are dying.	*They will die.*	*They died.*
KELIKO:	'bá-**rɪ-pɪ̀** àdra.	ko-**pɪ** drà-ra.	'bá-**rɪ** ɔ̀drà-kɪ-gɪ.
LUGBARA:		kó-**rɪ** drà-là-ra.	'bá-**rɪ** ɔ̀drà-kɪ-'bo.

	My cows are dead.	*My field.*
KELIKO:	ama-tí-**rɪ̀-pɪ** dra-kí-gɪ̀.	ámvú-**rì** mávénì.
LUGBARA:	àmatí-**rɪ** drà-'bo.	ámvá-**rí** mâni.

This man is good.
KELIKO: 'ba 'dà-**rɪ̀** ànyísì.
LUGBARA: 'ba 'dà-**rɪ̀** mʊkɛ.

657. When the noun is the object of the verb, the particle **rɪ** occurs alone.

KELIKO: mí-fɛ mání ópí adʒu-**rɪ**. Give me the chief's spear.
    „ „ mandripi a bɔ̀ŋgɔ-**rɪ**. Give me my brother's cloth.
ndrógó (adre) édrágo ru **rì**. The cat caught a mouse.
(nzɔ́rɔ́ údrúgú ru **nde**.—Lugbara).
*mi-le adi-**ri**?* What do you want?
LUGBARA: má-gba mvá 'dì-**rɪ**, má-gbà mɪ kʊ. I beat the child, not you.

658. Mention should be made at this point of the 'dead' suffix **pi** found in so many words denoting relationship, even in languages in which **pi**, as a relative, does not occur (cf. §§ 165–6).

	father	*brother*	*sister*	*friend*	*uncle*	*aunt*
LOGO:	atá	adrú(pi)	ämvúpi	arupi	adro(*pi*)	ao(*pi*)
MORU:	tăpi	ädrúpi	ämvúpi (Ä.)			

For use of the relative particles with adjectives, see §§ 701–3.

MORU: *ta se däsi* (what great things).
MADI: *bara **loso-rɪ-ɪ**, oja ro ba-zü tro ko.* The boy who is good does not quarrel with others.
    alo-(zo-)re-e (the first).
LOGO: *toko ave-le **pi**-ďi* (a beautiful woman).
LUGBARA: *nyaku oni-efi be **ri*** (stony ground).

659. Examples from various languages, compared:
Subject relative:

Cook.
MADI { Lo.: madí lényá ʊdɪ-re-rí'ì   *or* madí tá ʊ́dɪ-re.
       { Pa.: mo'dí línyá lo'di-re-rí'ì   „ la'di-re.
LUGBARA: 'ba ínyá a'di-le-pi.   „ akwá a'dí-le-pi, *or* 'dí-lé-pì-là-rì.
KELIKO: ('ba) ŋgá a'di-pè-ni.   „ ('ba) ŋgá a'di-pì.
LOGO: ('bá) ŋgá la'dí-lí-pì-'dì.
AVUKAYA: ('ba) ŋgá la'dí-lí-pì-'dì   „ ('ba) ŋgá la'dí-la'dí.
    (Cf. MORU: ŋgá la'di 'bá.)

Murderer.
MADI { Lo.: madí bà ʊdɪ-re-rì-'ɪ.
       { Pa.: mó'dí 'bá 'di-re-rɪ-'ì.
LUGBARA: 'bá 'bákɪ u'di-lɛ-rì.
KELIKO: 'bá 'bá ʊdì-pɪ-rì.

Poisoner.

LUGBARA: 'bá ɔtsá-lɛ-pì-'dì.
KELIKO: 'bá tsɔ-lɛ́-pì-'dì.
LOGO: 'bá a¹ tsó-lí-pì-'dì.
AVU. { Jl.: lédrɪ a tsó-**lí-pi-'di**, *or* olóko-'bá.
{ Jg.: lédrɪ a tsó-**lí-bè-'dì**, *or* olóko-'bá.
(Cf. MORU: oɽí-'ba.)

Examples from KELIKO (note difference between singular and plural):

*peti ga-**a**-pi* (wood-cutter). *peti ga-'**ba-ri**-pi* (wood-cutters).
*jo si-**i**-pi* (house builder). *jo si-'**ba-ri**-pi* (house builders).
*odri gbi-**i**-pi* (potter). *odri gbi-'**ba-ri**-pi* (potters).
'ba si-pi (traveller). *'ba si-'**ba-ri**-pi* (travellers).
'ba đu-pi (carrier). *'ba đu-'**ba-ri**-pi* (carriers).

I want a boy who speaks English.

LOGO: *ma-le mva-ago Aŋgelisi-ti **ta-le-pi**-'di.*
AVUKAYA: má-lɛ 'doí-mvá ŋgá-atra-ti **a ta-la-bɛ-ri-è**-'dì.
WA'DI: má-lɛ ndríŋgwa ŋgá-atra-ti **a tä-pi**-'di.

He who has ears to hear the word. (Mk. iv. 9.)
(lit. he who is with ears).

LOGO: '*Dia **adre-le-pi** bibale be ta yi 'di.*
LUGBARA: '*Ba nde **ovu-pi** bile be eyo eri-zu.*
MADI (Pa.): *Mađi ani bi tro, ani k-eri.*
MORU: *Anya **se** bi be ta ere-za.*

... and the seats of them that sold doves. (Mk. xi. 15.)

LOGO: *... ŋga liri-zo đii đia ko'bola **gi-le-pi** đii-ki-a be.*
LUGBARA: *... azini kiti 'ba abalao **ozi-pi-ri-ni** indi.*
MADI (Pa.): *... komi 'ba dri **nai** odze amomu.*
MORU: *... ndi giti ànya **se k-oge** tu'bu be **ana**-ro be.*

Object relative:

The words which the chief says are bad.

MADI { Lo.: ledzó ópí à dzo-lé-rìí, òndzi.
{ Pa.: lé'jó ópí **a** 'jó-le-rɪ, ńdʒwi.
LUGBARA: ídʒó ópí **ni** dʒó-lé-rɨ, ɔndʒɪ.
KELIKO: ta ópí **ní** 'jo-lɛ́-rɪ, òndʒɪ.

The dance which the ... dance is called ...

MADI { Lo.: lató Màdi à to-lé-rɪ, kàrúŋgwè 'mùrè'
{ Pa.: lató Mà'di a to-lé-rɪ, úluŋgwê ,,
LUGBARA: íŋgá Lúgbàrɪ **nɨ** tʊ-lɛ́-rɪ, ómvélɛ ,,
KELIKO: úŋgó Kèlìkó **ni** tʊ-lɛ́-rɪ, zikí òŋgó ,,

The boy whom you called is not here.

MADI { Lo.: bárá nyí-ɔŋgwé-lé-rɪ-'í, 'día iyu.
{ Pa.: 'bórá ny-á-luŋgwé-lé-ri, 'día iyu.
LUGBARA: ŋgótí mí **ni** ɔmvɛ-lé-rí, 'do yù.
KELIKO: mvá mí **ní** dʒwi-lé-rɪ, 'da yù.

¹ Note use of linking particle **a** in the *subject* relative in some languages. Such languages usually employ **ni** in the object relative.

The food which we have eaten was cooked by my mother.
MADI { Lo.: lényá àmà-nya-lɛ́-rì-í, mɛndrɛ ɔ̀di nì.
       Pa.: lényá àmà-nya-lé-rí-'ɪ, méndè 'dɪ nì.
LUGBARA: } ónyá 'bá **nì** nya-lɛ-ri, mándrǎpi a'di nì.
KELIKO: } (they)

I know not the man of whom ye speak. (Mk. xiv. 71.)
LOGO: *'Dia mi-dre* **adre-le** *ta* **ta-le ɖii**, *ma-ni ko kani'a.*
LUGBARA: *ma-ni-ni agu emi* **ni** *rua* **aji-le-ri** *ko.*
MADI (Pa.): *Ma-i a-ni ko maɖi* **nai** *any-edzo-le.*
MORU: *Mano se ny-***ata-na** *ata* **ono** *mä-ni ku-te.*

Tell them how great things the Lord hath done for thee. (Mk. v. 19.)
LOGO: *Dre ta muruŋgu Miri dre* **o-le** *mi-se* **ɖii**, *tepe-zo aii-dri.*
LUGBARA: *Mi-olo yi-tia eyo ambo-ro Muŋgu* **ni ye-le** *mi-be* **ri.**
MADI (Pa.): *Ny-edzo ai-ni e'bu retu-ndro Ruba ede nyi-driga.*
MORU: *Ago ny-iti ànya-ri ta se* **ɖäsi** *Opi* **k-oye-be** *mi-ri* **ono.**

What therefore God hath joined together. (Mk. x. 9.)
LUGBARA: *'Ba Muŋgu* **ni adi-le** *tu-alo* **ri.**
MADI (Pa.): *Ta Ruba* **oti-le ɖi-ni.**
MORU: *Tana ta ɖo-ro ŋga se Lu* **embe-be** *ono.*

Take heed what ye hear. (Mk. iv. 24.)
LOGO: *Mì-ko-lama ta mì-dre* **yi-le ɖi.**
LUGBARA: *Emi-ndre onyiro eyo emi* **ni eri-le-ri** **ɖi.**
MORU: *Ta se ny-ère* **na ono** *mì-'ba mi amiro komba kadu.*

660. Notice the difference between subject and object relative in the following:
The man who killed the lion is my brother.
MADI { Lo.: madí ebi dí-rɛ́-rɪ-i, mandrúpi 'e.
       Pa.: mo'dí ìbì 'di-rɛ-rɪ, máàdǎzì 'ɪ.
LUGBARA: 'bá òbì 'di-lɛ́-**pi**-ri, máàdrípì.
KELIKO: 'ba kemirú 'dí-í-**pi**-ri, máàdrípì.

The man whom the foreigner killed, is my brother.
MADI { Lo.: madí dzurugo à dí-lɛ́-rì-'ɪ, . . .
       Pa.: mo'dí   ,,   à 'dí-lɛ-rɪ-'ɪ, . . .
LUGBARA: 'bá 'báàzi **ni** 'dí-lɛ́-ri, . . .
KELIKO: 'bá mànya **ni** 'dì-le-ri, . . .

661. The relative is used in all languages in a peculiar construction to show cause or reason for an action. (Here the **se** is omitted in Moru.)
He died from snake-bite (lit. he who died a snake bit).
(Note verb postposition **ni.**)
MORU: ánya dra-bɛ́ ini sɪ-**nì.**
LUGBARA: 'ba drà-**pɪ**-'**dɪ-rɪ** ini ga-**nì.**
KELIKO: 'ba drà-**pɪ**-'**dɪ-rɪ** ini ga-**nì.**
LOGO: 'ba drà-**lɪ**-pɛ-'**di** ini tʃí-**nì.**
AVU. { Jl.: gúla drà-lɛ-bɪ-'**dɪ** ini tʃí-**nì.**
       Jg.: 'ba drà-lɪ-pɪ-'**dɪ** mì tʃí-**nì.**

Further examples from MORU:
ány(a) ɔi-bɛ́ ɔ̀pɪ 'bi-**ni.** He went because the chief beat him.
ánya { kwàdrà } -bɛ́ ɔ'du k-úfu-**ni** yà? He is dying because what is killing him?
      { (k-ɔ̀drà) }

CHAPTER XVIII

THE TONAL CONJUGATION OF VERBS

The Three Tone Classes

662. There are three classes of verbs in Moru-Madi when studied from the point of view of intonation, and these three classes have no connexion with the division of Moru-Madi verbs into the morphological classes already discussed in Chapter X. Each morphological class is represented in each tone class.

Owing to the complicated tonal behaviour of verb stems in sentence context, where words alternate in pitch according to the pitch of preceding or following words and particles, these three classes may only be distinguished by comparing verbs in similar contexts. Under these conditions verbs may easily be divided into:

verbs with relative *high* tone on the root.
,, ,, ,, *mid* ,, ,, ,,
,, ,, ,, *low* ,, ,, ,,

In this chapter the tonal patterns of some of the examples are given in tonic sol-fa. (See Chapter III.) This represents the actual intervals recorded from specific speakers.

TONE CLASSES IN MORU (MIZA).

663. In MORU this comparison is best arrived at by studying the verb when used with its characteristic vowel, i.e. in the General form of the Indefinite aspect. If one regards this vowel,[1] for the sake of argument, as having *mid* tone, the three classes are as follows:

High tone class: u-zí (to call); u'dú (to sleep); lerú (to light).
Mid tone class: u-'di (to dig); ɛkyi (to come); la'di (to cook).
Low tone class: ɔ-drà (to die); ɔzɔ̀ (to give); lɔgɔ̀ (to give back).

This fundamental relationship between tone of root and tone of characteristic vowel is always present, no matter what the actual pitch of the syllables may be. Thus, in some contexts, the actual tones may be:

High tone class: ù-zi, ù'du, lèru.
Mid tone class: ú-'dí, ɛ́kyí, lá'dí.
Low tone class: ɔ́-dra, ɔ́zɔ, lɔ́gɔ.

The verb stems are thus High, Mid (or equal), and Low in relation to the tone of the characteristic vowel, whatever pitch that may be.

Examples from MORU (Miza):

664. Morphological classes will be indicated in the margin.

	High tone verbs.	[tone pattern in tonic sol-fa]	
(Class I)	nyá ɔ̃'du ɔ̃yɛ yà?	m t, d t, d l,	What are you doing?
	má lòs(ɪ) ɔ̀yɛ.	m l, (d) l, d	I am doing work.
(Cl. III)	nyá ɔ̃'du **lerù** yà?	m t, d d de l,	What are you lighting?
	máá àsi **lėru**.	r-m l, d t, d	I'm lighting a fire.

[1] Or stem prefix in the case of Class III verbs.

THE TONAL CONJUGATION OF VERBS

(Cl. I)   má lómvó márɔ̀ ɔ̀trɪ.   I'm undressing myself.
         nyá ,,   mírɔ̀ ɔ̀trɪ.   You're ,,   yourself.
         ánya ká lómvó 'érɔ̀ ɔ̀trɪ.   He is ,,   himself.
         nyá andɪvɔ mɪ́rɔ̀ ɔ̀dzwa yà?   Are you washing yourself?
         máá ,,   márɔ ɔ̀dzwa.   I am ,,   myself.
         nyá à'dì ùzi ya?   Whom are you calling?
         má ŋgàgà ùzi.   I'm calling the boys.

Mid tone verbs.

(Cl. I)   nyá a'd(ù) u'di yà?   f d (de) d d ta₁   What are you digging?
         má 'bú u'di.   f f d d   I am digging a hole.
         nyá sandúku 'dó uŋgi gańwa yà?   Where are you carrying that box to?

(Cl. II)   má andívʊ már(ɔ) ɛ́dɛ́.   I am dressing myself.
         nyá ,,   mír(ɔ) ɛ́dɛ́.   You are ,,   yourself.
         ánya ká ,,   'ér(ɔ) ɛ́dɛ́.   He is ,,   himself.
         àmi tswíne nye-ekyi nòa.   All of you are coming.
         lédr ,,   ke-ekyi ,,   All the people are coming.
         ma ánya ɛ'bɛ.   I am leaving him.
         má gìí ɛmɛ.   I am heating water.
         nyá sandúku 'dó iŋgi niŋwa yà?   Where are you carrying that box from?
         —towards me.

Low tone verbs.

(Cl. II)   nyá ɔ̌'du ɔzɔ̀ yà?   m t₁ d d l₁ l₁   What are you giving?
         má ilì ɔzɔ̀.   m d re d l₁   I am giving a knife.
(Cl. III)   nyá ɔ̌'du lɔgɔ̀ yà?   m t₁ d d l₁ l₁   What are you giving back?
         má ilì lɔgɔ̀.   m d re d l₁   I am giving a knife back.

(Cl. II)   ánya ká gi ɛ́dà àma-drɔ.   He is pouring water on us.
(Cl. I)   (note, however: ánya ká gi ɔdà vru. He is pouring the water out.)

665. Sometimes in the Moroändri sub-group, Mid tone verbs are conjugated like Low tone verbs:

    MORU (Ä.):   àmi tsóni na-alì nia.   All of you are coming.
                 bèdr ,,   a-alì ,,   All the people are coming.
                 máró ídʒi ámɛ.   I am heating water.
(but:)   máró andívo máro ɛ́dɛ́.   I am dressing myself.)
                 ndáká sandùkù ändzì.   He is carrying a box—towards me.
(but:)   ndáká ,,   undzi.   ,,   ,,   ,, —away.)

666. It is sometimes difficult to discover whether some verbs are inherently High or Mid in tone. (Low tone verbs are easily distinguished.)

        nyá ǎ'di ɔ'bɪ̀ yà?   m t₁ d d re l₁   Whom are you beating?
        máá ŋgágà ɔ'bɪ.   m m l₁ d d   I am beating the boy.
        nyá ɔ̌'du la'dì yà?   m t₁ d d re l₁   What are you cooking?
        máá tórómó la'di.   m m m m d d   I am cooking maize.
        má dáwà umvu.   I am drinking medicine.
        nyá ígi mvu.   You are drinking water.
        lédr ka wá m̀vu.   The people are drinking beer.
        má éz(a) ɔnya.   I am eating meat.

Other Tonal Patterns of the Indefinite Aspect.

1. Influence of high tone pronoun immediately preceding verb:

667. The 'characteristic vowel' tone of High and Mid tone verbs is always high after such a pronoun, and the stem vowel relatively mid or low.

High tone class.

má-úzì-na. I am calling him. (Cf. má ŋgàgà ùzi. I am calling the boys.)
nyá-áta ɛŋʊnyɛ kala Mɔrʊ́ sı yà? How do you say it in Moru? (Cf. ánya ká-atà. He is speaking.)

Mid tone class.

nyí-íbi-na ıŋwa yà? Where are you pushing it? (towards). (Cf. ndá ká-**ibi** nà màrɛ. He is pushing it towards me.)
nyú-úŋgí-nà gáŋwa yà? Where are you carrying it? (Cf. nyá sandùku 'dóó uŋgi gaŋwa yà? Where are you carrying that box?)
nyá-**ú'di**-na ɔ'dutayà? Why are you digging? (Cf. má 'bú u'di. I'm digging a hole.)
nyɔ́i íŋwa yà? Where are you going?

The 'characteristic vowel' tone of·Low tone verbs, on the contrary, is low, and the stem vowel relatively mid or high.

Low tone class.

má-ɔ̀dra. I am dying. ánya kɔ́-ɔ̀dra. They are dying.

Note, however, the behaviour of the following Mid tone verbs:

nyá-**ubí**-na íŋwa yà?	Where are you pushing it? (away).
ndá ká-**ubi**-nà mîrɛ.	He is pushing it towards you.
nyé-ɛkpı ɔ'dʊtayà?	Why are you coughing.

668. In the MOROÄNDRI sub-groups, with intervening auxiliary particle **ro**, there is usually no such tonal assimilation:

Mid tone class.

(Cl. I)	mí-r(o)-**undʒi**-ná íŋgwa yà?	Where are you carrying it?
(Cl. II)	mí-rɔ́-ɔi íŋgwa yà?	Where are you going?
	mí-rɔ́-(a)ta íŋgɔtɪ kala Mɔrʊ́ sı yà?	How do you say it in Moru?

But note:

(Cl. I)	mí-r(ó)-**ú'di**-na (a)'dita yà?	Why are you digging?
	mí-ró -**úbi**-na ɛ́ŋwa ya?	Where are you pushing it (away)?
(Cl. II)	mí-ró-**äbi**-nà íŋwa yà?	Where are you pushing it (towards)?

Low tone class.

(Cl. I)	má-rɔ́-ɔ̀dra.	I am dying.
	andá rɔ́-ɔ̀dra.	They are dying.
(Cl. II)	mɪ-rɔ-ɛkpí a'dita ya?	Why are you coughing?

2. Influence of following suffix (on Mid and Low tone verbs):

669. Alternatively this may be called the 'Tone of the dependent forms', since even when the suffixes are lacking the tone is characteristic. The root syllable is higher in tone than the prefix (whether characteristic vowel or other prefix).

Mid tone verbs.

m-érɛ ŋgága te **lí**-vìa (or ká-**lii**). I heard a boy crying.
ɛmɛ́-nɪ́ mírí i'du.[1] You shall not boil it. (Cf. má gìi ɛ́mɛ̇. I am boiling water.)
mǎ-ni-ndí **là'di**-nɪ. I know (how) to cook.
má-'ba enyá tɛ lakázá yá **la'dí**-nɪ. I put food in the pot to boil. (Cf. máá tɔ́rɔ́mɔ́ **la'di**. I am cooking maize.)
m-ɔ́ìyɛ́ (e)za **ə̀nya**(-nɪ). I am going to eat meat.

Low tone verbs.

hakím pa ŋgágà te ni **ə̀drá**-vìa. The doctor saved the boy from dying.
má-lɛ̀ ku **ə̀dra**-nɪ. I don't want to die. (Cf. lédr ni **ə̀drà**-rɔ. Man is mortal.)

Note, however:

má-'ba gìí tɛ **la'di**-nì (or **usu**-nì.) I made the water boil.
má ndà ɔ̀'ba **ɛ́drɛ̇**-nì. I make him stop.
ndá turituri nì **íkyí**-vìa. He is afraid to come.
dófó (ɔ)nó lédr **ezà**-zá sɪ na. This stick is for punishing the man with.

Definite Aspect. General Tone Pattern.

670. The following three paradigms, in the general form with postposition **te**, illustrate best the three tonal classes as found in the definite conjugation. In High and Mid tone verbs the root syllable has usually mid tone; in Low tone verbs it has low tone. The tone of the characteristic vowel (in Class II verbs) is dependent on that of the preceding pronoun.

High tone class.

(Cl. II) mɛ́-**ɛ́sá**-te. [r r d] or m-**ɛ́sà**-te. [r d d] I arrived (here). m-**ú'du**-te. I slept.
ny-**ɛ́sá**-te. [r r d] or ny-**ɛ́sa**-te. [r d d] You arrived. ny-**ú'du**-te. You slept.
ópí **esá**-te. [r r d r d] ány-**ɛsa** te. [r d d d] The chief arrived. He arrived. ány-**u'du**-te. He slept.

(Cl. I) mǎ-**zi**-te. I called him.   máá-**sa**-te. I arrived (there).
mí-**zi**-te. You „   ópí **sa**-te. The chief arrived.
ányä **zi**-te. He „   mǎ-**mvu**-tė. I drank it.

Mid tone class.

(Cl. III) mí-**lii**-te. [r d d] I wept. mú-**luu**-te. I loved.
nyí-**lii**-te. [r d d] You „   nyú-**luu**-te. You „
ányä **lii**-te. [r d d d] He „   ányä **luu**-te. He „

(Cl. II) m-**ɛ́mɛ**-te. I boiled it. m-**ɛ̀mɛ**-te. We boiled it.
ny-**ɛ́mɛ**-te. You „   ny-**ɛ̀mɛ**-te. You „
ány-**ɛmɛ**-te. He „   any-**ɛmɛ**-tɛ. They „

Low tone class.

(Cl. I) má-**drà**-te. [r l̩ d]   I died.
mí-**drà**-te. [r l̩ d]   You „
ndá **drà**-te. [r l̩ d] but ánya **dra**-tė. [r d d l̩] He „
ànya **drà**-te. [l̩ d l̩ d]   They „

---

[1] Lit. To boil to you is not. See § 531.

671. In many cases, especially where an object is expressed or understood, there is no distinction between High tone and Mid tone verbs, but these are distinguished usually from Low tone verbs.

High tone class.

(Cl. I)	má-yɛ lɔsì te.	I have done the work.	
	mí-yɛ lɔsì te.	You ,, ,,	
	mǎ-'bwä lä'bí te.	I shot a waterbuck.	
	mí-'bwä lä'bí te.	You ,, ,,	
	má-trı lómvó márɔ tɛ.	I undressed myself.	
	mí-trı ,, mírɔ tɛ.	You ,, yourself.	
	ánya trı ,, 'ɛrɔ tɛ.	He ,, himself.	
(Cl. III)	mǎ-leru-te.	I lit it.	
	nyé-leru-te.	You ,,	
	ányä leru-te.	He ,,	

Mid tone class.

(Cl. I)	má-'bı ŋgwá te. r d r d	I beat the boy.	
	ópí 'bı mi 'dá yà?	Did the chief beat you?	
	zó 'dɛ-tɛ vùru.	The house fell down.	
(Cl. II)	zó ɛ́'dé-te mǎdrì.	The house fell on me.	
	m-ɛ́dɛ ru tɛ, or m-ɛ́dɛ andívʊ márɔ tɛ.	I dressed myself.	
	ny-ɛ́dɛ ,,	,, ,,	
	ány-ɛdɛ ,,	,, ,,	
(Cl. III)	ndí la'dí-gwo.	... and she cooked it.	

Low tone class.

(Cl. I)	mǎ-nì ŋgwá te. r l₁ r d	I knew the boy.	
(Cl. II)	m-ózɔ̀ ŋga ndǎrì.	I paid him (lit. gave thing to him).	
	ny-ózɔ̀ ,, ,,	,, ,,	
	ány-ɔzɔ̀ ,, ,,	,, ,,	

672. The following High and Mid tone verbs behave like Low tone verbs under certain circumstances (as yet undefined):

High tone class.

mǎ-sı̌- $\begin{cases} \text{ndi te, or má-sí-te, or mǎ-sí-tè.} \\ \text{'da.} \end{cases}$ I hit him.

mí-sı̣̌- ,, ,, ,,
ányä sı̣̌- ,, ,, ,,
mí-sì ndáá 'da yà?   Did you hit him?

má-sı̌- $\begin{cases} \text{ndi te, or má-sí-te.} \\ \text{'da.} \end{cases}$ I bit him.

mí-sı̣̌- ,, ,, ,,
ánya sı̣̌- ,, ,, ,,
mí-sı ndáá 'da yà?   Did you bite him?
má-sɔ̀ giní.   I hoed the ground.
  (Cf. má gìní ɔsɔ́. Indefinite.)

Mid tone class.

        ndá **bì**-te.   He pushed it.
        ányɛ-**ɛkyì**-te.   He arrived.
        ányɔ-**ɔ̀ì**-te.   He went.

But Low tone verbs are always relatively low in tone:

(Cl. II)   m-**ǎtì**-te. [m t₁ d] I held it.
                ny-**ǎtì**-te.   You held it.
                ány-**ǎtì**-te.   He held it.
(Cl. I)   ánya **dra**-bɛ́.   He who died.
           ánya **dra**-ndí ('dá) (té) yà? Did he die?
           lédr **dra**-ndì yà?   Was he dead?
           ndí **drà**-gɔ̀ (-gwo).   And he died.

Note. In the MOROÄNDRI sub-group the tendency is still more marked to conjugate all verbs as Low tone verbs in the Definite Aspect. Here, too, it is doubtful whether High tone verbs and Mid tone verbs are differentiated.

Other Tonal Patterns of the Definite Aspect.

673. These patterns occur in High and Mid tone verbs. The Low tone verbs are invariable in pattern.

1. *Influence of the negative postposition* **ku**.

High and Mid tone verbs.

The verb root syllable is invariably high in tone.

High tone class.

  má-**'bwǎ** èza ku. I didn't shoot the animal. (Cf. mǎ-**'bwä** lä'bí te. I shot a water-buck.)
  mǎ-**mvú** ku. I   didn't drink it.
  mí-**mvú** ku. You   „   „
  (Cf. mǎ-**mvu**-té. I drank it.)
  m-**ú'dú** ku. I   didn't sleep.
  ny-**ú'dú** ku. You „   „
  (Cf. m-**ú'du**-te. ány-**u'du**-te. I slept. He slept.)

Mid tone class.

  má-**nyá** (èza) ku. I   didn't eat (the meat).
  mí-**nyá** (èza) ku. You „   „
  (Cf. mí-**nya** eza té yà? Did you eat the meat?
  máá-**'bí** ku. I   didn't beat him.
  mí-**'bí** ku. You „   „
  (Cf. má-**'bɪ** ŋgwá te. I beat the boy.)
  m-**ɛ́mbɛ́** eba ku. I   didn't tie the rope.
  ny-**ɛ́mbɛ́** eba ku. You „   „
  (Cf. ny-**ɛ́mbɛ** ebà té yà? Did you tie the rope?)
    m-**ɛ́dɛ́** ru ku-tɛ. I   didn't dress myself.
    ny-**ɛ́dɛ́** „ „ You „   „   yourself.
    ány-**ɛdɛ́** „ „ He „   „   himself.
    (Cf. m-**ɛ́dɛ** ru tɛ. I dressed myself.)

má-**kandá** (tswɛ) ku.   I didn't shake (the tree).
nyá-**kandá**   You   ,,   ,,
ánya-**kandá**   He   ,,   ,,
mà-**kandá**   We   ,,   ,,
(Cf. má tswɛ̀ **kanda**. I shake the tree.)
má-'**dá** mi ku. I didn't insult you.
(Cf. mí-'**da** ma 'dá yà? Did you insult me?)
Low tone verbs. (Tone of root syllable unchanged.)
    mǎ-**nì** ku.   I don't know.
    ánya **drà** ku-tɛ̀. He didn't die.
    mó-**ləgə** ku.   I didn't give it back.

2. *The tone of the Subjunctive and Imperative.*

674. The Imperative and Subjunctive forms sometimes have a different intonation from the general form, and the influence of the negative particle **ku** is different here too.

High and Mid tone verbs.
High tone class.
 mɛ́-**ɛzi**. I must bring it. (Cf. m-ɛ́zi-gwo. And I brought it.)
 ányá-kɛ-**ɛzi**. He must bring it.
 ny-**ɛ́zi** mǎrì. Bring it to me.
 mí-'dɛ ma-**sə** vò. Let's hoe the ground.
 mí-'ba ánya k-**əsə̀** gìnɪ. Let him hoe the ground.
 (Cf. má-**sə̀** ginî. I hoed the ground.
  má gìní **əsə**. I hoe the ground.)
   mǎ-**ru**.   I must take it away.
   ányá k-**uru**.   He must take it away.
   mí-**dzwa** ŋgwá.   Wash the child.
   mí-**dzwà** ma.   Wash me.
 ny-**áta** kàlà Morò. Speak Moru.
 (Cf. m-**átá**-te ndäärì. I said to him.)

Mid tone class.
 nyá-**lasà** ŋgwa. m d t₁ d Wash the child.
 (Cf. nyá-**lasa** ŋgwá yà? Have you washed the child?)
 nyé-**émbɛ́** ɛba. Tie the rope.
 (Cf. ny-**émbe** ebǎ tè yà? Did you tie the rope?)
 mí-'dɛ m-**əì**. ⎫
 mɪ-'dɛ́ m-**ɔ́ì**. ⎭ Let's go.   ny-**ɔ́i**, pl. nyɔ-**ɔ́i**. Go!
 (Cf. ny-**ɔ́i**-te. You went.)
 mí-'ba m-**əì**. Let us go.
 mí-'ba ndá kʷ-**əì**. ⎫
 mí-'ba ánya kʷ-**oi**. ⎭ Let him go.
 (Cf. ány-**ɔi**-tɛ. He went.)

675. In many cases the Imperative and the General form are indistinguishable in tone. This is always the case in Low tone verbs.
High tone class.
 mí-**zi** ŋgàgà, pl. mì-**zi** ŋgàgà. Call the boys.
 (Cf. mí-**zi** ŋgàgà te. You called the boys.)

mí-yɛ lɔsì, pl. mì-yɛ lɔsì.   Do the work.
(Cf. mí-yɛ lɔsì te.)
mí-trɪ lómvó mírɔ̀.   Undress yourself.
(Cf. mí-trɪ lómvó mírɔ tɛ.)
mí-mvu dàwà.   Drink the medicine
(Cf. mǎ-mvu-té. I drank it.)
nyé-leru àsi, pl. nyè-leru àsi.   Light the fire.
(Cf. nyé-leru-te. You lit it.)
ny-ímu, pl. nyi-imu.   Run (to me).

Mid tone class.

nyá-la'di tɔ̀rɔ̀mɔ́, pl. nya-la'di tɔ̀rɔ̀mɔ́.   Cook the maize.
(Cf. nyá-la'di tɔ̀rɔ̀mɔ́ te yà? Did you cook the maize?)
ny-ékyi nòa, pl. ny-ekyi nòa.   Come here.
ny-ɛ́'bɛ̀ ánya.   Leave him alone.
ny-ɛ́d(ɛ) andívʊ mírɔ̀.   Dress yourself.
(Cf. ny-ɛ́dɛ mi tɛ. You dressed yourself.)
mí-nya èza.   Eat the meat.
(Cf. má-nya-gwɔ̀ ... and I ate it.)
mí-'bɪ ŋgágà.   Beat the boy.
(Cf. má-'bɪ ŋgwá te. I beat the boy.)
ny-émɛ gìí.   Heat the water.
(Cf. ny-émɛ gìi te. You heated the water.)

Low tone verbs.

    mí-dà vru.   Pour it away.
    ny-édà vru.   Pour it down.
    ny-ɔ́zə mǎrí.   Give it to me.
    ndá ɛkyɛ ny-ɔ́zə̀ i-ri.   He says you must give it to him.
    nyó-ləgə̀ ànyà.   m d l₁ r s₁   Take it back to him.
(but   nyó-ləgə miɛmbá'bǎ rì.   Take it back to your master.)

3. *Influence of negative postposition* ku *on the Imperative.*

676. Sometimes the root vowel of a High tone verb is relatively high before **ku**.
High and Mid tone verbs.

High tone class.

ánya kɛ-ɛzi ku. He must not bring it. (Cf. ánya kɛ-ɛzi.)
ányà k-urù kù. He must not take it away. (Cf. ányà k-uru.)
ndá kʷ-ə̀yɛ tàkù inyɛ̀. He shouldn't do it.
ny-ú'du ku. Don't sleep. (Cf. ny-ú'dú ku. (Negative past.) ny-ú'du-te. (Past positive.))

Mid tone class.

mí-nya (èza) ku.   Don't eat the meat.   (Cf. mí-nya èza. (Imperative.) mí-nyá (èza) ku. (Negative past.))
ny-ɛ́'bɛ ku.   Don't leave it.   (Cf. ny-ɛ́'bɛ̀ ánya. Leave him.)
nyá-lasa ku.   Don't wash it.   (Cf. nyá-lasà ŋgwa. Wash the child.)
ny-ɛ́'dɛ ku mǎdr.   Don't fall on me.
mí-'dɛ ku vùrʊ.   Don't fall down.

Low tone verbs.

nyó-lɔgɔ̀ ku. [m d t, d] Don't give it back. (Cf. mó-lɔgə ku. (Negative past.) nyó-lɔgɔ̀ ányà. (Imperative)).

4. *Future form.*

677. Compare these forms with forms of the same verbs already discussed (especially the negative past). Tone of root syllable is high.

High and Mid-tone verbs.-

(High).
   (Cl. I) mǎ-**zí**-na ŋgàgà 'da.   I shall call the boys.
   (Cl. I) má-**yɛ́**-na lɔsì 'da.   I shall do the work.
   (Cl. II) m-**ɛ́gɛ́**-na tɔ̀rɔ̀mɔ.   I shall buy maize.

(Mid).
   (Cl. I) . . . ma-**nyá**-na-gwò.   . . . and we shall eat it.
   (Cl. II) m-ɛ́'**bɛ́**-na Lúì ('da) ɔndɔ. I shall leave Lui to-morrow.
   (Cl. II) m-**ɛ́mbɛ́**-na ɛbà 'dà.   I shall tie the rope.
   (Cl. III) má-**la'dí**-na tɔ̀rɔ̀mɔ́ 'dá. I shall cook the maize.

(High).
   (Cl. II) ány-**u'dù**-a'da.   He will sleep.

(Mid).
   (Cl. II) ányɔ-**ɔí**-a'da.   He will go.
   (Cl. II) ány-**ekyí**-a'dà.   He will arrive.
   (Cl. III) . . . ánya **la'dí**-na-gwò. . . . and she will cook it.

(Mid).
   (Cl. II) ndá èkyè yé-**ékyí**-a'da. He says he will come.
   (Cl. II) anyá èkyè ye-**ekyí**-a'da. They say they will come.

(High).
   (Cl. I) ópí ɔ**sá**-na.   The chief will arrive
                                          (there).
   (Cl. II) ópí e**sá**-na.   The chief will arrive (here).

(Mid).
   (Cl. II) ópí **ekyí**-na.   The chief will come.
   (Cl. I) ópí ɔ'**bí**-na mí 'dá.   The chief will beat you.
   (Cl. II) lakázá ɛ̀'**dɛ**-'da mädɨ. d re re t, d d d s, The pot will fall on me.
   (Cl. I) lakázá ɔ̀'**dɛ**-'da ndädɨ. d re re s, d d d s, The pot will fall on him.

Low tone verbs.
   (Cl. I) má-**dà**-na-'da.   I shall pour it.
   (Cl. II) . . . m-**ɔ́zɔ**-ná-gwo tokó. . . . and I'll give it to my wife.

But note:
   (Cl. I) ànya **ɔ̀dra**-na-'dà.   They will die.

TONE CLASSES IN THE CENTRAL LANGUAGES

678. The following tonal data, though incomplete, show that there are three tone classes in the Central languages—except in Avukaya, which has only two, Mid and Low. The general form of the Definite Aspect (with postposition) gives clue to tone class.

High tone class.

LUGBARA	LOGO	KELIKO	AVUKAYA	
má-tsá-'bo.	má-tsá-drɛ.	má-tsá-gɪ. / má-tsa-gɪ.	má-tsa-trá.	I arrived.
[r r d]	[r r d]	[r r d] / [r d d]	[r d r]	

Mid tone class.

má-di-'bo.	má-di-drɛ.	mǎ-di-gɪ.	má-di-trá.	I hit him.
[r d d]	[m r d]	[re d de]	[r d r]	

Low tone class.

má-drà-'bo.	má-drà-drɛ.	má-drà-gɪ.	má-drà-tra.	I died.
[r l₁ d]	[m t₁ d]	[m t₁ d]	[r l₁ d]	
má-avì-ra.	má-vì-drɛ.	mâ-vì-gɪ.	má-vì-dra.	I forgot it.

679. With expressed object:

High tone class.

LUGBARA	LOGO		
mí-**sadria** makȧ.	mí-**lɛdɛ́** ma drɛ̇.		You helped me.
KELIKO	AVUKAYA		
mí-**ŋà**-rà mani.	n-ɛ́dɛ mǎ trȧ. (Jl.)		You helped me.
	mí-ɛ́dɛ ,, (Jg.)	,,	,,

Mid tone class.

LUGBARA	LOGO	KELIKO	
mǎ-**di** ŋgù tɛ̇ (drà-lɛ.)	mǎ-**di**-mvȧ drɛ̇.	mǎ-**di** mvȧ gi.	I hit the child.
[f d re re s₁ l₁]	[f d de si₁]	[re d de d]	

Low tone class.

LUGBARA	LOGO	KELIKO	AVUKAYA	
mí-**zù** ŋga.	mí-'**bà** ŋga.	m-ópì ŋga.	mí-lǎpì ŋga.	You hid the thing.

680. With negative postposition **ko**.

High tone class.

	LUGBARA	LOGO	KELIKO	AVUKAYA	
(Cl. I)	má-**rɪ** kʋ	má-**rí** ko.	máa-**rɪ** ku.	máa-**rí** kʋ.	I don't hear.
	[r d d]	[r r d]	[r-d d d]	[r-d r d]	
(Cl. III)	má-**k-u'dú** kɔ.	má-**kuyé** kɔ.	má-**kodù** kɔ̃.	má-**kẃodú** kɔ.	I'm not asleep.
	[r d r d]	[r d r d]	[re d de ta₁]	[r r-d r d]	

Low tone class.

	LUGBARA	LOGO	KELIKO	AVUKAYA	
(Cl. I)	mǎ-**nì** kʋ.	mǎ-**nì** kʋ.	mǎ-**nì** ku.	mǎ-**ní** kʋ.	I don't know.
	[m t₁ d]	[m t₁ d]	[m t₁ d]	[r r d]	

TONE CLASSES IN MADI.

681. As far as the material enables one to see, there are only two tone classes in Madi—High (corresponding to High and Mid in the other languages) and Low.

High tone class. The root syllable is relatively high in tone.

Indefinite.

Lo.: ma tî zà.
Pa.: má-zwá tí. } I am milking a cow.

má ta ὺmbɛ.
m-úmbɛ́ ŋga. } I am tying it.

Definite.

Lo.: á-tsa-rá.
Pa.: má-sa-rá. } I arrived (there).

mé-etsá-rá.
m-ésa-rá. } I arrived (here).

[m r re]
Lo.: á-zwa-rá. I milked it.

Lo.: á-tsá kʊ̀-rʊ̀.
Pa.: má-sá kʊ̀-rʊ̀. } I didn't arrive.

mé-etsá kʊ̀-rʊ̀.
m-ésá kʊ̀-rʊ̀. } I didn't arrive.

Lo.: ídré ɔtsí má a drì trɔ.
Pa.: ídé sí mà nɪ dì tɔ̀. } A mouse bit my finger.

Lo.: atsí lɛ̀dra.
Pa.: así lɛ̀da. } The fire flared up.

Imperative.

Lo.: nyi-zá.
Pa.:   zá. } Milk it.

Low tone class. Root syllable relatively low in tone. (Sometimes low-falling.)[1]

Indefinite.

má-dra. I am dying.   bá kákí-drà. They are dying.

Lo.: má bɔ̀ŋgo sì.
Pa.: má-tʃwí bɔ̀ŋgo. } I am tearing the cloth.

Definite.

Lo.: á-drà-ra.
Pa.: má-dà-ra. } I died.

á-sì-ra.   I tore it.   (m)ógù-ra. I stole it.
má-ndè-ra.   I milked it.

[m d r]

Lo.: á-drà kʊ (rʊ̀).
Pa.: má-dà kʊ (rʊ̀). } I didn't die.

Lo.: barángwá ɔsì máa.   [d m m d d-l₁ r-d]
Pa.: 'borángwà tʃwi mánɪ. [d m m   d   r d] } The boy hit me.

Lo.: lúkudó ɛdrà-ra.
Pa.: lóku'dó lɛdà-ra. } The pot broke.   atsí ɔ́drà-ra. The fire died.

Imperative (low-falling tone).

Lo.: nyi-sì. [m d-l] Hit it.
Pa.: tʃwì.   [d-l]   (nyi-) ndè [d d-l] Milk it.

---

[1] Not indicated by special diacritic, but shown in sol-fa notation.

682. Compare verbs **ndrέ** (to see) and **ndè** (to milk).
Indefinite.

   I am looking at a cow.   *I am milking a cow.*
Lo.:   má tí **ndè**.
Pa.: má-**ndέ** tí.   má-**ndέ** tí.

   The boy is looking at a cow.   *The boy is milking the cow.*
Lo.: bárá ká tî **ndrε**.   bárá ká tî **ndè**.
Pa.: 'borá k-**úndέ** tí.   'borá k-**úndέ** tí.

Definite.
   The boy saw a cow.   *The boy milked the cow.*
Lo.: bará əndrε tí rá.   bará **ondè** tí rá.
Pa.: 'borá **ndε** tí rá. [d r d r de] 'borá **ndè** tí rá. [d r l, r de]

   The boy did not see the cow.   *The boy did not milk the cow.*
Lo.: bárá əndrε (tǎ) tí (gá) ku.   bárá **ondè** tí kʊ.
Pa.: 'borá **ndε** (ŋgá) tí gí (ku).   'borá **ndè** tí ku.

As can be seen from the above, Pandikeri Madi shows tone-class distinction in the Definite conjugation, but not in the Indefinite.

Distribution of Tone Classes

683. Verbs which are etymologically related within the Moru-Madi language group usually show a tonal similarity also. This is especially the case of Low tone verbs, but there is considerable dialectal variation in the High and Mid tone verbs, while, in some languages, these merge into one tone class.

The two main dialects of Madi, however, show a startling variation of tone class in certain verbs.

MADI { Lo.: amá-**vù** drà-rε. } We are going to die. má-**sí**-ra. } I built it.
   { Pa.: ama-**vó** dà-rε. }   má-**sì**-ra. }

Lo.: á-**mù** ku. } I'm not going.   '**bà** } (to put) '**jà** } (to fight).
Pa.: mǎ-**mù** kʊ. }   '**bá** }   '**já** }

684. As said before, verb tone class is not dependent on morphological class. At the same time a verb root does not necessarily retain its inherent tone in all derived verb stems. Note the following examples:

MORU
(Cl. II) ánya ká gi **édà** àma-drɔ. He is pouring water over us.
(Cl. I)   ánya ká gi **ədà** vru.   He is pouring water away.
(Cl. I)   nyá-**ubí** na íŋwa yà ?   Where are you pushing it ? (away)
(Cl. II) nyí-íbi ,, ,, ,,   ,,   ,,   (towards)
(Cl. I)   M.: kú-**umú**. Äg.: kó-**ùmu**. } He is running.
(Cl. III) ká-**tumu**.   ká-**tumù**. }

MADI
(Cl. I)   ɔtsé **ɔtsɪ** ma ra.   The dog bit me.
(Cl. II) ɔtsé **ɔtsí** kwà ra.   The dog gnawed the bone.

CHAPTER XIX

ADJECTIVES

685. The following are the main qualifiers in Moru-Madi:
1. The possessive+postposition. (See Chapter VIII.)
    ɔpı ma-rɔ.   My chief.   (MORU.)
    ɔpı ma-dri.   ,,   ,,   (MADI.)
2. The demonstrative. (See Chapter VII.)
    lédr ɔnɔ.   This man.   (MORU.)
    ago niḍi.   ,,   ,,   (LOGO.)
3. The relative. (See Chapter XVII.)
    lédr sé ăfu bɛ.   The man who was killed. (MORU.)
    ago dra-le-pi-ḍi.   The man who died. (LOGO.)
    bara nyoŋgwe-le-rı'ı. The boy you called. (MADI.)
4. The adjective. The present chapter will deal exclusively with this form of qualifier.

686. There are forms of words specialized for qualifying, or what we may call adjectival function. Such forms are here termed 'Adjectives', and they fall into three types:
   A. Those with affixed *nominal* or *pronominal* particles:
      e.g. (MORU) giɽı-ŋwa (little); mba-go (old); mɔi-rú (poor).
   B. Those with affixed (i.e. prefixed or suffixed) *verbal* particles:
      e.g. k-ɔzí (bad); toro-rı'ı (little) (MADI).
   C. Those with no affixed particles. (These forms are relatively rare.)
      e.g. 'däsí (big); fɛrɛ̀ (few); sú (four).

Thus formally adjectives cannot be distinguished from nouns and verbs. The distinction lies in their application.

687. Adjectives may be used either attributively or predicatively. In most cases there is no formal distinction: e.g. *zo ḍäsi* = the big house or the house is big; but it has been found necessary to distinguish between these two uses, and this chapter will deal with adjectives in their attributive or qualifying sense only.

688. The adjective always follows the substantive it qualifies.

Many physicians. (Mk. v. 26.)   *All ye.* (Mk. xiv. 27.)
MORU: kʷozo **amba**.   vo amiro **cini**.
LOGO: alokoli-i **bi**.   ami **we-i**.
LUGBARA: ojo **obi-ro**.   emi **dria**.
MADI (Pa.): ojo **amgbu**.   anyi **podru**.

Sometimes a verbal postposition may intervene.

I bought one cow.   *We saw five men.*
MORU: ma-ge ti te **alo**.   mà-ndre ledri te **nji**.
KELIKO: ma-jɛ te **alo**.   ama-ndre 'ba **tau**.
MADI: ma-ze ti **alo** ra.   ama-ndre 'ba **tau** ra.
KELIKO: opi-ri jo be **su**. The chief has four houses (lit. chief house with four).

ADJECTIVES

A. ADJECTIVES WITH NOMINAL OR PRONOMINAL AFFIXES

l- *prefix*

689. In MORU the prefix l- is often used for ordinal numbers.

ŋgágà lírì or *riri-na* (the second boy).
ŋgágà lísu or *lisu-na* (the fourth boy).
ŋgágà lídzʷi or *linji-na* (the fifth boy).

-go, -ŋgwa *suffixes*

690. The augmentative and diminutive suffixes (see §§ 180–5) may occasionally be found with certain adjectives.

MORU: agɔmbago or agó àmba-**go**[1] (an old man).

M.: tɔkó àdra-**ŋwa**[2] ⎫
Ä.: ɔkó àdra-**va**   ⎬ (an old woman).
W., Jl.: akó ara-**ka** ⎭

M.: gɪɽɪŋwa ⎫ (small);   tsʷareŋwa ⎫ (narrow).
Ä.: gaáva   ⎭   sɛrɛva   ⎭

LOGO: *ca(-mva)* (small); *anyi (-mva)* (near).

KELIKO: *fe mani a'bogu* **ambo-go**. Give me a big banana.
andriga **abo-gu** *isa-gi*. A big palaver has come.

-'di *suffix*

691. This particle is found mostly after adjectives in LOGO. It may follow its adjective stem immediately, or it may be separated from it by other particles. The plural suffix -i, when used, follows it.

Mi adremakandra **konji-ɖi**. (Mt. xviii. 32.) Thou wicked servant.
mvamva **alo-ɖi** *dre* (Mt. x. 42) (to one of these little ones).
Aruka-na dre ɖe-zo vo **tani-ɖi** *mi*. (Mk. iv. 8.) Other fell on good ground.
Ago **konji-ɖi** *dre ŋga* **konji-ɖii** *do-zo aii-ŋga* **konji-ɖi** *ase*. (Mt. xii. 35.) An evil man out of evil treasure (lit. his things) bringeth forth evil things.
ɖia **erinyi-be-ɖi** *a jo na* (Mk. iii. 27) (into a strong man's house).
ago **mi-aku-ɖi** (blind man [lit. man without eyes]).
'Dia **mi-ako-ro-ɖi-i**. The blind (people).
'Dia **bi-ɖi-i** *k-ali-ki*. (Mk. xiii. 6.) Many (people) shall come.

Compare LUGBARA (rare):

mi-ndre yi aso so mi-rua **tre-ɖini**. (Mk. xv. 4.) Behold how many things they witness against thee.

Also in MORU (rare):

ànya fu koliya alo-ɖi.	They killed one monkey.
mà-fu ariaba alo-ɖi.	We killed one guinea-fowl.
Cf. *ma-ge ti te alo*.	I bought one cow.

692. Note its value as an adjective formative in the following:

LOGO: *aɖi laɖi ŋga konji*.	He cooks food badly.
aɖi laɖi ŋga konji-ɖi.	He cooks bad food.
aɖi si jo tani.	He builds a house well.
aɖi si jo tani-ɖi.	He builds a good house.
(*dridri* = before.)	(*dridri-ɖi* = former.)

---

[1] Cf. ɔmba = to grow.   [2] Cf. ɔdra = to die.

It is also used at the end of a sequence of adjectives:
    mi-no jo tani maligu-ɖi.   Look at that nice big house.
    mi-nda ama-boŋgo camva-ɖi.   Look for my small cloth.

693. It also serves as 'qualificative pronoun' (see Intro. § 416) formative:
    LOGO: *azi-ɖi* (another one); *tandi-ɖi* (another one).
           aruku-ɖi (some), pl. *aruka-'ba* (some people).

Compare also its use in the formation of verbal nouns (§§ 225, 535).
    ŋga fe-le-ɖi (gift); *ɖia kori ri-le-pi-ɖi* (sower).

Suffix -na (dial. lɛ)

694. In LULU'BA this particle is attached to most adjectives when used attributively:
    léti azó-**ná** (a long road).
    léti alí-**na** (a short road).
    mo'dí ágwí-**na** lê (that big man).

It occurs occasionally in LOGO:
    joale muruŋgu-ɖi kuru-na-ɖi (Mk. xiv. 15) = a large upper room.

In MORU it is sometimes used for ordinal numbers:
    ŋgágà 'bùtè-**na**.   The tenth boy.
    mina-**na** ledr ɖási.   The third is a big man.

Note also: '*Di-aza kadu-na iɖu.* (Lk. xviii. 19.) None is good (lit. another person good is absent).

695. In most languages, however, **na** is used to form qualificative pronouns. (See § 261.)

MORU { M.: má-lɛ kàdó-**na** àyan.
        Ä.: ,, andí-**na** yù.
        W.: ,, andí-**na** à'dɔ̀.
        Jl.: ,, tàndi-lɛ ì'dì. } I want a good one (indeed).

Cf. LOGO *azi-na, tandi-na* (another one).   *aruka-na* (something).

This suffix, however, is not essential in all instances of pronominal use.
    For many shall come (Mk. xiii. 6).   *Only two have come.*
    MORU: **amba** *eki-a-ɖa.*   *eki toto* **ri-tu**.
    MADI (Pa.): *aɖosi* **amgbu** *ai emu.*   (Torit): *eri emuki-ni.*
                                     KELIKO: *imuki iri.*

-ro, -ru (= body) suffix

696. This particle indicates the material from which a thing is made or the purpose for which it serves. Since in MORU it is apt to be confused with the genitive postposition **ro**,[1] the phenomenon is best studied from the point of view of LOGO:

    LOGO: *tigu fa-ro* (wooden door); *tigu aiya-ro* (iron door).
        fe aci-ro (fire wood); *vo kira-ro-'di* (stony ground).
    MORU: *tiza asi-ro* (fire-wood).
        ma-ndre vo siŋgo-ro ku. I don't see a sandy place.
        tori undi-ro (Mk. ix. 25) = foul spirit.
        ŋgá ŋgá-útu-**ru** = hammer (a thing-hitting thing).

It is more than probable that the two particles are identical in MORU.

ADJECTIVES

In MORU it is also used in tribal adjectives:
'dítókó Mɔró-rə (a Moru woman)   lá'bí Mɔró-rə (a Moru custom).
äzú Mɔró-rə (a Moru spear)   'bädr Mɔró-rə (the Moru country).
but: kala Mɔró (the Moru language).

697. In MORU and LUGBARA it may be attached to an existing adjective.[1]

MORU
- M.: *ma-le zo ǎdäsi(-ro)*. I want a big house.
  ledri ratara-ro (Mk. iii. 27) = strong man.
  ma-ndre ari oka-ro. I saw a red bird.
  boŋgo onje-ro (white garment).
- 'B.: *lédr 'di-pèi-rɔ* (a good man).

LUGBARA: *jo uru-le-ro ambo-ro* (Mk. xiv. 15) (a large upper room).
  eyo ambo-ro (Mk. v. 19) (how great things).
  afa onyi-ro (Mt. vii. 11) (good gifts).
  'ba koŋgoloko-ro (Mk. iii. 27) (strong man).
  boŋgo emve-ro izo-ro eri-ru a indi (Mk. xvi. 5) (clothed in a long white garment).

It is very much used in predicatives (see § 723 et seq.) in all languages.

-dro, -ndro

698. These suffixes seem to occur in MADI only.

Torit: *a-ndre anyi **ci-dro** ra.*
Opari: *ma-ndre anyi **ci-dro** ra.* } I saw you all.

Pa.: *jo **retu-ndro** uru* (Mk. xiv. 15) (a large upper room).
  *Ny-e'jo aini e'bu **retu-ndro** Ruba ede nyi-driga.* (Mk. v. 19.) Tell them how great things the Lord hath done for thee.
  *madi-ni **okpo-ndro*** (Mk. iii. 27) (a strong man).
  *e'bi **ga-dro*** (Mk. viii. 7) (a few fishes).

Adjectives formed by means of postpositions.

699. Many adjectives have the form: Nominal root+postposition.

LOGO: *ago **mi-ako-ǎi***
MADI (Pa.): *madi **mi-iyo*** } blind man (lit. man eyes without).

LOGO: *ǎia **irinyi-be-ǎi*** (strong man [lit. man strength with]).

LOGO: *ago **togo-mbamba-ǎi-be***
LUGBARA: *'ba **asi-mbaza-si*** } (a hard man [lit. man heart hard with]).

LOGO: *i adre ǎia kuli-ako-ǎi ledezo tai ta.* (Mk. vii. 37.) He maketh the dumb (people) to speak (words).

LUGBARA: *eri fe 'ba bile dirinya-ro be eyo eri.* (Mk. vii. 37.) He maketh the deaf (people) to hear (words).

MORU: *mano ŋgá dri ambá **be*** (Mk. x. 25) (a rich man).
  *moŋgu **be*** or *ɔsá **ké*** (fat); *rıti **bè*** (difficult).
  *mi ɔmbá **ké*** (clever, i.e. eyes strong).
  *avuzi **ŋga aku*** (Mk. xii. 42) (a poor widow).

MADI (Pa.): *izi **limi agotro iyo*** (a poor widow).

[1] In LOGO this only happens in predicatives. See § 725.
adi tali-ro. He is short.

B. ADJECTIVES WITH VERBAL AFFIXES

k-

700. In those dialects of MORU which have the auxiliary particle **ká** in the 3rd person (Indefinite Aspect), many adjectives may be found beginning with **k-**.

MORU
- M., W.: má-lɛ àzu kɜ̀zɪ ku.
- Ä., Jl.: má-lɛ àzu ɔnzí ku. } I don't want a bad spear.
- M.: *gini kadu* (good ground).
- Jl.: *odzɪla dɔ́* (a good man).

Note, however, the **k-** in other languages also:

AVUKAYA: ɔkyɛ́ **uku** (an old dog); ara **kä-ukú** (an old man).
LUGBARA: *'ba **kakao** yi ŋga-yo-ra.* (Mt. vii. 22.) Many (people) shall say.
  *'ba **ka-ra-karao** ŋga-emu.* (Mk. xiii. 6.) Many shall come.
LOGO: *boŋgo **kemve**[1] aḍi-ru* (Mk. xvi. 5) (clothed in a white garment).
  *ago **kacua*** (a tall man).
  *yi **kidri*** (Mt. x. 42) (cold water).

Adjectives with relative particles.

701. In MADI the attributive adjective usually has the relative ending **rɪ'ɪ**.

Lo.: *lenya loso-**re-e*** (good food); *oko onzi-**re-e*** (the bad woman).
Torit: *nyi-kwe mani rabolo ambugo-**re-e**.*
Opari: *ny-eke mani rabolo ndzago-**re-e**.* } Give me a big banana.
Torit: *maḍi ta'jo-re ndro-**re-e** emu-ni.*
Opari: *maḍi le'jo ezo-**re-re-e** kemu.* } A big palaver has come.
Torit: *a-ndre ariaŋgwa eka-**re-e** ra.*
Opari: *ma-ndre ariaŋgwa eka-**re-e**.* } I saw a red bird.
Torit: *opi dri zo ambugo-**re-e**.* The chief has a big house (lit. to the chief is a big house).
  *anidri zo toro-**re-e**.* He has a small house.

Note also after a demonstrative:
  *na-a-**re-e** ambago-dro.* That one is big.

This construction differs from the verbal relative construction in that there is usually no infinitive particle **rɛ**, **lɛ**, **ka**, or **zo**. (See §§ 647 et seq.)

Note also in LUGBARA:

*nyaku oni-efi be **ri*** (Mk. iv. 5) (stony ground [ground which with stones]).
*'ba mi-le dra-za be **ri*** (Mk. viii. 23) (blind man [man who with eyes dead]).

And in LOGO:
  *toko ave-le-**pi-ḍi*** (a beautiful woman).

Compare: *I want a strong bow.*

MADI
- Lo.: á-lɛ ósù ɔkpɔ́-**rí-'ɪ**.
- Pa.: má-lɛ ósù ɔkpɔ́-**rɪ-'ɪ**.

LUGBARA: má-lɛ úsù ɔkpɔ́-**rɪ-'ɪ**.
KELIKO: má-lɛ úsù ɔkpɔ́-**rɨ**.
MORU: má-lɛ äsu m̀ba-**ra**.

[1] In my vocabulary 'white' is translated **ɛmvɛ** or **kʸɛmvɛ**.

ADJECTIVES

702. The ordinals in MADI are similarly formed, though the verb suffix -zo may be used here at will.

alo-zo-re-e or *alo-re-e* (the first).
tou-zo-re-e or *tou-re-e* (the fifth).
mudri-zo-re-e or *mudri-re-e* (the tenth).

703. In MORU the relative pronoun *se* is often used to link the adjective to its noun.

mi-ndre ta se amba ànya k-oga-i mi-lomvo ono. (Mk. xv. 4.) Behold how many things they bear witness against thee.
ny-iti ànyäri ta se ɖäsi Opi k-oye-be miri ono. (Mk. v. 19.) Tell them what great things God hath done for thee.
ŋgaga (se) maro ono. This son of mine.
ta se ono. This thing.

-za (cf. §§ 571–2)

704. This particle occurs in LUGBARA adjectives only.

yi ambi-za-ro (Mt. x. 42) (cold water).
mi 'ba asi mba-za si. (Mt. xxv. 24.) Thou art a hard (hearted) man.
'ba mi-le dra-za be ri (Mk. viii. 23) (blind man).

C. EXAMPLES OF ADJECTIVES WITH NO AFFIXED PARTICLES

705. In all languages, adjectives with the simple form are to be found corresponding, even in neighbouring dialects, to forms with prefixes or suffixes.

MORU: *ya zo ro ɖäsi* (Mk. xiv. 15) (a large room).
*ŋga **amba*** (Lk. x. 41) (many things).
*ma-ndre ami te **cini**.* I see you all.
*anya ozo parata **fere** märi.* He gave me a little money.

AVUKAYA: *ɔndzɪla **dó*** (a good man).   *ɔndzɪla **pέ*** (a bad man).

MADI ⎰ Pa.: *vo **oni*** (Mk. iv. 5) (stony ground).
⎱ Op.: *ojo **amgbu*** (Mk. v. 26) (many doctors).
   *oke mani pese **ga**.* ⎱ He gave me a little money.
KELIKO: *eri fɛ mani farata **madaŋ**.* ⎰
*ma-ndrɛ ariŋa **ika**.* I saw a red bird.
*ma-ndrɛ imi **sere**.* I saw you all.

LUGBARA: *mi-i atibo-jeza **onzi**.* (Mt. xviii. 32.) Thou wicked servant (cf. LOGO konji-'di).
*eri i ecandi **ambo*** (Mk. v. 26) (suffered many things).

LOGO: *ma-no liwa **muruŋgu**.* I see a big elephant.
*ta **muruŋgu*** (Mk. v. 19) (great things).
*aii fe parata **we** tukutuku dre.* (Mt. xxviii. 12.) They gave large moneys to the soldiers.

THE FORMATION OF MORU-MADI NUMERALS

706. The MORU-MADI numeral system is a quinary one. The numbers 1–5 have distinct forms:

àlo, (e)rì, ná, sú (or isù), and njí (or tau)

The numbers 6–9 are compounds of 5 and the other numbers. The number 10 has a distinct form **'butì** or **mudrí**. 11–19 are compounds of 10 and the other numbers.

The number 20 is referred to either as two tens or by a phrase signifying 'eaten one man'. Counting is done on fingers and toes, and the above phrase indicates that one man's digits are exhausted.

Higher numbers may be, and in schools very often are, coined mechanically on the preceding principles, each number growing more involved than the last. The average Moru-Madi speaker, however, has no present need of them.

The numerals, like all other adjectives, follow their nouns.

Suffix -tu (numerals)

707. In most languages the numeral adjective follows the noun uninflected, but in the three Moru dialects, Miza, -ändri, and Kediru, it may take a suffix **-tu**. Mynors considers this a contraction of the word **lutu** = exactly. This suffix is only to be found after **iri** (two) and **na** (three).

MORU: *eki toto **ri-tu**.* Only two have come.

*mi'ba màmu mutuguri **nä-tu**.* (Lk. ix. 33.) Let us make three tabernacles.

Examples of numerals:

When he had taken the five loaves and the two fishes (Mk. vi. 41).   *The seven loaves* (Mk. viii. 6).

MORU: *Ago nda uru mapa **nji** gwo ndi ti'bi **ri-tu** be.*   *mapa **njidrieri***
LOGO: *Aḍi dre ambata **nji-ḍii** do-zo kosia **iri-ḍii** be.*   *ambata **njidriiri** nii*
LUGBARA: *Eri ŋga enya olimini **toi** du-ra, e'bi **iri** be.*   *enya olimini **aziri***

MADI ⎰ Pa.: *Lofo Yezu oko mugate **tou** e'bi **eri** tro.*   *mugate nai **tuderi***
       ⎱ Lo.: *... mugati ni ewo **tou** e'bi **eri** tro.*

*bara **alo** odra okolo si ra.* One boy (i.e. one of the boys) is dead from coughing.

LOGO: *mi-ko-fe za **mudri** lagi-se.* Pay ten cows.

THE POSITION OF QUALIFIERS IN A SENTENCE

708. In most languages a qualificative may not be separated from its substantive by any intervening particle. A noun postposition, therefore, follows the complete phrase.[1]

Examples from MORU (cf. § 685):

1.   MORU: *uḍu maro **vosi** (after my sleep).*
           *zo ledri ratararo ro **ya** (Mk. iii. 27) =* into a strong man's house.
   LUGBARA: *afa maniri **be** (Mt. xx. 15)* (with mine own).

2.   MORU: *masana 'bereŋwa se ana **ya** griḍa ya?* Shall I be able to reach yonder hill?
   LOGO: *mikota kira niḍi **dre**.* (Mt. xvii. 20.) Ye should say unto this mountain.

3.   MORU: *tokó lédr sé ăfubɛ aná **rǝ**.* The wife of the slain man.
   LUGBARA: *'ba emi ŋgupiri **madri** (Mt. v. 44)* (to them that hate you).

4.   MORU: *ce zo ḍäsi **ro**.* The wood of the big house.
        *male waraga onje ozonɪ ŋgaga giṛiŋwa **ri**.* I want white paper to give to the small boy.
   MORU: *gini kadu **ya** (Mk. iv. 20) =* on good ground.
   LOGO: *vo tani (ḍi) **mi**.*
   LUGBARA: *aŋgo onyiro **ma** alia.*

But: MADI (Pa.): *enyaku **a** loso* (on good ground).
            *ani oko dri maḍi **dri** mi iyo.* (Mk. viii. 23.) And he took the hand of the blind man.

---

[1] Madi Pandikeri shows the only exceptions to this rule.

709. When two or more qualificatives follow one substantive, the following are the main rules of precedence:

(*a*) A possessive usually precedes an adjective.
>MORU: *zo **miro** ḋäsi* (your big house).

>>*Thou art my beloved Son.* (Mk. i. 11.)
>MORU: *Mi-te Ŋgwa **se maro** molu tawi ono au.*
>LUGBARA: *Mi Mvi **mani** leletori i.*
>MADI (Pa.): *Nyi Aŋgwapi **madri** ale-ndro-ani-ra.*

>>*And he took with him Peter and the two sons of Zebedee.* (Mt. xxvi. 37.)
>LOGO: *Aḋi dre Petero anjia **Zebedayo aḋea iri-ḋii** be dri-zo li-le i-be.*
>LUGBARA: *Eri du Petero anzi **Zebedi ni iri-ḋi** yi-be.*

But note:
>MORU: *kokye **uni** toko **ḋäsi** odrupi maro **ro ri** drate.* The black dog of the head wife of my brother is dead.

(*b*) Demonstratives usually follow other qualificatives.

>>*For this my son was dead.* (Lk. xv. 24.)
>MORU: *Tana ŋgwa **se maro ono** dra je ndi.*
>LUGBARA: *Te mva **mani ḋi** dra-'bo.*

>>*Grant that these my two sons may sit.* (Mt. xx. 21.)
>LOGO: Mi-ko-ta togi anjia **iri nii ma-na 'dii** ko-liri-ro.
>LUGBARA: Mi-ece anzi **ma-ni iri 'di** ma-ri.

>>*But those mine enemies.* (Lk. xix. 27.)
>MORU: *Oko kila'bazi **se maro ono**.*
>LUGBARA: *Te aribo **mani ḋi**.*

>>*I have not found so great faith.* (Mt. viii. 10.)
>MORU: *m-usu taoma **amba** oso ḋo ronye ku te.*
>LUGBARA: *Dria ma-ndre aiita **ambo** ḋinile ko.*
>LOGO: *Ta kaile **muruŋgu** ŋgoro nitini ḋi ḋia . . . ma-kusu tejia ko.*
>MORU: *mi ruendu'ba **kozi ono**.* (Lk. xix. 22.) Thou wicked servant.
>LOGO: *mi-ko-no liwa **muruŋgu nda**.* Look at the big elephant.

(*c*) When two similar qualificatives are used with one substantive, the more accented one follows the less accented.

>>*Clothed in a long white garment* (lit. garment white long).
>MORU: *boŋgo **anjero ḋäsi** be lomvo ige.*
>LUGBARA: *boŋgo **emvero izoro** eriru a indi.*
>MADI (Pa.): *anikesu boŋgo **ŋgweri azo** tro.*

>MORU: *ago ànya ti'bi **geriŋwa fera** be.* (Mk. viii. 7.) They had a few small fishes.

>>*I saw many red birds.*
>MORU: *ma-ndre ari **amba te okaro*** (many red).
>MADI { Torit: *a-ndre arendzi **ekaree kareoko** ra* (red many).
>   Opari: *ma-ndre arendzi **ekaree kareako**.*

U

CHAPTER XX

PREDICATIVE CONSTRUCTIONS

710. As stated earlier (Introduction, § 421), a predicative may have either a verbal or a non-verbal form. This chapter will be devoted entirely to the various forms of non-verbal predication, which include:

Positively.
   i. Juxtaposition: The complement follows directly on its antecedent.
   ii. Linking particles: The complement is joined to its antecedent by an intervening particle.
   iii. Predicative suffix: The complement is followed by a particle.
   iv. Verb 'to be': The complement follows a verb (often defective).

The predicative of possession is found mainly under categories i and iv.

Negatively.
   i. The form **i'du** (or **iyo**): This form may follow the complement or may stand alone as a predicate.
   ii. The particle **ku.** This particle may either precede or follow the complement.

These two negative elements may be used with most of the above predicative constructions.

   iii. The postposition **aku**: Predicative of non-possession.

The complement may consist in a substantive (noun or pronoun), or a qualificative (including adjective), or a descriptive (including adverb), and the constructions binding it to its antecedent are practically identical for all kinds of complement. Note that the antecedent itself is very often 'understood', especially in replies to questions.

The predicative of comparison needs a separate section to itself. (§ 743.)

i. JUXTAPOSITION

A. *With noun complement.*

711. The complement immediately follows its antecedent.

MORU:	má Dɛŋgo. I am Dengo.	ru maro Kofi. My name is Kofi.
	ma ŋgwá Lofógó ro.	I am the son of Lofogo.
LUGBARA:	mí ugú. You are a thief.	
	Dɛŋgó-ri 'bá-àta. Dengo is a foreigner.	
	Dɛŋgó-ri Mòrúgó. Dengo is a Moru.	
MADI { Lo.:	ny(í) ógu nyi.	} You are a thief. (Note repetition of
{ Pa.:	ny(í) ógù-ŋga-lɛ nyì.	pronoun for emphasis.)
MADI (Torit):	ani 'ba eŋgwere'e.	He is a white man.
	ma-ru Kofi.	My name is Kofi.
KELIKO:	iri gilya-go.	He is a white man.

712. When the noun complement is followed by a postposition, the predicative construction may indicate possession.

MORU:	ánya äzú bè.	He has a spear (lit. He spear with).
	má mànyèrù bɛ.	I have scabies.
	má dr(ì)-ù'bá bɛ.	I have a headache.
	má yá-lú bè.	I have a stomach-ache.

PREDICATIVE CONSTRUCTIONS

    LOGO: *miri tie **be***.   The chief has cattle.
          *ŋga ma-drɪka **be***.   I have food (at home).
          *ta-tisile ɖi **be**?* (Mk. xii. 16.) Whose is the superscription?
    KELIKO: *opi-ri jo **be** ambogo*. ⎫ The chief has a big house.
    MADI (Torit): *opi **dri** zo ambugore'e.* ⎭ (lit. to the chief is a big house).

It may also indicate condition (i.e. possession of certain attributes).

    MADI ⎧ Lo.: *bárá 'dii andí **trɔ̀**.* ⎫ These boys are dirty. (andi = earth.)
           ⎩ Pa.: *'borá 'di andí **tɔ**.* ⎭
    MORU: *anya ya iɖwe **si***. He is glad (i.e. with cool belly).
    LOGO: *ama-ata irinyi **be***. My father is strong. (irinyi = strength.)

It may also indicate place.

    MORU: *Ago andivo ndaro regwo zevo **ya***. (Mk. iv. 38.) And he was in the hinder part of the ship.
    MADI ⎧ Torit: *anyokwa ambu ayi **a**.* ⎫ Plenty of animals are in the bush.
           ⎩ Opari: *ayi **a** anyokwa kareako.* ⎭
    LOGO: *Ama ata amvu **na***.   My father is in the field.
    KELIKO: *aria-ri pɛtɛ **sigɛ***.   Birds are on a tree.
          *ma-tɛpi-ri amvu **ge***. My father is on the farm.
          *oku-ri jo **aga***.   The woman is in the house.
          *anziriŋa-ri jo **ogaroga***. The children are behind the house.

B. *With qualificative complement.*

713. The complement may be an adjective or qualificative pronoun.

    LOGO: *fa niɖi **mana***. This stick is mine.   *niɖi **aɖiaɖia***. This is his.
         *fa nii **amakia***. These sticks are ours. *nii **aiikia ɖii***. These are theirs.

         What (thing) is this? (Mk. i. 27.)
         MORU: *'Do **oɖu** ya?*
         LOGO: *Niɖi **aɖo** ya?*
         LUGBARA: *'Di **aɖi** ya?*
         MADI (Pa.): *Ta ɖi **aɖo** ya?*

         MORU: ***aɖi-ro** ya?*   Whose (is it)?
         LUGBARA: *yi **aɖi-ni** ya?* Whose are they?

    Whose house is this?   *It is my grandfather's house.*
    MORU: *zo ono **aɖi-ro** ya?*   *zo ti'bi maro-ro.*
    KELIKO: *zo ɖi **aɖi-veni**?*   *ɛri ma-a'bipi-ri jo.*

714. An adjective complement may have almost any of the forms already discussed in the previous chapter.

    MORU: *bɔ̀ŋgó **wäṛi***. The cloth is clean.
          *ny-έdɛ bɔŋgó **wäṛi***. Clean the cloth (lit. make the cloth clean).
          *m-έdɛ bɔŋgó tè **wäṛi***. I cleaned the cloth.
          *Tana **k-iɖwi**.* (Jn. xviii. 18.) For it was cold.
          *Tana ama **du**.* (Mk. v. 9.) For we are many.
          *Mi-zi ma **kadu** o'duta ya?* (Lk. xviii. 19.) Why callest thou me good?
          *zo opi ro **ɖäsi***. The chief has a big house (lit. house chief of big).
          *zo opi ro **su***. The chief has four houses.

M.: äzú ɔnɔ **k-àtswa.** } This spear is long.
Ä.: äzú n(i) **àtswa.**
Ä.: lägú **àndi**; awóŋgo **ɔ̀nzi.** Laughing is good; crying is bad.
W.: ŋgá-lɛ **l-àndɪ.** Loving is good.
'B.: ání-andi **dɔ́** ya? Are you (lit. is your body) well?
ám-andi **dɔ́.** I am well.

AVUKAYA: má **dɔ́.**
mǎ **su-pé.**[1] } I am good.   ɔdzíla nɔ̀ **dɔ́.**
ɔdzíla nɔ̀ **su-pɛ.** } That man is good.
kúmu àmáka **dɔ̇.** Our chief is good.
Jl.: ɔkó kúmú kǎ **làzɨ̀làzɨ̀.**
Jg.: ɔkó kúmú kǎ **àzɨ̀làzɨ̀.** } The wife of the chief is ill.

LUGBARA: ɔkú mɔ̀kɔ̀tɔ̀ rú-'bǎ **ɔ̀ndzi.** The wife of the chief (body) is ill.
u'dú ubogu bɛ kó-r(i) **ùndʒɪ.** The leopard and the hyena (they) are bad.

MADI (Torit): *opi dri zo **su.*** The chief has four houses (lit. to chief four houses).
*na-a-re-e **ambago-dro.*** }
KELIKO: *ďir(i) alo **ambogo.*** } That one is big.

MADI (Pa.): *Aďosi ama **amgbu.*** (Mk. v. 9.) For we are many.
*mili ani **loso.*** (Mk. ix. 50.) Salt (it) is good.
*Asi Kerode dri **anya-ndro.*** (Mk. vi. 26.) The heart of Herod was grieved.

LOGO: *ami-mi **tani.*** You are clever (lit. your eyes good).
*liwa **muruŋgu** ya? aiya, aďi **muruŋgu.*** Is the elephant big? Yes, it is big.

Laughing is good; crying is bad.
LOGO: aríá **dɔ́**; awóŋgo **ɔ̀ndʒi.**
LUGBARA: agú-ŋa **múkɛ́-dɨ̀**; aá **ùnzi.**
KELIKO: ogú-ŋgárá **anyí-sì**; aáŋgɔ **ɔ̀nzi.**

	My arm is long.	His hair is white.	The salt is finished.
MORU:	dri maro **kaca.**	drikiri ndaro **nje-te.**	täi **ce-te.**
KELIKO:	ma-dri **aco.**	eri ve dri'bi-ri **imve.**	azi-ri **dɛ-gi.**
MADI:	ma-dri **azo.**	dri'bi-na **eŋgwe.**	ai **oko-ra.**

		That man is good.	The food is bad.
MADI	Lo.:	ma'dí nàɪ **lɔ̀sɔ.**	lényá **undzi.**
	Pa.:	mo'dí náná **nɔ̀sɔ.**	lényá **indʒwi.**
LUGBARA:		'bá 'dà-rɨ **mukɛ.**	ínya-rí **ùndʒi.**
KELIKO:		'bá 'dà-rɨ **anyí-sì.**	ísá-rɪ **ùndʒi.**

		Man is mortal.	God is immortal.
MADI	Lo.:	madí **drà-rɛ-rɨ̀-'ɪ.**	Rubaŋga **drà-rɛ-kù-rɪ-'ɪ.**
	Pa.:	mo'dí **dà-rɛ-rɨ̀-'ɪ.**	Lubaŋa **dà-rɛ-ku-rɪ-'ɪ.**
LUGBARA:		'bá **drà-la-ra.**	
KELIKO:		'bá-rɪ **drà-ra.**	

---

[1] Probably a verbal construction with postposition **pɛ**.

PREDICATIVE CONSTRUCTIONS

715. In LULU'BA there is no formal difference between a predicative adjective and an intransitive verb in its relation to its antecedent,[1] and the auxiliary particle k- is used for the third person.

    LULU'BA: m-əlíndʒwe. I am bad.   mí-n-ɔlíndʒwe. You are bad.
    mo'dí lέ-ní **k-ólíndʒwe.** That man is bad.
    léti **k-ólàli.** The road is short (or a short road).
    léti **k-ólàzɔ.** The road is long (or a long road).

C. *With adverbial complement.* (See also § 712 for 'place'.)

716.   *Where is your father?*   *His house is there.*
    MORU: *täpi miro gaŋwaro ya?*   *zo anyaro lau.*
    KELIKO: *mi-atepi-ri ŋga?*   *ɛri ve jo-ri ɖa.*
    MADI {Torit: *ny-ata iŋgwa ya?*   *zo-na naɖe.*
           {Opari: *ny-ata iŋgole?*   *zo anidri naa.*

ii. LINKING PARTICLES
a, ni, ndi

717. In many dialects a linking particle, similar to that in use in one of the genitive constructions (see § 269) intervenes between the predicative and its antecedent.

A. *With noun complement* (a) (ni).

    MORU: mí **a** Zánde yà? Are you a Zande?
    MADI {Lo.: Dɛŋgó **ni** dʒúrúgo. } Dengo is a foreigner.
           {Pa.: Dɛŋgó **ni** dʒurugo-i.}

B. *With adjective complement* (ni) (ndi).

    Loving is good.   M.: *mano-ɖo **ni** kado.* This is a good (man).
      M.: ŋgă-lu **ni** kàdo.   M.: *täyi **ni** kadu.* (Mk. ix. 50.) Salt is good.
MORU {L., K.: ŋgó-lɛ **ni** kàdo.   M.: *mɪ **ndi** kado(ro) ya?* Are you well?
      Jl.: ŋgá-lɛ **n(i)** àndɪrɔ.   M.: *ma **ndi** kado-ro.* I am well.
                                  M.: *adravo maro **ndi** kozi-ro.* My sickness is bad.

    The wife of our chief (her body) is sick.
    LOGO: tokwá mɔ̀kɔ̀tɔ̀ rú-'bá **ni** kɔ̀ndzi.
    KELIKO: mɔkɔtɔ okú rú-'bá **ni** ɔ̀ndzi.

iii. PREDICATIVE SUFFIXES

718. There are two predicative suffixes, **-i** and **-ro**. The former is used mostly with noun or pronoun complements and the latter mostly with adjective complements.

-i (-ɨ, -è)

A. *With noun or pronoun complements.*

719. This suffix offers considerable difficulty to the investigator because of its resemblance to the plural suffix (§ 191), and because it is hard to hear before the

---

[1] Note, however, that predicative adjectives have not the same range of tense forms as verbs, and that verbs cannot be used attributively in the same way as adjectives.

interrogative particle **ya**. It follows the complement, whether the latter be a single word or a phrase, but apparently may be omitted at will, in which case predication is effected by juxtaposition alone. Examples:

MORU: *ónó kitipárá-i yà?* Is this a stool. *má lédrì-í.* I am a man.
Ayílè àtra-i. Ayile is a foreigner. *anya ämgba-i.* He is a white man.
ánya Mòrɔ-ì. He is a Moru. *anyá Mòrɔ-ì.* They are Moru.
AVUKAYA: *má Odzíliwá-ì.* I am an Avukaya. *ama Odzíliwá-ì.* We are Avukaya.
gúlɔ nɔ lédr ònzí-'i. That man is a bad man.
KELIKO: *Dɛŋgó-ri 'bá-àtra(-i).* Dengo is a foreigner. *Dɛŋgó-ri Mòrú-i.* Dengo is a Moru.
mi-ru aďi-i? What is your name? *ma-ru Kofi-i.* My name is Kofi.
LOGO: *niďi kiti-e ya?* Is this a chair? *kiti-e.* It is a chair.
aďi toka-le-pi-ďi-e. He is a smith. *aii toka-le-pi-ďi-e.* They are smiths.
ma ago-e. I am a man.
MADI: *ny-a-ru aďi-i ya?* What is your name? *ma-ru Kofi-e.* My name is Kofi.
zo ďii aďi-i dri ya? Whose house is this? *zo m-ata dri-e.* It is my father's.
LUGBARA: *mi 'ba emu-pi mi-i?*
mi-i mi 'ba emu-pi-ri? } Art thou he that should come?

Compare:

		I am a Miza, &c.	*You are a thief.*
MORU	M.:	má Míza-í.	mí kugú-i.
	Ă.:	má Moroǎndrí-ì.	mí kugú-i.
AVUKAYA	Jl.:	má Odzílà(wá)-ì	ni ugú-i.
	Jg.:	má Ädzígù-ɪ.	mí ugù-'i.
LOGO		má Lógù-(y)e.	mí kugú-ru.
KELIKO		má Ma'dí-î.	mí ugú-ì.
LUGBARA		má Lúgbàr-ì.[1]	mí ugú.
LULU'BA		má Olu'bogo.	mí ogú-'i.
MADI		má Ma'dí.	ny(i) ógu nyi.

		Who are you?	*I am So-and-so.*	*I'm the son of So-and-so.*
MADI	Lo.:		má Lúgumà-'ɪ.	ma bara Ámólí drí-ɪ.
	Pa.:		má Oyúru-i.	ma 'bórá Sùmein dɪ-'ɪ.
				ma Súméin 'bora-ì.
AVUKAYA		mí a'dú-í yà?		
LOGO		mí a'dí-í yà?		
KELIKO		mí a'dí yà?	má Ayílè-i.	má Álúma mvá(-ì).
LUGBARA		mí a'dí yà?	má Arábà-i.	má Gbágbé ŋgoti.

	Who is there?	*I am.*	*Is it I?* (Mk. xiv. 19).	*It is I* (Mt. xiv. 27).
MADI (Lo.):	a'di ina?	ma-'ɪ.	(Pa.): *Ani ma-i?*	
LUGBARA:	a'di-rɪ 'dá nià?	ma-ɪ.	*Eri ma-i ani?*	ma-i ma do-i.
KELIKO:	a'di-rɪ 'dá nià?	ma-ɪ.	*Ma-e ya?*	ma-e.

[1] Or má Lúgbàrà-nî.

PREDICATIVE CONSTRUCTIONS

720. This suffix is also used to emphasize a noun in a given sentence. Compare the following two examples in LOGO:

mi-adre aɖo o ya? ma-i-dre mondo. And:
mi-adre aɖo i ya? ma-i-dre mondo-i.

The translations of the above are respectively:
'What are you doing?' 'I'm grinding grain.' And:
'What are you *grinding*?' 'I'm grinding *grain*' (not maize).

Further examples:

LOGO:	*ma-nya-dre ŋga-e.*	I was eating *food* (at the moment of speaking).
	zi tudru-e jiɖa be.	He called the bull-frog and the kicking-frog.
	ma-si ama-jo-e.	I'm building my house.
MADI { Lo.:	(m)á-lɛ mata-'ɪ. }	I love my father.
Pa.:	má-lɛ mata-'ɪ. }	
Lo.:	*nyí-'ɪ nyi-mu.*	*You* are going.

721. It often occurs after verbs of calling.

They call me So-and-so.

MADI { Lo.:	adi moŋgwe Lúgumà-ɪ.
Pa.:	úluŋgwé ma Äyurù.
LUGBARA:	zi-kí mà Araba-i.
KELIKO:	zi-kí ma Ayɛ́lɛ̀.
MORU:	ází ma Dɛŋgò.

B. *With adjective complement.*

722. Adjectives are very rarely found with the predicative suffix **-i**.

AVUKAYA: *latítrí ɔ̀nzí-'i.* Cursing is bad.
MORU ('B.): *lédr 'di pè-i-rɔ.* That man is good (or a good man).
LOGO: *'Dia alo tani-e.* (Mt. xix. 17.) One only is good.

ro or ru (= body)

A. *With noun (or verbal noun) complement.*

723. This suffix is much used in predicatives indicating condition, state, or similarity.

MORU: *bòŋgó ndi-rù.* The cloth is dirty. (ndi = earth.)
bòŋgó gi-ro. The cloth is wet. (gi = water.)
má kɪlá-rə ndá bɛ. I am angry with him. (kɪlá = war.)
ɔkɔ́ ɔ́pí rɔ àdra-vù-rɔ. The wife of the chief is sick. (àdra-vù = sickness, lit. death-place.)
nya-kanda ma ku ägbibi-ro. Don't shake me like an earthquake.
. . . kode mataza-ro te ini ro, kode mataza-ro te kitoni ro. . . . either as a prisoner of the snake, or as a prisoner of the scorpion. (Folktale.)

LOGO: *ma-adrupi adre dra-ro.* My brother is sick.
aɖi konji ako-ro. He is without badness.
ma komba-ro mi-dre. I am angry with you.
Yesu Kristo asi-dre anji-ro. Jesus Christ came down as a baby.
ami-lasu ŋgoro (<*ŋga-ro* 'thing') *ami-andre lasu tini.* Your appearance is like your mother's appearance.
mí kugú-ru. You are a thief.

He is not dead; he is still alive.
MORU: dra ku; drì lédri-rə. (lédri = person.)
LUGBARA: írí drà ku; ırı drì ídı-ru.
KELIKO: érí drà kuɛ; ırı ídrı-ru.

KELIKO: *mi ve boŋgo-ri iyi-ru.*   Your clothes are wet.
mi ve pa-ri indi-ru.   Your feet are dirty.

724. It also occurs after verbs of making and becoming:
LOGO: *adi mba ago-ro.* He grew into a man.
dre go-zo adre-le fa-ro. (Mt. xiii. 32) (and becometh a tree).

I will make you to become fishers of men. (Mk. i. 17.)
LOGO: *ma-ka-la-ro ami dia-be-le-pi-di-i-ro.*
LUGBARA: *Ma-ŋga emi 'ba obi 'ba-'ba-oko-pi-ri-ro.*
MORU: á'ba ndá te ópí-ró lédrı drì. He was made chief over the people.
méndzwe bòŋgó te ùndi-ru. I made (lit. spoilt) the cloth dirty.
ndi ko'ba adu-go toko-ro mui ri. So the Jackal became wife to the Hyena.

B. *With adjective complement.*

725. In LOGO the predicative adjective nearly always ends in **-ro**. In MORU and LUGBARA **-ro** is often used, but, as has already been seen in §§ 696 et seq., it is not confined to predicative forms. In the other languages **-ro** does not appear.

LOGO: *adi täli-ro.* He is short.
adi tovo-ro. He is lazy.
adi adre adi-mise konji-ro. He seemed bad to him.
MORU: *'bugʊ á'dó-tɛ ɔkȧ-rɔ́.* The bananas have turned red.
ópí àmarɔ mbara-rɔ. Our chief is strong.
ago anya nyagworaŋwa-ro. (Lk. xix. 3.) For he was little of stature.
opi kozi-ro. The chief is bad.
drikiri maro uni-ro. My hair is black.
kari oka-ro. Blood is red.
kowa ratara-ro. Bone is hard.
gi idwi-ro. The water is cold.
gi eme-ro. The water is hot. (Cf. *eme* = to heat.)

	The road is narrow.	Cutting things is bad.
MORU { M.:	líti tswàrè-ŋwa.	ŋgó-ɔ̀lɔ̀là kòzi-**ro**.
Ä.:	pavʊ tsware-va-**ro**.	ŋgó-alɔlɔ ɔ̀nzi-**ro**.
'B.:	pavʊ tswàrì-ŋgwa-rà.	

	This man is good;	that man is bad.
MORU { M.:	lédr 'dó kàdɔ;	lédr aná kʷɔ̀ⁱ-zi.
Ä.:	lédr 'dí àndi-rə;	lédr aná ɔ̀nzi-rə.
'B.:	lédr 'dí àndi-rə;	lédr ena'di kòzi-**ro**.

LUGBARA: *mokoto amaní kpǎ-rù.* Our chief is strong.
econi mini dri'bi efi alo obizaro ko, kani emve-ro kani ini-ro. (Mt. v. 36.)
Thou canst not make one hair white or black.
mva co-ra, orindi erini eca okpo-ro. (Lk. i. 80.) The child grew and (he) waxed strong.

iv. Verbs 'to be'

726. In all languages there are specific verbs 'to be'; although constructions with these verbs often stand as alternatives to the constructions already mentioned, the primary function of these verbs is to indicate *existential predication*, 'to be somewhere' rather than 'to be something'.

a (or ci) MADI, au MORU

727. Used mostly in existential predication.

MADI: *azeni waraga ga ma-a* (or *-ci*). Yesterday I was in the school.
ma-dri endri tou aa (or *be* or *ci*). I have five goats. (By me goats five are.)
MORU: *à'di* **l-au** *ya?* *ma-a*ú. Who is there? I am.
ma ni au ya? (Mk. xiv. 19.) Is it I? *Ono ma-au.* (Jn. vi. 20.) It is I.
gi alo ɖi ni wutedrieri ya . . . au. (Mk. xiv. 20.) It is one of the twelve.

But note:
mi aɖi ya? ma Matindi au? Who are you? I'm Matindi.
ma opi Ndarago au. I am chief Ndarago.
K.: *au ɖi.* That's right.

alú, ǝlú MADI

728. This verb is used only in existential predication.

MADI (Lo.): *obo nyi-alú bàru ya?*	To-morrow will you be at home?
búk ǝlú sanduk-'a.	The book is in the box.
Lo.: *ódrà kù-ru; adri ǝ̀lǝ lídri.*	He is not dead; he is still alive (lit. a
Pa.: *da kú-ru; ǝlú lídɪ.*	person).
Torit: *arendzi kolo kwe dri.*	Birds are on a tree.
m-ata kolo ganyi a.	My father is in the town.
oko olo zo ga.	The woman is in the house.
'borondzi olo jo mboro ga.	The children are behind the house.
Opari: *'borondzi olo zo a maraga.*	

be

729. In LOGO *be* has an existential function.

LOGO: *ama-andre be jo na.* My mother is in the house.
ti be ama-drika. I have a cow (lit. cow stays by us).
ŋga be ya? Is there any food? *ŋga be.* There is.
ŋga be mi-drɪka ya? Have you food? *ŋga be.* I have.

In MORU *be* is used impersonally in sentences like the following:

be *mǎ-rí giní ǝ̀sǝ-nɪ.* I must hoe the ground (lit. it is to me the ground to hoe).
be *ányä-ri giní ǝ̀sǝ-nɪ.* He must hoe the ground.
bé *giní ǝ̀sǝ-nɪ.* The ground must be hoed.

Note also in MORU:
ma-be noŋa. Here I am.
zo maro be ono. My house is here.
MADI: *nyi-dri au azia be* (or *ci* or *aa*). You have six fowls (lit. by you fowls six exist).

730.   **bo** MORU

'Di-aza alo ni ku Ŋgwa **bo** *aḋi ya.* (Lk. x. 22.) No man knoweth who the Son is.

dre, adre LOGO; edre MADI; adri LUGBARA

731. This form of verb to be, which is mostly to be found in LOGO, is used for all forms of predication.[1]

Existential function.

Mataya niḋi kicoa **adre-le** *ko.* (Mk. iii. 24.) That kingdom cannot stand (lit. exist).

k-adre nitini kitu na etu ḋi. (Mk. 1. 9.) It came to pass in those days (lit. it was thus in those days).

k-adre nitini kezia bi **adre-ki** *ŋga nya.* (Mk. v. 11.) Lit. It was thus pigs many were food eating.

Ami-ŋga vo-ni a mi-dre-le-le-ḋi **dre adre-le** *ḋise, ami-togo* **k-adre** *indi.* (Mt. vi. 21.) For where your treasure is (lit. your things' place which you love), there will your heart be also.

ama-ata (**adre**) *amvu na.* My father is in the field.

ama-andre **adre** *jo na.* My mother is in the house.

LUGBARA: drusi **médrɪ** 'bòru?
KELIKO: dru mí-**adri** 'bàru?   } To-morrow will you be at home?

Other functions.

   A. With noun complement.

      LOGO: *aii dre* **adre-le** *kosia-belepiḋiiro ḋise.* (Mk. i. 16.) For they were fishers.

            dre gozo **adre-le** *faro.* (Mt. xiii. 32) (and becometh a tree).

            miri **adre** *tie be.* The chief has cattle.

            amaandre **adre** *irinyi-aku.* My mother is weak (without strength).

            amaata (**adre**) *irinyi-be.* My father is strong.

   B. With adjective complement.

      LOGO: *mì-***adre-***le-pi konjiḋi.* (Mt. vii. 11.) Ye being evil.

            ma-adre lenzele mi-a we. (Mk. i. 11.) I am very pleased with thee.

            mà-dre **adre-le** *bi ḋise.* (Mk. v. 9.) For we are many.

            male ḋia bi aḋea kogo **adre-le** *yokoḋo.* (Mt. xxiv. 12.) The love of many shall wax cold.

            amimi adre konji, ma-dre **adre-le** *tani ḋise ya?* (Mt. xx. 15.) Is thine eye evil because I am good.

            midre kicoale dri'bi aloḋi ole **adre-le** *kemve ko ḋise, kini ko ḋise.* (Mt. v. 36.) Thou canst not make one hair white or black.

      KELIKO: *ibi-ri* **adri** *kuni.* The leaf is green.

gi MORU

732. This verb is only used in emphatic sentences.

    *mi-***gi** *aḋi ya?* Just who are you?

    ma-le **gi** *alo täyi (ayan).* I want only salt (lit. I want it is one salt indeed).

---

[1] The function of **dre** as a verbal auxiliary has already been discussed (§ 484).

ə-rɪ (to stay) MORU

733. This verb, which in predicative sentences is usually found in its 'participial' form ərɪ-via (ərɪ-vəya), is never used for other than existential predication.

*eza amba **ori-via** coa ya.* Plenty of animals are in the bush.
*kiano ledri **ori-via** nɔŋa, oko yau-ono dra-te cini.* Once there were people here, but now they are all dead.
ərí-vɪá yà? Is he here?
ŋgó-inyà ərí-vɪá ya? Is there (any) food?
'dí-azá ərí-vɪá láu ya? Is any one there?
M.: *ma ərí-vɪá nono.* } I am here.
Ä.: *ma ərí-vəyà* nɪa. }
*oko vo driba **ori-via**.* (Lk. xiv. 22.) And yet there is room.

Note:

*'Bädri se ana ni **ori** ku.* (Mk. iii. 24.) That kingdom cannot stand (lit. kingdom which that knows staying not).

Predicative of possession:

*Matindi **ori-via** ŋgwa be ya?* } Has Matindi any children?
*ŋgwa Matindi ro **ori-via** ya?* }
*parata Ayaŋwa ri **ori-via**.* Ayangwa has some money.

ovu LUGBARA

734. This verb may be used in all forms of predication.

Existential function.

*Econi suru ďini **ovu-zaro** ko.* (Mk. iii. 24.) Lit. Can kingdom that exist not.
*Eri ŋga **ovu** etu ďi si.* (Mk. i. 9.) It was (i.e. came to pass) days those in.
*Curuďo ezo karakarao **ovu** iribi nyaria va oni tia ogogo.* (Mk. v. 11.) Lit. Now pigs many were eating there the hill near.
*Afa mini pari **ovu-ria** asi mini eri **ovu** ďale.* (Mt. vi. 21.) Lit. Things your where are heart your it is there.
*Erini, eri **ovu** oďua oguru etia vile.* (Mk. iv. 38.) Lit. He, he was asleep the boat at the back.
*te ŋga ti pari **ovu-zu-ri** ace indi.* (Lk. xiv. 22) (and yet there is room).

Other functions:

A. *With noun complement.*

*Yi **ovu** 'ba-e'bi-okpo-pi-ri.* (Mk. i. 16.) They were fishers.
*azini eri **ovu** 'ba onzi-ni* (Lk. vii. 39) (for she is a sinner).
*eri **ovu** pati* (Mt. xiii. 32) ([it] becometh a tree).
*Oni ďi yi isu **ovu** oni mbili ambo ri.* (Mt. xxi. 42.) The same (stone) is become the head of the corner.
*Eri **ovu** daimoni be eri ma alia.* (Lk. vii. 33.) He hath a devil (lit. he is with a devil inside him).
*'Ba dri-le baro **ovu-pi** asi alio-ro be ri.* (Mt. v. 3.) Blessed be the poor in spirit (lit. people be blessed who are hearts sad with).
*Opi ŋga ani **ovu** candi si ambo.* (Mk. vi. 26.) Now the king was very sorry (lit. with great sorrow).
*e'bi gakandia-ro **ovu** yi-dri, were indi.* (Mk. viii. 7.) They had a few small fishes (lit. fish small were to them, few also).

B. *With adjective complement.*

Ama-ni **ovu-le** *obi-ro risi.* (Mk. v. 9.) For we are many.
aiiniri eri **ovu** *onyi-ro.* (Mk. ix. 50.) Salt (it) is good.
Awa fo mi-le mi-ni **ovu** *onzi ma-ni* **ovu-le** *onyi-ro risi ya?* (Mt. xx. 15.) Is thine eye evil because I am good?
Eri-ni **ovu-le** *aliŋa-ro risi.* (Lk. xix. 3.) For he was little of stature.
Eri **ovu** *gaŋa-ro ori azini dria aga erira.* (Mt. xiii. 32.) Which indeed is the least of all seeds.
'Ba azini indi dri erini **ovu** *ondri-za-ro.* (Mk. iii. 1.) There was a certain man there whose hand was withered.
le-za 'ba kakao eri ŋga **ovu** *koza-ro.* (Mt. xxiv. 12.) The love of many (people) (it) shall wax cold.

te (to stay)

735. This verb is used mostly in MORU with an adjective complement.

Existential function.

MORU: *Ago tu se kai si aḍu* **te** *inye.* (Mk. i. 9.) Now in those days it was thus.
MADI (Opari): *emukararee eri aḍi* **te**. Only two came (lit. those-who-came two there were).

With pronoun complement.

LUGBARA: *'Di* **te** *aḍi ya?* (Mk. iv. 41.) What manner of man is this?

With adjectival complement.

MORU: má-**te** kàdu. I am well.
   *ma-**te** kado ta miro si.* (Mk. i. 11.) I am pleased with thy affairs.
   ánya **te** mòyù-ru. He is poor.
   *ma-**te** moi-ru.* I am poor (or sad).
   *ondro kadu ami-**te** mi-aku.* (Jn. ix. 41.) If ye were blind.
   ami se **te** *kozi ono.* (Lk. xi. 13.) Ye being evil.
   *emba ka-**te** onje.* The moon is shining (i.e. white).

NEGATIVE PREDICATION.

736. On the whole there is a sharp distinction drawn in negation between the existential and non-existential aspects of predication. If the existence of an object in a given place is to be denied, the negative form is **i'du (iyo,** &c.). Otherwise the negative particle is **ku**.

i'du, iyo

737. This word may stand alone as a complete predicate, or it may follow the subject.

MORU: 'ɔrí-vɪá yà?' 'í'dú'. 'Is he here?' 'No'.
   'dí-azá **í'dú** nòa. Nobody is here (lit. other one absent here).
   Askeri **iḍu** *noŋa ya? Askeri* **iḍu**. Is there no policeman there? No.
MADI: *Azeni waraga ga ma* **iyo**. Yesterday I was not in the school.
LUGBARA and KELIKO: gɛ́-'da **yò** = no! (in answer to questions like 'Is he here?' 'Will you be at home to-morrow?', &c.)

There is no food.
LUGBARA: ŋga-nya 'da **yɔ̀**.
KELIKO: ŋga-nya **yɔ**.
LOGO: ŋga **yo**.

PREDICATIVE CONSTRUCTIONS

Note also (cf. § 531):

MORU: ɔnyá-ní mǎ-rí **i'du**. I shall not eat it (lit. eating to me not).
ɛmé-ní mí-rí **i'du**. You shall not boil it.
oi-nɪ Maridi ya **iɖu** mä-ri. I shall not go to Maridi.

738. Predicative of non-possession:

MORU: ŋgoinya **iɖu** toko ri. The woman has no food (lit. food not to the woman).
parata **iɖu** mi-ri (lit. money not to you). } You have no money.
parata miro **iɖu** (lit. money your not). }
LOGO: ti **yokoɖo** ama-drika. I have no cattle (at home) (lit. cattle not us by).
Logo ni ti **yokoɖo**. The Logo has no cattle (lit. Logo's cattle not).
ami-ta-nini **yokoɖo**. You are stupid (your knowledge is lacking).
ŋga ma-drɪka **yo**. } I have no food.
ŋga **yo**. }
LUGBARA: nyaku alenia ambo-ro **yo**. (Mk. iv. 5.) Lit. earth in it much not.
MADI (Pa.): vo enyaku amgbu **yo**. (Mk. iv. 5.) Where it had not much earth (lit. place earth much not).
Baritimao mi **iyo**. (Mk. x. 46.) Blind Bartimaeus.

739. Occasionally this particle is used in predicatives of a non-existential nature, where it alternates in function with **ku**.

MORU: ma idʒíliwá **i'du**. I am not an Avukaya.
ädrupi maro adravo-ro **iɖu**. My brother is not ill.
KELIKO: ɖipa tre **yo**. They are not many.

ku, ko

740. The negative particle **ku** may either precede (as in MORU) or follow (as in other languages) the complement. The predicative suffix **i** is sometimes heard and sometimes not. The linking particles are never heard.

A. With noun complement.

MORU: má **kó** Zándè-i. I am not a Zande.
ɔ́nɔ́ **kʊ** kitikpárá-i, ɔnɔ gíti-i. It is not a stool, it is a chair.
má **ku** ('di-)tɔkɔ́-ì. I am not a woman.
má **kú** kugú-i. I am not a thief.
AVUKAYA: má Makaraka-i kə-'dá. I am not a Zande.
mǎ ogú-i **ko**. I am not a thief.
MADI: ma Madi **ko**. I am not a Madi.
LULU'BA: mó ogú **ku**. I am not a thief.
LOGO: má kugú-i **kɔ**. I am not a thief.
kiti-e **ko**. It is not a chair.
ma toko-e **ko**. I am not a woman.
ago naɖi ru-fu-le-pi-ɖi-e **ko**. That man is not a warrior.
ago konae ru-fu-le-pi-ɖi-e **ko**. Those men are not warriors.
naɖi ago-e **ko**, aɖi toko-e. That is not a man, it is a woman.
konae ago-e **ko**, aii toko-e. Those are not men, they are women.

B. With adjective complement.

MORU (Ä.): má kʋ ɔndzí-rɔ́. I am not bad.
  (M.): ma ku kado-ro. I am not well.
AVUKAYA: má sú kú ('da). I am not good.
  àwɔ sú ko. Crying is bad (i.e. not good).
LOGO: awóŋgɔ sú kɔ̀. Crying is not good.
  yi ve ko. The water is not hot.
  adi tovo-ro ko. He is not lazy.
  adi konji ko-ro. He is not bad.
  adi muruŋgu ko, adi ca. It is not big, it is small.

LOGO (A.): nini ko andi. This is different (not the same).

MADI ⎰ Lo.: nyí lɔsó ko. You are not good.
     ⎱ Lo.: má ɔndzí ko. ⎱ I am not bad.
       Pa.: má indʒwí ko. ⎰
LULU'BA: mí ndʒwé-na ku, mí osú-na. You are not bad, you are good.

    I am not bad;   *you are not good.*
  LUGBARA: má ɔdʒí kʋ; mi múké kʋ.
  KELIKO: má ɔdʒí kʋ; mi múké kʋ.

  This banana is not big. *This iron is not hot.*
MORU: kogo ono ku däsi. logo ono ku eme-ro.
KELIKO: a'bogo dir(i) adri ambogo ko. aya dir(i) adri asiasi ku.
MADI (Opari): rabolo dii nza ko.

  This is my rice; it is not yours. *They are not many.*
MORU: ono ruzu maro; ku miro. ànya ku amba.
KELIKO: diri ma-mofuŋga; adri mini ku. dipa trɛ yo.
MADI (Torit): dii rusu madri; dii anyidri ko. ae kareako ko.

Where it had not much earth (Mk. iv. 5.)
  MORU: gini na ŋgi ku amba.
  LOGO: kini vo na mi we ko.

aku

741. When the complement is followed by the postposition **aku**, the predicative construction may indicate non-possession. (Note that the form **i'du** may also function in such sentences.)

MORU: *kiano ledri Moro-ro boŋgo aku, oko yau-ono ndaka boŋgo be.* Once the Moru people had no clothes, but now they have clothes.
MADI: *opi boronzi ako.* The chief has no sons.
LOGO: *ma-adre ŋganya ako-ro.* I am without food.
  adi konji ako-ro. He is without sin.

Note the number of adjectives formed with **aku** or **iyo**:

LOGO: *mi-ako-di* (blind); *irinyi-aku* (weak).
MADI (Pa.): *mi-iyo* (blind).

Negation of verbs 'to be'.

742. Where the verb 'to be' is retained in the negative sentence, its form is that found in the negative of any other verb.

MORU: **be** mă-rí **kù** giní ɔ̀sɔ-nɪ. I must not hoe the ground.
bé kú giní ɔ̀sɔ-nɪ. The ground must not be hoed.

LOGO: *kini dre **adre-le** we **ko** d̆ise.* (Mk. iv. 5.) Because it had no depth of earth (lit. earth was much not because).
*kosia **adre** bi **ko**, camva-d̆ii **be**.* (Mk. viii. 7.) They had a few small fishes (lit. fishes were big not, small and).

LUGBARA: *Emi-asi **ovu** ruru-ro eyo drusi **ko**.* (Mt. vi. 34.) Take therefore no thought for the morrow (lit. your hearts be worried things to-morrow not).

	I am not a Zande.	*I am not a thief.*
LOGO:	má-**ádrí** Mákáráká-ɪ kə.	
KELIKO:	má-**ádrɛ̀** Màdzɛndɛ kù.	má-**àdɛ̀** ugú-i kò.
LUGBARA:	má-**drɛ** Makárágá ko.	má-**drɛ** ùgú **ku**.
AVUKAYA { Jl.:	má-**á'dú** Makaraka-ì kə.	
Jg.:	má-**a'dó** Makaraka-ì kə.	

THE PREDICATIVE OF COMPARISON

743. There is no 'comparative' or 'superlative' in adjectives, but there are certain constructions whereby equality or superiority may be shown. This is usually obtained by the combined use of certain adjectives or verbs with certain postpositions.

MORU: *lidi miro ame-ro **oso** lidi maro **ronye**.* Your soup is as hot as my soup (lit. soup yours hot like soup mine thus).
*ma-le paleti märi **ojo** paleti Ayaŋwa ro **be rere**.* I want a reward for me equal to the reward of Ayangwa.
*iɽi maro kado **para**[1] (ni) ono **dri-si**.* My knife is better than that one (lit. knife mine good first that from).
*Maridi id̆wi-ro **ndra** Amadi **dri-si**.* Maridi is colder than Amadi (lit. Maridi cold great Amadi from).
*manod̆o kozi **para**.* That man is very bad.
*eza aruwa ro (kado) **para**.* Hippo meat is the best.
zo miro d̆äsi, zo maro giɽiŋwa. Your house is bigger than mine (lit. house yours big, house mine small).
*mi-omba anyaro **levu** (mi-omba) ledri (ro) cini.* His cunning excels (the cunning of) all people.
*ndrwa anyaro **sa** ku 'bute.* His years are less than ten (lit. have not reached ten).

LOGO: *lo'ba muruŋgu **ŋgoro** lä'bi **tini** ya?* Is a hartebeest as big as a water-buck?
*koko, **amba** lä'bi muruŋgu lo'ba **ruse**.* No, a water-buck is bigger than a hartebeest.
***amba** jo ni maligu minad̆i **ruse**.* This house is bigger than yours.
***amba** läti aŋgod̆i mvu **ni** ya?* Which path is farther?
*kiju si **lavu** keya si.* The white-ant's bite is worse than (i.e. surpasses) the pitching ant's bite.

[1] Para = first.

MADI: *baru opi dri* **onde** *madri ra.* The chief's village is bigger (or better) than mine.
nyi okwo, i-za ma ra. You are stronger than I.
labolo milimili, **oza** *kaata ra.* Bananas are sweeter than potatoes.

Compare:

     And taketh with himself seven other spirits more wicked than himself. (Mt. xii. 45.)
 MORU: *ndi uru tori azakai njidrieri anya be, koizi* **para ni** *andivo anyaro* **ri**.
 LOGO: *dre teri njidriiri* **amba** *i konji-ɖi* **ruse** *ɖii do-zo.*
 LUGBARA: *azini eri oko orindi onzi azini aziri eri-be, yi* **aga** *eri-onzi.* (Mt. xii. 45.)
    eri oko eri-vu orindi azini aziri onzi **aga** *eri-ni* **ra**. (Lk. xi. 26.)

    And the last state of that man is worse than the first. (Mt. xii. 45.)
 MORU: *ago ori ädu manana ro aɖugwo koizi* **para ni** *käti ana* **ri**.
 LOGO: *tai vele-ro ɖise-ɖi ago niɖi go adre-le konji* **amba** *akoɖia tai dri-dri-ɖi* **ruse**.
 LUGBARA: *afa vile 'ba nde eri* **aga** *onzi eyo oko-ri.* (Mt. xii. 45.)
    vile-risi 'ba ɖi-ri eri-mvi onzi **aga** *oko-ri* **ra**. (Lk. xi. 26.)

   The chief's house is bigger than my house. *He has more money than I.*
 MORU: *zo opi ro ɖäsi* **para** *maro drisi.* *parata ndaro* **para** *maro* **ri**.
 KELIKO: *opi ve ja-ri abagu* **aga** *ma-jo.* *iri farata ve trɛ* **aga** *mani.*
 MADI { Torit: *zo opi dri ambagoree* **oza** *madri* **ra**. *anidri pese* **oza** *madri* **ra**.
   { Opari: *zo opi dri* **oza** *madri* **ra**.   ,, ,, ,,

   There is no command greater than these. (Mk. xii. 31.)
 MORU: *Ta driota-ro aza* **para ni** *ɖo ri te iɖu.*
 LOGO: **Amba** *togi azina togi nii* **ruse** *ko.*
 LUGBARA: *Azita azini ɖi-ri* **aga-pi-ri** *yo.*
 MADI (Pa.): *Iyo tsara zi* **za-ka** *laɖi si.*

   It groweth up, and becometh greater than all herbs. (Mk. iv. 32.)
 MORU: *mba-go,* **levu** *ce nyagoraŋwa cini go.*
 LOGO: *dre mba-zo muruŋgu* **amba** *lanya wei ɖii* **ruse**.
 LUGBARA: *eri zo-ra, oconi* **aga** *afa vipi nyiri nyiri ri dria.*
 MADI (Pa.): *ozo amba-ndro ani retu-ndro* **oza** *hwe podru.*

   They had disputed who should be greatest. (Mk. ix. 34.)
 MORU: *ànya pe-i kala go ii-voya ta aɖu-ro* **para**.
 LUGBARA: *Yi ovu te agata ga kini: aɖi* **aga-ri** *yi agyi dri-lia ya?*

   Who is the greatest in the kingdom of heaven. (Mt. xviii. 1.)
 LOGO: **Amba** *aɖi mataya 'bu aɖea na ya?*
 LUGBARA: *Aɖi ŋga ovu* **ambo** *suru 'bu-a-ri* **be** *ni-a?*

   It is the greatest among herbs. (Mt. xiii. 32.)
 LOGO: *adre* **amba** *lanya wei-ɖi* **ruse**.
 LUGBARA: *eri* **aga** *ase dria.*

CHAPTER XXI

REDUPLICATION IN VERBS AND ADJECTIVES

744. Reduplication may be in whole or in part, i.e. a whole word stem (with initial vowel or prefix) may be repeated, or only a part of it.

Reduplication in Verbs

745. The following are instances when reduplication is mostly to be found. Note that the most common form in reduplicated sentences is: subject+verb+object (if any)+verb with characteristic vowel.

Impatient imperative.

MORU:	mi-mu-ri, mi-mu-ri!	Do run!
	mi-ru-ri, mi-ru-ri!	Do catch it!

Imperative with implication: 'Very well, do it!' or 'Do it, of course!'
With characteristic vowel:

MORU:	nyémbɛ-ɛmbɛ	Tie it.
	nyóndzwɪ-ɔndzwɪ.	Untie it.
	mí-la-ɔ́là.	Cut it.
	mí-dzwa-ɔ́dzwà.	Wash it.
	mì-'bɪ-ɔ'bí.	Beat him.
	mí-m(u)-ùmù.	Run (i.e. Don't walk).
LULU'BA:	ovù-r(i) óvû.	Blow away.

Without characteristic vowel:

MORU:	mí-vɔ-vɔ̀.	Beat him.
	mí-si-sì.	Punch him.
KELIKO:	mí-'bà-'bà.	Hide it.

After causative verbs.
Subjunctive form:

MORU:	mí-'ba kumu-úmù.	Make it run.
	mí-'ba ndá kɔnyá-ɔnyà.	Make him eat.
	mí-'ba gí ka-la'di-la'di. ,, kusi-usi.	Make the water boil.

Infinitive form:

	má-'ba ndá turi-ní turì.	I made him fear.
LOGO:	ma-'ba do aga-le agaga.	I put the fat to melt.

In passive constructions.

MORU: má-lìí (tana) á'bi ma ɔ'bì. I'm crying because I'm beaten.
liwa ɔnɔ äfu-äfu? 'ɔ 'ɔ, asu-asu. Was this elephant killed? No, it was found (dead).

In active constructions.

MORU: má-lìí tana täbírí fu mä fu (or ni). I'm crying because hunger kills me.
(AVUKAYA: ... fú mä fù-fù.)
má-tɛ kadó tana má ndá ɔ'bi-ɔ'bì. I'm happy because I've beaten him.
ma te kilaro, tana mi-'bi nda te ɔ'bi. I'm angry because you beat him.

        liwa ono, mɪ-ǎi te uǎi ya? *'ɔ 'ɔ, musu-usu.* This elephant, did you spear it? No, I found it (dead).
        mucu-na nda tata ucu. I'll just chastise him a bit.
        mú-túri ndá tùrì. I fear him.
        mú-turi-turi. I fear it.
LULU'BA: *mɔnd(ɛ)-óndɛ.* I see.
        logár(i) ogà? ewé, mugá-r(i) ogári. Are you chopping? I am.
        ziwá ku, kóŋgoŋgù. Don't bring it here, it smells!
        má mí gbagba. I'll beat you.
LOGO: *ndri lapa mbi-na lapa-lapa.* The goat runs off into the grass.
        za adre ra-le ra-ra. The cattle are running.
LUGBARA: *Te eri osu-osu.* (Lk. v. 9.) For he was astonished.

746. Reduplication is never found in negative verbs, and seldom in connexion with verbal postpositions.

MORU: *mí-nya ku.* Don't eat it.   *nye-turi ku.* Be not afraid.
        mi-si eba ku, mi-la ola. Don't bite the rope, cut it.
        mí-'bà tana kudzʷe kú. Don't forget it (lit. you let talk escape not).
        la'di ku dri.
        la'di dri ku. } It is not yet boiling.
LUGBARA: *indrí ri ésu-kí ku.* The goat is not found.
LOGO: *mi-ko-loga kokia, aǎi ko-o za ra-le ako.* Stop the dog from making the cattle run.
MORU: *má-'bà gyi tɛ la'di-nɪ . . . usi-nɪ.* I made the water boil.
        má-tɛ kadó tana má-'bi ndá tɛ̀. I'm happy because I beat him.
        á'bɪ ma tɛ. I am beaten.

REDUPLICATION IN ADJECTIVES

747. As may be expected, reduplication is used to emphasize the quality expressed by the adjective, which may be used attributively or predicatively. In many respects reduplication corresponds to the 'superlative' in English grammar. Note here, too, reduplication is seldom used in the negative.

MORU: *ambamba* (very many), *fereŋwa-fereŋwa*
                               fere-fere } (very small).
        ma-le täu ogye-nɪ ambamba. I want to buy a lot of hens.
        epe nderi-nderi. Honey is sweet.
LUGBARA: *aŋgo lúgbara ni múké-múkè.* The Lugbara country is very nice.
MADI: *lanyu limi-limi.* Honey is sweet.
LOGO: *paipai ka-ka.* The pawpaw is ripe.   *paipai ka ko.* The pawpaw is not ripe.
        yi ve-ve. The water is hot. *yi ve ko.* The water is not hot.
        kitu kanya-kanya. The sun is dazzling, or the dazzling sun.
        tai lego-lego, or *tai lelego.* Crooked words.
        muruŋgu-muruŋgu, or *muruŋguŋgu.* Very big.
        maligu-maligu, or *maligugu.*   „   in LOGO (A.)
        mi-ko-gi ndri to'yo-to'yo-ǎi ko, mi-ko-gi alo liŋga-liŋga. Don't buy a skinny goat, buy a plump one.
KELIKO: *fá-ri okpokpo.* Bone is hard. *anyu-ri ini-ini.* Honey is sweet.
        iyi-ri dri-dri. The water is cold. *iyi-ri ko-ko.* The water is hot.
        aya ǎir(i) adri asi-asi ku. This iron is not hot.

(307)

CHAPTER XXII

ADVERBS AND ADVERBIAL PHRASES

748. Doke defines an adverb thus: 'A word which describes a qualificative, predicative, or other adverb with respect to manner, place, or time.'

The *Oxford Dictionary* defines it: 'A word that modifies or qualifies an adjective verb or other adverb.'

With this definition in mind, it is easily seen that forms which may already function as nouns, verbs, adjectives, &c., may also be used adverbially.

749. Nominal and pronominal forms.
(Note locative suffix **le** in many cases. Cf. § 188.)

MORU: kuru(le) = sky = up. vùru(le) = ground = down.
kɔ(n)volɛ = back = backwards.
nana = that = there.

MADI (Lo.): oru = sky = up. vurú = ground = down.
aŋgwe = the bush = outside.

LOGO: *ndu* = bottom = below. *amvo* = field = outside.
lona = space below = below. *tugu-le* } = back = behind.
a-le = belly = inside. *ädu* (A.) }

750. Usually a combination is made of noun (or pronoun) and postposition, resulting in an *adverbial phrase*. Thus, just as in Moru one may say *äzu si* = with a spear, or *golo ya* = in the river, or *waraga be* = with a letter,
So one may say:

MORU: *kitu ono si* (to-day)   *kunduäsi* (behind)[1]
ko(n)vole si (afterwards)   *no si* (on this side)
tu aza si (another day)   *na si* (on that side)
ŋgäki si (by night)   *tääsi* or *tɛsì* (outside)
drikä si (day after to-morrow)   *dri ya* (forward)
tu se kɔi si[2] (nowadays)   *äise* (therefore)
emba ono si (this month)
emba azi si (next month)
ndrwa azi be (last year)
ŋgäki be (last night)
tandrube (yesterday)
drikäsi be (day before yesterday)
emba (azi) be (last month)
itu ya (when?)
itu be ya (when? past time)

MADI: *andraga* (before)   *asisi* (willingly)   *esadro* (in vain)
agaga (inside)   *okposi* (strongly)   *lokudru* (undoubtedly)
oguga (behind)   *aŋgusi* (in haste)
bitoga (beside)   *etu tro* (by day)
zelega (below)   *eniaga(si)* (by night)   *dia* (here)
karaloga (together)

[1] Contracted from *kundu ya si* (lit. back belly with).
[2] Lit. Days which go with.

LOGO: *kituse* (by day)
ŋgäcise (by night)
nolese (from here)
nalese (from there)
kandrase ⎫ (in front)
andrase (A.) ⎭
kuruse (above)
kurulese ⎫ (in the East)
urulese (A.) ⎭
tabulese ⎰ (below)
⎱ (in the West)
aďose (ya) (why?)
ďise (therefore)

The particle **ro** may also be used to form adverbs:
MORU: *ndrwa-ro ndrwa-ro* (year after year). (< *ndrwa* = year.)

751. Note how the interrogatives appear in:
MORU: *íŋgunyɛ (ya)* (how?) *íŋwa (yà)* (where?) *ɪŋɔtú (yà)* (when?).
niŋgwasi (ya) (whence?) *tana a'di ya* ⎫ (why?).
ɔ́'dú tá yà ⎭
MADI: *íŋgóni* (how?); *íŋgwá* (where?); *o'dósi* (why?).
LOGO: *(ta)ŋgíní (ya)* ⎫ *ɪŋga (yà)* (where?); *ǎŋgutú (yà)* (when?).
aŋgotini ya ⎬ (how?). *aďo si ya* (why?).
aŋgini ya ⎪
aďo tai ya ⎭
LUGBARA: (idʒu) *ŋgɔ-ni yà* (how?); *ŋga yà* (where?); *a'du tú-rɪ yà* (when?).

752. The following adverbials correspond in function to conjunctions in English, but are not conjunctions in MORU-MADI.
LUGBARA: *amani ovu-le obiro* **risi**. (Mk. v. 9.) For we are many.
LOGO: *mà-dre adre-le bi ďise*.
LOGO: *Tebiri dre ma o-le ďise*. (Mt. xxv. 35.) For I was hungry (lit. hunger was me hurting because).
MORU: *tana m-efu-be ono-ro* **ta-ďo-ro**. ⎱ (Mk. i. 38) = for therefore came I
LOGO: *ma-dre afo-le* **ta-niďi-se** *ďise*. ⎰ forth.

753. Other adverbial phrases are formed by adding an adjective or other qualifier to the noun, &c.
MORU: *pere (na) moda ya?* How often? (lit. times how many).[1]
pere (na) amba (often).
ɔndrɔ́ àlɔ. Every day (lit. to-day one).
pa toďi (na) (again) (lit. time different).
tana aďi ya? Why? (lit. talk of it what?)
ɔ'du ta ya? Why? (lit. what word?)
voaloya (altogether) (lit. place one in).
MADI: *voalo-voalo* (sometimes) (lit. place one place one).
druzi (< *dru*+*azi*) (day after to-morrow) (lit. to-morrow another).
LOGO: *vese alo* (once); *vese iri* (twice).

[1] Cf. Bari: *perok modâ*.

754. Verbal forms.
    MORU: *uḋu te ritu oko.* Two days later (lit. (they) slept twice afterwards).
    MADI: *te* or *tebe.* Just now (*te* = to remain).
    LOGO: *ka(y)ida* ⎫
            kuḋuda (A.) ⎬ Some time ago (lit. have slept).

Verbs are often found in adverbial expressions, which are in themselves complete sentences.
    MORU: *(ledri) uḋu te cini* = late at night (all (people) are asleep).
          gogo pe te = at dawn (cock has crowed).
          vo kiwi = at dawn (earth is growing light).
          vo kuni = at dusk (earth is growing black).
          vo ni te = after dusk (earth has grown black).

755. Adjectival forms.
    MORU: *a'bi ma te **kozi**(ro).*   I was badly beaten.
         *mi-ye losi miro **kadoro**.*[1] Do your work well.
    MADI (Lo.): *boronzi kede zipisi **loso**, zipisi **onzi**.* The boys do it sometimes well, sometimes badly.
    LOGO: *aḋi laḋi ŋga **konji**.*   He cooks food badly.
         *aḋi laḋi ŋga **tani**.*[2] He cooks food well.

        He hath done all things well.   They were greatly amazed.
              (Mk. vii. 37.)   (Mk. ix. 15.)
    MORU: *nda 'ba ŋga cini ni **kadu**.*   *laru-i-ge **amba**.*
    LUGBARA: *eri ye afa dria **yeke**.*   *yi ŋga osu-osu **ambo**.*
    LOGO: *akoḋi o tai wei **tani**.*
    MADI (Pa.): *edeki e'bu (k)podru **loso-ndro**.* *ai-ori-ki **loku-dro**.*

'True' adverbs.

756. There are, however, a number of words whose main (if not only) function is adverbial. The following are the most common. (Note that these, too, may be followed by postpositions or suffixes. Note also the frequent use of reduplication.)
    MORU: (Mynors):

		ele ya (why?)
		enye (thus)
madá ⎫ (for a long time)		*ayan* (indeed)
madámadá ⎭		
yau (ono) (now)	*lau* (there)	*eke* ⎫ (very)
		tawi ⎭
ndri (soon)	*loto* ⎫ (near)	*kiti* ⎫ (quite)
	ti(ti) ⎭	*kure* ⎭
dori (at once)		
foroforo (at once)	*kige* (inside)	*ndri* ⎫ (quickly)
		ndrindri ⎭
käti[3] (formerly)	*lozo* (for)	
kiano ⎫ (once upon a time)	*dii* (very far)	*lialia* ⎫ (slowly)
ro kiano ⎭		*liaro* ⎭
ondro (to-day)		*awi* ⎫ (for nothing)
		gini ⎭

[1] Cf. *mi-ye losi (se) kado miro ondro.* Do your good work to-day.
[2] Cf. *aḋi laḋi ŋga tani-ḋi.* He cooks good food.   [3] From Bari.

    tandrube (yesterday)   *wairo* (at random)
    ondo (to-morrow)   *toto* ⎫
    ondoro ondoro (always, continually)   *lutu* ⎭ (exactly)

For a fuller list, including times of the day and seasons of the year, see Mynors' *Moru Grammar*, Chapter VII.

 MADI (Molinaro):
    endro (to-day)   (*l*)*aka* (there)   *kwe* (in vain)
    o'bo ⎫   *anyi* ⎫   *pili* (quite)
    drusi ⎭ (to-morrow)   *ire* ⎭ (near)   *rie* (sufficiently)
              lolu (far)
    ati (formerly)
    mbembe (immediately)
    azeni (yesterday)
    andrani (day before yesterday)
    eze (once)
    para (always)

For a fuller list, with examples in context, see Molinaro's *Grammatica della Lingua Madi*, chapter v.

 LOGO. Since there is little likelihood of Miss Mozley's Logo grammar being published in the near future, the complete list of adverbs (whether 'true' or derived) is given here below from her manuscript.

  ŋgä(c)ise (at night)   *nole*   ⎫   *yaya* (slowly)
              nono   ⎬ (here)
  kituse (by day)   *konua* ⎭   *mbelembele* ⎫
                        geguo   ⎬ (quickly)
  abutise (A.) ⎫   *niŋga* ⎫   *foroforo* (A.) ⎭
  dribise   ⎬ (in the early   *nile* ⎭ (A.) (here)   *konji*   ⎫
  birise   ⎭   morning)   *be nono* ⎫   *vnji* (A.) ⎭ (badly)
               be ni (A.) ⎭ (is here)

  yendrose ⎫ (in the   *vele* (truly)
  lenjise (A.) ⎭ evening)   *nolese* (from here)   *allose ya* ⎫
               nilese ⎫ (A.) (from   *ase ya* ⎭ (why?)
  kiono   ⎫   *niŋgase* ⎭ here)
  äkú   ⎬ (formerly)   *tani*   ⎫
  walaka ⎭   *daǎi* ⎫   *doro* (A.) ⎬ (well)
               naǎi ⎬ (there)   *bucäki* (A.) ⎭
  ono   ⎫   *nana* ⎭
  ono dridri ⎭ (A.) (formerly)   *dale*   *titi*   ⎫
                          kırri (A.) ⎭ (quietly)
  dridri (before)   *daŋga* ⎫ (A.) (there)   *kolia* ⎫
              nale ⎭   *kice*   ⎬
  dribikiono ⎫ (before   *be da* ⎫   *kere*   ⎬ (always)
  bilikiono (A.) ⎭ sunrise)   *be nana* ⎭ (is there)   *du* (A.) ⎭

  velero ⎫   *aŋgini ya* ⎫ (how?)
  drandru ⎬   *dalese* ⎫ (from there)   *aŋgotini ya* ⎭
  ndo   ⎬ (afterwards)   *nalese* ⎭
  ädu (A.) ⎭   *kodia*   ⎫
               anyi   ⎫   *alo kodia* ⎬ (only)
               anyimva ⎭ (near)   *alo*   ⎬
                          ayo (A.) ⎭

ADVERBS AND ADVERBIAL PHRASES 311

amvutu (ndo)
velero ndo } (soon)
dre (already)

mvumvu
jeje (A.) } (far)

aŋgua ya
aŋgole ya } (where?)

laga (beside)

kitu kpacia (all day)
kitu vuse kolia
utu vuse du (A.) } (every day)

kandrase (in front)
andrase (A.) (of person)

kona vuse kolia
kona vuse du (A.) } (every year, for ever)

dridri (in front)

tugule
ädu } (behind)

aŋgutu ya (when?)

lana
ana-a (A.) } (inside)

amvena
amvele } (outside)
tevile

ale { (inside) (lining)

amvo { (outside) (surface)

ndu
lona } (underneath)

tile (at the front)
tabulese (below)
tabule(se) (in the West)
kuruse (above)
kurule(se)
urule(se) (A.) } (in the East)

THE POSITION OF ADVERBIALS IN THE SENTENCE

757. The most usual place for adverbials is at the end of the sentence or before the verb postposition. This is especially so in the case of interrogatives and adverbials of place.

MADI: *indre ma iŋgole?* (or *iŋga ya?*) Where did you see me?
ta dii karoŋgwe iŋgoni? How is this thing called?
anyi ro ti adosi ya? Why are you quarrelling?

Padre omu lolu ko, omba ogogo dia. The father has not gone far, he is stopping near here.

	Why did he not come?	Why is he angry?	I sit down.
MORU:	*nda eki ku tana adi ya?*	*anya kilaro tana adi ya?*	*mari vuru.*
KELIKO:	*eri imu k(u) asi ya?*	*eri adra asi?*	*marii viga.*
MADI:	*emu ko adosi ya?*	*aŋa adosi ya?*	*mari vuru.*

758. Adverbs of manner, and especially of time, may either precede the subject or follow the verb, according to emphasis to be placed on them.

MADI: *driadro ei kodi.* Rain is now falling.
odido ma nyi mba. Now I'll beat you.

nosi meŋgwi o'bo. Perhaps I'll return to-morrow.
kombako o'bo ei kod̄ira, **asi** *meŋgwi druzi.* But perhaps it will rain to-morrow, in which case I'll return the day after.
deso toroŋgadro anyindre ma **asi** *ko.* Again a little while and ye shall see me no more.
nyimu amvu a **azeze.** Go to the field quickly.
amemu waraga ga **ditri.** We go to school every day.
'boronzi waraga si-ka **loso** *re-e.* Boys who write (paper) well.

MORU: **kiano** *ma adravoro.* I was ill before.
ŋgwa se **kiano** *mbara aku,* **yauono** *ad̄ute kadoro.* The child who was formerly weak has now become well.
male Ndarago andivo ondreni **ondo.** I want to see Ndarago himself to-morrow.
manya eza te **tandrube,** *oko* **yauono** *anjokona ŋwate.* I ate the meat yesterday, but now the rest is rotten.

DESCRIPTIVE ADVERBS (IDEOPHONES)

759. In English we have a fair number of semi-interjections of an onomatopoeic nature to describe the results of an action. E.g., The branch broke, snap! It fell on the ground, thud! It fell into the water, splash!

In most African languages such interjections may accompany almost any verb, and they describe either the noise of the action (as in English) or the effect of the action either on the doer or the watcher.

MORU: gárà lifu-te, äpwuð̀! The bowl was broken, crash!
MADI: „ „ kpulumgbu! „ „ bump!
MORU: mí-za léi tí rɔ, tsɔ̀rɔ̀! tsɔ̀rɔ̀! Milk the cow.
túdrú kóɔ̀nga, ndzwa'du! ndzwa'du! The frog jumps, hop! hop!
ini kúdi á lèlèlèlè! The snake wriggles.
gyí te tiusí-ní syoooo! The water is just on boiling.

760. Adjectives are equally emphasized by these particles:
bɔŋgó uní gbírìkílí (M.) ⎫
  „   „ tsɔnì (Ä.)   ⎬ The cloth is as black as black can be.
  „   ítá nì kúdrú-kúdrú (Jl.) ⎭
uni dobani = black (and dirty).
d̄asi 'bokoto = big (and soft).
d̄asi mbitiri = big (and hard).
bɔŋgó ɔndzwa pìà (M.). The cloth is as white as white can be.
  „   „ rrrríkó (Ä.).

My body is feverish.
M.: lɔmvɔ márɔ ɛmɛ-ndí syoooo!
W.: ama-rúmvu amɛmɛ huaa!
Jl.: amorudzwa amɛmɛ gboo!

761. These 'descriptive adverbs' are the most varying of all the parts of speech. It is very rare to find two neighbouring dialects using the same descriptive adverbs, as can be seen from the preceding examples. It is possible that each social unit within any tribe has its own vocabulary of expletives, which may or may not coincide with that of its neighbours, but whose geographical range is extremely limited.

762. Another interesting point about these particles is that they often embody sounds foreign to the rest of the tribal vocabulary. Thus in Moroändri, an alternative to 'rrríkó', as descriptive adverb for 'white', is 'líá', the l-element of which is produced by placing the tongue-tip against the upper lip and flapping outwards. Another ideophone in the same dialect, to describe the noise of a stick striking somebody's head, is 'lui', the l-element of which is produced by placing one's tongue in one's cheek and flapping it across the mouth opening.

CHAPTER XXIII

CONJUNCTIONS

763. An important thing to note about conjunctions is their linking function. Consequently, only such words as link sentences, and consequently invariably stand at beginning of their sentences, are recognized here as conjunctions. Other forms, such as suffixes (see § 563 et seq.), postpositions (see § 595 et seq.), auxiliaries (see § 507), or adverbials (see § 752), may show consecutive or dependent action and correspond in function to conjunctions in European languages, but they must not be confused with Moru-Madi conjunctions.[1]

The following are the main (but by no means the only) conjunctions in Moru-Madi. Note that the forms used are very often to be found in other contexts as other parts of speech.

764.   **aba** MORU

aba *moigo Maridi ya, muduna eŋgwa ya?* Supposing I go to Maridi, where shall I sleep?
udru ga ma be, **aba** *madrate.* When the buffalo gored me, it was as if I died.

ago MORU

765. This conjugation is nearly always to be found in connexion with the narrative postposition **go**. The reader is referred to § 603 for examples.

ako, oko, ki MORU, LUGBARA, MADI

766. This conjunction in Moru usually corresponds to English 'but'; in Lugbara, on the other hand, it seems to correspond to 'because'.

MORU: *kiano ledri Moruro boŋgo aku,* **ako** *yau ndaka boŋgo be.* Once the Moru had no clothes, but now they have clothes.
MORU: *anya geṛiŋwaro* **oko** *anya ratararo.*
MADI: *ani toro* **ki** *(ani) okwo.* } He is little but he is strong.
LUGBARA: ma-gɔ vúlé **akə** ŋganya yɔ. I go back because there is no food.

---
[1] This is a mistake that Molinaro makes when he gives the name 'conjunction' to the **zo** of *tolu kwe ga-zo* (axe for chopping wood), and the **dro** of *ma-mu-dro* (that I may go). Op. cit., p. 44.

eke MORU; kidi LOGO

767. This form exists as a defective verb = to say, e.g. *anya eke* = he says. As a conjunction it is used in Moru to introduce a statement in oratio obliqua, even when other verbs of saying are used in the main clause. In Logo it introduces oratio recta.

MORU: *anya pe ta go mä-rı **eke** gyiga-te twi! golo ya.* He told me that the water had risen right up in the river.
*mere ta-aza te **eke** endre mi-ro adravoro.* I heard a report (lit. another word) that your mother was ill.

LOGO: *aii dreki ta-zo **kidi**: Aďi adre terikonjiďi be.* (Mt. xi. 18.) And they say He hath a devil.
*Aďi dre ta-le ďise **kidi**: Ma-ko-tabe . . .* (Mk. v. 28.) For she said: If I may touch . . .

768.   **mada le** MORU (cf. postposition **le**, § 298)
*miriandi noŋa, **mada le** ädrupi miro ezi parata te.* You will stay here until your brother has brought the money.
*male ku anya ondrenɪ, **mada le** anya konde losi iro te.* I don't want to see him until he should finish his work.

əndrə, də, dri, di, yi

769. This conjunction usually introduces the 'if' clause in a condition. In Lugbara a postposition is used.

If we stay here, the Makaraka will kill us.

MORU: **əndrə** ma-rɪ-té níá, Makaraká úfú-na àma ndi.
MADI { Lo.: **drɪ** ama-ɔló 'díà,   ,,   ká(kí) àma ù'dì-rá.
        { Pa.: **dɪ** ma-lɔ́ 'dià,   ,,   kú'dí àma ra.
LUGBARA: àma-di-də 'do,   ,,   kɪ àma u'di-ra.
KELIKO: **də** àmà-drí nə,   ,,   -rɪpɪ àmà 'di-ra.
LULU'BA: **yí** osí ekí-'o, móki 'ba. If the chief comes, I'll go home.
yí ki e'bwó'ɔ, mokwé míní gurú ni. If (you) work, I'll give you money.

If you die, I'll weep.   *If you don't go, I won't go.*
MADI { Lo.: **dzə** nyí-dra-rá, ma-wɔ.   (Torit): **zo** anyata kwe, ma-mu-ra kwe.
        { Pa.: **dɛ** ,, -da-kpó, ma-waù.   (Opari): **zo** nyi-mu ko, ma-mu se ko.
                                         KELIKO: **do** mi-mu ko, ma-mu ko.

In Moru this particle is followed by the verb in the Subjunctive:
***ondro** anya kosa-i-te 'bäru oko, anya uďu-go vuru.* When they reached home, they went to sleep.

770.   **kado (te)** MORU (cf. **kado** = good)
***kado** te anya oko, täpi aďu ku kilaro mɪbe ya?* Supposing it is so, won't (your) father get angry with you?
***kado** losi miro te koziro, ma'bi mi andi coda si.* If your work should be bad, I'll beat you with a whip.

771.   **ndi** MORU
*ópí 'ba ánya gʷo kámba yá, **ndi** dra-gʷo.* The chief put him in prison, and he died.
*ŋgaga ndre ma go, **ndi** mu-go.* The boy saw me and fled.

CONJUNCTIONS

ŋga and ta

772. Compare these forms with the indefinite pronouns (§ 237 et seq.).
I'm going back because there is no food.
LOGO: ma-gɔ andʒílí **ŋgá** ŋganya yɔ̀.
KELIKO: ma-gɔ vúlɛ́ **ŋga** ŋganya 'da yɔ̀.
MORU: **tana** *ama du.* (Mk. v. 9.) For we are many.
KELIKO: *ɛri madaŋa* **ta-alo** *ɛri okpo.* He is little but he is strong.

te LUGBARA

773. This conjunction seems to introduce an antithesis.
te *ma-yo emi-tia.* (Mt. v. 22.) But I say unto you.
te *'ba ɔŋɔlomuro ka-ndre-'bo.* (Mt. ix. 8.) But when the multitude saw (it).
te *eri yo eyo eri-asi si.* (Mt. ix. 21.) For she said within herself.

ukyi MORU

774. This conjunction may best be rendred by 'lest'. It is followed by the verb in the Subjunctive.
mátì tà ɔnɔ míri, **ukyí** nyúturi-'dà. I tell this thing to you, lest you should fear.
anya go-go 'bäru ndrindri, **uki** *kilazi anya-ro* **kufu** *anya te.* He returned home quickly lest his enemy should kill him.

775. The following list of conjunctions is taken from Mynors (for Moru) and Molinaro (for Madi).

MORU	MADI
oko (and, but)	ki, le
	kendre (as)
dooko (and so)	asi
ago (and so)	
ndi (and)	
teinye (and so, viz.)	ama(la)
	ama(ta)
anjioko (moreover, i.e.)	voa
(tu)se (when)	se
ondro (if)	dri
aba (if, supposing)	
(tu)se (when)	
... be (supposing)	
uki (lest)	ki (but)
... ro be (so that)	dro
tana (because)	a'dosi
kode[1] (whether)	
kado te (supposing)	
ca (although)	(zo)sa
mada le (until)	
	ambi(si) (instead)
	noni, nosi (perhaps)

[1] Borrowed from Bari.

SECTION III
ORTHOGRAPHY

CHAPTER XXIV
SUGGESTIONS FOR THE SPELLING OF MORU-MADI

776. At the time of the Rejaf Language Conference, Moru and Madi had not attained the literary status that they now enjoy, and consequently no alphabet was allotted to them. This forthcoming section will show how the principles and, as far as possible, the alphabet recommended at the Conference may be applied to this group of languages.

VOWELS

777. The five European vowel letters, *a, e, i, o, u*, are already in use. Owing to the great alternation between tense and lax vowels, it is of doubtful value to prescribe additional vowel symbols for the whole Moru-Madi group.

The lax vowel ɪ, however, is an exceptional sound with an apparent entity of its own, which has already given trouble to orthographists. English-speaking missions write it '*i*', sometimes '*ị*' (see Logo Gospels), because to their ears it approaches the sound in 'sit'; Italian-speaking missions often write it '*e*', because in their ears it approaches the sound in 'mese'. The symbol ɪ (cursive form—undotted '*i*') would probably be a useful addition to the alphabet, but should be used in specific cases only, such as the postposition drɪ (§ 292), the verb auxiliary drɪ (§ 486), the verb suffixes nɪ (§ 530), and rɪ (§ 646), and possibly the 2nd personal pronoun mɪ.

Central vowel.

778. Since in the majority of centralization cases the centralized vowel is related to the **a** vowel, the symbol '*ä*' is preferable to the Rejaf symbol '*ö*', as this would allow for those dialects in which **a** is not centralized—in which cases the diaeresis would be ignored.

e.g. ma (I)   *täpi* (MORU)   *ata* (MADI) = father.
                 märi   *madri*   = to me.

Vowel alternation.

779. Even with a limited vowel alphabet, the question of vowel alternation is not entirely overcome. For example, **o** alternates with **u** in many positions.

e.g. *siŋgo-ro* (sandy), but *ndi-ru* (dirty) in MORU.

In such cases the vowel alternation should be recognized, and one should write '*u*' where **u** is pronounced, rather than write '*o*', because in some actual or hypothetical 'ground form' of the word, **o** is heard. The spelling should, in this case, be phonetic rather than etymological.

CONSONANTS

The following remarks apply only to those consonants which might give trouble to the orthographist. Examples, except when otherwise stated, are from Moru.

Labial consonants: p, b, f, v, 'b, m.

780. It is true that in MORU MIZA and MADI, **p** and **f** could be amalgamated under one letter *p*, and **b** and **v** under one letter *b*, since the explosives occur only before front vowels, while the fricatives occur only before back vowels. Owing, however, to the large number of contiguous dialects in which **f** and **v** are found before all vowels, it would be safer to retain all four consonants *p, f, b, v* for use in all dialects. (There is no need, however, for *pf* and *bv* combinations. See § 48.)

e.g. (*k*)*ope* = guinea-fowl; (*e*)*ba* = rope; *torofo* = ashes; *vo* = place.

781. Implosive **'b** should be distinguished from explosive **b**, even in dialects, like Lokai Madi, where the distinction is not so often made. It is an easy matter to omit the ' diacritic in the cases of those who make no difference between the two sounds, and to insert it in the cases where the sound is implosive.

e.g. *bara* or *'bara* (Lokai Madi) = child; *ba* = breast; *'ba* = village.

Dental consonants: t, d, n.

782. There is no need to mark the dentality of **t** and **d** in these languages (as, for instance, in the Nilotic languages),[1] since there are no alveolar **t** and **d** sounds to be confused with them.

e.g. *ti* = cow; *ede* = make.

Alveolar consonants (liquid): r, l.

783. l and r should be distinguished. In most languages the flapped sound ɽ is obviously a variety of **l**, and should therefore be written *l*.

This principle, for the sake of uniformity, may also be extended to MORU, even though, as seen in § 51, a case could be made out for employing the symbol *ɽ* in that language.

Examples from MIZA:

l	r	flapped ɽ
lo (cut)	*ro* (noun postposition)	*lo* (verb postposition)
muluu (I love)	*uru* (to bring)	*älu* (blessing)
golo (river)	*koro* (well)	*gulo* (cat)
oli (wind)	*ori* (to sit)	*äli* (poison)
loli (to rest)	*tori* (spirit)	*koli* (basket)
milii (I weep)	*iri* (to him)	*ili* (knife)
rwali (rope)	*kari* (blood)	*gali* (left-hand)

Alveolar consonants (retroflex): tr, dr, ḍ.

784. The combinations *tr* and *dr* are already in use. These should be retained even in those languages where the **r**-element is weak, but should not be used in such dialects (like Pandikeri Madi) as pronounce *dental* **t** and **d** for these sounds (unless the students are being taught an approved 'standard' dialect containing **tr** and **dr**).

e.g. MADI: *tro* or *to* = with; *dri* or *di* = head.

Implosive **'d** should be distinguished from explosive **d**.

e.g. MORU: *aḍo* = what? *ido* = fat; *oḍa* = to insult; *oda* = to pour.

Alveolar consonants (sibilant and semi-sibilant); s, z, c, j.

785. *s* and *z* will cover all cases of alveolar fricatives, including Logo ʃ, since this sound occurs only before the vowel i. (There is no need for the special š-symbol of the Logo New Testament.) The intrusive **w**-element, which is found in some dialects, need not be shown.

e.g. (*i*)*su* = four; *si* = split; (*e*)*za* = meat; *azo* = long (Madi).

[1] Where the sounds are written *th* and *dh* (and *nh*).

786. *c* and *j* will cover the alveolar fricatives, even where they are not etymologically related. Thus:

    MORU: *c* and *j* stand for **ts^w** and **dz^w** (the w-element need not be shown).
        e.g. *ce* = tree; *keci* = seed; *uje* = burn; *onje* = white.
    MADI: *c* and *j* stand for **ts** and **dz** (**dʒ** in dialects), whether these sounds correspond to **s** and **z** or **k** and **ġ** elsewhere.
        e.g. *aci* = fire; *aco* = hoe; *aju* = spear; *jo* = hut.
    LOGO: *c* and *j* stand for **ts** and **dz** and **tʃ** and **dʒ** (the latter group occurring before **i** and **u**).
        e.g. *aca* = arrive; *ci* = bite; *kojwa* = wizard; *ji* = wash.
    LUGBARA: *c* and *j* stand for **ts** and **dz** and **tʃ** and **dʒ** (the latter group before **i** and **u**).
        e.g. *aca* = arrive; *ci* = bite; *ujogo* = wizard; *ju* = wash.

787. The nasal combination has hitherto caused divergence of spellings. The choice lies between *nz* and *nj*. In MORU and MADI *nz* is already in use, and to substitute *nj* for it would cause much trouble for little gain.[1] In LOGO and LUGBARA, on the other hand, where the post alveolar **dʒ** is heard before certain vowels, *nj* would be the better combination (not forgetting that the normal phonetic value of *j* is **dz**, not as in English).

Note. Since '*dz*' is not being used in any of the orthographies, there is no necessity for coining a new compound '*ndz*'.

    e.g. (MORU)   *enzo* = lies;   *onzi* = bad
        (MADI)   *enzo*   *unzi*
        (LOGO)   *njo*   *konji*
        (LUGBARA) *njo*   *onji*

Palatal consonants: ny (y, see § 793), 'j, 'y.

788. The 'glottal' palatals should be written '*j* or '*y* according to the most common pronunciation in the dialects concerned. These sounds exist only in Madi and the Central languages.

    e.g. (MADI) *o'ju* = horn;   '*jo* = speak.
        (LOGO) *ko'ya* = horn; *to'yo* = thin.

Velar consonants: k (ky), g (gy), ŋ.

789. *k* and *g* are already in use. For the palatalized varieties heard before front vowels in MORU, *k* and *g* are more appropriate symbols than *c* and *j*.[2] If felt necessary, the symbols may be amplified to *ky* and *gy*.

    e.g. *kuki* or *kukyi* (thorn); *gi* or *gyi* (water)
        koke or *kokye* (dog); *ge* or *gye* (to buy)

but this amplification is not desirable in the k-prefix. (See § 68.)

    e.g. *kemba* (net); *kini* (skin); *kembe* (neck)

---

[1] In Moru it would be definitely wrong, as *nj* stands for the palatalized sound **ndzw** as in *onje* (phon. ɔ̀ndz^{w}ɛ) = white, *nji* (phon. ńdz^{w}í) = five.

[2] I had ample proof of this in the MORU country, where I found that the spellings *kuci, koce, ji,* and *je* were actually responsible for a growing 'school-boy' pronunciation **kutswi, kɔtswɛ, dzwi,** and **dzwe** at the Mission, instead of the traditional pronunciation **kukyi, kɔkyɛ, gyi,** and **ġyɛ**.

790. ŋ is a necessary letter, in order to distinguish such doublets as—

> *kokye-ŋwa* (little dog); *kaŋwa* (flying ant)
> *kokye-ŋgwa* (young dog); *ŋga* (to fly) in MORU.
> *ŋo* (to break); *ɲa* (ground)
> *ŋgu* (to smell); *ŋga* (thing) in MADI.

Note. The nasal compound ŋ+g should be written 'ŋg' and not 'ng'.

Labio velar consonants: kp, gb (w, see § 793).

791. kp and gb are already in use, and should be retained in spite of the Rejaf Conference's recommendation of *kw* and *gw* (for Bari); such a recommendation would cause great confusion if carried out in Moru-Madi, since the sounds **kw** and **gw** already exist here.

Compare (in MADI) *ekpadru* = many, and *kwa* = bone;
> *logbi* = beads, and *gwe* = burn.

792. The nasal gb combination should be written *mgb*, rather than *ngb*, as the latter spelling might suggest a *dental* **n**. The Madi Gospel spells the sound *ɲb*, but this spelling has the disadvantage of not being applicable in such languages (like Zande) as do not ordinarily need the letter ɲ.

> e.g. *kätumgbu* (MORU) = rhinoceros; *amgbu* (MADI) = many.

The semi-vowels.

793. Where **w** and **y** occur merely as glide sounds between a close and an open vowel (or vice versa), they should not be written.

> e.g. *mɪa* (guinea-worm), not *mɪya*
> *käi* (grass), not *käyi*.

Similarly, where the **w** glide is the result of assimilation on the part of a back vowel, it should not be written.

> *kodra* (bamboo), not *kwodra*
> *zo* (hut), not *zwo*
> *go* (verb postposition), not *gwo*

Where also the **w** is a structural element in a sound, like **ts**^{w} and **dz**^{w}, it should not be written.

> *ɪcɪ* (bowels), not *ɪcwɪ*   *uje* (to burn), not *ujwe*
> *keci* (seed), not *kecwi*   *onje* (white), not *onjwe*
> *ce* (tree), not *cwe*

794. This narrows down the use of *w* and *y* to those occasions where they are real consonants or semi-vowels (i.e. close vowels pronounced too quickly to be classified as vowels).

e.g. *as consonants:*

> *wa* (beer); *tawi* (very); *lɪwa* (elephant)
> *ya* (belly); *kaya* (knee)

as semi-vowels:

> *kwa* or *koa* (bone); *kizwe* (pig)
> *lya(a)* or *lia* (slow)

and in Logo, before the suffix -a:

> *zoa* or *zwa* (hut); *tokoa* or *tokwa* (woman).
> *karia* or *karya* (leprosy); *tombia* or *tombya* (locust).

In addition, in Moru and Logo, *y* might be used to show the palatalization of *k* and *g*. (In Logo again before suffix *-a*.)

>MORU: *kokye* (dog); *gye* (to buy)
>LOGO: *kokya* or *kokia*; *gya* or *gia*

Laryngeal consonants: ' h.

795. Whether the enclitic glottal stop (as in MADI *a'u* = hen) should be recorded or not is hard to say. If the ' sign be used in this sense, then it should not be used to indicate elision of vowels (as in French 'l'enfant'). Some writers are inclined to use it in both senses, and the result is confusion.

Note that ' already occurs in the glottal consonants '*b*, '*d*, '*j*, '*y*, and as initial sound in some dialects in '*a* (belly), '*e* (to make).

796. Where h is merely an optional enclitic, it should not be written. It is, however, useful in certain Moru words—*ihwi* (wild dog), &c., and in Pandikeri Madi—*hwe* (tree), *hwi* (to enter).

INTONATION

797. In a practical orthography only one tone mark need be used, and that sparingly. The *low* tone mark ` will be found particularly useful in distinguishing between singular and plural pronouns. This distinction is most noticeable in Moru and Logo.

e.g. MORU:	*mamute*.	I went.	*màmute*.	We went.
	mimu.	Go!	*mìmu*.	Go! (pl.).
	anya mute.	He went.	*ànya mute*.	They went.
LOGO:	*mimu*.	Go!	*mìmu*.	Go! (pl.).

THE SUGGESTED MORU-MADI ALPHABET

798. The following are the symbols recommended:

a, ä, b, c, d, e, f, g, h (MORU and MADI Pa.), i, (I), j, k, l, m, n, ŋ, o, p, r, s, t, u, v, w, y, z, (').

The following combinations of existing symbols are also recommended:

'b, 'd, 'j (MADI), 'y (LOGO and LUGBARA).
kp, gb, tr, dr, ny, ky (MORU and LOGO), gy (MORU and LOGO).
mb, mv, nd, nv, nz (MORU and MADI), nj (LOGO and LUGBARA), ŋg, mgb.

N.B. The orthography of Lendu will be treated separately in an appendix.

CHAPTER XXV

WORD DIVISION

799. Although the Moru-Madi languages are fundamentally monosyllabic, it has been felt by most authorities that an ultra disjunctive system of writing would be unsatisfactory for any Moru-Madi language. It is obvious that certain particles, which in themselves have no separate existence in speech, should not be given an independent existence in writing, e.g. the *-pi*, *-zi* suffixes in nouns and the *-nɪ*, *-le*, *-ka* suffixes in verbs. On the other hand, these languages are characterized by the frequent compounding both of words and of particles to such an extent that an orthographical system, based on a rigid adherence to the conjunctive method, would frequently result in words of as many as twenty letters, and this, as is generally known, is a great hindrance to fluent reading. The following examples should illustrate this point:

LOGO[1]: Suppose, on account of vowel assimilation, it is felt necessary to attach postpositions to pronouns,

e.g. *mase* = from me (< *ma ase*). Then: *makandralese* = from before me.

Take now the word *kabiliki* = sheep, and the compound noun agent *kabiliki-likilepi(ɖi)* = shepherd. If we are to join all postpositions, then:

'from before the shepherd' = *kabilikilikilepikandralese*.

MADI[2]: Suppose it is felt necessary to attach the relative particles to the verb stem. (*so* = to hoe.)

e.g. *'ba leti sokarɪ'ɪ* = the men who are hoeing the road.

With the intrusion of the negative particle, little trouble would be experienced.

e.g. *'ba leti sokakorɪ'ɪ* = the men who are not hoeing the road.

But what about intruding adverbs?

e.g. *'ba leti soka-loso-rɪ'ɪ* = the men who are hoeing the road well.
'ba ecaka-azeni-rɪ'ɪ. = those who arrived yesterday.

800. It is obvious that some sort of compromise is called for; that which appears in the works of the MADI missions seems to be the most satisfactory, and the forthcoming tentative rules are based mostly on their practice, although the actual examples, unless otherwise stated, will be taken from MORU.

PRINCIPLES UNDERLYING WORD JOINING

A. *Sound assimilation*, &c.

801. Assimilation or elision of sounds is often a good reason for joining elements in a sentence; e.g. *nyozo* for *ny(a) ozo* (= you give).

Note, however, the following examples:

In MORU: má ŋgàgà ùzi (I am calling the boys), when spoken quickly, sounds like máŋgàgòzi.

In MADI: *ka ma uŋgwe* (He calls me), when spoken quickly, sounds like *kamoŋgwe*.

It would lead to great confusion if every such phrase or sentence were written exactly as it is spoken, even if extensive use of the apostrophe (e.g. *ka m'oŋgwe*) were made.[3] Sound assimilation, therefore, is a dangerous criterion for conjugation, if taken by itself; nor should its absence be arbitrarily taken as sole criterion for disjunction.

B. *Morphological function.*

802. The only safe criterion to follow is that which takes the morphological function of the speech units into account. The rules for conjunction and disjunction should rest upon a grammatical basis, with due regard to the sound assimilations found in normal speech. The categories of speech units, already set out in Section II, will serve as a useful basis for the discussion of word joining.

[1] Example furnished by Miss McCord.
[2] Example taken from Fr. Molinaro's Madi grammar.
[3] This latter practice is subject to heavy criticism on psychological grounds, besides being doubly unsuitable in the Moru-Madi languages on account of the 'glottal' value already given to the apostrophe.

Nouns.

803. Compound nouns should be written conjunctively.

liwasi (ivory); *dri'bi* (hair); *pakususu* (heel).

This also applies to nouns derived from verbs:

MORU: *ŋgɔinya* (food); *ŋgaladi'ba* (cook); *boŋgolosezo* (needle).
MADI: *lenyaudirerɪ'ɪ* (cook).
LOGO: *tatisiledi* (writing); *ŋgaladilipidi* (cook); *boŋgwalaseza* (needle).
LUGBARA: *asindriza* (compassion); *'baenyaadilepi(ri)* (cook); *boŋgogbijo* (needle).

804. Genitives, however, should *not* be joined, even when intimate.

MADI: *opi aju* (the chief's spear); *Sumein 'bura* (Sumein's son).
opi ni aju (the chief's spear); *opi a bara* (the chief's son).
bara opi dri (the son of the chief).
MORU: *äzu opi ro* (the spear of the chief).
LOGO: *ago ni dili* (the man's spear); *akodi a ŋga* (that man's things).
dilya miri adia (the spear of the chief).
LUGBARA: *oko Simonini ma andri* (Simon's wife's mother).

This is because in a compound noun a new entity is expressed, whereas in the genitive constructions, merely the relationship of two known entities is being given.

805. Noun suffixes should be joined:

ibiago (male lion); *ibiendre* (lioness); *ibiŋwa* (little lion); *ibiŋgwa* (lion cub).

806. Noun postpositions should not be joined unless the resultant form expresses a new entity. Thus:

MORU: *zo ya* (in the house)   *kɪtoreya* (in the midst)
MADI: *osu si* (with a bow)   *okposi* (strongly)
laki dri (over the people)   *vudri* (down)
LOGO: *amvu na* (in the field)   *amvena* (outside)
LUGBARA: *aiita si* (with faith)   *adisi* (why)

Pronouns.

807. Under 'pronouns' will fall many exceptions to the above rules, since the sound assimilation in the case of pronouns is often so great that disjunction would be almost impossible. This is particularly the case in the 1st and 2nd person pronouns.

808. Where the 1st and 2nd person genitive precedes the thing possessed, it should be joined, unless there is an unassimilated linking particle. Where the 3rd person possessor is represented by a noun, this should not be joined.

MADI: *amata* (our father); *anyendre* (your mother).

With contracted linking particle *a*:

mapa (my leg); *nyapa* (your leg); *napa* (his leg); *amapa* (our legs).

but: *ma ni dri* (my hands); *aɪ a pa* (their legs).

LUGBARA: *yi ma jo* (their house).
amakiadrupi (our brother).
LOGO: *amadrupi* (my brother); *amiadrupi* (your brother); *adiadrupi* (his brother); *aiadrupi* (his own brother).

but: *akodi a ŋga* (his things) because *akodi* is a noun (= that man).
adi ni tayilepidii (his disciples).

WORD DIVISION

809. Where the possessor follows the thing possessed, it should not be joined to it; it should, however, be joined to its genitive postposition.

    MORU: *toko maro* (my wife); *andivo ɪro* (his own body).
    MADI: *oko madri* (my wife); *amvu anidri* (his field).
    LOGO: *kisu mana(di)* (my bow); *mokoto amakia(di)* (our chief).
    LUGBARA: *zamva mani* (my little daughter).

810. Pronouns should be joined to the postpositions which follow them, with due attention to sound assimilation.

    MORU: *märi* (to me)   *malomvo* (against me)
            miri (to you)   *milaga* (towards you)
            anyäri (to him)   *sina*¹ (with it)
    MADI: *madri* (on me, of me)
           nyisɪ (from you)
           'bani (to them)
    LOGO: *madre* (to me)   *amadrika* (chez moi)
           mibe (with you)   *masɪdrɪ* (away from me)
           adivule (to him)
           lana (in it)   *adivulesɪ* (from him)
    LUGBARA: *mavuti* (after me)   *emidri* (unto you)
           *vunia*¹ (to him)

Verbs (Preceding elements).

811. Foregoing nouns should not be joined.

    MORU: *opi ndre ma.*   The chief sees me.
    MADI: *opi ondre ma.*
    LOGO: *komoko no ma.*
    LUGBARA: *opi ndre ma.*

812. Foregoing personal pronouns should be joined. This applies particularly to the 1st and 2nd person pronouns, to the 3rd person *referring* pronoun **i**, and to the 3rd person **k(a)** particle. (See § 216.)

Great attention should be paid to sound assimilation, especially that exercised by the characteristic vowel.

    MORU: *mamu(te)*. I ran.   *mudu(te)*. I slept.   *mumu*. I am running.
          mimu(te). You ran.   *nyudute*. You slept.   *nyumu*. You are running.
                                                      anya kumu. He is running.
    MADI: *amu(ra)*. I went.   *memu(ra)*. I came.   *mamu*. I am going.
          imu(ra). You went.   *nyemu(ra)*. You came.   *nyimu*. You are going.
          omu(ra). He went.   *emu(ra)*. He came.   *komu*. He is going.
          omuki(ra). They went.   *emuki(ra)*. They came.   *kakimu*. They are going.
    LOGO: *mata* (I say)   *amale ko* or *màle ko* (we don't want)
          mita (you say)   *amikoli* or *mìkoli* (Go! pl.)
    LUGBARA: *mamu* (I go)   *amamumu* (we go)
          mimu (you go)   *emimu* (go! pl.)

813. The joining or not of the 3rd person pronoun to the verb stem is a matter for discussion. In most languages the pronoun, when used, has a rather emphatic value, and is best kept apart² (except where sound assimilation occurs).

---

¹ Here the particle precedes. See § 263.
² The referring pronoun, **i**, should be joined, however.
    MORU: *Anya eke imute.*   He says he went.
    LOGO: *Jida tadi ikodo.*   The frog said he would take.
    MADI: *Izipi kinibe nile mu.*   His wife said she wished to go.

	MORU: *anya mute* (he ran)	*anya kumu* (he is running)
but:	*anyuḓute* (he slept)	
	MADI: *ani omura* (he went)	*ani komu* (he is going)
		ai kovovo (they are going)
	LOGO: *aḓi dre taza* (he said)	*aii dre taza* (they said)
	akoḓi kaḓedi (when she fell)	*aii koliki* (when they propitiated)
	LUGBARA: *eri ovu kuhani* (he was priest)	*yi ovu mva kokoro* (they were without child)

814. The particles *-ni* and *-ri* should be joined to the pronoun in Lugbara.

LUGBARA: *kori dralara.* They will die.
erini ovule meleki (when he was king); *yini yoria* (they saying)
eco mani emuzaro (I can come); *mini ovuria lizaro* (when thou art judged).

815. Where the pronouns do not immediately precede the verb stem, they should stand alone.

MORU:	*ma eza onya.*	I am eating meat.
	anya ka eza onya.	He is eating meat.
MADI:	*ma eza nya.*	I am eating meat.
	ani ka eza nya.	He is eating meat.
	kaki eza nya.	They are eating meat.
LOGO:	*ma za nya.*	I am eating meat.
	aḓi za nya.	He is eating meat.
LUGBARA:	*ma eza nya.*	I am eating meat.
	eri eza nya.	He is eating meat.

816. Foregoing particles should be joined when they immediately precede the main verb stem, and the pronouns that precede these should be joined also. (This does not apply to 3rd person pronouns. See § 813.)

	MORU: *anya katuḓu.*	He is sleeping.
but:	*ledri ka liti oso.*	The people cut a road.
	LOGO: *mikolaḓi.*	Cook (it).
	ai kovovo.	They are going.
	LUGBARA: *amamafi.*	That we may enter.
	'ba nde kadrara.	If a man should die.
	MADI: *kakidra.*	They are dying.
but:	*kaki ta no.*	They are seeing something.

817. Auxiliary verbs, however, should not be joined to the main verb stems, but the pronouns that precede them should be joined as to ordinary verbs. (See §§ 812–13.)

	MORU: *mɪ'ba kumumu.*	Make it run.
	mɪde maŋgo loŋgo.	Let us sing a song.
	madrɪ embana.	I am still tying it.
	magi aba.	I am just walking about.
	anya kate laḓi.	He is cooking.
but:	*anya katuḓu.*	He is sleeping.
	LOGO: *mio do agale.*	Make the fat melt.
	mao lile.	I am going.
	madre linya nya.	I am eating food.
	madre tecile.	I am walking. I walked.

LUGBARA:	*econi mini mbozaro.*	You can jump.
	eri adri fo.	He then went out.
	maŋga mi ɖura.	I'll carry you.
	eri ŋga fi.	And he entered.
MADI:	*oŋga onyara.*	He was eating.
	ifo emusi ko.	You didn't come.
	nye'be komu.	Let him go.
	nyi'ba komuki.	Make them go.

Verbs (following elements).

818. Following nouns or pronouns should not be joined.

            mandre mi.   I see you.
            mandre opi.   I see the chief.

819. Verb suffixes should always be joined.

MORU:	*male ku odranɪ.*	I don't want to die.
	anya ŋgonya onyavia.	He is eating food.
	male kodra zo omuza.	I want bamboos for building the house.
MADI:	*amavu drare.*	We are going to die.
	ale muka 'baru.	I want to go home.
	lenya loso nyale.	Food is good to eat.
LOGO:	*mani boŋgo dile ku.*	I don't know how to sew cloth.
	azi oleɖi adre tani.	To do work is good.
	akoɖi lidre yi mvuzo.	He has gone to drink water.
LUGBARA:	*Erini agaria.*	As he was walking.
	'Ba imbazu.	And taught people.

820. Verb postpositions should be joined only when they immediately follow the verb stem.

      MORU: *mämute.* I have gone.
but: *mandre mi te.* I saw you.
              ànya odranaɖa. They will die.
but: *mandrena Ndarago ɖa.* I shall see Ndarago.
              ledr se atra fube . . . (the man whom the foreigner killed).
but: *ledr se fu ibi be* (the man who killed the lion).

      MADI: *amura.* I have gone.
but: *ano nyi ra.* I saw you.
              mamura. I shall go.
and: *ma nyi nora.* I shall see you.
              'boronzi waraga sikarɪ'ɪ. The boys who write books.
but: *'boronzi waraga sika loso rɪ'ɪ.* The boys who write books well.

      LOGO: *manyadre.* I have eaten it.
but: *manya ŋga dre.* I have eaten food.
              manyaru ŋga. I shall eat food.
              maaliɖi. I am just coming.
              mvaago ŋgolepi(nda)ɖi. The boy who is crying.
but: *ago acalepi agia ɖi.* The man who arrived yesterday.
and: *ɖia adrelepi aɖilaga ɖi* (the people who were standing beside him).

LUGBARA: *mamu'bo.*   I have gone.
            kori dralara.   They will die.
            eri ŋga ecando.   It shall come.
but: *amanya eza 'bo.*   We have eaten the meat.

821. The negative postposition *ku*, because of its irregular behaviour, is best not attached to the verb.

            male ku.   I don't want it.
            ma ku nyana.   I'm not eating.

822. The interrogative particle (*y*)*a* is also best not attached to the verb, but there are certain interrogatives (pronominal and adverbial) where it will often be to one's advantage not to try to separate it out.

        aḍi(a)? (who?)   *ituya?* (when?)   *ɩŋwaya?* (where?)

Adjectives.

823. Adjectival suffixes should be joined to the adjectival stems, but adjectives should not be joined to the nouns they qualify.

    ledri koziro.   A bad man.   *ago miakoḍi.*   A blind man. (LOGO).

Predicatives.

824. Where predication is formed by juxtaposition of two substantives, &c., these should not be written together.

            ma Madi.   I am a Madi.
            ma kadoro.   I am well.

825. Predicative suffixes, however, should be joined to the words they follow.

     MORU: *ma ku tokoi.*   I am not a woman.
     MADI: *adi ma uŋgwe Lugumaɩ.*   I am called Luguma.
     LOGO: *ago naḍi ajubulepiḍiɩ.*   That man is a warrior.
     MORU: *oko opi ro adravuro.*   The wife of the chief is sick.
     LOGO: *aḍi mba agoro.*   He grew into a man.

826. But predicative auxiliaries, where they act as verbs, are attached only to pronouns.

     MORU: *mate kado.*   I am well.
but: *ma oriviya nono.*   I am here.
     MADI: *Deŋgo ni jurugo(i).*   Dengo is a foreigner.

Adverbs, prepositions, and conjugations.

827. Prepositions and conjunctions should be written separately, and not attached to the words they refer to. Compound conjunctions should be written as one word.

A distinction should be made between adverbs and adverbial phrases. Adverbs, even when composed of several elements, should be written as one word.

     MORU: *kɩtoreya* (in the midst)   *drukäsibe* (day before yesterday)
     MADI: *oḍosi* (why?)   *vudri* (down)
     LOGO: *amvena* (outside)   *kitukere* (always)
     LUGBARA: *aḍisi* (why?)   *aḍuturi* (when?)

CHAPTER XXVI

SPECIMEN TEXTS[1]

MORU

Two Miza folk-tales, contributed by T. H. B. Mynors
(Translation by phrases)

1. *Ŋgäri ndi Ko'ba be.*
   Ngori and the Jackal.

Ŋgäri ndi Ko'ba be oügo agba ya.   *Ndi 'bu esago, ndi ànya muigo zo Mui*
Ngori and the Jackal went for herbs.   And rain came, and they ran in house of

ro ya,   *ndi Mui esago ago ozo eza go ànyäri,*   *ago ànya reigo sina*
the Hyena, and the Hyena arrived and gave meat to them, and they stayed with

voaloya.   *Ago Ko'ba nya eza se Mui kozobe anyäri ana go, ago*
him together.   But the Jackal ate the meat which the Hyena gave her there, and

ondro ànya katoi oko, Mui eke:
when they were going just, the Hyena said:

'Nyòzo eza maro se mozobe amiri ǎo.'   *Ndi Ŋgäri ozo iro go, oko*
'Give (me) my meat which I gave to you this.'   So Ngori gave his, but the

Ko'ba nya iro te.   *Ndi Mui atago Ko'ba ri, eke:*   *'Yauono mite*
Jackal had eaten hers.   Then the Hyena said to the Jackal, (saying): 'Now you are

toko maro.'   *Ndi Ko'ba aǎugo tokoro Mui ri,*   *ndi Ko'ba ti ŋgwa go*
my wife.'   So the Jackal became wife to the Hyena, and the Jackal bore children

Mui ri 'butena nätu.   *Ago endre Ko'ba ro ek(y)igo*
for the Hyena thirty (lit. tens of them three).   Now the mother of the Jackal came

Ko'ba ondreni,   *ago Ko'ba atago endre anyaro ri, eke:*   *'Endre maro, ondro*
to see the Jackal, and the Jackal said to her mother, saying: 'My mother, when the

Mui kek(y)ite oko, nyata ku ndäri,   *tana anya ku kado.'*   *Ago ndri-*
Hyena comes, do not speak to him, because he (is) not good.'   And shortly

oko Mui esago,   *ago ondro Mui kesate oko,*   *Ko'ba ǎi 'bu te*
afterwards the Hyena arrived, and when the Hyena had arrived, the Jackal dug a

ǎäsi,   *ago ede asi te kige,*   *ndi Mui ǎego 'bu se ana ya.*   *ndi jego*
deep pit, and prepared fire in it, and the Hyena fell into that pit, and perished

asi ya.
in the fire.

2. *Muiambago ndi Kito be.*
   'Old-Hyena' and the Hare.

Uǎu alo oko Muiambago origo abanı,   *ndi usu kumu se ana pa go,*   *ndi*
One day   Muiambago went to hunt, and found honey that also, so (he)

---

[1] For the sake of clearness in distinguishing between singular and plural of pronouns and verbs, the low tone diacritic is used here. This would probably not be necessary in everyday Moru-Madi writing. It should further be noted that, since none of the contributors made any distinction in writing between explosive and implosive **b** and **d**, I can only guarantee the accuracy of the letters in those words which are actually known to me.

gogo kovole ndi zi Tafo go okinɪ anyäri sina kumu se ana onyanɪ.
returned back and called the Squirrel to go for him together to eat the honey which

    Dori ànya ɖeindi oinɪ kumu se ana onyanɪ,   *ago ànya*
(was) there. At once they began to go to eat the honey which (was) there, and they

saigo kige.   *Kito eke: 'Tafo, mutu!'*   *ago Tafo tugo,*
arrived at it. The Hare said: 'Squirrel, jump up!' and the Squirrel jumped up,

ago ndrioko Muiambago sago dori,   *ago nda ru Kito go,*   *ago ru Tafo pa*
and very soon Muiambago arrived at once, and he took the Hare, and took the

go,   *ndi vo ànya go komvo ya,*   *ŋgi ànya go 'bäru anyarige.*   *Ago*
Squirrel also, and threw them into a sack, carried them home to his place. And

nda koite ànya ufunɪ oko Kito eke:
he was going to kill them but the Hare said:

'Mifu ama ku, mi'ba ama teinye lukuɖu ya, tana ondro mifu ama te oko, laɖinɪ
'Do not kill us, put us like this in the pot, because if you kill us, you

amäri te iɖu,   *ago ondro miso gi te amadri oko,*
won't be able to cook us (lit. cooking of us is not); and if you pour water over us,

laɖinɪ amäri pa iɖu.   *Oko ondro miso le te amadri oko, màlaɖina-*
you won't be able to cook us either. But if you pour milk over us, we shall

ndi.'   *Ago Muiambago so le go ànyadri,*   *ago za käi go ànyazele.*
certainly cook.' So Muiambago poured milk over them, and burned grass under

   Ndi Muiambago oigo abanɪ.   *Ago ànya mvui le go cini,*
them. Then Muiambago went to walk (i.e. hunt). And they drank all the milk,

ndi ànya efuigo taasi ni lukuɖu ya, ndi fui endre Muiambago ro go,   *ago la*
and they came-out out of the pot, and killed the mother of Muiambago, and cut

ezana go lukuɖu ya,   *ndi 'ba asi go amba zelei ga,*   *ndi muigo.*   *Ago*
up her flesh into the pot, and put much fire to its bottom, and ran (away). And

ondro Muiambago kegote ni abaviya oko,   *nda usu eza laɖite.*   *Nda*   *eke*
when Muiambago returned from walking, he found the meat cooked. He said

iro   *kode eza Kito ro ndi Tafo be,*   *ndi nda nya*
to himself (i.e. thought) that (it was) meat of the Hare and Squirrel, and he ate

endre go,   *ago Kito ndi Tafo be*   *kondre ta ɖo nunye oko, dori*
(his) mother, and the Hare and the Squirrel (when) they saw this affair thus, at once

ànya trego lägu be.
they shouted with laughter.

     Extract from New Testament (Mark vi. 35–44)
    (The miracle of the loaves and the fishes). Literal translation.

   35. *Ago tandrulesi oko, taeri'bai ndaro eciigo ndare, eke:*   'Vo ono
      And setting-with when disciples His came Him to, saying: 'Place this

     vocoai,   *ago kitu te tandruleru;*   36. *nyepere*   *ànya,*
    (is) a desert-place, and the sun is low.   You-send them (away),

kuciiro   'ba   yasi   biki,   ŋga   og(y)e   ànyäri   onyanı.
that they may go   country   into   round about,   food   buy   them for   eat.
37. Oko nda atago ànyäri,   eke: 'Nyòzo   na ni   onyanı ànyäri.'
    But He said them to, saying: 'You-give something to eat them to.'
Ago ànya ataigo ndäri,   eke: 'Màk(y)ina mapa og(y)e parata kama-ritu
And they said Him to, saying: 'We go shall bread buy pence hundred-two
si, ozonı onyanı ànyäri ya?' 38. Ago nda atago ànyäri, eke: 'Amı mapa
for, give eat them to?'   And He said them to, saying: 'You loaves
be taŋwanye ya? Nyòi ondrenı.' Ago ànya ndreite oko, ànya eke: 'Nji,
with how-many? You-go see.'   And they saw   when, they said: 'Five,
ndi ti'bi ritu be.' 39. Ago nda ozo ata go ànyäri ledr(ı) oba orinı
and fishes two with.'   And He gave word them to people all sit
ŋgero käi dri v(u)ru. 40. Ago ànya rrigo deri deri, kama   si,
by-companies grass on down. And they sat rank rank, hundreds by,
ago pa 'butena-nji si. 41. Ago nda uru mapa nji go ndi ti'bi ritu be,
and also fifties by.   And He took loaves five and fishes two with,
ago pi mi te kuru oko, älugo, wa mapa go; ndi nda ozogo taeribai
and raised eyes up when, blessed, broke loaves; then He gave disciples
ri lanjinı[1] ànyäri; ago nda lanji ti'bi se ritu go ànya cini ri.
to distribute them-to; and He distributed fishes which two them all to.
42. Ago vona cini nyaigo, ago ojo ànya go. 43. Ago ànya urui
    And multitude all ate, and filled they.   And they gathered
anjokona 'boloto ro go   koli 'butedriari twi, ago ti'bi ro pa. 44. Ago ànya
fragments bread of   baskets twelve   full, and fishes of also.   And they
se konyai mapa be ana anjioko manago na kutu   nji.
that ate loaves of those about   men thousand five.

Logo

Two folk-tales, contributed by Miss Lucy McCord.

(Translation by phrases)

1. *Pidigo Logoki aḋi.*
   Fable of the Logo.

'Dia-ŋga-komvo-wei-'balepiḋi zi Tudruı   Jiḋa be,
The creator-of-all-things   called the Bull-frog and the (small Long-legged)
dre tazo, kiḋi: 'Mìkodo ŋga nie mundia drı,   ŋga naḋiikie
Frog, and said saying: 'Take these things to the people, those things (are)
mbalimbalıı, kafuı, aciı, ŋgakori weiḋi be.   Jiḋa taḋi ikodo
a sling,   a hoe, fire, all seed for planting with. The Long-legged Frog said he
mbalimbalıı,   aipa dre adrele kacua ḋise,   ikowaro yi
would take the sling (but), because his foot delayed long, he would jump (i.e. swim)

---

[1] This is probably a misprint in the original for '*laŋ(y)i*' or '*lanyi*'. (See 'divide' in vocabulary.)

mise aba ḋivo.　　　　　　*Tudru taḋi ini doaɪ,*　　　　*Tudru dre*
in the water by means of it(?) The Bull-frog said he would take it, and the Bull

mbalimbali dozo,　　*dre ḋezo aba yi na.*　　　　*Jiḋa*　　　　　　　　*dre*
frog took the sling, and fell with it in the water.　The Long-legged Frog then

kafu,　*aci, ŋgakori wei be ḋiiki dozo, ziazo aba,*　　　　　*fezo mundia edrɪ.*
the hoe, fire, seed　all and these took, passed over with them, gave to the people.

Andru kafu be,　　　　*aci be,*　*ŋgakori weiḋii be.*　　*Logo adreki tusua Logo*
To-day (there is) the hoe, the fire, and all the seed.　The Logo think the Logo

tusuki Tudru koo,　　　*ta mbalimbali ḋele ko ḋi,*　　　　*mundia kicoa*
think the Bull-frog should work, because if the sling had not fallen, the people need

amvu a ko,　　*mundia kicoa ta amvu vi mbalimbali se.*
not hoe the fields, the people could manage[1] their garden affairs with the sling.

2. Logo folk-lore.

Logoɪ taki toko aloḋi adre 'ba na.　　　　　　　*Toko nda taja aiikira*
The Logo say a certain woman stayed in a village.　This woman spread her stones

keru drina.　　*Kozia adre afile,*　　　　*toko nda dre razo, aikira awoa*
on the granary.　(When) the rain had come, that woman ran, to gather her stones

keru drina.　　*Idre adrera kera awoa ḋia,*　　　　*kozia dre ḋizo we, ŋga*
on the granary.　While she remained gathering the stones, the rain fell much, things

dre torizo we.　　*Toko nda dre ŋgatori sizo*　　　　*aḋezo vudrile.*
were very slippery.　This woman slipped (on) the slippery things fell on the ground.

Akoḋi kaḋe ḋi, dre tozo ago aloḋi ni keru zona.　　　　*Mundia konoki*
When she fell, (she) slid under a certain man's granary.　The people when (they)

akoḋi ni komve be akoḋi pa,　　*akoḋi ru'ba mundiaro ko,*　　*aii adre akoḋi*
saw from her anklets (on) her leg, (that) her body was not mortal, they propitiated

ru'ba tili tau se.　　*Aii koliki tau keka se ḋi.*　　　　*akoḋi lofo tau*
her person with a fowl.　When they propitiated with a red fowl, she became like a

niro, aikuli tau nise ḋi,　　*akoḋi lofo tau mvero.*　　*Aii koliki ndri se,*
fowl, her cry was (that) of a fowl, she became a white fowl. When they propitiated

　　　　ŋga we ḋise ḋi, akoḋi dre lofozo ŋga ndaro.　　*Aii dre lizo mundia se,*
with a goat, with all things, she became like those things.　They propitiated with a

　　　dre lofozo mundiaro,　　*dre adrezo kero lii ni mvatokoro,*
person, she became like a person, (and) abode (with) the granary's owner as daughter,

ago dre akoḋi ozo　　*dre anji tizo lezole we.*　　　*Aiiniiki a suru adre Wura*
the man married her and she bore many children.　Their tribe　　is Wura

Matafa ni vu na.
in Matafa's region.

Extract from the New Testament (Mark vi. 35-44)
(The miracle of the loaves and the fishes). Literal translation.

35. *Kitu*　*koo*　*ta*　*ndizo ḋi,*　　*ḋia*　*aḋi ni tayilepiḋii aliki aḋivuna,*
　　Sun　making　thing　setting,　people　His　disciples　came　Him to,

[1] Translation of 'vi' uncertain. 'Mbalimbali', too, needs closer definition.

dreki taza, '*Vo niḍi amgboro, kitu o ta ndizo nyanomvano;*
saying, 'Place this a desert-place, sun made thing setting already;

36. *mikomu ḍia aii koliro lau ase, 'ba ase kurukuru*
You-send them (away) they may-go country into villages into round about

ŋga gi aiidri nyale.' 37. *Aḍi ako ta tale dre taza aiidri,* '*Mɩ̀kofe*
food buy them-for eat.' He however word said saying them-to, 'You-give

ŋga aiidri nyale.' *Aii dreki taza aḍidri,* '*Màkoli ŋga gi, mokuta kama*
food them-to eat.' They said him to, 'We shall go food buy pence hundred

iri ḍiise, ŋga fezo aiidri nyale ya?' 38. *Aḍi dre taza aiidri,* '*Ambata be*
two for, it give them-to eat?' He said them to, 'Loaves are

amidrika aŋgopi ya? Mìli noa.' *Aii koniḍi aii dreki taza,* '*Ambata*
you by how-many? You-go see.' They when knew they said, 'Loaves

nji, kosia iri.' 39. *Aḍi dre ta tazo aiidri, ḍia weiḍii koliri*
five fishes two.' He was word saying them-to, people all should-sit

mbi solisoliḍi dri tɩrɩro. 40. *Aii dreki lirizo tɩrɩ, arukaba nyaḍinji*
grass green on in-ranks. They sat in-ranks, by fifty

nyaḍinji, arukaba nyaḍiri-dri-mudri nyaḍiri-dri-mudri. 41. *Aḍi dre ambata nji*
fifty, by hundred hundred. He was loaves five

ḍii dozo kosia iri ḍii be, dre mi dora'a kuru na i'ba beneditu
those taking fishes two those and, was eyes lifting heaven to he-made blessing

ŋga ru, dre ambata tupizo, dre fezoa ḍia aitayilepiḍii drɩ 'bale aiikandra;
food on, was loaves breaking, was giving people his-disciples to set them before;

aḍi dre kosia iri ḍii lanjizo aiidri wei. 42. *Aii nyadre wei, aii dre*
He was fishes two those dividing them-to all. They ate all, they were

pizo. 43. *Aii dre ambata-koronyo kuḍuzo kanji mudri-dri-iriḍii a tukuda,*
filled. They were bread-fragments gathering baskets twelve full(?),

kosia iri ḍiikia be. 44. *Ago ambata nyalepiḍii kutu nji.*
fishes two those and. Now loaf eaters thousand five.

LUGBARA

Lugbara folk-tale, written by K. T. Lanalana of Kampala Normal School, Uganda.[1]

(Translation by phrases)

Oduko. Aliko pi Odrudru be.
Story. The (Small) Frog and the Bull-frog.

Andradrio afa ovu nyaku a kakao,   'ba be, ti be ndri be, anyakpa
Long ago there were many things in the world, people, cattle, goats, and many

andini be kakao, afa dria ovu kakao. Etu alo Aliko pi 'ba agata ga Odrudru
wild animals too, all things were plentiful. One day the small Frog and the Bull-

be yi eselia eyo ḍiri si: Deŋga
frog they had an argument among themselves about this matter: (viz.) Before the

---

[1] Kindly contributed by Mr. A. Lush of the Uganda Education Department, at the request of Mr. R. A. Snoxall.

'bani ovuzu nyaku a kakao,   bini azo yi eselia aloni ko,
people were numerous in the world, (they) caught no single illness among them,

'ba drani¹ ko oḏu ḏasi.   Aliko yora,   'Aŋgo ḏori ovu onzi,
and people did not die in those days. The small Frog said, 'This place is bad,

amamazo yi tia aḏasi.'   Odrudru yora,   'Ka ḏini amani zoria,
let us cross to the other side of the water.' The Bull-frog said, 'If it is so that we cross,

male 'ba ori² ḏu mai,   maŋga mbo yi be yi tia aḏasi.'
I wish to carry the people's lineage myself, and I'll jump with them to the other

                    Aliko yora,   'Hai Odrudru! pa mini ovu omutrutruaro,
side of the water.' The small Frog said, 'Oh Bull-frog! your legs are very short,

econi mini mbozaro 'ba ori be yi tia aḏasi ŋgoni ŋgoni ya?'   Odru-
how will you be able to jump with the people's lineage to the other side?' The

dru yora,   'Maŋga mbora, ḏi eyo mani.'   Aliko yora,   'Yeke,
Bull-frog said, 'I shall jump, that is my affair.' The small Frog said, 'Good, for

mai maŋga anya ori ḏu anyakpa be.'   Yini 'baria azi ḏiri ŋgaria,
myself I shall carry seeds of food and animals.' When they began to do this work,

de isu 'ba kakao yini ovuria yi tia,   Aliko 'ba Odrudru ndro
there were many people who were at the edge of the sea, the Frog began to revile

kini   agu ḏiri ŋga mbo 'ba ori be ŋgoni ŋgoni ya?
the Bull-frog saying how was this one going to jump with the lineage of the people?

'Ba dria yi yora,   'Miko ḏi eyo erini.'   Vilerisi yi 'ba afa yini ḏuleri
The people all said, 'Leave him to his business.' After this they began to divide

awa.   Aliko ḏu anya ori anyakpa be.   Odru-
the things for them to carry. The little Frog took the seeds and animals. The

dru ḏu erini 'ba ori.   Yi yini lezu mbozu drinisiri
Bull-frog took for himself the ancestry of the people. The sea over which they wished
                                                                           [to jump

ovu ambo mileni ovu ekaro kile arile, azini alini to,   yi ka'ba toroalo
was big and was red like blood, moreover it was very deep, if one were to

'ba izuro alinia,   yi econi cazaro alini a ko.
place a hundred men lengthwise, they would not be able to reach the distance.

Curuḏo yi 'baḏi mbo.   Aliko si reka mbo yi tia aḏasi,
Now they began to jump. The little Frog drew back and jumped over the sea,

ori aloni panii ḏe yi a ko indikani anyakpani.   'Ba dria ovupi yi tia
and not even one seed fell in the water nor an animal. All the people who were at

ri,   yi kandre ḏinile,   yi dria ovu aiikosi to,   oŋga tozapie.
the sea, when they saw this, they were all very pleased, so that they danced (a song).

Curuḏo Odrudru eri 'ba mbo ori 'bani be,   eri si yibe reka,
Now the Bull-frog got ready to jump with the people's ancestry, he drew himself

     mbo yi a trua!   Aliko kandrera,   eri yora, 'Wo wo!
back, and jumped into the sea, plop! When the Frog saw it, he said, 'Wo wo!

---

¹ Or 'ba dra ni ko = People knew not death (?).
² Lit. People's seed; but 'ukoo wa watu' in accompanying Swahili translation.

Mayo tera, ɖi eyo Odrudru eyo mini.' Coti ovu candisi 'bani oɖele yi aliarisi,
I said, Bull-frog, it was your business.' Then he was sad (because) the people had

eri mbo yi alia,   eri oɖu 'ba ma joloko
fallen into the sea, he sprang in the sea, he picked up the people who were half of

acepi yi tiari amve.   Lugbara oduko yora
them drowning in the sea (taking them) out. (This) story of the Lugbara says that

'ba ye ndra odra ko Odrudru kandra ori 'bani be yi a ko.
the people would not have died if the Bull-frog had not dropped the ancestry of

Azini Aliko kandra 'ba acepiri opa ko,
the people into the sea. Also the little Frog if he had not helped the people who

te ɖo ori 'bani ovu nyaku dria yo.
were drowning, there would have been no ancestry of the people in the world.

Eyoɖisi 'ba yi ovu aiikosi Aliko vu,   yi ovu asi adra si Odrudru vu,
Therefore the people are pleased with the little Frog, (but) are angry with the Bull-

ecazu troa curuɖo yi ŋgu Odrudruni onzi ɖani.
frog, from then till now they hate the Bull-frog very much.

Extract from the New Testament (Mark vi. 35-44).

(The miracle of the loaves and the fishes). Literal translation.

35. *Etu kaeca ambo,   'Baerini   ŋga emu vunia ŋga yo tinia*
    Sun reached far, people his (i.e. disciples) came Him to said Him to

kini: 'Aŋgo ɖoa   aŋgo tokoni, etu curuɖo zo ambo 'bo; 36. *mipe   yi*
thus: 'Place this a place desert, day now passed far has;   You-send them

tiale,   yi mamu   aŋgo va   amaageia ɖoa   aku alesi ŋguluŋgulu nyaka
away, that they may go country into us-around here villages into everywhere food

je   yidri.' 37. *Yi ŋga yo yitia,   kini: 'Emife   yidri nyaka nya.'*
buy themselves for.'   He-said them to, thus: 'You give them to food eat.'

Yi ŋga yo tinia, kini: 'Amaɖi   mu nyaka je   siliŋi   torotoro-iri si fe
They-said Him to, thus: 'We (emph.) go food buy shillings hundred-two for give

yidri ani?' 38. *Eri yo   yitia dika, kini: 'Enya-olimini   emidri   si ya?*
them to?'   He said them to again, thus: 'Loaves you among how-many?

Emimu ndre.'   Yi kani'bo,   yi yora, kini: 'Toi, azini e'bi iri.' 39. *Eri*
You-go see.'   They when knew, they said, thus: 'Five, also fishes two.'   He

azi   yi ra kini 'ba mari vadria   irindi   dria eselesi eselesi.
commanded them thus they should sit down green (grass) all company company.

40. *Yi ŋga ri   dere dere, azini   toro   toro,   azini kalitoi kalitoi.* 41. *Eri*
    They (and) sat rank rank, also hundred hundred, also   fifty   fifty.   He

ŋga enya-olimini toi ɖura, e'bi iri be, eri ŋga aŋgo lu   'bua   uru,
then   loaves   five took, fishes two and, He then prayer said heaven to up,

eri ka   asi   ndriza aiidrinia 'bo, eri ŋga enya-olimini maale ati,   ŋga fe
He when blessing invoked them-on.   He then   bread   up broke, gave

'Baerini   madri   yi maasa   'ba   nde   palaa.   Azini   e'bi   iri   ďi   eri
people His   to   they might set people then before.   And fishes two those He

ŋga awa   yidri   dria.   42.   Yi   dria ŋga nya   ŋga trara.   43.   Yi
divided   them among   all.   They   all   ate   and were filled.   They

ŋga   joloko   oďu   abaka alia tre mudri-drini-iri, azini e'bi   jolokoni ndi.
and fragments gathered baskets in full   twelve   and fish fragments also.

44.   'Ba   nyaka nyapiri kalafe yini   kali   toro   toi agupi adule.
Those food that-ate given them to about thousand five men alone.

Madi

Madi story[1] (Translation by phrases).

Etawo ini Ewa be.

The Hare and the Elephant.

Anyi te cara,   *ba tataa edo ŋga aju ra.*   *Dee Etawo*
When the rainy-season had come, all people began hoeing things.   But when

edoni eri awo ŋga aju ko,   *Etawo izipi kinibe Etawo tia:*   '*Agu maovi*
the Hare had not begun to hoe yet,   the Hare's wife said to the Hare: 'Look here

la!   Mimu amayowo   ŋga ba aariaŋara ya?'   *Etawo kinibe ya*
my man! Are you going to our field when the people are hoeing?' The Hare said

yee.   Etawo ndee izipi ru Apuatei.   *Vini inibe Etawo ini*
very well.   Now the Hare's wife's name was Apuate. Thus she said to the

    ani olaria nyawua.   Kinibe izipi Apuatei   obhu tilebe eri
Hare as they lay in bed. He said to his wife Apuate in the morning that she should

tri oso,   izipi ŋgaindi tri oso ra,   *Etawo ŋgaindi*
give (him) some beans, and the wife forthwith gave the beans, the Hare at once

fi jo a,   du ebu   pu aja,   to oso maŋgala alea,
entered the house, picked up (his) hoe and went outside, put the beans into a bag,

kodri mu.   Etawo asi a eyo ga   kadri ava akua,
and set out.   The Hare deliberated the matter in his heart and returned home,

kinibe izipii   eri isi oso isi isika azile bha   te arani eri ŋga
and said to his wife that she should dry the beans in the fire so that when he

mbele   acici beni.   Izipi Apuate ŋgaindi isi oso ra,
planted them they should grow more quickly. The wife Apuate forthwith dried

       to maŋgala alia   fe Etawoi.   Etawo kodri mu
the beans, put (them) in the bag and gave them to the Hare. The Hare set out

asea   dhu oso indi,   te ca asea balini,   mu pati alowo osedro
into the bush carrying the beans, when he arrived in the bush, he went underneath

[1] Kindly obtained by Mr. A. Lush of the Uganda Education Department at the request of Mr. R. A. Snoxall. The dialect, which is very like Lugbara, is probably that of Aiivu County. Since some of the idioms of this language are unknown to me, only a general translation can be given. Spellings like *bh, th, ch*, are left as in the original, though the *h* is probably unnecessary. No attempt is made here to differentiate between explosive and implosive consonants.

SPECIMEN TEXTS 335

zelea   ŋgaindi ri nyawua,   ba oso dho,   te oso dho
a certain big tree and sat down (to rest), and began to munch the beans, when he

de baa,   ace de isu etu ca mudri.
had munched the beans, it now was (lit. found) the tenth hour of the day (4 p.m.).

Etawo ŋgaindi gani kaŋgua nyawu ci,   ba ru yo,   kinibe
The Hare then cut up small pieces of clay, and rubbed (them) on (his) body, mak-

te ebi ŋga ale.   Ŋgaindi mvi akua.   Izipii eri belea
ing out that he had been hoeing. Then he returned home. His wife had made

enya koci.   Izi ŋgaindi fe enya eriyhi,   ŋgaindi nyara. Izipi kinibe dru
food ready. His wife at once gave food to him, and he ate. His wife said she

nile mu ŋga co,   de izi nde gia mva ode iyani,
wished to go weeding the next day, and his wife would bring (her) young child

draru erini.   Etawo ŋgaindi ģasi, kinibe ya mva ru adra dru,
with her, and he was ill. The Hare objected, saying that the child's body was

nicote ŋga coti.   Dru vini bua izipi isi osu dih aju
very ill, and that he had finished weeding. In the morning therefore his wife dried
[more beans for planting

druzi bua izipi isi osu dih.   Etawo te izipini ole
(as) she had dried beans the other morning. After the Hare had deceived his wife

ca odu mudri ba,   kinibe izipii ace nia ŋga ti osedro baa,
while ten days passed, he said to his wife that he had hoed quite enough,

ace nile ambiju akua.   Odu te egati mudri ba ni, izipi zi eritia,
and wished to rest at home. After ten days had passed, his wife called to

kinibe: 'Oso ŋga onyibe a?'   Etawo kinibe: 'Ee, onyia
him, saying: 'Are the beans (growing) well?' The Hare said: 'Yes, very

mbani.' Mba te ca alo dria odu mudri dria towi,   Etawo izipi Apuate kinibe
well.' After one month and fifteen days had passed, the Hare's wife Apuate said

nile mu osobi edi nya avai,   te nindre wei zini ani ba osobi
she wished to go to gather the beans for eating, because she saw other women

nyanya.   Etawo kinibe yee,   nimu osobi edinii.   Etu te
eating beans. The Hare said very well, he would go and gather the beans. When

zora,   Etawo kinibe izipii   nimu osobi edi,
the sun rose, the Hare said to his wife that he would go and gather the beans,

ŋgaindi mura, dena mu osobi edi   ogidru   Ewa belea ŋgaa;   te osobi
and he went, but he went to gather beans like a thief in the Elephant's field; when he

edi baa,   kodri mvi akua, ji osobi fe izipii
had gathered the beans, he returned home, and brought the beans and gave

Apuate ŋgaindi adhira   nya Etawo ibe tataa.
(them) to his wife and Apuate cooked them and the Hare and his (family) all ate.

Etawo tela nyawua,   kinibee izipii,   'Apuateh, oso amayowo vi erimu ka
As the Hare lay down, he said to his wife, 'Apuate, our beans will yield a great

mbani.' Ace bha tata te ba oso nya bani,   Apuate kinibe Etawo
harvest.' Now when all the people began to eat their beans, Apuate said to the

tia nile mu oso ti.   *Etawo ŋgaindi gasi, kinibe*
Hare that she wished to go and pick the beans. The Hare objected, saying that

nimu oso ti nii,   *erigiamva abudro,*   *Etawo*
he would go and pick the beans himself, as his child was still ill. The Hare

dhu maŋgala   *mu oso ti*   *Ewa belea ogidru,*
took the basket and went to pick beans at the Elephant's (place) as a thief,

te osu ti bani,   *mvi akua ji oso fe izipii,*
after gathering the beans, he returned home bringing the beans and gave (them) to

         izipi ŋgaindi ovu oso ra   *nya Etawo ibe alo mva oko vii.*   *Ini*
his wife, and his wife had the beans and the Hare and his son and wife ate. Now

ani olaria nyawua Apuate kinibe   *ace mva ru a ati ace ba,*
when they were lying down Apuate said that the child had now recovered in body,

nile mu oso ti.   *Etawo ŋgaindi kinibe ni mili a*
and she wished to go and pick the beans. The Hare at once said that with his eyes

noa   *mva ru a ovu nani*   *nileni*   *eri aci mvani awo vi*
he saw that the child was still ill in body and that he wished that she would not

be etu a ko.   *Oso tizadru,*   *nimu tira nii.*
walk with his son in the sun. As for gathering the beans, he would go and gather

          Ewa tendre niawo bani oso ogiogi,
(them) himself. When the Elephant himself saw that he was robbed of his beans,

dro ace ŋga tia pati ci.   *Ewa ko leti aloadidi,*
he surrounded his field with wood (i.e. a hedge). The Elephant left a narrow path,

leti nde erini kole naa   *alea ba wichi ci,*   *azile baruo oso ogini*
and the path which he had left in it he set a trap, so that the man who was stealing

    eri ai beni wichi a.   *Aŋgo te bi bani*   *Etawo ŋgaindi*
beans so that he should get caught in the trap. The following night the Hare took

duh ogei mu oso ti   *Ewa belea ogidru,*   *te oso ti*
a basket and went to gather beans at the Elephant's (place) like a thief, and when

bani,   *ace erini oria puria,*   *ai agamile a wichi a*
he had gathered the beans, and when he was running away, he was caught by the

cot!   *aŋgo ati driya naa.*   *Aŋgo te atira*   *de etu nai*
loins in the trap fast, and stayed all night there. When the night broke and it was

    Arawo tata ri mu oŋgoka,   *ri tata egati leti nai.*   *Etawo tendre vini,*
day many Baboons came to dance, they all passed by that path. When the Hare

      rini ajyaajya kinibele a laraka larale.   *riji Arawo omvepai.*
saw this, he flung himself about as though playing while he called the Baboons.

Arawo tata egatira,   *alo ace ava.*   *Etawo te eri omvera*
The Baboons all passed on, but one lingered. When the Hare called him he

mu Etawo bu,   *Etawo riji oŋgo ŋgopai:*   '*Drile ba mani eri ma tro andru ra.*'
came to the Hare, while the Hare sang a song: 'My head will save me to-day.'

'Drile ba mani eri ma tro andru ra.' *Kinibe Arawo* *eri tro ŋga wichi*
'My head will save me to-day.'[1] (Then) he said to the Baboon that he should

ni agamili a ra, eri fi azile wichi alea,
loosen the trap from his loins, and that he (the Baboon) should enter the trap,[2]

te wichi tro Etawo agamili a bani, *ŋgaindi fi wichi alea.*
and when he had loosened the trap from the Hare's loins, he entered the trap.

Etawo ŋgaindi bhe cere: *'Madrile onyi mbani,* *madrile onyi mbani.'*
The Hare then made a noise: 'My head[3] is very good, my head is very good.'

Ewa te cere erina, *ca Etawo bu,* *Etawo olo*
When the Elephant heard the noise, he came up to the Hare, (and) the Hare ran

eyo Ewai nini *niisu Arawo* *ri oso ogi eriawo,*
and said to the Elephant that he had found the Baboon stealing beans himself,

niŋgaindi nini eri droria mu ace ai wichi a dii. *Ewa tendre Arawoni*
and when he chased him he went and was caught in that trap. When the Elephant

ba candi, *beni co eri co adule ko eri ra.* *Etawo kinibe*
saw the miserable Baboon, he merely beat him and left him. The Hare said to

Ewa tia: *'Adroma Ewa,* *maru ogiru o* *miawo oso ogiria di*
the Elephant: 'My uncle Elephant, I caught the thief robbing your own beans

de mimu mai ari afa fe a?' *Ewa kinibe lete* *nife erii ari afani*
now what thing are you going to give me?' The Elephant said what thing should

a? *Etawo kini* *nile* *eri sinii oso ŋga be,*
he give him? The Hare said he wished he would divide his field of beans,

Ewa ŋgaindi si oso ŋga be, *fe Etawoi.* *Etawo kinibe*
so the Elephant divided up his bean field, and gave the Hare (half). The Hare said

Ewai *eri ji eyo vi olo akua ko.* *'Mite ji*
to the Elephant that he should meanwhile not tell these matters at home. 'If you

eyo vi olo akuai, *Arawo imu oso ogi di.'*
say anything to the people at home, the Baboons will come and steal the beans

Etawo temvi akua, *izipi zi eria:* *'Etawo la,*
again.' When the Hare returned home, his wife called to him: 'Look here Hare,

miri ovu ŋgooa?' *Etawo kinibe* *nimu ndra adronia.* *Dru vini*
where have you been?' The Hare said he had gone to see his uncle. So in the

Etawo ji izipini *ece* *oso Ewa ni fele erii*
morning the Hare took his wife and showed (her) the beans the Elephant had given

Arawo ni ruleivia *Oso nde tini eroi tree.*
him for catching the Baboon. And the beans filled the granary (lit. were put in

the granary full).

---

[1] The Swahili translation gives: 'kwa bahati njema nitajiokoa leo' (with good luck I'll escape to-day)—which does not seem to fit the Madi wording at all.
[2] In order to be able to play like the Hare.
[3] 'My luck' according to the Swahili translation.

Madi-Lokai

Extract from 'Ofo oloree' (Madi Bible History), pp. 98–9.
(The miracle of the loaves and the fishes). Literal translation.

Mugati enyaika.
Loaves for eating (or feeding?)

'Ba   retu   emuki   anidri   le'jo   enire,   ma'jo   ojoki   anini,   'Nyoze
People many   came   Him to   words   learn,   disciples said   Him to 'You-send

'ba   ďii   'baru   pi   tanyaleri'ı ndrure, aďosi   oďu   ina   kakiolo
people these   home   away food   get,   because days   three   they suffer

amatro   abiri   si.'   Yesu   le o'jo: 'Anyidro   aı   pi   ko,   anyikwe
us with hunger from.' Jesus and said: 'You-drive them away not,   you-give

aını   tanyaleri'ı.'   Ma'jo   oceki: 'Amadri   dya   aı   mugati ni ewo tou
them   food.'   Disciples answered: 'Us among here they loaves of bread five

e'bi   eri   tro aďito,   ta   zii   iyo.'   Ani asi: 'Anyeji   ta   ďii   mani
fish   two   with only,   thing other not.'   He then   'You-bring things those me to

anyi'ba   'ba   koriki vuru   tro. Voa Yesu   onji   mina   oru   oco
you-make   people sit   down   and. Then Jesus raised eyes   his   up pronounced

tutu   tanyaleri'ı a   ruga   o'jo asi   ma'jo   ni kanjoki   ta   'ba
blessing   food   on   broke said then disciples   should distribute things people

ni.   Laka   otrakiro   'ba   ago   drorı'ı   elf   tou   pi   okonji   aı
among.   Now   amounted to   people men   all   thousand five   and   women   they

'boronji   tro.   Cidro onyaki   ta   tri   Yesu   o'jo   kotraki   anya
children   with.   All   ate   things but   Jesus said   they should gather meal

fofo   rebereri'ı.   Otrara,   esuro   rege   mudri-limbi-ri   fofo
remnants   left over.   Gathered,   were found   baskets   twelve   remnants

rebereri'ı   si.
left over   of.

Madi-Pandikeri

Extract from the New Testament (Mark vi. 35–44).
(The miracle of the loaves and the fishes). Literal translation.

35. *Lofo   ondrwe   laga   ma'jo   anidri kemu keanini.   Ai   o'jo,   ''Dia*
    When   evening   descended disciples His   came Him to.   They said,   'Here

aiiya   loku   etu   atera.   36. Nyeze   'ba   kohwi   eia   koje lonya   aďosi
desert and   sun   has set.   You-send them   away   they buy   food   because

lonya   aidri   iyo.'   37. Ani   keŋgwi   ofo   aidri, 'Anyekwe   'ba   lonya.'
food   them to is not.'   He   replied   then   them to, 'You-give them food.'

Ai   o'jo keanini, 'Amamu amaje lonya   siliŋi   mia-eri   okwe ai ra?'
They   said Him to   'We go we buy food   shillings   hundred two   give them?'

38. *Yezu   o'jo keaini, 'Aa mugate si?   Anyevo,   anyendre.'   Lofoďi   ai*
    Jesus said them to, 'Are loaves how-many?   You-go,   you-see.'   When   they

endre,	*ai*	*o'jo,*	'*Mugate*	*tou,*	*e'bi*	*eri.*'	39. *Ani ko'jo*	*ai podru anyirire*
saw,	they	said,	'Loaves	five	fish	two.'	He said	they all you-sit

vuru	*aise*	*a.*	40. *Ai*	*yori vuru*	*laini laini*	*mia mudi-tou*
down	grass	on.		They sat down	company company	hundreds fifties

tro.	41. *Lofo Yezu oko mugate tou e'bi eri tro,*					*ondre*	*'bua,*	*anjo,*
with.	When Jesus took loaves five fish two with,					looked	heaven to,	*blessed*,

oti	*mugate,*	*okwe*	*ma'jo*	*dri e'bi eri tro.*	*Ai*	*okwe*	*'ba moro.*
broke	loaves,	gave	disciples	to fish two with.	They	gave	people before.

42. *Posa*	*onyaki*	*aogandro.*	43. *Ai*	*odu evo*	*mudi-limbi-ri*
All	ate	and were filled.		They picked up	baskets twelve

mugate dri ti	*e'bi tro.*	44. *Ai*	*nai onya mugate*	*kendre*	*ai elefu*
loaves of and	fishes with.		They who ate loaves	seemed	they thousand

tou.
five.

SECTION IV
VOCABULARIES

Note that the verbs are given in the infinitive form without suffix. Where an object is incorporate in a verb, it will precede the verb root in the vocabulary, as in the infinitive form (except in Pandikeri Madi and Lulu'ba, where the word order is unchanged in the Indefinite Aspect, see §§ 426 and 430). Morphological class is shown as follows:

    Class I. ɔ-sɪ (to bite)—characteristic vowel (in such languages as use it) separated from root by hyphen.
    Class II. ɛzí (to bring)—characteristic vowel not separated.
    Class III. lerú (to kindle).

Tone class is shown as follows:

    High tone class: ɔ-vó / vó (to blow), ɛzí (to bring) lerú (to kindle).
    Mid tone class: ɔ̄-'bɪ̄ (to beat), ɛ̄kpɪ̄ (to cough), lā'dɪ̄ (to cook).
    Low tone class: ɔ-drà / drà (to die), ɛlè (to lick), turì (to fear).

Absence of tone marks on verb stems indicates uncertainty as to tone class. Such verbs in the Moru dialects at least seem to behave like Mid tone verbs.

There are many Moru-Madi words that have relationships in other languages. These will be indicated by the following figures:

    (2) relationships in Bongo-Baka.
    (3)   ,,   ,, Ndogo-Sere.
    (4)   ,,   ,, Zande.
    (5)   ,,   ,, Dinka.
    (6)   ,,   ,, Nuer.
    (7)   ,,   ,, Shilluk-Acholi.
    (8)   ,,   ,, Bari.

No attempt is made, however, to ascertain whether the word in question is a borrowing into or out of these languages. It is interesting to note that most of these words occur in Bongo-Baka and/or in Bari.

VOCABULARY
MORU

	Miza	Kediru	Lakama'di	-ägi	Wa'di	'Bälimbä	-ändri
animal	èza (2)	èza	èza	èza	èza	èza	èza
carnivore	koronya	koronya	tsitsí	tsɪtsí	tsɪtsí	tsɪtsí	tsɪtsí
ant (gen.)							
ant-hill (see *termite*)	koto	koto	koto	koto	koto	ɔtɔ	ɔtɔ
arrow	ätú	ätú	ätú	ätú	ätú	ätú	ätú
ashes	tórófɔ	tórófɔ	tórófɔ	kórófɔ	kófó	tórófò	órófó
axe	kólóŋwá	kólóŋwá	kólóŋwá	kólóŋwá	kɔlángwá	kólóŋgwá	óɽóvá
baboon	lɔré (8)	lɔré	lɔré	lɔré	lɔré	lɔré	lɔré
back	kundu	kundu	kundu		kwögú (2)	ugú	ugú
bamboo	kʷódrä̌	kódrä̌	kódrá	kódrá	kódrá	ódrá	ódrá
basket (gen.)	kóɽi	kóɽi	kóɽi	kóɽi	kóɽi	kóɽi	täbi
bat	'bí'bí (2)	'bí'bí	'bí'bí	'bíb'í	'bí'bí	'bí'bí	'bí'bí
beard	tivu	kǎsúsú-'bi	kǎsúsú-'bi	tilí-'bí	tilí-'bí	gbaŋgò	tili-'bi
beer	wá	wá	wá	wá	wá	wá	wá
belly	ya	ya	ya	kúɽù	kúɽù 'á	'a	úɽù ia
bird	àrɪ (2)	àrɪ	àrɪ	àrɪ-ŋwa	àrɪ-ŋgwa	àrɪ-ŋgwa	àrɪ-va
blacksmith	tòkǎ-'bå	tòkǎ-'bå	tòkǎ-'bå	kòkǎ-'bå	kòkǎ-'bå	òkǎ-'bå	òkǎ-'bå
blood	kàrɪ	kàrɪ	kàrɪ	kàrɪ	kàrɪ	àrɪ	àrɪ
body	ló(m)vó ro (2)	lóvó	lómvó	rúmvú	rúmvú	úmvǒ	rúmvú
bone	kɔwà	kɔwà	kɔwà	kwa	kwa	kwà	fà
bow	kúsu	kúsu	kúsu	kúsu	kwósu	úsu	úsu
bowels	ɪtsʷí (2)	etʃʷí	ɪtsʷí	ɪtsí	etsʷí	esʷí	ɪfí ɔfí
brains	kúmè	kúmè	kúmè	kúmè	kúmè	kúmè	kúmè
breast (*man*)	kótótì	kǎtǎtì	kótítì	ágá	ǎgǎsì	ágá	ágá
(*woman*)	bà (2)	bà	bà	bà	bà	bà	bà
brother	ädrúpi (2)	ädrúpi	ädrúpi	ädrúpi	ädrúpi	ädrúpi	ädrúpi
buffalo	udrú	odrú	udrú	udrú	ädrú	udrú	udrú
bull	'dauŋgò	'daŋò	'daŋò	raŋga	ití-agɔ		'daŋgò
buttocks	zɛvò	zɛvò	zɛlé	zɛrévò	zɛlévò	límè	límè

VOCABULARY

AVUKAYA					MADI			
Ojila	Ojiga	Logo	Keliko	Lugbara	Lokai	Pandikeri	Lulu'ba	Lendu
à'wa	à'wa	za *kawa*	za	èza	èza	za	èza	ezâ
tsɪtsí	ŋgóònzi ŋgáàtra	kalíjá	kalájí	anyukpá o'dógó *nyaraga*	anyukwá	anyukwá	anyukwá	aazanaza
	kyíkyɪwá	kyékyé	kyékyévá	kyéké	nyanyai	nyɛnyɛi	lɔŋíŋɪní	kaka
ótó	ótó	kótóa	ótó ɔ'dɔgɔ	ɔtógɔ a'dɔgɔ	ótó	ótó	ítú	tʃó
ɪ'yé	ɪ'yá	kɪ'yá	í'yɛ 'jɛ	'yɛ 'ɛ	ɛ'ɛ	ɛ'ɛ	ɛcí	mbrr
ɔfɔ̀	ófódró	tófórókó	ɔforago (=ash-heap)	ɔfɔra	ófúdrô	ofúdó	kúro	hu
ɔ́ɽóvá	ólówá	kòbâɽú	kâɽú ùbolu	túlu òbo'du	tólú	tólú	tólú	lo
lɔré	ogyɪ̀	ɔgia ɔgyà	ógyi ùdzigɔ	ódzigó idzigó	lɔré	dʒɔmî	ɔrwé	ŋgrr
ugúlé	ògule	gólé mvʊ	gólé ogɔrɔ	ògurɛ ogɔrɔ	ogu (2)	ogu	ogú	(le-)dzz
ɔdrá	(k)ódra	kɔdra	ódrá ganzi	ódrá ʊdra	ɔ̀dra	kwèda	kwɛda	bi
yevò	ívʊ̀	kánzià	ùvʊ kánzì	ùvʊ vwá	èvo	èvɔ	èbɔ	tyo
'bì'bìwä	'bɪbɪgúä	bibinya kyíri	purupuruŋá kyíri	sisi idiriɽi	'bí'bí	'bí'bí	nyákúlúli (8)	kiki lonyo
tili-'bi	tili-'bi	tílí-'bià túlú-'bià	tílí-'bí	tí'bí(-tî)	tí'bí	tí'bí	tílí-'bí	letsɔ-kákà
ɔ̀dra	odrá	ówá	ówa (l)éwa	ówá éwa	erá	ówá	ewa	wa
'a	'à	'á togó	'à	'ya 'à	'a	'a	'à	o
àrɪ-wa	àrɪ-wa	arɪ-á	arí-vá	arí-a arí-ŋá	arí-áŋgwá	arí-áŋgwá	àrɪ	rɛ
lɔrɪ-'ba	mondógó	tóká agúlágú	óká túmúnì (8)	óka bòdò (7)	ɛrɛmú	ɛrɛmú	èrɔmògɔ	jojuke
àrɪ	àrɪ	kariá *ari*	(k)àrɪ	àrɪ	àrɪ	èrɪ	èrɪ	ʒú
rú'bä	rú'ba	rú'ba *rumva*	rú'ba	ru'bâ	rú	rú	rú	le-róŋga
fà	fà	fà	fà	fa	kwà	kwà	kwà	kpa
úsu	úsu	úsu *kusu*	úsù kísù	ósù	ósu	ósu	ósu	sò
fî	fí	fí fɪa	(ɪ)fí órófɪ	fî ífɪ	ikwí	ikwí	ɪkwíí	zz
umè	úmè	kóme	óme úmì	óŋwì	kúdzwé	udʒê	ugyɛ	vi
ágăsi	ägäsi	tʃitʃi (ágá=armpit)	tʃitʃi	gìrìdzò	ágá	ágá	ágá	(le-)ba-jo
bà	bà	bà	bà	ebà	bà	ɪba	èba	(le-)ba
ädrúpi	ädrúpi	ädrúpi	ädrúpi adrípi	ädrúpi adrípi	ädrúpi	adäzi	adíŋá	àdʒɔ
drú	drú	drú	(u)drú	udrú	odrú	odú	odú	bi (2)
ití-agɔ	tí-agwa	tí-agwa (-ago) dru	tí-agɔ	tí-agɔ tí-mănì-go (8)	ti-agɔ	ti-agɔ mänigó	tí-ógó	tsz-kpa
elímì zɛvɛrè	àndu	àndu	ǹdu teri (Cf. 'back' in Moru)	ìndu	zɛlédrì	zɛlédrì	fɔli	(le-)'du

VOCABULARY

MORU

	Miza	Kediru	Lakama'di	-ägi	Wa'di	'Bälimbä	-ändri
boy	ŋgágà	ŋgágà	ŋágà	ndǎróŋgwa	ndríŋgwà	ŋgwágà	mvágà
son (cf. *child*)	ŋgwá	ŋgwá	ŋgwá	ŋgwá	ŋgwá	ŋgwá	mvá
canoe	tómgbó	tómgbó	tómgbó	kolómgbò (4)	kolómgbà	kolómgbò	kolómgbò
cat (*gen.*)	guṭó	goṭó	goṭó	goṭó	goṭó	bılıwà	gɔṭó
wild-cat	máòu	máòu	máòu	máòu	máòu	máòu	máòu
charcoal	kíriṭí (2)	kíriṭí	kíriṭí	kíriṭí	kílìrı	kíriṭí	kíriṭí
chief	ópí	ópí	ópí	kúmu mírì	ápí	ópí'	ópí
child	ŋ̇gwá	ŋ̇gwá	ŋ̇gwá	dríàŋgwa	dríàŋgwa	ŋ̇gwá	m̀vá
chin	tívu	kǎsósú	kǎsúsú	kǎsúsú	kǒmgbǒ	gbáŋgò	gbáŋgò
cloth	vɔŋgʷó (8)	lɔó (7)	lɔú	bɔŋgó ıta	ıta	bɔŋgó	bɔŋgó
cloud	'buänzǎ	buändʒé	fɔli (7)	mbara-mbasà	mbara-mbasà	'díkílo (8)	'díkolo
cotton	kɔdè	warò (8)	warò	katúà (4)	kodo	kɔdò	kɔdò
country	'bädrì (2)	'bädrì	'bädrì	'bädrì	'bädrì	'bädrì	'bädrì
cow	tí	tí	tí	tí	ití	tí	tí
crab	kyégà	kyégà		kégà	kıgà	ségà	kyígà
crocodile	kíí (8)	kyeyu		kei	kíǎ	íyí	yíí
land-crocodile	kínyì (8)	kyínyè	kínyì	kínyè'	kínyà		ínyì
dog	kɔkyé	kwakyé	kɔkyé	kɔtsé	kwatʃé	ɔkyé	ɔtsé
donkey	dɔŋgí	dɔŋgí	dɔŋgí	dɔŋgí	dɔŋgí	dɔŋgí	dɔŋgí
horse	kayanà	kayanà	kayanà	kayanà	kayanà	kayanà	kayanà
doorway	kǎlǎsi-kàlà zɔ-kàlà	kǎlǎsi-kàlà zɔ-kàlà	kǎlǎsi-kàlà zɔ-kàlà	zósi zɔretì	zɔretì	käjíti (8)	kǎlǎsi
door	lekyí	lekyí	lekyí	kǎtì	kǎtì	kǎti-kàlà	kǎǎtì ŋgisì
dove	tú'bú	tú'bú	tú'bú	à'bu'bu	tú'bú	tíí'bú	tú'bú
dream	tɔrí	tɔrí	tɔré	kwarı	kwarı	ɔrí	órí
drum	läri (8)	läri	läri	läri	läri	läri	läri
durra (cf. *food*)	ìnya	dìrı	enyá' derí	àdri	àdri	ènya	ènya
ear	bí (2)	bí	bí	bí	bí	bí	bí
earth	vurú	vurú	vurú	vurú	vurú	vurú	vurú
ground	gìní	gìní	gìní	kyiní	kyiní	ìni	ìni

VOCABULARY

AVUKAYA					MADI			Lendu
Ojila	Ojiga	Logo	Keliko	Lugbara	Lokai	Pandikeri	Lulu'ba	
'dənyímvá	'doyímvá	mvámva	mvaŋá	ŋgotiŋa	'bará-ŋgwa	'boráŋgwa	àdə	gbetsi-mgba
mvá	mvá	mvá	mvá	ŋgótí				du
kolómgbò	kolómgbà	kolómgbà atifa	kɔlómgbò ògo	kɔlómgbò go ki'bo (8)	i'bwo (8)	i'bwo	ɪ'bɔ	bu ('bu?)
alókókó máʊ̀ɔ	olókókó	gónzà	òloko nzóró ndrógò	ólógòlo	ɔló	ɔló	àbibi	nyamu
ɪlí ɪlɛndré	älé	kílla atsíkelá	ìlɛ atsíkɔló	ɪlé	àtsíkolo	àtsíkolo	àni	liti
kumu	kumu	mókótó mírɪ	mókótó mírɪ	mókótó ópí	ópí	ópí	ósí	pi
mva	dòimva	mvá(mvá)	mvá	mvá	'bàraŋgwa	'bòraŋgwa	'borá	(kalú)-mgba
ɪsísí ítʃu	ítʃíkɪ	kútʃɪka kétséŋgè	ótsókɔ̀	íkpíkpi	otsokpɔ̀	otsokpɔ̀	nyɛkɛmʊ (8)	letsɔkúkù
ɪta	ítá	bòŋgwa	bòŋgɔ	bɔ̀ŋɔ	là'bo	là'bo	bɔŋgó	ru
'díkolò mbarasara kòdò	igwä 'bu	nduruku 'bu	obwo	'bu	lafó (=mist) wórɔ̀ (8)	ru'bu wórɔ̀	rúdo lafú waratá	ndundu coka
'bälípi	vɔ aŋgɔ	bvɔ aŋgo lau	aŋgo	aŋgo	dzuruga	dʒuruga	gyuru	tsonaŋga
ití	ití	tí	tí	(i)tí	tí	tí	tí	tszź(ja)
ɪgarátatà égiritata (kí)yíá	ɪgéráku kíí	kígga kíí	ɪgérakó ííŋá	gárákɪɾɛ̀ kínyú-kúnyù	ɪgá dʒɔre ínyó	kágoré (8) ínyó	ɛyi	itha rasu
ínya	ínyàu	ínya						
ɔkyé		kɔkyí kɔkyá kokia	utsógó mɔ̀dza	utsógó	ɔtsé	ɔké	ɔkyé	tseé
dɔŋgí kayanà	kailo	kailo	kailo	kailo	kainɔ (cp. enkaina (LuNyoro))	kainɔ	kaina 'bayalà	
dzóti-liti	dzóti-liti	'bà'a jo-ti	dzóätí	titemí	dzóti	Bu. = kotúmì (8)	dzolätì	dza-tso
átì ŋgisì	átì	vologa tigua	kääti	irɛgɛ	rigi	rigi	rigi	dzatso-i
ätú'bú	ätí'bú	kɔ'bʷɔlà	'bàlògu	àlà'bu	oló'bò	gúrè (8) Bu. = gúrè	gúrè	bana
ɔvarɪ		torobi	ɔ̀rɔ̀bi		ɔrɔbí	ɔrɔbí	ɔrɔbí	nyu nyo
läri	läri	leri gudugudu	äri	äri	läri	läri Bu. = lárí	ari	idzz
ådrigʊ	ådrigʊ	nya	ànya	ànya	ígí	ådzí Bu. = 'dukwe	ɪnyá	
bí	bí	bí	bí	bíle	bí	bí	bí	(le)bi
vùdre anyókú	lɔdrí	vo	nyoku	nyoku	vúrú Bu. =vurú	vúrú	vwa bua	ŋgo
anyókú		kiní			ìŋa Bu. = oni iŋá	ìŋa	oni	dzz

VOCABULARY

MORU

	Miza	Kediru	Lakama'di	-ägi	Wa'di	'Bälimbä	-ändri
egg	täú-'bwǎ (2)	täú-'bwà	täú-'bwǎ	käú-'bwo		äú-'bwò	äú-'bwò
elephant	lìwa	lìwa	lìwa	ǹzıgo	ındzígwá	lìwa	lìwa
excrement	zè	zè	zè	zè	zʷè	zè	zè
dung	múrè			múrè			múrè
eye	mì	mì	mì	mì	(mìŋgetʃwí) mì	mì
face (cf. eye)	mì	milétí	mì	mì		mì	mì
fat	ıdó	ıdó	ıdó	àdɔ	àdɔ	ɔdó	ɔdó
				ıdó			
father	tépi	tǎpi	tǎpi	kǎpi	kǎpi	tǎpi	tǎpi
fence	kándà	kándà	kándà	kándà	kándà	kándrà	kándà
enclosure	agà	agà	rakyí (2)	agà	agà	agà	agà
field	ãmvu	ãvu	ãmvu	ãmvu	ãmvu	ãmvu	ãmvu
finger (cf. hand)	drí-ŋgwà	drí-ŋgwà	drí-ŋgwà	drí-ŋgwò'	drí-ŋgwà	kónyí-ŋgwa (8)	drí-mvà
thumb	drí-ágó	drí-ágó	drí-ágó	drí-ágó	drí-ágó	drí-ágó	drí-ágó
fire	así	así	así	así	así	así	así
flame	ka'bílíkà lèlè	ka'bílíkà	ka'bílíkà	ka'bílíkà	así-lɛdrɛ	'bílíkà	'bílíkà
fish	tì'bi	ke'bí	ke'bí	ke'bí	ke'bí	i'bí	i'bí
fly	kùmú	kùmú	úmú	kúmú	kwomú	úmú	úmú
food	ŋgʷónya	ŋgʷónya	ŋgʷónya	ŋgʷónya	ɽinya	ŋgónya	ŋgónya
foot } leg }	pá	pá	pá	pá	pá	pá	pá
foreigner	atrá	atrá	atrá	atrá	atrá	atrá	atrá
white man	ãmgbà	ãmgbà	jòkäni	túrù	(ŋgá)àtra	gãlã (8)	gãlã
fowl	täú	täú	täú	käú	kä'ú	äú	äú
frog	túdrù (2)	túdru	túdru	amgbà	amgbà	amgbà	amgbà
giraffe	kǎrì (8)	kǎrì	kǎrì	kǎrì	mányarà	mányarà	mányarà
girl daughter (cf. child)	ŋgùti	ŋgútíŋɔ	ŋgútí	ŋgútí	ŋgwǒtíŋgó	ŋgútí	mbǎti
goat	ìndri	ìndri	ìndri	ìndri	ìndri	ìndri	ìndri
sheep	tembélé	temélé	temélé	temélé	kǎbilíki (8)	temélé	temélé
God oracle	lùu dímití	lùu dímití	lùu dímití	bule'bwä dímití	avaré	'bule'bǎ dímití	lùu dímití
gourd	kúrú	kúrú	kúrú	kúrú	kúrú	gǎuǎ	gǎuǎ

VOCABULARY

AVUKAYA		MADI						
Ojila äú-'bú	Ojiga äú-'bú	Logo táú-'bú	Keliko oú-gbɛ	Lugbara a'ú-gbe	Lokai a'ú-ɛlɛ	Pandikeri a'ú-kɛlɛ	Lulu'ba a'ú-r-ɛlɛ	Lendu o-bi
ǹdʒɪgɔ	ɔnzígó	lìwa	lìwa ɛ̀wa	ɛ̀wa ɔ̀wa	lɛ(y)á	laá Bu. = làá	ɛ̀wa	eʒó
zwɛ̀	zʷɛ̀	zà	zɛ̀	zɛ̀	zɛ̀	zɛ̀ Bu. = zɛ tí-ni-zɛ̀ Bu. = wórɔ̀	zɛ̀ wórɔ̀ (8)	za
lifí nilé	mifí milé	mí kandraga mibali	mí andrɛti	mí andrɛti	mí ándra	mí ándasí Bu. = anda	mí ánda	(le-)nyɔ (le)nyotso
dɔ̀	dɔ̀	dɔ(a)	odo	adʊ	adó	adó Bu. = àdɔ	àdɔ	thu
ata	tá	atá	atắpi	átá	átá	átá Bu. = ata	átî	aba
kándà 'baraŋa	kándà 'baraŋa	kàla (5, 6, 7) maranya	kání márɪŋà	kaní mɛrɛ̀	gányì 'bú tí tswɛli	mɛ́rì Bu. = mɛ́rì tí tswɛli	kali	kala kala-naŋga
ấmvu	ấmvu	amvú	ämvu	amvu	amvu	amvu Bu. = amvu	ambu	nza
drí-mvä	dri-mva	drí-gandʒa drikanji	dri-anzi	ɔnyufa	dri-aŋgwa	di-ŋgwa Bu. = di-aŋgwa	dí-ni-ŋgwá	(le)θókpa
drí-ágó		dri-gagɔ	drí-àgɔ	drí-àgɔ		Bu. = dí-endɛ̀	dí-nànde	(le)thoja
lesí läsí-landra tsɔkɔ	atʃí atʃí-kòkò	atʃí(a) -árákɔ̀lɛ -kɔkɔ	atsí -arɛkɔlókʊ̀	atsí -rìdìdì	atsí	así Bu. = así	así	kazź kazz-dza-rotha
i'bí	i'bí	kòʃia	i̇'bi	i̇'bi	e'bí	e'bí Bu. = e'bi	e'bí	be ('be?)
ɛtrɛ̀	kùmú	kùmú	únyú	únyú	oɲú (2)	oɲú Bu. = aɲú	aɲú	vovo
nyasá	nyasá	lɛ́nyá	ɪnya esa	ɪnya	lenyɛ	lɪnya Bu. = línya	ínyá	nyúdzz 'jú
pá	pá	pá	pá	pá	pá	pá Bu. = pa	pá	ko
ŋgáatrá awa ŋgá àtra	'báledrɪ-tàkɔ ŋgá àtra	móndyé'dì terí-mva	'bárì gelia	'bá'dì gelia	dzurugo (5) mondú	dʒurugo mondú	dʒurugo gelagó (8)	sha teli
ä'ú	ä'ú	(t)ä'ú	ä'ú	a'ú	a'ú	a'ú	a'ú	oó
amgbà mányarà	túdrù mányarà	túdru dzi'dá mányarà	udrugudru dzɔdrɛ	udrugo	údru kúri	údu Bu. = udu kúri Bu. = kúrì	o'do'dú árì	da dʒítʃɛ kanyare
'dɔnyɔkówá ízáṁvá	(ízá) mvá-ǹdzwa	mvátòkwa	mvóòkɔ ízóɲá	ŋgútiòko izɔŋa	za	zʷa(ŋgwa)	izóɲá ŋgwá(nɪ-ŋwá)	simgba (le)tha
ìndri	ndrí	ndrí	ndrí	ndrí	indrí	indí Bu. = indí	indí	ndrr
kǎbilíki	kǎbilíki	kébɪlikyà kabiliki	kǎbɪlítɔ	kɔbɪlɔ	kǎbilítɔ	bilo Bu. = bílo	kɔbílù	cembu
ovaré 'bule'ba	woré	oré	adrógò	àdrogoɲa	rubaɲà (7)	orí Bu. = ɔrɪ	ɔrí	
òpuwä	kyɛrɛ	kuruku kega	kuluku	kuluku	kʸére	kérɛ Bu. = kérɛ	érɛ̀	

VOCABULARY

MORU

	Miza	Kediru	Lakama'di	-ägi	Wa'di	'Bälimbä	-ändri
granary	kʸɪró	kʸèrɔ	kɪrá	kɔró kwàra	kwàra	eró	eró
grandfather	tí'bí	tí'bí	té'bí	a'buo äópi	ä'buwa	aópí	aópí
grandmother	làdra	làdra	làdra	dèdä	dède	ädrắpi	ädrắpi dède
grass	käi	käi	käi	käi	käi	äyi	äyi
grave	'búdɨ	'búdɨ	'búdɨ	'búdɨ	'búdɨ	'búdɨ	'búdɨ
ground-nut	sɛremundi (8)	sɛremundi	seremundi	sämändì marakanda	särä-gbändì	sämändì	sämändì
guinea-fowl	kɔ̀pɛ ariabà	kɔ̀pɛ	kɔ̀pɛ	kwàpɛ	kwàpɛ	kɔ̀pɛ	kɔ̀pɛ
guinea-worm	mɪa	mɪa	mɪa	mɪa	mɪa	mɪa	mɪa
hair	(drɨ)kyɛ́rɪ (tà)'bi	(drɨ)kírɪ	(drɨ)'bí	(drɨ)'bí	(drɨ)'bí	(drɨ)'bí	(drɨ)'bí
feathers	taró'bí kapírɨ (8)	arí'bí	arí'bí	käpírɨ	käpírɨ		arí'bí
hand	drí	drí	drí	drí	drí	drí	drí
arm	drí						
hare	kɪtó (8)	kɪtó	kɪtóŋgó	komo	ɪtógó	ɪtógó	ɪtógó
hartebeest	ló'bʷɔ (8)	lá'ba	lá'ba	lá'ba	lá'ba	ló'ba	ló'ba
head	drɨ̀	drɨ̀	drɨ̀	drɨ̀	drɨ̀	drɨ̀	drɨ̀
heart, liver (seat of emotions)	karíbà	karíbà	karíbà	karíbà	tsótsóló	aríbà	aríbà
heel (cf. chin)	pákásusu	pákásusu	pákásusu	pákásusu	paidi	paisisi	pakasusu
hill	'bérɛ́ŋwá	kuni	'bérɛ́ŋó	kwöni	kwöni	kúní	únívá
hippo	aróà	aróà	aróà	aróà	aróà	aróà	aróà
hoe	kʸɛ'bo	kʸɛ'bo	kʸɛ'bo	kʸɛ'bo	kʸɛ'bo	ɪ'bo	ɪ'bo
honey	ɛpɛ	ɛpɛ	ɛpɛ	ɛpɛ	apɛ	apɛɛpɛ	apɛ
bee	kumé-ɛpɛ	kumé-ɛpɛ	komʊ-ɛpɛ	apɛ-tsi	apɛ-tsi	omu-ɛpɛ	omu-ɛpɛ
horn	kʷɔyí	kʷɔyí	kʷɔyí	kʷɔyí	kwa'ya	kɔí	kɔí
(instrument)	toro'ba	toro'ba	toro'ba wùdo	tɪrɪ'ba ŋguniwä	tɪrɪ'ba wùdo	tɪɽɪ'ba undílì	tɪrɪ'bá ŋgunivä́
house	zʷó	zó	zá	zó	zwa	zó	zó
home	'bà	'bà	'bà	'bà	'bà	'bà	'bà
hunger	täbírí	täbírí	täbírí	käbírí	käbírí	äbírí	äbírí
hyena	muí	muí	mä'däú (2)	lubägù (8)	läbogù	läbägù	läbägù
iron	wyítì	wyítì	wyítì	wyítì	wyítì	wyítì	wyítì

VOCABULARY

AVUKAYA						MADI		
Ojila	Ojiga	Logo	Keliko	Lugbara	Lokai	Pandikeri	Lulu'ba	Lendu
ìrɔ	eró	kero	èra	ìra	ɛró	ɛró Bu. = ɛrɔ	ɛró	dero
ä'biwa	ắbí	tắpi tepi	ä'bipì	a'bipì	á'bî	á'bî Bu. = a'bɪ	a'bí	(le)bu ('bu?)
dède	dède	adrắpi	ɪdrắpi	ɪdrắpi	ada	ada Bu. = adâ	dadâ	(le)ja
omà (2)	mbí	mbɪà kaisa	asɛ	äsɛ	a(y)ísé	a(y)í Bu. = aísé	áí	tso i
lɔ'dɛ	gulä (8)	mógwá mogo	mógó 'burädrì	mógó úidrì	'búdì	'búdì Bu. = i'bú	gúlù	'dódzɨ̀
särägbondì	suru- gbändì	bàgendi wandɪ ʃɪngwa	wandɛ tʃɛŋgɔ	seremendì	fúlù (Ar.)	fúlù (Ar.) Bu. = sere- mändì	kyɛrɛ- ŋwändì	
ɔ̀pɛ	ɔ̀pɛ	kɔ̀pɛ	ɔ̀pɛ	opé	ɔ̀pɛ	ɔ̀pɛ Bu. = ɔ̀pɛ	ɔ̀pɛ	'dei
mɪa	mɪa	madzaka (8)	madzaka	madzaka	mɛ(y)á	me(y)á Bu. = mɛ(y)á	mɛ(y)á	ɛ(y)a
(drì)'bí	(drì)'bí	dri'bi (drì)'bya	(drì)'bi	(drì)'bi	(drì)'bí	(di)'bí Bu. = dzi'bí	(di)'bí	(lédʒó)ká
arìwá'bi								o-ká
kupírì	kupírì	kùlä	kùlä	kùlä	sa			
drí	drí	drika drí	drígá	drí	drí	dí Bu. = dí	dí	(lɛ)θɔŋ
		drí	drígá	drí	owú	owú		(lɛ)kù
ɪtógóá	ɪtógwá	kìtɔ	ʋtógɔ	ùtɔgɔŋa	ɪtó	ɪtó Bu. = itó	ɪtó	co
ló'ba	ló'ba	ló'ba	ó'bórodʒi ä'bi	ó'bórodʒi lɔ'ba	kundrɔ	lɔ'bà Bu. = lɔ'bà	lɔ'bà	
drì	drì	drì	drì	drì	drì	dì Bu. = dì	dì	(le)dʒɔ (2)
tsótsóló lovolovo	tsòfo	kàrì'ba tògɔ karijo	ási àga	ásí	asi	asi Bu. = asidì	asidì	(lɛ)θì lègu
paidi paisisi	pämgbɪrì	kìlèda kalundra	ìdɛ	ònyinya	(pá)vùdu	Bu. = 'bódó	'bɔrɔdɔ	(le)kojuti
úní(älà)	írà	írà rovo, koŋgo	írà	írà oni	'bé	'bé Bu. = 'bé	'bé	ŋgo
gulúbà	arúwà	aríwa	aróà	aróà	robí	robí Bu. = yarʋ	yarʋ (8)	nya
àtsɔ	käfú	käfú kafu	käfú	àtsɔ	àtsɔ kefú	àso Bu. = asó	àsɔ	jo joju
ápɛ	ápé	ápá apesu	ànyu	ànyu	laŋú	laŋʋ Bu. = laŋúzɛ	ɪpɛ	ti
afífí apɛfí	apífí	àpɛkifyɛ apikifi	ànyu-fi	ànyu-fi	laŋú	laŋʋ Bu. = laŋú	laŋú	ti-ɖa
ɔ'ye	ó'yá	ko'yá	ó'jú	údze	o'ju	o'ju Bu. = ɔ'jɔ	o'ju	'yo
tɪrɪ'bá wùdo	tɪrɪ'bá goká	molya goká	sɪrɪ'ba goké	sɪrɪ'ba goké	túrulú kpere	bɪlà (7) Bu. = bɪlà àgʋra Bu. = tɔrɛ́ (8)	bɪla	lo
zo	dʒwó	dʒwá jo	dʒó	dzó	dzó	zó	gyó	dzá
bà	'bà	'bà	'bà	'bà	'bà	'bà	'bà	ba ('ba?)
ɔfó	äbírí	tabírí tebiri	àbiri	àbiri	abiri		vʷí	u
ɪ̀dímgbi	läbägù	ɪŋgílyà maŋgili	lubogù	ubogù	moyí	moyí	ŋaduo	nyaú
àfa	làfa	aya	wítì aya	wítì aya	aya	aya		mbu

VOCABULARY

MORU

	Miza	Kediru	Lakama'di	-ägi	Wa'di	'Bälimbä	-ändri
iron-ore	mò'di	mò'di	mò'di	ödi	ödi	mò'di	mo'di
implements of iron for trade	lógʷɔ̀	lógʷɔ̀	lakázà	lòkʷɔ	lakwá	lakázò	lógʷɔ̀
iron-stone	kàgwa				kagwá		
island	róŋga	róŋga		ráŋga 'bɪ'bɪ	ráŋga	róŋga	róŋga
jackal	kòba	kòba	kòba	kòba	kòba	òba	òba
fox	mútútú	mútútú	mútútú	mútútú	mútútú	mútútú	mútútú
knee	kàya	kàya	kàya	kà'ya	kà'ya	kàya	kàya
elbow	kuɾukosú (2)	kuɾukosú	gelɛmɛ	kuɾukusu	kuɾukusu	gelɛmɛ	kuɾukosi
knife	íɾí	íɾí	ílí	íɾígó	ɾígó	íɾí	íɾí
lake	fóló	fóló	påfå	fåfå	àpàpà	påfå	påfå
swamp	tái	téya	täi	kayaga	kayaga	áyágá	áyágá
pool	tsʷétsʷé	tsʷétsʷé	sesɛŋgwà	tsétsé	tsʷétsʷɛkɔ̀	sesɛŋgwà	tsʷétsʷé
leopard	kaá	kaá	kaá	kawá	kà'wa	kaá	kaá
leprosy (cf. blood)	karí	karí	karí	karí	karí	arí	karí
lion	ìbì	ìbì	äbì	kämì (8)	kämì	äbì	äbì
lips	bɪɾí	bɪɾí	kɪnɪ si ru	bɪɾí	tɪmbìɾi vòlɛ (lower)	bɪɾí	bɪɾí
lizard	käbi					käbi	käbi
chameleon							
locust	tombí	tombí	tombí	kombí	kombí	ɔmbí	ɔmbí
maize	dábàɾi		toɾomo	toɾomo	mbämu (8)	dábàɾi	dábàɾi
man (homo)	lédr	lédr	lédr	'dédr	'dédr	ɾédr	lédr
(vir) husband	'diàgo mánágo lédrago	'diàgo mánágo lédrago	'diàgo mánágo lédrago	'diàgo mánágo lédrago	'diàgo mánágo lédrago	'diàgo mánágo lédrago	'diàgo mánágo lédrago
meat (cf. animal)	èza (2)	èza	èza	èza	èza	èza	èza
medicine	kyérá	kyárá	kyéré	alókò	alókò	frá	frá
poison	äɾí	äɾí	äɾí	äɾí	äli		
milk	lɛi (8)	lɛi	lɛi	lɛi	lai	lɛi	lɛi
moon (month)	ìmba	ìmba	ìmba	ìmba	ìmba	ìmba	ìmba
mosquito	nyényé	nyényé	nyényé	nyényé	nyényé	nyényé	nyényé
mother	éndrè	éndrè	éndrè	éndrè	låpì	ndrúpì	ndrúpì

VOCABULARY

AVUKAYA					MADI			
Ojila	Ojiga	Logo	Keliko	Lugbara	Lokai	Pandikeri	Lulu'ba	Lendu
ädi	ädi	lumunyà	e'bufi	e'bufi		Bu.= o'dezè	o'dó	johwa
làfa		ayakifi						
rɔvɔ								
gändzírì	lʊmvʊ́-	iyí-gufálɛ́	yí-ɛsámvó	yí- ruŋa		ruŋa	pípí	ŋgodu
'bɪ'bɪ	lɔfálɛ́			édrɪdríŋe				
òba	òba	bóá	bòa	òbalɛgo	òba	òba	egigì	lu
		karo				Bu. = igigì		
mu'du'du	kätrkäträ	känyirà	zèŋgù			Bu. = gbɛ́	gbɛ́	
'a'ya	à'ya	korokᵂo	kòmo (8)	kòmo	à'ja	à'ja	anya	(le)ḍeti
à'i						Bu. = a'já		
kulúkusú	kulúkusú	kålèndru	limgbilimgbì	usukomì	kɔŋgú'	logʊlɛ̀	ísú	(le)ku-
		kalundra						ḍeti
ílígó	ílígó	lígó	íɽí	ílí	ílí	élí	ili	'jú
		älí				Bu. = ili		
àpàpà	àpàpà	täɽi	äɽi	äɽi	ápara	ápara	papa'da	zhuḍa
	gäli						à'bulu	
áyágá	yí-kafolɛ	cokwa	yí-dzondzo	yí-tsetse	ndzɛtɛ	ndzɛtɛ	tor	ḍaḍo
tsɛtsê	tápárà	yí-didì	atafara	oátá				ḍalu
kotsoko		tápárà						
		tadodoa						
àlɪgɪ	kalígyá	kalígyɛ́	lígí	u'dú	ɔ'dó	ɔ'dó	ɔ̀'dʊ	gɔaðà
		kaligi						
àrɪ	àrɪ	kàrya	àrɪ	àrɪ	àrɪ	èrɪ	emí	cokoro
		kari		ofo				
kämì	kämì	kämi	kämirú	kími	ɛbî	ibî	ɛbî	tʃu-
				ɛbì				mgburù
tɪ-mbìɽi	tí-mbìli	tí-fàni	kòkòfi	lɔ'biu (8)	tì'-o'bo	tì-'borokoto	tiri 'bódó	(le)tsojo
vòlɛ		ti-kini					lɔ'biu	
(lower)							(lower)	
härägägä	mbɪɽɪgyä	ambɪlɪdʒa	bilindʒì	lobudzì	imvúlú	opólóŋò	ɔkólɔŋò	landrrca
		mbiligi						
		lendri			makíkò	makíkò	ŋgéŋge	suligu
ɔmbí	ombí	tombyá	ómbì	ómbì	ombí	ombí	umbí	nju
		kesa						the
mbämu	mbomu	mʊndᵂó	kàka	kaká-	bombò	bombò	bemu (8)	kwi
		mondo		mʊ̀ndʊ				
ledr	ledr		ídrɪ	ídrɪ	lídri	lídɪ		
òdzílà		mondya	'bá	'bá	ma'dí	mo'dí	mo'dí	ke
'diàgo		mundia			pl. 'ba	pl. 'bálà	pl. bánàni	ndrú
mánágo	agó	agó	'bagɔ	agopi	agɔ	agɔ	ágona	gbetsi-ke
lédrago								
a'wá	a'wá	za	za	èza	èza	zá	èza	za
		kà'wa						
alókò	alókò	aloko	udzwó	udzwó	ɛrua	ɛrua	ɛrwa	rr
		lòdzwa						
alókò	ledzó	lojo	udzómva	adráki(?)	enyenya	enyenya	ɛrwanìnji	tsu
lɛ	lɛ	ti-lɛ	lɛ	lɛ	tí-lɛi	tí-ní-lɛi	ílɛ̂	ba
		tí-bà						
para	m̀ba	m̀ba	mba	ìmba	ìmba	ìmba	ombá	bi
							embá	
gyípírí(wá)	gyipírí	ŋòŋwa	kìmʊrʊ (8)	kìmʊrʊ	mäimäi	àmvuru	amburu	do
andrɛ	ándré	ándré	éndrắpi	ándrắpɪ	íắ	ɛndɛ̀	ande	i
bàbá						Bu. = ɛ́ndɛ		zha

352 VOCABULARY

MORU

	Miza	Kediru	Lakama'di	-ägi	Wa'di	'Bälimbä	-ändri
mouth	kàlà	kàlà	kàlà ti	kàlà	ti	kàlà	kàlà
mud	kʊrʊ́	kʊrʊ́	kurú	kurú	kuré	kuré'	kuré
nail	kʷónyí	kʷónyí	kónyí	kónyí	kwanya-ŋgwa	kónyí	ónyó
name	avúrú	ävúrú	avúrú	rú	rú	rú	rú
navel	kɔtó	kɔtó	kɔtó	kɔtó	kwató	ɔtó	ɔtó
neck	kyɛmbɛ	kyɛmbɛ	kyɛmbɛ	kɛmbɛ	kʸɛmbɛ	embɛ	embɛ
necklace beads	mayɛka	mayɛka	mayɛka	mayɛka	mayakà	'bíaàla	'bíaàla
net	kyémbá	kyémbá	kyémbá	kyémbá	kʸɪmbá	bɪrá (2)	embá
night	ŋgăkyi	ŋgăkyi	ŋgăkyi	ŋgătsi	ŋgătʃʷi	ŋgăkyi	ŋgătsi
nose	kʷɔmvó	kovó kövó	kɔmvó	kɔmvó	kwamvó	ɪmvɔ	ɔmvó
ostrich		arɪtsóro	arɪsʊrʊ̀			kútè (8)	kútè
paddle (spoon)	deɽi	deɽi	deɽi	mbitsé	mbiritsé	deɽi	deɽi
pig	kizwe	kɪzʊ̀	kɪzʊ̀	kɪzʊ̀	kɪzʊ̀	izɔ̀	izù
place	vo	vo	vo	vo	vo	vo	vo
pot (gen.)	làkazu	làkaza		làkaza		làkaza	làkaza
water-pot	lúkù'du		lúkù'du		lamvɔ	límvó	límvó
rain	'bù	'bù	'bù	koze	kuze	'bù	'bù
lightning	'busíá						usí
rat	nyedu	nyädu	nyedu	kɪdrɛ	kɪdra	édré	édré
rhino	kätumgbu	kätuŋu	kätumgbu	moŋgu (2)	moŋgù	tigigi (8)	tigigi
river	gólo	ìdʒi (= water)	gólo	ìdʒi	ìdzi	gólo	gólo
river-bank	kútʊ-tí						kútʊ-tí
road	líti	líti låti	líti	páti pávo	páti	ɽíti	pávʊ
rope	rɔali	rɔali	rɔali	gbulù	màgbeɽɛ	redʒɔ̀	redʒɔ̀
string	eba	eba	eba	eba	eba	eba	eba
sacrifice	tórí		tórí	arí-kwɔrí-tɪ			
act of sacrifice	ɔla	torí-lɔvɔ̀	ɔla		avarí	ɔrí-lɔfɔ̀	ɔrí-lɔfɔ̀
saliva	tɪ	tò	tù	tù	tù	tù	tù
salt	teyí	täyí	teyí	käyí	kä'í	täyí	täyí

VOCABULARY

AVUKAYA		Logo	Keliko	Lugbara	MADI			Lendu
Ojila	Ojiga				Lokai	Pandikeri	Lulu'ba	
ti	ti	ti	ti	ti	tí	tí	tí	(le)tso
rutɪ́	urútrã́	kùru	motrɛtrɛ	kɔtsɔtsɔ̀	nzɛtɛ	nzɛtɛ	papada	
àlutr		kurutra			oto	oto	'bɔ'dɔ'dɔ	do
							(8)	
ɔnyagɔ	ɔnyagɔ	kɔlizya	ɔnyɔfi	ʊnyʊka	tsokwa	tsokwa	anyukwɛ	
rú	rú	rú	rú	rú	rú	rú	rú	(lɛ)róðò
ɔtó	kòto	kùtwa	òto	òto	ɔtó	ɔtó	ɔtó	(le)teku
		koto						
ɛmbɛ	ɛmbɛ	kyımbɛ	ombɛ	ombɛ	ɛmbɛ	ɛmbɛ	ɛmbɛ	(le)cuti
		kembe						
mɔyí	mɔyí	magada	ŋalɪ	ŋalɪ	lésù	lésù	mìyo	ra
		ŋgalya			ɛmbɛga			
		maika			àlɔ	logbi		
embá	ìmba	kyìmba	ɪmbà	bìra (2)	ebá	ebá	ebá	njo (hunting) dou (fishing)
ŋgǎtʃi		ŋgǎtʃi						
ínɪ́kuruwa	ínírɪ́kúá	kimba	iniŋa	ini	ini	eni	ínìgɔ	kunaŋga
ɔmvó	omvó	komvó	umvú	umvú	ɔ̀mvɔ	ɔ̀mvɔ	ɔ̀mbɔ	enyíndò ndutu
olíndrɪnɪ̀	gbɔ	gbɔ	gbɔ	gbɔ	u'do	u'do	tútwò	
mbirɪtsé	kǎpí	fa (=stick)			atú	atú		kule
kǎpí								
ɪzò	ɪzya	kɪzya	ɪzògɔ	ɪzògɔ	ìzò	ìdzò	ɛzɔ	jo
vo	vo	vorà	vo	vorétò	vò	vò	ɔfó	ŋga
límvó	límvó	lìdrya	òdri	ómvo	tsopɛ	lo'bù	ɛgya	ca, de
		lidri						
límvó	límvó	mɔ'dà	lämvu	tíbídʒò	túbídʒo	lò'di		danju
ɔzɛ	'bu	'bù	yigɔ	ózɔgó	eyí	eyí	iyí	dʒí
		kózya			(= water)			
ɔzɛ	ɔzɛ	'bù-lèvɛ	òvi	àvi	eyíí-lòri	eyíí-lòri	íyí-lòvwɛ	vo
		'bu-lagulagu						
ɛdrɛgo	ɛdrɛgʊ	tédrágwá	edragɔ	edragɔ	idrɛ	idɛ	idɛ	'yo
		tédra	údrɔgɔ	údrɔgɔ				
tɪgigi	kɪŋgɪlì	tiŋgɪ́lì	tíŋgili	tíŋgili	idzidzì	igigì	egigí	
mɔŋgù								
kárá	lumvú		iyí	iyí	a'bú	golù	gólò	da
	(= water)	yi-andre		(= water)				(= water)
lomvú-tí	iyí-tí	iyí-ni-kòba	iyí-tí	iyí-tí	a'bú-tɪ	golù-ti		da-tsoŋga
		yi-tapara						
pávo	lǎti	lǎtɪ	létɪ	létɪ	léti	léti	léti	(lala)cu
			bítɪ	gàri				
màgbɛlɛ	màgbɛrɛ	bákadɪ	nɛkɛrɛ	nye- mgbɛlɛ	oŋgoli	oŋgoli		mbi
bagó	bagó	bá	bá	bá	ebá	ebá	ɪbá	mbi
		gálà-dezu	adrógɔ	ówá	á'dí-indílì-	á'dí-indílì-	rɪbu-lozó	letha
		ŋga-teri-lede			ɔrɪga	ɔrɪga		
ɔvarí	ovárí							
tʊ̀	tù	tísɪ̀ya	utúsú	tutu	tuzɛ̀	tuzɛ̀	làla	sadà
		tusu	täsú	tatú				sa'dà
ä'í	ä'í	te'í	ä'í	a'í	a'í	a'í	a'í	ku

A a

VOCABULARY

| | \multicolumn{7}{c}{MORU} |
	Miza	Kediru	Lakama'di	-ägi	Wa'di	'Bälimbä	-ändri
sand dust	sıŋgɔ durufu	sıŋgı durufu	sınyı durufu	sınyı durufu	sınyı kirifu	sınyı durufu	sınyı durufu
scorpion	kítənı (8) kítwa	kítənı	kítənı	kítənı	kítànì	ítɔ	ítɔ
seed	kɛtsʷi	ketʃʷi	kʸɛsi	kɛtsʷi	kɛtsʷi(na) kwarì	esi	efi
sesame	kånyú (8)	kånyú	kånyú	kånyú	kånyí	ånyú	ånyú
shadow spirit	lendr lendr	lendr	lendr	lendr	lendr	lendrɛ lendrɛ	lendr lendr
shield	daragà (Ar.)	mokägä (2)		mokägä		mogågå	mogågå
shoe	mvókà	mvókà	mvókà	mvókà	kámúkà (8)	kámúkà	kámúkà
shoulder	kufú	kufú	kufú	kufú	kwofú	ufú	ufú
side	lama	lama	lama	lama	lama	lama	lama
sister	ɛndréŋwá	ɛndréŋwá	ɛndréŋwá	ämvúpi	ämbŏpì	ämvúpi	ämvúpi
skin hide	kʸinì	inì	inì	inì	kʸını là'ú (7)	inì la'bó	inì la'bó
sky	'bukúrú vukúrú	'bukórú	'bukórú	'bukúrú	'bù	voúru	voúru
slave	àtı'ba	màrabà	àti'ba	àti'ba	kʸɛmvó	kòr'bɛ	àtı'ba
smoke	kätu		kätu		así-kà	kätúkå	kätúkå
snake python	inì kárà	inì kárà	inì kárà	inì kárà	inì kárà	inì kárà	inì kárà
spear	àzu	àzu	àzu	àzu	àzu	àzu	àzu
fish-spear	tsʷɛké pítí (5)	pété	pítí	tsʷɛké	biti suké	tsʷɛké	
star	'bı̀'bı	'bı̀'bı	'bı̀'bı	'bı̀'bı	'bı̀'bı	'bı̀'bı	'bı̀'bı
stick club	dámgbáɽá dɔfɔ	dámgbáɽá dɔfɔ	dáŋgúrá mɔvɔ̀	dáŋgúrá lɔrɔ	tʃɛŋwá lɔrɔ	dáŋgúrá dɔfɔ	dáŋgúrá dɔfɔ
stone	'bɛrɛŋwa	kúníŋwa	kúníŋgwa	kúníŋwa			únívä
rock (cf. hill)	kuni àlɛlɛ (8)		kuni	kwóní	kwöni	älå	
stool neck-rest	kìtìkpara	kòtòpara	kìtìkpara	mgbá'dá	mgbá'dá	kìtìkpara	kìtìkpara kɔtɔkpá
sun day (cf. sleep)	kitú ú'dú	kıtú o'du	kitú u'du	kitú o'du	kitú o'du	utú u'du	utú u'du

VOCABULARY

AVUKAYA					MADI			
Ojila	Ojiga	Logo	Keliko	Lugbara	Lokai	Pandikeri	Lulu'ba	Lendu
sınye	sínyá	sınya	tsínyáfà	ófórò(?)	tsʷinyagɔ	tsʷinyakwi	ıŋá	soro
äpílíndri	fàpùlindri	tàpùlindrya	fúrúndi	kú'dǎpù alíkùkù	äri	äri	àfula'bi	ho
ítɔnı ótɔnı					ítoni	ítoni	itoní	
efıla	ŋgáífí	(nya)kífya ŋgakisia	ıfı	(ànya)ıfı	(kwĕ)kwí	kwɛníákwí		
ɔrì	ɔrì	kori	ɔrì	ɔrì			ɔ̀ri	kpa
änú	änuŋ	känyi kenu kanyu	ǎnyú	anyu	anyu	anyu Bu. = anyú	ǎnyu(m)	nyokpa nyoce
lendrı	líndrı	líndrı	ındrı(ndr)	éndrlɛ̀ndr	líndrı	líndílìndi	indi	{ susuŋga lendʒídʒì le(thi) le(he)
lendrı	líndrı	teri	ındrı(ndr)	éndrlɛ̀ndr	líndrı	líndílìndi	indi	
ŋgisi	dáragà	ägbóù ŋgali ceŋgu		dáragà	'búkú (8)	'búkú	'búkú	agbau
kámúkà	kámúkà	kamuka 'bàkɛɛkà	kamuka	kamuka	mvuká	mvuká	kamukà	nyasu
ufú uú	ùwu	tùwu alara	kídi (8)	kídi	oúdì	oúlókódì	olu	(le)kujo
gara	gara	gàrà	gàrà	márákà	aŋgu		mɛrɛtɛ	lelajo lai
ezɔ	ämvúpi	ämvúpi	ämvúpi	ämvúfi	amvótì	ambázì Bu. = adozi	amboŋa	(le)ve
ınyırıku	ınyırıkɔ	kʸını	fnírfkɔ	fnírfkɔ	ɛnı	ɛnı	ɛnɛ	sɜ
gombɛri(kɔ)	gumbɛrɛ	kʸindri	la'bʊ	lɔ̀'bu	lɔ̀'bu	lɔ̀'bu	gɔbɛri (8)	ka
bùrùkù	pırí	kurúna 'bu	ùrù	ùrùgı	'bù	'bù	oru	ra
'bù	úrúla							
márabà mváànze auwa	mváànze auwa	kımváàndzi	gbaya	'báǹdıla 'bàzendʒırı	ɔpígó		ɔpyógó	nokpa noi
ɔtsí-kà	atsí-kà	atsí-ka	atsí-kà -ga	atsí-ka -ga	asíkà	así-kà	así-gà	koí
inì à'wagɔ(?)	mì kárà	{ mi nì kárà	nì arà	inì arà	inì arà	inì arà	inì arà	su ra-su
ädʒú	ädʒú	'dılyè ďili	àdzu	àdzu	adzú	azú	adʒú	li
agataù ŋgúrì	maga'da				mbéré'dè	mbéré'dè	bıdí	
'bì'bıä	'bi'biä	'bí'bínyà	lenyà(?)	'bí'bíŋa kàsiri (8)	lɛlɛgó	lɛlɛ	ı'bı'bí	dyodyo
femvá pıdrígú	(=tree) fɛ fɛ	{ fa kenzo kutu	ùdu	turɛ (8) fɛ-ilíle	pɛrɛ ɔtó	{ kɔ'bílì ɔ̀pɛpɛ béle	turɛ	tsi tsu
únimvä	unímva	kıramva kıra	frámva ùporafı ùdzigo	ırámva	uniaŋgwa gwɛny	uniŋgwa uníkwé ırà	uni toro	ju
{ kɔ̀baka kìtìkpara tokporo	kıtıkpáɾá gbólókó	kıtıkpálá lópa	kítíkpara lópa	kítíkpara lópa	kómí (7)	kómí	gàrà lakérê	thiŋga
yitú ai	utú ŋgǎtʃi	kıtú ŋgátsı	ıtú ŋgáki	etú o'dù	ıtú íná oďu	ıtákàli ó'dú	tékelí íní	'jí 'dɔ̃

VOCABULARY
MORU

	Miza	Kediru	Lakama'di	-ägi	Wa'di	'Bälimbä	-ändri
tail	taví	taví	taví	kaví	kaví	az^wí	aví
tear	mi-éndrè	mi-éndrè	mi-éndrè	mi-índrè	mi-índrè	mi-índrè	mi-índrè
termite (gen.)	kótó	kótó	kótó	kótó	kótó	ótó	ótó
(soldier)	kɪnzú	kɪnzú	kɪnzú	kízú	kízú	únzú	ízú
	lɛmgbɛrɛ	lɛmgbɛrɛ	lɛmgbɛrɛ	lɛmgbɛrɛ	lɛmgbɛrɛ	lɛmgbɛrɛ	lɛmgbɛrɛ
(edible)	káŋwà (2)	kótó	káŋwà	kótó	kawa	ɔŋa	óŋwa
thigh	turu'bu	turu'bu	turu'bu	kuru'bu	kworo'bu	kuru'bu	uru'bu
thing	ŋgá	ŋgá	ŋgá	ŋgá	ŋgá	ŋgá	ŋgá
thirst	(gyí-)lóò	(gyí-)lóò	(gyí-)lóò	(idz^wí-)lɔvó	-lavó	-lɔvó	-lóvó
thorn	kukyí	kɔkyí	kukyí	kutsí	kwötʃí	ukyí	uts^wí
tongue	làdra (2)	làdra	làdra	làdra	lèdrɛ	làdra	làdra
tooth	sí	sí	sí	sí	sí, ʃí	sí	sí
tree	{ kyè { ts^wè	ts^wè	ɪsɛ	ts^wɛ	ts^wɛ	ɪsé	fè
firewood	tízá	tízá	tízá	àsi	así	ézà	àsɪ
bush forest	k^wɔkyɛ äíaɽimi	kwakyɛ	kɔkyɛ	kɔkyɛ	kwatsè	kɔkyè	kɔkyè vɔtsúà
tribe (cf. country)	'bàdrì	'bàdrì	'bàdrì	'bàdrì	'bàdrì	'bàdrì	'bàdrì
twins	(ŋgwá)lèzɔ	(ŋgwá)lèzɔ	(ŋgwá)lèzɔ	(ŋgwá)lèzɔ	(ŋgwá)lèzɔ làzwe	lèzɔ	lèzɔ
udder (cf. breast)	bà (2)	bà	bà	bà	bà	bà	bà
urine	kudŕ (2)	kudŕ	kudŕ	kudŕ	kudŕ	udŕ	udŕ
vein	kídrwe (2)	kídru	kídru	kídrɛ	kédru	údrɛ	ídrɛ
sinew	riŋo	riŋo	riŋo	riŋo	riŋwö	riŋo	riŋo
village	'bà (2)	'bà	'bà	'bà	'bà	'bà	'bà
home	'bà (2)						
vulture	k^wɔi k^wɔi-dafálà	kwai	k^wɔi -dävöri	k^wɔi	lɔgúnò (8)	kwai -dafúrà	kwai
war	kìla	kìlà	kìla	kìla	kìla	kìla	kìla
warrior	kìla'ba						
warana (lizard)	lets^wɛ	mányà (6)	lɛsɛ	ts^wa	ɽítsó	ɽɪtse	lɪfɛ
water	gyìí	gií	gií	idz^wí	idʒí	igyi	ìdzì
water-buck	lä'bí	lä'bí	lä'bí	lä'bí	lä'bí	lɛ'bí	lä'bí
water-rat	täɽú	täɽú	täɽú	käɽú	käɽú	äɽú	äɽú
well	kòrò	kóró	kúrúŋwa	kóró	kóró	koro	kurʊ

VOCABULARY

AVUKAYA				MADI				
Ojila	Ojiga	Logo	Keliko	Lugbara	Lokai	Pandikeri	Lulu'ba	Lendu
avé	avé	tàvya kota		kótè (8)	sâ	ètsʷa	ekyá	vi-ti
iní-ndrɛ́	mí-ndrɛ	mi-ndrá	mí-ndrɛ	mí-ndrɛ	mí-ndra	mí-nda	mi-nda	lendʒ-'da dzz-'da
ótó							ɪto	θərózi
idʒuruku	údʒurukɔ	kɪdzú-(rúkwá)	idzúrúkó	udzúrúkó	idzúkɔlɔrɔ	idzúkɔlɔrɔ	okolorò (8)	
awa	oŋwa	kóŋwà	ɪfú	ónyà	óŋa	óŋa	óŋá	le
pä-uru'bu	pá-ndra	pá-ndra pa-andre	pa-dò (2)	i̯i̯i	melí	melí	'dɔ (2)	(le)dzu
ŋgá	ŋgá	ŋgá	ŋgá	ŋgá afá	ta	ŋga	ŋgáà	rítsz̀ ditsz
-lóvó	i-liɔvó	òlɛ yi-lavo	úɾe	úɾi	eyí-ví	eȳí-ví	vʷí	dzatyuŋga
asopá(?)	ukyí	kutʃí	kutsé ùtsɛ	utʃʷí ase	otsí	okí	ɔki	kpɛlɛ
làndra (2)	làndra	làdra	àdra	édrè ídrà	lɛdrá	lɛdá	lɛda	ledà
sí	sí	sí	sí { kpɛti fa	sí { piti fɛ	sí	sí	sí	lɛkú
fɛ	fɛ	fa			kwɛ	kwɛ	kwɛ	tsû
lèsi-fɛ	atsí-fɛ	atʃí-fá	ìdza	ìdzìdza	ízékékwé	ízékékwé	atʃú-kwé	kali
òkʸɪ̀	ɔkʸɛ omändú	kòkya gbíɛndúsì	rùdu (aŋgo)kpé-rínì	rùdu ase'dusì	aŋgwe		oké	-go
bädri aŋgwá	aŋgwá	'bà suru	aŋgu'ba	aŋgo	kwaí	kwaí	gyuru	tsi bu ('bu?)
làti	làti	làti	äti-kurudò	kurudò	lèdzu	lèdʒu	kúrúduä	zu
bà	bà	bà	bà	bà	tí-bà	tí-ni-bà	ebányà	debatiti
òdrɛ	udrɛ	kudryɛ kodri { kari-läti	udrɛ kɔdrɛ	udrɛ	ùdrwe	ùdwe	udwe idwe	nzè
ídre	(k)ɪdrɪ	kɪdrya	usu	isu	isu	isu	isyu	drr
riŋgo	(k)ɪdrɪ	kɪdrya	usu	isu				
'bà	'bà	'bà	'bèti	litsoga	é'í	'bà	'bá	ba ('ba?) (ba)gu
	kpúkpú lɔgunù	kpúkpú wala àla giri	púpu lɔgunù	fúfu nógúnù	aŋgɔfɔ ɔpɛrɪ	aŋgɔfɔ lɔgunúsɛ	pupu lɔgúlu	
lɔgúnò								
ɔmbà àdzu	ɔmbà	kɔmbà aju	ɔmbà	àgùbì	ɔ'ja	ɔ'ja	rɔ'diu	la
ɔmba'ba	ɔmba'ba	kɔmbà-mundya ajuđia	ɔmbà'ba	àgùbì'ba	ɔ'ja'ba	ɔ'ja'ba	rɔ'dí'bá ódikèléo	lathike
lɛfe manya	manya	manya	manya	manya	nyako	manya	manya	
lomvó	lumvú	iyí	iyí	iyí	eyí	iyí	iyí	'da
là'bí	là'bí	lɛ'bí	iɛrɛ	iɛrɛ	la'bí	le'bí	là'bi	ndʒei
äɾú älú	äɾú	tälú	älú	älú	alú	alú	alú	
óró	óró	korwa kɪ'dya (8)	kídɪ	kídɪ	ɪdɪ	ɪdɪ	a'dí	đabu

VOCABULARY

	Miza	Kediru	Lakama'di	-ägi	Wa'di	'Bälimbä	-ändri
wild dog	íhu	íku	ŏfu	ŏhu		ŏku	íhwi
wind	òlɪ (2) likuliku	òlɪ	òlɪ	lɪkulɪku	àɽɪ	òɽɪ	òlɪ
witch	kóz^wó	kóz^wó	kóz^wó	kwázwá	kózó / kwázwá	ózó	ózó
witchcraft	òdra	òdra	òdra	àdra	àdra	òdra	òdra
evil eye	kúlɛ̇	kúlɛ̇	kúlɛ̇	kúlɛ̇	kúlɛ̇	ólɛ̇	ólɛ̇
woman wife	tòkó	tòkó	tòkó	ɔkó	akó	ɔkó	okó
word	ta	ta	ta	ta	ta	ta	ta
work	lòsɪ̀	lòsɪ̀	lòsɪ̀	lòsɪ̀	làsɪ̀	lòsɪ̀	lòsɪ̀
yaws syphilis	ädábäri òdra	ädábäri òdra	kayaŋà (8) òdra	kayaŋgà' òdra	barakanyà àdra	nyarlɛ òdra	nyarlɛ òdra
year	ndrwa	ndrɔ	kíɲá (8)	ndrɔ	ndrɔa	kíɲá	kíɲá
PRONOUNS							
I	má (2)	má	má	má	má	má	má
you	mí	mí	mí	mí	mí	mí	mí
he	ndá ányà	ányà	ndána ányà	ndínà	ndána ányà	ndána	ndâ
she	ndá ányà	ányà	ndána ányà	ndínà	ndána ányà	ndána	ndâ
we	àma	àma	àma	àma	àma	àma	àma
you	àmɪ	àmɪ	àmɪ	àmɪ	ɛmɪ	ìmɪ	ìmɪ
they	ainya	ndàka ànya	ànya	ndíka	ɛndíka	ndàka	ndàka
he (referring)	í pl. ì						
it (referring) reference particle	na 'dó	'dó	'dó	'di	na 'di	'di	na, la 'di
self (refl.)	rú lúmvú						
self (emph.)	andí(vɔ)						
this	ònɔ	ònɔ	ɪnɔ	ni	ni / ea'dí	ni	ìnɪ
that	àna	àna	ɪna	ɪna	ena('dí)	'da'da	ìna àna
yonder		làna	léná	lɛɛná'di	ɪná'bá	lɛ'da'da	leìna
other	àza aki	àza	àza	àza	àza	àza	àza
who?	à'di(yà)	ò'di	ò'di	à'di	à'di	à'di	à'di

VOCABULARY

AVUKAYA		LOGO	Keliko	Lugbara	MADI			Lendu
Ojila	**Ojiga**	**Logo**	**Keliko**	**Lugbara**	**Lokai**	**Pandikeri**	**Lulu'ba**	**Lendu**
húhu	kåndí-kändr	ndróndrwa	àràkɪlà	àràkɪlà	owowia	lû (8) Bu. = lô	olô	rudu
iṛi		lía	òlɪ	alíkùkù	äri	ɔlí	ɔlí	vuvu
kägumâ	kägumâ							
òdzó	odzɔ	kɔdzwa	udzɔgo	udzɔgɔ	ódzó	ózó	ózó	uthaba (-'ba?) ndruba (-'ba?)
ɔdra								
ɔlɛ	ólɛ	kóllà	olè	olè	ollɛ	ollɛ	ólé	cethike
ɔkó	okó	tɔkwá	ɔkó	okó	òko	mo'dí-ízí	ezóṇá izi	isi ði
úṛí		kulí	atata	udúkɔ				lɔ̃
		ta(i)	edʒo	idʒó	le'jó	le'jó	e'jo	
(l)äsi		azi	azi		'bù	'bù	'bwo	nji
		azi						
barakanyà	manya	manya	manya	manya	lɔgbotó	lɔgbotó	lófúfurì	
dra	ŋgóŋgówá	marídrá	adúsì	adúsì	nyala	nyala	i'dwe	
ndrɔa	kʋna	kɔna	kɪŋa	kɪŋa	kɪnya	áyì	ki	co
má	má	má	má	má	má	má	má	má
mí	mí	mí	mí	mí	nyí	nyí	mi	
ni								ní
		'bá	'bá	'bá	àndá	àndá		
gúlà	gúlà	a'di ni	ɪrɪ	ɪrɪ	àni	àni	náṇi	ké
		'bá	'bá	'bá	àndá	àndá		
gúlà	gúlà	a'di ni	ɪrɪ	ɪrɪ	àni	àni	náṇi	le
àma	àma	àma	àma	amâ	àma	àma	amá	ma kò
amí	amí	amí	amí	imi	ànyi	ànyi	amí	
àni								nì
gúlèi	gúlèi	gúlè(?) aii	'bá	'bá	andráàpɪ à'ɪ	andápi à'ɪ		kpà ndru ndima
		í pl. ì	é	e, i	na(?)			
{ lɛ la		na		la	(n)a	(n)a	na	r(ɪ)
'di	'di	'di	'di	'di	'dí	'dí	lɛ	'di
		ru	ru	ru	rú	rú		ro
lúmvú		{ tandi ati (A)	tàndi	indi				ndi
{ ('dì)lɛ ('dì)nò	nɔ'di	{ 'diwà ni(ǎi)	nòrɛ	'dìrɪ	{ lɛ'di 'dí	{ ilé(ré) 'dí	{ lalya 'bàwa	iri
nà('dí)	na'di	{ 'dà'di na(ǎi)	'dàrɪ	'dàrɪ	na'i	ná'i	'bà . . . ná	{ cari furi
{ kpánnà na tònna na	na'di	naale					'bà . . . 'ná	cari
àza	àza('dì)	èzɛ('dì) azi(na)	àzi('dì))	àzi('dì)	zì	zì		nja
a'dú(yà)	a'dú(yà)	a'dí(yà)	a'dí(yà)	a'dí a'dú	à'di	à'di	à'di	ie (2)

VOCABULARY

	Miza	Kediru	Lakama'di	-ägi	Wa'di	'Bälimbä	-ändri
			MORU				
what?	a'dɔ	à'di	ɔ'di	à'di	à'di	à'di	à'di
	ɔ'di (2)						
which?	ɪŋgɔ						
how many?	táŋwànyɛ yà	táŋwànyɛ yà	mɔ̀da yà (8)	e'dé'dí yà	e'dye'diè	mɔ̀da yà	mɔ̀da yà
relative	sɛ ... bɛ				... pi		sɛ ... bɛ

VERBS

	Miza	Kediru	Lakama'di	-ägi	Wa'di	'Bälimbä	-ändri
arrive (here)	ɛsá	ɛsá	ɛsɛ	asa	asa	asa	asa
(there)	ɔ-sá	ɔ-sá	ɔ-sá	a-sá	a-tsa	ɔ-sá	ɔ-sá
be (something)	...ì	...ì	...ì	...ì	...ì	...ì	...ì
(somewhere)	ɔ-rí	a-rí	a-rí	a-rí	a-rí	a-rí	ɔ-rí
	ɔ-tɛ						
bear (child)	u-tí	u-tí	u-tí	u-tí	u-tí	u-tí	u-tí
(twins)	ɔ-só						ɔ-só
beat	ɔ́-'bɨ	ɔ́-'bɨ	ɔ́-'bɨ	ɔ́-'bɨ	a-'bi	ɔ-'bɪ	ɔ-'bɪ
punch	ɔ-vó (2)						ɔ-vó
strike	u-sí	u-sí	u-sí	u-sí		u-sí	u-sí
bite	ɔ-sɪ	a-sɪ	ɔ-sɪ	a-sɪ	a-sɪ	ɔ-sɪ	ɔ-sɪ
gnaw	ɔ-kwa						ɔ-fá
blow	ɔ-vó (2)	ɔ-vó	ɔ-vó	ɔ-vó	a-vó	ɔ-vɔ	ɔ-vɔ
break (stick)	ɔ-ŋgó	ɔ-ŋgó	ɔ-ŋgó	ɔ-ŋgó	a-ŋɔ	ɔ-ŋgó	ɔ-ŋgó
(bowl)	u-fú	u-fú	u-fú	u-fú	ä-fú	u-fú	u-fú
(cf. kill)							
bring (here)	ɛzí	ɛzí	ɛzí	azi	azɪ	azi	azi
(there)							
build	ɔ-mɔ	ɔ-mɔ	ɔ-mɔ	ɔ-mɔ	a-mó	ɔ-mɔ	ɔ-mɔ
burn (tr.)	ɔ-za			ɔ-zɔ	a-zá		ɔ-za
(intr.)	u-dzʷé	u-dzɛ	u-zè	ö-dzɛ	ɛdzé	u-zʷe	u-vé
kindle	lerú	lerú	lerú			lerú	lerú
buy	ɔ-gyé	ɔ-gyé	ɔ-gyé	ɔ-dʒɛ	a-dzé	ɔ-gyɛ	ɔ-dzwé
sell	ɛgyɛ			adʒɛ		agyɛ	adzɛ
call	u-zí	u-zí	u-zí	u-zí	ä-zi	u-zí	u-zí
carry (here)	ɨngyi	ɨngyi	ɨngyi	ändzi	ándzì		ändzì
(there)	ú-ŋgi	ú-ŋgi	ú-ŋgi	u-ndʒi	à-ndzì	u-ŋgyä	ú-ndzi
catch	ɔ-kó	ɔ-kó	ɔ-kó	a-kó	a-kó	ɔ-kó	ɔ-kó
hold	ătì	ătì	eti	äti	äti	äti	äti
cease!	nya'bʊ	nya'bʊ tí!	nya'bʊ tí!	nya'bʊ tí!	na'bö ti!	na'bʊ	na'bʊ
	kàlà!					kàlà!	kàlà!
stop (cf. stand)	ɛdré	ɛdré	ɛdré	ɛdré	adrɛ	adrɛ	adre

VOCABULARY 361

AVUKAYA					MADI			
Ojila	Ojiga	Logo	Keliko	Lugbara	Lokai	Pandikeri	Lulu'ba	Lendu
à'dɔ	a'dú	a'dú	a'dú	a'dú	a'du	a'du	à'dwi	mgba
à'dʊ(la)yà		aŋgo'di(ya)			iŋgo			
tèísí yà	tɛsi yà	áŋgʷɔpíyà	íŋgɔpíyà	íŋgɔpíyà	sí	sí	sí	thi
	áŋgopíyà				iŋgopi			
... pi }	... pi }	... pi	... pɪ	... pi	... rɪ'ɪ	... rɪ'ɪ		
... bɪ }	... bɛ }							
atsé	atsá	atsá	ɪtsá	atsá	etsá	esà	ɛsà	si
tsàá	tsá	tsa	tsa	tsá	tsá	sá		si
... ì	... ì	... ì	... ì	... ì	... ì	... ì		ku
a'do		adre	adrɛ		edre		lé	ŋgu
be		be			alú			
ti	ti	ti	ti	àti	tì	tì	ti	ro
sɔ	ti	ti	ti	àti				'ye (animals)
tso(a)	tswa	{ tso	gba	gbà	mgba (2)	mgba	mŋé	ti
		{ tswa	vi					ði
		'bɛ́						'bi (slap)
	si	sa	sì		di	di		
si	di	di	di	di	sì	sì	di	ɖu, te
tsɪɛ	tsi	tʃì, ta	tʃì, tɛ	tsi	tsí	sí	ɔsí	ká
	tsi	lèrè	fa	tsi	ɔtsí	ɔsí		ka
								a
vɔ	vò	vo	vò	vò	vó	vó	vɔvu	vu
ŋɔ	ŋɔ	{ ŋo	ŋɔ	nyú	ŋò	nò	ŋɔŋɔ	ko
drà(?)	fu	{ ŋwa	fu	api	edrà	ledà	ɛda	kwi
		fu						
(a)dʒi	(a)fɛ	{ ado	dzi	dzi	ɛdzí	ɛzí	{ ɛkwé	(a)bu
	(a)dzi	{ ɛfu	dzi		dzí	zí	{ ɛkú	(a)pu
		do					kwɛ	
mò	sì	sì	sì	mbɛ	sí	sì	u-si	ci
tɪ(a)								
'dì								
za	za	za	zà	aso	dò	dò	dɔ	bi
vὲ	vɛ	vé	vɛ́	vè	gwè	gwè		gbi
etʃwi		turu					ɛfɔ	co
'ji	ji	'di	'jù	edze	'jì	'jì		
gyi	ge	{ gi	{ dze	ogba	dzè	gè	ge	dzz
		{ gyɛ	{ gyɛ					dzz
zi	zi	zi	zi	mve	uŋgwe (8)	luŋgwɛ	uŋgwe	ndzz
		vi						
atru		ado						
tru	trɔ	dɔ	'du	'du	ndzì	ŋgì	gu	ɖu
								mgbe
(lo)kó	ru	ru	ru	ru	kɔ́	kɔ́	ru	lo
àtì	ru	ru	ru	ru				dzz
ru								
namù ti!	namɔ ti!	mítà'bu tì!	míru tì!	méku ti!	nyivu tsɪrɪ!	dì tʃirɛ!	abu ŋgálí!	
mɪrɪ ti!	miru ti!							
adrɛ	lɔvɔ	adre	adre	drɛdrɛ	mba	ɛdɛ	édè	tai

VOCABULARY

MORU

	Miza	Kediru	Lakama'di	-ägi	Wa'di	'Bälimbä	-ändri
clean	ɔ-yó	ɔ-yó	ɔ-yó	ɔ-tó	ɔ-tó ä-tri	ɔ-tó	ɔ-tó
come	ɛdɛ ɛ́kyi ɛ́ṛi	ɛdɛ ɛ́kyi	ɛdɛ ɛ́kyi	ɛdɛ aṛi	aṛi	ɛdɛ ɛkyi	I-dɛ áṛi
cook	là'di (2)	là'di	là'di	là'di	là'di	là'di	là'di
cough	ɛ́kpɨ	ɛ́kpɨ	ɛ́kpí	ä̊kpi	äkpö	ɛ́kpɛ̇	ɛ́kpɛ̇
count, read (cf. *call*)	ɔ-tí u-zí	ɔ-tí	ɔ-tí	a-ti	a-ti	ɔ-tí	ɔ-tí
cry	lii	ili	ilɪɪ	ɔ-ŋgaʊ (8)	(awɔ) ŋgwaó	ɔ-ŋgó	ɔ-ŋgó
curse	latrɪ ɔ-trí	ɔ-trí	ɔ-trí	ɔ-lɔ (?)	latri trí	latrɪ ɔ-trɪ	latrɪ ɔ-trɪ
insult	ɔ́-'dà	ɔ-'da	ɔ-'da	ɔ'-da	'da la'da	ɔ-'da	ɔ-'da
cut	ɔ-ló(a)	ɔ-lɔ	ɔ-la	ɔ-lɔ	ɔ-lɔ aɲo	ɔ-la	ɔ-la
saw chop	täṛi ɔ-ga (2)	täṛi ɔ-ga	täṛi ɔ-ga	täṛi a-ga	äṛi a-ga	täṛi ɔ-ga	täṛi ɔ-ga
dance	(läří) ɔ-tó	(läří) ɔ-tó	(läří) ɔ-tó	a-tó	a-tó	ɔ-tó	ɔ-tó
die	ɔ-drà	ɔ-drà	ɔ-drà	ɔ-drà	a-dra	ɔ-drà	ɔ-drà
dig	ú-'di	ú-'di	ú-'di	ä-dí	ä-dí	ò'dì	u-'dì
dive	ɔ-'dé	ɔ-'dé	ɔ-'dé	ɔ-'dé	a-'dɛ	ɔ-'dé	ɔ-'dé
divide split	ɔ-nyí (yana) u-fu ɔ-si	ɔ-nyí (yana) u-fu	ɔ-nyí (yana) u-fu	a-nyi (yana) u-fu ɔ-si	a-nyi (ana) ä-fu	kʊra (yana) u-fu pɛrɛ	kɔra (yana) u-fu
dress	(rú) ɛ́dɛ̇	(bɔŋgó) ɔ-sɔ	(lɔwó) ɔ-sɔ	(lɔwó) ɔ-sɔ	ä-su	ɔ-sɔ	(rúmvú) ɛ́dɛ̇
undress	(lómvó) ɔ-trí	(lómvó) ɔ-trí	(lɔwó) ɔ-trí	(lɔwó) ɔ-trí	a-ndzé	ɔ-trɪ	ɔ-trɪ
drink smoke	u-mvú ɔ-sɛ	u-mvú	u-mvú	u-mvú	ä-mvú	u-mvú	u-mvú
eat	ɔ́-nyà	ɔ́-nyà	ɔ́-nyà	a-nyá	a-nyá	ɔ-nya	ɔ-nya
fall	ɔ́-'dɛ̇ ɛ́'dɛ̇ (2) lada	ɔ́-'dɛ̇ ɛ́'dɛ̇	ɔ́-'dɛ̇ ɛ́'dɛ̇	a-'dɛ a'dɛ	a-'dɛ a'dɛ	ɔ-'dɛ a'dɛ	ɔ-'dɛ a'dɛ
of rain	u-'di						u-'di
drop (cf. *throw*)	ɔ-vɔ	ɔ-vɔ	ɔ-vɔ	a-vo	a-vo	ɔ-vɔ	ɔ-vɔ
fear	tʊrì	tärí	tʊrì	kʊrì	kwöri	urì	urì
fight (*make war*)	kɪlá ɔ̀-yɛ	kɪlá ɔ̀-yɛ	kɪlá ɔ̀-yɛ	kɪlá à-yɛ	kùmbà 'ɛ	kɪlá ɔ̀-yɛ	kɪlá ɔ̀-yɛ
fly ... *towards*	ɔ-ŋgá ɛŋgá	ɔ-ŋgá ɛŋgá	ɔ-ŋgá ɛŋgá	ɔ-ŋgá aŋga	a-ŋgá áŋgá	ɔ-ŋgá áŋgá	ɔ-ŋgá áŋgá

VOCABULARY

AVUKAYA					MADI			
Ojila	Ojiga	Logo	Keliko	Lugbara	Lokai	Pandikeri	Lulu'ba	Lendu
tɔ	fa	fa	fa	ufa	kwá	kwá		(a)u
tri			ti	ti	trí	tí		
adrɛ					sá	swá	swa	
					ekí	ekí	ɛkyi	(a)si
ani	ani	aṛi	aṛi		emu	emu		(a)ra
					ɛmba	ɛfu		
là'di	là'di	là'di	a'di	a'di	'dì	'dì	nɛ	ri
kpu		kipílà(ga)	ɔkélè(ga)	ɔkélè(ga)	ɔkólò	ɔkólò	ɛkʸéikʸi	ákru
								kpi
la		lálà	laflalà	lalà	lalà	lalà	lóluà	zo
		lálà			lalà		lóluà	zo
(àwɔ)ŋgɔ'ɔ		ŋgɔ	ɔŋgɔ	wáwó	ɔwó	ɔú	ɔú	dzz
			ɛmia	aá				
latítrí		tatri	tra	lu				
trí		(kɔ)ta	(ka)ta	tri	tali	ɛtali	lemi (5, 8)	thu
		litrí						
'da	'dá	'da	'dá	'dà	'da	'da	na	thu
la'dá								
mva		lwà, lo	làrɪ, ṛì	lì	lí	lí	li	ʒírɪ
			⎰ ṛiṛi					
ṛi		liré, si	⎱ liri	lirâ			ligyé	ʒɪrɪʒí
ga		ga	ga	ga	gá	gá	ga	tsa
								krr
(ändu) tò	(ändú) tòa	(läri) tó	(óŋgwó) tʊ	(ɪŋgà) tu	(lató) to	to lató	tɔ	be
drà		drà	drà	drà	drà	dà	da	ðɛ
'di	'di	'di	gagà	'di			'di	ji
							'dó'dì	
'dɛ		'dɛ			lwee	lwee	'de	
nyi	('ani) kù	lanji	dzadza	àdi(lɛ)	(asì) ɪdzá	zɛkɛ	ákyira kyì	ndo
(ala) fu		('ani)ku						
pɛrɛ	si	ʃì	sì	sisì	pì	pì	pirapi	tha
			ùsì					
(bɔŋgó) su	so	asɔ	sòzì	so	so	so	tɔ	tho
(étá) aŋgí	ŋgi	tri	ndʒɛ àmvɛ	trù	ǹdzɛ	ŋké	ɛtwé	klo
		avu		ndʒí				
mvu	mvu	mvú	mvú	mvú	mvu	mvu	mbú	⎰ 30
	sé	sé	sé	sé	sɛ	mvu	mbú	⎱ mbu
								ɖa
nya	nya	nyá	nyá	nyá	nya	nya	nya	nyo
'dɛ		'dɛ			ro lá	lá ro	lá ro	bu
a'dɛ		a'dɛ	a'dɛ	'dɛ'dɛ	'dé	'dé	'dɛ	'dɛ'dɛ
	gbä	'di	'di	rà	'dí	'dí	'dɛ	kɔ
			rá(=leak)					
vu			'bɛ					dze, ci
euri		tiri	dri	ourisi	orí	orí	ɔro	donji
rɔ		drí	rʊ				ru	
ʊmba'ɛ	'ɔmba	kumba'ɔ	ɔmbɔ fû	agubì'ɛ	'jà	'já	ésì	li
	furu	⎰ furu	'di'di	furu				gu
		⎱ lawa						
ŋga	ŋga	ŋga	ŋga	ŋgà	ŋgoru	ɛndzi	ŋgoru	tata
aŋgá	aŋga	aŋga	aŋga					

VOCABULARY

MORU

	Miza	Kediru	Lakama'di	-ägi	Wa'di	'Bälimbä	-ändri
forge	tɔká ù-di	tɔká ù-di	tɔká ù-di	kóká ä̀-di	kóká ä̀-di	ɔká ù-di	ɔká ù-di
forget	ʊ-dʒʷɪ	u-dʒe	u-ze	ɛdʒɪ̀	ädzi	u-zʷɛ	ʊ-vɪ
give	ɔzɔ̀	ɔzɔ̀	ɔzɔ̀	ɛtsɛ (to me) tsɛ (to him)	atsɛ (to me) tsɛ (to him)	azɔ	azɔ
go	ói u-kyí	ói u-kyí	ói u-kyí	ayi eṛi	ai ɪṛɪ	ɔyi ṛɪ	ɔyi ṛɪ
go out	ɔ-fɔ						fo
hate (neg. of love)	lɛ ... kɔ	lɛ ... kɔ	lɛ ... kɔ	lɛ ... kɔ	lɛ ... kɔ	lɛ ... kɔ	lɛ ... kɔ
hear	ɛrɪ	ɛrɪ	ɛrɪ	ari	ɪrɪ	arɪ	arɪ
listen	bí ɔ-ga	bí ɔ-ga	bí ɔ-ga		bí a-ga	bí ɔ-ga	
help	ɔ-pá	ɔ-pá	ɔ-pá	a-pa	a-pa	ɔ-pa	ɔ-pa
hide	dembí	lä́pi	lä́pi	lä́pi	lä́pi	lä́pi	lä́pi
hoe	ɔ-só						
interpret	kala lógɔ̀ ... ya	kala lógɔ̀ ... ya	kala lógɔ̀ ... ya	lagʊ	lagwa	lɔgɔ	lɔgɔ
kill	u-fú	u-fú	u-fú	ä-fu	ä-fu	u-fu	u-fu
know	u-nì	u-nì	u-nì	ä-ni	ä-ni	u-ni	u-ni
laugh	u-gu(gù) (2)	u-gu(gù)	u-gu(gù)	gu lägu	u-gu	u-gu	
leave allow	ɛ́'bɛ́ ɛ'dɛ	ɛ́'bɛ́	ɛ́'bɛ́	ɛ́'bɛ́	a'bɛ	a'bɛ	a'bɛ
lick	ɛlɛ̀	ɛlɛ̀	ɛlɛ̀	ɛlɛ̀	alɛ̀	ɪlɛ̀	ɪlɛ̀
lie	kuwé ɔ-gá (= cut)	kuwé ɔ-gá	kuwé ɔ-gá	ɛnzɔ ɔ-ga (=sleep)	kuya 'élé	usu ɔ-ga	usu ɔ-ga
lie (down)	ɔ-'dé (vùru)	ɔ-'dé (vùru)	ɔ-'dé (vùru)	ä'du	ä'di	ɔ-'dé	ɔ-'dé
lay	ɔ-'ba lalà	ɔ-'ba lalà	ɔ-'ba lalà	ɔ-'ba lalà	'ba lalà	ɔ-'ba lalà	ɔ-'ba lalà
love want	lúù ɔ-lɛ	ɔ-lɛ	ɔ-lɛ	a-lɛ	a-lɛ	ɔ-lɛ	ɔ-lɛ
make	ɛdé	ɛdé	ɛdé	adɛ	adɛ	ɪdɛ	ɪdɛ
do	ɔ-yé	ɔ-yé	ɔ-yé	a-'yé	a-'yé	ɔ-yé	ɔ-yé
marry	ɔ-gyé (2)	ɔ-gyé	ɔ-gyé	ɛdzé	a-dzɛ	ɔ-gyɛ	ɔ-dzé
meet	drɪ ɔ-'bɛ ... bɛ	drɪ ɔ-'bɛ ... bɛ	drɪ ɔ-'bɛ ... bɛ	drɪ ɔ-'bɛ ... bɛ	drɪ a-'bé	drɪ ɔ-'bɛ	drɪ ɔ-'bɛ
foregather	ɔ-tɔ	ɔ-tɔ	ɔ-tɔ	ɔ-tɔ		ɔ-tɔ	ɔ-tɔ
milk	(lɛi) ɔ-zá	(lɛi) ɔ-zá	(lɛi) ɔ-zá	a-zá	a-zá	ɔ-zá	ɔ-zá

VOCABULARY

AVUKAYA					MADI			
Ojila	Ojiga	Logo	Keliko	Lugbara	Lokai	Pandikeri	Lulu'ba	Lendu
ɔká di	ókála di	atsó di	di di	atsó di	di	di	dí	kajoŋga
ɔvi	vì	vì *avi*	àvì	avì	egwe	legwe	boŋo (8)	*vi*
afɛ	afe	afɛ̀ (to me)	afɛ̀	ɪfɛ (to me)	ɛkɛ	ɛkɛ	ɛkwé	'bu
fɛ (to him)		fɛ (to him)	fɛ	fɛ (to him)				
nì	nì	ŋga, nji		mú	mú	mú		(á)rà
lämu	gò	ṭí	ṭí	lʊ	vʊ	vɔ kí	kii	tu
			fó	fo	fó			
lɛ...kɔ	lɛ...kɔ	ze	ʊndʒi ndrɛ ('see bad')	lɛ...kɔ ŋgu	ɪmanà (5,7)	emána	imana	ndro
arí	rɪ	rí yi	rɨ̀ àrɨ̀	rí	ɛrɪ	ɛrɪ	ɛrɛ	rr
bilɛ ga								
pa ɛ̀dɛ̀	ɛ̀dɛ	*pa tedri ledé*	ŋàrà (8)	loku isadria aza, eto	ékónyi(5,7)	élóku	ŋara	go
lå̂pɨ	låpi	*zu 'bà* (ŋga) 'a	zù opɪ̀ (mvú) 'a	zù opi (mvú) 'a	zô (ŋga) ju	zô	amgbé	ru
lɔgo...'á	úlí atá	kuli ta kuli laja	'jɔ̀	údʒú lɛgá udʒú dʒû	ɪdrɪ 'di	edì 'di	ŋgwe	le
äfu		fu 'dɪ̀	fu 'dɪ̀	gbɨ 'di	'dí	'dí	'dí	hwi zhi
nì	nì yí	nì	nì	nì	nì	nì	nì	tʃu
gù	gù	gù gu ari	gù	gù	gu	gu	agu	gbo
arí	arí							
ayɛ	ayɛ	tái	yɛ kʊ	ɛ'bɛ kʊdzà	é'bé	é'bé	yi	(a)'ba
aǹdra								ɖa
mbɛ̀	mbɛ	mbɛ	mbɛ	mbé	mbé	mbé	ɔmbɛ	mbu
enzo ga enzo élé		kìndzɔ lí	kìndzɔ ṭi	ndzò ṭí	éndzó	éndzó	ozɔ	kali ti
äɪ (vudri)	åyi (bidri)	*ai (vudri)* la (mvùga)	lɔ (vùga)	la (vùru)	ro-la			ai (guna)
'ba...í	'ba	'ba	'ba	'ba				do
la(la)	lala	alala *laile*	alala	alala				
lè	lè	{lɛ né	lè	lè	lɛ	lɛ	lɛ	ʒi
ɛdɛ	lɛdɛ	lɛdɛ	ɔdɛ	idɛ	ɛdé	ɛdé		ndʒi
'ɛ		o ba	ɔ	'ɛ	'owɛ	'ɛ	wɛ	ndʒi
gyɪ	gyɛ	gyɛ mo	dzɛ	ogba	dzʷè	gyè	gɪ	thi ko
dri'bɛ ru isu ru e'be	su ru e'be	*ru kusu* ru kisu *ru kebe* ató náro	usu	fu	ru itsi ro emó	esi ru emó ro	riŋɔ esu	cu nju
za	zwa	zwa zɔ	zɔ	zá	zá ndrè	zwá ndè	ɔzwa	

VOCABULARY

	\multicolumn{7}{c}{MORU}						
	Miza	**Kediru**	**Lakama'di**	**-ägi**	**Wa'di**	**'Bälimbä**	**-ändri**
open	u-pì	u-pì	u-pì	ä-pi	ä-pi	u-pi	u-pi
pain	'bu'bà	'bo'bwe	'bu'bä	'bwä'bwä	'bä'bà	'bu'bä	'bu'bä
	lulu	lulu	lolo	loulou	loulou	lulu	lulu
pay (cf. give)	ɔ-zɔ	pa̧rí	tɛsɛ	atswɛ	tsɛ / atsɛ	ɪfɛ	ɔfɛ
pick (up)	ɛŋgá (kuru)	ɛŋgá (kuru)	ɛŋgá (kuru)	ɛŋgá (kuru)	aŋga	ɪŋga(uru)	ɪŋga(uru)
poison	a̧rí ɔ-zó	a̧rí ɔ-zó	emvu a̧rí si	a̧rí ɛtswɛ	äfu äli sì	kyo	tso
pray	mätu	mätu	medé	mätu	mätu	mätu	mätu
put	ɔ-'ba	ɔ-'ba	ɔ-'ba	ɔ-'ba	ɔ-'ba	ɔ-'ba	ɔ-'ba
set up	u-ti	uti		u-ti	eti	öti	u-ti
remain	ɔ-rɪ	ɔ-rɪ	ɔ-rɪ	ɔ-rɪ	ɔ-rɪ	ɔ-rɪ	ɔ-rɪ
wait	kɔtè	kɔtè	kɔtè	a-tɛ	a-tɛ	kɔtè	kɔtè
return: come back (here)	ɛgɔ (kõvɔlɛ)	ɛgɔ (kõvɔlɛ)	ɛgɔ (kõvɔlɛ)	ágɔ̀ (ndoa)	agɔ̀ (kóvúlé)	agɔ	agɔ
go back (there)	ɔ-gɔ	ɔ-gɔ	ɔ-gɔ	ɔ-gɔ	à-gɔ̀	ɔ-gɔ	ɔ-gɔ
return: give back (here) (there)	lɔgɔ̀						
run (here)	imú	imú	imú	ämu	ämu	ämu	ämu
(there)	u-mú	ó-mu	o-mú	u-mú		ä-mú	u-mú
say	(ta) átá	(ta) átá	(ta) átá		ta	(ta) átá	átá
talk	lɛdzi			ladzi	(ata) kwó-ri̧		lɛdzʷi
tell answer	ta iti	ta iti	ta iti	ta iti	tà äti	ta iti	ta iti
see	ɔ-ndré	ɔ-ndré	ɔ-ndré	ndrɛ	ndrɛ	ɔ-ndré	ɔ-ndré
watch	ɔ-kwà		ɔ-kwá	atɛ	atɛ	ɔ-kwa	ɔ-tɛ
shoot (gun)	o-'bwá	o-'bwá	o-'bwá	o-'bwá	ä-'bä	o-'bwä	o-'bwä
(bow)	o-'bwá	o-'bwá	o-'bwá	o-'bwá	ä-'bä	o-'bwä	o-'bwä
shut	ɔ-sé	ɔ-sé	ɛsɛ	a-sé ɛsɛ	asa	ɔ-sé	ɔ-sé
sing	(lɔŋgó) ɔ-ŋgɔ	(lɔŋgó) ɔ-ŋgɔ	(lɔŋgó) ɔ-ŋgɔ	(làŋgwa) ɔ-ŋgɔ	(lòŋgwa) ŋgwa	(làŋgɔ) ɔ-ŋgɔ	(làŋgɔ) ɔ-ŋgɔ
sit (cf. remain)	ɔ-rí	ɔ-rí	ɔ-rí	ɔ-rí	a-rɪ	ɔ-rí	ɔ-rí
sleep	u'dú	u'dú	o'du	u'du	ä'du	u'du	u'du
smell (tr.)	äŋgù	äŋgù	äŋgù	äŋgù	äŋgu	äŋgu	äŋgu
(intr.)	tägyí			tädzí	kädzí	ädzí	ädzí
sneeze	(kɔ̀mvɔ) ɔ-sì (= nose)	(kɔ̀mvɔ) ɔ-sì	(kɔ̀mvɔ) ɔ-sì	(kovɔ) ɔ-si	a-sɪ	(imvɔ) sì	(ɔ̀mvɔ) sì
spread	lara	lara	lara	lara	lara	lara	lara
	pɛrɛ	pɛrɛ	pɛrɛ	pɛrɛ	lapɛ	pɛrɛ	pɛrɛ
stand (cf. stop)	ɛdrɛ	ɛdrɛ	ɛdrɛ	ɛdrɛ	adrɛ	adrɛ	adrɛ

VOCABULARY

AVUKAYA					MADI			
Ojila	Ojiga	Logo	Keliko	Lugbara	Lokai	Pandikeri	Lulu'ba	Lendu
pi			zì	ázwì				
nzì		ŋgyì	ŋgyì		áfù	áfù	ufo	pu
						Bu. = lufo		(a)wɛ
'bu'bu		àdra swalɛ	àdra salasa	àzɔzɔ	azaza	ledʒwá-	áza	ɖro
lazilazi		'bulu'bulu	àdra gàlagà		(ó)fefè	ledʒwá		
						(ó)féfe		
fɛ	fɛ	fè	ufè	ufè	úkwɛ	lúkwɛ	ɪrɔpa (8)	ne
								'bu
trò (uru)	ŋga	ŋga	ŋga	ŋga	e'dú (òrù)	'dú	ɪnu	va
ŋga		tiŋga						
fu alókɔ sì	fu ledzó sì	fu lɔdzó sì	otso	otso	enya	enya érúá sì	isu	
					érúá sì			
ŋgwa ... dri		ŋgo ... drɪ			ɛlégì	ɛlégì		nzz
(= cry to)								
'bà	'bà	'bà	'bà	'bà	'bà	'bá	'ba	li
ti								
		{ liri						'bɔ
		{ adre	tɛ	tɛ	tè	tè	tè	di
tɛ	ta	tɛ	tɛ	tɛ	tè	tè	tè	ŋgu
		lete						
agò (vúlé)	agò (vúlé)	agò	ɪgò (vʊlɛ)	gò (ndɔ)	ɛŋgwé	éŋgwí	ɛŋgwí	aŋgu
		(àndʒɪlɛ)				(vulɛ)	(bulɛ)	
gɔ	gɔ	gù	gò	gò (vʊlɛ)	ŋgwè	ŋgwí	ŋgwí	aŋgu
				mvi				
		aji						aŋgu
		aji						aŋgu
		go						
ra	ára	ára		ɪtsɪ̀	ɛlò (2)	ɪfè	emu	co
	rà	rà	ndzù	tsɪ̀	ɔ-lò	fè	mu	nyi
ta	ta	ta	ta					po
			'jo					ŋga
(ta) úʈí			dza	dʒu	'jó	'jó	'jó	ti
ta ŋgo		loŋgo			'jó	'jó	e'jó	'dra
		ta ako			yeì	kà		ŋgulo
		{ nó		{ nɛ	{ nó			
ndré		{ ndre	ndré	{ ndrɛ́	{ ndrɛ́	ndé	ɔ-ndɛ	(a)ndʒa
tè		nda		ndɛ				'bo
		(= look for)						be
'bù	'bwo	'bú	'bu	gbí	bwí	bwé	'gbwé	(á)pɔ
'bù	'bwo	'bú	'bu	gbí	bwí	bwé	sɔ́	(á)sz
sɛ		asɛ			á'bú	ló'bú	umɔ	(á)tʃí
'ba		drɔ	ɔdrɔ	òpí		Bu. = afu		
(lòŋgo)	(lòŋgo)	(lòŋgɔ) ŋgɔ	(ʊŋgɔ) ŋgɔ	(ɪŋgɔ)	ru oŋgó	ŋgo	ŋgo	ŋgo
ŋgo	ŋgo			ŋgɔ		(loŋgó)		
ɔrɪ	ri	ʈiri	rɪ	rɪ	rɪ	rɪ	eri	(á)dí
				arɪ		Bu. = eri		(gùna)
(k)o'dú		kɛí	ko'dú	ku'dú	(k)o'dú	(k)o'dú	nonu	'dɔ
äi		ayi kò	ɛi	oɖu				
			làlà	la				
ŋgù	ŋgù	ŋgu	ŋgu	ŋgu	ŋgù	ŋgù	ŋgoŋgù	ŋgo
ädʒí		ŋguŋgu		ŋguŋgu	kóŋguŋgù	kúŋgúŋgù		ŋgoŋgo
(ɔmvɔ) tsě	(ɔmvu) tsɪ	(kɔmvɔ) syà	mvu tsò	mvu tsò	òmvo tso	tso òmvo	otʃwà	ndu ti
ladzwà	ladza	tadza	adzadza	adzadza	anyá	anyá	ìwe (?)	hu
lapɛ								yi
adrɛ	adrɛ	adrɪ		adrɪ	mba	ɛdɛ	ɛdɛ	to

VOCABULARY

MORU

	Miza	Kediru	Lakama'di	-ägi	Wa'di	'Bälimbä	-ändri
stand up							
steal	kugu (2)	kugu	kugu	kugu	kwogu	ugù	ugù
stoop	ändi	ändi	endi	ändi	ändi	ändi	ändi
crawl	tɛgatɛga (2)	tɛgatɛga	tɛgatɛga	tɪgatɪga	gàgà	égàegà	égàegà
suck	ɔ-ndró	ɔ-ndró	ɔ-ndró	ɔ-ndró	a-ndró	ɔ-ndró	ɔ-ndró
sweep	ɔ-wyá	ɔ-wyá	ɔ-ya	ɔ-tɔ / ɔtɔ		ɔ-tò	ɔ-tò
swim	ɛlɛ̀ (2)	ɛlɛ̀	ɪlɛ̀	ɛlɛ	ɛlɛ	ɪlɛ̀	ɪlɛ̀
take away	u-rú	u-rú	u-rú	u-rú	ä-ru	u-rú	u-rú
tear	ɔ-wa / ɔ-sî	ɔ-wa / ɔ-sî	ɔ-wa / ɔ-sî	ɔ-wa / ɔ-sî	a-wyɛ / a-sɪ	ɔ-wa / ɔ-si	ɔ-wa / ɔ-si
throw (away)	ɔ-vó	ɔ-vó	ɔ-vó	a-vu	ä-vu	ɔ-vɔ	ɔ-vɔ
(towards)	ɛvɔ	ɛvɔ	ɛvɔ	avɔ		avɔ	avɔ
tie	ɛ́mbɛ́	ɛ́mbɛ́	ɛ́mbɛ́	ɛ́mbɛ́	ambɛ	ɔmbɛ	ɔmbɛ
untie	ɔndʒʷì	ɔndʒʷì	ɔndʒʷì	andʒʷi	andzi	óndzʷi	óndzʷi
walk	abá	ɔba	ɔba	abá	ätʃi lämu	ɔbá	ɔbá
wash	ɔ-dzwá	ɔ-dzwä	ɔ-dʒu	ɔ-dʒu	a-dzɪ	ɔ-zi	ɔ-dzi
bathe	lásá	lasa	lasa	lasa	a-dzɪ	lasa	lasa
work (cf. make)	(lòsì) ɔ̀-yɛ	(lòsì) ɔ̀-yɛ	(lòsì) ɔ̀-yɛ	(lòsì) ɔ̀-yɛ	(làsì) à-yɛ	(lɔsi) ɔ̀-yɛ	(lɔsi) ɔ̀-yɛ
write	ɛgyɪ	ɛgyɪ	ɛgyɪ	ɛgi	adzi	egyɪ	ɪdzɪ
yawn	aʊ	aʊ	aʊ	aʊ	'o(a)	aʊ	aʊ

ADJECTIVES

	Miza	Kediru	Lakama'di	-ägi	Wa'di	'Bälimbä	-ändri
absent	i'du	i'du	i'du	i'duä	i'duä	i'du	i'du
angry	kìla-rɔ	kìla-rɔ	kìla-rɔ	kìla-rɔ	kumbá-rú	kìla-rɔ	kìla-rɔ
bad	kɔzí(-rʊ)	kozí-ro	kozí-ro	kozí-ro	kòzɪro	ɔnzí	ɔnzí
big	'dɛsí -(a)go	lɛsí -(a)go	'dɛsi -(a)go	'dɛsi -(a)go	ombá (2) -(a)go	'dɛsi -(a)go	'dɛsi -(a)go
bitter	ɔsó	ɔ̀sɔsɔ	ɔ̀sɔsɔ	dzìàdzì	kàdziro	ɔgyɪ	ɔdʒí
sour	ɔsó	äträträ	äträträ	äträträ	äträträ	äträträ	äträträ
black	ùni	ùni	ùni	ǒni	eni	ùni	ùni
blue	lú'búlí	lú'búlí	loú'búlí	lú'búlí	lä'buli	lä'buli	lo'buli
blind	mi akó (= without eyes)	mi akó	mi i'dú (= no eyes)	mi akó	miŋgétsi àkɔ	mi i'dú	mi i'dú
blunt	sí kʊ (= not cut)	sí kʊ	sí kʊ	sí kʊ	sɪ kʊ	si kʊ	si kʊ
clever	(mi) ɔmbáké (= eyes strong)	(mi) ɔmbáké	(mi) ɔmbáké	(mi) ɔmbáké	(ŋgetsí (na)) mbapɛ	(mi) ɔmbáké	(mi) ɔmbáké

VOCABULARY

AVUKAYA					MADI			
Ojila	Ojiga	Logo	Keliko	Lugbara	Lokai	Pandikeri	Lulu'ba	Lendu
		ŋgá (kuru)	ŋgá		ŋga (uru)	ŋga (uru)	ɛdɛ́ orúsì	ádáni rừnà
ugu	úgù	kúgù	úgù	úgù	ogù	ogù	ugu	gbu
ändi		tändi	övòvò		wowò	wówò	(ó)wowò	ko
gàgà		taga	agaga		gaagà	gáágà	(á)gagà	go
ndrɔ	ndro	ndro	ndru	ndrú	ndró	ndó	ndo	nju
		ndrundrù						
tò		wa	wè	wé	wé	wé	wɛ	tsu
kừ	kủ	awo						
ɛlɛ	(iyí) wɛ	(iyí) tswa	tu	(iyí) wè	'dɛ	'dɛ		vi
								gbithi
tru		agu		egu				tu
				wu				
wɔ	wè							tha
sɪ		sì	sisi	sì	sì	tʃwì	ɔkɛ́	drr
		lasí(á)		asíasi				
vù		be		be				bu
ävù								o
ɔmbɛ		tile	ʊmbé	ʊmbé	umbɛ	umbɛ	umbɛ	
ambɛ	ambɛ	lambé						
ɪndzɪ	indʒi	kɪndʒí	eyòyù	éyu	yu	yu	uŋgyi	klɔ
		tri	tri				(kɛ́lɛ́)	ŋga
lämu	etʃí (tòlɛ)	etʃí (tòra)	tʃí (tolɛ)	tʃí (legà)	mú (lalɛ)	mú (nàlɛ)	kyi	bi
		teci	kéki				(awala sì)	
		li						
dzí	dzí	ji	di	dʒi	dze	dze	udʒwe	u
da(?)		adʒi	dʒi					u
läsi 'ɛ		(azi) o	(azí) ŋgà	'a	('bù) 'ɛ	'ɛ́ ('bù)	kyi ('bwo)	nji
egyi	ósi(á)	tíʃɪ	sì	úru (8)	sì ,	sí	(kyi)	ndi
							wuru	
(si'bala)	(sí'balɛ) fä	wa'wà	a'a'	'wa'ú	'ò	'owá	a'ú	ga
à-va		(sibala) nzì	síláfäŋgi					
i'duä		yò	⎧'dayo	⎧'dayo			kéèwɛ	kừ ŋga
iyu	yo	yokɔ'dɔ	⎨yo	⎨yo	yo	yo		
			yekɔ'dɔ	ɔ'yu'yò				
wä-rú			kumba-ro		tò àtsi	nirùgé àsi	tàtwe	tho
							'do	
súkú'dá (2)	wòndʒi	kùndʒi	ɔ̀dʒi	ùndʒi	undzí	undʒwí	ɔlíndʒwé	tʃê
		kɔnzi	ɔnzi	ɔ̀ndzi	ondzí	ɔndʒwí	ndʒwé	
ambá (2)	mbá	mórúŋgú	àmbagɔ	ambágòrɔ	ndzá	ndzá(-réè)	gwi	bò ...
-(a)go	-(a)go	-(a)go	-(a)go	-(a)go				
		kadrɪ	lɔpừr					
gyɪgyɪ	gyɪgyɪ	kudʒíkudʒì	dràdrà	okoka	aŋá	aŋá	aŋa-na	dyadya
utruträ	ukoukä	àswaswa	dràdrà		owá (7)	owá		ŋgoŋgo
nìni	nini	kyini	(n)inì	(i)nirú	íní	íní	àni-na	titi
lä'buli	kini-kɪdr	kini-ca	ini-tsuru	lä'bule	lɔkɪrɪ̀'	lɔkɪrɪ̀'	aforɔ-na	titi
		pfarapfara						
lifi akó	lifi yu	mi yó	mi òkɔ	mi ìko	mi àkɔ	mi dàra	mi nakéwe	nyo
		mi kudu-				(= eyes dead)		tsutsu
		kudu						
tsíku'dá (2)	tsí kɔ	tsí kɔ	tsí kɔ	tsi ku	ɔ-tsi ko	si ko	erí-na	yuku
tsíla dràta								dhedhe
(lifi)	(lifi)	mì tʃítʃi	mì tʃitʃi	mi tʃí		mi tsiri	ambá-na	nyo'yu
mbatró	mbamba	cogiabe		mùkpó	mi ɔkpó	mi ɔkpó		(ke)

VOCABULARY

MORU

	Miza	Kediru	Lakama'di	-ägi	Wa'di	'Bälimbä	-ändri
cold	kí'dɪ (2) ɪ'dwɪ	ɪ'dwɪ	é'de	ɪ'dɪ	ä'di	ɛ'dwɛ	ŋge'de ʊ'dɪ
fresh	wäṛí						wäṛí
deaf	(= without ears) bí àkɔ	bí àkɔ	bí í'du	àsì- te	bí àkɔ	bí àkɔ	bí àkɔ
dumb	kàlà landɔ			kàlà landɔ		kàlà landɔ	kàlà landɔ
tongue-tied							
different		tɔ̀tɔ̀					
dry	wɪ-tɛ	wɪ-tɛ	wɪ-tɛ	wyi-tɛ	i-tra	wɪ-tɛ	wɪ-tɛ
equal	ódzó-rɛ̀rɛ̀	ódzó-rɛ̀rɛ̀	úzú-rɛɛɛ	ódzó-àlɔ	ŏdzwó 'dɛ̀rɛ̀	odzadzo rierie	odzadzo rierie
fast	ndrɪndrɪ fɔrɔfɔrɔ	ndrɪndrɪ	dìkèdìkè (2)	ndrɪndrɪ	'wa'wa	fɔrɔfɔrɔ	fɔrɔfɔrɔ
fat	ɔs(a) ékᵛé moŋgu be (2)			mpá-'desi	amba	mäŋgwà-kyɛ	mäŋgwä-éké
few	fɛ̀rɛ̀	fɛ̀rɛ̀	pɛrɪ	diŋwa	ediŋgwa	sɛrɪŋgwá	sèrè
finished	kyé-té	kyé-té	kyé-té	tswɛ-tɛ ndɛru-trá	tswe-tra	kyé-té	tswé-té
good	kàdʊ	kàdo-ro	kàdɔ	àndi-ro	supé	pɛɛ(-rɔ)	àndi
well	tandi(-ró)	(te)kadó	kàdo-ro	àndi-ro	táàndí-ró	(tɪ)pɛɪ-rɔ	tandi-ro
green	lúru	lúru	lúru	kébi-ru	kébi-ru äni-ru (= black)	lú-ru	lú-ru
hard	ṛatara-ró	ṛatara-ró	gbùrùkù-turu	ṛàtằrằ-rʊ	abara-kɔtɔró	ṛatara-ró	ṛatara-ró
strong	mbárá(-ro)	mbárá(-ro)	mbárá(-ro)	mbárá(-ro)	kombá-ró	mbárá-ro	
heavy	läŋÿi-läŋgyi	läŋÿi-läŋgyi	läŋÿi-läŋgyi	ländzi	ländzi	läŋgyi	ländʒi-ländʒi
difficult	rɪti bɛ̀	rɪti bɛ̀	rɪti bɛ̀	rɪti bɛ̀	rɪti bɛ̀	rɪti bɛ̀	rɪti bɛ̀
hot	ɛmé	ɛmé	ɛmé	amémé	amé	amé	amé
left hand	(drí)gàṛɪ (2)	(drí)gàṛɪ	(drí)gàṛɪ	(drí)gàṛɪ	(drí)gàṛɪ	(drí)gàṛɪ	(drí)gàṛɪ
light	toùtóu (2)	tévi	tévi	tǎvi	tǎvi	kyóù	tǎvi
easy	toùtóu (2)	tévi	tévi	tǎvi	tǎvi	kyóù	tǎvi
little	gɪṛí-ŋwá	gɪṛí-ŋwá	gɪṛí-ŋó	ɪ'dɪ-ŋgwa	ɪ'dí-áŋgwá	sɛré-ŋgwá	gaá-vá
long	katsó	katswá	sà	katswá	katswá	sàtɛtú	atswá
long-ago	ukú						
many } much }	àmba du	àmba	àmba	àmba	àmba	àmba	àmba

VOCABULARY

AVUKAYA		Logo	Keliko	Lugbara	MADI			Lendu
Ojila	Ojiga				Lokai	Pandikeri	Lulu'ba	
	kɪ'dɛ	kɪd'dya						
edrí-rú		kidi-ro	ɪgbɛ̀	igbɪ	e'bwé	i'bwe	i'due	grr
	dríkídrɪ	dríkídrɪ	drɪgɪdrɪ̀	gbigbi				o
		todia-ro						
bí akó		bibale ako						
gbili i'duwä	kudu	lédu	lédu	kóyà	abí yo	abílé yo	gbikɛ	bi tsutsu
tí lando		kuli ako			tì yo	tì yo		letso tsutsu
	gbulá-gbulá	gbulá-gbulá	ŋulubê	ŋulubê (8)			ŋulubɛ	
		ladra kikipa					lʊ'da	
náàŋgyi	náàndí	dìdìtwa toatoa	tóŋó	ìtono			'dúle	njonjo
ɪ-tra	va'í'i	tà kʊ yoyo	'gyɪ-ru	'í-ru	ɔ̀'wɪ-ra	ɔ̀'wɪ-ra	a'wé	'yu
étsá-'dɛ̀rɛ	tú-alɔ rɛra	tú dede	trɔ̀trɔ̀	tùtʊ̀	ɔmbarrɛ̀	ledzorrɛ̀	kóvɔ-jojo (8)	tʃéé didi
'wa'wa	'wa'wa	mbelembele siri		mbele-mbele	dzérɛ-dzɛ́rɛ̀	fefe	títɪ	tsetse lele
amba ävuävu	selípɪ	kadrí-gú liŋgaliŋga	osé-gúgú	ɔ̀sɛ-ru	osede	swede	àswɛ	thu(?)
finyɔaare gbiwetí dà	fínyówá	tsà	gaa-rò madane	gaa-rò wɛwɛ-rò	toro	gà	galû	rereno
kyɪ-trá nderu-trá	nde(ru)-trá	lande-dre	dɛ̀-gɪ	okó-'bɔ	ɔká-rà	okó-rá	kyɔwɔ	tsi nji-'blo
dó supé (tra) dódó	dó dó	tànì tànì	anyí-sì bokɛnyɛ	ɔnyi-ró mʊkɛ	lɔsɔ e'bwé	lɔsɔ e'bwé	osú	blɔ la
ibi-ru nini-ru	nini	ndrindri	ríbìli	iríbìli	lu'bulɛ̀	lu'bulɛ̀	a'bulɛ̀	zhu
kägä'dä mbámbà	mba	ɔmba	mba	mba	ɔkpó	ɔkpá	ambá	kpakpa ndi
tàmbàrà-ro	mba	lɔmbáwɛ irinyi be	mbámba	mbogu	ɔkpó	ɔkpá	ambá	sisi klo
ländzi	lɛndʒì-lɛndʒì	lɛndʒì-lɛndʒì	andzä-ndzì	andzä-ndzì	andzí	âŋgí	aŋgí	o-li
rɪti bɛ̀	kɪnɪkɔ	kɪnɪkɔ mvu	kpɔkpɔ	kpʊkpɔ	ɔkpó	ɔkpá	ambá	kpakpa 'ya
amémé	amɛamɛ	tʃetʃi aci-ro	así (=fire)	tsɛtsi	atsí	así	asi-ná kɔlási	kaka lili
ɽidzí	lidzí	lidʒí	idzí	idzí	ledzí	legí	legí kolépé	gru
fára'bá	toutóù	⎰ kaukau ⎱ yowiyówù	koukou	pɛrɛpɛrɛ	ɛpé	ɛpé	ɛpé	sese
fára'bá	mʊkɛ	dó-rɔ mvu ko	anyísì	mʊkɛ	ɛpé	ɛpé	amú'dwɛ-na	nye
daʋa fínyá-ri	bía-vá	tsaá-mvá-'di caḍi	màdà-ŋa màdà-va	gàá-rɔ wáría-rɔ wɛrɛ	tóró-rí-'ì	tóró-ré-è	kɛdi kɔtɔndɔ	rè... sésé...
atsʷɛrɛ	katswa	katsʋa	tsɔ	zɔ-rɔ	àzʷɔ	lolu	azʷó	(ʒa)'dá... nde
äkúrú	äkú	äkú	ukú	odula				
ámba du		ɽizówe bi, poya	pì bigo	kî áza-rò	ɛ̀kpadrú karakɔ		nágó a'bí-rù	birobiro krr

VOCABULARY
MORU

	Miza	Kediru	Lakama'di	-ägi	Wa'di	'Bälimbä	-ändri
(all)	tʃʷéni kítɪ	tsʷínnɪ	ɽíkítɪ̀	tsúnɪ kurɪ	tiɽiɽi	sónɪ kåɽå	tsónɪ kúrɪ mgbú
new	tɔ'dɪ	tɔ'dɪ	tu'dɪ	ku'di	ko'di	ɔ'di	ɔ'di
young	tɔ'dɪ	tɔ'dɪ	tu'dɪ	käríä ndríäŋgwå	ko'di	ɔ'di	agwanzi
old (things)	ukú	ukú	ukú	äkú	ukú	äkú	ukú
(people)	mba-go	mba-go	mba-go	mba-go	mba-go	mba-go	mba-go
pleased	(ya) i'dwe-te	(ya) i'dwe-te	i'de-ti	i'dwe-te	('a) o'di-tre	ä'de-ti	e'de-te
poor	mɔi-rú	mɔi-rú	tɪlɪmo-ró	moi-rú	tsúni	(tàkʊ)	(tàkʊ)
present	ɔrí-vìa	ɔrí-vìa	arí-vìa	arí-vìa	egbí	arí-vòya	ɔrí-vòa
red	ɔká	ɔká	ɔká	aká	aká	ɔká	ɔká
pink							
brown							
rich	ŋgá dri-ambá be		drígwó		ambá-ro		
right hand	(drí)gú	(drí)gwå	(drí)gó	(drí)gwå	(drí)gó	(drí)gó	(drí)gú
sharp	siɔsì	sí	síɔsì	síasì	ʃiaʃi	sisì	sisì
short	nyagʊrà	dʒúɽú	nyagʊrà	dʒúɽú	kuduŋgu	nyakurà	dʒúɽu kúdu
sick	adrávɔ-rɔ	adrávɔ-rɔ	adrávɔ-rɔ	adrávɔ-rɔ	loulou	odrávɔ-rɔ	odrávɔ-rɔ
slow	lya-rɔ lia	lya-rɔ	lyaa	lya-rɔ	maní sìì	lya-rɔ	lya-rɔ
soft	'bɔlɔtò	'bɔlɔtò	'bɔlɔtò	'bɔlɔtò	'bɔlɔtò	'bɔlɔtò	'bɔlɔtò
stupid	amamai	amamai	amamai lémò-ro	amamai	amamai ifónai	amamai	amamai
sweet	ndɛɽɪndɛɽɪ	ndɛɽɪndɛɽɪ	ndɪɽí	ndɪɽí	arɛrrɪ	ndíɽí	ndíɽí
nice				asʊasʊ	kurɛkurɛ-ni		asʊasʊ
thick	ŋgyiúŋgyi	ŋgyiúŋgyi	ŋgyiúŋgyi	ndzíändzi	ndʒíändʒi	ndzindzi	ndzindzi
thin (people) (objects)	rórè tʃwàrì	rwarwè	rorà sara	ywi-tè tswari	mbɪlɪ-ɪŋgonì	rɛrɛ	rɛrɛ
true real	ŋgyé módó	(ta)ŋgyé	(ta)ŋgyé	(kúɽí) àndiro	pätî	ɛndá-ró ífífíi	ɛndá-ró ífífíi
wet	adʒwa-tɛ tʃurutʃuru	adʒwa-tɛ tʃurutʃuru	gi-ru	surusúrù	adʒi-tra tsurù-tsúru	surusúrù	ádzì-te tʃurutʃuru
white	òndʒʷɛ	òndʒʷɛ	òndʒʷɛ	andzʷé	ándzʷɛ	òndʒʷɛ	òmvɛ

VOCABULARY

AVUKAYA		MADI						
Ojila	Ojiga	Logo	Keliko	Lugbara	Lokai	Pandikeri	Lulu'ba	Lendu
zi-àndrɛ		wéì	tsérɛ̀	dríyâ	kpɔ̂(də)	'bɔ̀rɔ̀(du)	kɛvɛvɔ̀	krú
'dəndrɪ		dra						
o'di	ó'dyé	toìli-ìli	ú'dí	'dí	'dí	'dí	unwa-nà	o
		tí'dyá						
mgbá-na	ó'dyé	tí'dyá	ú'dí	'dí				ìle
		toìli-aro						za
ukú	äkú	äkú	uku	dula	okú	okú	kɔlandí	ä̀rrä̀rr,
								ŋgo
sisi	ambá	agwáàga		modo-	dzali-gó	dzali-gó	agwí-na	ŋgo
arákà		maliga	àràkà-go	modo				
('a) ä'di-tra		lenzele			lɛndɔ̂	(nà) sí	(ye) mi	le-zhi-na
						'bwe	twɛ̀	
(ŋga gɛyù)	'bálàmu	lemere-ro	málimàlì	(ädʒúkú)	étsá ǹdirɛ	étsá ǹdirɛ	mokyokî	njetha
yo-ró		kɪdríkɪ̀drɪ						
bɛ(rìa)	bɛ̀	bɛ̀	bɛ̀	tʃí	ɔlú		wi	ku nî
	noŋgá	'á	gá	alagá	'à	'ǎ	'a	
kaáká	kakà	ká	ka-rɔ	ka-rɔ	ka	eka	kelí-na	kaka ...
		keka	eka-'de	eka			kóláàkeli	
	kakà	kakà	kakà	kakà				
		keka ca						
	wà	kini	'ba ìka	'ba ìka				kari kaka
		bälíbälì						
ŋgá bidù	lafɔ́lípí	ŋgäliyi	ŋgä'dipà	àku'dípi	koroni-go (8)	koroni-go	kworoni	ditszba (-'ba?)
ndaŋgáhò								
(drí)ágó	(drí)ágó	(drí)gó	(drí)ǹdäpi	andá	nyaré	(dí)andá	indá	tha
tsi-trá	tʃitʃi	tʃitʃi	tʃitʃi	tʃitʃi	lɔtsì	lɔsì	kólási	ka lili
kútuä	ànyɪ	tälí	älí	anyíǹá-rɔ	alí	títi	kóláli	du
tsɛ kɔ							kɛ'diru	
lazɪlazɪ	lazɪlazɪ	kobila-ro	dra bɛ		vù		kɔmbwɛ	dhe na
		dra be		rú'bɛ	ru ɔndzí	ru indzwí		
		rú'bá kɔ̀ndʒi		ɔ̀nzi				
		(=body bad)						
maní sìì	manyí sìì	ayiya	madää (8)	madaa	tsɛtsɛ	sɛsɛ	kɔzi	nyenye
		yaya					injɔ	dzodza
'bɔtʃí'bɔ́tʃi	kpɛtrò-	dɔ̀ladóla	monyá-	ɪnfînɪ	a'dú	a'dú	kɔla-	susu
	kpétrè	boliboli	mónya				mú'dwe	belebele
		menememe						
mí lífɔlífɔ								
mí yayɔì	àyɔ̀'i	màbvɔyɔ						ŋga nyo'yu
ɔfɔla'i		togi ako						
(k)urɛ(k)urɛ	kɪnikɪní	kɪnikɪní	àdiàdi	ɪgbé-ru	limílìmi	limí	kɛ'yupeli	mbu
ɔrɛrɛ		kadikadi						
asuasɔ								blo
ndʒindʒi		njinji			nzá		luswe	krrkrr
rɛrɛ	'ì'ì	to'yóto'yô	úyíyi	ndzúndzù	orwé	orwé	arwé	re
mbɪlɪwa èti		wolewole			ɔndzú (ra)	lowí (ra)		bleble
								gbagba
ta 'dí	tandí	tandí	tandí	tandí				
pätî	pätî	pätî		ndípɪ	lóku drɔ̀	andá dɔ̀	'diri (8)	bubu
dó							'diri	
adzi-trá					tsoma	tsoma	ɔ̀'wɛle	
surusúrù	lumvú-rú	yi-rú	yí-ru	yí-ru			kolú 'eyi	nduka-nduka
amvɛ	(k)ɛmvɛ	(ky)ɛmvɛ	(n)imvɛ	ímvè-rɔ	iŋgwi	iŋgwi	aŋgwé	sáwɔ ...

MORU

	Miza	Kediru	Lakama'di	-ägi	Wa'di	'Bälimbä	-ändri
yellow	fɔrɔla mgbɔrólɔ	fɔrɔla mgbɔrólɔ	fɔrɔla mgbɔrólɔ	fɔrɔla mgbɔrólɔ	fɔrɔla	mgbörölö	mgbɔrólɔ

NUMERALS

	Miza	Kediru	Lakama'di	-ägi	Wa'di	'Bälimbä	-ändri
one	àlɔ	àlɔ	àlɔ	àlɔa	àlɔ	(see Miza)	
two	ärrì	ärrì	ärrì	ɪrrì	ɪrrì	(see Miza)	
three	ṅnà	ṅnà	ṅnà	ɪna	ena	(see Miza)	
four	sú	sú	sú	sú	isu	(see Miza)	
five	ṅdzʷí	ṅdzʷí	ṅdzʷí	ṅdzʷí	idʒi	(see Miza)	
six	ndzʷí drì àlɔ́	ndzʷí drì àlɔ́	ndzʷí drì àlɔ́	ndzʷí drì àlɔ́	ndzʷí drì àlɔ́	ndzʷí drì àlɔ́	ndzʷí drì àlɔ́
seven	ndzʷí drì ɛrì	ndzʷí drì ɛrì	... äri	... eri	... näri	... ɛrì	... ɛrì
eight	ndzʷí drì ana	ndzʷí drì ana	ndzʷí drì ana	ndzʷí drì ana	... nana	... éná	... ɛna
nine	ndzʷí drì äsu	ndzʷí drì äsu	ndzʷí drì äsu	... esu	... näsu	... esu	... äsu
ten	'butɪ	'butɪ	'butɪ	'butɪ	'butɪ	'butɪ	'butɪ
eleven	'butɪ pá ŋga àlɔ	'butɪ pá ŋga àlɔ	'butɪ drà àlɔ	'butɪ pá àlɔ	'bute dri alɔ	(see Miza)	
fifteen	'butɪ pá ŋgà ndzʷi	'butɪ pá ŋgà ndzʷi	'butɪ dränzi	'butɪ ŋga pánzi	'bute pá ŋgónzi	(see Miza)	
sixteen	'butɪ pá ŋgà ndzʷi-dryàlɔ	'butɪ pá ŋgà ndzʷi-dryàlɔ	'butɪ drá-nánzídralɔ́	'butɪ ŋga-pánzidràlɔ	'bute páŋgónzi-dryàlɔ	(see Miza)	
twenty	'bútérɪ-tʊ	'bútérɪ-tʊ	'bútǻärì	kítinǻrì nya 'di-tra	kítinǻrì nya 'di-tra (= eaten one man)	(see Miza)	
twenty-one	'bútérɪ-tʊ drɪafàlɔ	'bútérɪ-tʊ drɪafàlɔ	'bútǻärì draŋgaalo	kítinǻrì drinángá-àlɔa		... ŋgo-ŋgáàlɔ	... drɪa-fàlɔ
twenty-three	'bútérɪ-tʊ drɪafuna	'bútérɪ-tʊ drɪafuna					
thirty	'butenätu	'butenätu	'bútàànà	kítinana	kítínana	'butena-ɾútu	'butena-ɾútu
forty	'bútéesu	'bútéesu	'bútéesu	kítínäsu	kítíäsu	(see Miza)	
fifty	'búté ndzʷi	'búté ndzʷi				(see Miza)	
hundred	'búté nä'butè	'búté nä'butè	'búté nä'butè	kítinä'bùtè	kítinä'bùtè	(see Miza)	

ADVERBS

	Miza	Kediru	Lakama'di	-ägi	Wa'di	'Bälimbä	-ändri
where? (cf. which)	íŋwa yà níŋwa gaṅwa	íŋwa yà	iŋgɔ yà uŋgɔ yà	íŋgwɔ yà aŋgwaga yà ɪ'dɪgé yà	ɛŋgwala yà	íŋgòlɛ yà	íŋgwa(ra) yà
here	nòa	nòŋwa	nòŋga	nìlɛ nìga	nìlɛ nìga	nɛénɔ	nìa
there	láʊ̀	láʊ̀	nàŋga	ìle	ìle	'daá'da	nanà
yonder	lɛ láʊ̀	lɛ láʊ̀	lɛ nàŋga	toànánà	ìlɛ́rɔ́	lɛ 'daá'da	lɛ́ na nà
far	lóózɔ	lózoa	lázá	dìle	dìle	lɛlóza	lóza

VOCABULARY

AVUKAYA		Logo	Keliko	Lugbara	MADI			Lendu
Ojila	Ojiga				Lokai	Pandikeri	Lulu'ba	
fɔrɔlà		pfɔró	fɔrɔfɔrɔ	fɔrɔ-ró	lɔfwarà	lɔfarà	afɔrɔ̀	tsudatso
mvɛlɛrɛ̀	mgbanyà							
àlɔ	àlɔ	àlɔ	àlɔ	àlʊ	àlʊ	àlʊ	alu(bé)	'di
ärrì	ärrì	írì	írì	írì	(e)rì	(e)rì	(e)rì	arɔ̃
ńná	ńná	(í)ná	ńná	ńná	ɪna	ɪna	nâ	(u)gbɔ̃
sú	ɪsʊ	(í)sú	ɪsù	ɪsù	isu	isu	su	θɔ̃
ńdʒʷí	ńdʒʷí	índʒwí	toú	táú	tòu	tòu	tòu	(u)mbú
		nji		toi				
nzɪ kázé		(ìntʃí)	ázíá	ázíá	ázíá	ázíá	ázíá	azá
		kázíá						
nzɪ lérì	nzi drɪ	(ìntʃí) dɨ̀	ăzíɨ̀	ázíɨ̀(i)	túderì	túdwerì	túdierì	arugbɔ̃
	äri	(n)írì						
nzɪ lana	nzi drɪ	(ìntʃí) dɨ̀	arò	arò	arò	arò	arrɔ	aru
	nna	na						
nzɪ läsu	nzi drɪ sʊ	(ìntʃí)	óromì	óromì	drítsàlɔ	drítsàlɔ	tɔ́rɔmè	dreði
		dräsu						
mudrí		mudrí	mudɨ́	mudɨ́	mudrí	mudrwí	mudúrí	dre
mudrí	mudrí	mudrí		mudɨ́	...límbí	...límbí	...ímbí	dre dir
drilágáàlɔ	drìalɔ	drìalɔ		drilu	àlɔ	nàlô	alò	na tszdhi
mudrí	mudrí	mudri			...alimbi			dre mbur
drilágănzí	drínd3í	dri nji			tou			na pidhi
⎧mudrí dri-	mudrí	mudri dri			...alimbi			dre azar
⎨lágănzíri,	drigalɔ	kazia			azia			na pi
⎩mudrí dri-	kazia							
gänzi								
nya 'di trá	nyá 'di ʒi	nya ɗia alo		mérîìrì	mudírì	mudírì	mudírì	dredreŋga-
								arɔ
nya 'di trá	nyá 'di ʒi	nya ɗia alo		mérîìrì	mudírì	mudírì	...ímbíalo	...ndijo
drilágáàlɔ	drɪalɔ	dri alo		drìlàlʊ	alímbíàlɔ	alímbíàlɔ		ɗirna
					mudírì			
					alimbi ina			
nya 'di trá		nya ɗia alo		⎧mérí	mùdina			dredreŋga
drilagá múdrí		dri mudri		⎨lana				ugbo
				⎩mudrína				
nya 'di ri		nya ɗia iri		mérí lasu	mudisu			dredreŋ
								tho
nya 'di ri		nya ɗia iri		mérí	muditou			dredreŋ
drɪ lɛga mudrí		dri mudri		tau				mbu
nya 'di ndzʷi		nya ɗia nji			mùdimudí	mùdimudí	mudu-	dredreŋga
					mudi-		mudúrí	dre
					mudri			
		aŋgoleya						
(l)aŋgɔléryà	aŋgu(lɛ)ya	aŋgu ya	ɪŋga yà	ŋga yà	íŋgwá	íŋgʋ̀a	ŋɔ	mgbaga
		ɪŋga yà						
nòlɛ	nòlɛ	nòlɛ	nòlɛ	'dòlɛ	(lɛ)'día	(lɛ)'día	wá	ʒúɽù
								iga
tɔlà	nàrɪ	nàlɛ	'dàlɛ	'dalɛ	ná'a	nàá	lyâ	caga
dʒà tólà		naale	gbú 'dàɽɪ	gbú 'dálé	lalé	nalé	na	tʃáɽù
dzɛdzeró	dzɛdzéŋgí	kógó(?)	rárɨ́aro	ällí	lolu	lolu	ɔ'de	dá
	nàna	mvumvu						

VOCABULARY

				MORU			
	Miza	**Kediru**	**Lakama'di**	**-ägi**	**Wa'di**	**'Bälimbä**	**-ändri**
near	lɔ̀tɔ̀(ti)	lɔ̀tɔ̀(ti)	lɔ̀tɔ̀(ti)	mgbäti	mgbäti	lɔ̀tɔ̀(ti)	lɔ̀tɔ̀(ti)
up	kuru	kuru	kuru	kwöru	kwöru	uru	uru
down	vùru	vùru	vùru	vùru	vùru	vùru	vùru
away	tɛsì	tɛsì	tɛsì	kyɛvì	kyɛvì	teesì teísì	tɛsì ivè
back again	kɔ̃(n)volɛ				kóvúlé	óvólé	óvólé
when?	ítú ya ɪŋɔtúyà	ítú yà	étí yà	ä'ditú yà	editú yà ɛŋutúyà	ätú yà	ätú yà
to-day	ɔndrɔ̀	ɔndrɔ̀	ɔndrɔ̀	andrɔ̀	andrɔ̀	andrɔ̀	andrɔ̀
to-morrow	ɔ́ndɔ́	ɔ́ndɔ́	ɔ́ndɔ́	ɪdrú	ɪdrú	idrúzɔ	udrú
day after next day	dru kăsì ... kaìsì	dru kăsì ... kaìsì	dru kăsì ... kaìsì	nätú drukăsì	inătú inásì	'da 'básì nätúnă	nätú tuke na'basì namasì
next day							túazá-kaínìsì
yesterday	tàndróbɛ	tàndróbɛ	tàndróbɛ	odzí	ädʒí	ädʒí	ädzí
day before previous day	drukăsì bɛ	drukăsì bɛ	drukăsì bɛ	nätúnä	nätúnä	'da 'dasì	nätú bɛ túkänä-'básìbɛ
previous day							túkazá-kásìbɛ
now	yáʊ̀	yáànɔ	yáànɔ	ìmgbano	ìmgbano	iyáàno	mgbanó
formerly	kianó	kianó	kyanó	kyánó	ökúnäi	énó	énóna
always	ɔndrɔ́ àlɔ óndɔrɔndɔrɔ́	ɔndrɔ́ àlɔ	ɔndɔ alɔ	ɪdrú àlɔ	tsetse	zurú alɔ	udrú àlɔ udrwá-udrwálɔ̀
often							
how?	íŋgʊ nyɛ(yà)	íŋgʊ nyɛ(yà)	íŋgʊ nyɛ(yà)		enöŋgu ni yà		ìŋgɔtí(yà)
thus	ìnyɛ́	enye	enye	ä'dírí yà eni	o'dírúyà ieni	a'díró yà eténà	étí
why?	ó'dú tá yà ɛlɛ yà	ó'dú tá yà	ó'dú tá yà	ä'du ta yà	ä'di tɛ sià e'delé yà	a'dí ta yà	a'dí ta yà
because	tana						

VOCABULARY

AVUKAYA					MADI			
Ojila	Ojiga	Logo	Keliko	Lugbara	Lokai	Pandikeri	Lulu'ba	Lendu
(m)'gbànyì	(m)'gbànyì	vàvà(?) (ny)anyímvá	vàvà(?) nyíŋáŋá	nyíŋá	ɪré	itíti	gɔgɔlyá	tʃotʃo
uru	uru	kúrú	urugägä	urugbí	oru	oru	orukɪ	runà arrna
vùru	bìdri	bvìdri tabule vudrile	vùdri vùga	vùru vàga	vurú	vugá Bu. = vùru	bwa	gunà dzzjɔ̃
ivyélà		amvena	àmve	àmve	àŋgwe	láŋgwe	àŋgwe	arugo
vʊlɛ	vʊlɛ	àndʒɛlɛ	vʊlɛ	vʊlɛ ndɔ̀ a'dutúrɪ yà	vʊlɛ a'dùŋgání	vuvu a'dùŋgání	búlɛ	mgbaŋgana
áŋgutúyà	áŋgutúyà	áŋgutúyà	áŋgotú yà ɪŋgotú yà	ŋgotú yà	etúíŋgɔsi			
andrɔ̀	ándrónʊ́	ándrɔ̀ andru	ándrɔ̀	ándrɔ̀ ɛndrɔ̀	éndrɔ̂	ándô	nínínisì	ńʒu
ɪdrú	udrú	kɪdrú tudru	udrʊ́ drù	drʊ̀ d(r)usì	drúzí ɔ'bú	dúzí ɔ'bú	à'i o'búti	bú(tsɔ)
inắtú	druzi	nätú	drúzí	d(r)úzí	drúzí èŋga	drúzí èŋa	ínínánisì	njaŋga
inásì	nắtú	na'disì	druzi 'dàsì	dúzíasí 'dasi	ɛŋgá nasì			njaŋga njaŋga
inásì	nàási	nalánasì	druzi 'dàsì	ú'dúosírisì	ɛŋgá nalénasì			
ägyí		ägyia	adzɛ ágyɛ	adzɛ	adzíni ándáni	agíni ándáni	andíní nànisì ó'bútííní nànisì	ndzz
inắtú	druzi	andratu drù	utúresè	d(r)uzi	ándáni èŋga	ándáni èŋga	o'búnínánisì	dica
{ inásì { indrắtú	nätu nasì	na'disi nalanasi	utúresè		ɛŋgá nasì			
indrắtúlasì					ɛŋgá nalénasì			
mgbàáno	tä'dú	ta'dú'dì nyaúmvá nyanomvánɔ̀	ú'dí'di ɔ'dɪvanì	andrɔ ú'dí'da ídʒutsá ú'dí'da	diá'do te (be)	duá'do	ɪlélénɪ	kpajɔ̀
ökúrú		kienɔ walaka (= all day long)	okô	ɔkórɪ	andé èzɛ	andé èzɛ	ɔgɔ	ʒádrrdrr
tsetsɛ	itúvú tsetsé	kitú kere	itú tsɛrɛ	ídʒu dʒʊmárɔ	ilítilitì	'díniŋòni	inia lubé	'jirɔ'jirɔ
ŋgou ŋgou		vese kolia	tigesi	áyuáyu				
	tà bɛ dú	tà('di)'dumäru	tà tre	ídʒú kárakara	'día karâkó	wé'dià karâkó	íníá 'bíru	bijaina
ɛláŋgɔtí yà	áŋgo tí yà	aŋgotini ya (ta)ŋgíní yà	ta ŋgónì ya	idʒu ŋgɔniyà	íŋgóni	sísí ni	sî	mgba bu
ɛ'ití ɛnɔ̀ti	ɔtí	ni tini 'dìnì	'dínì	ínì	'dínì	'dínì	lê	furbai
a'du tasɪ								aɖu ro
a'dɔ lé yà		esi yà	asi yà	òsi yà				
a'dɔ si yà	a'du(si) yà ŋgá	aɖo si ya ŋgá	ŋgá	akɔ	o'dósì nga	o'dósì nga		furiro

VOCABULARY

	MORU						
	Miza	**Kediru**	**Lakama'di**	**-ägi**	**Wa'di**	**'Bälimbä**	**-ändri**
very	táwí	táwí	táwí	táwí para	tri pé	táwí	táwí

CONJUNCTIONS

and	ágɔ̀						
but	òkò ndi...'bɛ						
if	ɔndrɔ						andrɔ

VOCABULARY

AVUKAYA					MADI			
Ojila	Ojiga	Logo	Keliko	Lugbara	Lokai	Pandikeri	Lulu'ba	Lendu
ódrà		we		to	karâkó		twê	'bo
pέ							ɔ'di	
		dre ... zo						
andrɔ								
tí		kodo	andrɔ	έndrù	ké	tí		ditʃú
								ndiro
andrɔ		... 'di			dzɔ̀	dὲ	yí	njati
àzaŋgásì								

379

APPENDIX
LENDU
CONTENTS

Chapter			
”	I.	The Phonetics of Lendu	380
”	II.	The Spelling of Lendu	386
”	III.	Nouns	388
”	IV.	Pronouns	391
”	V.	Qualificatives	395
”	VI.	Noun Postpositions	400
”	VII.	Verbs	402
”	VIII.	Verbal Auxiliaries	405
”	IX.	Verb Postpositions	408
”	X.	Predicative Constructions	412
”	XI.	Adverbs and Conjunctions	414
”	XII.	Specimen Text	416

LENDU

1. The language 'BALE-DHA or 'BAA-DHA (to give it its true name)[1] is closely related to the Moru-Madi languages etymologically, but this relationship is not superficially noticeable either in pronunciation or in grammar, in which many foreign elements are to be found. Consequently the language is studied separately here.

2. Most of the phonetic material I was able to acquire at first-hand from a visiting Lendu teacher at Aba. For most of the grammatical material I have had recourse to extracts from the Lendu Gospels and, most important, the Rev. B. L. Litchman's answers to my questionnaire. Material from these sources will be recorded in italics and according to suggested orthographical rules for the language.[2] There was not enough material for anything approaching an exhaustive study of the language, and the following short sketch is meant primarily to show in what respects Lendu conforms to the Moru-Madi language pattern.

CHAPTER I
THE PHONETICS OF LENDU
Vowels

3. From the few notes I was able to take, the vowel system of Lendu is very similar to that of other Sudanic languages already treated. Nine vowels may be distinguished—four 'tense' vowels, four 'lax' vowels, and the open vowel **a**.

Tense	i	isi (woman)	dí (to sit)	titi (black)	
Lax	ɪ	tsɪí (dog)	nɪ (you)	rítsɜ̀ (thing)	-rɪ indefinite pron. suffix

---
[1] Pronounced 'balèðà or 'báðà. The people are called 'BALE-NDRU. The name 'Lendu' was erroneously given to these people by Europeans who thought that the 'ba' was a Bantu class prefix, like Wa-Swahili, Aba-Ganda, &c.
[2] I was unfortunately unable to compare my results with those of Deleu's *Essai de Grammaire Kilendu*, as that work is now out of print.

THE PHONETICS OF LENDU

Tense e	le- (noun prefix)	dre (ten)	te (to strike)	tʃê (bad)
Lax ɛ	rɛ (bird)	kpɛlɛ (thorn)	wɛ (to open)	
Tense u	ru (cloth)	ʒú (blood)	ku (to be)	ditʃú (but)
Lax ʊ	ndrʊ́ (person)	gʊ̀na (down)	rʊ̀nà (up)	
Tense o	eʒó (elephant)	ʒo (to drink)	'bo (very)	òo (fowl)
Lax ɔ	àdʒɔ (brother)	pɔ (to shoot)	'bɔ (to stay)	bɔ̀ (big)
a	tata (to fly)	rà (to go)	kaka (red)	

4. Sometimes the **u** appears fronted and unrounded in certain words: e.g. gu (liver); ńju (to-day); gu (to refuse). Compare: 'jú (knife); kú (tooth) with pure vowels.

I have come across no case of centralization of **a** before a following **i** or **u**.

5. I was unable to note much alternation of tense and lax vowels. Note, however, the vowel in the noun prefix in the following examples:

> le-nyɔ (eye)   lɛ-kú (tooth)
> le-bi (ear)   lɛ-θì (heart)
> le-tsɔkúkù (chin)   lɛ-róðò (name)

6. In some words the vowels were pronounced with distinct nasalization by my informant:

> 'dɔ̃ (day); arɔ̃ (two); gbɔ̃ (three); θɔ̃ (four); dzz-jɔ̃ (down)

but there is nothing in the current orthography to suggest that this is standard.

7. When two vowels come together, the resultant sound is not a true diphthong, as the two distinct syllables are preserved:

> nyaú (hyena); tsɪí (dog); koí (smoke); tʃéé (equal)

CONSONANTS

8.	Labial	Dental	Alveolar	Post-alveolar	Palatal	Velar	Labio-Velar	Glottal
Explosive[1]	p b	t d	ts dz	c (tʃ) j (dʒ)	(j) 'j 'y	k g	kp gb	
Implosive	'b		'd					
Nasal	m	n			ny	(ŋ)		
Fricative	f v	θ ð	s z	ʃ ʒ				h
Liquids, &c.			r, l, (ɽ)		y		w	

Notes on the pronunciation of consonants

The explosives.

9. The explosives **p** and **b**, **t** and **d**, **k** and **g** are probably similar to those in French; the explosion on the **p, t, k** is not accompanied by as much aspiration as in English; at the same time, the general articulation is slacker than in normal French; **t** and **d** are dental.

Examples:

> pɔ (to shoot)   bɔ̀ (big)
> te (to strike) dá (far)
> ká (to bite)   gɔðà (leopard)

---

[1] i.e. pure explosives **p, t, k**, double-articulation explosives **kp** and **gb**, and affricates **ts, dz, tʃ, dʒ**.

The alveolar and post-alveolar affricates.

10. Contrary to Moru-Madi pronunciation, the two sounds **ts** (as in English 'its') and **tʃ** (as in English 'church') do not belong to the same phoneme, but have to be differentiated; the same applies to the voiced counterparts **dz** (pronounced as in 'bids') and **dʒ** (as in 'judge'). Thus:

tsrí (dog)); tsû (tree); tsa (to chop); bútsɔ (to-morrow)
tʃéé (equal); ditʃú (but); tʃága (there); tʃí (to shut); tʃotʃo (near)
dzá (house); dza (possessive particle); (*le*) *dzu* (thigh)
dʒɔ (head); dʒítʃɛ̀ (frog); dʒí (rain)

Whether the true palatal **j** exists as a separate phoneme from **dʒ** is doubtful. The only examples I have noted are: kpajɔ̀ (now); dzzjɔ̃ (down).

The labio-velars.

11. There is a likelihood that **kp** and **gb** are interchangeable with **kw** and **gw** in dialects. The word for 'man', for example, is written *bwetsike* by Litchman, but *kbetsike* in the Lendu Gospel.

Examples of labio-velars:

    kpɛlɛ (thorn)   gbɔ̃ (three)
    kpajɔ̀ (now)   arugbɔ̃ (seven)
    kpà (they)

The implosives.

12. As in other Eastern Sudanic languages, the implosion with these consonants is very weak. It is to be doubted if there is any at all with **'d**, as very often pronounced. This sound is differentiated from normal dental **d** by its retroflex tongue position.[1] In the case of **'j** the sound is very often more like **'y** (a palatal glide preceded by a slight glottal catch). The two sounds may, however, be distinct:

  'bi (to slap)   'dódzɛ̀ (grave)   'jú or 'yú (knife)
  'bu (to give)   'dei (guinea-fowl)   'jí (sun)
  'ba (to leave alone)   'dɔ̃ (day)   'jú (food)(?)
  'bɔ (to stay)   'da (water)   nyo'yu (clever)
  'bo (very)   'dɛ́'dɛ̀ (to drop)
    'dɔ (to sleep)
    'dá (long)
    'di (one)
    'dirɔ (always)

The nasals.

13. m and **n** are pronounced as in English, **ny** as in French 'montagne'. I have no examples of the velar nasal **ŋ** occurring as a separate sound.[2] It seems to occur only in combination with **g** (where the resulting sound is similar to the *ng* in 'finger').

Examples of nasal consonants:

    má (I)
    na (with)   ní (you)
    nyamu (cat)   nyu (to dream)

---

[1] The sounds seem to be interchangeable in one or two words, e.g. sa'dà or sadà (saliva). See Part I, § 73 et seq., for further differentiation between explosive and implosive sounds.

[2] Except in the word lɛθɔŋ = hand, which, however, is given '(le)tho' both by Litchman and the Lendu Gospel.

The fricatives.

14. **f** and **v** are presumably labio-dental as in English or French. I have no notes on the sounds, but Litchman gives:

    fu (that)   *vi* (brains)
                     vovo (fly)

15. θ and ð correspond to the unvoiced and voiced dental fricatives in the English words 'thin' and 'then':

    θɔ (hand)   ðɔ́ (name)
    θi (heart)   ði (wife)
    θɔrózi (termite)   gɔaðà (leopard)
    θà (to split)   ði (to beat)
    θɔ̃ (four)   ðɛ (to die)

16. **s** and **z** correspond roughly to **s** and **z** in English; the voiced variety is very rare. (For syllabic **z** see later.)

    sò (bow)   (e)zâ (animal)
    sáwɔ (white)
    sa'dà[1] (saliva)
    sɛ́sɛ́ (little)

17. Whether ʒ (the voiced sound found in English 'leisure', 'azure', 'pleasure', &c.) is a separate phoneme from **z** is uncertain.[2] This sound is by far the more common of the two:

    θɔrózi (termite)   ʒú (blood)   (e)ʒó (elephant)
    ʒí (to cut)   ʒi (to love)   ʒo (to drink)
    (ʒa)'dá (long)   ʒúɾù (there)   *mgbaraʒhiʒhi* (secretary bird)
    ʒádrrdrr (formerly)

This sound occasionally coincides with the **dʒ-** sound. Thus Litchman writes 'zha' for 'mother', but '-ja' when the word is used as a female suffix.

18. Whether the unvoiced counterpart ʃ is really indigenous to Lendu is another problem to be investigated. I found no examples of the sound myself, but Litchman gives *sha* = foreigner, and the Gospel gives *shinga* = life, *marasha* = ointment.

19. **h** seems a rare sound. I have not met it, but Litchman gives *hu* = ashes, *hwi* (also *kwi*) = to kill, *hu* = to spread, *hwe* = to skin.

The liquids.

20. As in the case of most Eastern Sudanic languages, there are three liquid sounds, a rolled **r**, a clear **l**, and a flapped l-sound, ɾ, the last named being rather rare:[3]

    aru (eight)   kalú (young one)   ʒúɾù (there)
    arɔ̃ (two)   kpɛlɛ (thorn)   tʃáɾù (yonder)
    rɛ (little)   le- (noun prefix)   tsúlàɾi (manioc)
    ru (cloth)   li (to put)

---

[1] The **s** in this word seemed to me to be particularly long.

[2] Litchman writes *zha* = bushbuck as opposed to *za* = meat. On the other hand, the word for 'to love' he sometimes writes *zi* and sometimes *zhi*. The Lendu Gospel gives *zi*, whereas I heard ʒi.

[3] This sound is probably a member of the l-phoneme.

Consonant combinations.

21. Lendu, in common with most African languages, contains nasal combinations; but it also contains combinations with the liquids, and here it differs from other African languages.[1]

Nasal combinations.

22. Cognate nasals may occur before any of the voiced explosive consonants. Thus:

mb   mbu (to drink); mbú (five); *cembu* (sheep); mbi (string).
nd   enyíndɔ̀ (nose); nde (and); *ndundu* (cloud).
n(d)z[2]   nzè (urine); nzá (negative particle); *nza* (field).
ndʒ   lendʒíndʒì (shadow); ndʒeí (water-buck); ndʒi (to make). ndʒa (to see); ń(d)ʒu (yesterday).
ng or ŋg[3] leróŋga (body); kalaŋgà (ground-nut); ŋgá (negative particle).
mgb   cumgburù (lion); mgbà (verb postposition); m̀gba (child).

Combinations with liquids.

23. In the **dr** combination the **d** is not dental but alveolar, as in Moru-Madi **dr**. Whereas, however, in Moru-Madi **dr** is to be regarded as a single sound-unit, in Lendu it should, I think, be regarded as a sound combination, like **kr** and **gr**:

r   dre (ten); kó drɔ̀ nì (to fall—of rain); ndrú (person); kru (to cough); krú (all); krû (to cook); *gru* (left-hand); *ăro*[4] (to pain); *ăra* (to tell).
l   blɔ (good); *'blo* (verb postposition); *klo* (to untie) (strong); *pli* (more) (?); *kplaka* (?) (frog).

Syllabic consonants.

24. One of the outstanding characteristics of Lendu is its 'spitting' pronunciation, caused by the number of words containing syllabic **z** and **r**. (In this respect the language reminds the listener of Czech.)

Syllabic z.

25. In several cases this sound is due to the elision of a vowel in syllables beginning with **s, z, ts, dz** or combination **nts, n(d)z**, with a corresponding lengthening of the fricative element.

Thus Litchman writes sometimes *bwetsike* and sometimes *bwetzke* for 'man'; and *kaza* and *kazz* for 'fire'; and *isi* and *isz* for 'woman'.

Other examples:

sz (to shoot).
zz (bowels); kaźź (fire); mbazz (tobacco).
tszź (cow); rítsż (thing).
dzz (ground) (flour); nyúdzż (food); 'dódzż (grave); dzz'da (tear).
dzz (to buy, to cry); (*le*)*dzz* (back); *idzz* (drum).
ndzz (to call); ndzż (yesterday)[5]

---

[1] I have met similar combinations in Kreish, but nowhere else in the S. Sudan.
[2] The d- element is so faint as hardly to warrant representation.
[3] In narrow script ŋg, but if it is found that ŋ does not exist in any other context, it may be treated here as part of the n- phoneme and the compound may be written *ng*. See §§ 13 and 38.
[4] What the exact pronunciation of 'dro and 'dra is I cannot say. Litchman, who supplied the examples, evidently felt that there was a difference between these sounds and normal **dr-**.
[5] The **d** element is stronger here than in words like **nza**.

Syllabic r.

26. This sound is found after r or compounds with r, and may occasionally be traced to the elision of a vowel with corresponding lengthening of the r-element. Thus:

    many = krú or *krr*.   *ra* or *rr* verbal auxiliary.
    eight = aru or *arr*.

Other examples:

    mbrr (arrow); brr (to jump); ndrr (goat) (cp. MORU: ìndri).

Tone.

27. There seem to be three tone levels—high, mid, and low. Since, as previously pointed out,[1] it is very difficult to specify the tone level of any syllable in a chain of speech, I have arrived at my conclusions by comparing individual word stems with their prefixes, assuming the prefixes to be constant.

28. Thus, assuming the noun prefix le- to have a constant mid tone, the following three tones are to be observed in the noun stem:

High	*Mid*	*Low*
lerɔ́ŋga (body)	lebi (ear)	lɛkù (arm)
lɛgú (liver)[2]	lenyɔ (eye)	lɛθì (heart)
lɛrɔ́ðɔ̀ (name)	ledʒɔ (head)	ledà (tongue)
lendʒíndʒì (spirit)	ledʒɔka (hair)[2]	
lɛkú (tooth)	lɛθɔŋ (arm)	

29. Similarly, assuming the verb imperative prefix a- to have a constant high tone, the following three tones are to be observed in the verb stem:

High	*Mid*	*Low*
átʃí (open)	ákru (cough)	árà (go)
ádí gùna (sit down)	ápɔ (shoot with gun)	áθà (split)
ádá ni rùnà (stand up)	ász (shoot with bow)	

The following verbs, however, have been noted with mid tone on both prefix and stem:

    andʒa (see); a'ba (leave alone); awɛ (open).

30. That tone plays an important semantic part in the language will be obvious from the following examples:

lɛkú (tooth)	nɪ or ní (you) (sg.)	'dá (long, to smoke)	m̀gba (child)
lɛkù (arm)	nì (you) (pl.)	'da (water)	mgbà (verb postposition)
ndzz (to call)	krú (all)	rɛ (bird)	mbú (fine)
ndzz̀ (yesterday)	kru (to cough)	rɛ̀ (little)	mbu (to drink)

There is no grammatical tone analysis to hand.

---

[1] See Part I, Chapter III, pp. 111 et seq.
[2] lègu and lédʒɔ́ká in my original notes.

CHAPTER II

THE SPELLING OF LENDU

31. The present system of spelling in Lendu is on the whole fairly satisfactory, and the following section will be devoted to indicating how best to improve on it within the already existing framework, borrowed material (including the Biblical quotations) being then written in this proposed new system.

Vowels.

32. Only five vowels are recognized, *a, e, i, o, u*. Owing to the Sudanic tendency to alternation between tense and lax, there is hardly anything to be gained by the introduction of further vowel letters, though ɔ might possibly be found useful.

Consonants.

33. The following is the spelling system suggested for the sounds set out in § 8:

	Labial	Dental	Alveolar	Post-alveolar	Palatal	Velar	Labio-velar	Laryngeal
Explosives, &c.	p b	t d	ts dz	c j	(j)	k g	kp gb	
Implosive	'b		'd		'j ('y)			
Nasal	m	n			ny	(ŋ)		
Fricative	f v	th dh	s z	(sh) (zh)				h
Liquids, &c.			r l		y		w	

This system differs from that of the Lendu Gospels in the following particulars:

34. The Gospels fail to show the difference between unvoiced and voiced dental fricative (θ and ð), writing *th* for both (as in English). This could easily be remedied by writing *th* for the former and *dh* for the latter as suggested at the Rejaf Conference. Thus:

    tho (hand)   dho (name)
    thi (heart)   dhi (wife)
    thorozhi (termite) goadha (leopard)
    tha (to split)   dhi (to beat)
    tho (four)   dhe (to die)
            dredhi (nine)

35. The Gospels ignore the implosives altogether. Litchman, however, uses the Rejaf system of noting these, viz. 'b, 'd, 'y (or better 'j), which is recommended here.[1] Thus:

    'bu (to give)   as opposed to butso (to-morrow)
    'bo (to stay)   ,, ,, bo (big)
    'blo (verb postposition) ,, ,, blo (good)
    'da (water)   ,, ,, da (far)
                     leda (tongue)
    'di (one)   ,, ,, dicu (but)
    'ji (sun)   ,, ,, ji (rain)
    'ju (knife)   ,, ,, nju (yesterday)

[1] Note that Litchman does not always hear implosive 'd, consequently the *d*-spellings in the grammar section are probably not all accurate.

36. The Gospels rightly use *c* and *j* for the sounds **tʃ** and **dʒ**, and employ the digraphs *sh* and *zh* for the sounds **ʃ** and **ʒ**. It is to be doubted whether there is any need to distinguish between **s** and **ʃ** or **z** and **ʒ**, as the sounds seem to be interchangeable; consequently the letters *s* and *z* will probably be found sufficient and the digraphs superfluous. (The digraphs will be used here, however.)

Since **ts** is an altogether different sound from **tʃ** and **dz** from **dʒ** (not as in Logo where they overlap, see Part I, § 59 et seq.), the digraphs *ts* and *dz* will need to be retained.

37. The Gospels write *kb* for *kp*. This is an unnecessary deviation from a spelling that has now almost universal acceptance.

Consonant compounds.

38. *mb, nd, nz, nj,* and *ng*[1] are logical ways of writing the nasal compounds with *b, d, z, j,* and *g.*

e.g. *mbu, nde, nza, nja, nga.* See § 22.

The compound with *gb*, however, has been written *nb*, thus: *nba* = child (for *mgba*).

This is unsatisfactory in two ways, first because *n* does not occur in the sound itself, and secondly because this spelling gives no clue to the labio-velar quality of the sound and its phonetic relationship to *kp* and *gb*. Consequently *mgb* is recommended here as elsewhere, e.g. *cumgburu, mgba.*

Syllabic consonants.

39. Here there is some confusion. If the syllabic **z** is to be regarded as doing the work of a vowel, it should be given a letter to itself. Thus:

bwets-z	as against	*bwets-i* (person)
dz-z	,,	*dz-a* (ground)
nz-z	,,	*nz-a* (to call)
z-z	,,	*z-a* (bowels)

Or else one could make use of a convention, as Litchman does, which ignores the preceding fricative element. Thus *bwet-z, d-z, n-z, z* (hyphens are my own). This method requires the reader to learn that *z* is syllabic when not followed by a vowel in the same word, but is a consonant or part of a consonant when a vowel follows, as in *dz-a, nz-a, z-a.*

The Lendu Gospel follows the first method in words like *ritsz* (thing), *kbetsz* (man), *iszle* (woman), but the second method in words like *dz, nz.* Litchman himself revokes his own convention in the word for 'fire', which he writes *kazz* instead of *kaz*, and 'skin', which he writes *szz* instead of *sz*.

40. The same applies to syllabic **r**, which occurs alone and after the compounds **br, gr, kr,** &c. Here Litchman follows the first method of doubling the letter in:—

mbrr (arrow); *ngrr* (baboon); *rr* (medicine); *krr* (much); *arr* (eight)

though inclines to the second method in:

dr (vein); *kr* (to chop—also written *krr*); *r* (to hear); *d̆r* (to tear up); *gr* (cold); *krkr* (thick); *d̆rd̆r* (old).

---

[1] Unless the sound ŋ is found to exist by itself in Lendu there is no need to introduce it into the velar nasal compound ŋg, which may otherwise be represented, quite unambiguously, by *ng*.

.The Lendu Gospel inclines to the first method in:
arr (eight)

but the second method in:
r (to hear)

41. In the following grammatical sketch I shall adhere to the first method for both sounds except in the case of the -r(ɪ) suffix (see § 66), where the vowel seems to be definitely elided without compensatory lengthening of the consonant. Thus:

bwetsz, dzz, nzz, zz, mbrr, rr, krr, arr.

CHAPTER III

NOUNS

42. As in Moru-Madi, nouns, in their simplest form, are of three kinds:

Monosyllabic, consisting in consonant (including consonant combination)+vowel (including syllabic z or r):

dʒɔ (head) *ko* (foot) *pi* (chief) *dzz* (ground)

Dissyllabic, consisting in vowel (+consonant)+vowel:

eʒó (elephant) oó (fowl) *isi* (woman) *idzz* (drum)

Dissyllabic, consisting in consonant+vowel+consonant+vowel:

kazź (fire) rítsż (thing) *liti* (charcoal) *teku* (navel)

Noun Prefixes

42. In the absence of comparative material for those Lendu word-roots which lie outside the Moru-Madi vocabulary, only such prefixes will be discussed here as may be added to or dropped from nouns within the language.

le-

43. This prefix is optional before noun stems indicating relationships or parts of the human body. It probably carries with it the idea of 'human'.

eye	= nyɔ or *lenyo*
ear	= bi or *lebi*
breast / half-brother	= ba-jo or *leba-jo*
sister	= ve or *leve*
half-sister	= veve or *leveve*
disciple	= *gotiranadike* or *legotiranadike*

Characteristic Vowel

44. Some noun stems begin with a vowel prefix, which may or may not be dropped at will.

za or *ezâ* (animal)	*itha* (crab)
jo or àdʒo (brother)	*aba* (father)
ʒo or eʒó (elephant)	*isi* (woman)
dzá or *adza* (house)	Cf. *si-mgba* (girl)

NOUNS

Note also the numerals:

    mbu or umbu (five)
    gbɔ̃ or ugbɔ̃ (three)
    'di or *aɖi* (one)
    azá (six)
    arr (eight)

a-

45. Whether this is a prefix or a grammatical particle needs further investigation. The following examples are insufficient:

dza = hut.   *i dza* (this hut).
aluti **adza** = behind the hut.
zha ku **adza**. My mother is in the house.
'ba = village.
ni-ka-nja e ie **a'ba**? Whom did you see at the village?
Cf. *aba ku ndi-'ba.* Father is at his home.
ma-kpa = my husband.   **akpa-ni** = your husband.
tsû or *tsz* = tree.
athu atsz bu na. Climb up the tree.
athu tsu ma-tho kuso. Climb down the tree to me.

Compound Nouns

46. As in all Sudanic languages, Lendu is capable of forming compound words to an almost unlimited degree:

cow = tszź or *tsz-ja* or *ndrr-tsz-ja.*
calf = *ndrr-tsz-kalu.*
water-pot = *ɖa-nju.*
tsu-jo = the top of the tree, i.e. tree head.
koi-ku-na-gali = train (lit. smoke-sits-*na*-cart).
'Bá-ðà or 'Ba-lɛ̀-ðà = the Lendu language.

Noun Suffixes

47. There are certain particles, many of which are recognizable as nouns, which have a particular function when compounded with other nouns. They may thus be regarded more as noun-suffixes or formative elements than as words in themselves.

-le

48. The function of this suffix is not at all clear. It seems to be attached to certain singular nouns or pronouns and to have an emphasizing value:

e.g. *aba ku 'Ba-le; zha ku Logo.* My father is a Lendu; my mother is a Logo.
   kɔ̀-kù 'Ba-le. We are Lendu.
   isi or *isz-le* = woman.
   fu-le = the man in question (cf. demonstrative *fu*).

as in

   ɖi-ke ce-'blo; bwetsz-mgba ce-ngue fu-le. The man woke up; the boy woke him up.

-ke

49. This word is used often as the pronoun for the third person singular. See § 56. As a suffix it is used to express singular of nouns relating to human beings:

bwetsz-ke = a man.
nyorithi-ke = a cook.
gbunjithi-ke = a thief.

It may also be attached to demonstratives and numerals:

i-ke. This man. *fu-ke*. That man.

e.g. *fu-ke ku lathi-ke*. That man is a warrior.

di-ke (one man, or the man in question).

-kpa

50. This suffix seems to have the following functions:

(a) Plurality:

cembu (sheep), pl. *cembu-kpa(r)*   *nyori-kpa* (cooks)
bwetsz-ke (man), pl. *bwetsz-kpa(r)*   *gbunjithi-kpa* (thieves)
ritsz (thing), pl. *ritsz-kpa(r)*   *ca*; pl. *ca-kpa(r)* (pot)

It may be attached to demonstratives or numerals:

fu-kpa ku lathi-kpa. Those men are warriors.
aro-kpa ce-ngue ndima. The two (men) killed each other.

(b) Male sex in animals:

cumgburu (lion)   *cumgbur-kpa* (male lion)
njei (water-buck)   *njei-kpa* (male water-buck)
tsii (dog)   *tsi-kpa* (male dog)
oo (fowl)   *o-kpa* (cock)
tszz (bull or cow) *tsz-kpa* (bull)

Note *ma-kpa* = my husband. *akpa-ni* = your husband.

(c) Augmentative:

(e)zho (elephant)   *kelo-zho-kpa* (monster elephant)
tsii (dog)   *kele-tsi-kpa* (very large dog)

(d) Other uses:

di ku di-kpa le-u-na lo tho. It (i.e. this stone) is for grinding corn. (vb. = *u*)

Cf. *kpa-jo*   now

-ja

51. This suffix shows female sex in animals:

cumgbur-ja (female lion)
njei-ja (female water-buck)
tsi-ja (bitch)
o-ja (hen)
tsz-ja (cow)

It is probably related to *zha* = mother.

-i

52. As far as can be made out, this is a feminine suffix applied to nouns or pronouns denoting human beings:

ke 'bi a-i-ndi-jo tsu na. He hit his wife on the head with a stick (lit. he hit wife-his-head stick with).

Masai-i ka-ra aḍu nji? What do the Masai women do?

Note, however:

dza-tso (doorway) (hut-entrance)
dza-tso-i (door)

fu ritsz-kpar ma-por-i dzzjo. These things I speak in the world.
Abrahamu nji-ngue fur-ba-i nza. This (i.e. thus) did not Abraham.

-mgba (= child)

53. This suffix is added occasionally to form the diminutive:

    bwetsi-ke (man)   *bwetsi-mgba* (boy)
    isi (woman)   *si-mgba* (girl)

-tha

54. The function of this suffix is to indicate the young female of a species:

    cumgbur-tha (young lioness)   *o-tha* (pullet)
    njei-tha (young female water-buck)   *tsi-tha* (young bitch)

-ba ('ba?)

55. This suffix is the Moru-Madi 'personal' suffix. (See Part I, § 186.)

    kali (nji) (to tell lies)   *kali-ba*, pl. *kali-kpa* (liar)
    ndru (man)   *ndru-ba* (wizard)
                         itha-ba or *utha-ba* (doctor)
                         ro-ba (sorcerer)

CHAPTER IV

PRONOUNS

Personal Pronouns

56. *ma,*   pl. *ko*   1st person   Phonetically: má   kɔ̀
     ni,   pl. *ni*   2nd person   ní   nì
     ke (= person), pl. *kpa* (= people) 3rd person   kɛ́   kpà
                         ndru (= people) 3rd person
     nganga   reflexive

     ndi, pl. *ndima*   referring pronoun for 3rd person[1] (cf. MORU andi)
     di ('di) and *i*   reference demonstrative   (cf. MORU 'di)

---

[1] Litchman is inclined to regard *ndi* and *ndima* as *feminine* or *common* pronouns, but his examples seem to support the 'referring' theory.

Examples:

ma-nja ni.	I see you.	*ni-nja ma.*	You see me.
ma-nja ke.	I see him.	*ni-nja ke.*	You see him.
ke nja ma.	He sees me.	*ke nja ke.*	He sees him.
ke nja ni.	He sees you.	*ke nja ke-nganga.*	He sees himself.
ma-zhi ni.	I love you (pl.)	*ni-zhi ma.*	You (pl.) love me.
ma-zhi ndru.	I love them.	*ndru zhi ma.*	They love me.
kpa zhi ke.	They love him.		
ke zhi kpa.	He loves them.		
ko-rr ni.	We hear you (pl.)	*ni-rr ko.*	You (pl.) hear us.
ko-rr ndru.	We hear them.	*ndru rr ko.*	They hear us.

57. Sometimes the 3rd person pronoun **ke** is used in an impersonal manner:

ke ká-kù zá nà ni? ke ku zá nà nga. Is there any meat? There is none (lit. He *ka* is meat with *ni*? He is meat with not).

58. Examples of the referring pronoun **ndi** (cf. Part I, § 198):

ma-jo por **ndi** *ku-dhe.* My brother says he is sick.
zha por ke ku-dhe na nga. My mother says he is not sick.

ke ku nga bwetsike; **ndi** *ku iszle.* That is not a man; it is a woman.
Fu ndru ku nga bwetsikpa; **ndima** *ku isz-ndru.* They are not men, they are women.

Note, however:

ke ku nga lathi-ke; ke ku jojuke. He is not a warrior; he is a smith.
kpa ku nga lathikpa; **kpa** *ku jojukpa.* They are not warriors; they are smiths.
ike kwi-ngue **ndi, ndiro.** The man killed himself.
aro kpa ce-ngue **ndima.** The two men killed each other.

59. Examples of **di** ('di?) and **i**. Cf. § 77:

o, ari ďi. All right, cook it.
za ka mgbaga? ďi le-a-'blo. Where is the meat? It is eaten.
ni-dza tsi ka mgbaga? ďi dhe-'blo. Where is your dog? He is dead.
zho ka-ku titi? oro, ďi ku titi. Is the elephant black? Yes it is.
í kaka búkù. It is a red book.

Interrogative Pronouns

60.   **ie** (= who)

ni-ka-ku ie?	Who art thou?
ni-ka ie ne?	Whom seek ye?
ni-ri ie tho, ka?	Whom are you cooking for?
di ka ie a-ri?	Who ate it?

PRONOUNS

à'du (= what)

61. This particle may also be used adverbially for 'why'. See § 150:

ní-ká **à'du** njì? What are you doing?
ni-ka a'du ri? What are you cooking?
ni-ka hwi-e a'du butso? What did you kill this morning?
ma-ka-ka a'du ri? What shall I cook?
ni-ka a'du nji fu krrkrrnaritsz? What are you doing with that chopper?
ni-ka a'du ne? What seek ye?

Cf. *ni-ka a'du gbo?* What are you laughing at?
   mgba ka-dzz a'du-jo? Why is the boy crying?
      (*a'du-ro*)

mgbá (= what, which (?))

62. It is hard to determine the difference between **mgba** and **a'du**, as witness the following sentences:

fu ju ka-ku **mgba** *lo-tho?* What is this stone for?

ma-dza ndrrtszja dhe-'blo; ma-ka-ver nji **mgba?** My cow is dead; what shall I do?
   ni-ka-ver nji **mgba?** What will you do?

For qualifying use, see § 79.

With relative effect:

mgba *rr di na ndru.* They that hear.

Many adverbs may be formed from this root. See § 150.

Pronoun Suffixes

-ro (= body)

63. This particle is attached to the pronoun to give a reflexive or emphasizing force:

*ko-ka-ve ko kwi, ko-***ro**. We shall kill ourselves.
*i ke kwi-ngue ndi ndi-***ro**. The man killed himself.

ma-ve por, za dzz-ngue tso-na-nyamu. Aba por ndi po kali, ke du-ngue ndi **ndiro**.
   My sister says the meat was taken (by) a wild-cat. My father says she lies, she took (it) herself.

-ma

64. This particle also may have a reflexive function, though referring to a plural subject. It may also show reciprocal action:

*bwetsz-nzo dhi ndi-***ma**. The boys are beating themselves.
*bwetsz-nzo ndi-***ma** *dhi, di mgba na.* The boys are beating each other (lit. themselves with that boy).
*kpa ndi-***ma** *thu.* They curse each other.
*aro kpa ce-ngue ndi-***ma**. The two men killed each other.

65. In the following sentences the function of **ma** is uncertain:

*fu ndru ku nga bwetsikpa; ndi-***ma** *ku isz-ndru.* Those people are not men; they are women.
*bwetsi-kpa zhi za-zho-tha tho-***ma** *'be-lo-tha na di.* Men love hunting and fishing.
*ndi-***ma** *ngu wago naro.* They return from the woods.
kareno **ma** *nga.* Not at all.

-r(1)

66. This suffix, which usually appears as **-r,** has many functions, some of which are still uncertain.

Its most easily discernible function is that of the English indefinite pronoun 'one', pl. 'ones':

i tsu ku ma-dza-r. ni-dza-r ka-ku mgbaga? This stick is mine (i.e. my one). Yours is where?

ma-dza-r ku nga; i-ri ku ke-dza-r. I have none; this one is his.

and in the plural:

fu tsu-kpa-r ku ko-thi-r; ni-thi-r ka-ku mgbaga? These sticks are ours; where are yours?

ko-thi-r ku nga; fu-r ku kpa-thi-r. We have none; these are theirs.

Compare:

ma-ka-ka o ri? o, ari-r. Shall I cook a chicken? Yes, cook one.

ma-ka-ka fu ni-sz na ẻe ri? o, ari ẻi. Shall I cook the guinea-fowl you shot? Yes, cook it.

ni-ka-nja motokar calu? o, ma-nja-r mgba. nza, ma-nja-r nza. Do you see a motor-car over there? Yes, I see one. No, I don't see one.

ni-ka-nja ajo nzz nza? o, ma-nja ke mgba. Did you see my brother yesterday? Yes, I saw him.

67. It is very often attached to the plural suffix **-kpa** when apparently referring to an unspecified number or to plurality in general:

>*bwetsz-ke* (the man, a man)
>*bwetsz-kpa* (the men)
>*bwetsz-kpa-r* (several men, men in general)
>*ko-thi tsu-kpa-r* (our sticks)

Attached to adjectives:

blo-r nji na ndru. They that have done good (things).

ce-r nji na ndru. They that have done evil (things) (lit.) evil doing people.

68. Or it can be used when no specific object is mentioned:

ari-r! ma-ka-ka aẻu ri? ari o. Cook (something)! What shall I cook? Cook a chicken.

ko-ka na di ngo nzi? nzi, nzi ngo-r. May we not sing? No, don't sing (anything).

ʒí-rɪ (to cut); *ʒí-rɪ-ʒí* (to saw).

69. Sometimes it seems to overlap in function with **'di** in referring to something already mentioned:

ni-ka aẻu nji fu krrkrrnaritsz? ma-krr tsu ẻi-r na. What are you doing with that chopper? I'm cutting wood with it.

abu 'yu lehwe za-r na. Give me a knife for cutting meat with.

amba ẻa ma-tho. angu na-r. Bring me some water. Take it away.

atu i nyo iga-ro. angu-r na. Take this food away. Bring it back (lit. return it with).

70. Very often, however, and especially when attached to verbs, its function is impossible to define: cf. **ri** in Lugbara (Part I, § 168):

tszkpar rr nyinyi. nzi ni-'ba tsi li-r tsz nyi-r. The cows are running. Don't let the dog make the cows run.

má-tsa tsû. I chop the tree. má-tsa-r tsá. I chop (lots of trees, &c.).
ma-jo po-r: ... My brother says: ...
pi po-ngue-r: ... The chief said: ...
ni-ka-ve-r nji mgba? What will you do?
(cf. *ma-ka-ve nja ritsz nji nzi.* I shall do nothing.)
ma-gu-rí gu-r. I refuse.
ko (ko nga ni-r). We (we excluding thee).
fu-r ka nga Yesu, Yosepa du-r? Is not this Jesus, the son of Joseph?
kaka (red); kaka-r (redness).[1]
blɔ (good); blɔ-r (goodness).
vivi (to lose); vivi-r ('lostness').

CHAPTER V
QUALIFICATIVES
A. ADJECTIVES

71. There is nothing formal to distinguish an adjective from a noun (many words being capable of functioning as both), except that adjectives are capable of reduplication and are never given the plural suffix -**kpa**. The adjective precedes the noun it qualifies:

ma-nja bo zho. I see the big elephant.
anja bo zho. Look at the big elephant.
nde bo tso-kpa ngue fuga ni. Now there was much grass in the place.
ma-zhi bo 'ju nza, ma-zhi re 'ju. I don't want a big knife, I want a small knife.
re zho (little elephant); *re tsi.* (little dog).
blo isz-le (a good woman); *krú ndru* (all the people).

Compare:
bo dza-tso (a big door).
tsu dza-tso (a wooden door) (*tsu* = tree).
mbo dza-tso (an iron door) (*mbu* = iron).

72. With reduplication (chiefly in colour adjectives):
sasau tsz-kpa (a white bull); *kaka tsz-ja* (a red cow).
titi tsz-kpa (a black bull); *tanga tsz-ja* (a spotted cow).

B. NUMERALS

73. Numeral adjectives seem capable of both preceding and following the noun:
di ke (one man, lit. one he); *aro ndru* (two men).
aro kpa ce-ngue ndima. The two men killed each other.
nde arr 'ji goti ... And after eight days ...
a'bu tsz dre. Pay ten cows.
nde ju-dza-ḋa-nju-kpa-r aza ngue fuga ni ... And there were set there six water-pots of stone ...

[1] I am doubtful of the validity of this note of mine.

C. Qualificatives with Linking Particles

na

74. The linking particle **na** may be used when the qualificative is formed from a nominal root or verbal root (where it corresponds to the relative or participle in other languages).

From nominal root:

tso **na** *nyamu* (wild cat; lit. grass *na* cat).
tso **na** *za* (game; lit. grass *na* animal).
lɛ́tsɔ **ná** sa'dà (spittle; lit. mouth *na* saliva).

Note, however, *tsu dza-tso* (wooden door) without linking particle.

From verbal root (root usually reduplicated):

nzi   ni-dzz gloglo **na** ndrr, adzz thu **na**-r.
Don't buy   thin   goat, buy fat one.

blo ɖani **na** *iszle* (a beautiful woman). (Here 'blo' qualifies "dani'.)

With participial effect (note reduplication in verb root):

dhedhe **na** *ke* (a dead man); *ɖoɖo* **na** *tsi* (a sleeping dog).
dhedhe **na** *ke ngue ma-jo*. The man who died was my brother.
nzi ni-ce ɖoɖo **na** *tsi*. Don't wake the dog which is sleeping.

With relative effect:

fu ni-sz **na** *za*. That animal which you shot (lit. that you-shoot *na* animal).
aco ma-tho dzzdzz **na** *bwetsimgba*. Send to me the boy who is crying.
aco ma-tho Ingeleza-tha po **na** *bwetsimgba*. Send me a boy who knows English (lit. English-language speak *na* boy).
ma-dza lo rr **na** *ndi-le*. He that heareth my word (my-word hear *na* he).
keke-na-ritsz, pl. *keke-na-ritszkpar* (pincers; lit. pinch *na* thing).
krr-na-ritsz (chopper).
a-a-za-na-za (carnivore; lit. eat-animal *na* animal, i.e. animal which eats animals).

dza

75. This linking particle, besides being part of the genitive construction, may be used with qualificatives formed from nominal roots:

tsi **dza** *mgba* (puppy; lit. dog *dza* child).
kpele **dza** *klo* (thorny crown; lit. thorn *dza* crown).
ju **dza** *ɖa-nju-kpar* (stone water-pots; lit. stone *dza* water-pot-*kpar*).

thi

76. This linking particle, besides being part of the genitive construction, may be used with qualificatives formed from verbal roots:

kpakpa **thi** *iszle* (a jealous woman).
be **thi** *dyi* (a dancing song).
wa mbu-tha **thi** *dyi* (a drinking song; lit. beer drink *tha thi* song).
za zho **thi** *ke* (a hunter; lit. animal hunt *thi* person).
za zho **thi** *kpa* (hunters; lit. animal hunt *thi* people).

QUALIFICATIVES

D. PRONOMINAL QUALIFICATIVES

Demonstratives

77. The demonstratives behave in the same way as adjectives in that they precede the noun qualified. There are three degrees of distance:

i ke	This man (near me)	*i kpa*	These men
fu ke	That man (near you)	*fu kpa*	Those men
ca ke	Yonder man	*ca kpa*	Yonder men
i iszle	This woman	*i iszndru*	These women
fu iszle	That woman	*fu iszndru*	Those women
ca iszle	Yonder women	*ca iszndru*	Yonder women
i li	This spear	*i likpa*	These spears
fu li	That spear	*fu likpa*	Those spears
ca li	Yonder spear	*ca likpa*	Yonder spears

78. Note that the reference form **di** (§ 56) never seems to function as a qualificative (as in Moru-Madi), but that **i** and **fu** may sometimes function as a reference pronoun:

i búku ku kákà. The book is red.
í kaka búkù. It is a red book.

For the use of demonstrative forms in the formation of adverbs see § 150.

Interrogative

79. The interrogative form **a'du** seems to be incapable of qualifying, but **mgba** may qualify nouns:

mgba ditsz? Which thing?
di ka-ku mgba bwetsike? What man is this?

Relative cu

80. The relative sentence is often expressed by means of a circumlocution with **na** (see § 74) and the following examples of **cu** are found only in the Lendu Gospel:

ɖi ka-ku mgba bwetsike cu por ni-tho. What man is that which said unto thee:
ɖi ku nja ke cu ma-dza lo tho. There is another that beareth witness of me.

Indefinite

81. The following indefinite qualifiers are most common:

... *kpa ndro nja kpa di.* ... and despised others.
... *ma-ku didi nja ndru bai nga.* ... that I am not as other men are.
nde ke po-ngue-r nja ke-tho. Then said he to another (he).

ke tsu-ngue ɖi bagu; ɖi isz-le... He entered into a certain village; and a certain woman ...

(Cf. **'di** = one—numeral, § 73.)

E. POSSESSIVE QUALIFICATIVES (GENITIVE CONSTRUCTION)

82. The genitive construction is in many cases identical with the compound noun construction already discussed. When the possession is intimate, i.e. as in the case of one's bodily members, or the integral parts of a whole (and sometimes one's relations), the possessor (whether noun or pronoun) precedes the thing possessed, and the two words combine to form one unity:

ma-jo (my head or my brother)[1]   *ma-bi* (my ear)
ni-jo (your head or your brother)   *ne-bí* (your ear)
ke-jo his head or his brother)   *kɛ-bí* (his ear)
ndi-jo (his own head or her[2] brother)   *ndrú bi* (the man's ear)
ko-jo-kpar (our heads)
ni-jo-kpar (your heads)
kpa-jo-kpar (their heads) (masc.)
ndima-jo-kpar (their heads) (common)[2]

má-ra **má**-'bà. I am going home (i.e. my house).
aba ku **ndi**-'ba. Father is at home (i.e. his own home).
ko-si-ngue **ko**-'ba naro. We come from home (i.e. our home).

bwetsike jo. The man's head.
le-jo. A human head.
bi-jo. A buffalo-head, or the buffalo's head.

bwetsike jo. The man's brother.   *bwetsike jokpar.* The man's brothers.
bwetsikpa jo. The men's brother.   *bwetsikpa jokpar.* The men's brothers.

zhakpa-ka. Antelope-skin.

83. In some cases, not yet fully investigated, the possessor *follows* the thing possessed:[3]

nzi ni-bi nza aba-ni tho. Don't hoe the field for your father.
ni-ri-ngue akpa-ni tho? Have you cooked for your husband?
ke-le'bi-ngue. ie tho? aba-ndi tho. He was beaten. By whom? By his father.

Cf. *ma-ri* **ma**-*kpa tho*. I'm cooking for my husband.

Linking Particles

-dza-, -thi- (*Non-intimate genitive*)

84. When possession is non-intimate, i.e. when the thing possessed is merely held by the owner, and may be transferred to another owner, the possessor does not immediately precede the thing possessed, but is separated from it by the particle **dzá** if the possessor is singular, and **thí** if the possessor is plural:

ma-dza li (or *likpar*) (my spear, or spears)   *ma-dzá 'jú* (my knife)
ni-dza li   ,,   (thy ,,   ,,)   *ni-dzá*   ,, (your ,,
ke-dza li   ,,   (his ,,   ,,)   *kɛ-dzá*   ,, (his ,,
ndi dza   ,,   (her[4] ,, ,,)
ko-thi li   ,,   (our ,,   ,,)   *kɔ-θí lɔ* (our word)
ni-thi li   ,,   (your ,,   ,,)   *ni-θí lɔ̀* (your ,,)
kpa-thi li   ,,   (their (masc.) spear, or spears)   *kpa-θí lɔ* (their word)
ndru thi li   ,,   (their (com.) spear, or spears)

---

[1] Head = (le)dʒɔ; brother = (à)dʒɔ.
[2] Litchman's rendering.
[3] My own notes give: **ma**-dʒɔ (my brother); adʒɔ-**ni** (your brother); kɛ-dʒɔ (his brother).
[4] Litchman's rendering. See, however, § 58.

QUALIFICATIVES

bwetsike dza li. The man's spear. *bwetsi-kpa thi nji.* Men's work.
'Bale-thi-ke dza li. A Lendu's spear. *iszndru thi nji.* Women's work.
'Bale dza li. A Lendu spear.
tsú dzá kpɛlɛ. The tree's thorn(s).

Note the difference between intimate and non-intimate genitive in the following:

*tsi ka **ndrrtsz-kpa**.* The dog is eating a cow-bone.
*bu gbunji **tsi dza kpa** na.* The monkey stole the dog's bone.

85. Note the use of **-r(i)** when the thing possessed is not stated:
i tsu ku ma-dza-r. ni-dza-r ka-ku mgbaga? This stick is mine. Yours is where?
ma-dza-r ku nga; i-ri ku ke-dza-r. Mine is not (i.e. I have none); this is his.

and in the plural:

fu tsukpar ku ko-thi-r. ni-thi-r ka-ku mgbaga? These sticks are ours. Where are yours?
ko-thi-r ku nga; fu-r ku kpa-thi-r. We have none; these are theirs.

86. This genitive construction, as already shown (§§ 75–6), may have a qualifying function in the treatment of diminutives or the young of a species, or in showing the material from which a thing is made:

tsi dza mgba = puppy, i.e. dog's child.
zho dza mgba = baby elephant.
kpele dza klo (crown of thorns; lit. thorn *dza* crown).
ju dza ɖa-nju-kpar = 'water-pots of stone' (i.e. stone *dza* water-pot (pl.))[1]

It is also one way of expressing possession. See also predicatives, § 144.

ma-dza ndrrtszja ku ni. I have a cow; lit. my cow is present.
nokpa dza ndrrtszjakpar ku nga. The slave has no cattle; lit. the slaves cattle are not.
ni-dza vi ku nga. You have no brains.

-thi-

87. This plural suffix is also widely used as a noun agent formative. Here it is usually followed by **-ke** or **-kpa**, according to whether the noun is singular or plural:

nji-thi-ke, pl. *nji-thi-kpa* = worker
za-zho-thi-ke, pl. *za-zho-thi-kpa* = hunter (animal-killer)
'be-lo-thi-ke, pl. *'be-lo-thi-kpa* = fisher (fish-catcher)
ru-to-thi-ke, pl. *ru-to-thi-kpa* = tailor (cloth-piercer)
nyo-ri-thi-ke = cook (food-cooker)

88. Non-possessive qualificatives may also be formed in this way, as already mentioned:

'ya thi iszle (a jealous woman).
kpakpa thi iszle (a hard-hearted woman).
'Bale-thi-ke (a Lendu man).
kali-thi-ke (or *kali-ba*) (a liar, i.e lies *thi* man).
be-thi-dyi (a dancing song).
wa-mbu-tha-thi-dyi (a drinking song; lit. bear-drink-*tha-thi*-song).

[1] Note, however, tsu dzatso = wooden door, i.e. wood hut-entrance.

CHAPTER VI
NOUN POSTPOSITIONS

jo (= head)

89. This particle retains its original meaning of 'head' in: *tsu-jo* = top of the tree, where it is probably component part of a compound noun. As a postposition it occurs:

*ma-jo ra-ngue ɖa **jo**.*	My brother has gone in the direction of the river.

Adverbial compounds with **jo** are seen in the following:

*mgba lego-ngue-'blo kpa-**jo**.*	A child has just been born.
*mgba ka-dzz aɖu-**jo**?*	Why is the child crying? (i.e. for what).
*njei sisi ba **jo**-lu.*	A water-buck is bigger than a cob.

kuso

90. This compound postposition implies 'next to':

*ato iga ma-**kuso**.*	Stand here, next to me.
*ato fuga ke-**kuso**.*	Stand there, next to him.
*ada tsu ma-tho **kuso**.*	Pull the log towards me.
*ada tsu ma-**kusu** roro.*	Pull the log away from me.
*ada ɖi fu ke-tho **kuso**.*	Pull it towards that man.
*athu tsu ma-tho **kuso**.*	Climb down the tree to me.
*ní-ku ma-**kusɔ** tʃotʃo.* *ní-ku ma-ró tʃotʃo.*	You are near to me.

lo tho

91. The exact function of **lo** in this compound postposition is uncertain (**lo** = 'word'):

*fu nju ka-ku mgba **lo-tho**?* What's this stone for (for what word)?
*ɖi ku dikpa le-u-na **lo-tho**.* It's for grinding corn (for corn-grinding word).

Cf. *'di-tho* = because:

ɖitho ke nji-ngue fu ritsz sabiti-dyi na (because he had done these things on the Sabbath day).

ma

92. This particle (cf. pronoun suffix **-ma**) is used for connecting words and phrases, and corresponds to a conjunction in English:

*. . . nganyondru **ma**, tsukotsundru **ma** tsubai **ma** na di. . . .* of blind, halt, withered.
*ni-rr ke-cu di ca **ma** nza, ni-nja ke-rozi **ma** nza di.* Ye have neither heard his voice, nor seen his shape.

It also occurs in the formation of adverbs:

*gu-**ma*** = above.

na

93. This particle imparts to the noun it follows a locative significance usually, though it has also an instrumental use. The following examples are arranged according to the English prepositions which have to be used to translate it:

*zho ku wago **na**.*	There is an elephant in the woods.
*aba ku nzagu **na**.*	Father is in the field.
*rasu ku ɖa **na**.*	There is a crocodile in the river.

NOUN POSTPOSITIONS

*bo glu tse-**na**.*   At the foot of the big hill.
*ju tsz-**na**.*   Under the stone.
*athu atsz bu **na**.*   Climb up the tree.
*ni-u wago **na**?*   Are you going to the woods?

*koi-ku-na-gali tu-ngue nzz Kilo, ďi ka-si iga bu ma-**na**.* The train left Kilo yesterday, it will arrive here to-morrow.
*koi-ku-na-gali tu-ngue nzz iga, ďi ka-si Kilo **na** bu.* The train left here yesterday, it will reach Kilo to-morrow.
*ke 'bi ai-ndi jo tsu **na**.* He hit his wife's head with a stick.
*bwetsike to-ngue to ma-ko 'ju **na**.* The man stabbed my leg with a knife.
*ďi lehwi li **na**.* He (referring here to a dog) was killed by a spear.
*abu 'yu lehwe za-r **na**.* Give me a knife to skin the animal with.
*ara ma-**na**.* Come with me.
*ko (ni ma-**na**).* We (you and I).
*ko (ni ko-**na** kru).* We (you and all of us).
*isí ku hwé-**nà**.* This woman is beautiful (i.e. with beauty).
*bwetsikpa zhi zazhotha tho ma 'belotha **na** di.* Men like hunting and fishing, i.e. hunting and fishing with it.
angu **na**-r. Take it back (lit. return with it).

Cf. angu-r **na**. Bring it back (lit. return it with).

ro

94. This particle, which usually occurs reduplicated or in combination with other particles, gives the impression of motion away from somewhere:

*ada tsu ma-kusu **roro**.*   Pull the log away from me.
*atu i nyo iga-**ro**.*   Take this food away.
*ko-si-ngue ko-'ba na-**ro**.*   We come from home.
*ndima ngu wago na-**ro**.*   They return from the woods.
*ndru ngusi ďa na-**ro**.*   The people are coming from the river.
*aji bu na-**ro**.*   Climb up out of the well.

tho

95. This particle has many implications:

*aco ma-**tho** Paulo.* Send to me Paulo.
*amba ďa ma-**tho**.* Bring me some water.

*ke le'bi'bi. ie **tho**? aba-ndi **tho**.* He is being beaten. By whom? By his father.

*ke dzz ni-dza li 'blo, za zhotha **tho**.* He has taken your spear for killing game.
*li nji-ni Logo **tho** la **tho**.* Spears are used by the Logo for fighting.
*ni-ri ie **tho**, ka?* Whom are you cooking for?
*ma-ri ma-kpa **tho**.* I am cooking for my husband.

*ni-ka-ve nzz roba nzi, ďi-dza dhitha **tho**?* Won't you see a witch-doctor about its death?

Its function is vague in the following examples, where it seems to supplement the gerund particle -tha (see § 108):

*nyo ritha-**tho** ku iszndru thi nji.* Cooking food is woman's work.
*bwetsikpa zhi zazhotha-**tho** ma 'belotha na di.* Men like hunting and fishing.

CHAPTER VII
VERBS

96. Verbs are mostly monosyllabic. A few seem to be dissyllabic, beginning with the vowel **a-**, which may be dropped on occasions. For examples, see vocabulary, as contexts are lacking. It is probable that such verbs correspond to the directional verbs in **a-** in Logo. (See Part I, § 445.)

97. There are a few compound verbs. Thus the verb *ti* = to say, occurs in compounds like
  kali-ti (to tell lies)
  ndu-ti (to sneeze)
and the verb *nji* = to do, occurs optionally in
  za-zho (nji) (to hunt game; lit. game hunt do)
  'be-lo (nji) (to catch fish; lit. fish catch do)
  nji (nji) (to work; lit. do do)
  gbu (nji) (to steal; lit. steal do)
Other compounds:
  ngusi (to return here) <*ngu* (return) *si* (arrive)

Aspect

The distinction between Definite and Indefinite Aspect (see Part I, § 339) is shown in the word order only.

98. *Definite aspect.* Subj.+verb+obj. (+postposition):
  ari o. Cook a chicken.
  ma-nja bo zho. I see a big elephant.
  ma-krr tsu. I cut the wood.
  ma-zhi tsu. I sawed the wood.
  má-tra 'Balɛ̀-ðà. I speak Lendu.
  a-bi nza pi tho. Hoe the field for the chief.
  nzi ni-bi nza aba-ni tho. Don't hoe the field for your father.

99. The verbal postpositions may follow either the verb or the object:
  ma-tha-ngue ru.   I tore the cloth.
  laka ka-ngue tsu.   The mouse gnawed the wood.
  ma-nja ke mgba.   I saw him.
  ke dzz ni-dza li 'blo. He has taken your spear.

100. *Indefinite aspect.* Subj. (+aux.)+obj.+verb:
  ni-ka aðu nji?   What are you doing?
  ma nga o.   I'm hoeing something.
  nzo ra tsz-ba mbu.   Children drink cow-milk (habitually).
  má 'da ʒú.   I am drinking water.
  má mbazz 'dá.   I am smoking tobacco.
Compare thus:
  má 'ou krû.   I'm cooking a chicken.
  ma-krú 'où.   I've cooked a chicken.
  má 'ou 'á.   I'm eating a chicken.
  má-'a 'où.   I've eaten a chicken.

VERBS

101. Note that in the dependent constructions, suffixes are not as common in Lendu as in the other Moru-Madi languages, and the unchanged verb stem is used here in contexts which demand suffixes in other languages. (See, however, § 108.)

(vb. = bi) *ni-u nza **bi** pi tho ka?* Are you going to hoe the field for the chief?
(vb. = nja) *ma-si ma-ve **nja** 'blo.* I have come to see my sister.

REDUPLICATION

102. Reduplication in verbs serves the following purposes (note that it may occur in negative sentences):

Continued action:
  bwetsimgba ɖoɖo. The boy is asleep.
  ni-ɖoɖo? nzi, ma-ɖoɖo nzi. Are you asleep? No, I'm not.
  ke le'bi'bi. He is being beaten.
  tszkpar rr nyinyi. The cattle are running.

Habitual action:
  bwetsimgba ra ɖoɖo nzz. The boy sleeps every day.

Imperative (rare):
  ani-ngongo! Sing! (pl.).
  adu ni-dza ra, abibi di. Take up thy bed and walk.

Past time:
  di dhedhe mgbar bai? How did he die?
  bwetsike to-ngue to ma-ko 'ju na. The man stabbed me in the leg with a knife.
  njati ni-zho-ngue fu tsu, ni-dhe-ngue dhe. If you had drunk that medicine, you would have died.

State:
  ni-dza semisi tha-ni tha. Your shirt is torn.
  kazź ðèðè. The fire is dead.
  ma-njɛ ma-njɛ. I am tired.
  ni-njɛ ni-njɛ. You are tired.

Noun derivatives:
  ke-ke-na-ritsz, pl. ke-ke-na-ritszkpar = pincers.
  krr-krr-na-ritsz = chopper.

Participials and relatives:
  dhedhe na ke (a dead man).
  ɖoɖo na tsi (a sleeping dog).
  gloglo na ndrr (a thin goat).
  kpakpa thi iszle (a hard-hearted woman).
  aco ma-tho dzzdzz na bwetsimgba. Send me the boy who is crying.

VERB STEM PREFIXES
á- (imperative)

103. This vowel is prefixed to the verb stem in the imperative singular. The second person pronoun is not normally used (as in other Moru-Madi languages):

  átsa fu tsû. Chop that tree.   áθa tsú ngà. Split the wood.
  ango dyi. Sing a song.   avu kazz. Blow the fire.
  adi tsztsz-ro. Keep quiet.
  ari za. Cook meat.

atu-ni! Go away! (Whether 'ni' is the second person pronoun or a locative
      suffix is not known. See also § 132.)
   ada-ni! Rise!

Note however: *nzi ni-nji ce nji ki*. Sin no more (lit. don't you do bad deed again).

104. In the plural the 2nd person pronoun is used before the verb stem, and the vowel a- precedes the pronoun:
   ani-ngongo! Sing ye!
   ani-ra! Come!
   ani-pu i ritsz iga-ro! Take these things hence!

Sometimes, however, the singular form is used with plural meaning:
   ko-ka-ka adi ngo? ango be-thi-dyi. What shall we sing? Sing a dancing song.

le-

105. This prefix forms the passive stem, which may have both Definite and Indefinite aspect.

Definite:
   ke le-'bi-ngue. He has been beaten.
   za ka mgbaga? ǎi le-a-'blo. Where is the meat? It is eaten.
   ǎi le-hwi li na. It was killed by a spear.
   ma-le-go-ngue 'blo, drrdrr njina. I was born long ago.
   abu 'yu le-hwe za-r na. Give me a knife to skin the animal with. (Note verb in passive.)

Indefinite:
   ke le-'bi'bi. He is being beaten.

106. There is another passive construction, however, in which the verb stem has no prefix. The word order here is significant: Sufferer+agent+verb.
   ǎi ka ie a-ri? It was eaten by whom? (lit. It (interrog.) who ate?).
   ma-gbogbo furiro ma-jo ke ti sz-ngue-ro. I am laughing because my brother was stung by a bee (lit. I-laugh because my-brother he bee stung).

Cf.: *ma-dzá mgbà* **vivi**. My child is lost.
   ma-ví ma-dzá mgbà **vi**. I lost my child.

107. Yet another passive construction makes use of the postposition **-ni** instead of a prefix, but the word order is not altered. (See § 132.)
   liti nji-ni Logo tho koi tho. Charcoal is used by the Logo for smoking.
   li nji-ni Logo tho la tho. Spears are used by the Logo for fighting.
   ni-dza semisi tha-ni tha. Your shirt is torn.

VERB SUFFIX
-tha

108. Perhaps the best equivalent of this particle in English is the *-ing* of the gerund. The object, when present, precedes the verb stem:
   nji-tha ku blo. Working is good.
   gbunji-tha ku ce. Stealing is bad.
   nja-ke zhi ǎo-tha. So-and-so loves sleeping.
   nza-nga-o-tha ku bwetsikpa thi nji. Hoeing fields is men's work.
   ma-zhi nza nza-nga-o-tha. I don't like hoeing fields.

Sometimes the verbal noun is assisted by the postposition **tho**, whose function here is rather vague:

*nyo-ri-**tha**-**tho** ku iszndru thi nji.* Cooking food is women's work.
*bwetsikpa zhi za-zho-**tha**-**tho** ma 'be-lo-**tha** na di.* Men love hunting and fishing.

Occasionally this construction indicates a noun instrument:

to (to pierce); *to-**tha**,* pl. *to-**tha**-kpar* (piercing instrument).

109. The particle may also be used in 'purpose' sentences (where it corresponds to **za** in Moru-Madi):

*ke dzz ni-dza li 'blo, za-zho-**tha** tho.* He has taken your spear to go after game (i.e. for killing game).

Usually, however, no suffixed particle is needed:

ke ra-ngue da zho 'blo. He has gone to drink water.
ma-si ma-ve nja 'blo. I have come to see my sister.

Note the following two gerund examples, in which the **tha** particle is missing:

*liti nji-ni Logo tho **koi** tho.* Charcoal is used by the Logo for smoking.
*li nji-ni Logo tho **la** tho.* Spears are used by the Logo for fighting.

CHAPTER VIII

VERBAL AUXILIARIES

110. As in Moru-Madi, the verbal auxiliary forms stand between the subject of the sentence and the verb, usually immediately after the subject. Some auxiliaries seem to be merely particles, but others are formed from verbal roots which themselves may function as independent verbs in other contexts. In such cases the English equivalent of the verb will be given.

111. 'ba (= to leave). Causative auxiliary. See **li**, § 119.

'de

112. This particle seems to be used in negative sentences with the sense of 'not yet':

(vb. = *si*) *ni-ka-si ni-dza nji 'blo? nza, ma-'de si nji nza go.* Have you finished your work? No, I have not finished the work.

(vb. = *we*) *ni-ka-we e zha-kpa-ka? nza, na^1-'de zhakpa-ka we nza.* Have you skinned the buck? No, I have not skinned the buck yet (lit. removed the buckskin).

Note in the second reply the word order suggests an Indefinite construction.

ke ka-ve dhe nja nzi, nza ke 'de Kristo Pi nja-go-ro. He should not see death until he had seen the Lord Christ (lit. not he yet Christ Chief seen-had).

[1] *ma*(?)

ká

113. This particle seems to accompany all interrogative sentences, no matter what form or tense.

Indefinite:

ní-ká à'du njì?	What are you doing?
ní-ká à'du ri?	,, ,, cooking?
ní-ká za rí?	Are you cooking meat?
(Note, however: ni-dodo?	Are you asleep?)
ni-ka adu gbo?	What are you laughing at?
mgba ka-dzz adu-jo?	Why is the boy crying?

Definite:

ni-ka-nja motokar calu?	Do you see a motor-car over there?
ni-ka-nji adu butso?	What were you doing yesterday?
ni-ka-hwi e adu butso?	What did you kill yesterday?
ni-ka-si ni-dza nji 'blo?	Have you finished your work.
zho ka-ku bo?	Is the elephant big?

114. Occasionally **ka** may end a sentence (cf. **ya** in Moru):

ni-ri ie tho, **ka?**	Whom are you cooking for?
ni-u nza bi pi tho, **ka?**	Are you hoeing for the chief?

115. In the reply to these questions, there is no **ka** particle:

ma-nji ritsz nza.	I'm not doing anything (definite constr.).
ma nyo ri.	I'm cooking food (indefinite constr.).
ma-gbogbo furiro ...	I'm laughing because ...
o, ma-nja-mgba.	Yes I see (it).
ma-u e kwi.	I was grinding corn.
ma-hwi e zha.	I killed a bush-buck.
nza, ma-de si nji nza go.	No, I didn't finish the work.
oro, di ku bo.	Yes, it is big.
ma-ri makpa tho.	I'm cooking for my husband.

ka (= to be able)

116. This auxiliary is used in the Definite construction, and is followed by the main verb in the Indefinite or Definite construction, or by a dependent sentence. Its function corresponds with that of the English auxiliaries 'can', 'may', 'must', 'shall'.

(Note, in interrogative sentences, this **ka** is often preceded by the **ka** of interrogation.)

Definite construction:

ni-ka-ka-mgba ni-nja motokar calu? o, ma-ka-mgba. Can you see the motor-car over there? (lit. you ka can p.t. you see motor there)? Yes, I can.

nza, ma-**ka** nza. No, I can't.

ma-**ka** nza ma-u ni-na. I cannot go with you (lit. I can not I go you with).

zha por ... aba ka ke 'bi te. My mother says ... my father must beat him (lit. mother says father must he beat te).

pi po-nguer ma-ka-bu tsz dre te. The chief said I must pay ten head of cattle (lit. chief say p.t. I must pay cattle ten te).

VERBAL AUXILIARIES

117. It may also have a future significance, although in some respects it approaches more the 'volition' **ko** of Logo in function (see Part I, § 509).

Indefinite construction:

ma-ka-ka aḋu ngo?	What shall I sing?
ko-ka-ka aḋu ngo?	What shall we sing?
ma-ka-ka aḋu ri?	What shall I cook?
ma-ka-ka o ri?	Shall I cook a chicken?
ma-ka-ka fu ni-sz-na-ḋe ri?	Shall I cook the guinea-fowl which you shot?

Note: In the replies to these questions there is no **ka** (whereas Logo imperatives would contain **ko**):

ango be-thi-dyi.	Sing a dancing-song (sg. and plural).
ari o.	Cook a chicken.
o, ari-r.	Yes, cook one.
o, ari ḋi.	Yes, cook it.

njati ni-vi cembu, aba-ni ka ni 'bi. If you lose the sheep, your father will beat you.

njati mgba dzzdzz, ma-ka tsz-ba 'bu nzi ndi-tho. If the child cries, I shall not give cow-milk to him.

njati mgba dzz nza, ma-ka tsz-ba 'bu ndi-tho. If the child does not cry, I shall give cow-milk to him.

ato calungi, ma-ka-ka nza ni nja nde. Go far off, where I cannot see you.

118. It is often combined with **ve**.

Definite construction:

(vb. = *nji*) *ni-dza ndrrtszja dhe-'blo; ni-ka-ve-r nji mgba?* Your cow is dead; what will you do?

ma-ka-ve nja ritsz nji nzi. I shall do nothing.

ma-dza ndrrtszja dhe-'blo; ma-ka-ve-r nji mgba? My cow is dead; what shall I do?

(vb. = *nzz*) *ni-ka-ve nzz roba nzi, ḋi-dza dhi-tha tho?* Won't you see the medicine-man about its death?

(vb. = *si*) *ke ka-na-ve si iga bu? o, ke ka-ve si nio.* Will he arrive here to-morrow? Yes, he will.

(vb. = 1st *nji*; 2nd *nji* = sb.) *ni-ka-ve nji nji pi tho nju inga bu?* Will you work for the chief to-day or to-morrow?

ma-ka-ve nji nji ke-tho bu; nju ma-ka ma-ro nga cu. I'll work for him to-morrow; to-day I shall rest.

Compare the following with § 117.

(vb = *'bu*) *njati mgba dzz-ngue, ma-ka-ve 'bu-ngue tsz-ba ndi-tho nza.* If the child had cried, I should not have given cow-milk to him.

njati mgba dzz-ngue nza, ma-ka-ve 'bu-ngue tsz-ba ndi-tho. If the child had not cried, I would have given cow-milk to him.

li, 'ba (to leave), **'bu** (to give). Causative auxiliaries.

119. There is insufficient data to distinguish between these causative auxiliaries. **li** probably implies forcing, and **'ba** and **'bu** allowing or permitting:

nzi ni-'ba tsi li-r tsz nyi-r. Don't let the dog make the cattle run.

bwetszmgba ḍa mbu. ma-li bwetszmgba zho ḍa. The boy is drinking water. I make the boy drink water.

mgba ba nju. mgbai 'bu ba mgba nju. The baby sucks milk (or the breast). The mother suckles the baby.

alir ndru ku guna. Make the men sit down.

na

120. Only a few instances of this particle are to hand, where it seems to have a future significance, as in Moru (Part I, § 628).

ke ka-na-ve si iga bu? Will he arrive here to-morrow?
ma-ka-na-di ngo nzi? May I sing?[1]
ko-ka-na-di ngo nzi? May we sing?[1]

ra (to go)

121. This auxiliary is reminiscent of Moroändri **ro** and Logo **dre**, but in Lendu it seems to confine itself to sentences implying habitual action only. It is used with the Indefinite form:

kpa ka-ra aḍu nji?   *kpa ra tsz tso 'ya.*
What do the men do?   The men herd cattle.

nzo ka-ra aḍu mbu?   *nzo ra tsz-ba mbu.*
What do children drink?   Children drink milk.

nzo ka-ra wa mbu?   *nzi, nzo ra wa mbu nzi.*
Do children drink beer?   No, children do not drink beer.

bwetsimgba ra ḍoḍo nzz.   The boy sleeps every day.

The syllabic **r** in the following sentence is probably a form of this auxiliary:

tszkpar rr nyinyi.   The cattle are running.

u (to go)

122. Whether this is a genuine auxiliary of present progressive time or not, cannot be determined at this point:

ni-u nza bi pi tho, ka? nzi, ma-u nza bi pi tho nzi; ma-u nza bi aba tho. Are you hoeing the field for the chief? No, I am not hoeing for the chief, I am hoeing for my father.[2]

123. ve. See under ka, § 118.

CHAPTER IX

VERBAL POSTPOSITIONS

124. As in the Moru-Madi languages, these are very numerous, and are found mostly in the Definite Aspect. Some of the forms, in different contexts, are capable of functioning as independent verbs. In such cases the English equivalent of such verbs will be shown in brackets.

---

[1] These sentences seem to be negatively expressed. Probable translation should be, 'mayn't I sing?'

[2] The sentences could be translated equally well: 'Are you *going* to hoe the field for the chief?' &c.

'blo

125. This seems the most common postposition for past time, and it is probably related to Lugbara **'bo**. It indicates completed action:

ni-ka-si ni-dza nji 'blo? Have you finished your work?
ma-dza ndrrtszja dhe-'blo. My cow is dead (i.e. has just died).
ni-dza tsi ka mgbaga? ďi dhe-'blo. Where is your dog? Dead.
za ka mgbaga? ďi le-a-'blo. Where is the meat? It is eaten.

ndrrtszja go-'blo. The cow gave birth.
iszle go-'blo. The women gave birth.
ma-go-'blo. I gave birth.

It may be used after **ngue** to indicate state entered upon:

ke ra-ngue ďa zho 'blo. He has gone to drink water.
ndrrtszkalu le-go-ngue-'blo kpajo. A calf has just been born.

de

126. This postposition is used with the verb in the Indefinite aspect, and carries with it the same 'purpose' implication of **dro** and **ro** in MORU-MADI. (See Part I, § 595 et seq.):

ni-ka shinga ko-de. That ye might have life.
ko-ka-ka dzz-dzz mgbaga ro, i ndru ka-nyo-de? Whence shall we buy bread, that these may eat?
ndima ka-ve ke 'bu Pi tho de. That they might present him to the Lord.

mgba

127. This postposition seems to be used only in affirmative answers to questions.

ni-ka-nja ajo nzz nza? o, ma-nja ke mgba. Did[1] you see my brother yesterday? Yes, I saw him.
ni-ka-nja motokar calu? o, ma-nja-r mgba. Do you see a motor-car over there? Yes, I see one.
ni-ka-ka-mgba ni-nja motokar calu? o, ma-ka-mgba. Can you see a motor-car over there? Yes, I can.
ni-a-ďo-mgba? ma-ďo-mgba. Have you slept? I have (greeting).
dicu ma-cu ni mgba. But I know you.

nga

128. This is a negative postposition used only with the verb to be, **ku**. In some respects it is the negative counterpart of **ni**; see § 132. Alone, it means 'no':

í mba kù blɔ̃ ṅga, ku tʃê. This child is not good, (he) is bad.
ma-dza ndrrtszja ku nga. I have no cow (lit. my cow is not).
nokpa dza ndrrtszjakpar ku nga. The slave has no cattle.
ni-dza vi ku nga. You have no brains.
ke ku nga bwetsike; ndi ku iszle. That is not a man; it is a woman.
njegu ka-ku bo? nga, njegu ku bo nga. Is a digdig big? No, it is not big.

Note also:

nga-nyo-ndru (the blind (lit. without-eyes-people)).

---

[1] (?)Didn't you see . . .

ngue (= to be)

129. This postposition may best be described as indicating present state entered upon as the result of past action. It is used mostly with intransitive and passive verbs.

Intransitive:

*ko-si-**ngue** ko-ba na ro.* We (have) come from home.
*ke ra-**ngue** ďa zho 'blo.* He has gone to drink water.
*pi po-**ngue**-r:* The chief said:
*meri tu-**ngue** nzz i-ga.* The boat left here yesterday.
*dhedhe na ke **ngue** ma-jo.* The man who died was my brother (lit. die-die *na* man *ngue* my-brother).

Passive:

*ke le'bi-**ngue**.* He has been beaten.
ndrrtszkalu⎫
mgba   ⎬ *lego-**ngue**-'blo.* The calf⎫
ma   ⎭   The child⎬ was born.
                                   I   ⎭
ma-ve por za dzz-nge¹ tso-na-nyamu. My sister says the meat was taken by a wild-cat.
*aba por ndi po kali, ke ďu-**ngue** ndi ndiro.* My father says she is lying, she took it herself.
*ma-gbogbo furiro ma-jo ke ti sz-**ngue** ro.* I'm laughing because my brother has been stung by a bee.

130. It is, however, not uncommon with active verbs:

*ma-hwa-**ngue** ru.* I folded the cloth.
*ma-tha-**ngue** ru.* I tore the cloth.
*laka ka-**ngue** ma-tho-'bi-li.* A mouse bit my finger.
*bwetsike to-**ngue** to ma-ko 'ju na.* The man stabbed my leg with a knife.
*ni-ri-**ngue** akpa-ni tho?* Have you cooked for your husband?
*i-ke hwi-**ngue** ndi ndiro.* The man killed himself.
*aro kpa ce-**ngue** ndima.* The two men stabbed each other.
*ďi-ke ce-'blo; bwetszmgba ce-**ngue** fu-le.* The man woke up; the boy woke him up.

131. It is very much used in impossible condition sentences:

*njati ni-vi-**ngue** cembu, aba-ni 'bi-**ngue** ni.* If you had lost the sheep your father would have beaten you.
*njati ni-zho-**ngue** fu tsu, ni-dhe-**ngue** dhe.* If you had drunk that medicine you would have died.
*njati ni-ra-**ngue** fulu, ni-**ngue** hwini . . . dhini.* If you had gone there you would have been killed . . . beaten.

ni

132. This postposition, which also seems to indicate state entered upon, occurs usually after the verb to be '**ku**', and after verbs with passive implication.

With verb to be: . . . (ká-)ku-**nî**.

*ma-dza ndrrtszja ku-**ni**.* I have a cow (lit. my cow is *ni*).
*pi dza ndrrtszjakpar ku-**ni**.* The chief has cattle.
*ni-ku-**ni**? ma-ku-**ni**.* Are you present? I am (greeting).
*nga-lele na nar ku ke-tho na **ni**.* Whose fan is in his hand.

¹ (?)*ngue.*

VERBAL POSTPOSITIONS

In the passive construction, note that the passive prefix **le-** is lacking (cf. § 107).

*liti nji-**ni** Logo tho koi tho.* Charcoal is used by the Logo for smoking.
*njati ni-ra fulu, ni-ka-hwi-**ni** ... dhi-**ni**.* If you go there you will be killed ... beaten.
*njati ni-ra-ngue fulu, ni-ngue hwi-**ni** ... dhi-**ni**.* If you had gone there you would have been killed ... beaten.
*ni-dza semisi tha-**ni** tha.* Your shirt ('chemise') is torn.
*ni-dza semisi ḋri-**ni** vi.* „   „   „   „ tattered.

Examples with active verbs:
*ko-ka-ve hwi-**ni**.* We shall kill each other.
*Yesu dza nyoyu nya-ngue-**ni** nya.* Jesus' wisdom increased.
*dicu ma-jolu si na kpakpangaba si-**ni**.* But one cometh (vb. = *si*) mightier than I.
*ke tu-ngue-**ni** ke-ro ro nji.* He departed from him for a season.

nzá

133. This is the negative particle for the Definite construction, and usually occurs finally in a phrase, although it may occasionally be followed by the object or another postposition. (It corresponds in function to the **ko** or **ku** of Moru-Madi.[1]) It may be used alone, signifying 'no':

*má-tra Lógo **nzá**.* I do not speak Logo.
*má-'bí mgba **nzá**.* I am not beating (didn't beat) the child.
*ma-zhi **nza** nza-nga-o-tha.* I do not like hoeing.
***nza**, ma-nja-r **nza**.* No, I don't see one.
***nza**, ma-ka **nza**.* No, I cannot (see it).
*ma-hwi e ditsz **nza**.* I didn't kill a thing.
*ma-zi bo 'ju **nza**.* I don't want a big knife.
*ma-ḋe si nji **nza** go.* I haven't (yet) finished the work.

nzi

134. This is the negative particle for the Indefinite construction, and it occurs finally in a phrase. It may be used alone, however, signifying 'no':

(vb. = *nji*) *ma-ka-ve nja ritsz nji **nzi**.* I shall not do anything.
(vb. = *nzz*) *ni-ka-ve nzz roba **nzi**, ḋi-dza dhi-tha tho?* Won't you see the witch-doctor, about its death?
(vb. = *si*) ***nzi**, ndi ka-ve si iga bu **nzi**.* No, he won't arrive here to-morrow.
(vb. = *ri*) *ni-ka za ri?* ***nzi**, ma za ri zi,*[2] *ma 'be ri.* Are you cooking meat? No, I am not cooking meat, I'm cooking fish.
ni-ḋoḋo? ***nzi**, ma-ḋoḋo **nzi**, ma-i pa.* Are you asleep? No, I'm not asleep, I'm just lying down.

135. It is also used initially in a phrase when negativing the Imperative.[3] The 2nd person pronoun may precede the verb here:

$\left.\begin{array}{l}ma\\ko\end{array}\right\}$ *-ka-na di ngo nzi?* ***nzi**, **nzi** ngo-r!* $\left.\begin{array}{l}\text{May I}\\ \text{May we}\end{array}\right\}$ (not?) sing? No, don't sing!

***nzi** ni-bi nza aba-ni tho, a-bi nza pi tho.* Don't hoe the field for your father, hoe the field for the chief.
***nzi** ni-'ba tsi lir tsz nyir.* Don't let the dog make the cattle run.

---
[1] Phonetically, it corresponds to the negative particle **nja** of Bongo-Baka.
[2] (?)*nzi*.
[3] According to my notes, the vowel in the negative imperative particle is -ɛ: *ndzέ dzὲ*. Don't cry.

o[1]

136. This postposition seems to be used in affirmative answers to questions:
mí-'bi mgbá? má-'bí mgba ɔ. Are you beating the child? I am.

ri

137. This postposition seems to be used only in questions and their answers. (Cf. **ni** in Moru, Part I, § 617.)
ďi ka ie a-ri? tsi a-ri. Who ate it? The dog ate it.

ro

138. One of the functions of this particle is to indicate subordinate adverbial clauses:
ma-gbogbo furiro ma-jo ke ti sz-ngue-ro. I'm laughing because my brother has been stung by a bee.
adi tsztsz-ro, aba ďo-'blo-ro. Sit still, (for) father is sleeping.
njati ni-zho fu tsu ro, ni-ka-ve-dhe. If you drink that medicine you will die.
dicu-ni ma-si-ro. While I am coming.
mgba Yesu nja-ngue ke i ro . . . When Jesus saw him lie . . .
ko-ka-ka dzz-dzz mgbaga ro? Whence shall we buy bread?

139. In the following examples **ro** seems to be an adverbial or predicative formative:
adi tsztsz-ro. Sit still.
furi-ro (because).
kɔ̀-kù ndru, kɔ-ku ngá tsɪ-rɪ̀ (or rɔ̀). We are people, we are not dogs.
ni Pontio Pilato ngue Yudaya dzzjo pija-ro. Pontius Pilate being governor of Judaea.

te

140. This postposition occurs only after **ka** when it implies obligation:
pi po-nguer ma-ka 'bu tsz dre te. The chief said I must pay ten cows.
zha por . . . aba ka ke 'bi te. My mother says my father must beat him.

CHAPTER X
PREDICATIVE CONSTRUCTIONS

141. As in Moru-Madi, non-verbal predication may be affected largely by *juxtaposition*:
í kaka búkù. It (is) a red book.

142. In questions the interrogative auxiliary may be used in the same way as it is used before verbs. (See § 113.)
za ka mgbaga?   Where is the meat?
ni-dza tsi ka mgbaga?   Where is your dog?

Verbs to be

143. The verb **ku** (= to be) is very much in use, both for predication implying existence in space and for other kinds of predication.
Noun complement:
aba ku 'Bale, zha ku Logo. My father is a Lendu, my mother is a Logo.
fu ke ku lathike. That man is a warrior.
fu kpa ku lathikpa. Those men are warriors.

[1] Phonetically: ɔ.

PREDICATIVE CONSTRUCTIONS 413

Adjectival complement:
zho ka-ku bo? Is an elephant big?
oro, ďi ku bo. Yes it is big.
ma-nyo **ku** blo. My eyes are good.
í mgba **kù** blɔ̃. This child is good.
tsɪ **kù** tʃɛ̂. The dog is bad.
aba ku kpakpa, zha ku belebele. My father is strong, my mother is weak.
njegu ka-ku titi? Is a digdig black?
i búku **ku** kàkà. This book is red.

Adverbial complement:
aba ku nzagu na. My father is in the field.
zha ku adza. My mother is at home.
rasu ku ďa na. There is a crocodile in the river.
ma-ku tho na. I am angry (lit. with anger).

144. The verb to be may also be used in sentences describing possession:
ma-dza ndrrtszja ku-ni. I have a cow (lit. my cow is).
pi dza ndrrtszjakpar ku-ni. The chief has cattle.

145. The verb **ngue** (= to be) is used mostly in existential predication:
nde bo tsokpa ngue fuga ni. Now there was much grass in the place.
ni Pontio Pilato ngue Yudaya dzzjo pija-ro.[1] Pontius Pilate being governor of Judaea.

Predicative particle e

146. This particle is strongly reminiscent of the Moru-Madi suffix ɪ (Part I, § 719), except that it *precedes* the complement:
fu ni-sz na za ka-ku bo inga karno? ďi e karno. Was the animal you shot big or little? It was little.

147. It is sometimes used to introduce an object (cf. Part I, § 720). This usually happens in describing past action:
ni-ka-nji aďu butso? What were you doing this morning?
ma-u e hwi. I was grinding corn.
ni-ka-u e aďu butso? What were you *grinding* this morning?
ma-u e hwi. I was grinding corn.
ni-ka-hwi e aďu butso? What did you kill this morning?
ma-hwi e ditsz nza. I killed nothing.
ma-hwi e zha. I killed a bush-buck.
ni-ka-nja e ie a'ba? Whom did you see at the village?
ma-nja e ngo-ke cu dicukpa. I saw only one old man.
ni-ka-we e zha-kpa-ka? Have you taken off the buck's skin?

Negative predicative

148. The negative of the verb to be (ku) is effected by means of the postposition **nga**.

Noun complement:
ke ku nga bwetsike, ndi ku iszle. That is not a man, it is a woman.
kpa ku nga lathikpa, kpa ku jojukpa. Those are not warriors, they are smiths.
kɔ̀-**kù** ndru, kɔ-**ku** ngá tsɪ-rɔ̀ (or-rɨ̀).[1] We are people, we are not dogs.

[1] Note predicative suffix **ro**. Cf. Part I, § 723.

Adjective complement:

í mgba **kù** blɔ̃ **ṅga, ku** tʃê. This child is not good, he is bad.
*nga, njegu **ku** titi **nga**, d̃i ku uzar.* No, a digdig is not black, it is grey.

Negative possession:

*ma-dza ndrrtszja **ku nga**.* I have no cow (lit. my cow is not).
*nokpa dza ndrrtszjakpar **ku nga**.* The slave has no cattle.
*ni-dza vi **ku nga**.* You have no brains.

Predicative of comparison

149. The forms **didi ... tsz**, and **sisi ... jolu**, are used with the predicative to show equality and superiority respectively:

*ba **ka-ku** bo **didi** njei **tsz**?* Is a cob as big as a water-buck?
*nga, njei **sisi** ba **jolu**.* No, a water-buck is bigger than a cob.
*di **sisi** aro ndru **jolu**.* More than two people.

Compare also:

didi *ma-rr-ri bai ma-lo* **di**. As I hear I judge.

CHAPTER XI

ADVERBS AND CONJUNCTIONS

150. As in Moru-Madi, adverbs and adverbial expressions may be built up from forms which, in other contexts, function as nouns, verbs, adjectives, &c.

Adverbs from nominal or pronominal forms:

*ato **i-ga*** (ma-kuso). Stand here, next to me.
*ato **fu-ga*** (ke-kuso). Stand there, next to him.
*ato **ca-ga**.* Stand over yonder.
*ato **ca-lungi**, ma-ka-ka nza ni nja nde.* Stand right over there where I can't see you.
*nde bo tsokpa ngue **fuga** ni.* Now there was much grass in the place.
*angu **alo-ti**.* Come back.
*fu lokpa **go-ti**.* After these things.
ru-na (up); ***gu-na*** or ***dzz-jo*** (down); ***kpa-jo*** (now).
*ní-ra **mgba-ga**?* Where are you going?
*ni-ka-r u **mgba-cu**?* How can ye believe?
mgba-bu (how?) ***mgba-nga-ba*** (when?)
ad̃u-ro and ***ad̃u-jo*** (why?)
*njati ni-ra **fu-lu** ...* If you go there ...
*njei sisi ba **jo-lu**.* A water-buck is bigger than a cob.
*ara **zhu-lu**.* Come here. ***ca-lu*** (yonder).
*angu **a-lu-ti**.* Come back. (Cf. *a-lu-ti a-dza.* Behind the hut.)
(Cf. postposition in: *kpa ra ma-**ulu-di**.* They follow me.)

Adverbs from verbal forms:

*adi **tsztsz-ro**.* Sit still.

ADVERBS AND CONJUNCTIONS

151. Many forms are capable of acting both as adverbs and conjunctions:

fu-r-bai (thus)   *fu-ri-ro* (because, therefore)
fu-lo-jo
fu-lo-tho } (therefore)   *fu-r-go-ti* (after this)

As Adverb:

*ditho le-co-ngue ma **fu-lo-tho**.* For therefore am I sent.
*ni-dza tsi ka **mgba-ga**?* Where is your dog?

As Conjunction:

*ma-gbogbo **furiro** majo ke ti sz-ngue ro.* I'm laughing because my brother was stung by a bee.
*pi po-nguer: 'ma-ku tho na, **furiro** ni-ku kalithike.'* The chief said: 'I am angry because you are a liar.'
***furiro** iszle 'ba-ngue ndi-dza danju.* Then the woman left her water-pot.
***furiro** ma-po-nguer ni-tho . . .* I said therefore unto you . . .
***furiro** mgba Yesu cunguer ndiro . . .* When Jesus therefore perceived . . .

152. There are other forms which do not seem to be derived from nominal or verbal roots, and which may also act as adverbs or conjunctions (and often as both). Owing to lack of material, these forms are treated here very superficially.

153. cu, dicu

As Adverb:

*ma-ka-ve nji nji ke-tho bu; nju ma-ka ma-ronga **cu**.* I shall work for him to-morrow; to-day I shall just rest.
*ma-nja e ngo ke **cu dicu**-kpa.* I saw only one old man.

As Conjunction:

*zha por ke ku dhe-na nga, **dicu** vi **cu** dhe.* My mother says he is not sick, but only lazy.
*ndi ka-ve si iga bu nzi, **dicu** nja-na-nga.* He won't arrive here to-morrow, but the day after.

154. inga

*ni-ka-ve nji nji pi tho nju **inga** bu?* Are you going to work for the chief to-day or to-morrow?
*fu ni-sz na za ka-ku bo **inga** karno?* Was the animal you shot big or little?

nde

155. This particle is used throughout the Lendu Gospel to translate 'and then', 'thereupon', &c. It seems to have a narrative significance:

***nde** kpa po-nguer: . . .* and they said: . . .
***nde** bo tsokpa ngue fuga ni.* Now there was much grass in this place.
***nde** furgoti kpa ne-nguer ndima ka ke lo.* Then they sought to take him.
***nde** kpa thu-nguer ke-tso . . .* Then they asked him . . .

Whether the final particle in the following sentence is the same as the above, cannot be said at this stage:

*ato calungi, ma-ka-ka nza ni nja **nde**.* Stand far away, where I cannot see you.

pa

156. Whether this is a postposition or an adverb is yet to be determined:

*ni-ka aḍu nji? ma-didi **pa**. ma-bibi **pa**.* What are you doing? I'm just sitting. I'm just walking.

*ni-ḍoḍo? nzi, ma-ḍoḍo nzi, ma-i **pa**.* Are you asleep? No, I'm not asleep, I'm just lying down.

CHAPTER XII

SPECIMEN TEXT

157. Extract from the New Testament (John vi. 5–13):

(The miracle of the loaves and the fishes)

5. *Furiro mgba Yesu mgbengue ndinyo aronaro, nde ke njanguerni bo*
   Then when Jesus lifted his-eyes up, and he saw many
ndrukpar ngusi ndinanga naro, nde ke ponguer Pilipo tho: 'Kokaka dzzdzz
   people return-come him-unto, then he said Philip to: 'We-shall buy
mgbaga ro, i ndru kanyode?' 6. *Ke ponguer fu lo kethi dza mbuthatho*
   how, these people may-eat?' He said this word his of proving
ḍitho,[1] ke ndiro cungue ndi kanji na ritsz mgbar tho. 7. *Pilipo ngungue*
   for, he himself knew he would-do (rel.) thing what. Philip replied
lo ketho: 'Faranka mia aro na ledzz na ledzz
   word him-to: 'Pennies hundred two (rel.) is bought (rel.) is bought (i.e. that
                                        ka-ka ndru tho nzi, ndiro
   which is bought for two hundred pence) will-be-sufficient people for not, he
kru ndi kru kar lo ninima de.' 8. *Ke*
   every he every (i.e. each one) can take a little.' A certain
gotiranadike,[2] Andareya, Simona Petero jo, ponguer ketho: 9. *"Di*
   disciple, Andrew, Simon Peter's brother, said him-to: 'One
zadake ku iga ni, cu ndidza blu le blu tso na dzz ku mbu ni, dijo[3] 'be[4]
   boy is here, who his loaves(?) grass-earth (barley?) are five, and fish
ku aro di[3]: dicu fur ka-ku mgba ritsz birobiro i ndru kana?'
   are two: but these (things) are what thing many these people among?'
10. *Nde Yesu ponguer: 'Alir ndru ku guna.' Nde bo tsokpa ngue*
    Then Jesus said: 'Make people be on-ground.' Now much grass was
fuga ni. Nde fu ndru kungue guna, kpa ngue inga elfu mbu nanga tsz.
   there. And those people sat down, they were or thousand five about (?)
11. *Nde Yesu longue fu dzz, mgba ke 'bungue mersi Mungu tho 'blo-ro, ke*
    And Jesus took that food, when he gave thanks God to, he

---

[1] *ditho* (?)
[2] Lit. after-come-*na*-that-person (rel. form; see § 74).
[3] *ḍijo* (?) *ḍi* (?)
[4] *be* (?)

SPECIMEN TEXT

ndonguer legotiranakpa tholu, nde legotiranakpa ndonguer guna kungue na
distributed disciples to, and disciples distributed down seated (rel.)
ndru tho. 12. *Mgba ndru oliro, ke ponguer ndigotiranakpa tho:*
people to. When people were-filled, he said his-disciples to:
'*Aso kekeni dzz gumar, nzi dicukpa ritszro ma kaviviro.*'
'Gather fragments (of) food up, not mere (-things) things shall-escape.'
13. *Furiro kpa songuer, nde kpa lingue yo dre-ndijo-aro-na fu kekeni*
Therefore they gathered, and they filled baskets twelve those fragments
na mbu ngue na dzz
(rel.) five were (rel.) food (i.e. food fragments which remained of the five loaves)
guma mgba nyonguer na kpa tho rori.
above what ate (rel.) people unto.

POSTSCRIPT

158. Father L. Hertsens' excellent monograph on the phonetics of Lendu[1] only appeared when the present work was in the press. Consequently only passing reference can be given to it here, but the reader is advised to study it in conjunction with this work. Certain points of interest may be noted here, however.

Vowels.

159. The author distinguishes three sorts of **i**-sound (two of them being retracted) and four sorts of **u**-sound (two of them being unrounded). His retracted **i**-sounds correspond in the main to ɪ in the present work, but his distribution of rounded and unrounded **u**-sounds does not correspond to that found here.

The distribution of **o** and **ɔ** corresponds with that given here, but not always the distribution of **e** and **ɛ**. Compare:

ke (he) with kɛ; *tʃɛ* (bad) with tʃê.

The vowels **e** and **a** have centralized varieties not noticed by the present writer. Compare:

dzə (tear) with dzz; *dzə* (earth) with dzz.

In the second syllable of *da:dha* (smoke), he notes a centralized vowel of a different sort.

Consonants.

160. The most outstanding divergence of the author's consonant system from that given here is that in the former a sharp distinction is made between normal and 'ejective' explosives (both unvoiced and voiced), but no distinction is made between explosive and implosive voiced consonants. Note the following examples, compared with words from the present work where available:

	Normal	*Ejective*
Unvoiced consonants:		
	pɪ (to press)	*p'ɪ* (greatly)
	pu[2] (to flower)	*p'u*[2] (to reject)
	ta (to tear)	*t'a* (to burst)

[1] 'Quelques notes sur la phonétique lendu' (*Africa*, vol. xiii, no. 3).   [2] Fronted **u**.

Voiced consonants:

bɔ: (big)	cp. bɔ	*b'a* (to leave)	cp. 'ba
bi[1] (ear)	cp. bi	*b'i*[1] (egg)	
bu (to give)	cp. 'bu		
da: (water)	cp. 'da	*d'ɔ* (to pour)	
da (to smoke)	cp. 'dá	*d'u* (to steal)	
ḍi (guinea-fowl)	cp. 'dei	*d'i*[1] (equal)	
dyi (sun)	cp. 'jí	*'yo* (rat)	
gbɪ (to knock)		*gb'ɪ* (to knock)	cp. 'bi (to slap)

161. Less important points are:

He describes *th* and *dh* as interdental *explosives* and not as *fricatives*, and warns his readers not to confuse the sounds with *th* in English.

He describes as a velar fricative (**x**) the sound represented by Litchman by the letter *h*.

He distinguishes two **w**-sounds, one being fronted.

He notes syllabic **l** as well as syllabic **r**, but does not mention syllabic **z**. (Words containing syllabic **z** in the present work have the vowels *i* or *ə* with him.)

In other respects the two systems agree.

Orthography.

162. At the end of his article the author suggests a practical alphabet for Lendu which may well be compared with that suggested here:

Hertsens: a e i o u ü b b'   p p' d d'   dy t t' dh th k g kp gb gb'
Present work: a e i o u   b   'b p   d   'd   'j t   dh th k g kp gb

Hertsens: dz ts ch dj m n ny l ll r rr   s z   sh j   x h w y
Present work: dz ts c   j m n ny l   r rr f v s z zz sh zh   h   w y

[1] Retracted **i**.

TRIBAL AND HISTORICAL INDEX

(Preface, Chapters I–III of Introduction)

Aba, 4, 5, 18 & n.
Ababua (Babua), 21, 23, 24, 27, 28, 31.
Abadule, 28.
Abagwa, 23.
Abambia, 25.
Abandia (Abandya, Bandiya), 17, 23, 24, 29, 30, 31, 50, 52.
Abangwinda, 23 & n., 28, 30.
Abarambo (Barambo), 17 & n., 23, 26, 27, 29, 30, 31.
Abare (Bare), 15, 47; *see also* Belanda.
Abaza (Baza), 23, 31.
Abd-el-Samath, 32.
Abèlè, 23, 27, 29, 31.
Aboguru (Bukuru, Babuckur), 10, 17 & n., 23, 28, 30, 32, 37, 41 n.
Abokaya, *see* Avukaya.
Abomo, 54.
Abonga, Chief, 39.
Abou Semen, 14.
Abuku, R., 5.
Abwaya, *see* Kreish.
Abyssinia, vii, 24, 25, 35.
Acholi, vii, 22, 25, 26, 35 n., 37, 38, 39.
Adio (Makaraka), 16, 17, 23, 27, 28, 30, 31, 37, 39, 41.
Adjenge, *see* Dinka.
Africa Inland Mission, x n., xii.
Agabu, 30, 50.
Agambi (Logo), 5, 37, 38.
Agamoro, 4.
Agangwa, Chief, 3, 4.
Agar (Dinka), 10.
Aiivu (Madi), 7.
Aija, R., 41.
Aja, 11, 14.
Ajigo (Avukaya), 4.
Aka (Pygmy), 23.
Aka, R., 17, 36, 37, 41.
Akare, 23, 25, 28, 31.
Akbwambi, 23.
Akbwaya (Baya), *see* Kreish.
Albert, L., 8 & n., 26, 34, 37.
Alingi, *see* Kreish.
Alulu, *see* Alur.
Aluma, Chief, 5.
Alur, 5 & n., 7 n., 8, 21, 26 & n., 38, 39.
Amadi (Madyo, Amago, Aogo), 16 n., 17, 23, 26, 27 & n., 29, 30, 31, 37, 41.
Amadi, District or town (Southern Sudan), viii, 3, 4, 8, 9, 10, 16, 22, 34, 36, 37, 38, 39.
Amadi, District or town (Belgian Congo), 15, 16, 25, 27 n.
Amago, *see* Amadi.
Ambadi, L., 47.
Ambia, R., 5.
Ambomu, *see* Mbomu.

Am Dina (Kouka), 14.
Angada, 23, 27, 29, 31.
Ankole, 25.
Anunga, *see* Nunga.
Aogo, *see* Amadi.
Aoro, *see* Kreish.
Aouk, R., 11, 12.
Apambia (Pambia), 17 & n., 25, 30, 31, 49, 54.
Api, R., 17, 27.
Arabi Pasha, 34.
Arabs, 22, 23, 24, 29, 30, 31, 32 & n., 35, 40.
Arkell, A. J., 11 n.
Aro, R. (Aru), 5 n., 6 n.
Arua, 6.
Aruwimi, R., 25, 28.
Asa, R., 25, 27.
Ashton, Mrs. E. O., xiv.
Aswa, R., 7 n.
Atogbo, *see* Kreish.
Attiak, 22.
Atwa, R., 9 n.
Atwot, 10.
Aungba, 5.
Auro, 23, 27, 29, 31.
Avongara (Avungara), 17, 24, 28, 29, 31, 37, 38, 41, 52, 54.
Avukaya, viii, 4, 6, 8, 22; *see also* Ojila, Ojigä, Ajigo.
Avungara, *see* Avongara.
Ayak, 32.
Ayuru clan, 5.
Azande, *see* Zande.
Azenge, *see* Dinka.

'Baadha, *see* Lendu.
Babalia, 11, 13, 45.
Babiker, Chief, 18, 52.
Babira, 21.
Babua, *see* Ababua.
Babuckur, Babukur, *see* Aboguru.
Bafuka, Chief, 30.
Baganda, 25 n., 36.
Bagirmi, vii, viii, ix, 8, 12 & n., 14, 19, 29 n., 41, 42, 43.
Bagpwa, Hill, 5 n.
Baguirmi, *see* Bagirmi.
Bahima, 24.
Bahr el Arab, 26, 52.
Bahr el Ghazal (Southern Sudan; river and province), vii, viii & n., 18 n., 26, 30, 31, 32, 33, 34, 41, 44, 46 & n., 48, 49, 50, 53.
Bahr el Ghazal (Lake Tchad; river and province), 42 & n., 45.
Bahr el Jebel, *see* Nile.
Bai (Belanda clan), 15 n.; *see also* Belanda.
Bai, 15, 48, 49, 50, 51.
Baï, Sara (Mbaï), 11, 15 n., 45.

TRIBAL AND HISTORICAL INDEX

Baka, vii, viii, ix, 4, 8, 9, 14, 18 & n., 19, 20, 22, 26, 27 & n., 28, 30, 36, 37, 39, 41 & n., 54.
Bakango, 16 n.
Baker, Sir Samuel, 33.
Bakinda, Chief, 9.
Bakumu, 21.
Balambo, 53.
'Bale, see Lendu.
'Baledha, see Lendu.
'Balendru, see Lendu.
'Bälimbä, 4.
Bamanga, 21.
Bambili, 16.
Bamboy (Bomboi), 17, 28.
Ba Mingui, 12.
Bamingui, R., 53.
Bamvurugba, Chief, 31, 47.
Banda, ix, xii, 11, 17, 19, 20, 24, 29, 42, 50, 52 & n., 53.
Banda (Amadi), 27.
Bandas Vito Umbili, Chief, 50.
Bandiya, see Abandia.
Bandjia, see Abandia.
Bangassou, Bangaso, 17, 29, 32.
Bangba, 16, 18 n., 23, 26 n., 30, 31, 36, 54.
Bangenze, Mt., 36.
Bangoran, R., 53.
Bangui, 15, 53.
Bantu, 17 n., 23, 24, 25, 27, 28, 31.
Banwanda, see Auro.
Banyikondo, Chief, 47.
Banza, 27.
Banziri, 20.
Barain, 13, 44.
Barambo, see Abarambo.
Bare, see Abare.
Bari (Bai), see Bai.
Bari (Nilo-Hamitic), vii, 5 n., 7, 8, 15 n., 25 n., 37.
Bari-Logo, 5 & n., 15 n., 23, 25 & n.
Barma (Bârma), 11, 13, 14, 42, 45; see also Bagirmi.
Barth, Dr. H., xiv, 11 n., 12, 14.
Barumbi, 21.
Basili Mopwaya, see Kreish.
Basiri, see Sere.
Bate, Chief, 27.
Batutsi, 24.
Bay, Rev. Fr., xiii.
Bayoko, Chief, 30.
Baza, see Abaza.
Bazimbi, Chief, 30.
Beden, 38.
Beir, viii.
Belanda (Abare, Bare), viii, 15, 20, 26, 32, 46, 47, 48; see also Biri & Bor.
'Beli (Rumbek Jur), xiii, 10, 14, 41.
Bere, 18, 26 n., 36.
Bere, R., 18.
Berri, see Böri.
Bertrand, Col., 23.
Bethell, D. J., xi, xiii, 11 n., 18 n., 19, 20, 52.
Bidio, 13.
Bigbi, Chief, 41.

Biki, 13.
Bile, 17.
Bili, Chief, 30.
Bima, R., 16 & n., 17, 41.
Binga, 11, 54.
Birguid Kirdi, 13.
Biri (Bviri, Mve Gumba, Gamba); see also Belanda, 15, 20, 46, 47, 48, 50, 51.
Biri, R., 19.
Birri, 17, 25, 31.
Biselli, 49.
Biti (Moro), 9.
Bo, R., 8, 46, 47, 48, 51.
Bobali, 21.
Bodama, 27.
Bodho, see Dombo.
Bodo, 27, 53.
Bodue, see Gbudwe.
Bogwa, Chief, 30, 31.
Boko, 18, 52.
Bokoio, Bokoyo, Chief, 39.
Boku, R., 15, 27, 31, 49, 51.
Böliba, see 'Bälimbä.
Bomboi, see Bamboy.
Bomokandi, R., 16 & n., 18, 28, 29, 30.
Bomu, R., see Mbomu.
de Bonchamps, 35.
Bonvalet, Capt., 30.
Bondo, 17.
Bongo, vii, viii, ix, 4, 8, 9, 10, 12, 14, 15, 19, 20, 21, 22, 24, 26, 32, 33, 40, 41 & n., 51, 54.
Bongo (Banda), 53.
Bor (Mve Rodi, Mberidi), 15, 31, 46, 47, 48, 51.
Bora, 5.
Böri (Berri), 5, 8.
Bornu, 42, 43.
Boro, R., 18, 52.
Boruba, see Bamvurugba.
Bosé, 27.
Bote, 28.
Boua-Kara, 13.
Boubou, 20.
Boulala, see Bulala.
Bousso, 13.
Brazzaville, 34.
Broadbent, P. B., xiii, 11 n.
Brock, Major R. G. C., x.
Brown, Major L. N. F., xi, xii, 4 n., 9.
Budama, see Jopadhola.
Bufi, see Nyamusa.
Buganda, see Uganda.
Bukuru, see Aboguru.
Bulala (Boulala), 11, 12 & n., 13, 14, 42, 43, 45.
Bungö, 8.
Bunguru, Chief, 47, 48.
Bunyoro, 25, 33, 34.
Burssens, Prof. A., xiv.
Burton, 33.
'Burulo (Madi), 7.
Busoga, 25.
Bussere, R., 8, 47, 48, 50, 51.

TRIBAL AND HISTORICAL INDEX

Buta, 16.
Bviri, *see* Biri.
Bwaka, 23.
Bwere, R., 17, 27, 28, 36.

de Calonne Beaufaict, A., viii, xiv, 5, 15 & n., 18 n., 19, 22, 23, 24, 25, 26, 27, 29 & n., 30 n., 31, 36, 40 n., 41, 46, 47 n., 48 n., 50, 52 n.
Cann, Capt., G. P., xi.
Casati, G., xiv, 27, 28, 32, 34, 40.
Chala, 54.
Chaltin, 30, 34.
Chari, R., 11, 12, 14, 43, 44, 53, 54.
Chopi, *see* Jopaluo.
Chua district, 25.
Church Missionary Society, x n., xiii.
Clark, W. T., xi.
Comte, 53.
Congo (Belgian), viii, 3, 4, 5, 7 & n., 8, 9, 15, 16, 19 & n., 22, 25, 32, 35 & n., 36, 41, 49.
Congo (French), 47.
Congo, R., 24, 25, 28.
Congo Free State, 34, 35 n., 37, 38.
Crazzolara, Fr. P., xii.
Cureau, 53.
Czekanowski, J., xi, xiv, 8, 23, 24, 25, 26, 27 n., 33, 35 n., 36, 37.

Dagba, *see* Dakpa.
Dai, *see* Day.
Daï, Sara, 11, 12, 45.
Dakpa, 19, 46.
Dar, Chief, 7, 22.
Damara, 15.
Dar Banda, 27, 52, 53, 54.
Dar Fertit, 18 n.
Dar Fur, vii n., 11, 29 & n., 32, 33, 34, 42, 43, 52, 54, 55.
Dar Mara, 44.
Dar Nuba, vii n.
Day (Dai), 18, 39.
Daya, 46.
Decorse, M., ix, xiv, 11 & n., 12, 14, 42, 43, 44 & n., 50, 53.
Delafosse, M., xiv, 11–14, 42–4, 52–4.
Dem Arkab, 49.
Dem Bekir, 31, 49, 50, 51.
Dem Idris, *see* Ganda.
Dem Zubeir, viii, 15, 18, 20, 22, 31, 48, 49, 50, 51, 52.
Dembo, *see* Dombo.
Demi, Sara, *see* Ndémé.
Dendi, 24.
Denjé, Sara, 11.
Dervish, *see* Mahdi.
Devos, Lt., 30.
Didinga, viii.
Dinka, vii, 23, 26, 30 & n., 31, 40, 41, 49, 54 & n.
Diongor, 13.
Dissa, 11, 12, 46.
Djema, 50.
Djimtilo, 13.

Djingé, Sara Kaba, 12.
Djinjeboa, 11.
Djonkour, Kirdi, 13.
Djugu, 8.
Djulu, Chief, 39.
Do, *see* Ndo.
Doke, Prof. C. M., xiv.
Doko, 46.
Dokobo, Chief, 9, 10.
Dokolo, Chief, 9.
Dombo (Dembo, Bodho), 19, 26, 46.
Dongo, *see* Ndo.
Dongo (Dango), Jebel, 52.
Dongola, 26, 32.
Doromo, Chief, *see* Ndoruma.
Doromo (place), *see* Ndoruma.
Dufile, 7, 21, 27 n.
Duma, R., 30, 51.
Dumbo, Chief, 47.
Dungu, 16 & n., 22.
Dungu, R., 5 & n., 17, 18 & n., 36, 38.
Dupwa, 30, 37.
Duru, R., 32, 36.
Duwal, Chief, 41.

Éboué, Félix, xiv, 20.
Efe (Pygmy), viii, 21.
El Fung, vii n.
Eliwa, *see* Liwa.
Emin Pasha (Schnitzer), 10, 21, 33, 34, 35.
Equatorial Province, vii, viii & n., 3, 18.
Evans, I. L., xiv, 32 n.
Evans-Pritchard, E. E., xiv, 9, 10, 15, 16 n., 40, 41 & n., 46, 47 & n., 48.
Ezo, Chief, 30.

Fafa, R., 53.
Fajelu, *see* Päjulu.
Fan, 24.
Faradje, 4, 5, 9, 27.
Faradje, Chief, 38.
Fashoda, 35.
Fazogli, 32.
Feroghe, 20, 54.
Firth, J. R., x.
Fitri, L., 12, 13, 42.
Fort Archambault, 11, 12, 14.
Fort Crampel, 52.
Fort Lamy, 13.
Fraser, Dr. K. G., xi, xii.
Fraser, Mrs., xi, xii.
French Equatorial Africa, viii, 11, 15, 18, 20, 40, 52.
Fulbe (Ful, Peul), 42, 43.
Fung, 26 & n.
Fur, 50.

Gabéri, 45.
Gabu, *see* Agabu.
Gada, R., 26.
Gadago, 45.
Gaden, H., xiv, 12, 14, 42, 43.
Galia, Chief, 31.
Galla, 24.

Gamba, see Biri.
Ganda (Dem Idris), 48, 49, 51.
Gango, 40.
Garamba, R., 27, 36, 37, 41.
Gatanga, Chief, 15.
Gaudefroy-Demombynes, M., xiv, 11.
Gbaya, see Kreish.
Gberi (Rumbek Jur), 10, 41.
Gbudwe (Mbio, Bodue), 40.
Gedaref, 34.
Gede, Chief, 40.
Geri, Chief, 7.
Gessi Pasha, 33, 34, 48, 49.
Geti, R. (Getti), 15, 49, 51.
Gnop, 10.
Gima, Chief, 31.
Ginda, Chief, see Nindu.
Gobu, 17.
Gok (Dinka), 10.
Golkidja, 11.
Golo, 20 & n., 30, 48, 49 & n., 50, 52.
Golo, R., 51.
Gondokoro, 25, 27 n., 32, 33.
Gordon, 33, 34.
Gore, Canon E. C., xiv.
Goudoungou, 14.
Gouflé, 11.
Goula, see Gula.
Goulaye, Goulei, see Gulei.
de Graer, Fr. A., 15 n.
Grant, 33.
Gray, Major D. Logan, xi, xiii, 5, 8, 27 n., 36, 38, 39.
Great Lake area, 24, 26.
Gribingui, R., 12, 53.
Gulei, Sara, 11, 45.
Gula, Sara Kaba, 12, 44, 46.
Gulu district, 7, 25.
Gulumbi, 5.
Gungo, Chief, 9.
Gura, Chief, 29.
Gurba, R., 17, 30, 49.
Guruguru, 52.
Gwan, R., 27.

Hamilton, J. A. de C., xiv.
Hamitic, viii & n., 25.
Hanolet, 50.
Hassan, Chief, 3, 9.
Haute Sangha-M'poko, 15.
Hibbert, xi, 11 n.
Hofra, 18, 52.
Hofrat el Nahas, 18 n.
van Holsbeek, 30.
Home, R., 6 n.
Horo, 11, 45.
Huma, 17.
Hutereau, A., xiv, 5, 9 n., 15, 16, 18 & n., 23, 26 n., 27 n., 29 n., 30 & n., 31 n., 37, 39, 49.

Iba, R., 9, 41.
Iberu, Chief, 7.
Ikpiro, Chief, 49.

Indri, 20.
International Institute of African Languages and Cultures, x.
Iro, L., 11, 12, 44.
Ismael Pasha, 33.
Ito Gaperi, Chief, 7.

Jakalia, Chief, 22.
Jaluo, 25, 37.
Jambo, Chief, 4.
Janssens, Cpt., 30.
Jespersen, O., xiv.
Jopadhola (Budama), 25.
Jopaluo (Chopi), 25.
Juba, 8, 22.
Juba, R., 35.
Julukunda, Chief, 47.
Junker, W., xiv, 27, 35.
Jur (Luo), 10 n., 26, 31, 48.
Jur (Rumbek), 10, 40, 41.
Jur, R., 26, 51.

Kabba (Kaba), Sara, 11, 12, 44, 46.
Kafia Kingi, 50, 52, 54.
Kaiserswaldau, Capt. von Wiese und, 53.
Kajo-Kaji, 7, 22, 37.
Kakajin, 22.
Kakwa, 5, 25, 28, 30, 37, 38, 39.
Kaliko, see Ma'di.
Kanuri, 43.
Kapili, R., 32, 36.
Kara (Kare), 11, 14, 53.
Karagwe, 25.
Karamalla, Emir, 34, 41, 50.
Kare, see Kara.
Katuaka, 50.
Kaya, R., 7 n., 37.
Kayango, 20, 49, 51.
Kayango, Chief, 48, 49.
Kazibati, 5.
Kebo, 5.
Kediru (Moru), 3, 4.
Keita, R., 12.
Keliko, see Ma'di.
Kenga, 12, 13, 43, 45.
Kenga, Mts., 42.
Kenya, 25.
Kerasit, Chief, 8.
Kere, R., 15, 27, 30, 31, 49, 51.
Khartoum, 32 & n., 34, 35, 40.
Kibali, R., 5, 6 n., 17, 26, 27 n., 29, 36, 39, 40, 52 n.
Kimandogo, Chief, 18, 52.
Kipa, 17.
Kitchener, 35.
Konango, R., 53.
Kordofan, vii n., 32.
Koshi, R., 7.
Kosho, Chief, 18, 19, 52.
Kotoko, 13, 43, 45.
Kotto, R. (Koto), 50, 53.
Koubar, 14, 42, 43.
Kouka (Aouni), 14.
Koumi, R., 53.

TRIBAL AND HISTORICAL INDEX

Koung (Kouang), 45.
Kouka, *see* Kuka.
Kounjouroux, Kouka, 14.
Kouta, R., 52.
Kouti, 12.
Kpaile, Chief (Peili), 47, 48.
Kpala, *see* Kreish.
Kredj, *see* Kreish.
Kpango, Chief, 48.
Kpango, R., *see* Pongo.
Kreich, *see* Kreish.
Kreish (Kpala, Gbaya, Baya, Abwaya, Akpwaya), 5, 18 & n., 19, 20 & n., 25, 36, 48, 50, 51, 52, 54.
Kuka (Kouka), 12 & n., 13, 14, 42, 43, 45.
Kuku, 7, 25, 37, 39.
Kulu'ba, 6.
Kuru, R., 19, 48, 49, 51.
Kutowaka, 18.

Labongo, 7.
Labouret, Prof. H., xii, 13.
Lado, 32, 34, 35, 41.
Lag, *see* Lak.
Lagae, C. R., xiv, 17.
Lak, Sara (Lag), 11, 45.
Lakama'di, 3, 9.
Lake, *see* Lak.
Lali (Rumbek Jur), 10.
Lalieux, 53.
'Landekere', R., 22.
Lango, 25.
Lanzima, Chief, 9.
Larken, P. M., xiv.
Larongo, 8.
Laverick, Rev. F. G., xii.
Laverick, Mrs., xii.
Lay, Hills, 5 n.
Lemgbo, Chief, 49.
Lendu ('Bale, -ndru, -dha, 'Baadha), viii, 3, 5, 8, 15 n., 21, 25.
Lese, 26.
Lesi, 10.
Lesi (place), 22.
Lesi, R., 41.
Libo, Hill, 5 n.
Likati, R., 16 & n.
Linda, 19.
Lingala, 8, 36.
Litchman, Rev. B. L., xii.
Liwa, Chief (Eliwa), 31, 37, 48.
Lloyd James, Prof. A., x.
Loa, *see* Lowa.
Loa, Roman Catholic Mission, xiii.
Loggo, *see* Logo.
Logo, viii, xii, 5, 6, 8, 18 n., 21, 22, 23, 26, 36, 37, 38, 39, 41; *see also* Bari-Logo, Agambi.
Logone, R., 11, 43.
Logware, *see* Lugbara.
Lokai (Madi), 7, 8, 22.
Lokaliri, 8.
Lokoya (Oxoriok), 7, 8, 22.
Lomax, D., xi.
Lori (Rumbek Jur), 10.

Lorilo Kombo, Chief, 7.
Lotuko, vii.
Lowa, R., 5 n., 6 n., 27 n., 39.
Lugbara, viii, 5, 6, 7 & n., 8, 15 n., 21, 22, 25, 27 n., 36, 37 & n., 38, 39.
Lugwari, *see* Lugbara.
Lukas, J., xiv, 12 n., 13 n., 20 n.
Lukulu, 22.
Luluba, *see* Ulu'bo.
Luluba, Hills, 8, 37.
Lumer, 8.
Luo, 48; *see also* Jur.
Lupton Bey, 31, 34.
Lyria, 7.

M. J. W., xv, 46, 47 & n.
Maba, 46.
Mabadi, 23, 28.
Mabenge, Chief, 28, 29, 30, 31.
Mabinza, 21, 28.
Mabisanga, 28.
Mabudu, 21.
Mabuturu, Chief, 19.
McCord, Miss L., xi, xii.
MacMichael, H., xiv.
Ma'de, 6.
Madi (Ma'di), vii, viii, ix, xiii, 3, 4, 6, 7, 8, 9 n., 20, 21, 22, 25 & n., 26, 27 & n., 35 n., 36, 37, 38, 39, 54; *see also* Lokai, Pandikeri, 'Burulo.
Ma'di (Keliko, Kaliko), 5, 37.
Ma'di (Mittu), 9, 27 n.
Madjingaye, Sara, 12.
Madjo, 28.
Madjuku, R., 41.
Madragi, Chief, 4, 9.
Mä'du, 9.
Madyo, *see* Amadi.
Madzu, 28.
Maes et Boone, xi, xiv, 8 n., 9 n., 15 n., 18 n.
Mahaji, 8 n.
Mahdi, Mahdists, Dervish, 30, 31, 34, 35, 38.
Mair, L. P., xiv, 35 n.
Malinowski, Prof., x n.
Makaraka, *see* Adio.
Makere, 18, 21, 22, 23, 24, 25, 28, 29.
Makèrè Mapaya, *see* Kreish.
Makongo, R., 16 & n.
Makraka, *see* Adio.
Makraka (place), 32.
Makua, 32.
Makua, R., 39.
Maku'ba, *see* Kediru.
Malele, Maleli, 21, 28.
Mambe, Chief, 4.
Mambettu, *see* Mangbetu.
Mamvu, *see* Momvu.
Mandala, 54.
Mandjia, 29, 42, 53.
Mando, 28.
Mandugba, *see* Kreish.
Mangbele, 16 n., 23, 39.
Mangbetu, 20, 21, 23, 24, 26, 27, 28, 29, 30, 32, 33, 41 & n.

TRIBAL AND HISTORICAL INDEX

Mange, Chief, 30, 40, 41.
Mararit, 46.
Marba, 45.
Marchand, 34, 35, 41.
Maridi (Meridi), viii, 3, 4, 9, 16, 18, 22, 28, 36, 37, 38, 39, 41.
Maridi, R., 17, 21, 30, 41.
Marongo, Hill, 52.
Masai, viii.
Massa, 45.
Massakory, 42.
Massenya, 14, 42, 43.
Maturungbu, R., 41.
Mayeka, 23.
Mayogo, 23, 26, 36, 54.
Maze, *see* Medje.
Mbaï, *see* Baï.
Mbandakaï, 44.
M'banga, Sara Kaba, 12.
M'baye, *see* Baï.
Mbili, R., 28, 29.
Mbio, *see* Gbudwe.
Mbio, *see* Yambio.
Mbomu (Ambomu), 17, 23, 29, 30, 40, 41.
Mbomu, R. (Bomu), viii, 15, 16 & n., 17, 23, 24, 25, 26, 27, 28, 29, 30, 31, 36, 46, 49, 50, 51, 54.
Mboro, 48, 50.
Mbwaka, 20.
Medje, 28, 39.
Mèdjè Mapaya, *see* Kreish.
Mèdjè Mokpwaya, *see* Kreish.
Medogo, *see* Mudogo.
Meillet et Cohen, xiv.
Meinhof, C., xiv.
Melfi, 13.
Melzian, Dr. H. C., xiii, 14.
Mendele (Kouka), 14.
Meridi, *see* Maridi.
Meroe, 26.
Meshra el Rek, 47.
Miani, 32.
Migi, Hills, 52.
Mili, Mt. (Mela, Milah), 52, 53.
Miltou, 45.
Minibolo, 40.
Missioni Africane of Verona, x n.
Mittu (Wetu), 40, 41, 54.
Mittu, R., 27 n.
Miyayama, Chief, 52.
Miza (Moru), 3, 4, 22.
Mobenge, 21, 23, 28.
Modat, 50.
Modo, 10.
Mogororo, 11.
Mohammed Ali, 32.
Molinaro, Fr. L., xiv.
Mombutu, 21, 25, 26, 28 n.
Momvu (Mamvu, Monfu), viii, ix, 8, 21, 23, 24, 25, 26, 28 & n., 29, 31, 41, 54.
Monbutu, *see* Mombutu.
Mondari, 3, 9, 22, 27.
Monfu, *see* Momvu.
Mongaiyat, 20.

Mongalla Province, vii, viii & n., 5.
Mongbwandi (Mongbandi), 23, 24, 27 n., 31.
Mongelima, 21.
Monjombo, 20.
Mopoi-Banzegino, Chief, 31, 49.
Mopoi-Mokru, Chief, 31, 49 n.
Mopwaya, *see* Kreish.
Morali, 7.
Moro, 42.
Moroägi, 3, 4.
Moroändri, 3, 4, 7, 8.
Morokodo, 3, 4, 9, 10, 14, 22, 41.
Moru, vii, viii, ix, 3, 5, 6, 8, 9, 20, 21, 22, 23, 26, 27, 30, 32, 36, 37, 38, 39, 54 & n.; *see also* Miza, Kediru, Lakama'di, Moroändri, 'Balimbä, Moroägi, Wa'di.
Mousgou, 45.
Moyo (Madi), 7.
Mozley, Miss M., xii.
Mudogo, 12 n., 13, 14.
Mundu, ix, 4, 9, 10, 14, 15, 18 & n., 22, 26 & n., 27, 28, 36, 37, 39, 41 & n., 54.
Mundu, R., 18.
Munza, Chief, 29.
Mve-Gumba, *see* Biri.
Mve-Rodi, *see* Bor.
M'volo, 10.
Mynors, T. H. B., xi, xii, xiii, 4 n., 5.

Naam, R., 4.
Nachtigal, 11 n., 14, 42, 43.
Naka (Kreish), 18.
Nalder, L. F., x, xi, xiv, 27 n.
Nandi, viii.
Nasir, Sultan, 49.
Nava, R., 25.
N'dam, 45.
Ndarago, Chief, 3, 4.
Ndedegumbva, 49.
Ndele (N'dele), 44, 50, 53.
N'deme (Demi), Sara Kaba, 11, 12, 45.
Ndo (Ndogo, Do, Dongo), 5, 15 n., 21, 25, 48 n., 52 n.
Ndogo, Nduggo (Kreish), 15 n., 18 & n., 25, 52.
Ndogo, vii, viii, ix, xiii, 15, 16, 18, 20 & n., 36, 46, 48, 49, 51, 54.
Ndoka, 12.
Ndokile, Chief, 48.
Ndoruma, Chief (Doromo), 30.
Ndoruma District (Doruma), 15, 25, 28.
Nduggo, *see* Kreish.
Nduka, 12.
Nekiri, 27.
Nekongo, Chief, 26.
Ngama, Sara, 11, 12, 46.
Ngamande (Bilal) Chief, 18.
Nganzio, Chief, 9, 41.
Ngapou, 19.
Ngere, Chief, 3, 4.
Ngok (Dinka), 10.
Ngoku, Stream, 50, 51.
Ngoli, Chief, 40.
Ngoni, R., 47, 51.
Ngulguli, 11.

TRIBAL AND HISTORICAL INDEX

Ngura, Chief, *see* Gura.
Niangara, 16 n., 18, 26.
Niapu, 27.
Niellim, 45.
Nile, R. (Bahr el Jebel), 7 n., 22, 24, 25, 31, 32 n., 34, 37, 38, 39, 43.
Nile-Congo Divide (watershed), vii, 24, 32, 34, 52.
Nilotic, vii, viii n., 26, 54.
Nimule, 7, 22, 32.
Nindu, Chief (Ginda), 27, 30 & n., 31.
Nsakkara, *see* Nzakara.
Nuer, vii.
Nunga (Anunga), 23, 27, 29, 30, 31, 40, 47, 49.
Nunga, Chief, 30, 31, 47, 48, 50.
Nyamusa, 9, 10, 14, 22, 41.
Nyanga, 5.
Nyangwara, 3, 37, 39.
Nyani-Kuyu, Chief, 7.
Nye, 5.
Nyepo, 39.
Nyifwa, 37.
Nzakara (Nsakkara), 20, 53.
Nzoro, R., 5 n., 6 n., 16 n., 18 n.

Obi, R., *see* Nzoro.
Odego, Chief, 7.
Ojigä (Avukaya), 4, 6.
Ojila (Avukaya), 4, 6, 8.
Okabo (Okebu), 5.
Okupoi, Chief, 4, 9.
Olivetti, Fr., xi.
Olo, R., 4.
Omar Saleh, 34.
Opari, viii, 3, 7, 8, 9, 35 & n., 37.
Origo, Chief, 38.
Oru, R., 5 n.
Oruleo-ti, 6, 7.
Orugu, 5.
Ouadäi, *see* Wadai.
Oubangui-Chari, viii, 11, 18, 19, 55.
Oxoriok, *see* Lokoya.

Pajulu (Lugbara dialect), 6, 7.
Päjulu (Fajelu, Bari tribe), 4, 5, 6, 7, 8, 18 n., 22, 37.
Pambia, *see* Apambia.
Pandikeri (Madi), 7, 8.
Panyana, 5.
Patri, 53.
Pedersen, H., xiv.
Peili, Chief, *see* Kpaile.
Peul, *see* Fulbe.
Poko, R., 16 & n.
Pongo, R. (Kpango), 15, 49, 50, 51.
Poni, 5.
Popoi, 21.
Poro, 27.
Poutrin, Dr., xiv, 19, 20, 44, 52.
Pygmy, 21, 23, 24, 25, 28.

Rabah (Rabeh), 33, 42, 44, 53.
Rafai, 16 n., 17.

Raga, 49.
Raga, R., 19, 52.
Ramponi, Fr. E., xii, 6.
Rauf Pasha, 35.
Rejaf, 5 n., 30, 32, 34, 37, 38.
Renzi, Chief, 30, 47, 48.
Rhino Camp, 6.
Ribero, P., xv.
Rikita, Chief, 9, 40.
Roba, Chief, 3, 4.
Rohl, R., 32.
Ruanda, 25.
Rubi, R., 16, 17.
Rumbek, 9, 10.
Runga, 11.
Ruwenzori, 23, 25.

Saba, 13, 45.
Sabanga, 19.
Sabba, *see* Saba.
Sabun, Chief, 8.
Sahara, 24.
Said Bandas (Bundas), 18, 52.
Said bin Selis, 50.
Said, Pasha, 32.
Salamat, R., 11, 12, 46.
Sandeh, *see* Zande.
Santandrea, Fr. S., xi, xiii, xv, 11 n., 15 & n., 20 & n., 46, 47 & n., 48, 49, 50, 51.
Sara, viii, 11, 12, 13, 14, 24, 29, 42, 43, 44, 45, 46.
Sara, R., 12, 45.
Sarago, Mt., 49.
Sarouo (Seroua, Sarrouo), 13, 45.
Sayid Akidima, Chief, 18.
Schebesta, P., 21.
Schnitzer, *see* Emin Pasha.
School of Oriental and African Studies, x.
Schweinfurth, G., xv, 8, 9 n., 10, 12, 15 n., 18 n., 27 n., 28 n., 30, 31, 33, 48, 50.
Seligman, Prof. C. G. and Mrs. B. Z., vii n., x n., xv, 26 n.
Selimi, Chief, 41.
Semio, *see* Zamoi Epira.
Semitic, 24.
Senambia, Chief, 9.
Sennar, 26.
Senoussi, Sultan, 50, 53.
Sere (Basiri), vii, viii, ix, xiii, 15, 17 n., 18 & n., 23, 26, 27, 30, 31, 32, 36, 46, 47, 48, 49, 50, 51, 53.
Seroua, *see* Sarouo.
Shambe, 41.
Shatt (Thuri), 19.
Shayu, 20.
Shilluk, vii, 15, 19, 23, 25, 26 & n., 27, 31, 46, 54.
Shinko, R., 16 n., 29, 31.
Sili, R., 49.
Simpson, S. R., xi.
Sinyar, 11.
Slatin, R. C., xiv, 34.
Smith, E. W., 21.
Sofi, *see* Sopi.

Sokoro, 13, 44.
Solongoh, see Sonango.
Somrai, 45.
Sonango, Chief, 31, 47.
Sopi (Rumbek Jur), 10, 41.
Sopo, R., 20.
Speke, 33.
Stam, H., xi.
Stanley, 34.
Sueh, R., 17, 21, 25, 26, 27, 30, 36, 41, 42, 46, 47, 48, 51.
Suleiman, 33, 53.
Surango, 27 n.
Surur, Chief, 7, 22.

Tané, 11.
Tapari, R., 3.
Tar-Bârma, see Bagirmi.
Tar-Bàgrimma, see Bagirmi.
Taweish, L., 29.
Tchad, L., viii & n., 8, 12, 13, 25, 26, 29, 33, 43, 54.
Tchad, Province or Colony, viii, 42, 45, 46.
Télé, 11.
Teli, R. (Tely), 16.
Tembura, Chief (Tombora), 31, 40, 41, 47, 48, 49, 50.
Tembura (place) (Tombora), 15, 16, 22, 31, 47, 48, 50, 51.
Tendebi, Hill, 5 n.
Thomas and Scott, 25.
Thonner, F., xv.
Thuri, see Shatt.
Tié, Sara, 12.
Tikima, Chief, 31.
Tindalu, 3.
Titule, 16 & n.
Todo, 18.
Togbo, 20.
Toi, 22.
Toin, Chief, 40.
Toinya Post, 10, 32.
Tombo (son of Gura), 29, 30.
Tombo (son of Renzi), 30.
Tombora, Chief, see Tembura.
Tombora (place), see Tembura.
Topotha, vii.
Tonj, 8, 9, 22, 40, 41.
Toram, Kirdi, 13.
Torday, E., xv.
Tori, R. (Tore), 16, 28.
Toumak, Sara, 12, 45.
Tounia, Sara, 11, 12.
Turkana, vii.
Tuyugi (Tuji), Chief, 47 & n.

Ubangi, R., 15, 27 n., 53.
Ubangi-Chari, see Oubangui-Chari.
Uganda, vii, viii, 3, 6, 7, 8, 25, 34, 35, 36.
Ukwa, Chief, 39.
Ulu, R., 41.
Ulu'bo (Luluba), 7, 8, 22, 37 n., 38, 39.
Upper Nile Province, vii.

Urundi, 25.
Uziboko, Chief, 47.

Valé, Sara, 11, 12.
Van den Plas, H. V., xiv, 16 n., 17 & n., 23, 29.
Van Kerckhoven, 31, 34.
Vankerckovenville, 18 n.
Vekens, A., xv, 20 n.
Victoria, L., 25, 37.
Vumani, 27.
Vurra, 6, 7.

Wadai (Ouadaï), 12, 13, 35, 42, 43, 44.
Wadelai, 7 n., 27 n., 31, 34.
Wadi (Wa'di) (Moru), 4, 22.
Wagaya, 37.
Wajo, Chief, 3, 4.
Wala, Chief, 3, 4, 9.
Walese, 21, 25, 26.
Wallis, C. A. G., xi, 49.
Wambuti, 25.
Wanande, 21.
Wandi, 34.
Wando, Avuru-, 17.
Wando, Chief, 39, 41.
Wando (place), 32.
Wara, R., 31.
Wati, Mt., 6.
Watsa, 5.
Wau, viii, 8, 15 & n., 16, 20, 31, 48, 49, 50, 51.
Wau, R., 51.
Wele, R. and district, viii, ix, 6 n., 16 & n., 17, 21, 23, 24, 25, 28, 30, 31, 33, 36, 37, 40, 53, 54.
Were, R., 27, 29, 31, 41.
Werner, Prof. A., xv.
West Nile District, 6, 7, 8, 35.
Westermann, Prof. D., ix, x n., xiii, xv, 14, 20 n.
Wetu (see also Mittu), 10.
Wils, J., xv.
Winder, J., xi.
Wira (Moro), 9, 10, 22.
Woro (Kreish), 19, 48, 49, 51.

Yakoma, 20.
Yakoma (place), 28.
Yakpwa, 19.
Yakpwati, Chief, see Yapiti.
Yakululu, 28.
Yalo, R., 18 n.
Yambio (district or town), 16, 48.
Yambio, Chief, 30.
Yanderika, see Indri.
Yapate, Chief, see Yapiti.
Yapiti, Chief, 30, 41, 48.
Yei (district or town), viii, 3, 4, 5, 6, 7, 8, 9, 16, 17, 18, 22, 37, 38, 39.
Yei, R., 16 n., 27, 28, 41.
Yembio, Chief, see Yambio.
Yessié, 45.
Yo, 18 n.

Yobo, 31.
Yongo, Chief, 31.
Young, G., xv.
Yubu, 51.
Yubu, R., 51.
Yulu, 11, 14, 18 n., 54.

Zaga, Chief, 47.
Zamoi Epira, Chief, 31, 49.

Zangabiru, Chief, 31.
Zande, vii, viii, ix, 4, 9, 15, 16, 17, 18, 20 & n., 21, 22, 23, 24, 26, 27, 28, 29, 30, 32, 33, 35, 36, 37, 38, 39, 40, 41, 46, 47, 48, 49, 50, 51, 52, 53, 54, 55.
Zemio, 17, 25, 31.
Zibeir, *see* Zubeir.
Zobia, 16 n.
Zubeir, Sultan (Zibeir), 31, 33, 35, 50, 53.

LINGUISTIC INDEX

a, suffix (noun), 109–10, 127–8.
— (verb), 109–10, 178, 246.
prefix, 140, 160, 236 n., 237 n.
auxiliary, 220.
linking particle, 161, 293.
'a, postposition, see ya.
a'di, a'du, interrogative, 147–8.
Adjective, 57–8, 60, 73, 75, 79, 80 & n., 164, 235, 240, 282–9, 291–3, 295–6, 298, 300, 302–4, 306, 307, 308, 309, 312, 326, 368–75, 395, see also Qualificatives.
adre, adri, are, auxiliary, see dre.
Adverb, 75, 76, 77, 78, 79, 81, 82–3, 148–9, 172, 307–13, 326, 374–9, 414–16, see also Descriptives.
Adverb, interrogative, 308–9, 148–9.
Adverbial expression, phrase, 307–13, 414–16.
Affix, 83, 285–7.
Affricate, 100–1, 105, 115, 382.
AGAMBI, see LOGO.
Agglutinative, 90.
AIIVU, see MADI.
aki, adee, pronominal form, 155.
aku, ako, postposition, 116, 255, 302.
alia, postposition, see ya.
Alveolar, consonant, 101–5, 116–17, 317–18, 382.
anda, nde, pronominal form, 155–6.
andi, tandi, ndi, pronoun, 149, 151.
ARABIC, 58.
Armstrong, Miss L. E., 102 n.
Ashton, Mrs. E. O., xiv, 74 n.
Aspect, definite, 71–2, 98–9, 141–2, 144, 180–3, 185, 206, 210, 219 n., 220, 226, 229–30, 245–8, 253–4, 260, 262–3, 273–81, 402–5.
indefinite, 71–2, 95–6, 98, 142–4, 180, 183–4, 186–95, 197–207, 210, 216–17, 219–21, 223–5, 228–9, 231–2, 234–8, 251, 254–5, 261–3, 270–3, 279–81, 285, 402–5.
Augmentative, 133, 282–3.
Auxiliary, a, 220.
particle, 69, 181–3, 185–7, 189–93, 197, 201, 203–4, 219–34, 249, 272, 285, 405–8.
causative, 220, 223, 230–2, 405.
prefix, 198–9.
progressive, 221–2, 231–2, 237.
Auxiliary verb, 59, 75, 78, 83, 180, 190, 191 & n., 192, 217, 219–34, 245, 259 n., 324–5.
AVUKAYA, viii, 6, 8.
phonetics, 94–6, 101 n., 104–5, 107, 115–23.
intonation, 111, 136, 141, 279.
noun, 129, 133–6.
genitive, 159–60, 162, 164–5.
preposition, 175.
postposition, 166–8, 171, 173–5, 247, 251, 254, 257–60.
verb, 179, 196–7, 202, 208–10, 213, 215, 218, 221, 225, 232 n., 233–4, 236–7, 243, 247, 251, 254, 257–60.
relative, 262 n., 269, 277–9.
adjective, 286–7.
predicative, 292, 294–5, 301–3.
ideophone, 312.
reduplication, 305.
AVUKAYA, OJIGA, 6, 116, 135, 138 n., 142–3, 153, 160, 164, 171, 173–4, 196, 209, 211, 221, 233, 236–7, 243, 257, 260, 262 n., 268–9, 279, 292, 294, 303.
AVUKAYA, OJILA, 6, 8, 96, 103, 116–17, 131, 135, 138, 142–6, 149–50, 153, 157–8, 160, 164, 167–8, 171, 173–4, 196, 202, 209, 211–13, 216, 218, 220–1, 223, 225, 232 n., 233, 236–7, 243, 251, 257, 259, 279, 283–4, 286, 292–4, 303, 312.
aza, azi, zi, pronominal form, 154.

'ba, auxiliary, 220–1.
BAGIRMI, 14, 62, 63 & n., 64, 66–73, 75–7, 82–4.
BAKA, vii, viii, ix, 4, 14, 18, 62–3, 65, 67, 70, 84.
'BĂLIMBĂ, see MORU.
BANDA, ix, 20, 65.
BANTU, 17 n., 56–7, 59–60, 70, 72, 78.
BARI, 92 n., 308 n., 315 n., 319.
'bɛ, postposition, 167–8, 247, 262–3.
'BELI, xiii, 10, 14, 65, 68.
BITI, 64.
'bo, postposition, 248.
BONGO, vii, viii, xiii, 4, 14, 20, 21, 62–71, 73–81, 83–4.
Bradley, 82.
'BURULO, see MADI.
BUSHMAN, 56 & n.
Butlin, R. T., 108 n.

ca, postposition, 248.
Case, 57–9, 67–8, 166.
Causative prefix, 211, 217.
Characteristic vowel, 72, 74 & n., 95–100, 126, 142, 177, 180–3, 185–6, 193 n., 195–7, 200 n., 204–14, 225–6, 229, 233, 270–3, 323, 388–9.
Cohen, M., 56 n.
Combination of consonants, 108–11, 121–3, 384.
Comparison of adjectives, 303–4.
Compound noun, see Noun compounds.
Concords, 59–60.
Conditional, 249.
Conjunction, 76, 78–9, 82, 156, 224, 313–15, 326, 378–9, 414–16.
Consonant prefixes, 126–7, 204, 216–19.
Consonants, 100–11, 115–24, 316–20, 381–5.
elided initial, 141–2, 192.
alternation of, 116–17.

LINGUISTIC INDEX

Copulative, *see* Predicative.

'da, 'do, do, auxiliary, 221.
'dɛ, auxiliary, 223.
Definite aspect, *see* Aspect.
De Lacy Evans O'Leary, 56 n.
Delafosse, M., xiv, 70 n., 73, 74, 374.
Deleu, 380 n.
Demonstrative, 145–7, 265, 286, 289, 358, 397.
  near and far, 145.
  reference, 146–7, 265, 358.
Dental consonants, 101, 116, 317.
Dependent forms, 184, 186–92, 194–5.
  verb, 237–8.
  clause, 248, 256.
  see also Subordinate clause.
Derivative verb species, 57–9, 68.
Descriptive adverb, *see* Ideophone.
Descriptives, 76, 77, 79; *see also* Adverb.
di, 'di, prefixed nominal form, 131.
'di, 'do, reference demonstrative, 145–7, 236.
di, postposition, 248–9.
'di, suffix, 283.
Diminutive, 57, 133–4, 282–3.
Dissyllabic verbs (Class II and Class III), *see* Verb classes.
Doke, C. M., xiv, 59 & n., 60, 74 & n., 75, 78, 79 & n., 80 & n., 81 & n., 82–4, 108 n., 307.
dre, auxiliary, 221–2.
  postposition, 257.
drɪ, adrɪ, auxiliary, 222–3.
drì, drì, postposition, 162, 167–8.
drí, postposition, 168–9.
dro, ro, postposition, 249–51.
  suffix, 285.

e, i, plural suffix, 128, 136–7, 144, 178, 181, 183, 245.
  predicative suffix, 293–5.
eco, auxiliary, 223–4.
Emphasizing particle, 157–8.
Emphatic sounds, 58.
esi, auxiliary, 224.
Exhortative, 187, 203.
Explosive (plosive), 100–1, 105–7, 115–16, 120, 317, 381.

Feminine, *see* Gender.
Firth, J. R., 56 & n.
Flexional, *see* Inflexional.
fo, auxiliary, 224.
Fraser, Mrs., xi, xii, 137 n.
Fricative, 104, 115, 383.
Future, 182, 185, 188, 202 & n., 203–5, 209, 231, 258–9.
Future postposition, 187, 189, 258–60.

ga, postposition, 169, 251; *see also* ya.
ga'a, postposition, *see* ya.
Gaden, H., xiv, 14, 42–3, 63 n.
gbi, auxiliary, 225.
ge, postposition, 251.
Gender, 57–9, 66, *see also* Sex.
General form (verb), 181–95.
General interrogative, *see* Interrogative.

Genitive construction, 57–8, 60, 134, 139–40, 159–66, 176, 264, 322–3, 397–8.
Genitive, *see* Possessor.
Genitive particle, 57.
German, comparison with, 234.
Gerund, *see* Noun, verbal.
Glottal, *see* Laryngeal.
go, auxiliary, 224.
  postposition, 252.
  suffix, 283.
Gore, E. C., xiv, 62 n.
Guttural, 58.

Habitual, 221–2, 251.
Hailey, Lord, 56 n.
HAMITIC, 56–60.
HAMITO-SEMITIC, 56 n.
Hertsens, Fr. L., 417–18.
HOTTENTOT, 56 n.
Humboldt, 60, 61 n.

ı suffix (noun), 136–7.
— (verb), 245.
  predicative, 293–5.
ı suffix (verb), 178.
Ideophone (Descriptive adverb), 60, 74, 79, 81 & n., 312–13.
i'du, negative particle, 300.
Imperative, 71, 79, 183, 186–7, 189–91, 193–4, 197, 201–3, 206, 209–11, 229, 276–7, 280, 305.
Implosive, 101–2, 105, 107–8, 115–17, 119, 317, 382.
Incorporating, 60, 61.
Indefinite aspect, *see* Aspect, indefinite.
Infinitive, 199, 201–2, 216, 220–1, 224, 230, 232, 234–41, 263.
Infix, 83, 208.
Inflexional, inflecting, 58, 60–1, 65.
Inseparable particles, 77.
Instrument, 171.
Interjection, 78–9, 82.
Intensive prefix, 217.
Interrogative forms, 147–9, 308, 358–61, 392–3, 397.
  adverb, *see* Adverb.
  particle, 70, 80.
Intervening particle, *see* Linking particle.
Intonation, 57–9, 65, 111–14, 124–5, 136, 140–2, 198, 214, 225, 270–81, 320.
Intransitive conjugation, 181–2, 184–6, 188–9, 191–2, 194–5, 202–4.
Isolating, 57, 60, 61, 63.

Jespersen, O., xiv, 60 & n., 61 & n., 78, 82.

k prefix (noun), 126.
— (verb), 217.
  auxiliary, 226–8.
ka suffix (noun), 128.
— (verb), 179, 238–9, 241, 286–7.
  particle, 137, 143–4, 163–4, 183, 187.
  auxiliary, 225–6, 228–9.
  postposition, 252.
KEDIRU, *see* MORU.

LINGUISTIC INDEX

KELIKO, 5.
  phonetics, 94, 100, 104–5, 107, 115–16, 119–20, 122–4.
  intonation, 124, 141, 279.
  noun, 126, 128–9, 130–4, 136–7.
  pronoun, 138–40, 142–54, 150 n.
  genitive, 159–62, 164–5.
  postposition, 167–72, 247, 250–1, 254, 256–8, 260.
  verb, 179, 199 & n., 200–1, 203 n., 208–10, 213–15, 220–4, 226, 228, 239–41, 243, 245, 267–9, 279, 305.
  adjective, 283, 286–7, 306.
  predicative, 290–6, 298, 300–4.
  reduplication, 305–6.
  adverb, 311.
  conjunction, 314–15.
KHOISAN, 56 n.
kɪ suffix (noun), 128, 136–7.
— (verb), 178, 187, 189, 192, 245.
  particle, 144, 205.
ko, auxiliary, 189, 229–30.
ko, ku, neg. particle, 253–5, 301–2, see Negative.
kpɔ, kyɔ, postposition, 252–3.
KREISH, 19, 65.
kwɛ, ki, fɛ, auxiliary, 230.

l prefix (noun), 127.
  (verb), 216–19.
  (adjective), 283.
Labial consonants, 100–1, 115–16, 316–17.
Labialization, 121–2.
Labio-velar consonants, 106–7, 120, 319, 382.
Lagae, C. R., xiv, 68.
LAKAMA'DI, see MORU.
Lanalana, K. T., 331.
lɛ suffix (noun), 135.
— (verb), 179, 234, 236, 238–9.
  postposition, 170.
le suffix (verb), 239.
LENDU, viii, 3, 8, 102, 134–5, 138, 143, 146, 148, 151, 159–60, 170, 219–22, 229, 231, 248, 250, 253.
  phonetics, 380–4, 417–18.
  intonation, 385.
  orthography, 386–8, 418.
  noun, 388–91.
  pronoun, 391–5.
  qualificative, 395–9.
  postposition, 400–1, 408–12.
  verb, 402–12.
  predicative, 412–14.
  adverb and conjunction, 414–16.
  text, 416–17.
li, auxiliary, 231.
Linking particle, 73, 77, 80 n., 83 & n., 98, 129–30, 161–2, 164, 174, 176, 264, 266, 268 n., 283, 396, 398–9.
Liquid consonants, 116–17, 383.
liri, nili, ri, auxiliary, 231.
Litchman, Rev. B. L., xii, 87, 380, 382 & n., 383 & n., 384 & n., 386 & n., 387, 391 n., 398 n., 418.

LOGO, xii, 5–6, 8, 63, 67, 75–6, 82.
  phonetics, 87–111, 114–24.
  intonation, 111, 124, 141, 142, 279, 320.
  noun, 126–38.
  pronoun, 138–58.
  genitive, 159–65.
  postposition, 166–76, 247–81.
  preposition, 176.
  verb, 177–81, 189–92, 208–10, 213, 215–34, 236–7, 241–6, 247–81.
  adjective, 283–9.
  predicative, 290–304.
  reduplication, 305–6.
  adverb, 307–13.
  conjunction, 314–15.
  orthography, 316–26.
  text, 329–31.
LOGO, AGAMBI, 5, 138, 151, 162–3, 169, 172, 199–200, 201 & n., 231, 233, 255, 257, 308, 310–11.
LUGBARA, xii, 6, 7, 8, 83, 84.
  phonetics, 89–111, 114–24.
  intonation, 124–5, 141, 279.
  noun, 126–38.
  pronoun, 139–57.
  genitive, 159–65.
  postposition, 166–75, 247–81.
  verb, 177–81, 192–5, 199–201, 203–4, 208–10, 213, 215, 216–19, 239–81.
  adjective, 283–9.
  predicative, 290–304.
  reduplication, 306.
  adverb, 307–13.
  conjunction, 313–15.
  orthography, 316–26.
  text, 331–4.
Lukas, J., xiv, 12 n., 13 n., 20 n., 56 n.
LULU'BA, see MADI.
Lush, A., 331 n., 334 n.

ma, auxiliary, 231.
  linking particle, 162.
McCord, Miss L., xi, xii, 87, 246 n., 321 n., 329.
MADI (general), xiii, 7, 8, 62–3, 65 & n., 66–71, 71 n., 73, 77, 80, 83–4.
MADI:
  AIIVU, 7, 334.
  'BURULO, 7, 94, 115, 118, 138, 162.
  LOKAI
    phonetics, 90–111, 116–24.
    intonation, 111, 124, 136, 280–1.
    noun, 126–38.
    pronoun, 138–58.
    genitive, 161–5.
    postposition, 166–74, 247–81.
    verb, 177–81, 186–9, 198–9, 201–4, 207, 209–13, 215–19, 238–9, 241–81.
    adjective, 283–9.
    predicative, 290–304.
    reduplication, 306.
    adverb, 307–13.
    ideophone, 312.
    conjunction, 313–15.

MADI: LOKAI (cont.)
orthography, 316–26.
text, 338.
LULU'BA:
phonetics, 94, 105, 115, 117, 118 & n., 119, 121–4.
noun, 127–30, 132–8.
pronoun, 143–8, 151.
genitive, 160–2.
postposition, 167–8, 171, 174, 252–4, 256, 260–1.
verb, 199, 207, 209–10, 213, 215, 226, 228, 230, 246, 252–4, 256, 260–1, 305–6.
adjective, 284.
predicative, 293–4, 301.
reduplication, 305–6.
conjugation, 314.
OPARI-MADI, 135, 156, 241, 238, 285–7, 289, 291, 293, 297, 300–2, 304, 314.
PANDIKERI:
phonetics, 93, 99, 107, 115, 117–22, 124.
intonation, 136, 198, 280–1.
noun, 127–8, 130–2, 134, 136–8.
pronoun, 141–4, 148–50, 153–4, 157.
genitive, 159 & n., 161–5.
postposition, 177, 189, 198–9, 201, 203–4, 207, 209–13, 215, 217–19, 223–4, 226, 228, 232, 238–9, 246, 249–51, 253–4, 256–8, 261.
relative, 262, 264–5, 267–81.
adjective, 284–9.
predicative, 290–5, 297, 301–2, 304.
adverb, 308.
conjunction, 314.
orthography, 317, 320.
text, 338–9.
TORIT-MADI, 156, 214, 238, 264, 284–6, 289–93, 297, 302, 304, 314.
MANGBETU, 20–1.
Marouzeau, 75.
Masculine, see Sex.
Meillet et Cohen, xiv, 61.
Meinhof, C., xiv, 56 n.
Mitterrutzner, 90 n.
Monosyllabic verbs, 177, 340, 345, 347–8.
Mood, 57, 59, 181.
Molinaro, Fr. L., xiv, 87, 146, 187 n., 188 n., 230, 259 n., 310, 313 n., 315, 321 n.
MOROKODO, 67.
Morphological and Semantic suffixes, &c., 63–4, 84, 127–30.
Morphology, 57–9, 66–72.
MORU, 3–4, 5–6, 8, 20, 21, 62–3, 65 & n., 66 & n., 67–70, 71 & n., 72–84, 175.
'BÄLIMBÄ:
phonetics, 95, 107, 116, 122–3.
noun, 126, 133–4, 136.
pronoun, 138, 142–5, 147, 149, 157.
postposition, 168, 256, 259–60.
verb, 196–7, 202, 206, 209, 211, 214, 217–18, 220, 225, 232–3, 236, 256, 259–60.
adjective, 284.
predicative, 292, 295–6.

KEDIRU:
phonetics, 92, 95, 101 n., 116–17, 121–3.
noun, 126, 133 & n.
pronoun, 138, 142–5, 147.
postposition, 168, 171, 259–60.
verb, 178, 196–7, 202, 206, 209, 211, 214, 217–18, 223, 225, 236, 259–60.
adjective, 287.
predicative, 293, 297.
LAKAMA'DI:
phonetics, 95, 116–17, 121–3.
noun, 126, 133–4, 136.
pronoun, 138, 142–5.
postposition, 173, 256–7.
verb, 196–7, 211, 214, 220, 225, 236, 256–7.
predicative, 293.
MIZA:
phonetics, 89–111, 114–24.
intonation, 65, 111–14, 124–5, 136, 140, 141, 214, 270–8, 320.
noun, 126–38.
pronoun, 138–58.
genitive, 159–60.
postposition, 166–75, 247–81.
preposition, 175–6.
verb, 177–86, 197–8, 200–7, 209, 211–12, 214, 216–19, 220–36, 241–81.
adjective, 283–9.
predicative, 290–304.
reduplication, 305–6.
adverb, 307–13.
ideophone, 312.
conjunction, 313–15.
orthography, 316–26.
text, 327–9.
MOROÄGI:
phonetics, 94–5, 116–17, 121–3.
noun, 126, 134, 136.
pronoun, 138, 142–5, 147, 149.
genitive, 160.
postposition, 168, 257, 259.
verb, 196–7, 202, 206, 209, 211, 213–14, 225, 232 & n., 233, 236, 257, 259, 281.
MOROÄNDRI:
phonetics, 93–6, 101 n., 107, 115–17, 120–4.
intonation, 111, 140, 271.
noun, 126, 131, 133–4, 136–7.
pronoun, 139–40, 142–6, 148–9, 151, 153–4, 156, 158.
genitive, 165.
postposition, 167–8, 171, 173–4, 247–8, 250, 254, 256, 259–60.
verb, 196–8, 200–2, 204–5, 206, 208–9, 211–12, 214, 217–18, 220, 222–3, 225–8, 232–3, 245, 247–8, 250, 254–6, 259–60.
relative, 264, 267, 271–2, 275.
adjective, 283–4, 286–7.
predicative, 292, 294, 296, 299, 302.
ideophone, 312–13.
WA'DI:
phonetics, 92, 95, 105, 116–17, 121–3.
noun, 126, 131, 133–4, 136.

LINGUISTIC INDEX

MORU: WA'DI (*cont.*)
   pronoun, 142–6, 153, 157–8.
   genitive, 159–60.
   postposition, 168, 247, 251, 257.
   verb, 196–7, 202 & n., 211–14, 216–18, 223, 225, 234, 236, 247, 251, 257.
   relative, 268.
   adjective, 283–4, 286.
   predicative, 292.
   ideophone, 312.
Mozley, Miss M., xii, 87, 157 n., 180 n., 181, 216, 221 n., 231, 248 n., 310.
Müller, Max, 60–1.
Mynors, T. H. B., xii, xiii, 87, 109, 211, 216, 218, 248 n., 257, 287, 309, 315, 327.

na, particle, 157–8, 166, 396.
   suffix, 245–6, 284.
   postposition, 170, 400–1.
Narrative form, 252.
Nasal compounds, 107–9, 121, 318, 384.
Nasal consonants, 100–1, 105–6, 382.
ndi, postposition, 255.
   linking particle, 293.
NDOGO, vii, viii, ix, xiii, 16, 18, 62, 64–71, 73–84.
ndo, postposition, 255.
ndrɔ, postposition, 256.
Negative (with ku), 181–4, 186–8, 189–91, 192–3, 224, 236, 238, 253–5, 275–6, 277–8, 301–3, 306.
   (with i'du, &c.), 169, 235, 300–1.
Neuter-passive prefix, 218–19.
ŋga, suffix (verb), 239–41.
   auxiliary, 231–2.
ŋga, ŋgɔ, pronoun, 131, 153–4.
ŋgɔ, interrogative, 147–8.
ni, suffix (verb), 179, 234–6.
ni, suffix (noun), 128.
   linking particle, 161–2, 164, 293.
   postposition, 165, 169, 256.
   preposition, 175.
ni, nɔ, na, demonstrative, 145.
   suffix (verb), 246.
NILOTIC, vii, 26 & n., 54 n., 56 n.
Nomen rectum, *see* Possessor.
Nomen regens, *see* Possessed.
Nominal prefixes (Prefixed nominal forms), 131.
Nominal roots, 75–6, 79–82.
Noun, 58, 75–6, 78–81, 79 n., 80 n., 126–38, 342–58, 388–91.
   abstract, 130–1.
   compounds, 66, 130–2, 322, 389.
   formatives, 57–9, 61.
   prefix, 126–7, 388.
   suffix, 127–30, 322, 389–91.
   verbal (gerund), 127–8, 130–1, 153, 235–6, 238–41, 243–4, 283.
Number, 59, 69, 136–7.
Numeral, 67, 78–80, 282, 286–8, 374–5, 395.
nya form, 81, 142–3, 183.
NZAKARA, 20, 53, 64 & n., 77, 84.
nzi, suffix (noun), 129, 138.

o, auxiliary, 232.
'o, postposition, 256.
Object, 57–8, 60, 72–3, 139.
OJIGA, *see* AVUKAYA.
OJILA, *see* AVUKAYA.
oko, postposition, 256.
OPARI, *see* MADI.
Orthography, 316–26, 386–8, 418.
Oxford English Dictionary, 75, 79, 80 & n., 81–4, 307.

pa, postposition, 257.
Palatal consonants, 105, 119, 318.
Palatalization, 122–4, 128, 178, 319.
PANDIKERI, *see* MADI.
Particles (general), 74, 77–8, 81–4, 180–1.
Passive, 57–9, 70 & n., 71 & n., 72–3, 214–15, 263–4, 305.
Past, 200, 202–3, 209, 221–2, 240, 256–8, 262.
Pedersen, H., xiv, 60.
Perfect, 206.
Person, 140–4.
Personal suffix, 134.
Phonetics, 57–9, 65–6, 87–111, 106–24, 380–5, 417–18.
pi, suffix (noun), 129–30.
   — (verb), 179.
   postposition, 257.
   relative particle, 265–9.
Plosive, *see* Explosive.
Plurality, 128–9.
Plural particle, 225–6.
   suffix, 136–8, 178, 181–3, 186–7, 189, 192, 245, 283.
Polarity, 58.
Possessed, 57–8, 60, 73, 159–66.
Possession, 167–8, 173.
Possessive, 79–80.
   particle, 157.
   pronoun prefix, 160.
Possessor, 57–8, 60, 73, 139, 157, 159–66.
Postposition (general), 57, 67, 69–70, 72–3, 75–7, 82–3, 129, 140, 156, 159, 162–75, 181–2, 185–6, 188–90, 192–4, 199, 214, 224, 237, 247–69, 273, 275–9, 282, 285, 288, 302–3, 322–3, 325–6, 400–1, 408–12.
   relative, 262.
   interrogative, 262.
   potential, 261.
   emphatic, 255–6, 261.
   past, 248, 251, 257–8, 263.
   negative, 181, 183, 186–7, 189–90, 193, 253–5, 263, 275–9.
Potentiality, 223.
Predication, 80–1.
   negative, 300–3.
   juxtaposition, 290–4.
   existential, 297–300.
   comparison, 303–4.
   noun complement, 290–1, 293–6, 298–9, 301.
   qualificative complement, 291–3, 295–6, 298, 300, 302.
   adverb complement, 293.
   pronoun complement, 300.

Predicative, 79, 80 & n., 81 & n., 82, 163, 167, 169, 173, 248, 254, 285, 290–304, 307, 326, 412–14.
Prefix (general), 58, 77, 83, 126–7, 204–34.
  causative, 211, 217.
  intensive, 217.
  plural action, 210–11, 216–17.
  neuter passive, 218–19.
Prefixed nominal form, *see* Nominal prefixes; *see also* Noun prefix, Verb prefix.
Preposition, 57, 67, 73, 75–8, 81–3, 83 n., 171, 175, 244, 326.
Present, 201–3, 209, 221, 232, 262.
Pronominal particle, na, 157–8, 163, 166, 245.
  roots, 79, 81, 108–9.
Pronoun (general), 77–80, 82, 138–58, 322–5, 358–61, 391–5.
  demonstrative, *see* Demonstrative.
  emphasizing, 151–3, 239.
  indefinite, 152–6, 397.
  interrogative, *see* Interrogative.
  personal, 138–44, 391–2.
  qualificative, 79, 158, 163, 283–4.
  referring, 139, 152, 358.

Qualificatives, qualifiers, 75, 80 & n., 282–3, 288–9, 291–3, 307, 308, 395–9, *see also* Adjective and numeral.
Qualificative pronoun, *see* Pronoun.

ra, auxiliary, 221–2.
ra, tra, postposition, 257–60.
ra'a, ria, suffix, 244–5; *and see under* via, vɔya.
rɛ, suffix (verb), 179, 238.
  postposition, 170.
Reduplication (verb), 183, 185, 207, 214–15, 220, 305–6.
  (adjective), 306.
Reflexive, reciprocal pronoun, 150–4, 163.
Rejaf Language Conference, 316, 319, 386.
Relative (general), 79–80, 129–30, 136, 145, 156, 161, 262–9, 286, 332, 397.
  object, 161, 266, 268–9.
  pronoun, 156, 286.
  plural, 264, 268.
  singular, 264, 268.
  subject, 265–8.
Retroflex consonants, 102, 117, 317.
ri, suffix (noun), 130.
  — (verb), 234.
  postposition, *see* drí.
rɪ, postposition, 260.
  auxiliary, 233.
  relative practice, 263–5.
Ribero, Fr. P., xv, 65 n.
ro, ru, romvu, pronoun, 150.
  postposition, 171.
rɔ, suffix, 284–5, 295–7, 308–9, 393.
  postposition, 162, 401.
  auxiliary, 232–3.
ru, postposition, 260.
ruka, pronominal form, 154.
ɽɛ, postposition, 260.
ɽɔ, postposition, 260.

SARA, viii, 11, 14, 64, 67, 69, 71 n., 74.
Schleicher, 60–1.
se, relative particle, 156, 262–3.
selective interrogative, *see* Interrogative.
Semantic and morphological prefixes and suffixes, 63–4, 84, 127, 178.
SEMITIC, 56 & n., 58.
Sentence order, 57–8, 60, 71–3, 158, 180–1, 183–4, 186–7, 189–90, 192–3, 198, 214, 219, 225, 288–9, 311–12.
Separable particles, 77–8.
SERE, vii, ix, 15, 17 n., 18 & n., 62, 64–71, 73–4.
Sex, 132–3.
SHILLUK, 56.
sì, sí, sè, postposition, 171–2.
Sibilant and semi-sibilant consonants, 102–5, 118–19, 317–18.
Singular and plural, 57–8, 67, 136–7.
Size, *see* Augmentative and Diminutive.
Snoxall, R. A., 331 n., 334 n.
SOMALI, 102 n.
Stem, prefixes and suffixes, 63–4, 84.
Stress, 58.
Subject, 57–8, 60, 72–3, 140.
Subjunctive, 183, 185, 187–9, 191–2, 197, 202–4, 220, 223, 226–8, 230–1, 235, 255, 263, 276–7.
  postposition, 183, 187, 190.
Subordinate clauses, 226–30, 234, 244.
Subsequent action or State, 222, 224, 226, 228, 231.
Substantive, 78, 79 & n., 80–2, 282, 288–9, 290, *see also* Noun and Pronoun.
SUDANIC, 56 n., 56–60, 62, 71 n., 74.
Suffix (general), 58, 77, 83, 127–30, 178, 182, 234–46, 272, 282–5.
  infinitive, 179, 234–41, 251.
  participial, 179, 243–5.
  predicative, 293–6, 301.
SWAHILI, 59, 108 n., 322 n., 337 n.
Syllabic consonant, 384–5, 387–8.
Syntax, 57–8, 60, 72–4.

t, prefix (noun), 126.
  — (verb), 216–17.
ta, prefix (noun), 131.
te, auxiliary, 234.
  postposition, 260–1.
tɛ, auxiliary, 233–4.
  postposition, 247, 260.
Tense, 57–72, 180–1.
ti, suffix (noun), 130.
  postposition, 172.
Tone, *see* Intonation.
  grammatical (morphological), 65, 111–13, 125, 136, 140–1, 141–2, 198, 214.
  lexical, 65, 111, 124.
  syntactic, 114, 125.
Tonal conjugation of verbs, 270–81.
TORIT, *see* MADI.
Transitive conjugation, 181–94, 200–1.
trɔ, tɔ, postposition, 172–3.
trɔ, postposition, 261.
tsa, auxiliary, 234.

tu, suffix, 287–8.
'True' Adverbs, 309–10.

ve, linking particle, 162.
Velar consonant, 105–6, 120, 318–19.
Verb (general), 57–8, 60, 68, 73, 75–6, 78–9, 80–2, 81 n., 95–100, 177–281, 323–7, 360–8, 402–4.
Verb classes, 93, 95–100, 177–80, 180–99, 204–19, 341.
Verb, auxiliary, see Auxiliary verbs.
   causative, 211, 217, 235, 305.
   directional, 205–10, 213.
   of motion, 238, 257.
   postpositions, 75, 76, 82, 247–62.
   prefixes, 178, 204–34, 403–4.
   plural action, 210–11, 216–17, 233.
   suffixes, 178–80, 190, 234–46, 325, 404–5.
Verbal roots, 75–6, 79–83, 180.
Verbs to be, 297–300.
via, vɔya, suffix, 179, 244–5; see also under ra'a.
Vocabulary, 19, 20–1, 341–79.
Volition, 189–91, 261.
   imperative, 190–1, 199, 208, 220.
   particle, 229.
Vowel, 89–100, 114, 316, 380–1, 417.
   alternation, 316.
   central, 89, 92, 316.
   centralized, 66, 94, 141–3.
   coalescence and elision, 97–100, 141–3, 181, 186, 189.
   characteristic, see Characteristic Vowel.
   harmony, 89, 92–100, 181–2, 211, 214, 225, 233.
   lax, 60, 89, 92–3, 95–6, 205.
   prefixes, 126, 204–16.
   — causative, 211.
   — passive, 214–15.
   — infinitive, 215.
   tense, 66, 89, 92–3, 95–6, 205.
vu, postposition, 173.
Vycihl, Werner, 56 n.

w and y, compounds, 119.
WA'DI, see MORU.
Werner, A., xv, 56 n., 59 n.
Westermann, Prof. D., ix, x n., xiii, xv, 14, 20 n., 56 n., 87, 159.
Westermann and Ward, 94 n.
Whitney, 60.
WIRA, 64.
Word-Roots, 74–7.
Word division, 320–6.
Word order, see Sentence order.

ya, postposition, 173–4, 262.
ye, auxiliary, 234.

z-, suffix (verbs), 179, 241–3, 287.
za, zɔ, suffix (noun), 130.
ZANDE, vii, ix, 9, 15, 17, 18, 20 n., 62 & n., 64 & n., 65 & n., 66–84, 319.
zo, suffix (verb), 241, 243.
zu, suffix (verb), 243.
ZULU, 60–1 & n., 74.

For Product Safety Concerns and Information please contact our EU
representative GPSR@taylorandfrancis.com
Taylor & Francis Verlag GmbH, Kaufingerstraße 24, 80331 München, Germany

www.ingramcontent.com/pod-product-compliance
Lightning Source LLC
Chambersburg PA
CBHW071234300426
44116CB00008B/1032